The 2002 ASTD Training and Performance Yearbook

The 2002 ASTD Training and Performance Yearbook

John A. Woods
James W. Cortada

McGraw-Hill
New York   Chicago   San Francisco   Lisbon   Madrid
Mexico City   Milan   New Delhi   San Juan
Seoul   Singapore   Sydney   Toronto

McGraw-Hill

*A Division of The **McGraw·Hill** Companies*

Copyright © 2002 by The McGraw-Hill Companies, Inc. All rights reserved. Printed in the United States of America. Except as permitted under the United States Copyright Act of 1976, no part of this publication may be reproduced or distributed in any form or by any means or stored in a data base or retrieval system, without the prior written permission of the publisher.

1 2 3 4 5 6 7 8 9 0 AGM/AGM 0 9 8 7 6 5 4 3 2 1

ISBN: 0-07-138021-3

The sponsoring editor for this book is Richard Narramore. Tama Harris was the production and editing supervisor. Design and Production services were provided by CWL Publishing Enterprises, Madison, WI, www.cwlpub.com.

Printed and bound by Quebecor World/Martinsburg.

To order multiple copies of this book at a discount, call the McGraw-Hill Special Sales Department at 800-842-3075, or 212-904-5427.

To ask a question about the book, contact the author, or report a mistake in the text, please write to Richard Narramore, Senior Editor, at richard_narramore@mcgraw-hill.com.

Contents

Foreword	ix
Preface	xi
Acknowledgments	xv

PART ONE **The State of Training: Industry Data, Trends, and Statistics**

Introduction	1
Why Conventional Training and Education Are Dead, *Delphi Group*	3
State of the Industry Report: How Much Training Do Organizations Provide? *Mark E. Van Buren*	13
State of the Industry Report: How Do Organizations Deliver Training? *Mark E. Van Buren*	21
New Employee Orientation Survey: Summary Report, *Jean Barbazette*	37
Industry Report 2000 The People: Who Controls, Benefits From, and Delivers Training, *TRAINING Magazine*	42
Industry Report 2000 The Money: U.S. Organizations' Annual Expenditures on Employee Training, *TRAINING Magazine*	48
What Happens When Employees Telecommute?—Some Research Findings, *Lisa H. Cree and Richard C. Sorenson*	52
E-Learning: The Market Survey and Analysis, *Delphi Group*	56

PART TWO **The Cutting Edge of Training: E-Learning and Other New Training Technology**

Introduction	73
The E-Learning Revolution, *Patricia Galagan*	75
E-Learning: Are You a Tortoise or a Hare? *Marvin Gottlieb*	83
Integrating E-Learning with Busines Goals, *Delphi Group*	92
E-Learning: New Twist on CBT, *Bill Roberts*	99

Audience Analysis and Instructional System Design for
Successful Online Learning and Performance,
Margaret Martinez 104
A Primer on Tracking Web-Based Training, *Janeen Rossi* 115

PART THREE **Approaches to Organizational and Individual Performance Improvement**

Introduction 123

Organizational Performance

Creating and Sustaining the High Performance Organization,
Keith Owen, Ron Mundy, Will Guild, and Robert Guild 125
Motivate Managers to Review Performance,
Lin Grensing-Pophal 143
Serial Knowledge Transfer: How Groups Learn from
Themselves, *Nancy M. Dixon* 148
Dare to Share: Using Extranets to Exchange Knowledge,
Bill Roberts 162
Companies Need Well-Defined Electronic Monitoring
Policies, *Carrie Garcia* 169

Individual Performance

Reinforcing Professional Self-Management for Improved
Service Quality, *Baird K. Brightman* 174
Emotional Intelligence: Training People to Be Affective So
They Can Be Effective, *Mike Bagshaw* 188
The Key to Leadership Today, *Marlene Caroselli* 195
86 Your Appraisal Process? *Jonathan A. Segal* 200
When Stress Won't Go Away, *William Atkinson* 208
Retaining Peak Performers by Individualizing Employee
Recognition, *Cindy Ventrice* 215
The Manager's Role in Setting Goals, *Lynn Summers,
Diane Cox, and Jack Zigon* 223

PART FOUR **Implementing Performance Improvement Interventions**

Introduction 233

Analysis and Design

Design Training So People Learn Easily, Quickly, *and* with
High Retention! *Carolyn B. Thompson* 235

	Build It Backwards: Begin with the Outcomes, *The Final Copy Group, Inc.*	241
	Seven Surefire Steps to Getting Approval for Training Projects, *Peter Meyer*	246
	Is a Video in Your Vision? *Betty Sosnin*	249
	General Tips for Training, *Pete Blair*	255
	Training and Other Performance Interventions	
	People Development Strategies in the New Economy, *Greg Wang*	261
	Time to Treat Learners as Consumers, *Stephen L. Cohen, David W. Dove, and Edward L. Bachelder*	271
	The Lighter Side of Learning, *Kathleen McLaughlin*	280
	Make New Employee Orientation a Success, *Jean Barbazette*	285
	True Confessions: Adventures in Training, *Dave Zielinski*	289
	Designing a Buddy Program, *J. Leslie McKeown*	295
	Tactics for the New Guerrilla Trainer, *Phil Mershon*	302
	Teaching Diagnostic Steps vs. Teaching Situational Steps, *Michael O. Thomas*	307
	Expert Advice on Setting Up a Conflict Resolution Training Program, *Editors, Managing Training & Development*	312
	Evaluation of Intervention Success	
	Measuring the Training Department, *Stanley E. Malcolm*	317
	Liberating the Lamppost: Shedding Light on Training Evaluation, *Peter Bregman and Howie Jacobson*	326
	Evaluating E-Degrees, *Shari Caudron*	333
	Calculating Training Efficiency, *Scotty C. DeClue*	339
PART FIVE	**Focusing on People to Drive Organizational Strategy**	
	Introduction	343
	The Learning Organization in Practice: New Principles for Effective Training, *Mark Mallinger*	345
	Beyond Training: Reconceptualizing Learning at Work, *Patricia Bryans and Richard Smith*	351
	Leadership DNA: The Ford Motor Story, *Stewart D. Friedman*	364
	The Little Airplane That Could, *Sarah Fister Gale*	375

Managing Dispersed Work Effectively: A Primer
John D. Adams   381
A Seat at the Table, *Kristine Ellis and Sarah Fister Gale*   392
Turning Passion into Organizational Performance,
Richard Chang   397

PART SIX   **Training and Performance Resource Almanac**
Introduction   405
Training and Performance Resources Online,
Robert Magnan   407
Directory of Magazines, Journals, and Newsletters
Dealing with Training and Performance Issues   431
A Glossary of Performance Management Terms,
Lynn Summers   461
Directory of Training and Performance Associations and
Organizations   475
Calendar of Conferences and Events, 2002   497
Index   507

Foreword

The question "how do we improve performance?" is of foremost importance to companies today. Customer demand for speed, customization, timeliness, quality, and variety of products and services requires continuously improving performance by people at every level of the organization. Managers understand the importance of investing in a wide variety of interventions to upgrade skills and performance to remain competitive. Further, computer and communications technology both speeds up the pace of change and alters the skills that working people need.

The American Society for Training and Development's goals regarding performance are to raise awareness of performance improvement methods, to promote the development of new models and tools, to support their testing in the workplace, and to help practitioners master these critical workplace tools.

To be a player in the high-stakes game of performance requires a perspective that focuses not on how much training is delivered but on how fast people gain more capability to improve performance and how much of that capability the organization is able to use for strategic purposes. It is a perspective that measures success in terms of results, not how much skill or knowledge employees are exposed to. It is a perspective that sees training as one of many ways to reach a performance goal.

Many performance improvement specialists started out as trainers who began to ask if training was the best way to close a performance gap. The bigger-picture thinking necessitates a new set of skills and interventions to analyze the causes of performance gaps, select appropriate interventions to address the cause of the gaps, take actions to ensure interventions are implemented, and evaluate the achievement of desired results.

To deepen the training community's perspectives on current critical writings in the field of training and human resource development and to broaden the perspective to include a performance mindset, ASTD is pleased to continue sponsoring *The ASTD Training and Performance Yearbook*. This is the sixth edition of the yearbook, and it has evolved substantially since it was first published in 1997. It includes a new emphasis on current data and trends of interest to those working in our field, and there is more emphasis on e-learning than in previous editions. The materials included here have been screened and selected from hundreds of possibilities by the editors. They have compiled for easy reference essential materials and ideas for keeping you up-to-date in the changing work of training and performance.

Tina Sung
President
American Society for Training and Development
Alexandria, Virginia

Preface

Welcome to the 2002 edition of *The ASTD Training and Performance Yearbook*, a resource designed to help you keep current on what's going on in training and performance improvement. We have three purposes for this yearbook:

1. To provide a review of current data and statistics dealing with the state of training and human resource development (part one of this yearbook).
2. To provide an annual documentation of the most useful ideas, techniques, and case studies in the field of training and performance technology, including all types of training from classroom and on-the-job to the many iterations of e-learning.
3. To serve as an *annually updated reference* to publications, Web sites, organizations, and other information that will help you efficiently and effectively do your job.

We set various objectives for ourselves in developing this book. The most important include:

Create a Compilation of Statistical Data. As a yearbook, we have decided this publication should include current data on such items as how much money is invested in and in what types of training, who controls training, the trend toward e-learning, and more. To that end, we have brought such information together from various publications and studies. By putting it all in one place (with information on how you can learn more), we think this will enhance the value of this book to our users.

Create a Clearinghouse. Because there is so much coming out in the area of training and performance technology, ASTD, McGraw-Hill, and the editors perceived a need for a kind of "clearinghouse" to which people from all different organizations might turn as a starting place to learn about current thinking in these fields. *The ASTD Training and Performance Yearbook* is that clearinghouse and includes a comprehensive selection of articles from magazines and journals directly and indirectly related to this field. We want to save you the time of finding what might be useful to you in performing your job and put it all in one convenient compendium.

Create a Book of Lasting Value. Because it is revised annually, *The ASTD Training and Performance Yearbook* focuses on information that has come out in the year immediately preceding its publication. While currency is one of its strengths in this fast-changing field, we also intend each edition to have lasting value. You will find articles throughout the book that will continue to be applicable for years to come as you go about devising effective training programs and performance interventions to help people be more productive.

However, a value of each year's new edition is that it also updates you on all the book's content areas plus selected new topics that reflect the latest developments in the field.

Develop an Authoritative Review. Yet another goal for *The ASTD Training and Performance Yearbook* is to contribute to clearer thinking about and implementation of actions that will improve performance. Human resource and performance improvement are broad fields. By systematically including the latest discussion of applications of training and performance principles, we hope to provide a way to standardize how you think about and keep up with the field. Our goal is for you to have a resource that you can confidently use, knowing it is current, reliable, and authoritative.

Organization

To make it easy to find material, we have divided this yearbook into six parts:

Part One, The State of Training: Industry Data, Trends, and Statistics, provides a statistical portrait of the field of training and human resource development. We've excerpted data from different publications and reports designed to help you understand just where the field of training fits in the world of public and private organizations and businesses and the directions things are heading as we move into the 21st century.

Part Two, The Cutting Edge of Training: E-Learning and Other New Training Technology, provides a review of the latest developments in e-learning and the use of computers and other technology in the field of training. We include six different articles that range from trends in the field to an original article that provides detailed direction on how to design an e-learning course for different types of learners.

Part Three, Approaches to Organizational and Individual Performance Improvement, focuses on a broad array of issues involved in improving performance, both at the individual and the organizational levels. We've selected 12 articles dealing with the policies and practices that generate high performance across the organization and that describe specific best practices that can help individuals improve their performance. The point of this section is to emphasize not just training, but many different approaches to performance improvement that you may want to consider adapting to your organization.

Part Four, Implementing Performance Improvement Interventions, focuses on training and other specific interventions you might find helpful to consider for your organization. This part is organized around the paradigm of analysis and design, implementation, and evaluation. You'll find pieces providing insights on designing effective training programs, whether to use video in your training, guerrilla tactics for trainers, and new findings on how to evaluate your training program and the effectiveness of the training department.

Part Five, Focusing on People to Drive Organizational Strategy, emphasizes how people are at the core of any successful organizational strategy. We include seven articles that

PREFACE

deal with topics like the learning organization and its relation to training, how Ford creates leaders and the strategic importance of their leadership training program, how people at Boeing made an unprofitable plane profitable, and how training directors are becoming involved in the development of strategy.

Part Six, Training and Performance Resource Almanac, includes five sections that we think you will turn to often. You'll find our completely updated and annotated directory for online training and performance sites plus lots of other information on how to effectively use the Web to gather information and communicate with peers. You'll also find a similar directory of magazines, journals, and newsletters that either are devoted to this field or regularly carry articles dealing with training and performance issues—with subscription information. This edition includes a glossary of performance management terms that is a kind of mini-textbook on the subject. We conclude with an updated and annotated directory of associations and organizations, and a calendar, organized by months, of many organizational conferences and events for 2002.

Criteria for Selection of Articles

We applied three criteria in choosing material for inclusion in *The ASTD Training and Performance Yearbook*:

1. **Articles must be current.** Because this is an annual publication, part of its value comes from the timeliness of its content. Therefore, nearly all the articles included were published in 2001 or late 2000.
2. **Articles must be practical** and help trainers and performance technologists solve problems and do their work more efficiently and effectively. Articles selected represent the best thinking about how to understand and implement training and performance interventions. We want this book to be used, not sit on the shelf.
3. **Articles must be authoritative.** There is a great deal to choose from in putting this type of book together. The articles that made the cut are the ones that represent the best in their class, providing you with a standard for reading and judging other materials.

Using *The ASTD Training and Performance Yearbook*

This book is not meant to be read cover to cover (though that would be a valuable exercise). We suggest that you peruse the table of contents and read those articles of most interest and relevance to the situations in which you find yourself. Here are some examples of how various individuals might use it:

- **In-house training professionals** may use it to read about training case studies in different industries to see how those might apply in their particular situations.
- A **consultant** may use it to keep up with and review the latest thinking in the area of performance improvement.

- **Executives** who need more background in training and improving human resource performance will find this book a convenient source of information on how to do that.
- **Students** who are entering this field will find this a valuable resource for getting a feel for what their career will involve.
- **Performance technologists** will find it a valuable tool for determining what interventions they might try to bring about measurable performance improvement.

Vision for the Book

We envision this yearbook as the first resource you turn to whenever you have a question or problem that involves issues surrounding training and performance. We want this to be a problem-solving resource for you. If you can't find a suggested solution here, we hope it will guide you to where you can find the solution you're looking for. This book is an evolving documentation of the changes going on in the field of training and performance management. We designed it to help people like you understand and even shape these changes.

Feedback from You

As with all constantly changing products, this book is a kind of ongoing experiment. With its publication, we want to learn how well we are helping our customers and how we can make improvements. To do that, we need and invite your feedback. You can write to us at McGraw-Hill, 2 Penn Plaza, New York, NY 10121 or contact us by e-mail at jwoods@cwlpub.com or jwcorta@us.ibm.com. We look forward to hearing what you have to say and to serving your needs for many editions in the future.

Acknowledgments

This book was a big undertaking for us, and we are indebted to many people who have played a role in bringing it together. At McGraw-Hill, Richard Narramore has been a supportive partner in its undertaking. At ASTD, we have worked with Nancy Olson in organizing the book and selecting articles. Robert Magnan of CWL Publishing Enterprises has been an important part of our team in completing this book. He helped extensively in compiling information for the resources section. Nancy Woods also at CWL was in charge of permissions and took care of several other tasks that have resulted in the book you now hold.

We want to thank Carolyn Thompson for her article on designing training, and Janeen Roberts for her piece on tracking Web-based training. We also want to thank Les McKeown for his contribution on creating a buddy program. And thanks as well to Margaret Martinez for her article on designing online learning programs, a throughtful and practical contribution.

Finally, we want to thank you who purchased this book. We hope it lives up to your expectations, and that you will take the time to give us feedback on how we can make it even more useful. Contact us at McGraw-Hill at 2 Penn Plaza, New York, NY 10121 or via e-mail at jwoods@cwlpub.com and jwcorta@us.ibm.com.

John Woods
Jim Cortada

PART ONE

The State of Training: Industry Data, Trends, and Statistics

Part One of the yearbook is devoted to information on the state of the industry and is a kind of digest of several studies and reports that have been published in 2000 and 2001. Our goal is to give practitioners information they need to understand what's going on in this field. This part provides a frame of reference for what you are doing in your organization or, if you are a training supplier, where the best opportunities lie for selling your services. Of course, a major trend continues to be the move toward e-learning, and we document that move thoroughly here. We also include material from ASTD and *TRAINING* Magazine studies on what types of training are being delivered, who's receiving it, the level of investment in different types of training, and more. Here's what you'll find:

- *Why Conventional Training and Education Are Dead.* This piece does not leave much to the imagination about where Delphi Group stands with regard to the future of e-learning. This article is excerpted from the company's extensive study, *Enterprise E-Learning 2001.*

- *State of the Industry Report: How Much Training Do Organizations Provide?* This is part of the ASTD study and provides information on what types and how much training organizations are delivering. It's especially useful in that it compares companies from their benchmarking studies with the world at alarge.

- *State of the Industry Report: How Do Organizations Deliver Training?* This also comes from the ASTD study and of special interst includes statistics on trends in outsourcing.

- *New Employee Orientation Survey: Summary Report.* One of the more important training programs in any organization is orientation. This piece reports on a study undertaken to find how companies are doing this and what changes they'd like to institute.
- *Industry Report 2000 The People.* This is part of *TRAINING* Magazine's annual survey on the training industry. This section looks at who controls training purchases, dollars spent on training, and includes more good information on outsourcing.
- *Industry Report 2000 The Money.* More from *TRAINING*'s report, this time on how much organizations are spending on training.
- *What Happens When Employees Telecommute?—Some Research Findings.* Telecommuting is a trend, and it's useful to know if working from home affects performance and how to enhance the performance of telecommuters.
- *E-Learning: The Market Survey and Analysis.* This is more from the Delphi Group report that provided the first article in Part One. Here you'll find the statistics on which they make their case.

Why Conventional Training and Education Are Dead

Delphi Group

This article comes from Module I of a study prepared by Delphi Group on the state of e-learning in organizations today. This particular piece is both controversial and explores the trend toward enterprise e-learning. You may not agree with all the points raised here, but we believe this will provoke your thinking about e-learning and give you some insights into the conclusions one large consulting company has reached about trends in training and performance interventions.

Training, as it has been traditionally defined and deployed, has reached the end of its lifecycle. It is rooted in time and space, the two commodities modern enterprises do not have in sufficient quantities. It has simply become impractical to take workers away from their work for days or weeks at a time to train them. Management cannot afford it, and the worker does not wish it. In fact, workers prefer to learn in shorter, smaller, increments, on a need to know schedule.

Across America and around the world, trainers are looking at their field of work and setting about redefining it. Technology has, once again, changed a work landscape: training and education. What's more, it has happened three times in the last decade, first with computer-based training, then with Web-based distance learning, then with e-learning. Now, in the new millennium, enterprise e-learning is changing it once again. No longer can we think of training as an end in itself. No training is a means to an end: training creates knowledge which can be captured, reused, and turned into a corporate asset for great return on our training investment. This is the essence of enterprise e-learning.

In order to understand where we are going, it might be helpful to understand how we have gotten to this point.

Reprinted with permission from Module I of *Enterprise E-Learning 2001*. Copyright © 2001 by Delphi Group. All rights reserved.

The Training and Education Crisis

Public education in the United States is in deep trouble. After years of budget cuts and intellectual neglect, educators, politicians, and government officials are admitting that we have a problem: students are insufficiently educated to meet the needs of the New Economy. "The Power of the Internet for Learning: Moving from Promise to Practice," a recent report to the President and Congress from the Web-Based Education Commission, states:

> At the dawn of the 21st Century, the education landscape is changing. Elementary and secondary schools are experiencing growing enrollments, coping with critical shortages of teachers, facing overcrowded, and decaying buildings, and responding to demands for higher standards. On college campuses, there is an influx of older, part-time students seeking the skills vital to success in an Information Age. Corporations are dealing with the shortage of skill d workers and the necessity of providing continuous training to their employees.

The U.S. Bureau of Labor Statistics projects the most employment growth in service sectors through the year 2008, with most of those jobs for professional specialists and managers, whose stock in trade is ideas and knowledge. All other labor sectors, such as manufacturing, are expected to decline. With regard to education and training, the BLS states:

> Employment in all education and training categories that generally require an associate degree or more education is projected to grow faster than the 14 percent average for all occupations.

What this means to enterprises literally around the world is that the emerging labor pool is ill-equipped to learn, while at the same time the demand for better educated, highly skilled knowledge workers is on the rise. The upshot is that an overwhelming responsibility falls upon the shoulders of enterprise to train and educate its workers.

Several even greater challenges loom:

- to train and educate those with whom the enterprise conducts business.
- to capture this incredible reservoir of expertise and knowledge so that it can be reused in other aspects of the business.

The Delphi Group recently completed a survey of approximately 700 firms to assess their current e-learning initiatives. The respondents were primarily executives, project managers, line-of-business (LOB) managers, and information technology (IT) managers. The consensus was that there is a great need for more and better e-learning initiatives, but significant hurdles, lingering from the days of training, still remain.

What Is E-Learning?

E-learning is a suite of technologies used in organizations for a variety of skills development initiatives. *E-learning* is the application and deployment of just the right amount of training (or skills development) at just the right time, to those who have a need to possess the requisite knowledge or learn the specific skill.

Without a doubt, e-learning has its roots in traditional training and education which, based as they are on Industrial Era precepts, simply cannot meet the needs of today's Information and Internet Era enterprise. When we think of training, we generally think of developing the skills in individuals to perform specific tasks. Military training is probably the finest example, based on the concept of "tell them what you're going to teach them, teach them, and then tell them what you've taught them." When we think of education, we generally think of a teacher, a classroom, and a text, where instruction in ideas, concepts, points of view, and illustrative examples are used to convey information that is intended to at least instill the ability to learn and, at best, create a modicum of knowledge. Testing, in order to assure learning efficacy, remains an important aspect of both training and education.

Enterprise e-learning involves taking the knowledge acquired through e-learning initiatives and reusing it throughout the organization. Enterprise e-learning captures the tacit and explicit knowledge from training and from the operations of the entire value chain and cycles it into a knowledge management system, where it is captured and available for reuse. Ideally, this knowledge can be made available via portal technology to management, employees, business partners, and even customers, on a need-to-know basis. In its finest iteration, enterprise e-learning also captures tacit and explicit knowledge from business partners, suppliers, and customers from the portal and cycles that back through the knowledge management system.

Enterprise e-learning is emerging as the corporate response to the shortcomings of public education and the learning gaps endemic in traditional enterprise training. Enterprise e-learning takes complete responsibility and ownership for training and educating people who must work together to accomplish business objectives, both within and without the organization. It does not turn its back on traditional training and educational methods; rather, it extracts what is best about them and synthesizes them with cutting-edge technologies to create a new learning paradigm based on this premise:

> Any knowledge worker associated with the value chain, whether a professional, manager, employee, business partner, supplier, or customer, has a need to acquire understanding or knowledge about the way your firm does business, at some time. The means of acquiring the training or education necessary to know or understand that particular information must be available to knowledge workers on an *anywhere, anytime,* for *any reason,* basis. The means of delivering that

Without a doubt, e-learning has its roots in traditional training and education which, based as they are on Industrial Era precepts, simply cannot meet the needs of today's Information and Internet Era enterprise.

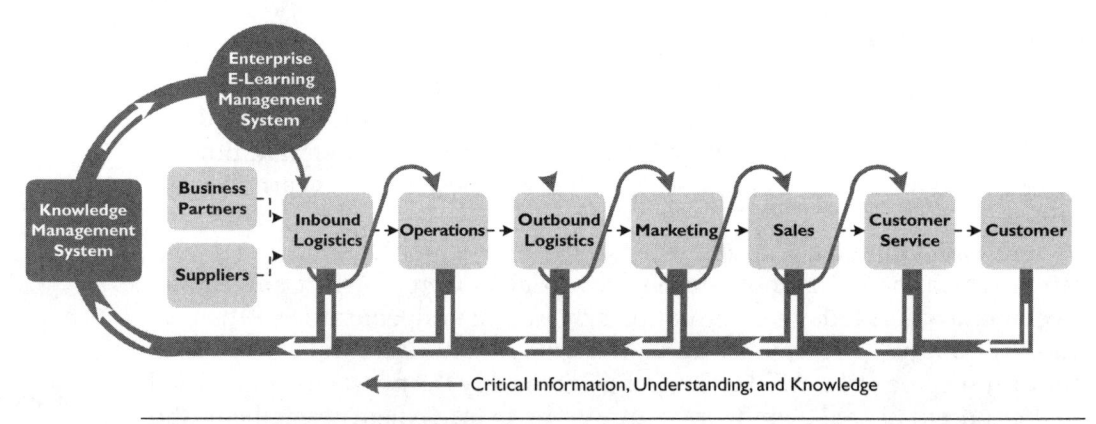

Figure 1. **Enterprise e-learning informs the value chain in new ways**

training or education must be ubiquitous and multi-faceted, so that learners can study and comprehend it on their own terms.

Conventional Training vs. E-Learning

One salient feature of e-learning is that the distinction between training and education has blurred. This is due in part to our shift from the Industrial Economy to the 21st century New Economy. An Industrial Economy worker needed only know how to pull a lever or perform a repetitive task. Work today is far more complex, often requiring an understanding of the overall process or goal. Unfortunately, we no longer have the time to spend days or weeks training a worker in every nuance of their job; moreover, it is impractical, for up to 70 percent of what the worker learns is quickly forgotten.

Today's knowledge worker needs the skills to perform a specific task while working, for example how to create a macro with a spreadsheet program or how to configure a network interface. Yet often the skillsets are cumulative, as in understanding how to design and produce complex, content-rich multimedia documents. In a word, knowledge workers need to understand not just-in-time steps but *processes*. This becomes increasingly important as we examine and refine those same processes embedded in the value chain—and use our understanding of those processes to first deconstruct and then reconstruct the value chain to adapt to changing business internal strategies or external conditions. And that change, once intermittent, is now a constant.

It is essential to understand that the differences between training and e-learning are not just semantic. There are eight distinct ways in which training of any sort, be it classroom or computer-based, and e-learning differ. In toto, they represent a state of the art e-learning system; most organizations, however, will likely undertake only one or two of these conversions from training to e-learning at a time.

Conventional Training

E-Learning Lifecycle

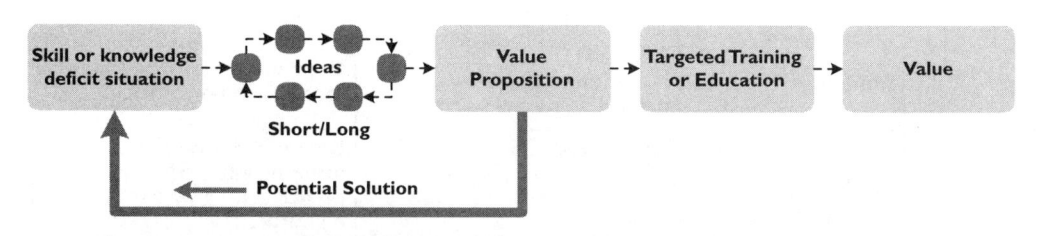

Figure 2. **All ideas have a learning lifecycle—some very short and some very long**

- *Delivery:* Training determines when the learner will learn. E-learning puts the learner in control of the learning process.
- *Responsiveness:* Training presumes to know what the learner ought to learn. E-learning lets the learner set the agenda and solve their own learning problems.
- *Access:* Training is sequential, like studying from a text or script. E-learning allows the learner to set the order and agenda.
- *Symmetry:* Training is physically and mentally separated from the work experience. E-learning helps make learning part of the work or task.
- *Modality:* Training has a clearly defined beginning, middle, and end. E-learning takes place whenever, however, in just the right amounts.
- *Authority:* Training places content responsibility on the educator or administrator. E-learning lets the learners and educators determine content collaboratively.
- *Personalization:* Training conveys little if any sense of relationship between the learner and the material. E-learning is intensely targeted at the individual learner.
- *Adaptivity:* Training is fixed in time and space, until the training stops and new materials replace the old. E-learning materials change whenever the need, learning environment, or situation changes.

	Training	E-Learning
Delivery	Push—Instructor determines agenda	Pull—Student determines agenda
Responsiveness	Anticipatory—Assumes to know the problem	Reactionary—Responds to problem at hand
Access	Linear—Has defined progression of knowledge	Non-linear—Allows direct access to knowledge in whatever sequence makes sense to the situation at hand
Symmetry	Asymmetric—Training occurs as a separate activity	Symmetric—Learning occurs as an integrated activity
Modality	Discrete—Training takes place in dedicated chunks with defined stops and starts	Continuous—Learning runs in parallel and never stops
Authority	Centralized—Content is selected from a library of materials developed by the educators	Distributed—Content comes from the interaction of the participants as well as the educators
Personalization	Mass produced—Content must satisfy the needs of many	Personalized—Content is determined by the individual user's need to know in order to satisfy the needs of one
Adaptivity	Static—Content and organization/taxonomy remains in their original authored form without regard to environmental changes	Dynamic—Content changes constantly through user input, experiences, new practices, business rules, and heuristics

Figure 3. **Eight critical distinctions between training and e-learning**

E-learning places the learner at the center of the learning process, giving them control over both content and process.

Another interesting aspect of enterprise e-learning is its democratizing influence. We see organizations flattening, people collaborating in teams, the rise of peer-to-peer technologies, and a new respect for the ideas and perceptions, not just of executives, but of all workers. In the past, only those being groomed for more responsibility were given the opportunity for training or education. Today, progressive organizations recognize the value in training or educating anyone who expresses a desire or interest in on-the-job improvement. The fact that it is less expensive to retain and train an existing worker than to hire and train a new one has never been more true. This awareness is quickly translating into e-learning initiatives sponsored by various governments around the globe, designed to lift public education and awareness.

E-learning is not a blanket replacement for classroom or instructor-led training. The dominant trend is toward blended learning, simply defined as

What Is the X-Economy?

Think of your last great idea, or that product or service that was sure to revolutionize the world and make you or your company millions. What stopped you from making it a reality? Capital? Time? Let's say you had plenty of both. What obstacles would remain?

As an entrepreneur, business manager, or *Fortune* 100 CEO, the greatest challenge for all good ideas is identifying, establishing and coordinating the network of suppliers, partners, and delivery channels required to get from concept to cash.

Building these intricate networks for producing and delivering goods, called a supply chain, is not trivial. Successful companies are those who have created a fortress of supply chains and who can effectively rebuild them for new innovations.

But building or rebuilding a supply chain assumes that the community of competent suppliers is known. In today's global markets, this is unlikely. The volume of innovation and the volatility of markets in the 21st century virtually assures that you will not know who the best prepared, most competent, and least costly supplier is for any specific task at any given time. Even when you know who your possible suppliers are and have established confidence in their ability to deliver their products or services, there is the lengthy process of evaluation and negotiation, such as issuing requests for proposals, getting pricing, and comparing quotations.

What if there was a way to do this instantaneously: to exhaustively identify partners, suppliers and buyers; coordinate and rebuild intricate value chains (the collection of businesses, resources, and tasks that go into producing and delivering any product or service); respond to market needs that consumers cannot yet even express? What might that mean to innovation, competition, quality consumer options, and the free market?

The new exchange economy, or X-Economy, is the environment in which this kind of instant innovation can occur. The Internet is the tool for this exchange, providing the opportunity for unprecedented flexibility, collaboration, and speed. This is the commerce of the future.

Why an "X" economy? X has a multitude of connotations. It is the symbol for a generation of Americans, the unknown variable of an equation, the restricted territory outside of the social norm; in short, X is the terra incognito that lies forever just outside of our grasp.

First and foremost, the X is about the online exchanges that will rule our markets and our economies. These are global exchanges where communities of trade will form and through which virtually all commerce will flow in only a few short years. Most of the focus of this book is on how these online exchanges will shorten the time it takes to form supply chains, partnerships, and products.

> The X refers to the unknown variable that is now systemic to our economic models. Economies have always been unpredictable, but at least they had durations of certainty. Like weather patterns, economies moved in large, slow arcs. Today, that luxury is lost. Markets, economies, and value chains move as microclimates—constantly volatile, constantly changing. There is no safe haven, no escape from the deluge of information on which to make economic decisions, no refuge in the maelstrom of alternatives, partnerships, and opportunities. We must find ways to manage this uncertainty and the ensuing global attention deficit disorder, using mechanisms that infuse markets with the ability to engender trust, create time, and ultimately establish new forms of community.
>
> X represents the extremities of markets, as well as the emerging economy to which power has been slowly but surely shifting for centuries. Every social, political and economic system is being further decentralized into entities that are apparently uncontrolled by conventional authority, ruled instead by their own unique communities of interest.
>
> Finally, the X represents the unlimited potential of an economy to flourish through the creation of the mechanisms that extend prosperity to a global community. This new kind of liquidity will have a significant impact on the economic prosperity of the individual as well as the enterprise.
>
> What is most important to understand is that the X-Economy is more than just networking an industry so that information can be shared electronically. There are certainly significant challenges in creating an instantaneous, extended enterprise made by piecing together all of the requirements, schedules, availability, pricing, logistical, and contractual issues that each partner in the value chain must take into consideration. But there is much more. The X-Economy is in fact a molecular economy of infinitely malleable and instantly responsive enterprises.

"the right tool for the right job." Neither is e-learning necessarily less expensive. It is subject to the same rules of development and implementation as traditional education and training; in other words, it's not going to teach itself without the framework created with instructional design. E-learning cannot be allowed to develop solely as a technology solution, or without embedding traditional pedagogical practices. If it does, it risks becoming yet another piece of technological detritus along the information highway.

E-learning has created the need for more training administrators, trainers, instructional designers and technology implementers. What's more, they need more skills and abilities and—yes, education and training themselves. For example, at the Center for Graduate Studies at Marlboro College in Vermont, the mission is "to train individuals to lead the Internet and online strategies of corporate, non-profit and educational institutions." The Center offers three Master of Science degrees: Internet Strategy Management, Internet Engineering, and Teaching with Internet Technologies.

E-learning lends itself to an innovative, modular approach to learning that helps develop new visions for the training curriculum, course contents, and the means of delivering training to your community. Online course delivery is very similar to just-in-time (JIT) manufacturing: Learners learn only what they need for current requirements, but then may enroll in additional modules as required. E-learning content can be updated, revised, and re-broadcast in far less time than conventional learning media, such as books. Multimedia or blended content improves learning; humans are visual learners—up to 83% of learning occurs visually. And studies have proven that the process approach to online learning, combined with multimedia learning tools, can improve retention by as much as 50 percent.

Enterprise E-Learning for Competitive Advantage

Low unemployment and a near dearth of available skilled workers have moved talent acquisition and retention to the top of every organization's list of critical success factors. The next logical step in mitigating the current circumstances is to maximize the utility of existing human capital. This involves educating the work force in a manner that tailors the methods and content to current needs while accurately anticipating future requirements.

As the individual worker becomes more valuable and at the same time more transitory, these problems only increase. Retention issues and internal reward systems are only part of the solution. In a free-agent economy, the onus will increasingly be on the employer to ensure the necessary tools and strategies are in place to remain competitive. Relying on heuristics and random knowledge exchanges offers little means of keeping pace with rapidly evolving skill requirements. In today's hyper-competitive market, the proverbial water cooler is an insufficient replacement for the formal classroom. The void left between formalized training and serendipitous discovery underscores the need for a "just-in-time" enterprise e-learning environment, where knowledge is dispensed as it is needed, rather than on a prescriptive basis. Ideas, talent, products, and opportunities become lost or abandoned without proper infrastructure to deliver appropriately filtered knowledge to those who need it. A brilliant idea may occur in an instant, but mobilizing an uninitiated work force can take months or years.

The rapidity with which required skill sets change and time-to-market cycles shrink has begun to shift the notion of corporate education in the 21st century from the realm of classroom training to continuous education. This, in turn, has redefined the concept of competitive advantage. In the Industrial Economy, having a leg up on the competition was defined by the product or service. In the New Economy, competitive advantage relies on the enterprise's ability to bring new ideas to market more quickly, and often in a more targeted manner. In the Industrial Economy, competitive advantage ended

> The void left between formalized training and serendipitous discovery underscores the need for a "just-in-time" enterprise e-learning environment, where knowledge is dispensed as it is needed, rather than on a prescriptive basis.

once a market was saturated. In the New Economy, the enterprise has moved on to the next idea or innovation and new windows of opportunity long before they see the end of the market in sight.

All this is contingent on e-learning. Without the right people possessed with the appropriate skills, it is difficult to have an environment that continually gestates new ideas and innovation. Therefore, e-learning's raison d'être means:

- In the short term, having the right employee trained and available for the right task or job is a competitive advantage.
- In the longer term, having the enterprise e-learning systems in place to train people at the right time, with just the right amount of learning dispensed and resulting in a process improvement, is a distinctively competitive advantage.

This realization has led to a new corporate imperative: aligning knowledge gathering and dissemination from enterprise e-learning efforts with the underlying corporate mission. The increased complexity of operations, coupled with the miasma of opportunities for new ideas and innovation, has rendered traditional prescriptive training obsolete. It is unwieldy, imprecise, and out of step with corporate needs. We expect to see training replaced by what we term the enterprise e-learning lifecycle.

Delphi Group delivers strategic advantage at the intersection of business and IT. Its thought leadership has assisted more than 20,000 professionals in the Global 2000. Its core competencies are in the emerging technologies of collaborative commerce, portals, content, and knowledge management, enterprise wireless, and e-learning. Visit their Web site at www.delphigroup.com.

State of the Industry Report: How Much Training Do Organizations Provide?

Mark E. Van Buren

Each year, ASTD undertakes a major survey to determine the state of the training industry. This piece and the one that follows it are from that report. This part provides a breakdown on how much training organizations provide. This information not only helps you understand better how organizations approach training today but hints at trends in this industry.

Introduction

The *2001 ASTD State of the Industry Report* continues ASTD's tradition of compiling and providing the most comprehensive set of statistics available regarding employer-provided training in the United States. The report is based on the findings of ASTD's Benchmarking Service, an annual process that collects information from all types of organizations on the nature of their training expenditures and practices. This year's report shares findings from 365 U.S. organizations that participated in the Benchmarking Service in 2000 by providing data on training activities for 1999.

In addition to reporting on how firms met the challenge of training their employees in 1999, *The 2001 ASTD State of the Industry Report* provides comparisons to data from previous years' surveys to assess how the training industry may be changing.

The comparisons with previous years' data revealed some unexpected findings. As a result, we conducted follow-up interviews with about 20 Benchmarking Service participants who reported changes similar to those seen in the overall data sample. The information gathered in these interviews was used to enhance our understanding of some of the reasons for the

Reprinted with permission from *The 2001 ASTD State of the Industry Report*. Copyright © 2001 by the American Society for Training and Development. All rights reserved.

changes observed. References to the insights we obtained are mentioned throughout the report where relevant.

The 2001 ASTD State of the Industry Report also serves as the primary source of publicly available statistics from the ASTD Benchmarking Forum. Created in 1991, the Forum provides a venue for world-class organizations to benchmark and share information on their training, learning, and performance improvement processes, practices, and services.

Summary of Key Findings

The following are some of the key findings from *The 2001 ASTD State of the Industry Report*:

Spending on Employer-Provided Training Falls. The key finding was a small overall decrease—the first since 1996—in employer-provided training, as measured by the amount spent on training. Among the figures were the following:

- Total training expenditures decreased from 2.0 percent of payroll in 1998 to 1.8 percent in 1999.
- Projections for 2000 indicate that the decline may be temporary. Asked about anticipated increases in expenditures between 1999 and 2000, Benchmarking Service participants projected a 28 percent jump on average, a larger increase than predicted any year in the past.

Nevertheless, the growth rate in spending on training has been slowing for several years. Between 1996 and 1997, for example, firms went from spending about 1.5 percent of payroll on training to spending just over 1.8 percent—a 20 percent increase. By 1997-1998, the increase in spending as a percentage of payroll was only 11 percent.

In addition, last year we reported that the 14 percent projected increase in total training expenditures for 1998-1999 was significantly lower than the actual and projected rates of change reported the previous year. With hindsight, it is clear that last year's lower projections hinted that spending might decrease in 1999.

Growth in Payments to Outside Firms Is Down. Last year, firms projected a lower rate of growth in payments to outside training firms for the 1998–1999 period (9 percent compared to 13 percent a year earlier). This year's findings provide strong evidence that firms are increasingly interested in bringing more of the training function "in house." For example, *The 2001 ASTD State of the Industry Report* shows that firms are spending a decreasing percentage of payroll on payments to outside training companies (19.9 percent in 1999 versus 24.4 percent in 1998) and an increasing percentage of their training expenditures on wages and salaries for training staff (50.0 percent in 1999 versus 45.6 percent in 1998).

HOW MUCH TRAINING DO ORGANIZATIONS PROVIDE?

Use of Learning Technologies Shows No Growth. Last year's survey showed that the average firm in ASTD's Benchmarking Service delivered 78.4 percent of its training in the classroom and 8.5 percent via learning technologies. In this year's survey, these figures changed very little, with the percentage of training delivered via classroom edging up to 79.9 percent and technology-delivered training holding steady at 8.4 percent.

The percentage of training delivered via technology in 1999 remains below the high-water mark of 9.1 percent reported in 1997. This leveling off in the growth of technology as a training tool suggests that organizations are finding the obstacles to implementing technology-based training difficult to overcome. We find this to be especially true among small to mid-size organizations.

Identifying Training Investment Leaders

Many of the major trends identified for the larger group of Benchmarking Service participants also were reflected in data provided by a select group of participants that ASTD identified as Training Investment Leaders. These were organizations that provided data to ASTD indicating they had made a dedicated commitment in 1999 to developing the knowledge, skills, and abilities of their employees.

To identify the Training Investment Leaders, ASTD ranked all U.S. firms in the Benchmarking Service and the Benchmarking Forum (with sufficient data) in the following four categories of training measures:

- Investment—a combination of two measures, weighted equally: 1999 training expenditures as a percentage of payroll and 1999 training expenditures per employee eligible for training (Maximum: 25 points)
- Time—total training hours per employee eligible for training in 1999 (Maximum: 25 points)
- Reach—percentage of employees eligible for training who received training in 1999 (Maximum: 25 points)
- Sophistication—percentage of training time in 1999 delivered using learning technologies (Maximum: 25 points).

The 10 percent of organizations with the highest combined scores across the four categories (out of a total maximum score of 100 points) were identified as Training Investment Leaders. On the basis of the number of firms submitting data in 2000, we identified 37 Training Investment Leaders. Data from this group are used throughout this report as an indication of what it takes for an organization to "separate itself from the pack" and make learning a central focus of an organization's efforts to stay competitive.

Adding It Up: How Much Training Do Organizations Provide?

Overall Expenditures

Of course, the dollar amount that an organization spends on training says nothing about the quality of the training it provides. Nevertheless, an assessment of training expenditures can provide important clues about the relative emphasis on training and employee development across organizations and industries.

The Benchmarking Service

In Table 1, we compare an organization's expenditures on training with the total payroll to obtain a reliable measure of year-to-year changes in expenditures—as well as differences across organizations and industries (not shown). Table 2 shows that for the average Benchmarking Service participant, total training expenditures decreased from 2.0 percent in 1998 to 1.8 percent of payroll in 1999, the same level as reported in 1997.

	Total Training Expenditures ($ Millions)	Wages and Salaries of Full- and Part-Time Training Staff as % of Expenditures	Payments to Outside Companies as % of Expenditures	Tuition Reimbursement as % of Expenditures	% Expenditures on Learning Technologies	Other Expenses as % of Expenditures
Benchmarking Service	1.2	50.0	19.9	12.5	3.5	14.3
Training Investment Leaders	33.0	50.2	17.6	9.3	2.3	20.0
Benchmarking Forum	75.7	36.2	30.4	12.0	4.3	17.0

Table 1. **Training expenditure distributions**

Some of the reasons for this drop in spending were evident from interviews conducted with participants in the 2000 Benchmarking Service. In some cases, the decline was caused by general belt-tightening or cost-cutting combined with an inability to demonstrate the value of firms' investments in training. In other cases, it was caused by cost savings realized from the related trend of relying on less outsourcing, which reportedly was often more expensive. Indeed, the biggest drop across the categories of spending was in the percentage of payments devoted to outside providers, which declined almost 20 percent from 1998 to 1999.

HOW MUCH TRAINING DO ORGANIZATIONS PROVIDE?

	Total Training Expenditures per Training-Eligible Employee ($)	Total Training Expenditures as % of Payroll	Percent of Training-Eligible Employees Trained	Training-Eligible Employees to Trainer Ratio	Percent of Training Time Via Classroom	Percent of Training Time Via Learning Technologies	Payments to Outside Companies as % of Expenditures	Total Training Hours per Training-Eligible Employee
Benchmarking Service								
1999	677	1.8	78.6	370	79.9	8.4	19.9	26.3
1998	770	2.0	75.9	317	78.4	8.5	24.4	29.0
1997	NA	1.8	NA	NA	77.6	9.1	27.1	NA
1996	NA	1.5	NA	NA	83.8	5.8	27.3	NA
1999 (Median)	550	1.3	90.0	200	90.0	5.0	10.2	16.0
1998 (Median)	522	1.4	85.0	199	85.0	5.0	15.8	20.0
Training Investment Leaders								
1999	1,655	3.5	98.4	155	77.0	14.9	17.6	62.5
1998	1,616	3.6	96.9	146	70.3	18.3	25.4	58.0
1999 (Median)	1,225	2.8	100.0	98	80.0	13.0	13.5	53.2
1998 (Median)	1,360	3.4	100.0	86	75.0	15.0	24.6	56.0
Benchmarking Forum								
1999	1,153	2.7	82.0	499	79.1	13.8	30.4	37.0
1998	1,147	2.6	81.2	361	78.7	12.3	25.0	36.0
1997	NA	2.3	NA	NA	66.1	NA	NA	NA
1996	NA	2.4	NA	NA	NA	NA	NA	NA
1999 (Median)	1,005	2.4	95.0	187	80.0	10.0	27.1	28.1
1998 (Median)	1,021	2.4	85.0	174	80.0	10.0	23.2	31.0
Benchmarking Service by Size								
1-499	922	2.4	81.9	147	81.0	8.0	21.1	29.8
500-1,999	592	1.6	79.1	378	80.3	8.2	20.1	26.0
2,000+	497	1.3	73.6	569	78.3	11.1	16.5	22.4
Benchmarking Service by Industry								
AMC	1,123	2.7	78.0	516	81.6	4.3	18.0	39.1
Technology	1,132	2.5	73.6	284	77.8	10.3	24.3	27.3
Nondurables	545	2.0	86.4	230	77.4	9.5	22.5	23.8
Durables	377	1.1	81.7	489	83.5	6.0	24.1	19.0
TPU	612	1.5	87.6	259	71.6	13.8	12.7	29.9
Trade	778	1.6	64.7	522	64.5	6.0	11.1	14.5
FIRE	664	2.2	78.9	175	87.4	6.7	17.4	31.2
Services	711	1.7	69.9	494	81.2	10.9	17.9	23.1
Health Care	424	1.2	92.1	396	77.2	10.3	12.2	21.9
Government	569	1.4	76.2	528	79.8	6.7	27.0	38.7

The Key Ratios

As in last year's *ASTD State of the Industry Report*, we calculated the eight key ratios that offer a quick snapshot of training investments and practices across organizations. These calculations illustrate the level of spending on training; the amount of training provided; the size of the training staff; the pervasiveness of outsourcing; and the amount of traditional, classroom-based training versus technology-delivered training. We created ratios (or percentages) for each of these measures to enable us to produce statistics that are comparable across the wide variety of organizations around the world that participate in the ASTD Benchmarking Service and the ASTD Benchmarking Forum. **NA** = Not Available

Table 2. **The key ratios**

Looking at specific industry sectors, those spending the most on training as a percentage of payroll included agriculture, mining, and construction; technology; and finance, insurance, and real estate. Those spending the least were from the durable manufacturing, health care, and government sectors. Figures on training expenditures per employee yielded nearly identical findings.

Training Investment Leaders

ASTD's Training Investment Leaders significantly outpaced their Benchmarking Service counterparts in spending on training in 1999. (This is true almost by definition.)

On average, the Training Investment Leaders each spent an amazing $33 million to train their employees (in great part because these companies tended to be larger than other participant companies). And, while training accounted for 1.8 percent of payroll for the average Benchmarking Service participant, for Training Investment Leaders the figure was a remarkable 3.5 percent, as shown in Table 2. Training Investment Leaders spent an average of $1,655 on training per eligible employee, compared with $677 for the average Benchmarking Service organization.

The Benchmarking Forum

Members of ASTD's Benchmarking Forum, true to their billing as organizations dedicated to enhancing their training efforts, spent significant sums on training in 1999. The average Benchmarking Forum organization reported total training expenditures of $75.7 million in 1999, up sharply from $46.2 million in 1998 and more than 40 times the industry average.

For Benchmarking Forum members, training expenditures were 2.7 percent of payroll, above the average for Benchmarking Service participants (1.8 percent) and above the average for the Service's large organizations of 2,000 or more employees (1.3 percent). Still, the Benchmarking Forum average on this score fell well short of the average for the Training Investment Leaders (3.5 percent).

The average Benchmarking Forum member spent $1,153 per eligible employee on training in 1999, versus $677 for the average Benchmarking Service participant and $1,655 for the average Training Investment Leader.

Spending Projections and Trends

The four straight years of comparable data gathered by ASTD's Benchmarking Service offer important information on year-to-year changes in training expenditures and other areas. A review of these changes—both in overall expenditures and in expenditures devoted to specific categories of training—can help spotlight industry trends that merit attention.

Asked about anticipated increases in training expenditures between 1999 and 2000, Benchmarking Service participants projected a 28 percent jump on average (see Figure 1). Across industries, the organizations projecting the largest increases in total training expenditures between 1999 and 2000 were in the government and trade sectors (37.5 and 35.3 percent, respectively).

This reflects a change from last year, when the technology sector led with projections of an average increase of 30 percent.

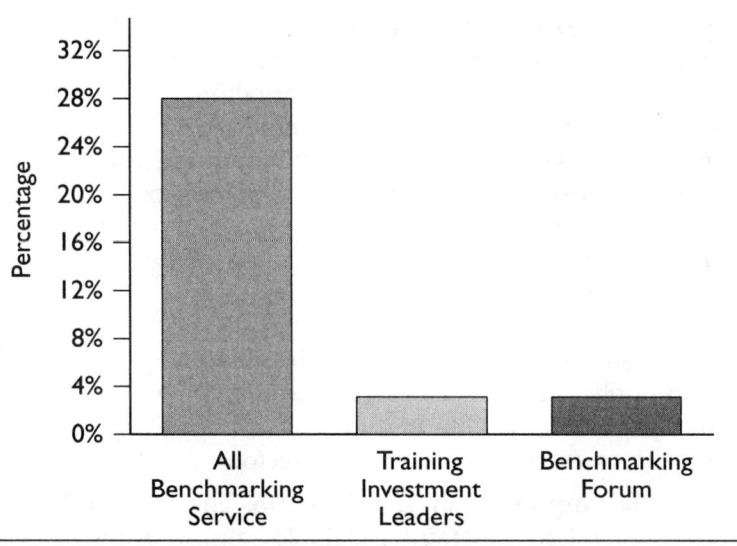

Figure 1. **Average estimated change in total expenditures, 1999-2000**

Combined with the finding that the average Benchmarking Service organization went from spending 2.0 percent of payroll on training in 1998 to 1.8 percent in 1999, the 28 percent projected gain in total training expenditures for 1999–2000 suggests that 2000 figures may show a healthy rebound from 1999. However, we note that in previous years, the actual changes in expenditures have typically fallen 50 percent or more short of projections. Our conversations with participants in the Benchmarking Service suggest that spending may have increased in 2000, but it is not significantly higher than spending in 1999.

Perhaps not coincidentally, Training Investment Leaders continued to project only modest increases in total training expenditures for the 1999–2000 period (3.2 percent). In fact, this figure is down from the 4.6 percent projection reported last year. Likewise, the companies in the Benchmarking Forum projected only a 3.0 percent increase between 1999 and 2000. A comparison of the gains projected by Benchmarking Service participants, the Benchmarking Forum, and the Training Investment Leaders suggests that, while the typical firm may spend more on training in 2000, firms investing the most in training are not likely to show a similar increase, if any.

Other Measures

Among the other key ratios ASTD uses to track the extent of employer-provided training among Benchmarking Service participants are the percentage of eligible employees who receive training, the ratio of training-eligible employees to trainers, and the hours of training per training-eligible employee (see Table 2).

Percentage of Eligible Employees Trained. In 1999, the average Benchmarking Service organization provided training for 79 percent of eligible employees, up from 75.9 percent the year before. Thus, despite cutbacks in training expenditures, the percentage of employees receiving training continued to grow. The average Benchmarking Forum organization did slightly better on this score, providing training to 82.0 percent of eligible employees.

By comparison, the Training Investment Leaders provided training for 98.4 percent of eligible employees on average, up 1.5 percent from the previous year. Translation: At these leading firms, very few employees are not being trained.

Across industry sectors, firms in the health care sector and the transportation and public utilities sector outpaced their peers in the percentage of eligible employees who received training in 1999. Bringing up the rear in this category were the services and technology sectors.

Training-Eligible Employees to Trainer Ratio. The average Benchmarking Service organization had 370 training-eligible employees for every trainer in 1999, an increase from 317 in 1998. Among Training Investment Leaders, the number of eligible employees per trainer (155) was more than 200 employees fewer than the total for the larger group. By comparison, the average ratio for Benchmarking Forum members was 499 to 1, lower than the 569 to 1 average of the largest Benchmarking Service organizations.

The industry sectors reporting the smallest number of training-eligible employees per trainer, on average, were finance, insurance, and real estate (175:1); nondurable manufacturing (230:1); and transportation and public utilities (259:1). Those reporting the largest ratios were government (528:1) and trade (522:1).

Hours of Training per Eligible Employee. On average, Benchmarking Service organizations provided 26.3 hours of training per eligible employee in 1999. The comparable figure for Training Investment Leaders was 62.5 hours. Benchmarking Forum members provided 37.0 hours of training, on average, per eligible employee. The Benchmarking Service number was down from an average of 29.0 hours in 1998. Our conversations with Benchmarking Service participants suggested that some of the observed reduction in training time could be attributed to a shift toward less time-intensive, more outcome-oriented training and quicker delivery methods.

The industry sectors providing the most hours of training per eligible employee, on average, were agriculture, mining, and construction (39 hours); government (39 hours); and finance, insurance, and real estate (31 hours). Those providing the least were durables manufacturing (19 hours) and trade (14 hours).

Mark E. Van Buren is Director of Research for the American Society for Training and Development (mvanburen@astd.org).

State of the Industry Report: How Do Organizations Deliver Training?

Mark E. Van Buren

This is the second excerpt of two from The 2001 ASTD State of the Industry Report, *this one providing an explanation and statistics on how organizations deliver training. You'll learn about the amount of outsourcing organizations use, what types of skills organizations are emphasizing in training, delivery methods, types of learning technologies being used and more. This is an excellent snapshot of training today.*

Delivering Training: Major Expenditure Categories

Figures from the Benchmarking Service show remarkably similar findings between Benchmarking Service participants and the select group of Training Investment Leaders in how much was spent on wages and salaries of training staff versus payments to outside companies in 1999 (see Table 1 in preceding article).

- Benchmarking Service participants reported spending 50.0 percent of training expenditures on wages and salaries; the comparable figure for Training Investment Leaders was 50.2 percent.
- On average, the Training Investment Leaders reported that payments to outside companies represented 17.6 percent of all training expenditures in 1999, compared to 19.9 percent for all Benchmarking Service participants.

The expenditure category showing the most pronounced difference between Training Investment Leaders and all Benchmarking Service participants was the residual category of "Other Expenses." This category includes expenses such as the cost of facilities, course materials, travel expenses for training staff, and other administrative costs. While the larger group reported spending 14.3 percent of expenditures on this category, Training Investment Leaders spent 20 percent of their training dollars on these types

Reprinted with permission from *The 2001 ASTD State of the Industry Report.* Copyright © 2001 by the American Society for Training and Development. All rights reserved.

of expenses. These leading companies appear to support their training investment through overhead costs higher than those of the typical firm.

By comparison, members of ASTD's Benchmarking Forum reported spending 36.2 percent of training expenditures on wages and salaries, 30.4 percent on payments to outside companies, and 17.0 percent on other expenses. Benchmarking Forum participants fell between the other two groups regarding these overhead administrative costs.

Trends in Outsourcing

For the third straight year, we saw evidence of a downward trend in outsourcing for the industry as a whole. Data gathered for the current report show that this trend continued between 1998 and 1999.

This decline in outsourcing has been coupled with an increase in the percentage spent on wages and salaries of training staff. Participants in the Benchmarking Service reported spending 24.4 percent of expenditures on payments to outside companies in 1998; in 1999, participants reported spending 19.9 percent (see Table 1 in preceding article). In contrast, wages and salaries made up 45.6 percent of training expenditures on average in 1998 versus 50.0 percent in 1999.

Unlike in previous years, not only did the share of dollars going to outside companies shrink between 1998 and 1999, but so did the absolute amount of outside spending. The decline was so large that, while total training expenditures dropped by about 12 percent, spending on outside companies dropped by over twice that amount (25 percent). The cutback in outsourcing was especially dramatic at small firms with fewer than 500 employees, going from 31 percent of spending in 1998 to 21.1 percent in 1999 (see Table 2 in preceding article).

By contrast, the level of outsourcing at the largest Benchmarking Service companies, while lower than in smaller firms, remained constant (about 16.5 percent). This, combined with the finding that the level of outside spending among Benchmarking Forum companies actually grew from 25.0 to 30.4 percent over the same period, suggests that especially large companies continued to find value in using outside providers (Table 2, preceding article).

Across industries, organizations in the government, technology, and durable manufacturing sectors devoted a larger share of their training dollars on average to outside contractors than did their peers (Table 2, preceding article).

Other conversations with Benchmarking Service participants shed some light on the reasons most firms are bringing more of the training function "in house." The primary factor appears to be a desire to obtain greater control of the training offered. Companies told us that the training they received from outside vendors tended to not meet their needs or their employees' specific needs. They wanted training that is more individualized, customized, and timely than vendors could provide. Moreover, they often found the training

HOW DO ORGANIZATIONS DELIVER TRAINING?

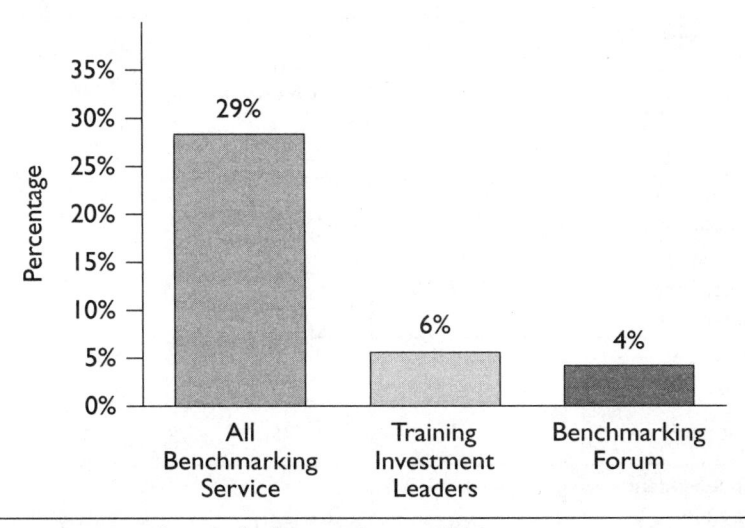

Figure 1. **Average estimated change in outside payments, 1999-2000**

services provided by outside vendors to be more expensive than performing the same tasks in-house would be.

Projections concerning the level of outsourcing in 2000 mirrored those of training expenditures overall (see Figure 1). Benchmarking Service participants forecasted large increases in outsourcing between 1999 and 2000 (29 percent, on average), while Training Investment Leaders and Benchmarking Forum companies predicted much smaller growth levels (6 percent and 4 percent, respectively). Nevertheless, these projections suggest that the trend toward less outsourcing may slow in 2000.

Types of Outsourcing. The pattern of the Training Investment Leaders' answers tend to correspond to that of the larger Benchmarking Service group (see Table 1). Private training and consulting firms ("Other Firms") were used by the vast majority of both groups. Coming in next were independent training consultants or contractors, four-year colleges and universities, and product suppliers.

Among Benchmarking Forum members, the findings were similar, although independent training consultants and contractors were used by slightly more companies than were private training and consulting firms. Coming in next were four-year colleges and universities and product suppliers.

The least commonly used providers of training for all three groups were federal, state, and local government organizations. Nevertheless, even these providers were used for some training by a significant percentage of organizations in each category—at least one in four.

Training Investment Leaders were more likely than their peers in the larger group to use every type of outside provider. The largest difference between

Percent of Organizations Using:	Benchmarking Service	Training Investment Leaders	Benchmarking Forum
4-Year Colleges and Universities	74.7	89.7	85.7
Community and Junior Colleges	64.2	75.9	73.8
Technical and Vocational Institutions	53.7	65.5	64.3
Product Suppliers	69.1	86.2	78.6
Other Firms	84.6	96.6	90.5
Independent Training Consultants or Contractors	80.9	86.2	92.9
Unions, Trade or Professional Associations	35.2	62.1	64.3
Government Organizations	34.0	37.9	23.8

Table 1. **Use of other training providers**

Training Investment Leaders and all Benchmarking Service participants in the use of other training providers concerned unions and trade or professional associations; these were used by 62.1 percent of Training Investment Leaders versus 35.2 percent of Benchmarking Service participants.

Consistent with the data suggesting that organizations spent less overall on outside training in 1999, two types of providers were used less than in the previous year. Among Benchmarking Service companies, the use of community and junior colleges dropped 5 percentage points and the use of product suppliers fell more than 3 percentage points.

Course Type Expenditures. Yet another way to gauge how organizations are dividing their training dollars is to examine the subject matter, or course types, on which they spend the most or least. As shown in Figure 2 (page 24), the largest share of the typical Benchmarking Service firm's training expenditures for 1999 went to training in technical processes and procedures, and in professional skills. These categories claimed 13 percent and 11 percent, respectively, of the average organization's training expenditures for the year.

Coming in next among the course types benefiting from a relatively high level of investment in 1999 were information technology (IT) skills, new

HOW DO ORGANIZATIONS DELIVER TRAINING?

employee orientation, and interpersonal communications skills, all around 9 percent of expenditures. Bringing up the rear were executive development, basic skills, and sales and dealer training. These statistics also indicate that, for the first time, spending on professional skills training has surpassed spending on both IT skills and managerial/supervisory skills training.

Interestingly, the pattern of spending for the Benchmarking Service participants is very similar to spending among the more select group of Training Investment Leaders. The major differences are that Training Investment Leaders report significantly higher spending on a percentage basis on new employee orientation and lower spending on interpersonal communication skills. Training in technical processes and procedures dropped from 23 percent of total training expenditures in 1998 to 13 percent in 1999.

Such changes are likely due to differences in the companies making up the group of Training Investment Leaders. This year's group is overrepresented by technology companies and transportation and public utility firms. Among all firms, the ones that spent a larger share than their peers on training in technical processes and procedures were more likely to be in the nondurables manufacturing, technology, and transportation and public utilities industries and were less likely to come from the health care sector.

Spending on IT Training

Given the increasing use of computers in the workplace and the well-publicized shortage of IT workers in the United States, we were especially surprised by the 3.8 percentage point drop in the share of dollars going to IT skills training between 1998 and 1999 (from 12.6 to 8.8 percent). The industry sector spending the most on IT training, on a percentage basis, was trade (20.4 percent of total spending). The sector spending the least was the government sector (5.4 percent).

Benchmarking Service participants were asked how they divided their spending on IT skills training among specific employee groups (see Figure 3). Predictably, we found that the group getting the most IT training as measured by expenditures were IT staff themselves (28 percent). Next were administrative employees and production employees (12 percent each). Executives and senior managers received the smallest portion of the IT training dollar for the second year in a row.

Results for the Training Investment Leaders were somewhat different, with non-IT professionals and customer service employees each receiving about 16 percent of the IT training dollars. By contrast, administrative employees in these firms received only a 9 percent share. The Benchmarking Forum members appeared to be a hybrid of the two other groups: After IT professionals, non-IT professionals and administrative employees received the largest portions (30, 17, and 13 percent, respectively).

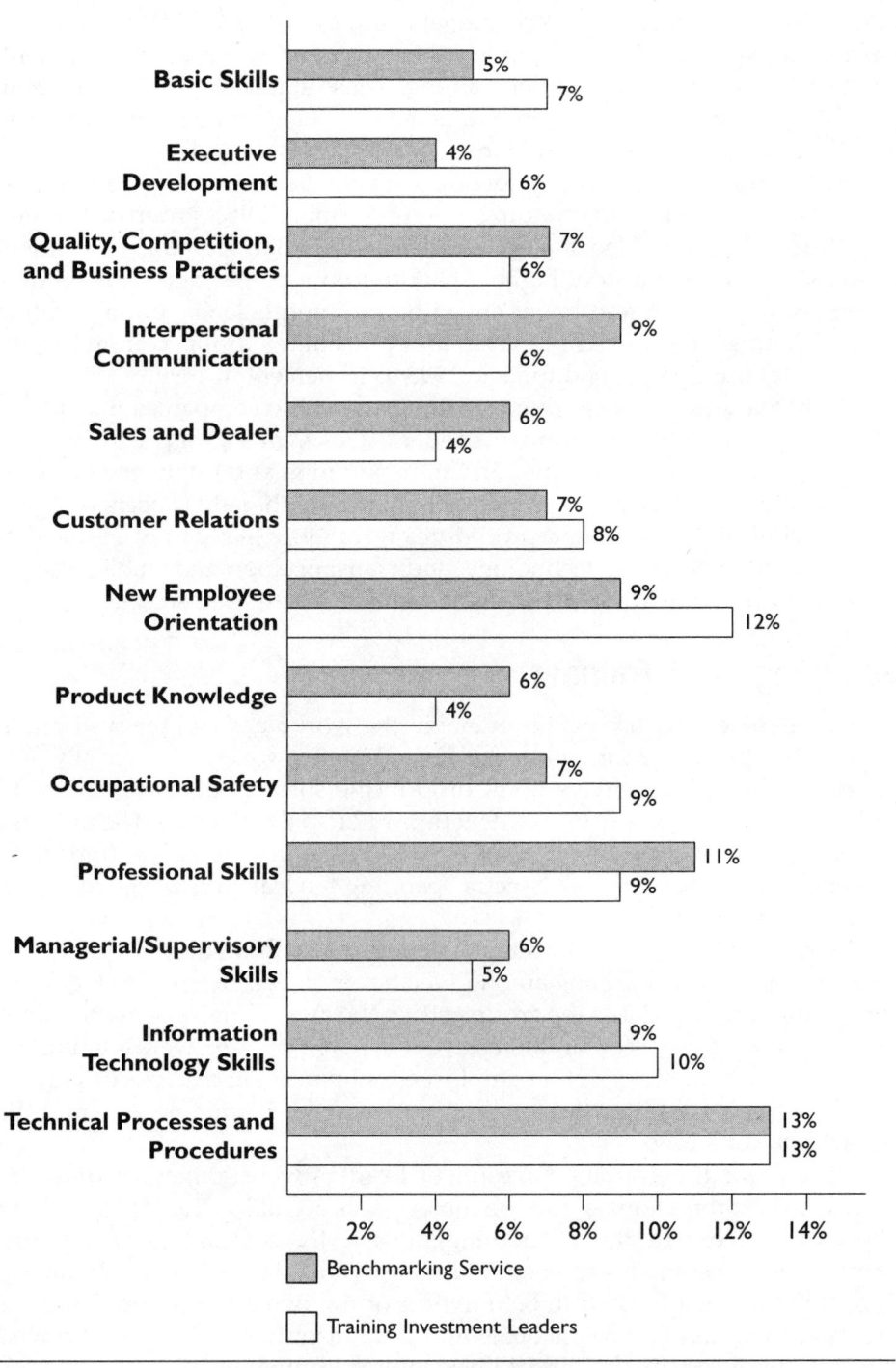

Course Type	Benchmarking Service	Training Investment Leaders
Basic Skills	5%	7%
Executive Development	4%	6%
Quality, Competition, and Business Practices	7%	6%
Interpersonal Communication	9%	6%
Sales and Dealer	6%	4%
Customer Relations	7%	8%
New Employee Orientation	9%	12%
Product Knowledge	6%	4%
Occupational Safety	7%	9%
Professional Skills	11%	9%
Managerial/Supervisory Skills	6%	5%
Information Technology Skills	9%	10%
Technical Processes and Procedures	13%	13%

Figure 2. **Course types as a percentage of training expenditures**

How do organizations deliver training?

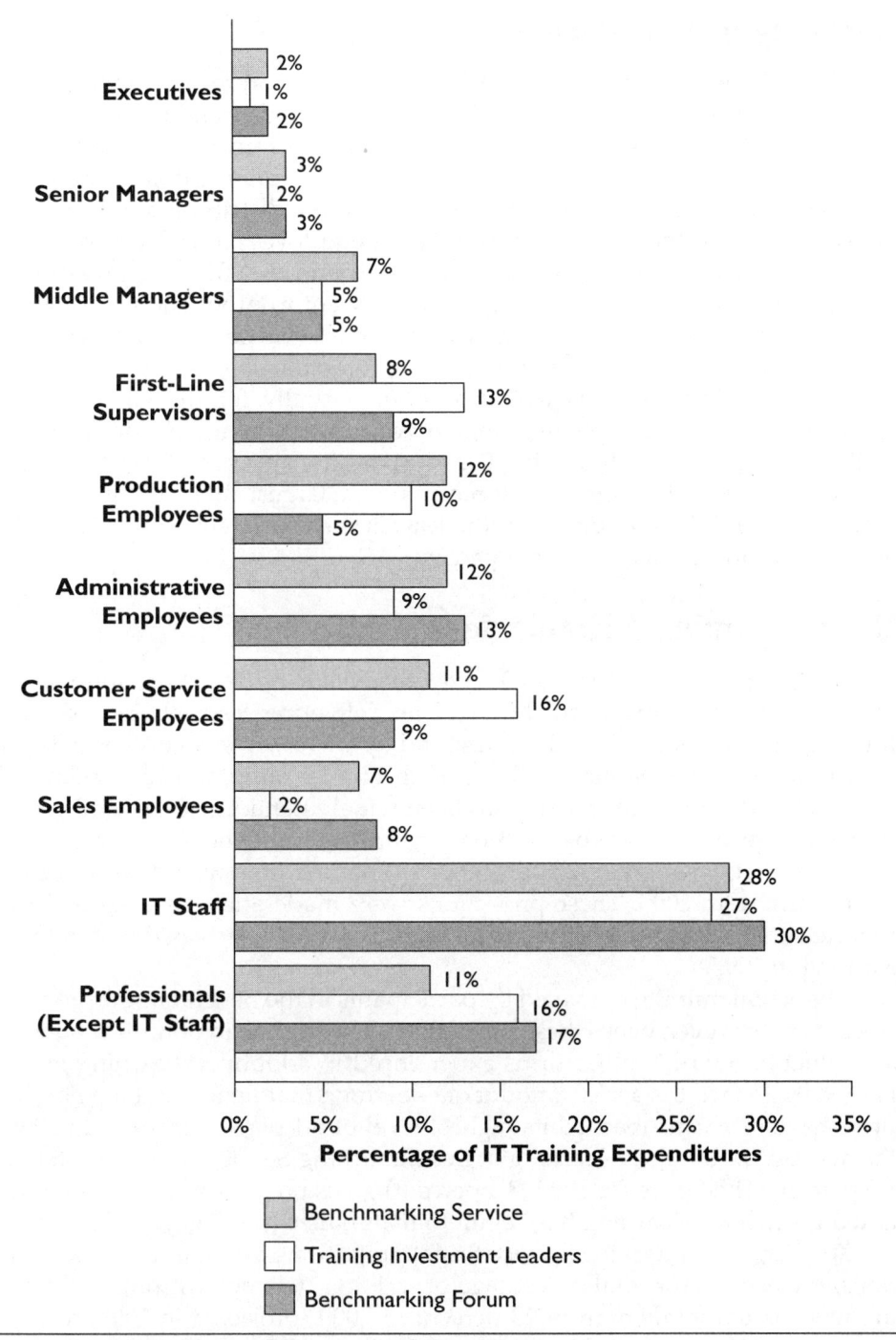

Employee Group	Benchmarking Service	Training Investment Leaders	Benchmarking Forum
Executives	2%	1%	2%
Senior Managers	3%	2%	3%
Middle Managers	7%	5%	5%
First-Line Supervisors	8%	13%	9%
Production Employees	12%	10%	5%
Administrative Employees	12%	9%	13%
Customer Service Employees	11%	16%	9%
Sales Employees	7%	2%	8%
IT Staff	28%	27%	30%
Professionals (Except IT Staff)	11%	16%	17%

Figure 3. **Spending on IT training by employee group**

Spending by Employee Group

In 2000, Benchmarking Service and Benchmarking Forum participants were asked for the first time how they divided their total spending on training among specific employee groups (see Figure 4). This information sheds more light on why certain types of courses received more training dollars than others. It must be read carefully, however, because the distribution of spending is likely to mirror the distribution of types of employees in U.S. companies.

Among Benchmarking Service companies and the Training Investment Leaders, the largest share of training dollars went to production employees (18 and 21 percent, respectively), followed by customer service employees (15 and 18 percent, respectively) and non-IT professionals (14 and 18 percent, respectively). These figures would account partially for the high level of spending on technical processes and procedures training and professional skills training. The Benchmarking Forum spending appears more evenly distributed, with non-IT professionals receiving the largest share of training dollars (17 percent). Not surprisingly, the least is spent on training executives in all three groups (between 2 and 3 percent).

Use of Learning Technologies

For several years now, *The ASTD State of the Industry Report* has found that organizations have projected they will be delivering less and less of their training in the classroom with corresponding increases in technology-delivered training or "e-learning." The growth of e-learning and the decline of instructor-led classroom training has been widely heralded for several years. Indeed, projections made by 1998 participants in the Benchmarking Service predicted that, on average, 23 percent of all training time would be delivered via e-learning in 2000. These projections were made after these same firms reported that an average of 9.1 percent of training time was devoted to e-learning in 1997.

The actual training delivered by participants in the Benchmarking Service since then, however, belies these projections. The decline in optimism may be a product of the difficulties firms experienced in adopting e-learning in the late 1990s. In fact, the actual amount of e-learning that Benchmarking Service firms have provided reached its highest level of 9.1 percent in 1997. In 1998, the average amount of e-learning at Benchmarking Service companies fell to 8.5 percent. The figure for 1999 (8.4 percent) gives no indication that the projected growth in e-learning has begun to materialize (see Figure 5).

Further, Benchmarking Service firms' projections provide similar indications. Projections for total percentage of training delivered through e-learning have actually fallen, from 23 percent in 2000 (projected in 1998) to 19.8 percent for 2001 (projected in 1999) and finally to 18.2 percent for 2002 (projected in 2000). These figures suggest that, while firms still remain hopeful

HOW DO ORGANIZATIONS DELIVER TRAINING?

Employee Group	Benchmarking Service	Training Investment Leaders	Benchmarking Forum
Executives	3%	2%	2%
Senior Managers	5%	6%	4%
Middle Managers	10%	6%	8%
First-Line Supervisors	11%	9%	10%
Production Employees	18%	21%	13%
Administrative Employees	8%	7%	14%
Customer Service Employees	15%	18%	10%
Sales Employees	10%	8%	12%
IT Staff	8%	5%	11%
Professionals (Except IT Staff)	14%	18%	17%

Percentage of Total IT Training Expenditures

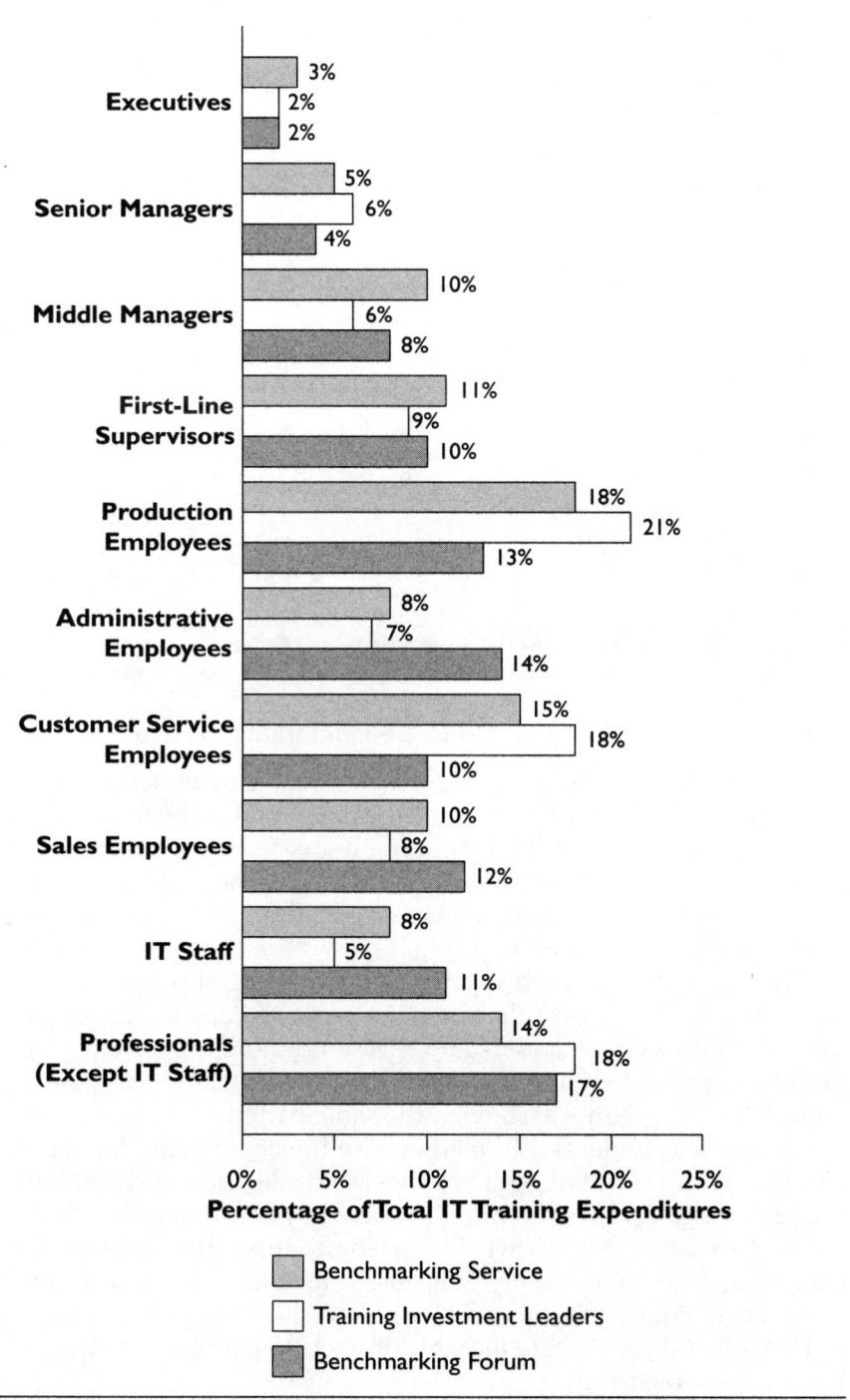

Figure 4. **Percentage of total training expenditures by employee group**

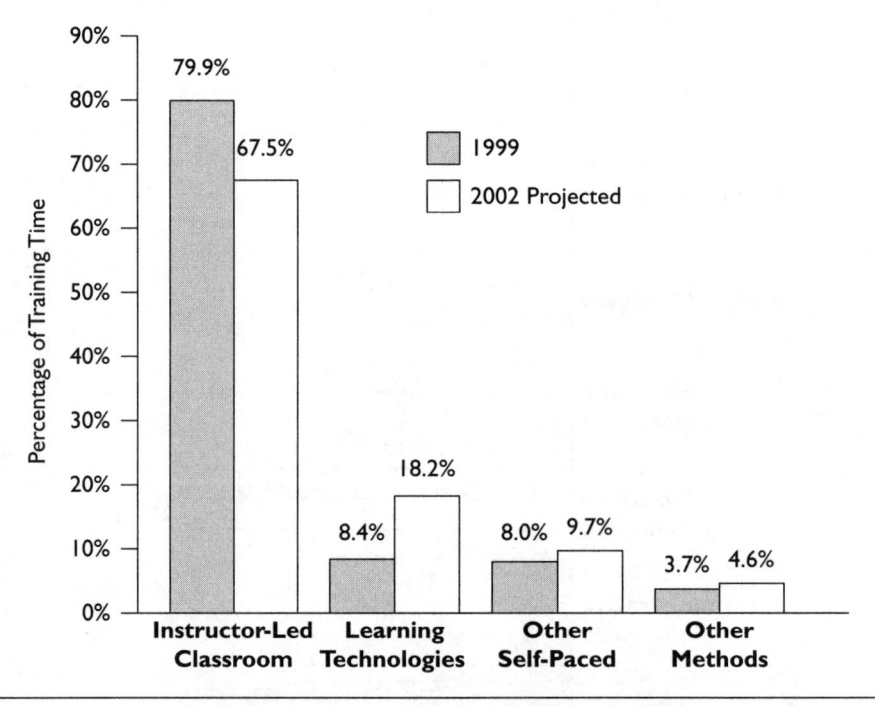

Figure 5. Use of delivery methods, Benchmarking Service

Method	1999	2002 Projected
Instructor-Led Classroom	79.9%	67.5%
Learning Technologies	8.4%	18.2%
Other Self-Paced	8.0%	9.7%
Other Methods	3.7%	4.6%

about the future of e-learning, they have been growing less optimistic.

At the same time, the average firm in ASTD's Benchmarking Service increased the percentage of its training delivered in the classroom from 77.6 percent in 1997 to 79.9 percent in 1999. Likewise, the projection for how much training would take place in the classroom three years from the survey year rose from 61 percent to 67.5 percent.

The continued growth of classroom training supports conjectures we raised in our 2000 report that perhaps organizations are finding e-learning difficult to do well. To understand this trend more fully, we contacted some of the companies that participated in the Benchmarking Service in both 1999 and 2000 whose numbers showed the same pattern.

Several respondents told us they faced declining enrollments in e-learning courses as a result of negative experiences learners had had with e-learning previously. A study recently conducted by ASTD and the MASIE Center, in fact, found that learners who reported negative previous experiences with e-learning were significantly less likely to take future e-learning courses offered to them. This finding emphasizes the importance of getting e-learning right the first time. We fear that this obstacle to e-learning will be particularly difficult to overcome.

Other companies attributed the growth of their classroom training to a rise in training using some form of technology but still occurring in a classroom or learning center setting. Given a choice between e-learning and classroom training, these firms reported these as instances of the latter. This form of training, which is neither clearly e-learning nor clearly classroom training, is one of a number of emerging forms of training that combine more than one form of learning. Such "blended learning," not e-learning, we believe, is the more likely successor to traditional instructor-led classroom training.

Finally, we found evidence that perhaps e-learning is not destined for the history pages but is only taking a breather. Some firms indicated that in 1999, they held the amount of e-learning steady while making significant new investments in e-learning systems and courseware. These firms told us that their e-learning levels had since grown in 2000. However, it is increasingly clear that firms that wish to provide large amounts of e-learning to their employees must first overcome significant up-front development and implementation costs to realize their ambitions.

The e-learning picture for the Training Investment Leaders is much the same (see Figure 6). Although selected partly for their e-learning levels, this year's group of leading firms reported significantly less e-learning in 1999 than did last year's group (14.9 percent and 18.3 percent, respectively). Likewise, their e-learning projections for three years from the survey year fell sharply from 30.0 percent to 24.4 percent.

By contrast, members of the Benchmarking Forum exhibited the opposite trend (see Figure 7). The percentage of training time spent on e-learning grew from 12.3 percent in 1998 to 13.8 percent in 1999, just short of the level of the average Training Investment Leader. In fact, their three-year e-learning projection (27.4 percent) was several percentage points higher than that of the leaders.

The results from the Benchmarking Forum lend support to the notion that, thus far, the growth of e-learning is occurring primarily at large companies. The e-learning figures for Benchmarking Forum companies, most of which are very large, mirror the averages at the largest Benchmarking Service firms (see Table 2, preceding article). The latter reported 11.1 percent e-learning in 1999 and projected 21.6 percent e-learning in 2002. Similarly, classroom training among large organizations was projected to drop to 63 percent of all training by 2002. We suspect that the foremost advantages of the present forms of e-learning accrue mostly to large firms. Because they have many employees, they can reap savings in distribution costs and travel expenses thanks to economies of scale.

When examined by industry (see Table 2, preceding article), ASTD's data show that the sectors reporting the highest levels of e-learning technologies included transportation and public utilities (13.8 percent of training time), services (10.9 percent), and technology (10.3 percent). Bringing up the rear was the agriculture, mining, and construction sector (4.3 percent of training time). The health care sector experienced a notable increase in e-learning from 5.0 percent in 1998 to 10.3 percent the following year.

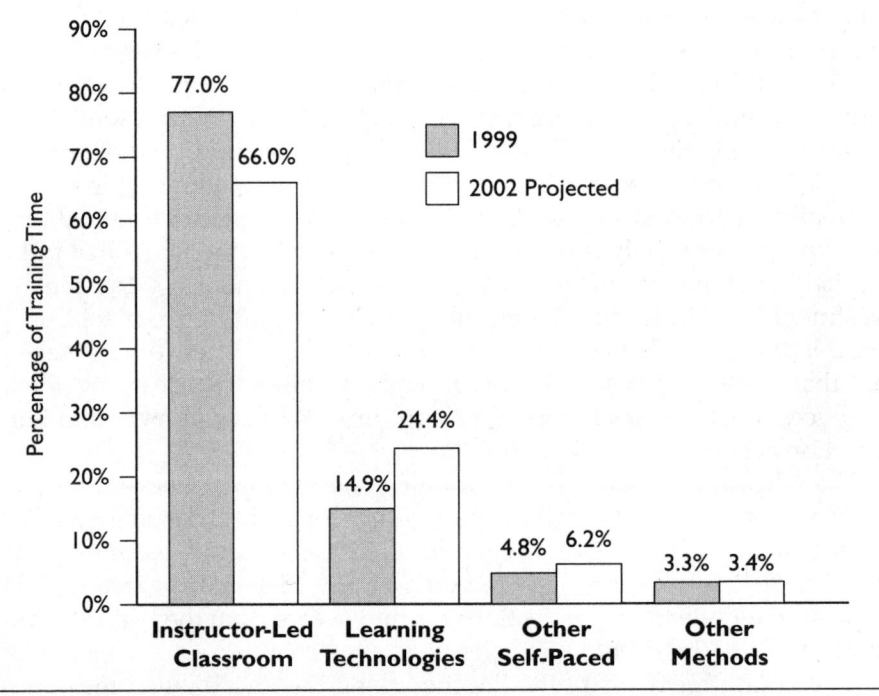

Figure 6. Use of delivery methods, Training Investment Leaders

Method	1999	2002 Projected
Instructor-Led Classroom	77.0%	66.0%
Learning Technologies	14.9%	24.4%
Other Self-Paced	4.8%	6.2%
Other Methods	3.3%	3.4%

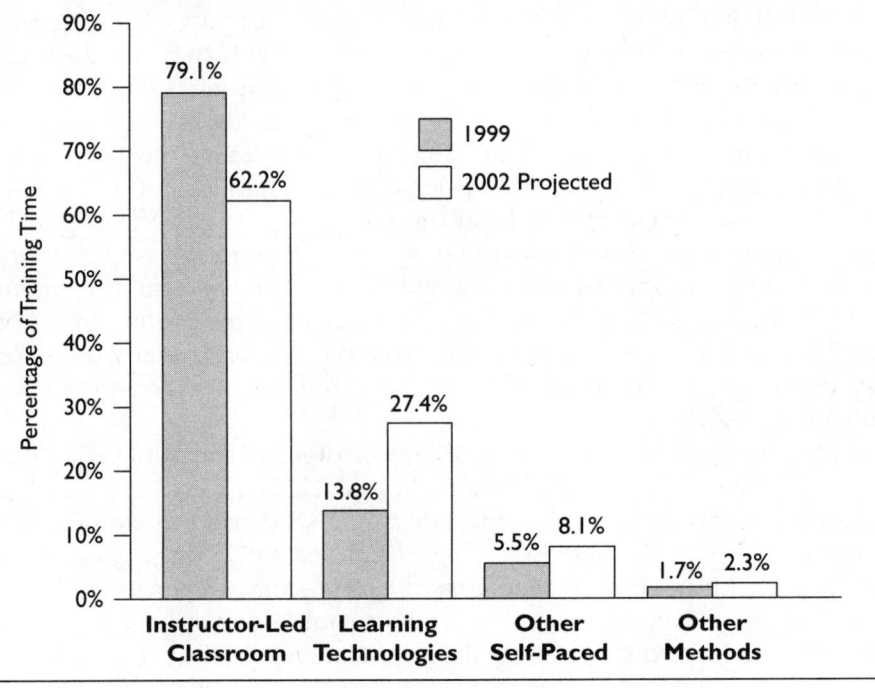

Figure 7. Use of delivery methods, Benchmarking Forum

Method	1999	2002 Projected
Instructor-Led Classroom	79.1%	62.2%
Learning Technologies	13.8%	27.4%
Other Self-Paced	5.5%	8.1%
Other Methods	1.7%	2.3%

Types of Learning Technologies

In addition to measuring the extent to which organizations are using learning technologies, ASTD's Benchmarking Service data reveal what types of technologies are being used (see Table 2). For clarity's sake, we have split learning technologies into two categories. The first includes technologies that relate to the format in which training is *presented*, or "presentation methods," such as computer-based training and multimedia. The second category includes technologies that are used to *distribute* training, or "distribution methods." Examples are cable TV, CD-ROM, and company intranets.

As shown in Table 2, the most popular technology among the presentation methods remained multimedia—used by 64.9 percent of Benchmarking Service organizations in 1999. This was closely followed by text-only computer-based training applications (64.4 percent). Training Investment Leaders also reported these two categories as their top presentation technologies, although the percentage of these organizations using both technologies was markedly higher (80.0 percent each).

Among distribution methods, the most frequently mentioned technology among all Benchmarking Service participants remained CD-ROMs, which were used by 61.5 percent of organizations. Coming in next were e-mail (46.5 percent), local area networks (40.9 percent), and intranets (39.8 percent). The greatest growth in distribution methods between 1998 and 1999 occurred in the percentage of companies using the Internet and intranets for training (increases of 15.5 and 7.5 percentage points, respectively).

The averages for the Training Investment Leaders were notably different from those of the larger group. Although CD-ROMs held the top position

Percentage of Organizations Using:	Benchmarking Service, 1999	Project Benchmarking Service, 2002	Training Investment Leaders, 1999	Projected Training Investment Leaders, 2002	Benchmarking Forum, 1999	Projected Benchmarking Forum, 2002
Top 3 Presentation Methods						
Multimedia	64.9	91.0	80.0	92.0	95.2	100
Computer-Based Training	64.4	79.3	80.0	83.3	83.3	81.0
Teleconferencing	35.9	63.0	44.0	65.2	66.7	81.0
Top 5 Distribution Methods						
CD-ROM	61.5	82.7	84.0	83.3	95.2	95.2
E-Mail	46.5	62.1	32.0	39.1	50.0	52.4
Local Area Network	40.9	62.0	45.8	45.5	57.1	52.4
Intranet	39.8	83.3	60.0	91.7	71.4	100
Internet	38.0	70.5	36.0	63.6	57.1	52.4

Table 2. **Use of learning technologies**

(84.0 percent), intranets were the second most popular distribution method, used by a full 60.0 percent. E-mail, in contrast, ranked seventh in use at 32.0 percent, while simulators were being used by a healthy percentage of companies (43.5 percent). The percentage of Benchmarking Forum companies using these presentation and distribution methods was higher in most categories, with 95.2 percent using CD-ROMs and 71.4 percent using intranets.

Projections for 2002 suggest that the spread of these technologies across organizations is likely to continue. By the end of 2002, significant majorities of all three groups expect to be using multimedia. Anywhere between 23 to 26 percent of courses are projected to have a multimedia component. Among distribution methods, for the first time, more companies in all three groups expect intranets to be the most widely used technology.

Use of Training Practices

Another important indication of how organizations approach the challenge of training their employees is the extent to which they use various training practices, from providing tuition reimbursement to sponsoring mentoring or coaching programs. As we have in previous years, ASTD asked Benchmarking Service participants which training practices they used, and the results were very similar to those reported in last year's *ASTD State of the Industry Report*.

As shown in Figure 8, the training practices most often used were employer-supported conference attendance (used by 97 percent of Benchmarking Service participants) and tuition reimbursement (90 percent). Also used by a significant percentage of the organizations were training resource centers (80 percent) and train-the-trainer courses (75 percent). Ranking at or near the bottom were line-on-loan or rotational training staff (40 percent) and mandatory annual training time (57 percent).

The Benchmarking Forum had higher usage of virtually all of the training practices than both the Training Investment Leaders and the Benchmarking Service, a fact that can be explained in part by the larger average size of the Forum's members. Both groups showed remarkable, double-digit percentage point increases in the use of apprenticeship training between 1998 and 1999.

Use of Evaluation Methods

As part of its effort to assess how organizations respond to the training challenge, ASTD asked participants in the Benchmarking Service to report on their evaluation methods using Kirkpatrick's four levels of evaluation and other forms of evaluation (see Figure 9).

These data reveal that more than three-fourths of the Benchmarking Service organizations (77 percent) were using reaction measures in 1999. In addition, more than a third (38 percent) were using learning evaluations, and

HOW DO ORGANIZATIONS DELIVER TRAINING?

Practice	Benchmarking Service	Training Investment Leaders	Benchmarking Forum
Tuition Reimbursement	90%	97%	100%
Employer-Supported Conference Attendance	97%	94%	100%
Line-on-Loan or Rotational Training Staff	40%	47%	64%
Train-the-Trainer Courses	75%	86%	100%
Training Resource Center	80%	97%	95%
Apprenticeship Training	62%	75%	83%
Mentoring or Coaching Programs	72%	75%	79%
Mandatory Annual Training Time	57%	61%	50%

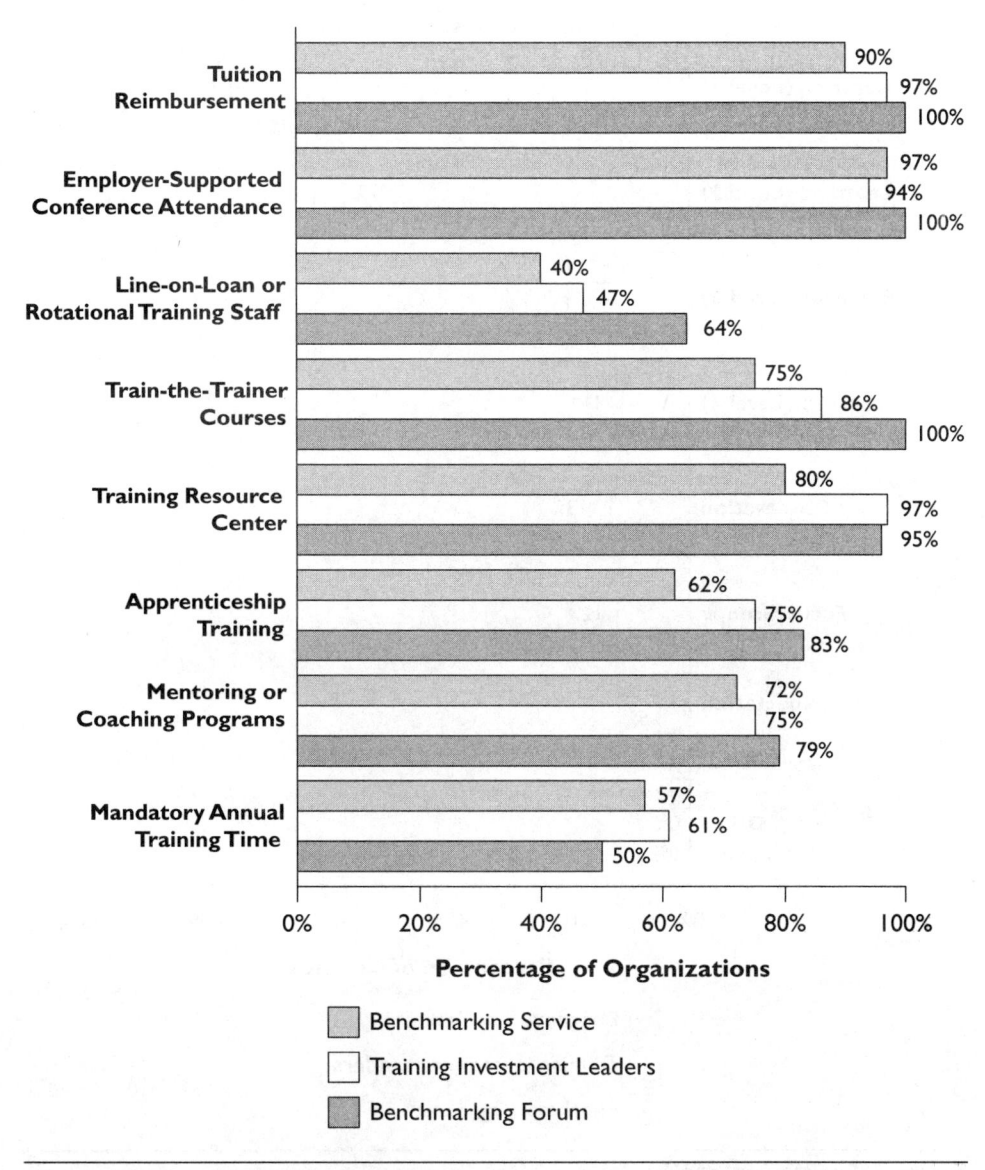

Figure 8. **Use of training practices**

behavior and results were used by a small minority of organizations (14 percent and 7 percent, respectively). Only the use of learning measures was up slightly from last year's findings.

Responses for 1999 from the ASTD Training Investment Leaders were very similar, although this group reported significantly higher use of learning evaluations (47 percent) than did the larger sample. Members of ASTD's Benchmarking Forum were more likely to use reaction measures, although

Evaluation methods

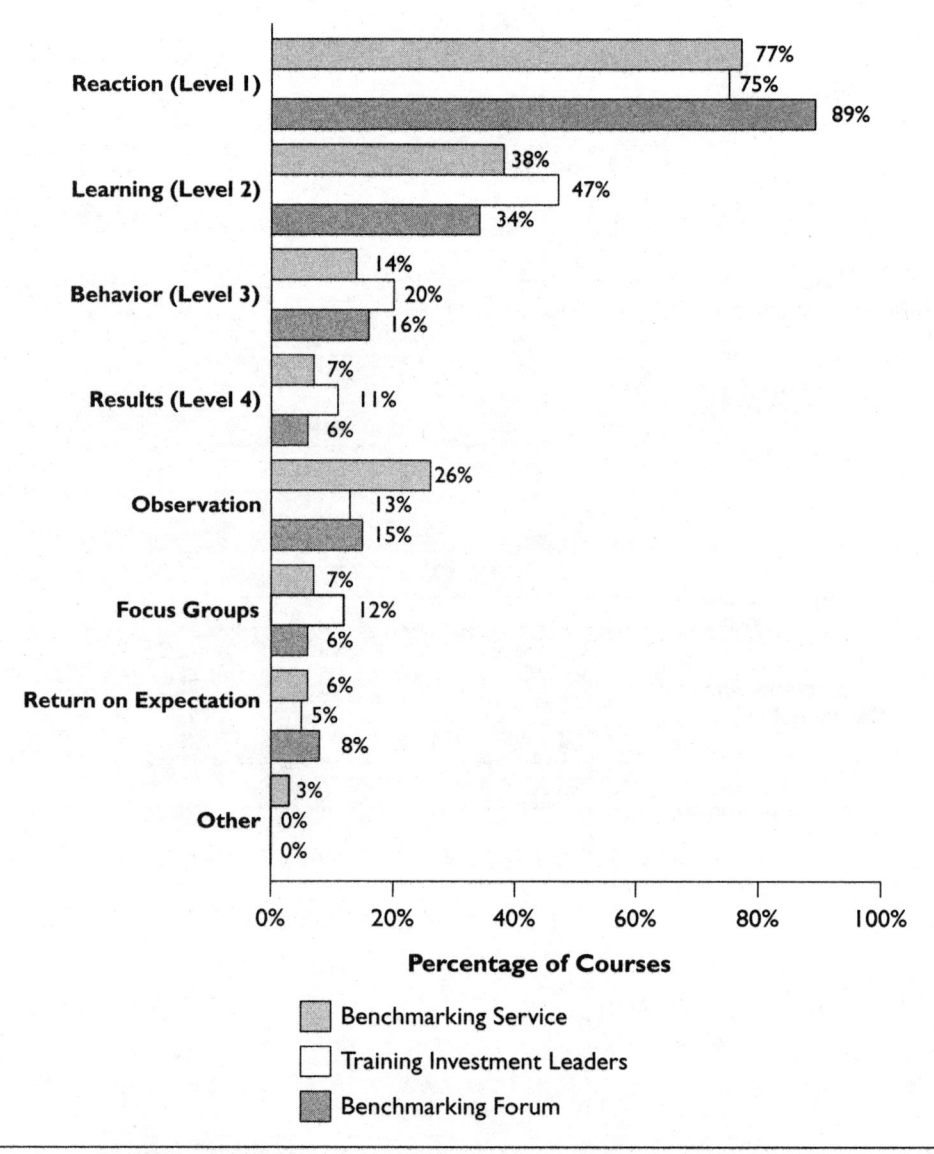

Method	Benchmarking Service	Training Investment Leaders	Benchmarking Forum
Reaction (Level 1)	77%	75%	89%
Learning (Level 2)	38%	47%	34%
Behavior (Level 3)	14%	20%	16%
Results (Level 4)	7%	11%	6%
Observation	26%	13%	15%
Focus Groups	7%	12%	6%
Return on Expectation	6%	5%	8%
Other	3%	0%	0%

Figure 7. **Evaluation methods**

the percentage dropped from 95 percent in 1998 to 89 percent in 1999.

The most commonly used form of evaluation in Benchmarking Service companies was "Observation." Over a quarter of these companies reported using observation, twice the rate of the Training Investment Leaders.

Mark E. Van Buren is Director of Research for the American Society for Training and Development (mvanburen@astd.org).

New Employee Orientation Survey: Summary Report

Jean Barbazette

What are organizations doing to orient their new employees? The Training Clinic has conducted three surveys of new employee orientation. This article sums up the results from the latest survey, with references to results from the 1993 survey. The results can help organizations benchmark their orientation efforts and perhaps inspire new initiatives.

Following are findings in the ongoing research The Training Clinic began in 1985. A few new trends are noted in this year's survey. Fifty organizations responded to the survey and represent an even split of manufacturing (including high tech manufacturing) and the not-for-profit sector (including government organizations, public transportation and utilities). Over half of the respondents have more than 1000 employees, while 45% represent employers of less than 500 employees.

The survey results that follow are compared to a similar survey conducted in 1993.

General Impression of Orientation

The general impression and quality of the new employee orientation (NEO) conducted in these organizations was said to be "excellent" to "good" by 90%. The 1993 survey reported "excellent" to "good" by 75%. All 1999 respondents said NEO is very important/important to both the organization and the new employees. The 1993 respondents said the same. In 1999, 75% reported "strong" to "good" management support for NEO. In 1993, 70% reported "strong" to "good" management support for NEO.

Reprinted with permission from *The Training Clinic*, www.thetrainingclinic.com. Copyright © 1999 by the author. All rights reserved.

Program Details

Number of employees who attend orientation?

Orientation seems to be a personalized process with 40% reporting groups of 1-5 employees attending orientation together. 30% had groups of 6-12 new employees while another 30% had more than 12 employees attend an orientation. Similar information was reported in 1993.

Who conducts orientation?

Human Resources conducts 95% of all orientations, while half of the organizations had the additional participation of operational personnel. Similar information was reported in 1993.

How often is orientation held? How long is orientation and over what period of time is it conducted?

Orientation was held most often on a weekly basis. Over 64% said they conducted orientation on an "as needed" basis. The majority of organizations held orientation in one day or less, while 34% conducted an orientation over 2-5+ days. This supports The Training Clinic's recommended view of orientation as a process, rather than an event. For those who conducted orientation over time, 12% reported a 2-4 week period for orientation, 8% over six months, and 6% over 12 months. Similar information was reported in 1993.

When does orientation start?

64% reported that orientation begins on the first day of employment. The remainder reported orientation being conducted when hired, during the first week, or during the first month. The 1993 survey reported 80% of orientation beginning during the first week and most of that during the first day.

Where is orientation held?

In the 1999 survey, 86% conducted orientation in a classroom setting, while 28% conducted NEO at the job site and the remainder used an off-site location.

Who attends orientation?

When asked which employee groups attend orientation, 100% said full-time professional employees, 98% said full-time hourly, 76% reported attendance by part-time employees, 44% reported temporary employees attend orientation, and 30% reported "transferred" employees attend orientation. One organization reported external vendors are permitted to attend NEO. The increased attendance of part-time and temporary employees at NEO from previous surveys will be interesting to track as an emerging trend.

Who are guest speakers?

78% of respondents use guest speakers to address new employees. These speakers usually addressed benefits and safety personnel most often. 36% used executives (CEO/CFO) as guest speakers. This figure is up from the 1993 survey, which reported executive participation at 30%.

NEW EMPLOYEE ORIENTATION SURVEY: SUMMARY REPORT

What is done prior to the first day of work?

Greater preparation for the arrival of new employees seems more evident than in past surveys. The 1993 survey showed 18% of the organizations making no preparations prior to the first day. In the 1999 survey all organizations did some preparation including, 80% receive a welcome letter while additional internal preparation is completed. Different preparation techniques include:

- 62% prepare the work area and schedule training for the new employee
- 64% have a computer and credit cards ordered
- 42-46% of companies provide relocation kits and order business cards and other supplies.

What types of materials are sent before the first day?

62-68% sent information to the new employee prior to the first day that included reporting directions and confirmation of their position and salary. Only 6% of companies sent no information prior to the first day. The practice of sending information prior to the first day seems to be on the increase from other survey years. In 1993 16% of organizations reported not sending any information to the employee before the first day.

What materials are given during orientation?

In the 1999 survey results, when asked what written materials were provided during orientation, 72-96% of companies provided written materials from human resources about benefits, vacation, retirement, and employee assistance programs. 72% provided organizational history and an employee handbook. 2% reported no materials distributed during orientation. In the 1993 survey results, 69% received an employee handbook and 59% received information about the organization's history. 4% received no written materials in 1993.

Who is responsible for covering specific topics?

When identifying who is responsible for presenting specific parts of orientation, human resources was most often responsible for benefits, induction paperwork, organizational history, policies and procedures, corporate culture, and organizational structure. The new employee's supervisor was most often responsible for relating performance expectations, department function, computer, and skills and/or customer service training, as well as an overview of any quality programs. Shared responsibilities included safety briefings, tours, and information about products/services.

How critical is the supervisor's role in NEO? What support do supervisors provide?

98% said the supervisor's role was very critical to the success of NEO. However, only 28% said supervisory support was "great." 66% said there was "some" support and 14% said there was little support for orientation. Past surveys have noted the importance of supervisory support.

What methods are used during NEO?

The most frequently used methods to transmit NEO information are lecture and a tour. From past surveys, there was an increase in organizations using self-study methods, with 30% encouraging new employees to take the lead in orienting themselves. 40% of organizations report use of the Internet/intranet for orientation.

How is NEO evaluated?

One of the most interesting trends since The Training Clinic has reported NEO survey information is the increase in organizations that measure the results of NEO for bottom line results. 16% review turnover statistics, 6% review accident/safety records, and 6% review increased productivity indicators, with 2% tracking grievance statistics.

Design Considerations

Survey respondents were asked: "If you could redesign your orientation program from scratch without concern for time or cost, what would you do?" They replied ("✔" represents repetition of the idea):

Video, redo video, multimedia approach, redo visuals ✔✔✔✔
More professional looking materials ✔✔✔✔
Use guest speakers, executive participation, experts ✔✔✔✔
Making it more of a process ✔✔✔✔
More interactive ✔✔✔
Allow tour of major facilities ✔✔
Train supervisors, supervisory involvement ✔
Special lunch, provide food ✔
Reduce time, simplify ✔
Use computer-based orientation, use Internet/intranet ✔
Minimum 2-day program before employee is released to work site
More interactive
Organization chart with key executive photos displayed
Spanish translation
Get everyone together at same time
Hire in batches
Goals and objectives
Incorporate skills training during first week
More efficient way to handle paperwork
Evaluate to see if we are improving

When was your program initially designed?
    22% before 1990
    20% between 1991-1995
    41% between 1996-1999

When was your program redesigned?
  12% before 1997
  26% in 1998
  42% in 1999

What resources were used?
  38% internal resources only
  54% combination of internal and external resources

What did it cost to develop your orientation program?
  Only 20% kept track of expenses.
  Of those, 7 organizations spent between $100-$2,000.
  Three organizations spent $10,000 or more.
  In 1993 the average "out-of-pocket" for internally designed programs was $6420.

How many design or development hours did it take to create your program?
  40% kept track of development hours.
  Ten organizations spent 20 hours or less.
  Three organizations took between 21-50 hours and seven organizations took between 50 and 160 development hours.
  Three organizations reported a development process that occurred over one to two years and reported no specific estimate of development hours.
  In 1993, the average number of design hours was 82 for internal personnel. Fewer than 20% kept track of design time.

Jean Barbazette is President of The Training Clinic in Seal Beach, CA, a training consulting firm she founded in 1977 (www.thetrainingclinic.com), and author of Successful New Employee Orientation *(Pfeiffer & Co., 1994; Jossey-Bass, 2001). Contact her at (800) 937-4698 or info@thetrainingclinic.com.*

Industry Report 2000
The People
Who Controls, Benefits From, and Delivers Training

TRAINING Magazine

This piece is an excerpt from TRAINING Magazine's Industry Report 2000. It explores and documents who makes training decisions, who gets the training, whether internal or external trainers are used, which industries outsource and more. These data are especially useful to consultants and trainers as they plan who to market their services to and what types of training are most popular today.

In the age of the Internet, who will decide which training courses employees take? If anyone can browse the Web and access online programs from dozens (or hundreds) of suppliers, won't individual employees gain more control over the courses they choose to take? That's what the conventional wisdom says, but it doesn't appear to be happening yet.

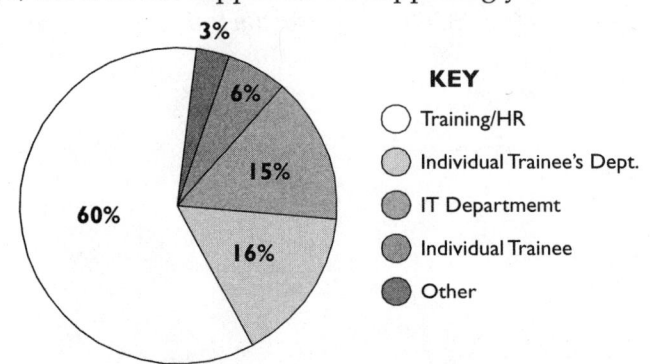

KEY
- Training/HR — 60%
- Individual Trainee's Dept. — 16%
- IT Departmemt — 15%
- Individual Trainee — 6%
- Other — 3%

Respondents were asked to distribute 100 points among four groups to indicate the amount of control over the purchase of training from outside suppliers. The "trainee's department" is the one in which the trainee works.

Figure 1. Who controls the training purchases (overall survey)

Reprinted with permission from *TRANING* Magazine, October 2000. Copyright © 2000 Bill Communications, Minneapolis, MN. All rights reserved.

INDUSTRY REPORT 2000 THE PEOPLE

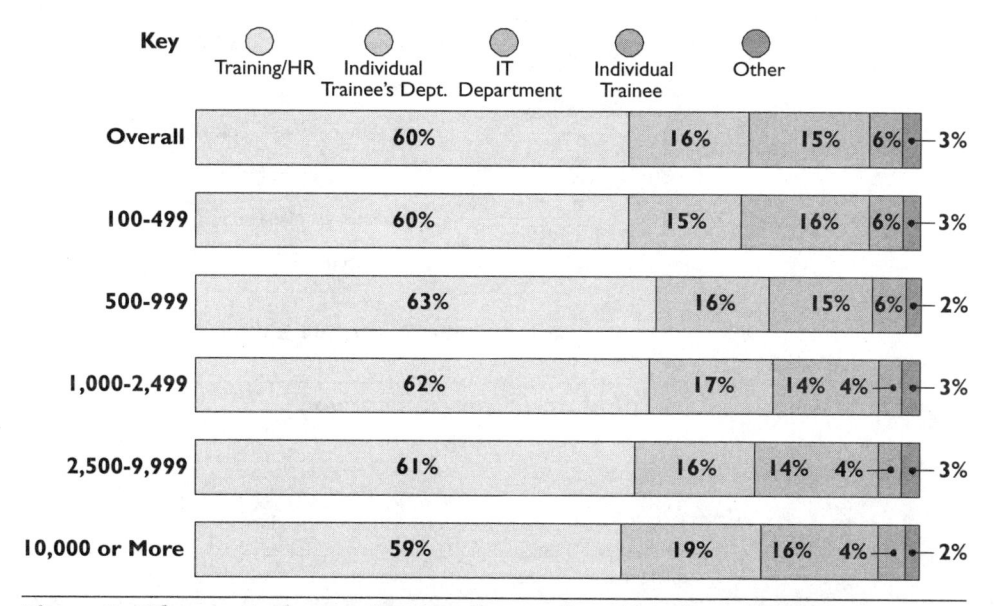

Key: Training/HR | Individual Trainee's Dept. | IT Department | Individual Trainee | Other

Size	Training/HR	Individual Trainee's Dept.	IT Department	Individual Trainee	Other
Overall	60%	16%	15%	6%	3%
100-499	60%	15%	16%	6%	3%
500-999	63%	16%	15%	6%	2%
1,000-2,499	62%	17%	14%	4%	3%
2,500-9,999	61%	16%	14%	4%	3%
10,000 or More	59%	19%	16%	4%	2%

Figure 2. **Who controls training purchases (by size of organization)**

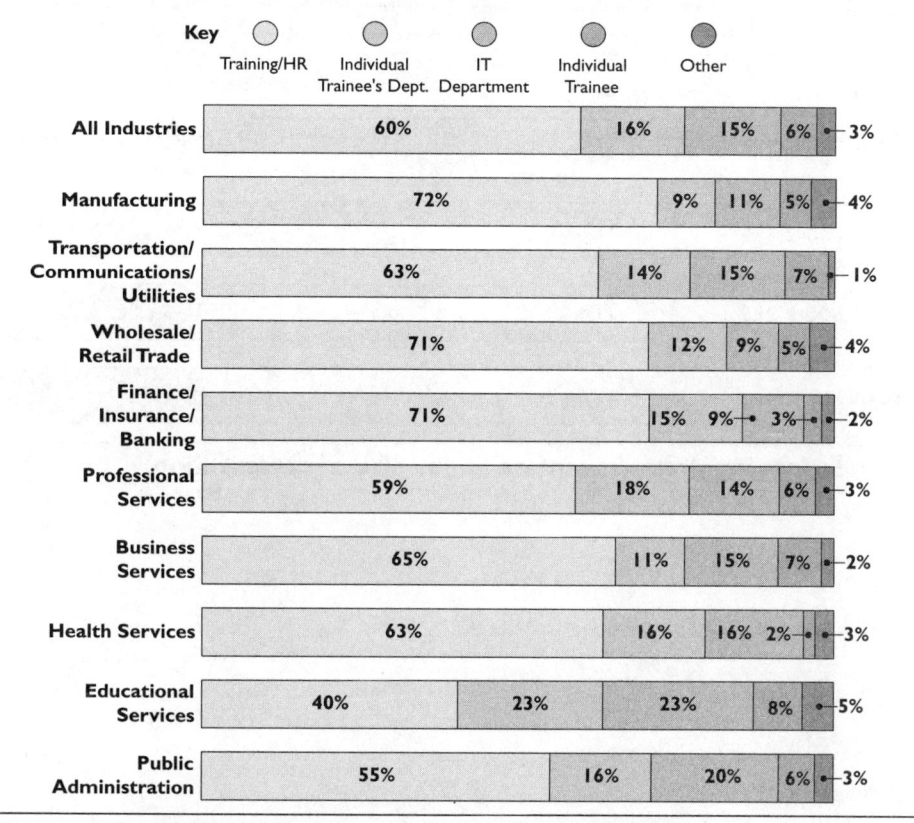

Key: Training/HR | Individual Trainee's Dept. | IT Department | Individual Trainee | Other

Industry	Training/HR	Individual Trainee's Dept.	IT Department	Individual Trainee	Other
All Industries	60%	16%	15%	6%	3%
Manufacturing	72%	9%	11%	5%	4%
Transportation/Communications/Utilities	63%	14%	15%	7%	1%
Wholesale/Retail Trade	71%	12%	9%	5%	4%
Finance/Insurance/Banking	71%	15%	9%	3%	2%
Professional Services	59%	18%	14%	6%	3%
Business Services	65%	11%	15%	7%	2%
Health Services	63%	16%	16%	2%	3%
Educational Services	40%	23%	23%	8%	5%
Public Administration	55%	16%	20%	6%	3%

Figure 3. **Who controls training purchases (by industry)**

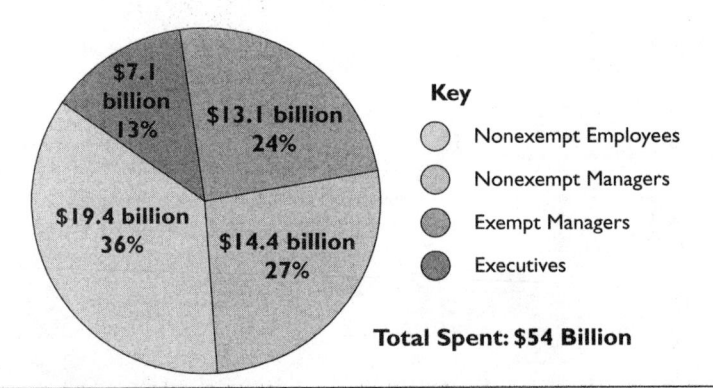

Figure 4. Training dollars spent on ... (overall survey)

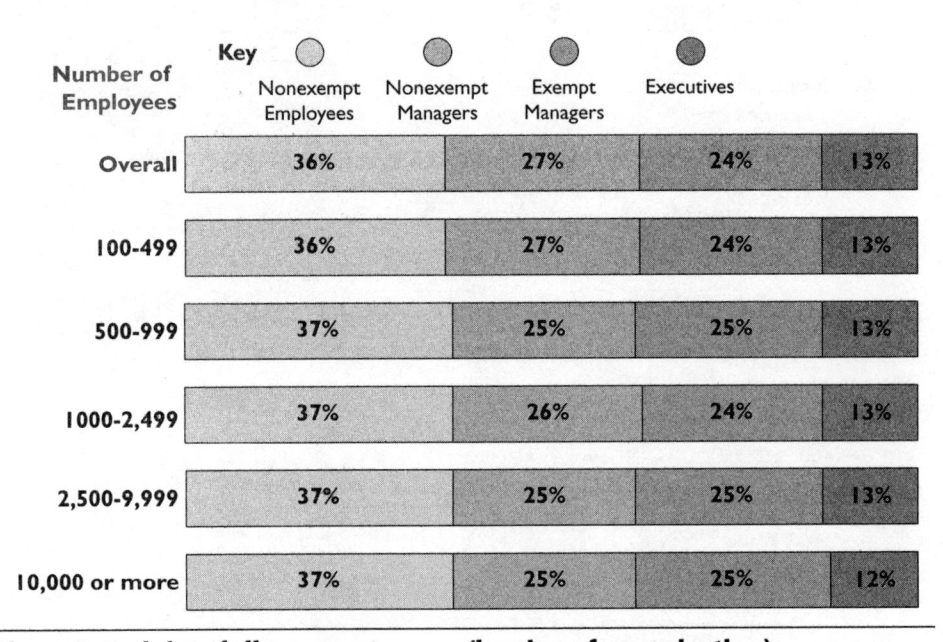

Total Spent: $54 Billion

- Nonexempt Employees: $19.4 billion (36%)
- Nonexempt Managers: $14.4 billion (27%)
- Exempt Managers: $13.1 billion (24%)
- Executives: $7.1 billion (13%)

Figure 5. Training dollars spent on ... (by size of organization)

Number of Employees	Nonexempt Employees	Nonexempt Managers	Exempt Managers	Executives
Overall	36%	27%	24%	13%
100-499	36%	27%	24%	13%
500-999	37%	25%	25%	13%
1000-2,499	37%	26%	24%	13%
2,500-9,999	37%	25%	25%	13%
10,000 or more	37%	25%	25%	12%

INDUSTRY REPORT 2000 THE PEOPLE

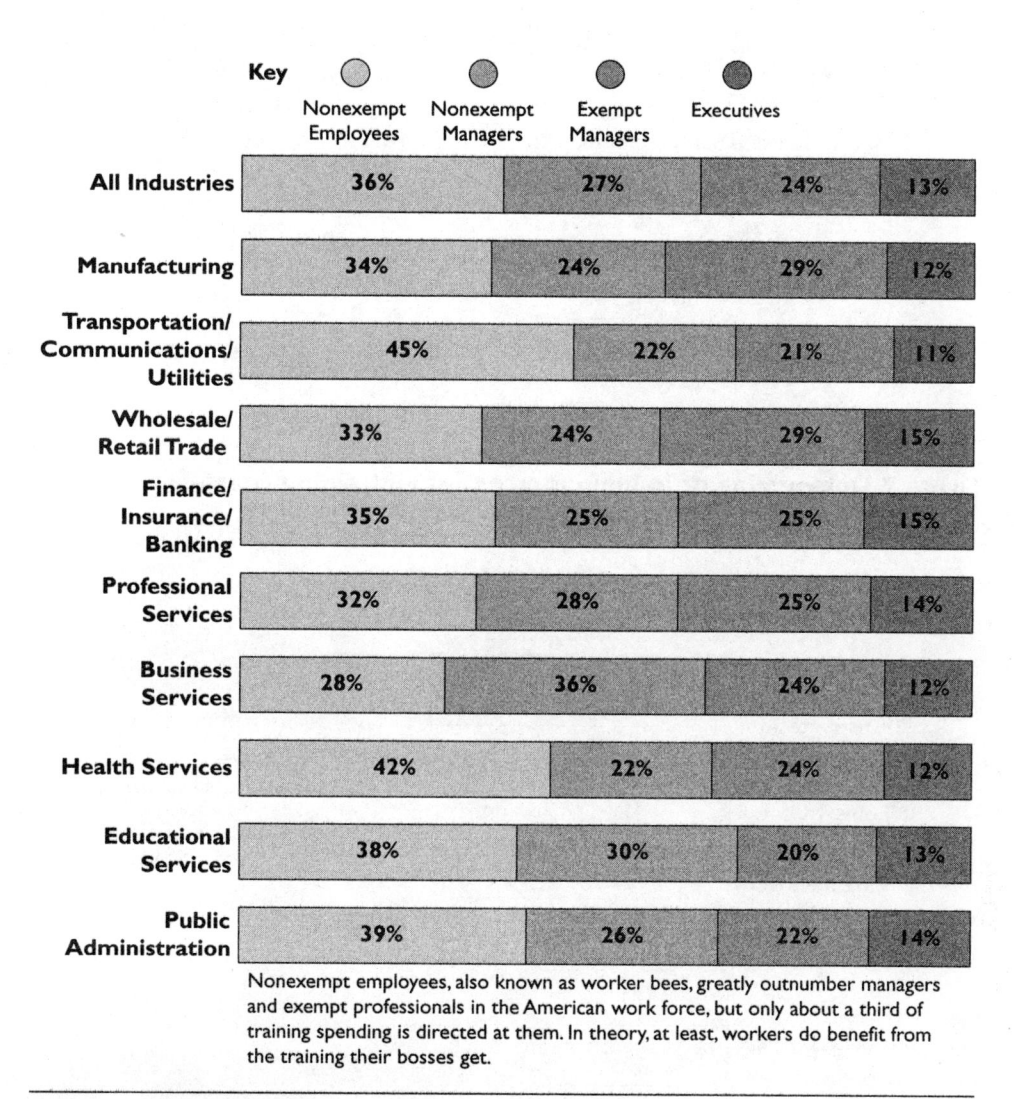

Key	Nonexempt Employees	Nonexempt Managers	Exempt Managers	Executives

Industry	Nonexempt Employees	Nonexempt Managers	Exempt Managers	Executives
All Industries	36%	27%	24%	13%
Manufacturing	34%	24%	29%	12%
Transportation/Communications/Utilities	45%	22%	21%	11%
Wholesale/Retail Trade	33%	24%	29%	15%
Finance/Insurance/Banking	35%	25%	25%	15%
Professional Services	32%	28%	25%	14%
Business Services	28%	36%	24%	12%
Health Services	42%	22%	24%	12%
Educational Services	38%	30%	20%	13%
Public Administration	39%	26%	22%	14%

Nonexempt employees, also known as worker bees, greatly outnumber managers and exempt professionals in the American work force, but only about a third of training spending is directed at them. In theory, at least, workers do benefit from the training their bosses get.

Figure 6. **Training dollars spent on ... (by industry)**

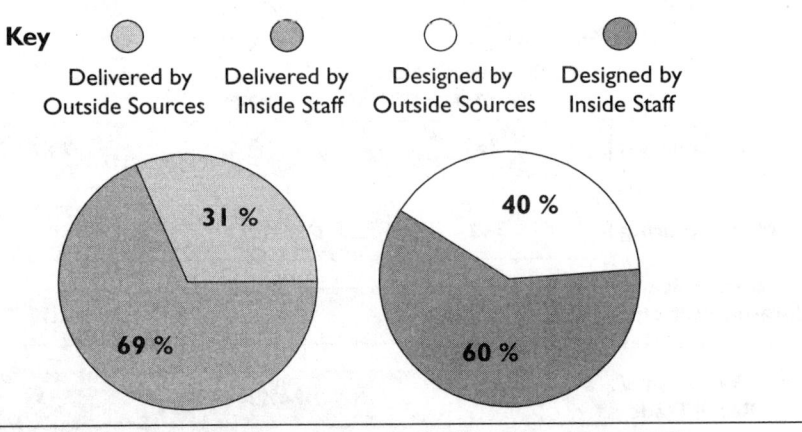

Key
- Delivered by Outside Sources
- Delivered by Inside Staff
- Designed by Outside Sources
- Designed by Inside Staff

Pie chart 1: 31% / 69%
Pie chart 2: 40% / 60%

Figure 7. **Outsourcing of training (percent of all training courses)**

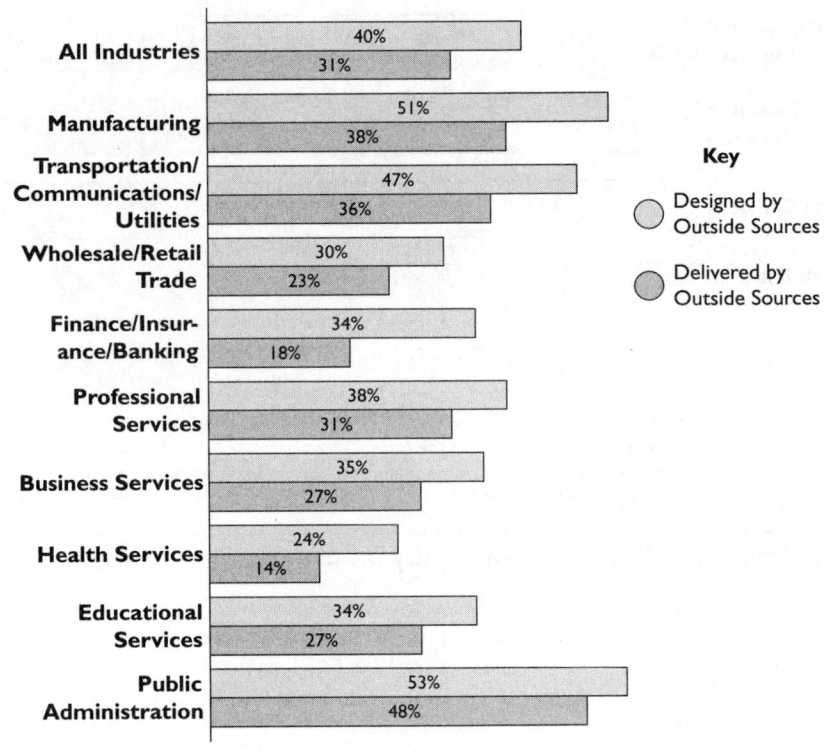

Industry	Designed by Outside Sources	Delivered by Outside Sources
All Industries	40%	31%
Manufacturing	51%	38%
Transportation/Communications/Utilities	47%	36%
Wholesale/Retail Trade	30%	23%
Finance/Insurance/Banking	34%	18%
Professional Services	38%	31%
Business Services	35%	27%
Health Services	24%	14%
Educational Services	34%	27%
Public Administration	53%	48%

Key
- Designed by Outside Sources
- Delivered by Outside Sources

About 40% of all training that employees receive is designed by outside sources, respondents estimate. The formats include public seminars, off-the-shelf and customized classroom programs, computer courseware, videos, manuals, and more.

Since in-house trainers, managers, and other staff often teach or facilitate courses developed by outside providers, the figure for delivery by outsiders is lower, at 31%.

Figure 8. **Outsourcing of training (by industry)**

INDUSTRY REPORT 2000 THE PEOPLE

Key — Outside Sources / Inside Staff

Percent of all training courses... Designed by

Size	Outside Sources	Inside Staff
100-499 Employees	41%	59%
500-999 Employees	41%	59%
1,000-2,499 Employees	36%	64%
2,500-9,999 Employees	37%	63%
10,000 or more Employees	37%	63%

Percent of all training courses... Delivered by

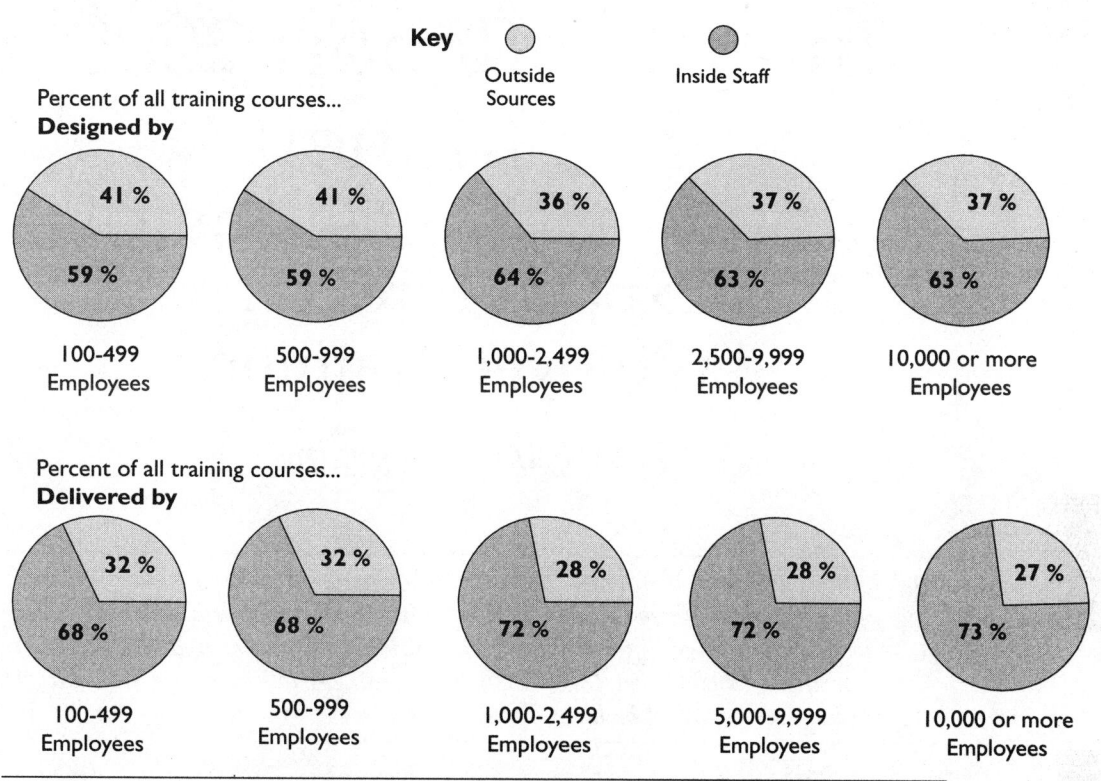

Size	Outside Sources	Inside Staff
100-499 Employees	32%	68%
500-999 Employees	32%	68%
1,000-2,499 Employees	28%	72%
5,000-9,999 Employees	28%	72%
10,000 or more Employees	27%	73%

Figure 9. **Outsourcing of training (by size)**

Industry Report 2000
The Money
U.S. Organizations' Annual Expenditures on Employee Training

TRAINING Magazine

The charts here are also from TRAINING Magazine's Industry Report 2000. It reviews the types of training in which organizations for different industries invested, as well as budgets of different size organizations, and more. Again this piece is useful for those who market their services as trainers to determine the markets where their services might be most favorably received.

U.S. employers will spend $54 billion on formal training during 2000 in the categories shown in Figure 1. Most of the money pays the salaries of in-house training specialists, but more than $19 billion will flow into the outside market for materials, courses, and services. Beneficiaries include everyone from book publishers, video producers, and computer-courseware suppliers to consultants, community colleges, and the sponsors of public seminars and conferences.

Definitions

Training Staff Salaries: Salaries paid to internal trainers and administrative support staff in the training department.

Total Outside Expenditures: Dollars budgeted for the following categories:
- *Custom Materials:* Materials tailored/designed by outside suppliers specifically for an organization, for example, A/V, video, film, classroom programs, computer courseware, etc.
- *Seminars/Conferences:* Training provided by outside providers/contractors either at an organization's location or off-site, including public seminars, but not trainee travel and per diem costs.

Reprinted with permission from *TRAINING* Magazine, October 2000. Copyright © 2000 Bill Communications, Minneapolis, MN. All rights reserved.

- *Off-the-Shelf Materials:* Prepackaged materials purchased from outside suppliers, for example, computer courseware, books, videos, classroom programs, etc.
- *Other Expenditures:* Other training products or services from outside suppliers.

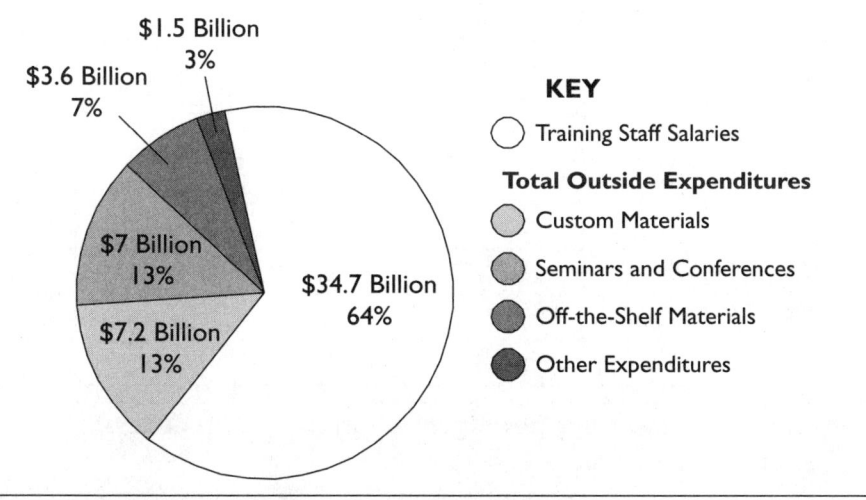

Figure 1. **2000 training budgets (total: $54 billion)**

Organization Size (Number of Employees)	Salaries	Custom Materials	Seminars & Conferences	Off-the-Shelf Materials	Other Expenditures	Total Budget
100-249	$5,278	$888	$1,416	$338	$226	$8,346
250-499	2,701	423	746	503	116	4,489
500-749	1,199	273	283	283	99	2,137
750-999	696	146	205	228	57	1,332
1,000-2,499	5,232	384	563	310	212	6,701
2,500-4,999	3,359	534	435	392	139	4,859
5,000-9,999	4,457	321	394	267	92	5,531
10,000-24,999	3,330	2,382	353	310	199	6,565
25,000-49,999	2,720	825	921	297	201	4,965
50,000 or more	5,765	1,005	1,650	468	209	9,094
Total	$34,737	$7,182	$6,966	$3,596	$1,538	$54,019

Figure 2. **The contribution of different-sized organizations to total training expenditures of $54 billion (projected totals in millions)**

Organization Size (Number of Employees)	Salaries	Custom Materials	Seminars & Conferences	Off-the-Shelf Materials	Other Expenditures	Total Budget
100-249	$60,054	$10,102	16,112	$6,124	$2,566	$94,958
250-499	91,544	14,354	25,280	17,044	3,940	152,162
500-749	111,902	25,487	26,403	26,454	9,210	199,456
750-999	144,271	30,361	42,448	47,191	11,889	276,160
1,000-2,499	512,523	37,634	55,137	30,351	20,776	656,421
2,500-4,999	898,451	142,841	116,471	104,915	37,148	1,299,826
5,000-9,999	2,362,078	170,357	208,968	141,353	48,912	2,931,668
10,000-24,999	2,672,291	1,911,749	283,156	248,444	152,188	5,267,828
25,000-49,999	7,533,421	2,287,506	2,552,425	822,202	557,558	13,753,112
50,000 or more	19,476,120	3,395,604	5,575,505	1,579,659	695,854	30,722,742

Figure 3. **Average spending per organization by size (in dollars)**

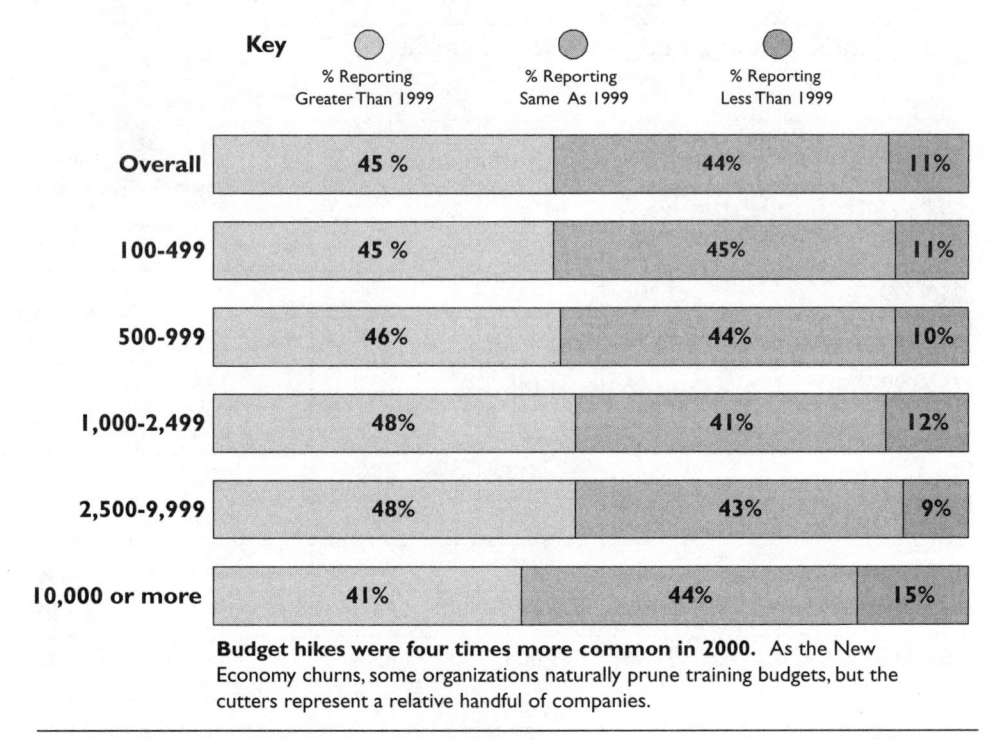

Key: % Reporting Greater Than 1999 | % Reporting Same As 1999 | % Reporting Less Than 1999

	% Greater	% Same	% Less
Overall	45%	44%	11%
100-499	45%	45%	11%
500-999	46%	44%	10%
1,000-2,499	48%	41%	12%
2,500-9,999	48%	43%	9%
10,000 or more	41%	44%	15%

Budget hikes were four times more common in 2000. As the New Economy churns, some organizations naturally prune training budgets, but the cutters represent a relative handful of companies.

Figure 4. **Reported changes in 2000 budgets (by size of organization)**

INDUSTRY REPORT 2000 THE MONEY

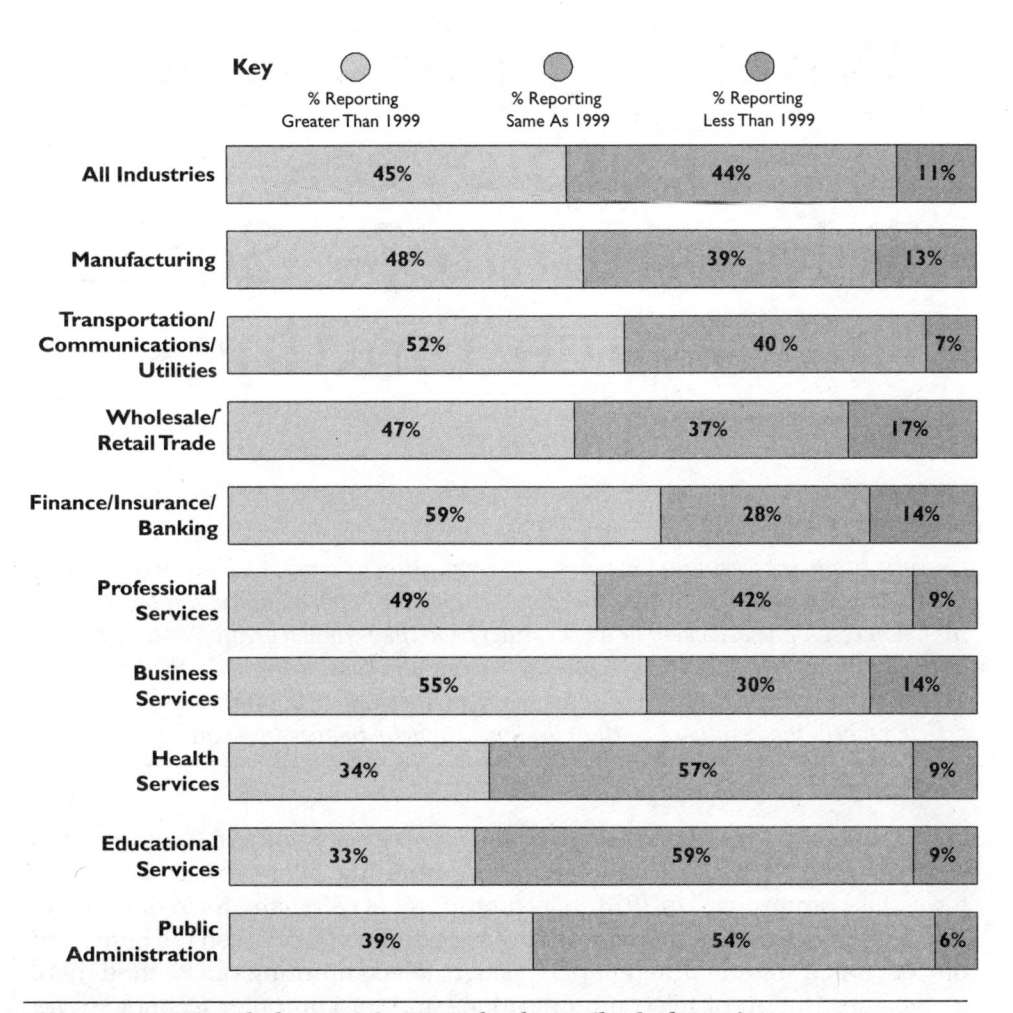

Industry	% Reporting Greater Than 1999	% Reporting Same As 1999	% Reporting Less Than 1999
All Industries	45%	44%	11%
Manufacturing	48%	39%	13%
Transportation/Communications/Utilities	52%	40%	7%
Wholesale/Retail Trade	47%	37%	17%
Finance/Insurance/Banking	59%	28%	14%
Professional Services	49%	42%	9%
Business Services	55%	30%	14%
Health Services	34%	57%	9%
Educational Services	33%	59%	9%
Public Administration	39%	54%	6%

Figure 5. **Reported changes in 2000 budgets (by industry)**

What Happens When Employees Telecommute?—Some Research Findings

Lisa H. Cree and Richard C. Sorenson

Organizations increasingly are using telecommuting as a practical means of dealing with a number of issues in the workplace. But what happens when employees work from home? Do they slack off or work harder? Do they enjoy a greater, or lesser, sense of flexibility and of balance between their work and family lives? Is their performance and job satisfaction better or worse than their office-bound co-workers? This article reports the results of a study designed to help answer these questions.

Jack Nilles who was a professor at the University of Southern California and involved in the first documented telecommuting pilot project[1] coined the term "telecommuting" in 1973. Telecommuting is using any form of telecommunication equipment at home and transferring work between the home and office. From a slightly different perspective, telecommuting can be thought of as the substitution of telecommunications and/or computer technology for commuting to work.[2] An associated term, "telework," means substituting any form of technology for work-related travel.

According to the definitions, all telecommuters are teleworkers, but not all teleworkers are telecommuters. Telecommuting is strictly based at the home-office. Telework includes telecommuting, but also includes linking workers located at other work sites away from the main office, such as working from one's car, satellite office close to home (in a center that resembles the conventional office), hotel room, or hotel conference center.[3] The telecommuters we studied all had an alternative work site at their homes, were employed for at least one year full-time with the same organization, and had been telecommuting at least 12 months.

Reprinted by permission of the authors. Copyright © 2000 by the authors. All rights reserved. This is a revision of a paper, "The Effectiveness of Telecommuting as an OD Intervention," presented at The 20th Organizational Development World Congress, Goa, India, July 2000.

Businesses implement telecommuting because they anticipate certain benefits, including enhanced ability to recruit and retain employees, reduced absenteeism and turnover, and improved worker productivity.[4] In addition, administrative expenses may be reduced through fewer office space requirements, while output may be increased through fewer interruptions.[5] Another rationale for the growing trend in telecommuting arose from environmental concerns—traffic and overcrowding. This new way of working may help transportation and urban planers move the traffic pattern away from the central office district in large cities.[6] This would reduce air pollution while saving time and money. For the individual, there is also the possibility of reduction in (or elimination of) commute time, as well as other costs associated with working, such as the upkeep of an automobile, clothing, and food.[7]

Method

In this study, we looked at the differences between telecommuters and office workers in terms of total hours worked, their sense of flexibility and of balance between work and family, performance, and job satisfaction. To address these questions a Work and Life Issues Survey was administered in 1996 to 13,019 U. S. employees of a large multinational corporation. The self-report survey was developed to gather information to improve "work and life balance" programs. It included 13 sections dealing with topics such as career opportunities, balancing work and personal-family life; manager-work group relationships; dependent children and elders; work schedules, locations, and flexibility; self and spouse/partner demographics; and telework.

The survey was administered online. An access code was provided in the survey invitation, which was sent via e-mail. Participation in the survey was voluntary and employees were assured that their responses would be anonymous. Overall, 7,586 of the 13,019 potential respondents completed the survey, for a response rate of 58%. To assure representativeness, a sub-sample of 6,451 full-time employees was created which included proportional samples from categories of employees as defined by the organization's human resources department.

We asked four experts in the area of work and family balance to review the survey items to determine whether they adequately sampled the content domains. In addition, we conducted a factor analysis on the survey data. We then used in our analysis of the research questions only those items that both the experts and the factor analysis results validated.

Among the respondents, we identified 221 telecommuters who had been employed full time for at least a year and indicated that they engaged in telecommuting at least 25% of their work time. For purposes of comparison, we randomly selected a group of 255 "office workers" from those respondents who had been employed full time for at least a year and who indicated that they did not engage in telecommuting at all. In addition to these comparisons, we also did regression analyses based on the entire sample.

Results

In comparing the telecommuters with the office workers we found that the telecommuters were working on average more hours per week than office workers. Telecommuters reported that they worked 56.4 hours while office workers reported logging an average of 47.1 hours per week. This difference is large and highly significant statistically. Further analysis of the full data set indicated that the more employees telecommute, the more hours they work.

We also found that telecommuters perceive that they have greater flexibility than do office workers. This difference is also large and highly significant. And it is also true that the more employees telecommute, the greater sense of flexibility they have.

With regard to work/family balance we were surprised to find that, while the difference between telecommuters and office workers was statistically significant, it favored the office workers. However, this relationship is affected by other variables such as total hours worked. When these variables are statistically controlled, there is a positive relationship between telecommuting and work/family balance.

Lacking an objective measure of productivity, we turned to self-reported performance appraisal ratings that were asked for as part of the survey. Comparing the telecommuters with the office workers, we found the difference statistically significant. In the regression analyses, we found a small but statistically significant positive relationship between hours spent telecommuting and performance. We can say that those involved in telecommuting report no lower performance evaluations than do office workers. Similar relationships were found for job satisfaction.

Conclusions

This study of telecommuting was done in the U.S. within a major multinational business enterprise. The more time telecommuters spent working at home, the more hours they worked in total. Managers should not be too concerned with whether employees involved in telecommuting are working. Probably they are working more than the office workers. Once total hours worked and other confounds are controlled, telecommuting is positively related to a sense of flexibility, work and family balance, performance, and job satisfaction, although the relationships with performance and job satisfaction are weak. Nevertheless, we interpret these findings to be positive regarding telecommuting.

The changing work environment, which includes technology as well as the demographics of the work force, currently influences the trend in telecommuting. Telecommuting is becoming a widespread business practice. By adopting telecommuting, organizations are striving to achieve many goals; one, in being able to provide their employees with a means to balance their work and family lives. There is a potential positive influence on work and family balance when employees are involved in telecommuting if overwork is avoided.

References

1. J.Nilles, *Managing telework: Strategies for managing the virtual workplace*, New York: Wiley and Sons, 1998.

2. D.C. Bacon, "Look who's working at home," *Nation's Business*, 1989, 77(10), pp. 20-31. L.F. McGee, "Setting up work at home," *Personnel Administrator*, 1988, 33(12), pp. 58-62. D.A. Newman, "Telecommuters bring the office home," *Management Review*, 1989, 78 (12), pp. 40-43. M.H. Olson, "The potential of remote work for professionals," in National Research Council, *Office workstation in the home*, pp. 125-132, Washington DC: National Academy Press, 1985. M. Pitt-Catsouphes and A. Marchetta, *A coming of age: Telework*, Boston: Boston University Center on Work and Family, 1991. United States Department of Transportation, *Transportation implications of telecommuting*, Washington, DC, 1993.

3. N.B. Kurland and D.E. Bailey, "The advantages and challenges of working here, there, anywhere, and anytime," *Organizational Dynamics*, 1999, 28 (2), pp. 53-68.

4. A.J. DuBrin, "Comparison of the job satisfaction and productivity of telecommuters versus in-house employees: a research note on work in progress," *Psychological Reports*, 1991, 68(3), pp. 1223-1234. E. J. Hill, B. C. Miller, S. P. Weiner, and J. Colihan, "Influences of the virtual office on aspects of work and work/life balance," *Personnel Psychology*, 1998, 51(3), pp. 667-683. E.W. Martin, *The IBM-Indiana telecommunications project*, Bloomington, IN: Indiana University School of Business, 1994.

5. S. Shellenbarger, "Overwork low morale vex the mobile office," *The Wall Street Journal*, August 17, 1994, p. B1.

6. Kurland and Bailey, 1999, op cit. S. McClelland, "Telework's global reach," *Telecommunications* (International Edition), 1995, 29, pp. 184-188.

7. B. Schepp, *The Telecommuter's Handbook: How to Work for a Salary Without Ever Leaving the House*, New York: Pharos Books, 1990.

Lisa H. Cree, Ph.D., is a consulting psychologist headquartered in New York City. Contact her at lcree@nyc.rr.com.

Richard C. Sorenson, Ph.D., is a professor at Alliant International University, San Diego, CA . Contact him at rsorenson@cspp.edu.

E-Learning: The Market Survey and Analysis

Delphi Group

The first article in this part of the yearbook was from the Enterprise E-Learning 2001 report issued by Delphi Group. We now conclude Part One with the summary of statistical findings from that study. It includes a number of figures that summarize the findings described in the report, and reading through these tables provides yet another perspective on the state of the training industry today, especially the emphasis on e-learning.

Survey Overview

Drivers

The drivers for e-learning have changed dramatically over the past ten years. What was once perceived as little more than a name change from computer-based training (CBT) to electronic learning—in large part reflecting the inclusion of various multimedia—has truly blossomed into an entirely new software industry with over 400 players.

In the beginning, the most obvious drivers were to use more technology for more efficient training. As the Internet grew more public and the Web was introduced, the driver was a new market niche: distance education. Multimedia and the Web eventually merged, and as they did so they subsumed a vast market segment: video training. In a stunning example, a few years ago a state Public Broadcasting channel abandoned a $3 million distance education Introduction to Computers college videocourse project. After a year of initial work, research indicated that by the time they completed the series, two years hence, Web-based distance education would have killed the for-sale videotape market. They were right.

Today, e-learning involves educating the right employee on an anywhere, anytime, for any reason basis, and is a vehicle for delivering skills development. E-learning drivers have replicated many of the best aspects of training, while addressing an entirely new market focus: the corporate infrastructure. This fundamental new focus is described throughout this report and does not need to be covered again here.

Reprinted with permission from Module X of *Enterprise e-Learning 2001*. Copyright © 2001 by Delphi Group. All rights reserved.

Obstacles

The major hurdles are time and distance. Technology vendors naturally encourage and support using the best technology available, and tend to believe that technology solves most, if not all, problems. This view is far from universal, especially in the academic community where course content often lags as much as five years behind the times. The same is true of corporate training, which is often reactive rather than proactive.

From the user's perspective, e-learning doesn't need much selling. People want to learn; lifelong learning is widely embraced by the population, and is often regarded by employees as a perk. If senior management perceives a hurdle to e-learning, it is likely because it's still defined as a cost center that does not demonstrate a value return. But there are other hurdles and they are discussed herein as they are gleaned from the survey.

Needs

Most enterprises recognize the need to deliver skills development resources in order to attract, develop, and retain excellent workers. Most of those surveyed are beginning to shift emphasis from traditional training and static in-house education programs to an emphasis on e-learning deliverables. A need that had not previously been ascertained was the ability to capture and reconfigure learning materials from a variety of in-house, as well as external, sources, a task for which e-learning tools are ideally suited.

Spending

Most of the companies surveyed are not spending enough on either traditional training or on new e-learning initiatives. This may in fact reflect the mistaken belief that e-learning, like old-line training, is a cost and not a source of revenue. This attitude must be set aside so that e-learning initiatives can be pursued with vigor, so that it can demonstrate its many positive returns to the enterprise.

Results

E-learning is definitely gaining momentum, but the training mindset is too often still in place and is hindering its potential, especially in using it to advance the interests of the value chain. It is probably unrealistic at this point in time to see a full implementation of e-learning with a knowledge management system, deployed across the value chain and delivered through a bi-directional portal, however, this should be the goal.

About the Research

The research used a Web-based survey that collected the views of over 700 corporate senior management, information technology (IT) management, line-of-business management, project management, and other professionals. In terms of annual revenue, 6% of the companies had revenues over $1 billion, while 60% had under $100 million. The number of employees at the respondents' locations were as follows:

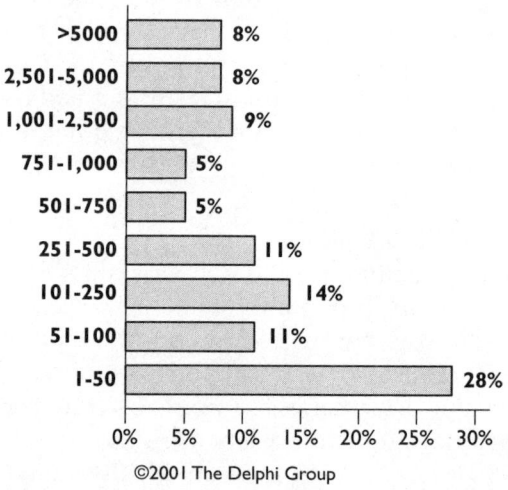

Employees	Percentage
>5000	8%
2,501-5,000	8%
1,001-2,500	9%
751-1,000	5%
501-750	5%
251-500	11%
101-250	14%
51-100	11%
1-50	28%

©2001 The Delphi Group

The survey targeted a broad cross-section of global businesses including aerospace, banking, business consulting, computing and electronics, finance and investing, government, healthcare, insurance, manufacturing, and retail. The location breakdown:

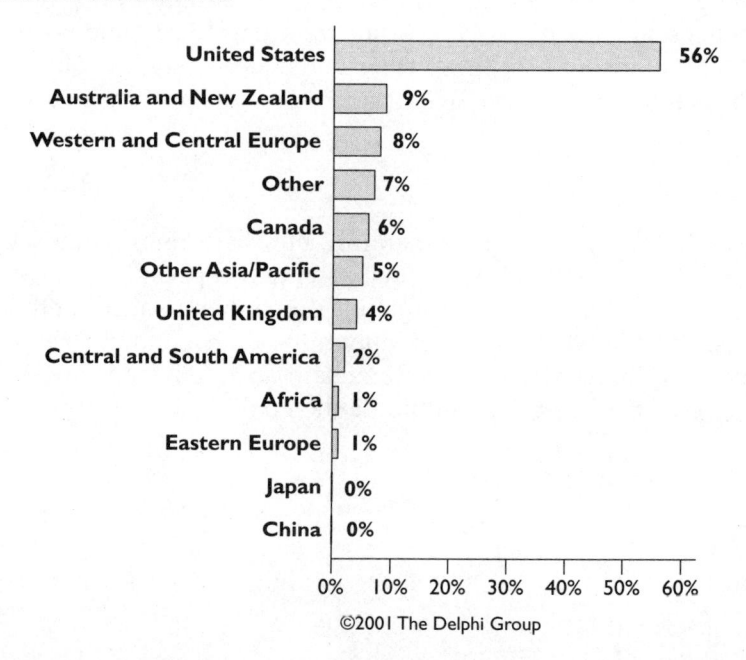

Location	Percentage
United States	56%
Australia and New Zealand	9%
Western and Central Europe	8%
Other	7%
Canada	6%
Other Asia/Pacific	5%
United Kingdom	4%
Central and South America	2%
Africa	1%
Eastern Europe	1%
Japan	0%
China	0%

©2001 The Delphi Group

Generally, U.S. companies with less than 500 employees and less than $100 million in annual revenues displayed stronger interest in e-learning than any other demographics.

E-Learning: A Definition

Almost half the respondents define e-learning as educational content available online. Others defined it as the means to leverage corporate knowledge or the tools to communicate complex concepts. E-learning had its origins in computer-based training (CBT), which attempted to replace paid instructors to reduce organizational costs; however, e-learning has continued to differentiate itself from traditional forms of CBT, as only 8% still make that association. Here's the breakdown on how respondents defined e-learning:

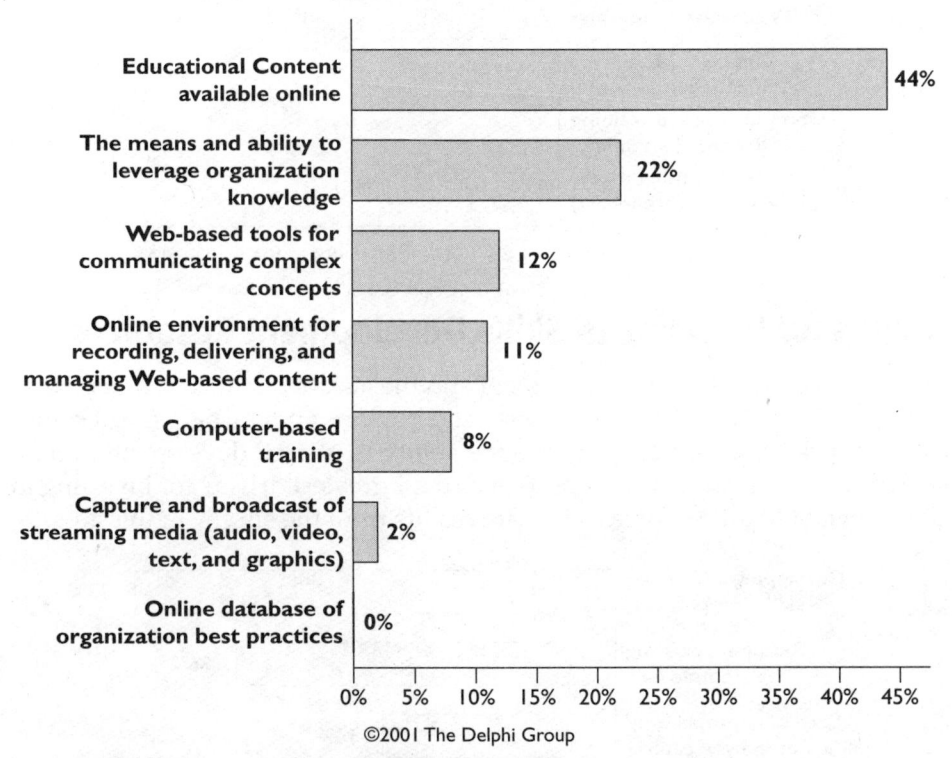

Definition	Percentage
Educational Content available online	44%
The means and ability to leverage organization knowledge	22%
Web-based tools for communicating complex concepts	12%
Online environment for recording, delivering, and managing Web-based content	11%
Computer-based training	8%
Capture and broadcast of streaming media (audio, video, text, and graphics)	2%
Online database of organization best practices	0%

©2001 The Delphi Group

Essential E-Learning Components

E-learning has many components, including course, media, and content delivery of reusable knowledge objects, but content and course management and collaborative components are the most essential. Organizations must be able to easily integrate the necessary components into their e-learning platform. As such, the industry will likely consolidate around providing a single platform of integrated solutions through partnerships. Here are some results on this subject from the survey:

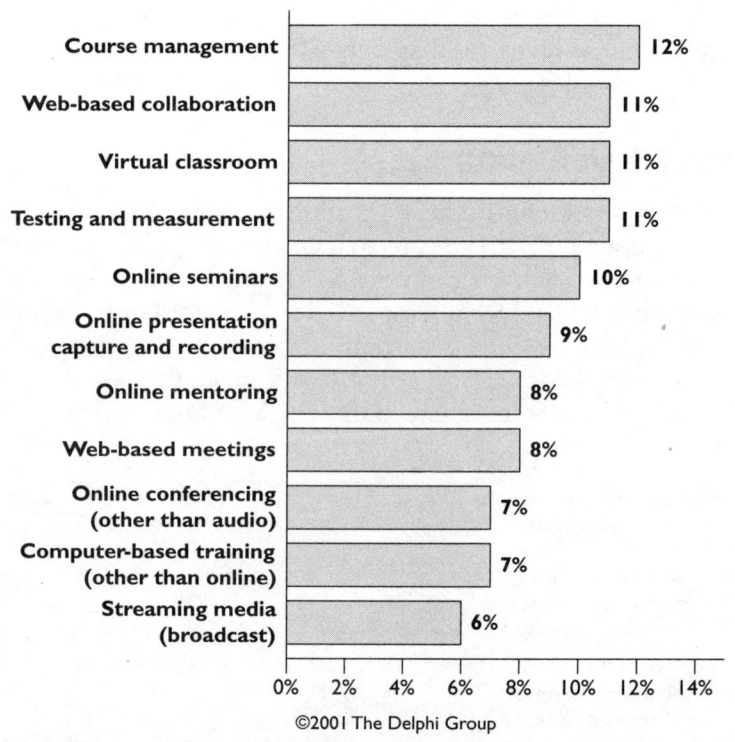

Category	Percentage
Course management	12%
Web-based collaboration	11%
Virtual classroom	11%
Testing and measurement	11%
Online seminars	10%
Online presentation capture and recording	9%
Online mentoring	8%
Web-based meetings	8%
Online conferencing (other than audio)	7%
Computer-based training (other than online)	7%
Streaming media (broadcast)	6%

©2001 The Delphi Group

Drivers for Investing in Skills Development Resources

In the 21st century, low unemployment and the lack of qualified workers have put a premium on intellectual property and human capital. Therefore, it comes as no surprise that respondents cite the ability to attract, develop, and retain skilled workers in a tight labor market as their greatest drivers for investing in skills development resources. Here are results from the survey in this area:

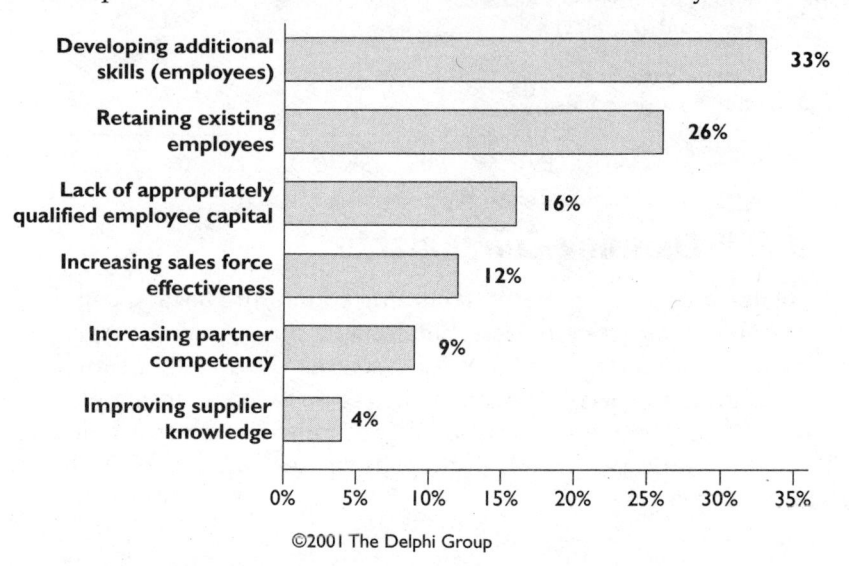

Driver	Percentage
Developing additional skills (employees)	33%
Retaining existing employees	26%
Lack of appropriately qualified employee capital	16%
Increasing sales force effectiveness	12%
Increasing partner competency	9%
Improving supplier knowledge	4%

©2001 The Delphi Group

How Skills Get Updated

Companies need to maximize existing human capital as a revenue-generating function in order to gain competitive advantage in this rapidly evolving market. Their strategic imperative must integrate e-learning into the enterprise infrastructure to develop better trained and more loyal knowledge workers. Respondents indicated that the following were their most commonly used tools for updating skills:

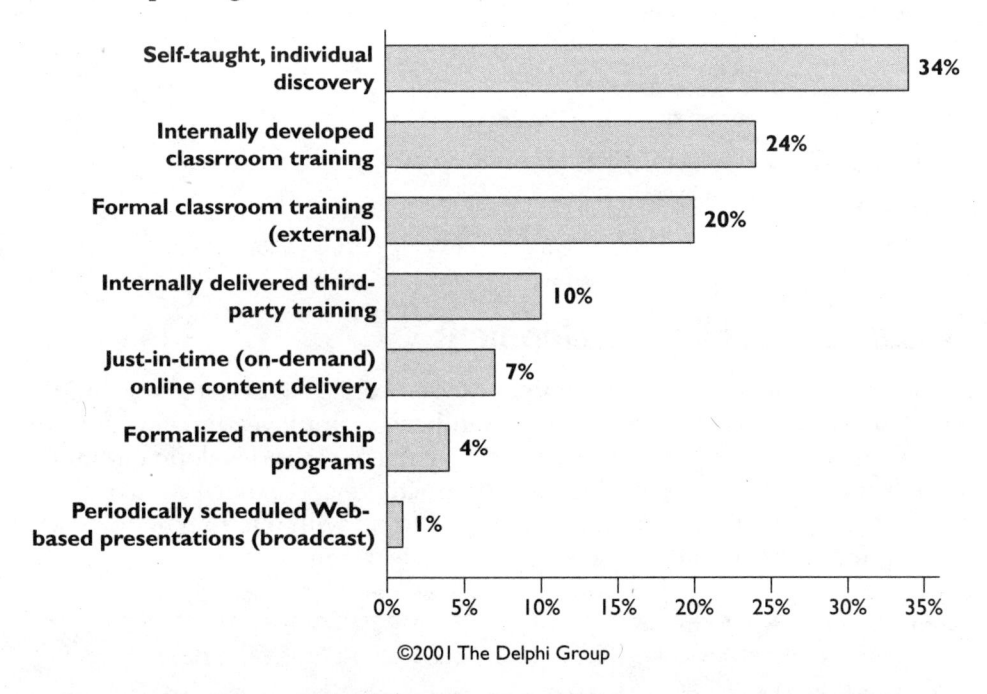

Tool	Percentage
Self-taught, individual discovery	34%
Internally developed classrroom training	24%
Formal classroom training (external)	20%
Internally delivered third-party training	10%
Just-in-time (on-demand) online content delivery	7%
Formalized mentorship programs	4%
Periodically scheduled Web-based presentations (broadcast)	1%

©2001 The Delphi Group

Companies must capture the large portion of individual self-discovery that takes place in organizations, and then integrate and reuse that knowledge throughout the value chain using e-learning.

Skills Development Programs

The term skills development appears to be replacing training, which has augered a remedial connotation in recent years. E-learning is used to facilitate skills development programs. It is not independent from existing education or training, but rather leverages both with new technology. E-learning is, however, superior because it is continuous learning and redefines the concept of competitive advantage by adding value to existing business processes. Most organizations are creating and delivering proprietary content to develop their human capital. Here's what the survey showed specifically:

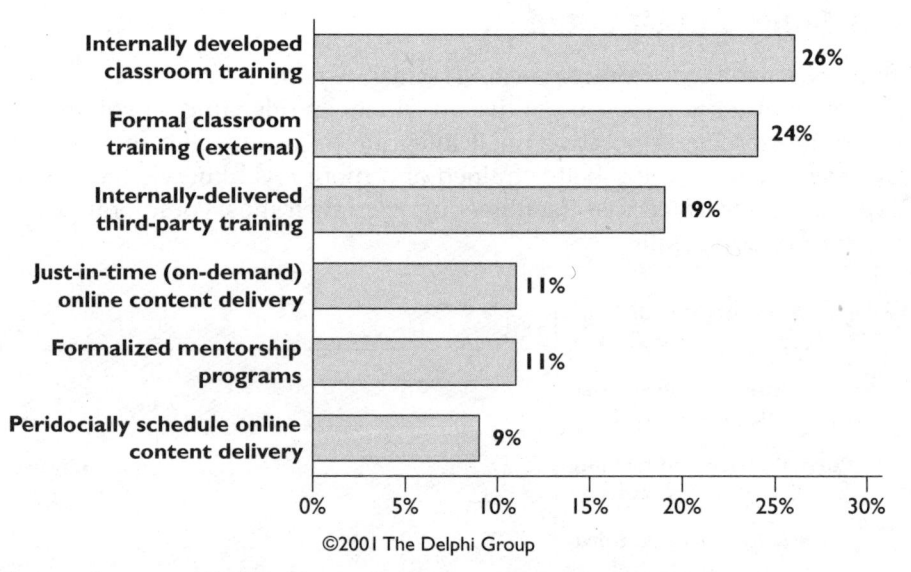

Category	Percentage
Internally developed classroom training	26%
Formal classroom training (external)	24%
Internally-delivered third-party training	19%
Just-in-time (on-demand) online content delivery	11%
Formalized mentorship programs	11%
Peridocially schedule online content delivery	9%

©2001 The Delphi Group

Obstacles to Skills Development

Classroom training is the most commonly used vehicle to update skills in 44% of organizations. Correspondingly, 43% indicated employee time away from the job as the greatest hurdle to expanding current skills development initiatives. The challenge is to justify the lost productivity and explicit costs of classroom training to the executives. This is hard to do within a training mindset, but is quite another matter when viewed as e-learning.

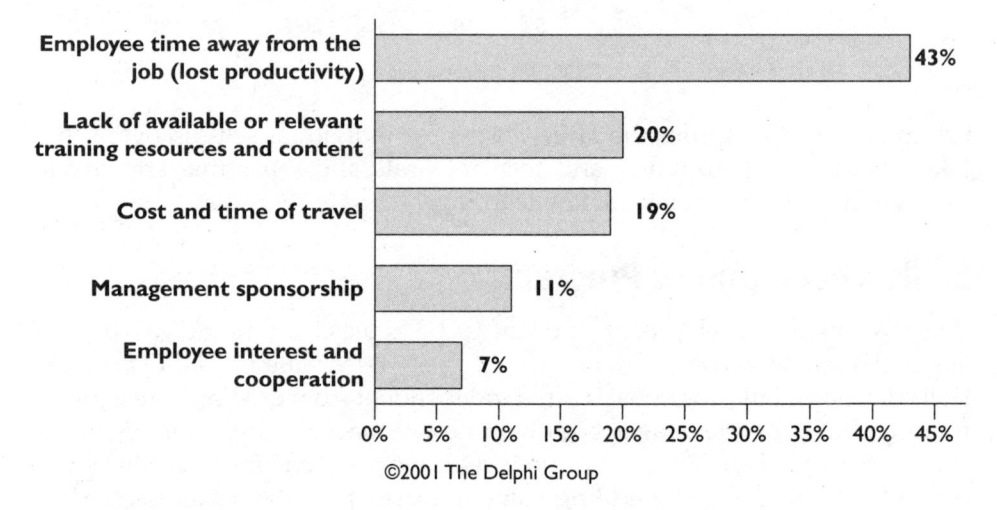

Category	Percentage
Employee time away from the job (lost productivity)	43%
Lack of available or relevant training resources and content	20%
Cost and time of travel	19%
Management sponsorship	11%
Employee interest and cooperation	7%

©2001 The Delphi Group

E-learning challenges the traditional notion of skills development as a cost center. It does so by eliminating the barriers of time and distance to provide the tools and knowledge needed to perform work. The right tools for the right job are moved to the workers—wherever and whomever they are—instead of the workers attending a training program. Personalized skills development can be integrated into the enterprise value chain to maximize human capital. Executives must view e-learning as a revenue-generating function, not a cost-reduction function.

Skills Development Spending This Year vs. Next Year

Survey results regarding expenditures on skills development were not altogether encouraging. Sixty-four percent of organizations spent $100,000 or less while 20% spent over $500,000.

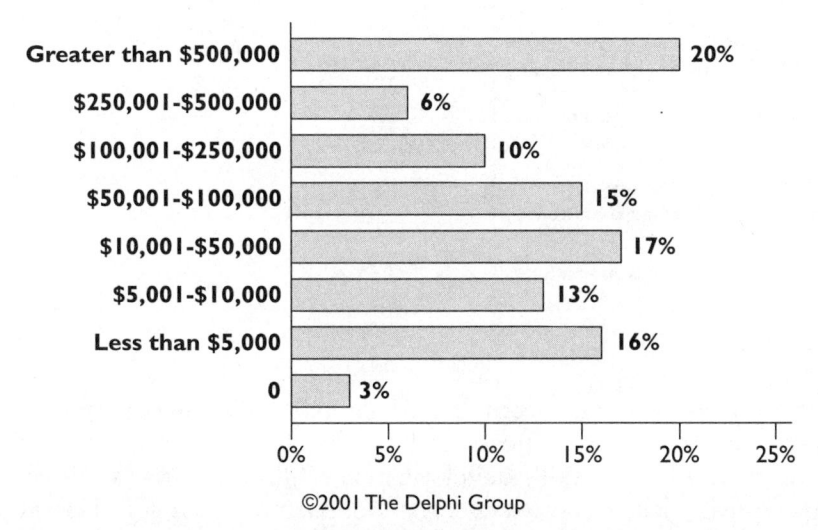

Spending	Percentage
Greater than $500,000	20%
$250,001-$500,000	6%
$100,001-$250,000	10%
$50,001-$100,000	15%
$10,001-$50,000	17%
$5,001-$10,000	13%
Less than $5,000	16%
0	3%

©2001 The Delphi Group

Ninety percent indicated that this trend will be about the same or substantially more than the last year's expenditures, which indicates a shift in purchase from content to more expensive e-learning tools and integration services.

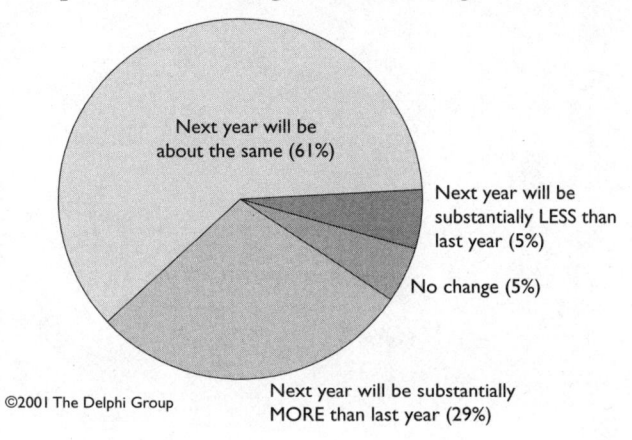

- Next year will be about the same (61%)
- Next year will be substantially LESS than last year (5%)
- No change (5%)
- Next year will be substantially MORE than last year (29%)

©2001 The Delphi Group

Areas Most in Need of Skills Development

The two areas with the most apparent need for skills development in organizations are technical skills and knowledge of organizational best practices. These core skills differentiate one organization from another in the marketplace to generate revenue.

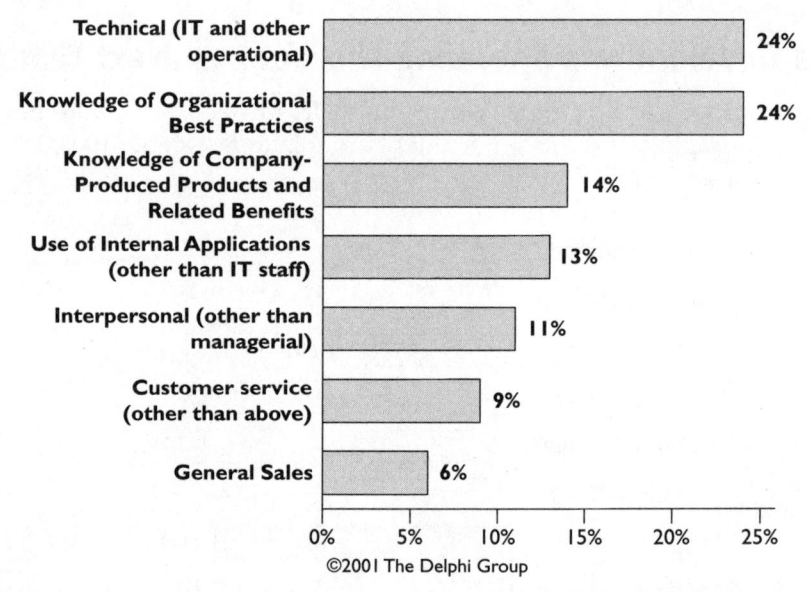

Area	Percentage
Technical (IT and other operational)	24%
Knowledge of Organizational Best Practices	24%
Knowledge of Company-Produced Products and Related Benefits	14%
Use of Internal Applications (other than IT staff)	13%
Interpersonal (other than managerial)	11%
Customer service (other than above)	9%
General Sales	6%

©2001 The Delphi Group

Most organizations have successfully delivered skills development tools to the identified weak areas. Those in need of technical or best practice skills have the most access to skills development. While enterprise skills development is critical, those of customers, channel partners, and suppliers must be addressed as well. The percentage of the extended enterprise with access to skills development resources is inefficiently low:

Audience	%
Technical Staff (IT and other operational)	22%
Senior Management	19%
Line-of-Business Management	17%
Sales	13%
Customer Service (other than above)	11%
Field Technicians	9%
Customers	4%
Channel Partners	3%
Suppliers	2%

©2001 The Delphi Group

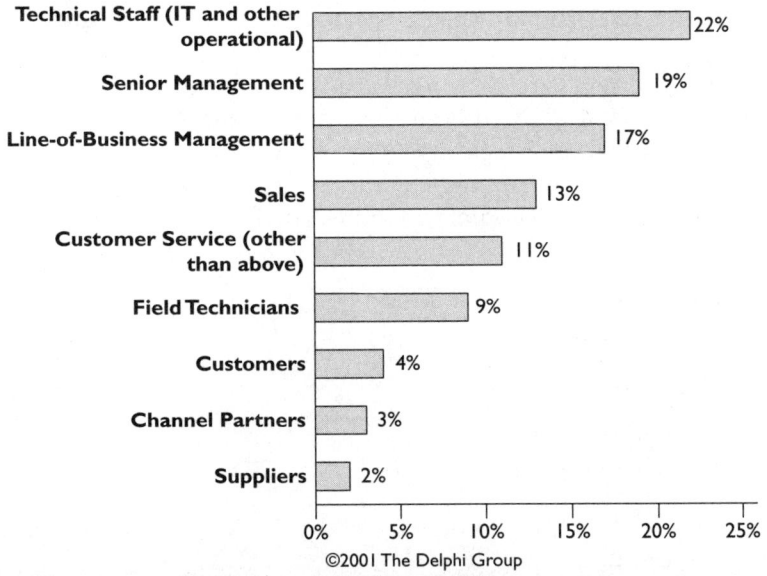

Integrating E-Learning and Channel Strategy

Most companies have yet to integrate e-learning throughout the enterprise in order to provide a viable means for their channel partners to proactively engage the market. They pursue strategies that provide inconsistent support or no support at all to their channels. The following graph shows the existing channel strategy components:

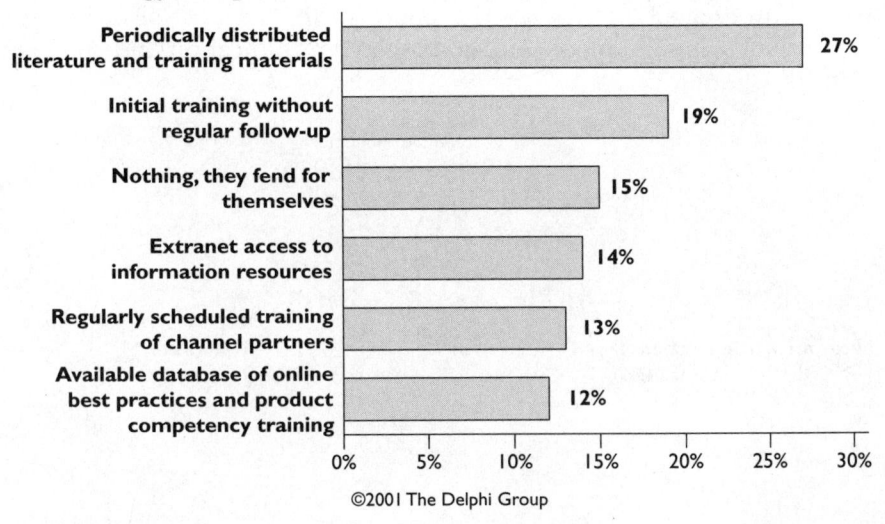

Strategy	%
Periodically distributed literature and training materials	27%
Initial training without regular follow-up	19%
Nothing, they fend for themselves	15%
Extranet access to information resources	14%
Regularly scheduled training of channel partners	13%
Available database of online best practices and product competency training	12%

©2001 The Delphi Group

E-learning should be used to create synergy between partners, salespeople, or various teams by providing a shared set of experiences and tools for collaboration. This is more powerful than periodic distribution of literature that may become outdated, or static classroom training solutions.

Web-based Communication and Conference Tools Spending

The most commonly used method to communicate significant developments within the organization is electronic memo, followed by the company intranet. Last year, 63% of the organizations spent less than $50,000 on Web-based communication and conference tools, such as online meetings and collaboration tools.

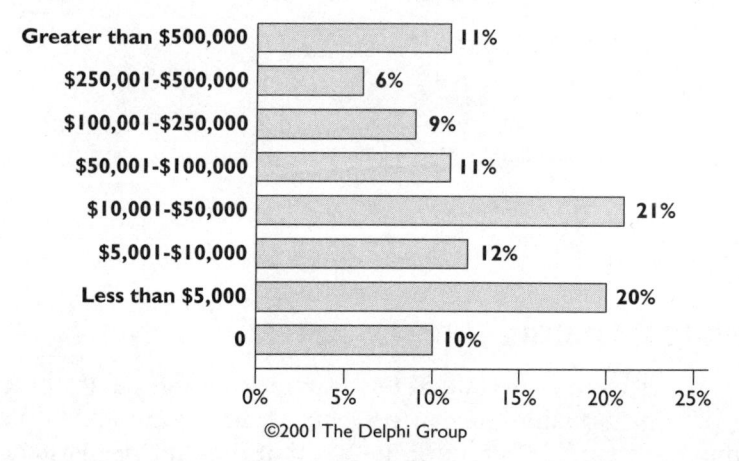

Spending Range	Percentage
Greater than $500,000	11%
$250,001-$500,000	6%
$100,001-$250,000	9%
$50,001-$100,000	11%
$10,001-$50,000	21%
$5,001-$10,000	12%
Less than $5,000	20%
0	10%

©2001 The Delphi Group

There were nearly as many organizations that did not spend any money on these areas as those that spent either between $50,001-$100,000 or greater than $500,000; however, 43% of the respondents anticipate that their organization will spend substantially more on Web-based communication and conference tools in 2001.

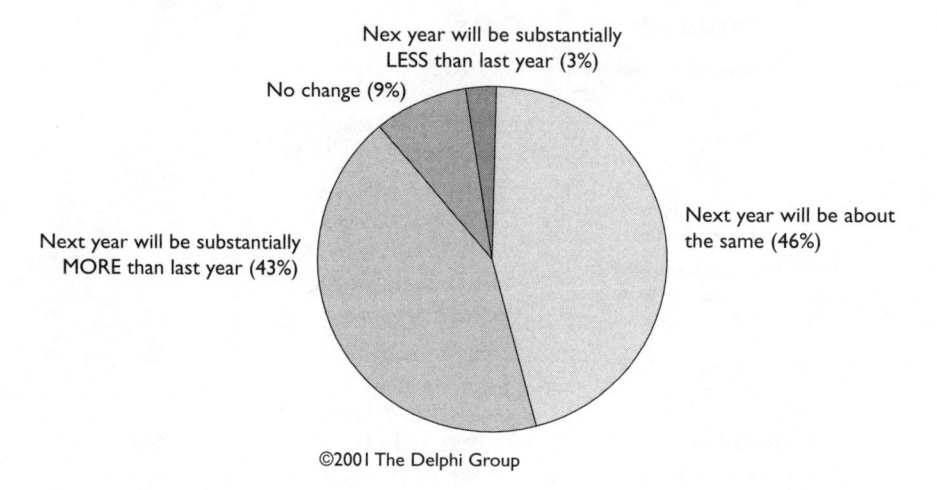

Category	Percentage
Nex year will be substantially LESS than last year	3%
No change	9%
Next year will be substantially MORE than last year	43%
Next year will be about the same	46%

©2001 The Delphi Group

Perceived Benefits of E-Learning Technology

Survey respondents said that the greatest perceived benefit of e-learning technology is its ability to access externally developed educational materials. But at the same time, respondents also reported that more content is being developed internally. While these two responses may seem to contradict each other, in fact they represent the rapidly evolving role e-learning is assuming in the enterprise. We believe the trend toward capturing internal expertise with e-learning systems will continue.

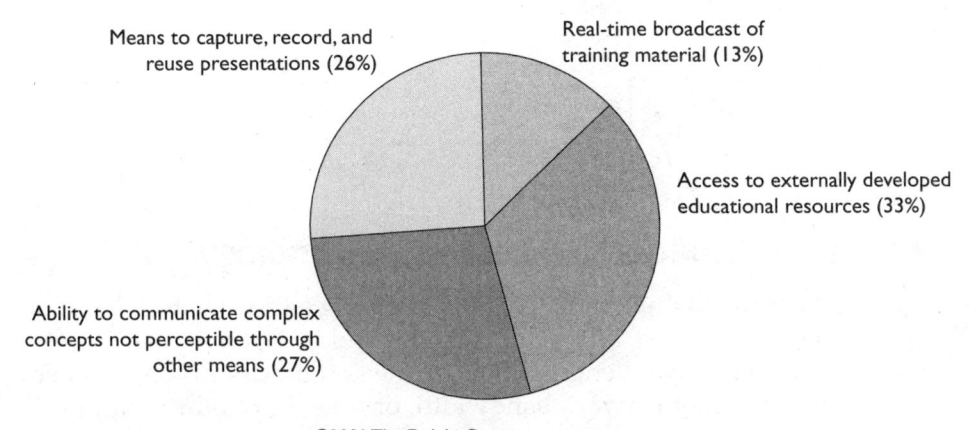

Means to capture, record, and reuse presentations (26%)

Real-time broadcast of training material (13%)

Access to externally developed educational resources (33%)

Ability to communicate complex concepts not perceptible through other means (27%)

©2001 The Delphi Group

Who Benefits from E-Learning

Thirty-four percent of the respondents indicated that sales and marketing would yield the greatest return from e-learning technology, followed by engineering and product development at 33% and executive management at 15%. Even so, other data suggest that many early e-learning initiatives are found in the IT organization, where skills upgrading and development are critical for implementing new technologies. This is most likely a good thing, as IT tends to be a group whose emissaries work throughout the enterprise. Their positive experiences with e-learning can serve to showcase it to senior management and other organizations.

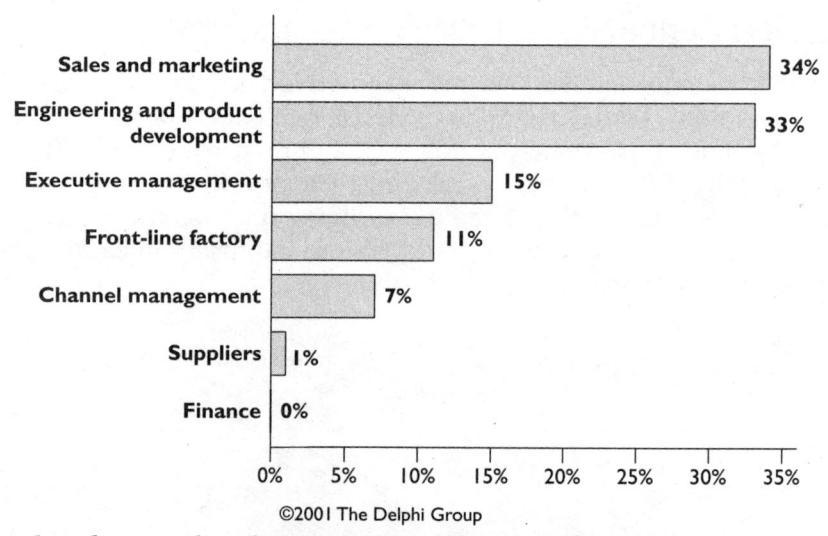

Category	Percentage
Sales and marketing	34%
Engineering and product development	33%
Executive management	15%
Front-line factory	11%
Channel management	7%
Suppliers	1%
Finance	0%

©2001 The Delphi Group

Perceived Drawbacks to E-Learning Technology

The greatest perceived impediment to implementing e-learning technology is not cost, which ranked last, but rather technical and integration issues. Forty-four percent of the respondents said either the complexity of development environments, a lack of network bandwidth, or absence of other computing resources, as their perceived impediments to deploying e-learning technology. The other challenge exists in the "soft," or organizational, perceptions of e-learning technology, as 39% indicated either a lack of management sponsorship or a lack of perceived need. E-learning technologies need to present ROI analysis to convince and market that demand.

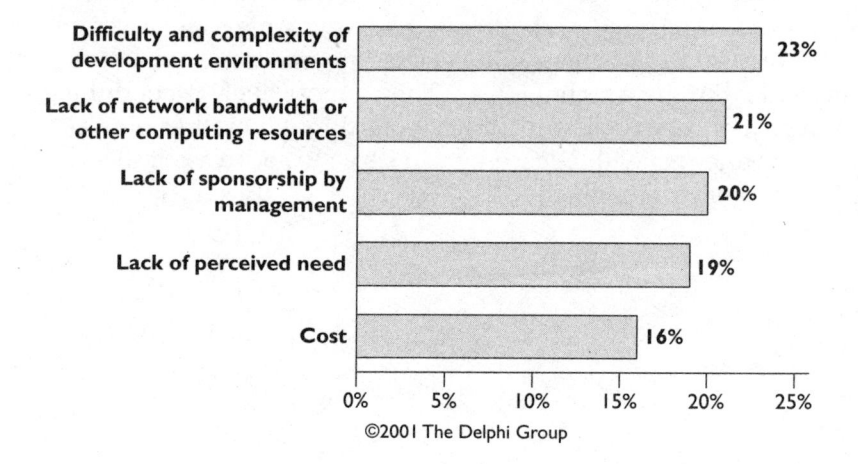

Category	Percentage
Difficulty and complexity of development environments	23%
Lack of network bandwidth or other computing resources	21%
Lack of sponsorship by management	20%
Lack of perceived need	19%
Cost	16%

©2001 The Delphi Group

E-Learning Content Resources

Much e-learning content is custom-designed to provide the critical personalization elements. E-learning targets the individual learner to bridge the synergy between the learner and the material. Custom content services will continue to play an integral role in providing e-learning resources.

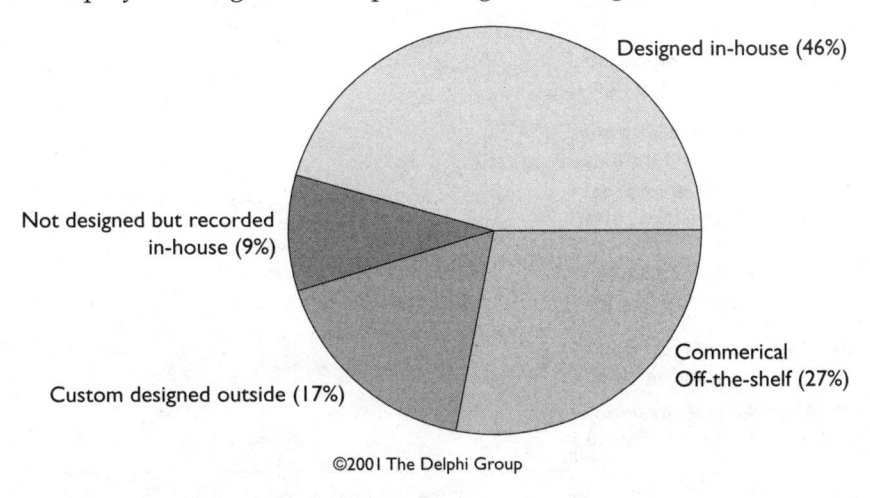

- Designed in-house (46%)
- Commerical Off-the-shelf (27%)
- Custom designed outside (17%)
- Not designed but recorded in-house (9%)

©2001 The Delphi Group

How E-Learning Is Developed

Thirty-two percent of respondents said converting PowerPoint presentations to content best describes their organizations' process for developing e-learning content. While it is not uncommon for a business initiative to begin with what is easiest, converting presentations certainly ranks up there with the good ideas. One caveat: a presentation may lack the necessary learning structure, or pedagogy, to easily translate into course content or a learning module. Any content being prepared for e-learning needs to be examined and evaluated for its learning attributes.

Category	Percentage
Developing PowerPoint presentations	32%
Structured course development and design	26%
Does not develop content	20%
Capture and codification of company best practices	7%
Multimedia content development	6%
Ad hoc capture of internal presentations (such as sales training)	6%
Preparation for a teleconference	2%
Development of industrial-grade training video	0%
Production of Hollywood-caliber movie	0%

©2001 The Delphi Group

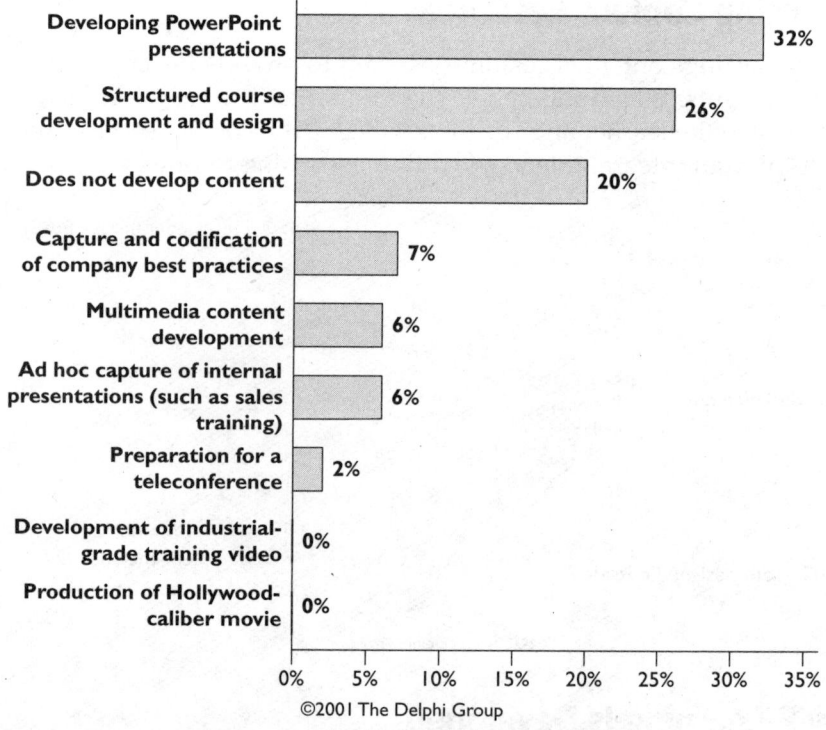

Most Common Use of E-Learning Materials

The most common use of e-learning materials is to capture, record, and reuse presentations. However, e-learning also is used to extract knowledge embedded in the value chain to help managers determine strengths and weaknesses in the enterprise's business processes. Most enterprises ought to be using e-learning for both purposes, as well as many others up and down the value chain.

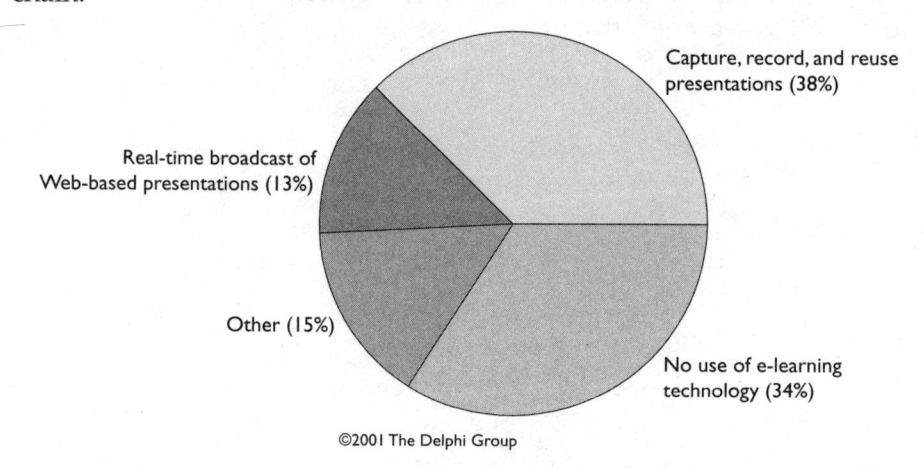

- Capture, record, and reuse presentations (38%)
- No use of e-learning technology (34%)
- Other (15%)
- Real-time broadcast of Web-based presentations (13%)

©2001 The Delphi Group

Platform Access to E-Learning Tools

Currently, 70% of the organizations access e-learning tools internally via a server or installed on a desktop. Twenty-two percent use application service providers (ASP), most likely because their software applications are either delivered or managed from ASP platforms and/or servers.

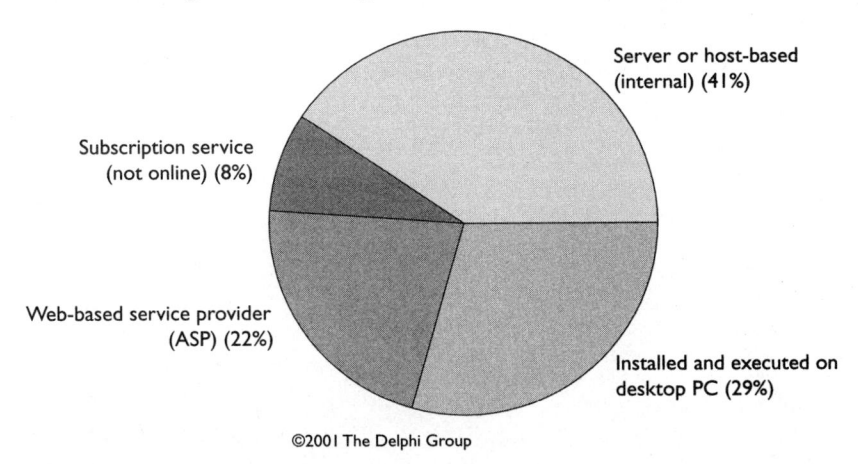

Server or host-based (internal) (41%)
Subscription service (not online) (8%)
Web-based service provider (ASP) (22%)
Installed and executed on desktop PC (29%)

©2001 The Delphi Group

Future Access to E-Learning Tools

Although most organizations access e-learning tools internally, preference for access via ASP is twice as great—22% compared to 52%—by those that are not currently using e-learning tools. This obviously reflects a preference for outsourcing. The maintenance expense of the e-learning tools over the lifecycle often exceeds the initial installation and startup expenses. This issue of lifecycle management will be an important criteria in future e-learning purchases.

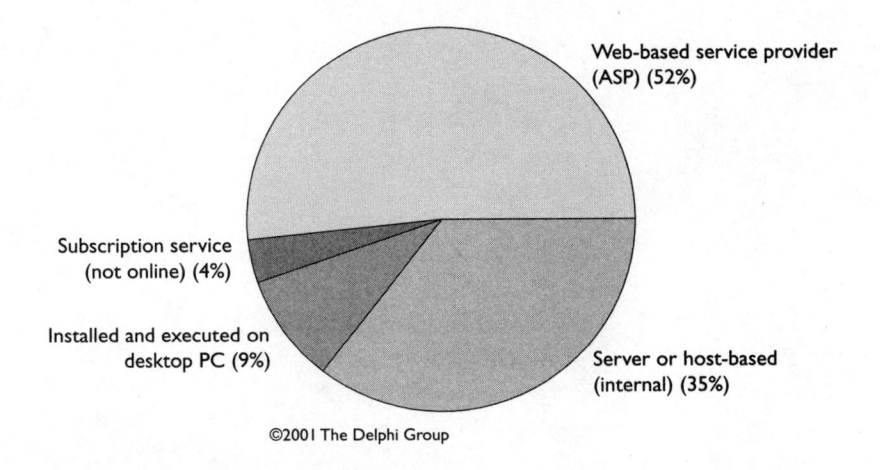

Web-based service provider (ASP) (52%)
Subscription service (not online) (4%)
Installed and executed on desktop PC (9%)
Server or host-based (internal) (35%)

©2001 The Delphi Group

PART TWO

The Cutting Edge of Training: E-Learning and Other New Training Technology

The use of the Internet, computers, and other electronic technology are, as surveys seem to show, the performance improvement technique of choice. The purpose of Part Two is to help you keep up to date with what's involved in understanding and using these new training technologies. To this end, we include six articles that provide an overview of the changes this technology has wrought and how to make use of it effectively.

We start with "The E-Learning Revolution" by Patricia Galagan. In it she documents the move to e-learning and how this is affecting those who work in training. It includes a sidebar with insightful comments from Peter Drucker.

Next we include a piece from Marvin Gottlieb's *Communication Project Magazine*: "E-Learning: Are You a Tortoise or a Hare?" In it he describes the state of flux brought about by the move to e-learning, and reviews a series of questions trainers should ask as they make the transition to these technologies.

We next include another excerpt from the Delphi Group study, *Enterprise E-Learning 2001*, "Integrating E-Learning with Business Goals." The whole point of e-learning is to help organizations improve performance in line with their overall goals and strategy. This article will help you learn how to do that.

From *HR Magazine*, we have included Bill Roberts' "E-Learning: New Twist on CBT." He explains what's involved in implementing CBT, the problems that can occur, and the patience required to see the payoff over other alternative approaches to training.

Next we include an original article written for the yearbook by Margaret Martinez with the long but descriptive title, "Audience Analysis and Instructional System Design for Successful Online Learning and Performance." This provides practical assistance on how to design an e-learning course with detailed direction on how to do this for different types of learners.

We conclude Part Two with "A Primer on Tracking Web-Based Training" by Janeen Rossi, written especially for the yearbook. In it she provides practical instruction on how to track learners' progress when they are engaged in WBT. She describes different scenarios for doing this and what to look for when making a decision about which WBT tracking software solution will work best for you.

The E-Learning Revolution

Patricia Galagan

In this article by the editor of Training & Development, *we learn more about what she contends is the future of training and, by not-so-subtle implication, the future of trainers as well. Traditional trainers still have important roles to play, but technology is changing things dramatically. Traditional classroom learning is under siege, and appropriately so, as increasingly sophisticated technology becomes a one-to-one teacher, always available when and where needed.*

"Let me lay my cards on the table face up," says Peter Drucker, venerable author, consultant, and professor of management, when asked if e-learning is changing the training profession. "I am the author of several online learning tools."

That piece of news says it all. Drucker, born well before World War I, recently worked with Corpedia Training Technologies to offer some of his management courses online. That move hastened his appreciation of two of e-learning's most compelling features: accessibility and scalability. Drucker, now 91 and still one of the most sought-after teachers of our time, knows he can reach only so many people through the classroom.

But e-learning has done far more than make knowledge easy to access by a large number of people. Its effects on the training profession are nothing short of revolutionary, challenging most of its basic tenets—from the classic instructional model, to who "owns" learning in an organization, to its strategic role. The profession is in the midst of a revolution generated not from within but by new players from other disciplines, by forces in the supplier market, and by the kind of learning that technology makes possible. Those are the tough truths facing training's fundamentalists.

Drucker agrees, cautioning that "as things are going, the trainer will be left high and dry. There will, of course, still be training as we have traditionally understood it—training in skills. But it is not a growth sector. The growth sector is learning, especially concept learning." Drucker maintains that his own foray into the e-learning world is based on the assumption that the trainer is obsolete. "The trainer is built into the teaching (or learning) device."

Reprinted with permission from *Training & Development*, December 2000. Copyright © 2000 by the American Society for Training and Development. All rights reserved.

No more pencils, no more books, no more teachers' dirty looks. That old song lyric by the 1970s group Alice Cooper could be the revolution's anthem. Goodbye and good riddance to the classroom and its artifacts—the test, the lecture, and the semester system, says Roger C. Schank, a vocal critic of traditional teaching methods. Schank is director of the Institute for Learning Sciences at Northwestern University and founder of Cognitive Arts, a company that pursues the commercial use of software-based teaching. He's also the author of *Coloring Outside the Lines: How to Raise a Smarter Kid by Breaking All the Rules.*

"Classrooms couldn't possibly work today," says Schank. "Centuries ago, they made sense: one literate person reading to the illiterate from what might have been the town's only book." But technology and times have changed. The ideal of one-on-one instruction is not practical in today's classrooms. "A computer can give you more one-on-one interaction than a human can when that human has 30 other humans to deal with," he says. "In a classroom, people who are curious, inquisitive, and questioning take up too much time."

The best things that technology has given training, says Schank, are "the possibility of one-on-one for every learner, the ability to simulate, and the chance to try stuff out and fail in private without the fear of ridicule from other students."

Schank believes that the strongest impetus for effective learning comes not from schools but from business organizations. "It doesn't matter to the school if you learn the Pythagorean Theorem, but it really does matter to your company that you learn to do your job," he says. It is corporate learning programs, many made possible on a large scale by e-learning, that are finding new ways to put human interaction into computer-based programs.

"Corporate trainers better figure out how to be part of that," warns Schank. "The ones who are part of the ancient system [of classroom training] are going to watch that ancient system disappear on them."

Clark Aldrich, a training market analyst for the GartnerGroup, has a different perspective on the origins of the classroom, but reaches the same conclusion: Trainers need to move on.

"The modern classroom is based on tenets of the Industrial Revolution," says Aldrich. "In that industrial model, instructors are the blue-collar line workers and students are the widgets moving through the assembly line." But, the GartnerGroup predicts, the traditional classroom model will represent less than 30 percent of all formal corporate learning programs by 2003.

Aldrich has been an early herald of a sea change in the role of training in business organizations. When e-learning and outsourcing began to change the training topography, Aldrich articulated this warning: "Companies must reexamine their core processes, including customer service and employee management, through the lens of an e-learning strategy. Primary responsibility for the execution against those goals cannot be the sole responsibility of the traditional training organization. CKOs, CLOs, and even COOs will have to drive the activities."

Strategic at Last

The rise of e-learning is dividing training into two streams: corporate learning—usually owned by HR or corporate training departments—and training for a variety of strategic purposes, usually owned at a level just below the CEO. The strategy-linked learning programs may target people beyond the company such as partners, suppliers, and hoped-for customers. But companies are also using e-learning to change direction quickly, such as going from a traditional business to an e-business.

A hallmark of such strategic learning initiatives is that they are company-wide and built onto existing technology systems at great cost. That makes them different in scope and visibility from most other training. Consequently, they are high-stakes and high-risk projects whose owners are reluctant to entrust them to traditional training units. That has produced a booming line of business for large consulting firms poised to guide a strategic initiative with a major e-learning component.

Jeff Schwartz, a partner at PricewaterhouseCoopers and global leader of e-learning services, confirms that such strategic initiatives are his unit's fastest-growing business area. "We're seeing more major supply-chain projects and lots of e-business projects, especially around building e-marketplaces. Increasingly, the foundations of those learning programs are e-learning based." At PWC, such projects are labeled "extended enterprise solutions."

Although solutions is an overused buzzword, it does convey one important characteristic of such programs: they address real business issues and do what training programs of the past have often failed to achieve, which is to help deliver value that a CEO can appreciate—such as new customers, additional business channels, or rapid product rollouts. In corporate-speak, they are known as value plays.

By contrast, says Schwartz, "Corporate learning focuses on efficiency and effectiveness in implementing learning. There's no question that in helping to administer learning and develop and deliver content, e-learning is a huge efficiency and a very effective way to go. But it's a cost-based argument."

The status boost for e-learning, says Schwartz, stems in part from the explosion during the 1990s of such companywide processes as enterprise resource planning (ERP) and customer resource management (CRM). "Companies are now in the second and third generation of those projects, and they're looking for e-learning platforms to support ongoing training for them."

For one such company, PricewaterhouseCoopers is helping piece together a learning platform to support an ERP overhaul that includes the installation of SAP (an ERP package), I2 (a supply chain package), and Siebel (a CRM package). The e-learning platform is a combination of KP2000, a learning management system from KnowledgePlanet.com, and Knowledge Warehouse, which is SAP's content management system. A learning portal, created with Knowledge Warehouse, is hosted on KnowledgePlanet's learning management system.

"This is a good example of a companywide strategic initiative that's leading a major learning effort," says Schwartz. "We expect to see a lot more of that."

Strangers in a Strange Land

What do a former junk bond king, a real estate tycoon, and a Wayne Huzenga wannabe have in common? They're all major stakeholders in new companies that have entered the training market in the past five years. And they are just the tip of the iceberg. A flood of entrepreneurs and their management teams are emigrating from formerly hot market niches in the industrial economy to superheated niches in the knowledge economy.

In the United States, the education enterprise, from cradle to gray hair, is the second-largest segment of the economy after health care. The education market is estimated by the investment firm W.R. Hambrecht + Company to total $772 billion.

Hardly anything is more telling of the new face of the learning market than a visit to a corporate training industry trade show. The Levittown-like booths of five years ago—a table, a chair, some brochures, and a guy in a nice blue suit—have disappeared from expo floors. In their place are towering constructions that feature espresso bars, leather sofas, second stories, and enough electronics to dim the lights of Las Vegas. They're staffed by Gen Xers in khakis and company-monogrammed polo shirts. With hastily acquired training lingo and sales skills honed at other dot.coms, these men and women are reaping the generous commissions that come with the sale of "enterprise-wide, end-to-end solutions." Front and center are companies that wouldn't have exhibited at a training show a few years ago—IBM, Intel, Oracle—and other companies that have changed their names so often you need a skip tracer to figure out who they really are.

Behind the scenes, you'll find some of training's founding fathers serving as discreet tour guides to the newcomers. Their management teams rarely include training pros. Instead, you'll find execs from other fields: toys, games, publishing, soft-drink bottling—all old-economy moneymakers. But as any geneticist knows, marrying outside of the clan enriches the gene pool.

Is Nothing Sacred?

What could be more sacrosanct to a trainer than the instructional systems design process? Yet, it too is being challenged by e-learning, whose essence is speed—the antithesis of ISD's cover-all-bases approach.

"The way we were taught to implement ISD 20 years ago often doesn't work anymore," says Diane Gayeski, principal in Omnicom Associates and professor in the Park School of Communications at Ithaca College. "It's too slow. By the time you find master performers and attempt to clone them, or by the time you write exquisitely detailed behavioral objectives, the business problem has changed. Trainers are trying to achieve a kind of perfection, and in that slow process you can miss the business opportunity."

The Internet has blurred the distinction between who is a content user and who is a content provider, throwing off balance another pillar of training—the role of instructor. "A lot of e-learning is a collaborative sharing of knowledge rather than an information dump," says Gayeski.

ISD models don't address the task of managing conversation and collaboration, she notes. "They are meant for something very different—project management and problem solving, which are applied very rigidly. It's not that ISD models are bad but that, typically, they are applied badly and their limitations aren't acknowledged. They may be good aids in learning instructional design, but master designers tend to be more fluid and rapid in the processes they use.

"In new training approaches, you should be able to address emerging problems and expect that some of your participants are actually the content experts. The just-in-time capability of the e-learning medium allows us to capitalize on new ideas."

E-learning also allows learners to displace the trainer at the center of the learning experience, says Joe Miller, president and chief learning officer at KnowledgePlanet.com. "The science and the instructional methodology and the standards are emerging now for an individual to be at the center of the experience, instead of being at the end of a flow of information from a subject matter expert or a trainer. That not only energizes the learner, but also shortens the time to mastery, making training time more efficient."

Miller continues, "I think the training industry will embrace that over the next 10 years and that it will appear in multiple modalities of training, not just e-learning, because trainers will see it as both valuable and doable."

"Technology is the great enabler," says Karen Vander Linde, a PricewaterhouseCoopers partner and the lead for outsourcing learning for PWC's clients. "It's creating new opportunities for learning professionals in how we can deliver learning." She sees knowledge management systems as prime examples of how technology can make learning continual rather than event-based. "CBT promised to do that, but it was really just a book on a screen. Now there is the capability to do much more."

Jeff Schwartz also sees technology enabling new things, but says the more important point for the profession is that "what we're doing in the learning space mirrors what businesses are doing as they restructure around the Internet."

Adds Schwartz, "We're seeing a much more pronounced interest in learning from senior executives beyond the HR or training worlds. In boardrooms around the world, the same question is being asked: How can I reinvent my company around the Internet before some Internet company takes me out?" E-learning enters the picture when CEOs realize they must transform their companies in 12 to 18 months, not in the three to five years it typically takes with a classroom model of learning.

Few CEOs, or their training advisors, choose a cold-turkey move away from classroom training. Most efforts are a blend of c-learning and e-learning. Yet, Schwartz still sees many training execs looking for ways to complement large instructor-led approaches with technology instead of looking at how things could be done differently with e-learning. "We encourage our [trainer] clients to really focus on the technology part," says Schwartz.

Counting What Matters

It has always been tough to isolate and measure the results of training. The decades-old Kirkpatrick evaluation model is still the blueprint for many trainers, even those who admit that its Level 4 (measuring the return-on-investment) is a nirvana seldom reached. The GartnerGroup has found that doing a Level 4 analysis costs at least twice as much as the training it measures. Will such classic measures as student reaction and even ROI be swept aside by the e-learning revolution?

KnowledgePlanet's Miller sees traditional measures of ROI changing "as we move toward knowledge-based businesses and a workforce that is measured by its ability to convert ideas into services, not products. But it's not happening yet." Pressure will come when companies have "mission-critical issues they really want driven by individuals, not by a corporate-mandated training program. Then you may see companies rewarding people for taking the initiative to acquire and use new skills and for aligning that effort with corporate goals."

Some of the most interesting developments in corporate learning are coming from new entrants to the training supplier market, especially those with lots of capital and corporate officers who come from fields other than training, such as games, systems development, and entrepreneuralism. As these new players rush to brand themselves and fight off competitors, they are attempting to invent better learning models, give learners more control, and integrate learning management into other business systems.

In the process, they're questioning many of training's oldest assumptions. Everything from what constitutes a basic unit of instruction to how to evaluate the success of learning programs is being reexamined in the light of what technology permits, and what matters to the business. That is bound to produce some innovations, and some discomfort, for training fundamentalists.

GartnerGroup's Aldrich notes the parallels with IT departments of five years ago and warns that history may repeat itself for training units. "Top officers are paying attention to strategic learning initiatives but not to train-

The Long View

Comments by Peter F. Drucker

I see the new technologies as only the trigger for the changes taking place in training. The root causes are elsewhere. One is the radical shift in the structure of the workforce.

Another root cause is the rapid restructuring of traditional work, whether in the factory or in large-scale repetitive clerical operations, which are actually production work. The application of systems analysis to mass production underlies the rapid decline in the number and proportion of blue-collar manufacturing workers in the U.S. labor force. It also underlies the upgrading of the blue-collar worker—something that traditional training does not yet understand and does not so far handle well.

A third root cause is new learning theory. Let me explain: Traditional training is a product of World War I, perfected in World War II. It arose out of the application of the basic concepts of Frederick Taylor's scientific management to the German invention around 1840 of apprenticeship. The first modern training was developed by Henry Ford's early partner, James Couzens, about 1914.

That kind of training hasn't become obsolete—far from it. But it is being transformed by the application of learning theories developed in the past 30 to 40 years, particularly in connection with Deming's total quality management. I could summarize that by saying that learning as we practice it still puts the teaching process at the center. Increasingly, we must instead put the learning process at the center.

There will, of course, still be training as we have traditionally understood it—predominantly for blue-collar and clerical people. But the growth sector is learning—still skills but, increasingly, concepts that must be learned by knowledge workers at all levels. GE's Crotonville, which I helped found 50 years ago, is the prototype for this new kind of learning for managers.

Now, new technologies make it possible to reach learners wherever they are and whenever they find it convenient, instead of bringing inadequately small groups to a central location away from their work. The learning devices we need for the new learning aren't first-rate college courses or even the first-rate seminars that so many universities are trying to market. They have to be designed for the new learning, which is what Corpedia and I tried to do with my online modules.

There will still be a need for skills training and for skills training that must be delivered where the workers' machines are. My knowledgeable friends say that can already be simulated, and I am certain that such developments will radically change the role and the performance of the skills trainer.

> But more and more of learning will be concept learning, and even more of that will be on the part of knowledge workers whether they are blue-collar or white-collar. So far, new learning is not being left to trainers, and as far as I can tell, traditional trainers are not reaching for it. In many institutions, both businesses and large nonprofits that I know, learning is the province of either the CEO or the senior HR executive.
>
> There is one thing that should be said loudly and clearly: trainers need to realize that things are going on that don't fit their assumptions, their own training backgrounds, and the way they typically have been doing their jobs.

ing departments," he says. "Virtually none of the IT innovations of that period, such as supply-chain management, intranets, ERP implementation, sales-force automation, and data warehousing, to name just a few, was introduced or championed effectively by the IT department. Instead, they were pushed by product vendors, systems integrators, and the consulting community. IT's involvement, if any, became maintenance."

He adds, "That upheaval is not unique to training departments. Trainers face the same revolutionary challenges as do banks, retailers, and even governments.

"Training is not going away, especially group training for customers. The part of the curriculum that is the same for all groups will be automated, freeing up trainers to be more like consultants."

Aldrich foresees a day when high-profile training, such as that which supports a new product or sets a new corporate direction, will be broadcast, not rolled out.

"The training organization will resemble CNN covering a war, working 24 hours a day for two to three weeks," he says. "If part of the program falls flat at 6 in the evening in Paris, it will be fixed in real time so that it's ready for the people on the East Coast of the United States when they get up."

When a profession finds its cherished practices under close scrutiny, there's often a tendency to circle the wagons and repel innovation. But for many trainers, that could be a career-limiting move. While traditionalists wring their hands about preserving instructional integrity, the new guard will forge ahead to reinvent learning so that it works with technology and supports corporate goals.

In the end, what trainers want may not matter. The growth of online high schools and colleges, plus the abundant opportunities to pursue learning online from Staples to Powered, may shape the expectations of the next generation of learners and the companies that employ them. Even in the knowledge economy, the market speaks.

Patricia A. Galagan is editor-in-chief of ASTD Magazines Group. Contact her at pgalagan@astd.org.

E-Learning: Are You a Tortoise or a Hare?

Marvin Gottlieb

To describe the e-learning industry as unstable is an understatement. There are a lot of questions facing any organization considering an e-learning option. This article discusses several of those questions, then suggests four "rules of engagement" for organizations and their training professionals for making it through the transition.

You know the story. The eager rabbit tears away from the starting line and in a short time perceives that he is so far ahead that he can focus on a variety of other things and still finish the race well ahead of the hapless, plodding turtle. The single-minded turtle pushes ahead step by step and ultimately wins the race by staying the course. No doubt there is a moral and lesson here that applies to the Internet in general and e-learning in specific.

The January 15, 2001 edition of *The New York Times* Business Section headlined and documented the demise of several dot-com rabbits, and we know there is much more to come. After running separate races, several companies that own content are either partnering with or buying companies providing learning management systems (LMSs). SmartForce is partnering with Docent, DigitalThink bought Arista, THINQ bought TrainingSoft, ElementK is partnering with Isopia, and there are many other consolidations completed or in the works.

This and other newsworthy items are included in the very interesting and informative January 2001 issue of *OnlineLearning Magazine*. In one article, entitled "The End of the Beginning," Clark Aldrich discusses the challenge of committing to a platform in an environment that is cluttered with competing standards. After stating, "… no one thinks today's HTML-based content is cutting it," he points out what he sees as an irony. "… creating platform-specific content today would limit the amount a vendor would be willing to invest in an individual course, defeating much of the purpose of e-learning platforms in the first place." On the other hand, if e-learning companies move too slowly, "…they'll end up with offerings that are built around tell-and-test slide shows with few just-in-time learning, virtual classroom simulation and knowledge management capabilities."

Reprinted with permission from *Communication Project Magazine*, Vol. 4.1, Winter 2001. Copyright © 2001 The Communication Project, Inc.

The Questions

Aldrich is speaking to and about vendors of training content and platforms, but the issue is even more complex for clients. These are just some of the questions that become part of the e-learning equation for a company considering an e-learning option:

- Why are we doing this? Because we think it will save money? Because everyone else seems to be doing it? Because it's just a logical extension of our enterprise-wide e-commerce strategy?
- Do we try to develop our programs in-house using our existing intranet and platforms? In this case, who owns the initiative? Training? IT?
- What do we do with all the content we currently have? Toss it? Add a second layer of development by trying to recondition it?
- If we decide to use a vendor, how do we choose one? They all appear to do the same things, so what are the differentiators?
- Are we best served with a thin-client platform? Do we need more data base and knowledge management support provided by a thick client?
- How do we know the one we commit to will be here to support our efforts down the line? Many of these vendors have changed names more than a few times already.
- What happens to the sunk costs we already have in other platforms and media—like Teleconferencing, CBT, electronic white boards? Can they somehow be integrated with the e-learning?

Let's address a few of these questions that are most widely shared by e-learning initiates.

1. Why are we doing this? At the risk of ruffling feathers of true devotees, there is only one reason that makes any sense—cost. Perhaps we should say "perceived cost," since most equations simply back out T&E and training materials like workbooks or other visual support items. Some more sophisticated analyses ascribe a value to trainee time and add that to the plus column. The assumption here is that if the e-learning is provided asynchronously, the trainees will get it on their own time without taking time away from revenue-generating activities.

Is this approach a good way to teach? Undoubtedly, there are subject areas and content that seem to fare quite well using electronic delivery. Does that mean it is the best way? While embracing components of the Internet that provide access to an increasing universe of information, most educators resist the practice of e-learning in the contemporary sense largely because most instructional content is still built on the "teaching machine" concept of B.F. Skinner, E.K. Thorndike, and others proposed in the 1950s. ("A Hypertext

> **OPERANT CONDITIONING**
>
> B.F. Skinner, the father of operant conditioning, is usually credited with the development of programmed instruction. In his classic 1954 article, "The Science of Learning and the Art of Teaching," Skinner described the conditions of the typical classroom as particularly adverse to learning. A single teacher cannot individually and appropriately reinforce thirty or more students at the same time.
>
> In this article Skinner first conceptualized a teaching machine for the classroom for use by individual students. This machine could present information, reinforce appropriately, and then branch to the next level of difficulty depending on the individual's performance. The roots of computer-assisted instruction can be easily seen in Skinner's teaching machine. (Karin M. Wiburg, "An Historical Perspective on Instructional Design: Is It Time to Exchange Skinner's Teaching Machine for Dewey's Toolbox?" http://www-cscl95.indiana.edu/cscl95/wiburg.html).

History of Instructional Design," www.coe.uh.edu/courses/cuin6373/idhistory/1950.html. Also see sidebar above.)

The need for a more constructivist approach to instructional design has been argued in an earlier edition of this magazine and will not be repeated here (Marvin Gottlieb, "Foundations of E-Learning," *Communication Project Magazine*, Volume 3.1 Summer 2000). However, it is interesting to learn what Internet "visionaries" have to say about e-learning. The same issue of *OnlineLearning* polled six individuals who are referred to as "'outsiders'—visionaries who have pondered technology's place in society but who aren't considered e-learning gurus." Each of them had reservations or warnings about the use of e-learning. (See sidebar, "The 'Outsiders.'")

The e-learning community is not the only communication-related segment to seek salvation on the web. *The New York Times* January 15, 2001 edition highlighted an article "Rethinking Internet News as a Business Proposition" about news organizations pulling back their commitment to web-based delivery. The article quotes Eric K. Meyer, a managing partner at NewsLink Associates, which conducts research into online journalism. He could be talking about e-retailing, travel, or other experiments including e-learning when he says, "This has been an industry that has been based on me-tooism and fads. Whenever someone did something, everyone else had to do it."

Internet Grammar

Also quoted is Christopher Feola, chief of technology at Belo Interactive, the online division of Belo Corporation of Dallas. Sounding like a latter-day disciple of Marshall McLuhan, he says, "… a period of overreaching attends the infancy of every new technology. Then you have business plans that bear no

THE OUTSIDERS

"With time people will recognize that e-learning is a fair to middling way of transmitting facts to a lot of people, but it's not a great way to actually get people inspired and pumped up about a subject."..."The more human the skill that you're trying to teach, the less applicable electronic means are."
Cliff Stoll—Author of *Silicon Snake Oil: Second Thoughts on the Information Superhighway and High-Tech Heretic: Reflections of a Computer Contrarian*

"I'd love to see dot-edu returning to the plate and seeing itself not just as a consumer of technical content, but creating a [teaching] platform designed to reach a lot of people."
Jonathan Zittrain—Assistant Professor of Law at Harvard, faculty co-director of the Berkman Center for Internet and Society at Harvard Law School

"In the post-Napster world, packaging something and selling it isn't the way you make money. Instead, you make money by being the preferred connector of people."
Jaron Lanier—Lead scientist for the National Tele-Immersion Initiative and creator of virtual reality programming language (VPL)

"I think the last thing people want is education anytime, anywhere. Who wants to be going to classes and doing homework everywhere, anywhere, around the clock? Education is not fun. Education is work, and it's about the hardest work people ever do. So we are not going to do ourselves any favors, speaking for the technology and education worlds both, by telling people this is going to be a pervasive thing in their world. Because that suggests that we don't know what education is and we don't really take it seriously as something that requires energy and effort."
David Gelertner—Professor of Computer Science at Yale University, chief scientist at Mirror Worlds technology, author of *Mirror Worlds* and *Drawing a Life: Surviving the Unabomber*

"The value added by the Internet is choice. And there is no such thing as Internet learning; there is only in-your-head learning. We're not going to have this magical training that's going to make everyone productive."
Esther Dyson—Chair of Edventure Holdings and author of *Release 2.0: A Design for Living in the Digital Age*

"...if something was published by Harvard University Press you tended to believe it because you knew it had gone through a serious editing process. Information published on the Net doesn't give you that feeling of security."
John Seely Brown—Chief scientist at Xerox, chief innovation officer of 12 Entrepreneuring, author of *Seeing Differently: Insights on Innovation,* and coauthor of *The Social Life of Information*

relationship to reality. The people who thought that the telephone was going to enable people to listen to symphonies look silly in retrospect."

And, as others have pointed out, sounding like McLuhan is not a bad thing when discussing the Internet. One of McLuhan's points that resonates with me is the notion that the content of a new medium initially incorporates the content of the previous medium. The content of movies was essentially books, newspapers, and Broadway until Fellini, Kurisawa, Antonioni, and others began to expand the "grammar" of film to create new images unique to the medium that could not be emulated by print or live performance. In the same way, the content of television was movies until we learned that TV is at its best as an extension of the eyes and ears: watching a live sporting event or O.J. Simpson traveling down the freeway with the law in soft pursuit. It is ironic that despite many experiments and millions of dollars spent developing television infrastructures as a vehicle for learning, the best (and most frequent) TV application for instruction is the "talking head."

> An age in rapid transition is one which exists on the frontier between two cultures and between conflicting technologies. Every moment of its consciousness is an act of translation of each of these cultures into the other. Today we live on the frontier between five centuries of mechanism and the new electronics.
> —Marshall McLuhan

I don't think we yet know what the "grammar" of the Internet is. But I'm almost certain that it's not television, or radio, or books. And yet I frequently have conversations with corporate people in charge of developing e-learning initiatives who long for the moment when bandwidth will allow for streaming video that doesn't jump, and two-way audio without the inherent delay. The longing is pragmatic because (a) we understand the old medium, and (b) we have all this stuff that we've already built or bought. Which brings us to the second key question.

2. What Do We Do with Our Existing Content?

If you're talking about training that's built on classroom or workshop models, you have to ask another question. What is the nature of the content? Are we getting a bunch of people in a room to teach them how to use Windows? To get the sales team up on the new enhancements to a core product? If so, there are opportunities to redesign the material to be presented electronically in both synchronous and asynchronous packages. If, however, the content involves human dynamics like interviewing, coaching, negotiation, and the whole range of management and leadership competencies, you are severely limited as far as what you can do electronically.

Does that mean that you can't use e-learning for soft skills development? Of course not. It's just that you're using it as part of the package and not the whole. In fact, if you have a three-day program that is 1/3 content and 2/3 activity, you can cut one day from the program along with the corresponding costs by delivering the "content" portion of the program as pre-work online. The up side is that you deliver to the classroom a participant fully prepared and certified to move forward with the discussion and practice aspects of your instructional objective. The down side is getting participants to do the pre-work.

It is not surprising that the majority of our work in e-learning at The Communication Project, Inc. (TCPI) involves the reconditioning or "repurposing" of clients' existing material. And after doing it for nearly ten years, first on proprietary networks and now on the Net, I can tell you, "it ain't easy."

While there are similarities between programs of the same type, each program and client will have specific requirements or idiosyncrasies that require a custom solution. Is the program being delivered locally? Nationally? Globally? If globally, what are the connectivity problems? What platforms can be supported? If certification of learning is desired or required (as in the case of our financial services clients) how do we collect the data? Store it? Ensure that a test is being taken by the person being certified? Do we allow participants to print out materials? If so, how can we be sure that they remain in compliance if something changes? How will the e-learning platforms integrate with our existing systems (a key concern for our technology companies)? Do we run from our servers or do we need a server devoted to the e-learning platform? If we use a host, what are the scheduling concerns? Security issues? Can the program get through our firewall? How do we promote and schedule the training to ensure a high level of participation (a big issue for our consulting firm clients).

Of course there are answers to these and other questions. It's just that very often the people driving the initiative have an unrealistic "wishful thinking" view of the ease and promise of e-learning and end up abandoning the whole effort when reality hits. Among those who have had experience trying to solve some of the problems of costs and logistics with other technology platforms, and are, therefore, more realistic about the obstacles, there is a desire to leverage their previous investments; which brings us to the third and final question to be considered here.

3. What Happens to Our Existing Platforms?

What happens to the sunk costs we already have in other platforms and media like Teleconferencing, PictureTel, CBT, electronic white boards?

In some ways, the answer here is simpler. Look at your content first. As part of any training reengineering, it needs to be divided into three categories regardless of platform: (1) content that is current and accurate; (2) content that is important but needs updating; and (3) content that needs complete revision or doesn't currently exist.

Many organizations driven by the thirst for economy are placing much of their redesign efforts and thrust toward e-learning on content and programs that are currently working well. Clearly there is a need for continuous improvement, but, as Henny Youngman might say, "Don't do that." You will likely spend as much or more money and end up with a less than satisfactory result. So, unless there is a compelling reason to do otherwise, you should continue to support the platform the program is currently using.

The second category offers some opportunities assuming that the content is currently platform independent; that is, it wasn't created specifically to be presented as CBT or on videotape. Paper-based and classroom programs generally provide opportunities to incorporate electronic enhancements like prework, follow-up, e-mail support, and chat communities to name a few. Since you needed to tamper with them anyway, you might take the opportunity to explore e-learning platform options.

The third category presents the most opportunity for innovation. However, a key driver here is the amount of time you have to get a program to the field. With short time frames you will do best to stay with platforms you already know. As seductive as it seems, e-learning takes a long time to prepare and deliver, and the learning curve on both the presenter and participant side is fairly steep—regardless of the platform.

Weathering the Transitional Storm

> After three thousand years of explosion, by means of fragmentary and mechanical technologies, the Western world is imploding. During the mechanical ages we had extended our bodies in space. Today, after more than a century of electric technology, we have extended our central nervous system itself in a global embrace, abolishing both space and time as far as our planet is concerned. Rapidly, we approach the final phase of the extensions of man—the technological simulation of consciousness, when the creative process of knowing will be collectively and corporately extended to the whole of human society, much as we have already extended our senses and our nerves by the various media.
>
> —Marshall McLuhan

While it's true that we can do things electronically today that were part of science fiction lore only a few years ago, we can't do all of the things we want to. Some day—maybe soon—the Net will connect us so seamlessly that it will stand out as the only logical solution to many of our communication and knowledge transfer challenges. We aren't there. So, in this transitional phase I suggest the following rules of engagement for companies and their training professionals who are the generals and soldiers in this engagement between technology and teaching.

Rule 1—Don't join the stampede.

Many companies who charged out of the gate have stumbled on some key hurdles. While finding that the percentage of companies offering e-learning for employees will double in the next two years, A Forum Corp. survey (www.forum.com) gathered a list of the most common obstacles faced by learning professionals. These included:

- Employee time for training/learning.
- Cost vs. value.
- Content quality.
- Perceived difficulty of e-learning.
- Lack of technology infrastructure.
- Internal resistance to technology/change.

Any one of these hurdles will trip up an e-learning effort. More than one will shut it down. Check your environment for the most effective ways to gain acceptance for e-learning technology in your culture.

Rule 2—Don't commit to one platform.

It is seductive to envision handling all of your e-learning needs by selecting one of the many vendor platforms with embedded authoring systems. By and large, they all do the same things. Many of the available platforms are feature-rich and enable you to present content in some manner, offer chat or conferencing options, register and track participants, and include a testing engine. However, selecting a platform to manage all of your e-learning needs requires that you conform to the limitations of that platform. I'm willing to bet that the first time you try to put up a program, you will want to do one thing that the platform won't accommodate. Also, can you be sure that the platform provider will remain at the cutting edge of what's happening in the rapidly changing environment?

As much as possible you need to remain "platform independent." While this may require more development work on your end, design training that is easily adaptable to different vendor platforms. Avoid complex branching screens and pop-ups that are more the province of CBT, and are usually annoying in Web environments. It is also advisable to have a separate vendor for registration and tracking if you can't manage the database in-house. This allows you to change e-learning platforms easily, or combine more that one platform in your training—like asynchronous training combined with periodic live training using a thin-client provider.

Rule 3—Make sure you have the full support and understanding of your stakeholders, and, if possible, your participant constituency.

Every design and implementation process must have a pilot component. You need to assemble a task force that compiles both enthusiasts and skeptics. Provide opportunities for your target audience to interact with the program and provide input. Conduct a force field analysis of your implementation strategy. What are the drivers? What are the restrainers? How can you enhance the drivers and reduce or eliminate the restrainers? E-learning will not sell itself, and giving orders will not make people learn.

Rule 4—Reach for the moon and settle for the tops of the trees.

Challenge your designers and e-learning providers with your highest goals. Many technical people are resistant to tampering with the machine once they get it running a particular way. However, when presented with a particular request, they often rise to the occasion and come up with excellent solutions. Often your idea will not be technically feasible. However, if you limit your thinking at the outset you are almost assured of coming up with less than you might have if you allowed your imagination to roam.

So, it seems to me that the winner's cup still goes to the tortoise. Get into the race, but take your time—the best is yet to come.

Marvin Gottlieb, Ph.D., is the president of The Communication Project, Inc. in Greenwich, Connecticut. This consulting group provides instructional design for workshops, seminars, self-instruction and e-learning, human resources development, and basic target market and organizational research. He is also an Associate Professor of Communication at the City University of New York, a frequent speaker on communication issues, and the author of five books: Getting Things Done in Today's Organizations: The Influencing Executive *(1999),* Managing the Workplace Survivors: Organizational Downsizing and the Commitment Gap, *with Lori Conkling (1995),* Making Deals: The Business of Negotiating, *with William J. Healy (1990),* Interview *(1986), and* Oral Interpretation *(1980).*

Integrating E-Learning with Business Goals

Delphi Group

Two of the major concerns of everyone involved in training today have to be with the implementation of e-learning and the alignment of training with organizational goals and strategies. This article, actually Module VII from the report "Enterprise E-Learning," written from an extensive survey undertaken by the Delphi Group, addresses these two concerns and shows how e-learning methods and strategy can be aligned.

The Business Justification for E-Learning

Given the growing demand for continuous training and education in today's tight labor market, it is easy to associate e-learning solutions with limited focus internal training initiatives. The market conditions also make it easy to associate e-learning solutions with limited-focus internal training initiatives. To do either at the expense of building business development and channel management is to miss the real benefit of this new generation of technology. Internal training is typically linked to operational issues and cost control, not revenue generation. Unfortunately, many organizations already using e-learning practices as if they were training are not fully leveraging its capabilities. The true business justification is applying e-learning to revenue-generating functions.

E-learning is one way to give both business partners and customers the ability to be proactive, rather than putting your organization in the position of constantly reacting and responding to their needs for precise information. Moreover, taking ownership creates greater immediacy for outside parties. Some of the business benefits of e-learning include:

- Keeping indirect channel participants current on product capabilities.
- Winning mind share with sales reps who push competing products (read "you sell what you know best").
- Promoting optimal utilization of products sold through indirect channels.

Reprinted with permission from *Enterprise E-Learning 2001*. Copyright © 2001 Delphi Group. All rights reserved.

- Educating supply chain partners in the end use of products.

Delphi Group research points out that more than half of the Global 2000 organizations surveyed stated that their collaborative commerce initiatives centered on communicating with partners and customers, using an electronic means other than the telephone. Within this group, one of the most frequently cited mediums for doing this involved creating a knowledge base of best practices, company, and product knowledge.

Identifying E-Learners

As the individual worker becomes more valuable and at the same time more transitory, training problems only increase. Retention issues and internal reward systems are only part of the solution. In a free-agent economy, the onus will increasingly be on the employer to ensure that the necessary people and systems are in place in order to remain competitive. Ideas, talent, products, and opportunities become lost or abandoned without proper infrastructure to deliver appropriately filtered knowledge to those who need it. A brilliant idea may occur in an instant, but mobilizing it to an uninitiated work force can take months or years.

The rapidity with which required skill sets change and time-to-market cycles shrink has begun to shift the notion of corporate education in the 21st century from the realm of classroom training to continuous education. The systems that used to support on-the-job learning, such as apprenticeship and mentoring, have been decimated by the discontinuity of today's workplace. This realization has led to a new corporate imperative: to align the dissemination of knowledge with the underlying corporate mission. The increased complexity of operations and opportunities obsoletes the traditional approach of prescriptive education, where workers are expected to learn in advance the bulk of what is required to fulfill their jobs. It also means that more people have access to more knowledge, signaling the end of the "knowledge is power" hegemony. Knowledge is yet another force that is flattening the organization.

Yet simply relying on heuristics and random knowledge exchanges offers little means of keeping pace with rapidly evolving skill requirements. In today's hyper-competitive market, the proverbial water cooler is an insufficient replacement for the formal classroom. The void left between formalized training and serendipitous discovery underscores the need for a "just-in-time" e-learning environment, where knowledge is dispensed as-needed rather than on a prescriptive basis. Again, this means continuous learning. Any employee may be learning at any given moment, while performing their assigned work. Simultaneously, that employee may be recycling their newly acquired and synthesized knowledge back into the business processes. E-learning recycles knowledge in continuous loops.

Markets Aren't Always So Smart

One way in which e-learning can have a profound impact on an enterprise's ability to recognize new opportunities is to quickly rally people around a new idea. Products for today's market, due to ever-decreasing lifecycles, must be continuously reinvented. Market forces which seem distressingly similar to Adam Smith's invisible hand, are commonly believed to drive business.

These purportedly blind, raging market forces present an enormous challenge to organizations: to continuously ramp up human resources on the latest trend, technology, or product. It is what management expert Peter Drucker refers to as organized abandonment, the ability to literally cannibalize your greatest successes in order to deliver the next successful product before your competitors do. In truth, sometimes the market prevails over what is seemingly a good idea for a product or service; one is reminded of how e-commerce was going to put bricks-and-mortar retail out to pasture. But other times an idea will rush into the market like a tsunami, as did the Razor scooter, completely baffling every industry and marketing prognosticator.

Enterprises that do not have a strong e-learning program in place are unlikely to be able to practice organized abandonment; lacking the tools for and focus on continuous reinvention, they are likely to drive everyone to extreme frustration as they constantly change the rules of the game.

On the other hand, successful enterprises that have incorporated e-learning as part of their strategies and processes think of supply chain awareness in terms of "What did we learn?" as opposed to "What do we make?" or "What did we sell?" For example, an architect's work may be described as either to design buildings or to translate human needs into aesthetically pleasing and functionally responsive structures. It's a lot easier to say that a residential architect designs ranch houses or split-levels, especially in these times that accentuate specialization. But what happens to the architect if demand for these types of homes declines, or even disappears? Clearly, someone or something must quickly provide the shift in focus or requisite skills needed to morph the competencies into new products and services.

The comfort in this is that core competencies always outlive specific products, despite the volatility of markets; the Coca-Cola company did not go out of business because New Coke was a market dud. E-learning, because it stresses continuity and incessant learning feedback loops, helps imbue workers and organizations with confidence in their ability to keep up with the market.

In many organizations, existing training systems and educational institutions actually undermine idea opportunities and organized abandonment.

> They are geared to react to, not to initiate, change. One might say they are not marketing-oriented. E-learning provides essential infrastructure support systems for high-velocity innovators. It can be especially valuable when it is deeply integrated into the marketing business processes, extending out to your business partners and customers, where it becomes a catalyst for innovation and an infinite generator of new ideas. Thus marketing itself becomes a student of e-learning initiatives, and gets smarter in the bargain.

Tactical Aspects of E-Learning

On the tactical side, e-learning can save time, money, and instructional resources:

- Saving time. E-learning delivers on the promise of anytime, anyplace learning. Education takes place at the learner's convenience. In many cases, the enterprise can provide education and training on an as-needed basis—for example to bring a team up to speed in order to launch a new product.
- Saving money. After initial startup costs, e-learning can be more cost-effective, especially when self-directed instruction is the learning mode. When the Web is used for delivery, it is the sole source of the media content delivery. Anytime, anywhere delivery saves costs, and employees don't necessarily miss work.
- Conserving instructional resources. E-learning utilizes the existing infrastructure of networks, intranets and PCs, while conserving and helping better utilize other corporate or organizational resources. For example, a new employee can begin study on his or her own and, once prepared, can move into the active learning phase with an instructor or mentor. That employee may, in fact, end up teaching others.
- Reuse of learning content. Learning no longer occurs in the vacuum of the classroom or seminar. What the individual learner retains from the learning experience can be returned to the organization through e-learning feedback loops and a knowledge management system.

Strategic Aspects of E-Learning

On the strategic side, organizations can use e-learning like other corporate resources. It can be an asset in launching new services or products, building quick-response teams, and developing new initiatives. E-learning, integrated into the value chain, should be especially integral to your organization's plans, business processes, information technology, and human relations.

- E-learning is about your core competencies and content management. Your organization's ability to train and educate people is as important as its manufactured product or delivered services. The better you train and educate your people, the better your core competencies. Likewise, information that comes from e-learning can be integrated and fed back into the organization to refine processes, improve systems, and train or educate others. When properly stored and organized, that information becomes tacit knowledge that can be disseminated and reused.
- E-learning inputs to your knowledge management systems. Tacit information from course materials and student work, along with information collected and stored in content management systems, are KM resources. These information assets might be anything from policies and procedures, business plans, product designs, or what-have you, and can be directed into the KMS and then re-deployed as needed.
- E-learning is part of your collaborative commerce strategy. Every time you bring people together, they are collaborating and learning from one another. That experience, regard less of how formal or informal, needs to be identified as part of your e-learning collaborative strategy. Knowing that their learning productivity is as important as their work productivity can be empowering for the individuals involved. Assessment is an important aspect of your e-learning collaboration strategy, both for participants and those who work with the information at a later date.
- E-learning is integral to your business processes and knowledge chain. An e-learning component should be a click away on every one of your Web portals—a virtual classroom, if you will. These clicks can be as simple as a product descriptor, as sophisticated as procedures for a supplier doing business with you, or an online instruction manual for your customers. In specific instances, you may want to have a standalone e-learning portal, where a diversity of instructional resources are available. You can deploy e-learning here, as well as creating an e-learning infrastructure that is deeply integrated into your business process and value chain.

E-Learning and the Value Chain

As enterprise value chains continue to increase in their complexity and their interaction with each other, chaos and unpredictability will enhance the value of time. What this really means is your enterprise has ever less time to accomplish its goals. The result is that you must attempt to leverage an ever-increasing amount of opportunity with an ever-decreasing duration of time.

With every timely idea, the clock is ticking from the moment of concep-

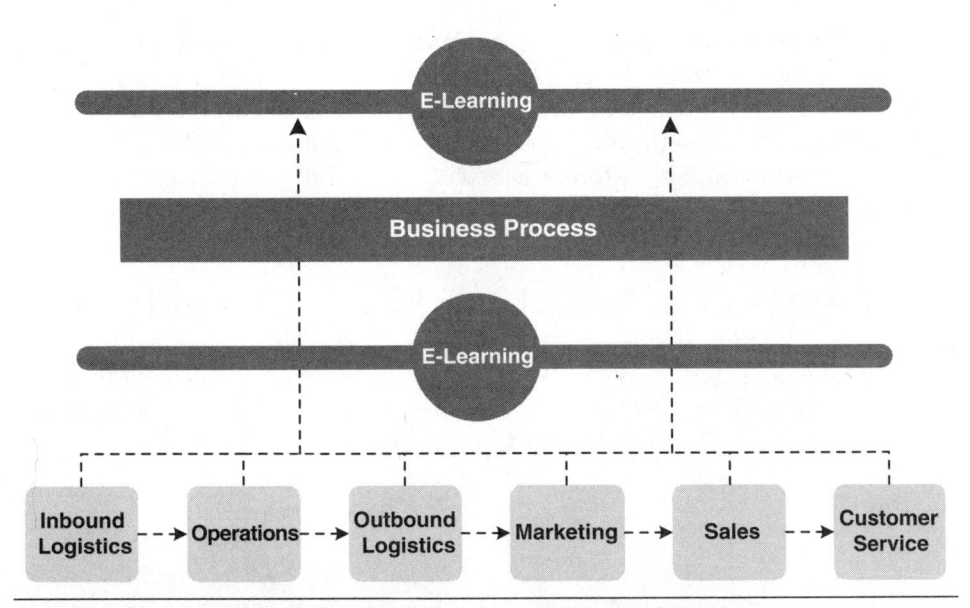

Figure 1. **The basic building blocks of enterprise e-learning**

tion. All content follows a utility curve where the value erodes as time progresses. The inherent latency in the process of creating complex communications, or having to follow-up to add further information, destroys the value of time sensitive content.

Within the span of a single career, we have shifted from a world where a week's delay was an acceptable response time to an "urgent request," to a world where we take for granted the 24x7 accessibility of information by partners and customers. In the face of this, the challenges of rapidly imparting knowledge throughout the value chain must be all but resolved by now, right? Unfortunately for most organizations the answer is "no." The fact is that this process is less about delivery than it is about creation.

It is a basic precept that although business opportunities in today's economy increase by orders of magnitude, the duration of any specific opportunity to match a time-based service with a time-based demand gets that much shorter. In this market space, market cycles are measure in intervals of days rather than months and years. It is here that e-learning provides its greatest payback: by manipulating time in such a way that an organization can more efficiently traverse the essential stages of bringing a new product or service to the market. The value chain becomes like an accordion, shrinking and expanding as the product or service makes its way.

In this context, it is reasonable to say the Internet is part of the value chain. It has shifted the burden of managing the time-sensitivity of content, which has in the past been placed at the foot of information delivery. Seemingly overnight, the Internet has changed by orders of magnitude the speed and expense of communicating on a "real-time" basis. Chat rooms have replaced conference calls and teleconferences. Document delivery used to take a day and cost upwards of $15; now, with e-mail, it is nearly instantaneous and free. Moreover, the supplier or business partner is often at one end of the value chain, using the Web and e-mail, and the customer is usually at the other end, doing the same thing. That is why it is so critical to incorporate portal technology with your e-learning and knowledge management systems.

Delphi Group delivers strategic advantage at the intersection of business and IT. Its thought leadership has assisted more than 20,000 professionals in the Global 2000. Its core competencies are in the emerging technologies of collaborative commerce, portals, content, and knowledge management, enterprise wireless, and e-learning. Visit their Web site at www.delphigroup.com.

E-Learning: New Twist on CBT

Bill Roberts

The Internet is helping employers take computer-based training initiatives to the next level. But it's not easy and it's not all a matter of technology. This article discusses various CBT initiatives and offers several recommendations: don't expect that e-learning will save a lot of money (at least at the beginning), focus on your business objectives, get your training specialists to decide on methods and technology, and do some smart internal marketing to prepare employees for your initiatives.

Another employer has joined the ranks of those using Internet-based technology to enhance their computer-based training (CBT) initiatives: the U.S. Army. Within the next year, the U.S. Army Recruiting Command (USAREC), based in Fort Knox, Ky., plans to launch a Web-based USAREC University that will handle much of the training for its 15,000-member staff.

USAREC University will offer online courses for entry-level recruiters, mid-career recruitment leaders and faculty who train recruiting specialists. A consultant involved with USAREC estimates the system could cut by at least 30 percent the time recruiters spend in school at Fort Jackson, S.C., potentially saving the Army millions of dollars.

"Most of the training now is done by instructors," says David Dawson, a retired master sergeant and training consultant to USAREC. When USAREC University launches, Dawson says, it will offer thousands of hours of training, focusing primarily on the sales techniques used by recruiters. The program also will allow students to schedule classroom training at Fort Jackson and will provide a database to track recruiter competency, certification and career progression.

Last year, the recruiting command made its first foray into CBT. It put onto CD-ROM 18 hours of instruction to train staff in a new recruitment information system. Learners completed the CD at their own pace before receiving an additional 16 hours of instructor-led training. Dawson, who was still in service and the ranking non-commissioned officer for the project, says the content is designed to be moved to the Web when the infrastructure is ready.

Reprinted with the permission of *HR Magazine*, April 2001. Copyright © 2001. Published by the Society for Human Resource Management, Alexandria, VA. All rights reserved.

Web-based training—also known as online training or e-learning—is the latest evolution in CBT. Instead of putting a CD-ROM on every desktop, e-learning allows organizations to post training courses on a Web site, which then can be visited by workers and easily revised by instructors. Gone are the days when CDs had to be updated, reissued and distributed each time curriculum changed.

"As Internet bandwidth increases, companies can distribute material around the country and the world on the Web," says Paul Jeffries, CEO of Logic Bay Corp. in Minneapolis. Logic Bay served as the contractor for the Army's CBT project and is vying for the USAREC University contract. Two years ago Logic Bay put 80 percent of its clients' content on CD-ROMs and 20 percent on the Web. Today, he says, the ratios are reversed.

Latest Wrinkle in CBT

However, experts say e-learning initiatives face significant challenges—many of which are not technology-related. Proponents of Web-based teaching programs must prove they can meet business objectives, be cost-effective and effectively train learners.

That may be why the number of corporate training programs delivered through technology, including the Web and CD-ROM, remains relatively small, says Mark Van Buren, director of research at the American Society for Training and Development (ASTD) in Alexandria, Va.

ASTD's most recent survey of CBT, conducted in 1999, found that only 8.5 percent of all training was delivered via some kind of technology. Van Buren estimates that today, only about 10 percent of training programs are computer-based. "People continue to tell us that in two to three years as much as 20 percent of learning will be delivered through technology," he says.

Brandon Hall, CEO of brandonhall.com, an e-learning consulting firm in Sunnyvale, Calif., predicts an even higher percentage. "It might not be that big right now, maybe 8 to 10 percent. But I think it will become half of all training in the next few years."

What has been holding back the technology? Van Buren says, "There are various reasons why more progress hasn't been made."

Among the reasons: some companies didn't put enough resources into their Web-based e-learning pilot projects; hence the results were less than satisfactory. Some earlier (pre-Web) CBT programs were not positive experiences for learners because the programs were not well thought out; it is not easy to woo these learners to try the newer e-learning programs. Also, implementation of e-learning programs requires high levels of executive buy-in and change management, never simple propositions. And, the jury is still out on the effectiveness and cost-savings of CBT.

In addition, says Van Buren, "There isn't strong evidence that it is superior to instructor-led learning. But, there's no evidence that it is inferior either."

Maybe that's why some companies take the attributes of e-learning and combine them with instructor-led training, not to replace it, but to enhance it.

For instance, IBM's online training focuses on management development. Hall estimates IBM has moved about 80 percent of this instruction online. But, he says, IBM still brings managers into the classroom for role-playing, team building and other group experiences. "The implication is that training specialists will have to figure out what you do online and what you do in the classroom," Hall says.

At Logic Bay, Jeffries agrees that some types of training dictate more traditional teaching methods. "Some skills are best taught in a human environment," he says." At some point the learner must pick up the wrench and change the tire. Any training aimed at building culture or leadership skills is best done in the classroom."

Steve McMillen, director of executive leadership development at Hillenbrand Industries Inc., a funeral and health care services company based in Batesville, Ind., agrees. McMillen has seen too many executives awestruck and led astray by technology. "The allure, cachet and sexiness wags the dog a lot of times," he says. "It gets people focused on the technology instead of looking at what they're trying to accomplish."

McMillen keeps that in mind as he leads a pilot program to develop a leadership program for Hillenbrand's top 200 executives. He believes executives learn best by doing. So the company has a number of opportunities for managers to work in temporary assignments to learn the competencies they don't have. The company also offers appropriate content to these executives on the Web.

Jeffries and others agree that the future is likely to see this kind of blending of traditional and high-tech teaching methods. The use of chat rooms and other Internet-based collaboration tools can bring to e-learning a level of human interaction that was absent from early CBT efforts. Van Buren believes that as more companies operate with virtual teams of geographically dispersed, Internet-linked workers, e-learning will emerge as a natural way to teach teamwork.

Linking Global Learners

Finding the right mix of e-learning and classroom training may depend on other factors, such as company size and your staff's training preferences.

For many organizations, CBT programs, enhanced by Web-based technology, represent the only feasible means of implementing companywide training initiatives. Cisco Systems Inc., based in San Jose, Calif., is in the middle of an enterprisewide e-learning rollout. Continuous learning is an integral part of Cisco's corporate culture, says, Bill Souders, Cisco's information technology (IT) director of global e-learning technologies. But with the size of its staff increasing tenfold over the past five years, Cisco found that traditional classroom training methods quickly were becoming impractical. "It became clear that a lot of the formal training we provide wouldn't scale," says Souders.

Cisco also discovered that e-learning works well for its employee population. The fast-growing technology company, which has 35,000 employees in 160 countries, began its e-learning initiative with a small experiment. It offered training to 200 field salespeople, using two different methods: one group of 100 received classroom-based training, while the other group did the coursework via e-learning. The e-learners retained slightly more material than the others, and they reported a much higher level of satisfaction with the training. Souders says that's because the e-learning students could go through the training on their own time, at their own pace.

Even before the experiment, individual business units at Cisco had launched their own e-learning initiatives. Initially, each unit set up its own learning management system (LMS) to handle the administration of training events. Experts agree that a robust LMS is essential for an enterprisewide Web-based e-learning program. It registers users, tracks their performance and provides links to courses as well as appropriate reports to management.

The enterprisewide initiative led by Souders was primarily aimed at adopting e-learning standards for Cisco, including a standard LMS platform. With the support of CEO John Chambers and key executives, the company formed a unit specializing in e-learning. That unit chose an LMS from Saba Software Inc., of Redwood City, Calif.

Souders says it is too early to tell what the savings from adopting an e-learning-based program will be, but he expects they will be substantial.

Elusive ROI

ASTD's Van Buren is skeptical of big claims of cost savings from e-learning programs. Not only are the results of a successful training program often hard to quantify, many organizations fail to accurately tally the costs of e-learning implementation. Van Buren says he has seen very few reliable return-on-investment (ROI) analyses. Although he believes e-learning programs will catch on, he cautions, "People should go in with their eyes open."

For one thing, it can be expensive, costing an average of $500 million for 8,000 students. Hall believes that, although it is costly to set up, e-learning can save companies money on training in the long run. Hall recently conducted a best-practices study of a dozen companies with e-learning programs. While half of the firms in the report said it was too early to judge whether e-learning had resulted in significant savings, one—IBM—estimated that online training programs had saved the company $200 million in one year.

One way to get a better ROI may be to outsource. An LMS either can be installed on company servers, or outsourced to a third-party provider—often a less expensive option. For example, Saba and Logic Bay, in addition to selling the software, also offer hosting services for clients.

Sell It

A key ingredient for a successful CBT initiative is effective internal marketing. The experiences of the companies in Hall's best practices study attest to this fact. "If you don't have a serious marketing program, you find the inverse of "If you build it they will come," Hall says.

David Dawson says that is what the USAREC experienced when it initially launched its CD-ROM-based training program. Even in the military, where training can be mandated, Dawson says they spent too little time promoting the new training method.

"It takes a lot of effort to get the old guys who are now in leadership roles to support these efforts," he says.

Bill Roberts, a freelance writer based in Los Altos, Calif., writes about business, technology and management.

Audience Analysis and Instructional System Design for Successful Online Learning and Performance

Margaret Martinez

This original article is aimed at readers who recognize that traditional classroom design methodologies may not always work for online learning, especially when an instructor is not available to facilitate learning. It discusses two important areas for designing personalized online learning solutions. The first deals with understanding that learning environments strongly influence how we learn, especially online. The second discusses how to create instruction that recognizes, matches, and supports how individuals want and intend to learn differently.

It's not enough to use traditional classroom methodologies to design today's online and distance learning solutions. Today's solutions need to enable individuals to learn independent of the instructor as they continually improve to meet rapidly evolving challenges. Unfortunately, many learners coming from the traditional classroom setting do not learn as well without an instructor. For these learners, the transition to online learning is not always an easy process. The transition is eased if instructional design methodologies consider how individuals want or intend to learn online differently. This perspective focuses on the impact of emotions and intentions. Technology focused or primarily cognitive-based solutions (processing, building, and storing knowledge) that do not consider the impact of emotions and intentions may not always be suitable for online learning, especially when an instructor is not available to manage learning direction, progress, and outcomes.

Reprinted with permission of the author. Copyright © 2001 Margaret Martinez. All rights reserved.

New Requirements for Online Learning

Designers are striving to design online learning environments and instruction that encourage and enable learners to stay abreast and comfortable with new technology, constant change, and continual learning and performance improvement. However, after years of instructor-directed learning, too many learners have been trained to be dependent on an instructor. As individuals move online, many learning solutions may not work well with learners who are not self-directed, self-assessed, or self-motivated enough for learning online independently.

To address today's sophisticated online learning and performance needs, the consideration of a comprehensive set of human factors from a whole-person perspective is critical—especially the psychological differences that the instructor tapped into in the classroom. This perspective considers how emotions and intentions impact learning and performance improvement. The question is how do we put the instructor in the box and emulate what the instructor intuitively does in the classroom?

Traditionally, designers have focused on cognitive factors (e.g., how people build, process, and store knowledge). These primarily cognitive designs often overlooked other sources for individual learning differences, such as emotions and intentions. If considered, these important factors are often relegated to a secondary role. Historically, the cognitive approaches reflect the industrial-age perspective that assumes that an instructor is available in the classroom and can respond to the audience's diverse range of complex human needs. As a result, instructors have often unintentionally nurtured a learning dependence that detracts from the learner's ability to self-motivate, self-manage, and self-assess online learning.

How and Why You Learn Differently

As learners move online, how can we use our instructional designs to attend to the basic human attraction for individualized attention? How can we support more self-motivated, independent, and self-directed online learning? How do we provide designs that acknowledge learners as feeling, intentional, thinking, and social human beings, each who can self-manage a diverse set of personal traits that influence learning? How do we provide environments and instruction that match how individuals want and intend to learn differently, improve learning ability, and continually foster increasing expertise and satisfactory learning relationships?

Many individual difference theories and models exist today to address how individuals learn differently. One seldom-recognized learning model considers the dominant impact of emotions and intentions on how humans learn online. Good instructors in the classroom intuitively considered these human factors (e.g., gratification, satisfaction, and rewards). Online or for distance education these factors are too often overlooked.

By considering the impact of emotions and intentions, learners can better understand how and why they learn differently. For example, some learners are happiest learning in collaborative, facilitated environments with learning tasks accomplished in a structured or linear fashion. Other learners thrive in competitive environments that focus on specific details, tasks, and projects. Some learners are passionate about exploring new challenges and taking risks, and enjoy using learning to achieve long-term personal goals. Finally, some learners are formally or situationally resistant to any kind of learning that appears to have little value or benefit.

Few online learning models consider these important distinctions. Translating this kind of psychological information into learning strategies helps individuals create and manage learning situations that work best for them. Using this information, learners can practice using personalized strategies (i.e., increasing self-motivation, self-direction, and learning autonomy) for greater online learning success.

Designers can translate this kind of psychological information into learning and design strategies as they take steps to personalize solutions. More importantly, they can help learners increase self-motivation, learning autonomy, and overall chances for online learning success.

Learning Orientations Research Foundations

Recent advances in the neurosciences have revealed the extraordinary complexities of learning and brain activity dynamically interacting with internal and external influences. Similarly, the learning orientation research (based on this brain research) creates a whole-person theoretical foundation to understand the complex psychological sources influencing learning. It considers the *dominant impact of emotions* and *intentions* on brain activity to explain how individuals respond differently in various learning situations.

In comparison, conventional primarily cognitive models have typically emphasized how people think or process information as the dominant influence on learning. Primarily cognitive learning models are solutions (e.g., learning styles or learning modalities) that often subjugate or overlook the influence of emotions and intentions. Traditionally, they have relied on instructor intervention in the classroom to manage emotions, intentions, and social issues, in addition to the cognitive aspects. Table 1 highlights significant differences between learning orientations and a typical cognitive model that describes learning styles.

Four Learning Orientations

The learning orientation research describes four distinct learner types, called learning orientations. Learning orientations generally describe how learners want and intend to approach learn. The four types are transforming, performing, conforming, and resistant learning orientations. The learning orien-

Learning Orientations	Learning Styles
Considers how individuals learn differently, using a comprehensive set of influences and sources for individual learning differences, including affective, connotative, social, and cognitive factors.	Considers how individuals learn differently by focusing primarily on cognitive ability, preferences, and differences in how learners prefer to think or process information.
Considers emotions and intentions as a dominant influence on learning (i.e., key influences that may develop, guide, or manage how we use cognitive ability).	Considers cognitive ability and preferences as the dominant influence on learning.
Considers how learners generally relate and respond to key internal and external influences in their environment.	Considers how learners use cognitive ability to process content, often regardless of the environment.
Provides measures to assess online learning ability.	Estimates cognitive preferences.

Table 1. **Describing key differences between learning orientations and learning styles**

tations model provides specific scales for measuring common learner attributes. This model adds other higher-order psychological factors (affective, connotative, and social) to the traditional, primary cognitive understanding about learning. Most learners will typically identify themselves as one or sometimes a combination of the following learning orientations. Note: since this is an article about successful online learning, the resistant learning orientation is not included.

Transforming learners are likely successful online learners with sophisticated online learning skills (i.e., highly self-motivated, self-directed, self-assessed, and independent). They use self-directed, strategic planning, and holistic thinking to apply great effort to achieve long-term goals. These learners are generally risk takers, innovators, and passionate, highly committed learners. They most often:

- place great importance on self-managed learning, committed effort, independence, and long-term vision.
- use personal strengths, ability, persistence, challenging strategies, high-standards, learning efficacy, and positive expectations to manage learning successfully.
- lose motivation and may become frustrated or resistant in environments or conditions that interfere with their aggressive learning patterns and challenging goals.

To be more successful, these learners should focus more on details to ensure task and project completion and practical application of theories and concepts.

Performing learners are skilled online learners who are typically self-directed in areas that they value, otherwise they rely to a greater degree on external support (instructors, coaching, fast tracks) to set goals for them. Similarly, these learners are self-motivated generally in learning situations that interest them; otherwise they seek extrinsic rewards (external sources for motivation) for accomplishing objectives. Typically, these learners are short-term, project-oriented thinkers who systematically and capably achieve average to above standard learning goals and tasks. They may:

- minimize or streamline learning effort by meeting (clearly acknowledged) only the stated objectives, getting the grade, and avoiding exploratory steps or effort beyond the requirements of the situation and learning task. These learners lose motivation or may even get angry if too much effort is required and the rewards are not enough to compensate the perceived effort.
- prefer interactive (hands-on), competitive or team environments.
- take less control and responsibility for their learning and often rely on others (external resources) for coaching, motivation, goal setting, schedules, and direction.

To be more successful, these learners should acquire more long-term, holistic thinking skills to find reasons to self-motivate and self-direct more challenging efforts.

Conforming learners are less successful online learners because they depend largely on the quality of and support from the environment and social relationships. They prefer to rely on explicit guidance and simple steps provided by an instructor. Complex online learning environments will frustrate them. These learners are concerned with safety, security, and acceptance. Conforming learners generally:

- are less skilled learners.
- react strongly to external influences.
- depend on supportive, structured environments.
- have less desire to control or manage their learning or initiate change in their jobs or environment.
- take fewer risks.
- have difficulty learning in open learning environments, which focus on high learner control, discovery or exploratory learning, complex.

To be more successful, these learners should acquire more independent thinking, risk-taking skills that enable them to trust themselves and take greater responsibility for their own learning.

Learning Orientations	Mass Customized Environments
Transforming Learners	For transforming learners, design environments that are sophisticated, discovery-oriented, mentoring environments. They prefer loosely structured, flexible environments that promote challenging goals, discovery, strategies, problem solving, and self-managed learning orientations. These learners want to be assertive, challenged by complex problem solving, and able to control, self-manage, and self-monitor learning and progress to attain higher standard, long-term goals.
Performing Learners	For performing learners, design semi-structured, interactive (hands on) environments that stimulate personal values, encourage teamwork, and provide details, tasks, processes, and project completion. These learners prefer task oriented, energizing, competitive, environments. These environments should use coaching, practice, and feedback to encourage self-motivation, problem solving, self-monitoring, and task sequencing—while minimizing the need for exploration, extra effort, and difficult standards.
Conforming Learnings	For conforming learners, design safe, low-learner controlled, structured environments that help learners achieve comfortable, low-risk learning goals in a linear fashion. These learners prefer environments that are simple, scaffolded, non-risk environments that use explicit, careful guidance that helps individuals learn comfortably in an easy, step-wise fashion.

Table 2. **Descriptions for mass customized learning environments**

Online Learning Environments

The first step in improving online learning designs is to consider the learning environment that works best for different learners—with or without an instructor or facilitator. While sophisticated learning technology is available, much still needs to be understood about the impact of online learning environments (technically, psychologically, and pedagogically).

Years ago in 1957, Lee Cronbach challenged the educational field to find "for each individual the treatment [solution or environment] which he can most easily adapt." Cronbach suggested that consideration of the treatments and individual together would determine the best payoff because we "can expect some attributes of a person to have strong interactions with treatment variables."

In the '80s, Carl Bereiter and Marlene Scardamalia, from the Ontario Institute for Studies in Education, suggested "learners in supportive environments have high levels of self efficacy and self-motivation and use learning as a primary transformative force." Today's challenge is for you, the online learner, to identify which elements in an online learning environment best support your interests, values, and expectations and match your successful learning attributes for strong interactions. More importantly, which elements will help you improve online learning ability (over time). One way to accomplish this challenge is to use learning orientations to estimate your online learning ability and identify areas for improvement.

Personalized (Mass-Customized) Learning Environments

The strategies for building learning environments should support the broad variability in learning from a whole-person perspective, not simply in cognitive terms. They should consider how emotions and intentions influence learning, thinking, and performance. The personalization strategies described in Table 2 suggest that a closely matched learning environment will have a positive impact. It is important to note that these strategies promote the use of sophisticated technology to create one learning environment that can flexibly adapt to create separate presentations (e.g., for transforming, performing, or conforming learners). Moreover, these strategies do not promote the creation of separate or distinct environments for three different learning orientations.

Design Strategies for Instructional Solutions

This section presents the second important area of consideration for designing online learning solutions. This set of strategies for design instruction highlight the three learner-difference factors that can strongly influence how we learn: self-motivation, self-direction, and learning autonomy.

As you design your online instruction, consider the additional strategies in Table 3 to enhance your current instructional and assessment strategies.

Summary

After reading this article, I hope you'll find that I have given the kind of information you need to expand your understanding about learning by considering (a) the influence of a comprehensive set of key psychological factors (connotative, affective, social, and cognitive) that influence learning differently, (b) the often overlooked dominant impact of emotions and intentions on learning, (c) critical human relationships between learning environments, key psychological sources that influence learning, accomplishment, and online learning ability, and (d) new design strategies for supportive learning environments and instruction that can individually adapt to how people want to learn.

Learning Strategies	Transforming Learners	Performing Learners	Conforming Learners
Self-Motivation			
User Interface	Achieve in an open learning interface that can stimulate exploration, discovery, problem solving, and complex, high-capacity processing.	Achieve in a competitive, simulated (hands-on) learning interface that focuses on external values and keen interest for medium stimulation and processing capacity.	Achieve in a consistent and simple interface for minimal stimulation and processing capacity.
Interaction	Achieve with occasional mentoring and stimulating interaction for achieving long-term goals (*Mentoring*). (Note: continually seek and use resources that help learner achieve best effort).	Achieve with consistent coaching and interaction for achieving short-term goals (*Coaching*). (Note: continually seek coaching to raise standards and call forth best effort).	Achieve with continual, explicit guidance and reinforcement for achieving short-term goals (*Guiding*). (Note: continually seek guidance to take greater risks and call forth best effort).
Feedback	Achieve with inferential, discovery feedback.	Achieve with concise, team-building, sometimes competitive feedback.	Prefer explicit, conforming, trust-building feedback.
Rewards and Recognition	Be inspired by added personal value increased by self-directed, instrinsically competitive standards, newly acquired knowledge to accomplish challenging, long-term goals, praise and recognition by mentors, and continual opportunity for innovation and improvement.	Be inspired by added personal value increased by external influences, immediate praise and recognition of expertise and accomplishment by higher ups and peers, competitive or team reward structures, and continuing opportunity for striving, increasing expertise, and project completion. Encourage learner to look for ways to increase self-motivation.	Be inspired by added personal value increased by stability, conformance, acceptance, and immediate praise and recognition by peers for incremental achievement of guided accomplishments. Look forward to guided opportunities to apply and reinforce newly acquired expertise. Encourage learner to look for ways to increase self-motivation.
Information Need	Seek holistic, theoretical information to solve long-term problems, discover new challenges, and achieve personal goals. Enhance information gathering with increasing specification and practical application.	Seek practical, specific information to solve short-term problems, complete projects, and demonstrate expertise. Enhance information gathering with increasing holistic or conceptual information (coached/rewarded by others).	Receive simple, guided information to solve short-term problems, complete assignments, and show accomplishment. Enhance information gathering with increasing levels of problem solving (supported by others).

Table 3. **Description of instructional strategies supporting different learning orientations (continued on next page)**

Learning Strategies	Transforming Learners	Performing Learners	Conforming Learners
Content Structuring	Achieve with freedom to construct own content structure and opportunities for new knowledge and innovation.	Achieve with freedom to accomplish tasks and projects well with minimal effort.	Achieve with freedom to rely on help from others to guide content structure, progress, and outcomes.
Collaboration & Peer Interaction	Achieve in a high-standard, complex environment with sophisticated goals and challenging accomplishments. (Note: may be frustrated by too much focus on detail, short-term goals, and lack of long-term accomplishment).	Achieve in a competitive team, interactive environment that supports intrinsic and extrinsic values focused on project completion and increased expertise. (Note: may easily be frustrated by extra time and effort required for slow peer interaction, long-term goals, or unmet needs).	Achieve in a guided participative environment with direction and answers provided by the instructor. Rely on a "sense of community" and combined achievement. (Note: may be frustrated or left behind by fast pace, complex processes, and high-level standards and achievement).
Learning Autonomy			
Independent Learning	Assume learning responsibility, self-select goals, self-manage learning, progress and outcomes—independent of the instructor. (Note: avoid frustration if placed in restricted environments with limited learner control).	Assume all learning responsibility in areas of keen interest. (Note: Try not to relinquish learning control and extend less effort for topics of less interest or in restrictive environments. Consider long-term implications and benefits).	Trust themselves to make decision about learning and rely less on guidance from others. Use structured environments to acquire self-directed learning skills. (Note: try not to relinquish all responsibility for learning to accomplish assigned learning goals).
Relationship to Instructors or Facilitators	Work with mentors as an added resource to explore and expand knowledge-building opportunities and attainment of long-term personal goals.	Use coaching from instructors or facilitators and interaction with peers as an added resource to enhance expertise, accomplishment, and project completion.	Use coaching and guidance from instructors or facilitators and careful interaction with peers as an added resource to increase achievement of low-risk goals.

Table 3. **(Continued)**

Learning Strategies	Transforming Learners	Performing Learners	Conforming Learners
Self-Direction			
Goal-Setting and Standards	Set and achieve personal short- and long-term, challenging goals. Maximize discovery and effort to attain personal, long-term goals and increasingly difficult standards, beyond those set by others.	Set and achieve short-term, project-oriented goals that meet average-to-high standards. Situationally minimize or maximize efforts and standards to reach assigned or negotiated standards. Consider long-term goals and consequences.	Follow and achieve simple, task-oriented goals. Take incrementally difficult steps and risks and increase effort (over time) in supportive environments with safe, manageable standards.
Task Sequencing	Sequence tasks according to performance needs, personal learning requirements, holistic information expectations, and varying levels of expertise. Use hypertext or multiple-levels to allow precise access to content and problem solving to accomplish objectives. (Note: consider influences on intrinsic values and benefits).	Sequence tasks according to interactive performance needs, detailed information needs, and increasing levels of expertise, and effort. Use semi-linear, logical branching (accessed by subtopic). (Note: consider influences on external values and benefits (e.g., using competition, adventure, or creativity) to guide task sequencing.	Sequence tasks according to manageable steps, low-risk performance requirements, and less complex, safety-based information needs. Use linear representations to provide simple, selective access to increasing levels of expertise. (Note: consider influences on stability and conformance to guide accomplishments).
Knowledge Building	Commit great effort to discover, elaborate, and build new knowledge and meaning. Consider practical application of new knowledge and innovation.	Increase effort to assimilate and apply relevant, valued knowledge and meaning. Develop interest in exploring related issues and discovering long-term consequences.	Accept and reproduce knowledge to meet external requirements. Develop trust in assimilating and experimenting with application of new knowledge.
Problem Solving	Learn using complex, whole (holistic)-to-part, problem-solving opportunities that lead to new content. Alternatively, consider part to whole solutions and practical applications.	Learn with competitive part-to-whole problem solving for specific projects and tasks. Develop trust in conceptual ability and long-term thinking. Alternatively, consider whole (holistic) to part opportunities.	Learn with scaffolded support for simple problem solving opportunities that reconfirm achievement and acceptance. Work with guide to improve problem solving ability and develop trust in own learning and problem solving ability.

Table 3. **(Continued)**

Learning Strategies	Transforming Learners	Performing Learners	Conforming Learners
Practice	Achieve using one good example and one bad example. Take time to consider practical application and apply knowledge towards project completion.	Achieve using a few good and bad examples. Take time to consider conceptual knowledge and long-term implications.	Achieve using multiple good and bad examples. Take time to consider related, increasingly difficult problems and achievement accomplished through increased effort.
Progress Monitoring	Self-assess and review achievements based on challenging standards and long-term personal goals.	Self-assess, seek assessment from others, and review achievements based on short-term goals and negotiated standards. Improve self-assessment skills.	Accept assessment and review from others and consider accomplishments based on short-term goals and standards aligned with stability and conformance. Improve self-assessment skills.
Questioning	Ask probing, in-depth questions to expand knowledge. To improve, seek opportunities to apply new knowledge and consider practical details.	Ask pivotal questions to solve problems and complete projects. To improve, seek opportunities to understand related concepts and long-term consequences.	Ask functional questions to accomplish assignments. To improve, seek opportunities to understand related concepts and long-term consequences.

Table 3. **(Concluded)**

References

Bereiter, C., and Scardamalia, M. (1993), *Surpassing Ourselves: Inquiry into the Nature and Implications of Expertise* (Chicago: Open Court).

Cronbach, L. (1957), "The Two Disciplines of Scientific Psychology," *American Psychologist*, (12), 671-684.

Margaret Martinez is CEO of The Training Place. Reach her at mmartinez@trainingplace.com.

A Primer on Tracking Web-Based Training

Janeen Rossi

How can you tell how well people are doing when taking a Web-based training course? That's the question this original article by Janeen Rossi of e-learning Objects LLC addresses. The technology for doing such tracking can be tricky, and the author explains how to make it work. She tells you about integrating WBT pages to database systems so managers can follow the online training progress of their direct reports. This is a topic not frequently discussed, so this article should be useful to you.

Is there a way for your managers to find out how well their direct reports are doing when they take a Web-based training (WBT) course? There can be. There *should* be. It is time to enable your WBT to tell managers if their direct reports have passed the course. After all, if the employee does not invest the time and effort to learn new material, the company is not getting its money's worth from installing and offering such courses.

More Reasons to Track WBT Progress

In addition to the business need described above, here are more arguments for tracking WBT learner progress:

- Learners need feedback on how well they are understanding the material in the WBT
- Managers need to know which employees have passed courses that are part of employee development plans or the company's new learning initiative
- HR needs to know which employees have which skill sets as part of your human capital management
- Training developers need to know if any section of their content or tests are consistently giving trouble to the learners and must be revised
- C-level executives (e.g. CEO, COO, CIO) need to know that the sales force comprehends and is prepared to put into action the company's newest strategy

Reprinted with permission of the author. Copyright © 2001 Janeen Rossi. All rights reserved.

It is possible to track nearly any piece of information about WBT progress that you define. You need only answer the question, "What do you want to track?" For starters, you can collect e-learning metrics such as learner status by WBT, learner achievement, WBT enrollments and completions, dates of access, and dates of completion. The resulting WBT tracking data can be an essential element of your ROI measurements. WBT score and status information gives you the hard data you need to make strategic decisions about your learning operation and justify budget levels. It can also give you notice that a correction in strategy is needed. Progress data can be correlated to determine learning effectiveness, training cost, and business results of learning.

The Technology Challenge

Technology you have purchased and installed may be able to help you achieve your WBT tracking goals. But WBT tracking solutions are not in the category commonly referred to as "out–of–the–box." There will be technology gaps to fill. As in most cases where enterprise level data collection and content integration is involved, it can be difficult. But if you have made the enterprise decision to deploy WBT, you have already signed up for technical challenges that far exceed how to get the ceiling mounted projection system to hook up to your guest instructor's laptop. This primer will prepare you for the road ahead so that you can avoid the pitfalls that those who have gone before you are still crawling out of.

From a technology standpoint, basic ingredients include WBT files, a learning management system (LMS), and a database (if you have an LMS, then there is a database associated with it). Bear in mind that if you have an LMS that shows learner transcripts with course scores and status, *the LMS plays no role in creating or gathering the WBT completion information it displays*. An LMS can only run reports on data that it has been sent by e-learning content. In most cases, the only data an LMS will report on are the course status, score, and date of completion—nothing more detailed than these.

Some LMS software programs enable the submission of WBT completion data by providing frame-based content development tools with preset communication paths to the LMS. The drawbacks are that these tools force a "page-turner" WBT structure and the extent of their ability to track progress is a kind of bookmarking function that allows the learner to resume the WBT on the page last *browsed*. This hardly constitutes completion data. To justify training expenditures and prove return on investment, you need hard data like scores on lesson assessment tests, results of scenario-based exercises, and a quantitative achievement measure on the course final exam.

And although there are content development tools that are billed as producing "plug and play" content, using them does not guarantee successful communication with your particular LMS. Many of these development tools are set to produce content that will communicate with specific LMS software.

If yours is not the named LMS, you will need to build connectors or "bridges" between the content and the LMS that will complete the communication path. If you are not using an LMS, you will need to design and deploy these connectors that enable database storage in any case.

Two Options

Converting your WBT from flat pages, pages that are comprised of text and graphics, to content that is fully integrated with a database and reporting mechanism is not simple. It requires a collection of HTML pages to become a fully functional Web application. Doing that will likely require a Web application engineer (someone probably not on staff in the training department).

Consider the two basic options below along with their benefits and drawbacks. The primary division lies in whether you use an LMS.

Scenario 1

- WBT
- No LMS
- An independent database (not related to an LMS)

Enabling direct communication of completion data from a WBT to a database is easy enough, provided that you have permission to connect and save data to the database. You need to provide a mechanism to identify learners to ensure that their completion data is stored and credited to them, and you need to devise a way for the completion data to persist from one learning session with the WBT to the next. Running reports on the database involves a standard set of skills that most database administrators have, but someone will have to design the database table structures that will store learner progress data.

Advantages. Saving data to the database and reporting on that data is simpler in this scenario than in the case of using an LMS because LMS software does not permit direct access to the database where it stores other learning-related data such as the learner's identity, role descriptions, and learning history (transcript).

Disadvantages. Devising a means to identify employees and verify those identities against data from the HR database can be complex for the programmer, and bothersome to the learner in the form of a login screen. If more than one WBT is tracked, that adds to the complexity of the situation as there are now multiple WBTs and multiple learners. For every possible combination of WBT and learner, a unique record identifier must be created to keep all the records straight. Also, there is no convenient way to see results of WBT sessions because all reports are a manual process.

Scenario 2

- WBT
- An LMS
- A database associated with an LMS

Adding an LMS to the equation exponentially adds functionality that benefits your entire organization—such as automated registration for all courses, a single portal for all learning related information and tasks, and employee skills and competency management. With regard to WBT tracking, the LMS will render the WBT tracking data instantly useful by showing learners and their managers WBT scores on personalized transcripts and automatically crediting learners with the skills that are associated with each course they complete. An LMS also provides easy Web-based reporting of nearly all data that it creates or collects. With this option, you are still required to produce content that can send completion data to the LMS. The LMS is completely blind to anything that goes on in the learner's browser.

Advantages. There are no additional databases to maintain or tables to design because all data is stored and managed within the LMS and its associated database for which you have a support contract with the LMS provider. Since most LMS providers now build to meet e-learning industry standards, the content that you intend to communicate with the LMS will also have to conform to standards. The emerging standards promoted by organizations such as AICC (Aviation Industry CBT Committee) and SCORM™ (Sharable Content Object Reference Model) are excellent and increase the likelihood that your content will be "plug and play" with other standards-compliant e-learning software that you implement in future versions of your e-learning infrastructure.

Disadvantages. Ironically, the last item in the advantages section above is also a disadvantage of this option. The downside of building to standards is that it is a much more difficult task than building to meet your unique requirements in your own (known) environment, the latter of which is undoubtedly a subset of the full set of requirements specified by the standards committees. To meet specifications identified by the standards organizations, you must first research hundreds of pages of documentation from the various organizations and choose your approach to achieving standards compliance. It is an arduous time-consuming process that requires the full time dedication of software developers.

In both scenarios described in the previous section, the most common technology gaps in this content integration project occur in the following three locations: (1) the WBT pages, (2) the Web server, and (3) the database.

- At the page level, WBT needs to create meaningful progress data—such as quiz scores or record of successfully completing practice exercises—as the learner interacts with the WBT. At the Web server level, progress information such as "passed" or "failed" needs to be translated into data streams that can be understood by the database. A second common technology gap at the Web server level is the lack of access to the database so that the data can be submitted for storage; a task that is made more difficult if an LMS is involved. Lastly, company personnel need to run reports on the progress data in the database.

The Differentiating Factor: Creating Meaningful Progress Data

Challenges at the Web server and database junctions are software engineering problems that are outside the scope of most training roles. When you do consult a software engineer to design a WBT tracking solution, the first question you will be asked is "What do you want to track?" The most essential piece of WBT tracking—and the element that makes or breaks effective WBT—is creating the meaningful interactions and completion data that together comprise the measurement of a learner's achievement in a course.

Most foundation level attempts at WBT production consist entirely of graphics and text with perhaps a test that is a grouping of multiple-choice questions. Enhancing your current WBT development processes to include the creation of scored interactions is an exciting and rewarding undertaking. Embedding scored interactions from which completion data is collected completes the learning cycle that in many cases was broken when training moved out of the environment in which instructors gave learners real-time feedback on their participation.

Scripting and DHTML is the most common way to add the functionality of answer judging, feedback, and scoring (all separate functions) to a question. Scripting can be in visual basic script, JavaScript and certain interactive behaviors can be created by script with Dynamic HTML enabled browsers. The next step up would be Java™ applets, ActiveX™ controls, and Flash™ movies embedded into a Web page.

Most of these technologies are out of the skills set of a training developer turned WBT developer. There are many software programs that automate the creation of fully functional questions for WBT authors such that no scripting knowledge or skill is required.

Creating complex practice exercises that are scenario-based and involve dynamic branching in response to a learner's progressive set of choices is not a standard output of the typical quiz question software. But this is precisely the type of interaction that should be the basis of WBT and will result in the learning and on-the-job proficiency that is the goal of training. Instructional designers in your group can generalize complex scenario-based interactions into design requirements for custom templates that a multimedia consultant can build for your group. It is well worth the investment. Simpler versions of this type of interaction can be achieved by following a scenario presentation with a set of multiple-choice questions.

The scores from any or all of these judged and scored interactions constitute the objective measurement of the learner's achievement and must comprise the final WBT course score that is communicated to the LMS (or the database in the case that there is no LMS). A word of caution: once you install the capability to create and track score and completion data, you may need to curb some instances of militant progress tracking. There is such a thing as too much information, even in WBT tracking.

What to Look For in WBT Tracking Solutions

When searching for WBT tracking solutions or designing one of your own, keep these basic requirements in mind:

Applicable to All Content. Take into account all the types of WBT that are part of your course catalog currently as well as planned future WBT offerings. Include pre-packaged WBT courses that you purchase from outside vendors and custom WBT courses that you outsource to consultants in your needs assessment. Ensure that the WBT tracking solution you choose will work with all of them or in the case of outsourced WBT production, require that the finished product communicate with your LMS. Go the detailed level of taking into consideration the various structures of WBT sites. If you find that no single solution will meet all the WBT tracking needs, consider instituting some parameters that narrow the variations on WBT structure or source.

Standards-Compliant. Content that is designed to meet standards such as AICC (Aviation Industry CBT Committee) or SCORM (Shareable Course Object Reference Model) will win half the battle of meeting the first requirement described above but does not guarantee victory. When you purchase WBT that is AICC-compliant, require that the content provider perform a demonstration of their content on your delivery environment that proves it will communicate to your AICC-compliant LMS. Most certainly, content developed by external vendors will not communicate completion data to a progress database developed in-house, so plan for extra project expense and time to port the content to your tracking solution, even if it is standards-compliant.

Require No Programming Skills. In order for the WBT tracking solution to be sustainable, it can not require your WBT authors to become software engineers. This is a tall order as the task really is to convert flat Web sites to mini Web applications. E-learning software providers have been working on this problem for at least one year now and we will begin to see the results of that focus in the coming months.

The best approach would be to survey the available tools, choose the one that meets most of your organization's needs, and then put internal or contract resources on filling in the technology gaps. Once you devise a solution to the WBT tracking problem in your organization, you can codify it and install it into your company processes and standards. The key to success is to have clear business and learning requirements in mind. And it all starts with that question, "What do you want to track?"

Janeen Rossi is CEO of e-learning Objects, LLC, which focuses on e-learning methods and technologies. Contact her at janeen@e-learningobjects.com and on the Web at www.e-learningobjects.com.

PART THREE

Approaches to Organizational and Individual Performance Improvement

As performance improvement specialists, it is appropriate for trainers to be familiar with and understand many different approaches to achieve their improvement goals. It's the purpose of Part Three to examine a variety of techniques for doing this aimed at enhancing both individual and organizational productivity. To that end, we have included 12 articles that share the experience and insights of practitioners and researchers. We've broken this into two subparts: *organizational performance* and *individual performance*.

Organizational Performance

We start this group of articles with a kind of global look at organizational performance improvement: "Creating and Sustaining the High Performance Organization" by Keith Owen, Ron Mundy, Will Guild and Robert Guild. It looks at five key success factors for creating sustainable high performance and then looks at five gaps that get in the way of this and how to close those gaps and then concludes with some hints on how to get started.

Among the other articles in this section, we include Lin Grensing-Pophal's "Motivate Managers to Review Performance," which looks at how to help managers use performance appraisals to actually improve performance (see more on this subject just below in the individual performance section).

From Nancy Dixon's *Common Knowledge: How Companies Share What They Know*, we include the excerpt "Serial Knowledge Transfer: How Groups Learn From Themselves." It includes several examples from different organizations that demonstrate both the value of sharing knowledge to improve performance and techniques for doing this. On the same theme is Bill Roberts' "Dare to Share: Using Extranets to Exchange Knowledge," which explains the use of a particular technology, extranets, to assist in the sharing of knowledge and explains, as well, how this technology facilitates collaboration.

Finally, we conclude with a piece that also looks at technology and how it can have a negative effect on organization performance if not well managed. This is because technology can distract employees from their main tasks. The article "Companies Need Well-Defined Electronic Monitoring Policies" by Carrie Garcia looks at how to deal with this potential problem in a positive and forthright manner.

Individual Performance

Managing professionals and helping them improve their performance can be a daunting task. The first article in this section, "Reinforcing Professional Self-Management for Improved Service Quality" by Baird K. Brightman looks at this issue and includes a number of techniques for doing what the title suggests.

Emotional intelligence continues to be an important area of study for improving performance and creating harmony on the job. How can you enhance EI? That's the question the article "Emotional Intelligence: Training People to Be Affective So They Can Be Effective" by Mike Bagshaw examines, and it includes several ideas for training in EI.

Leadership clearly has a direct influence on individual performance. In the original article "The Key to Leadership Today" by Marlene Caroselli, the author describes how to positively influence employees. She places special emphasis on the notion of cognitive dissonance, which can directly interfere with employee motivation and cause problems on the job.

In the next article, we revisit performance appraisal in "86 Your Appraisal Process?" by Jonathan A. Segal. In this article, Segal looks at all the reasons why people say performance appraisal doesn't work. He explains how each of these complaints is often a manifestation of how appraisals have not been properly administered and then what to do about it.

The final three articles in this section look at dealing with stress and how it can affect performance, how to retain peak performers by individualizing employee recognition programs, and how managers can work with employees to set goals that help improve performance. Each of these takes a practical, how-to approach, providing specific ideas for helping individuals improve in several different ways.

Organizational Performance

Creating and Sustaining the High Performance Organization

Keith Owen, Ron Mundy, Will Guild, and Robert Guild

This article shares what the authors have learned about developing and sustaining an organizational culture that is capable of high performance, of delivering quality products and services. It starts with a brief discussion of the concept of culture, presents a model for managing the organization toward sustainable high performance, and concludes with some practical steps for improving organizational performance.

The ability of an organization to sustain the delivery of quality products and services is essential to its long-term success. We believe this ability is a learnable organizational competence. If the capacity to sustain high performance is a learnable competence, why do many organizations fail to do so? We have observed three major deterrents to sustaining high performance:

1. Often the senior leadership of an organization has an inaccurate understanding of the marketplace in which the organization must compete. When this is the case, it almost inevitably leads to vision, mission, and strategy that are inappropriate. Often, even when leadership does have an accurate understanding of the market, they may fail to translate the organization's vision, mission, and values into the strategies and processes that will enable them to compete successfully. As a result the organization's culture, systems, and infrastructures may not be adequately aligned with the realities of the marketplace.

Reprinted from *Managing Service Quality*, Vol. 11, No. 1, 2001. Copyright © 2001 MCB University Press. All rights reserved.

2. Often the behaviors required to successfully implement the business strategy are out of alignment with customer and marketplace requirements. This can be true for leadership or employee behaviors. For example, leaders often succeed by exercising unilateral control of decision making. Such behavior is typically at variance with the behaviors required to create sustainable high performance, which must focus on empowerment, responsiveness, and accountability at the lowest levels possible.
3. Organization systems and process often fail to support the organization vision and strategy. As a result, organizations focus on, and measure, the wrong things. For example, the performance management system may rely on general measures that communicate little information, and thus it may not recognize or hold people accountable for the specific behaviors required to respond to customer needs.

Responsiveness to the marketplace, leadership and employee behaviors, and systems and infrastructure design and deployment serve to create the organization's culture, the set of shared beliefs and experiences that define the identity of an organization and serve to guide its behavior. Culture evolves over time and serves to guide the perception of what is important (value), what is possible (opportunity), and what is real (reality). This set of beliefs comes to be expressed through the routines that become normative in the organization and reinforced through the rewards and punishments meted out by the organization. One belief that impedes sustainable high performance is that hard measures of performance are adequate; however, this belief is contrary to sustainable high performance because it is the soft stuff of culture which, in reality, drives the hard measures upward.

In this paper we will share the results of our studies of the determinants of an organization's ability to develop and sustain a culture capable of delivering quality products and services over time. Such studies have enabled us to identify and understand the general requirements for sustaining high performance and provide insight into how to do it.

We start with a brief discussion of the concept of culture, which is followed by a model of how to manage the organization toward sustainable high performance. The paper concludes with a discussion of some practical steps you can take to improve your own organization's performance.

The Keys to Creating Sustainable High Performance

The Five Success Factors

The sustainable high performance organization is one that is able to:
- remain responsive to marketplace expectations; and
- sustain the behaviors required to meet marketplace expectations.

Organizations go into business to create long-term performance and values. So, a sustainable organization is one that thrives over the long haul, not just the short haul. This does not mean that it is a static organization; rather it implies that it is an organization that is much like a highly adaptive organism, one that beats the evolutionary odds and survives through adaptation.

This concept is not theoretical; rather it grew out of attempts to help clients develop and sustain high performance. We found the same set of variables emerged time and again as the drivers of sustainable performance.

If you, as a manager, wish to increase the odds that your organization's performance is sustainable, what do you do? What are the factors that will ensure your success? There is a set of core elements that drive the organization's ability to maintain high performance. Success is determined by bringing about the alignment of these core elements, as illustrated in the model shown in Figure 1. The model shows that the organization's ability to provide quality products and services and create value is determined by bringing about the alignment of five key factors:

1. Senior leaders' perception of the marketplace.
2. A shared vision, mission, values, and strategies which are aligned with the realities of the marketplace.
3. Leadership practices that are congruent with the vision, mission, values, and strategies.
4. Infrastructures which support and reinforce the vision, mission, values, and strategies.
5. Employee behaviors that meet customer needs.

Further, the model indicates that there is a cause and effect relationship among these factors, that is, when the factors are aligned, business performance will improve measurably. These relationships can be managed by creating and sustaining the alignment of five key success factors.

1. Senior Leaders' Perception of the Marketplace. Organizations produce sustainable performance as long as senior leaders understand and effectively respond to their market. Markets change over time due to factors such as

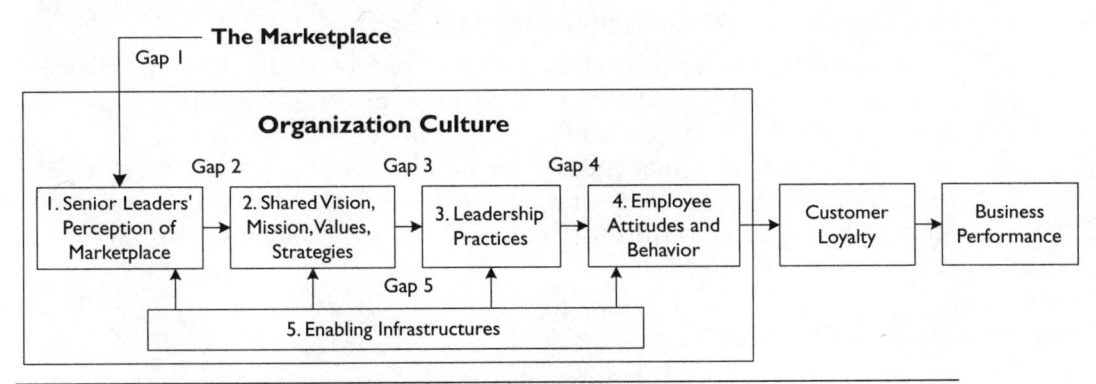

Figure 1. **Sustainable high performance culture model**

competition, technological change, and the economic environment. Successful organizations are able to anticipate and adapt to these changes.

When organizations offer products and services that meet market needs in terms of reliability, quality, and customer service, at a price that is considered reasonable and with payment terms that are affordable, they are likely to establish customers who are loyal and committed to the organization.

To excel, organizational structures, processes, and behavioral patterns must be continually and totally aligned with the type of market the organization is designed to serve. Who are your prospects and customers? What do they want? At what level of service will they be more than satisfied? What kind of organization do we need to create in order to acquire and retain profitable customers? These are the kinds of questions leaders must be able to correctly answer.

2. A Shared Vision, Mission, Values, and Strategies Which Are Aligned with the Marketplace. To build a high performing organization requires the organization to create structures and develop processes aligned with the requirements of the market the organization is striving to capture. The organization's vision, mission, values, and strategies are the foundations on which these structures and processes are built. Many messages are implicit in the vision, mission, values, and strategy statements. They tell people what is important, what counts in the organization, what gets rewarded, and what gets punished. Most importantly, they tell decision makers from the top to the bottom of the organization what they are expected to produce and what is acceptable in doing so.

It is easy to trivialize the concepts of vision and values, but research by Baum *et al.* (1998) has shown that the way in which the vision and values of the organization are framed and communicated impacts the bottom line. Companies' vision statements that were specific, targeted toward a specific strategic intent (e.g. to be the number-one maker of fine custom cabinets), and emphasized growth and learning, outperformed (in terms of market share, return on investment, and perceived market value) those whose visions were less carefully crafted and communicated.

3. Leadership Practices That Are Congruent with the Vision, Mission, Values, and Strategies. The term "leadership practice" describes what managers, from the very top to the very bottom of the organization, do. Every moment of every day, managers are making decisions and solving problems to meet goals. Our studies of sustainable performance have consistently shown that in high performing cultures effective managers, through their behaviors:

- ensure clear expectations;
- promote belonging;
- foster employee involvement in decision making and problem solving;

- place an emphasis on and reinforce the importance of quality;
- promote a consistent focus on meeting customer needs and requirements;
- encourage and reward learning and skill development.

If the vision, mission, values, and strategies of an organization describe what the organization aspires to be, then leadership practices describe what the organization actually is. In a recent study of the "drivers" of profit growth, the behavior of immediate supervisors was the most powerful determinant of employee engagement, productivity, and customer satisfaction and loyalty (Buckingham and Coffman, 1999).

4. Enabling Infrastructures Which Support and Reinforce the Vision, Mission, Values, and Strategies. Enabling infrastructures are the systems which select, develop, recognize, reward, terminate, and protect people, as well as the technical and operational sub-systems which enable employees to produce the products and services customers desire. The infrastructures serve to keep culture, climate, and tasks fully aligned and working toward the set of organizational goals.

Some examples of infrastructures are:

- goal-setting system;
- the measurement systems;
- the performance management system;
- the leadership evaluation system;
- the rewards and recognition system.

By measurement systems, we refer to all those elements of the organization that are deployed to provide data to employees that tell them what they are aiming at and how close they are to hitting the target. Some examples of measurement systems are:

- Systems to tell you who your best customer prospects are, to monitor the cost-effectiveness of your marketing efforts, to assess customer loyalty, and to help you identify and deal with barriers to sales growth.
- Systems to monitor how direct managers are behaving and to provide them feedback.

5. Employee Behaviors That Meet Customer Needs. Sustainable high performance is possible only when you have the right people in the right roles with the right manager. To ensure that you have the right people in the right jobs you must first identify the strengths of the individual employee. Second, you must position the individual in a role that capitalizes on these strengths, and third, you must engage the employee such that they are actively using their talents. When organizations do this successfully, employees exhibit:

- competence;
- cost-effectiveness;

- commitment;
- congruence with the organization's core values;
- desire to serve customers.

These are the behaviors required to maintain sustainable performance because they enable employees to respond to the ever-changing world of customer needs and expectations. Now let us examine the gaps that sometimes prevent organizations from attaining sustainable high performance.

The Five Performance Gaps

Often there is a gap between what is and what needs to be with respect to the five performance factors. For example, the available infrastructures may not be responsive to employees' needs for information; leaders may exhibit behaviors that are inconsistent with high performance and the values of the company.

Whatever the cause, when there is a gap in practice, the result is a reduction in the organization's capacity for sustainable high performance. Next we will discuss the causes of such gaps and suggest methods for identifying and eliminating them.

Gap 1. Marketplace and Senior Leaders' Perception of the Marketplace. *Causes.* One thing that differentiates companies is their ability to sustain performance over time. It is one thing to create strategy, it is another thing to continually modify and execute it effectively. An excellent example of this is now occurring in the utility industry. The leadership in many electric utilities had been convinced that the slight increase in rates that would be required to add renewable resources would eliminate customer demand for these resources. However, many managers in a client organization believed customers might be willing to accept such increases and extensive customer research validated this position. In this example, senior leaders failed or refused to listen to the marketplace as it demanded that more of its energy needs be met from renewable energy sources. The list below shows some causes for gap 1 we have observed in our work:

- Leadership has not successfully assessed marketplace expectations.
- The organization does not know who its real customers are, nor what they require to be satisfied and loyal.
- Customers' preferences have changed, but leadership fails to understand this.
- The processes for aligning the organization's strategies, processes and people are ineffective.
- Leaders lack confidence in the available market research.
- Pressure from short-term financial markets influences leaders to adopt short-term solutions.

Closing gap 1. Challenge: create processes that enable you to stay on the leading edge of emerging trends in customers' needs and buying preferences by providing product and service offerings that will be successful.

In our experience there are three strategies that produce results:

1. *Evaluating customer loyalty.* Customers are one of the most important assets of any business because they provide two economic advantages. Repeat sales to current customers cost much less than acquiring new customers, so they are more profitable. Loyal customers can provide a dependable revenue stream, providing financial stability that the organization can build on to grow.

Many companies attempt to get input from customers. Some do this simply by having a method of recording complaints. However, from years of research we know that 90 percent of customers who are dissatisfied will not tell you. Other companies have a formal process of measuring customer satisfaction. But customer satisfaction is not the same thing as customer loyalty. In many cases customers who claim to be generally satisfied are all too willing to go to a competitor.

What you need to seek are tools that not only assess the level of satisfaction and loyalty but also provide information about what the organization can do to create more loyal customers. Asking the right questions is important in continually monitoring how well the company is meeting customer needs. Focusing on the wrong questions can lead to disaster.

Several years ago we did a study for a company that manufactured video boards for personal computers. This company was focusing on quality. Our study established that newer technologies, already on the market, were rendering the product obsolete. This company had the right idea about monitoring the market but was asking the wrong questions; as a result it failed and closed its doors.

2. *Evaluating the marketplace.* Markets are made up of individual buyers. This is stating the obvious, but it leads to all sorts of implications that are not so obvious. Because markets are made up of individual buyers we must assign relative importance to individual preferences such as price, quality, reliability, level of service, technical innovation, marketing channels, and availability.

We can only treat individuals as a single entity if we can group them into homogeneous segments based on common preferences. For example, individuals might be grouped into "risk takers" and "risk avoiders." If you are selling a new technology, "risk avoiders" might focus on potential problems, while "risk takers" might relish the benefits.

Since we cannot profitably be all things to all people, our mission is to identify and quantify market segments whose preference patterns we can most profitably match. We occasionally read of some genius who is wildly successful because he had a clear vision of a market and took advantage of it. Since we cannot all be geniuses, we must look for a methodology to obtain a vision of our potential market with enough confidence that we are willing to bet our company on it.

3. *Seeking informed opinions.* Survey research can provide this vision and, with the use of statistical sampling, can provide objective confidence levels that the findings truly reflect the market. But useful research is not just about surveys and statistics. It is also about asking the right questions, the ones whose answers will allow us to set strategies and direct action. For example, we used a technique called Deliberative Polling® to enable executives at a company to observe and interact with customers. This technique is designed to elicit informed opinions from stakeholder groups including customers. By enabling this direct interaction, decision makers are able to understand two facts they had overlooked through more traditional forms of research: customers wanted energy from renewable resources; and they were willing to pay for the difference in cost.

Gap 2. Senior Leaders' Perception of the Marketplace and the Organization's Vision, Mission, Values, and Strategies. *Causes.* Once leaders understand the marketplace, they must be able to shape and deploy a vision, mission, strategies, and values that effectively encapsulate and communicate what needs to be done in order to attain high performance. This involves not only shaping the vision, but also creating a sense of urgency about what must be done to attain it, creating a dedicated leadership who believe in it, mobilizing commitment, and institutionalizing it. Proper alignment of the vision, mission, values, strategies, structures, and processes is crucial to sustainable high performance.

Even so, there is often a gap between the nature of the marketplace and the vision and strategies of the organization. As a consequence, critical decisions about structure, processes and people are based on invalid criteria. Some symptoms of this gap are shown below:

- Processes are ill-matched for the kinds of things the customers want.
- There is a lack of understanding of customers' needs and desires.
- People are rewarded for the wrong kinds of behaviors.
- The vision does not reflect the realities of the marketplace.
- Customers' needs have changed.
- Corporate vision is ill-matched to requirements of the marketplace.
- Leaders' true values are incongruent with the customers' needs.

Closing gap 2. Challenge: the challenge confronting leaders at all levels of the organization is to use valid information from the marketplace, translate it into sound strategy, and ensure that the organization is continually aligned with the strategy.

What can you as a manager do to ensure that your organization has functionally aligned a shared vision and business strategy? The first order of business is to develop a sound vision and mission of the kind of organization you want, while the second task is to manage the vision deployment process.

Shaping the vision and mission. There are two aspects to shaping a vision:

1. design; and
2. communication.

In terms of design, a recent study by Baum *et al.* (1998) showed that visions communicated by the CEO with the following attributes were associated with venture growth:

- brevity,
- clarity,
- entrepreneurial challenge,
- future orientation,
- stability,
- ability to inspire,
- abstractness.

Managing the deployment process. Once the vision and strategy have been shaped, the problem shifts from design to deployment. In their book, *Change at Work,* Mink *et al.* (1993) discuss the process of planned change as moving through phases:

- creating the need and readiness for change,
- mobilizing widespread commitment for change by explaining the desired future in terms of the present state of the organization,
- shaping and communicating the vision and change strategy,
- developing a leadership cadre to manage the deployment process,
- institutionalizing the change by developing enabling infrastructures,
- measuring and monitoring progress toward full deployment,
- making it last by rewarding and recognizing successes and correcting failures.

Gap 3. The Vision, Mission, Values, and Strategies and Direct Leadership Practices. *Causes.* Sometimes, a gap exists between the messages of the vision, mission, values, and strategies and how leaders lead and managers manage. Thus, quality may be a core value, but managers ship defective products; treating people fairly may be a stated value but a manager promotes his favorite, but less skilled, subordinate, etc. This situation is damaging in two ways. First, leadership is not adhering to its own blueprint of what it wants to achieve. Second, this situation is also demoralizing for employees.

One client of ours invested a lot of money implementing a new training process for developing direct managers. The program focused on developing a core set of leadership skills that were thought to be important to driving change. Every individual who supervised others went through the training program.

We were called in to evaluate the business impact of this extensive and expensive program. We found that the training program seemed to work for some managers but not for others. What we found was that the performance of teams led by managers whose behavior was congruent with the values and strategies of the company was significantly higher than the performance of those teams whose managers did not really believe in the values and strategies of the company. This difference translated to hundreds of thousands of dollars in revenue gained and/or lost, depending on how you look at it. The list below shows some of the typical symptoms and causes of the gap between vision, mission, and strategy and direct leadership practices:

- The vision, mission, values and strategies have been poorly communicated and deployed.
- There is a mismatch between the stated values and the actual values of the organization.
- Low level of leadership support.
- Poor role modeling.
- Lack of accountability.
- Lack of an effective measurement system that provides real time data regarding leadership behavior.

Closing gap 3. Challenge: the challenge is to identify the core leadership behaviors that actually operationalize core attitudes, values, and drivers of organizational performance, provide direct leaders regular feedback about their behavior, provide them opportunities for learning and development, and hold them accountable for their actions.

Defining quality leadership. Ensuring that leaders from the top to the bottom of the organization act consistently with the vision is basically a process of defining the key indicators of leadership effectiveness in your organization. Many organizations think that leadership capacity is defined by a set of attributes or traits, which if possessed produce an effective leader. Our studies have shown that this is an over-simplification. Effective leadership is an outcome of the interaction between attributes and the ability to achieve results.

Simply put, there is not a single model of leadership that applies to all organizations; rather, each organization must identify those behaviors required to drive the employee actions that produce value for, and loyalty from, customers.

Operationalizing your leadership process. One way to define the leadership practices that are the key effectiveness indicators for your organization's leaders is to define empirically the set of leadership practices that drive team performance. For example, in a study for a high technology company, we found that in the context of the organization's vision, mission, values, and strategies, there was a core set of leadership practices that were significantly and consistently correlated with team performance. Included in this set of behaviors were:

- modeling the values,
- making data available to the team,
- giving timely corrective and confirmatory feedback,
- removing obstacles to team performance,

- demonstrating a willingness to empower,
- focusing on learning,
- focusing on customers,
- focusing on quality,
- being willing to hold himself/herself accountable for team results.

These values, attitudes, and behaviors were made operative by developing and implementing a feedback system which enabled subordinates to evaluate their manager two to three times a year on these behaviors. When leaders were then provided ongoing and actionable feedback about their practices, provided opportunities to develop these behaviors, and were held accountable for them, both team and organizational performance improved substantially.

Gap 4. Leadership Practices and Employee Behaviors That Meet Customer Needs. *Causes.* To meet customer needs, employees must have the skills, capacity, resources (including information), incentive, and opportunity to do so. In other words, employees must be involved both technically and psychologically to be able to respond to customers' needs.

Direct managers can either enable or inhibit this level of involvement through their actions. When those in leadership roles do not act in a manner that is congruent with sustainable high performance, they may (inadvertently on occasion, deliberately on others) compromise quality in order to attain a production quota, ask for but then fail to listen to employee opinions, discount the organization's vision and mission, engage in double talk about the mission, or fail to fully engage employees in the process of meeting customers' needs.

Whatever the exact cause, ineffective leadership practices produce a significant performance gap between those practices and the kinds of employee behaviors required to meet and exceed customer expectations. The list below summarizes the potential causes of this gap:

- selection process does not screen out those who lack the skill to supervise;
- leaders are rewarded for factors unrelated to actual goals of the organization;
- the feedback and measurement system does not provide leaders valid data;
- leaders are unclear about what is really expected of them;
- leaders are not held accountable for their behavior and/or team performance;
- leaders do not take the time to communicate with employees.

Closing gap 4. Challenge: the challenge is to create friendly, yet highly usable, infrastructures that enable employees to align their day-to-day activities with core business strategies and to focus performance improvement efforts on activities that produce value.

Aligning individual and team performance with the organization's vision, values, and strategies. Many managers wrestle with how to align individual and team performance with the organization's core strategies. One way is to create a performance management framework that links the organization's core business strategies with day-to-day operations. This is often referred to as a "results scorecard." The results scorecard consists of a set of performance metrics that provide a balanced view of the organization based on four perspectives:

1. The financial perspective (consists of traditional financial measures such as revenue growth, return on investment).
2. The customer perspective (consists of measures of importance to customers such as cost, timeliness, quality, performance, service).
3. The internal business process perspective (effectiveness of processes used to meet customer needs).
4. The learning and innovation perspective (consists of measures of the organization's ability to adapt and innovate).

The scorecard provides a multi-level view of the organization which balances the internal and external perspectives, current versus future needs, and leading versus lagging indicators. It provides managers and leaders a tool for translating core business strategies into action and measurable performance.

Managing performance around your core values and business strategies. A four-step process is very effective for the purpose of managing your organization's performance around core values and business strategies:

1. Create a balanced set of performance measures from the top to the bottom of the organization. Each measure is specifically linked to one or more of the organization-level strategies and targets, and for each measure there is a target level of attainment and specific initiatives to translate the goals into action. Such results scorecards communicate how well each person and team is performing and then specifically link performance improvement needs to the corporate strategy. As a consequence the scorecards become an integral performance and strategic management system.
2. Link leadership practice to the balanced scorecard measures. As mentioned above, one way to do this is to define empirically the set of leadership practices that drive team performance.
3. Provide leaders and their teams actionable feedback.
4. Make rewards and recognitions contingent on performance.

Figure 2 shows what we refer to as the "2 x 2 performance matrix." The matrix illustrates one way in which leaders' rewards and recognitions are linked to team performance.

Gap 5. Enabling Infrastructures and Support of Behaviors Compatible with Sustainable High Performance. *Causes.* Infrastructures include organi-

	Ineffective	Effective
Excellent (Team Performance)	Coach	Incent
Poor (Team Performance)	De-Select	Coach

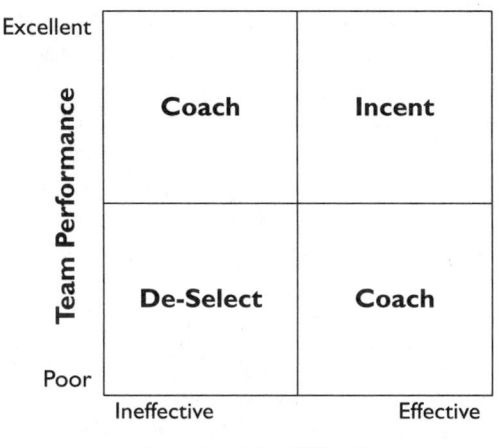

Leadership Effectiveness

Figure 2. **The 2 x 2 performance matrix**

zational policies, procedures and mechanisms put in place to monitor and provide feedback on organization systems. They ensure that the customers are being served by the right people

Creating and sustaining the high performance organization using the right technology at the right level. They also provide data about how well the organization and its parts are doing with respect to its vision, mission, values, and strategies.

Sometimes, however, there is a gap between what needs to be measured and what is being measured, or how the data are being collected, or even how the data are being fed back into the organization and used to make decisions. For example, in a software company we studied, managers were being rewarded for meeting delivery schedules for customers rather than providing leading-edge technology, even though the latter value was espoused as one of three core value propositions by which the company operated. In reality there was so much pressure to deliver on time that the level of innovation declined significantly.

In any case, the organization either does not get valid data about its progress relative to its vision, mission, values, and strategies or, getting such data, fails to use them properly. This situation creates a gap between the infrastructures and the behaviors required for sustainable performance. Some symptoms and potential causes of such gaps are summarized as follows:

- The behaviors required of sustainable performance are not known or not being measured.
- Leaders are not held accountable for improving their performance or their team's performance.
- Employees are rewarded even when the quality of their work is below expectation.

Closing gap 5. Challenge: create infrastructures that provide the right mechanisms, tools, and information to motivate, reward, and enable employees to improve quality.

Understanding your organization's capabilities. To successfully implement change, an organization must have the capability to execute the strategy. By capabilities we refer to the individual, process, and organizational tools, skills, and knowledge required to successfully implement change. What capabilities have been shown to impact the success with which change is managed? The discussion in this paper suggests that the performance capabilities needed to be continually assessed and improved:

- vision, mission, values, and strategy,
- system design,
- leadership practices,
- infrastructure capacity,
- expertise,
- motivation and climate, including rewards and recognitions.

The performance audit. One way to get a handle on the capabilities of your organization is to conduct a "performance or capability audit." Many studies have documented that organizations having timely, precise data from key stakeholders on which to base important change decisions outperform those that do not. While many companies have such information from financial and operational databases, few have such information from employee and customer databases. And, even when the information is potentially available, decision makers do not use it because they have serious doubts about the information's:

- relevance,
- timeliness,
- credibility, and
- accessibility.

A well-designed performance audit process can provide the data that link employee attitudes and behaviors with the organization's strategic performance indicators. So, when organizations measure the key employee dimensions which affect these performance "gauges" and then link these measurements to the goal setting and goal measurement systems, the organization will increase its ability to use this information as a change management tool.

This can be accomplished in a very straightforward manner:

- First, develop some kind of picture or model of your organization. Many people refer to this model as a "system architecture." The term "architecture" refers to the factors that are key to producing value in your organization.
- Second, measure where your organization is on each of these factors in order to define gaps between the required performance and the

actual performance relative to each of the factors in the architecture.
- Third, translate the data into actions that will improve functioning in the targeted performance factor.
- Fourth, manage the change process through providing leadership and mobilizing commitment.

Creating enabling infrastructures. At its most simplistic level, a business operation is a series of coordinated tasks. How well these tasks are coordinated within the organization is crucial to cost-effective and time-efficient operations. How well these tasks are coordinated with customer and prospect needs is crucial to survival.

We organize these tasks into job functions and departments but we should not lose sight of the fact that they are all interrelated and interdependent in creating a successful operation. If the sales department brings in a huge order, a series of interdependent tasks might have to take place as follows.

The sales department needs to give the customer a delivery date. To provide sales a delivery date the production department needs the purchasing department to provide delivery dates for raw materials and the human resources department to provide additional production staff. The finance department needs to arrange a bank loan to fund the project until the customer pays for the order. To do this they need a project budget from production. For the project to be successfully completed two things need to happen:

1. All departments must work together to develop an action plan, recognizing that some tasks cannot be completed until others are done.
2. All departments coordinate tasks and instantly communicate when a task is either ahead of or behind schedule.

To allow these things to happen, the corporate infrastructure must provide a means of motivating cooperation, of resolving differences, of prioritizing tasks when conflicts exist, of rapidly disseminating information to maintain a coordinated effort, and of measuring performance and communicating these measurements. In other words, the infrastructure involves a well-defined set of policies and procedures and the tools and systems necessary to measure compliance and performance.

The balanced scorecard method is a tool, used on an ongoing basis, to evaluate and control the effectiveness of managers in achieving established goals. Computers and computer software are tools that have allowed us to collect, analyze, and share information on a real-time basis. Both tools create "information systems." These systems allow us to use information in two important ways:

1. As feedback/measurement tools—obtain feedback about the results of our efforts so that we can learn how to improve.
2. As enabling tools—obtain information to facilitate coordination of efforts to maximize efficiency.

Developing information systems. For any information system to be sustainable it must provide a benefit that is greater than its cost. This would seem to be stating the obvious and, yet, many business information systems fail because the authors have ignored this axiom.

What is an information system? For our purposes this is a corporate database and application programs to manage input, maintenance, and information retrieval necessary to facilitate and evaluate the results of tasks or transactions.

Some information systems, such as financial accounting, are so important that a full-time staff is employed to ensure that information is timely and accurate. Other information systems, which might be equally important, might be assigned to individuals as an adjunct to their primary tasks. It is these latter systems that most often fail.

For example, a sales manager might want to implement an information system to facilitate and track sales efforts. While the sales manager might derive great benefit from such a system he is dependent on the sales staff to conscientiously maintain prospect profiles and record their contact/sales attempts and the results. This is not a matter of hiring someone to perform data entry. The sales staff control the detailed information about their efforts and they must make an investment of time to passing that information on.

Therefore, for this information system to succeed each salesman must perceive significant benefits in meeting the primary task to justify their commitment to maintain the system. Below are some examples that illustrate file maintenance tasks and immediate benefits to be derived (see Table I).

On the instruction of senior management of a national hospital corporation, we installed marketing management software in 38 hospital sites from Florida to northern California. The home office management saw three major benefits to be derived by the marketing system:

Time Investment	Benefit to User	Benefit to User and Manager
Log a call attempt to a prospect.	Computer dials the number for you.	A history of attempts and results becomes available for review.
Pend a task for future follow-up.	Computer will display a reminder of specified date and time.	A task history for this contact becomes available for review.
Log appointment information.	Computer will display a monthly appointment calendar for reference and display a reminder on specified date and time.	A task history for this contact becomes available for review.

Table 1. **Benefits of the typical file maintenance tables**

1. It would allow staff to greatly enhance physician loyalty by helping them bring in new patients, usually people new to the community.
2. The direction of newcomers to loyal hospital physicians would lead to increased admissions and hospital revenues.
3. The ability to tap into the hospital accounting system to assign revenues to products would bring accountability to marketing efforts.

This software provided:

- Enabling tools to facilitate such processes as physician referral, membership program management, health screenings, and work injury programs.
- Measurement tools, including an interface with the hospital accounting system to measure revenues.

During the next three years all but three sites abandoned the use of this software. Of the three remaining sites, one site had extraordinary success. Why could only one hospital in 38 succeed?

Senior hospital managers did not believe that the direct marketing efforts could significantly improve the bottom line. Because of this, only one would commit the level of personnel required to make the program succeed.

In the evaluation of any information system it is critical to obtain a clear idea of the cost of successfully applying it when you weigh the benefits of implementation against the cost. We have experienced a tendency among managers to see an application or methodology as a solution rather than a tool to be used to create a solution. Like other tools, it is an inanimate object, obtaining its value by how it is used.

Where to Start

One implication of the model presented in this paper is that the place to begin is to fully understand the current environment in which you are conducting business. How do employees perceive the organization? How closely do the organization's espoused values match its actions? How do current and potential customers view your organization? How do customers view your ability to provide them the products and services they need and want?

Since employee and customer attitudes are grounded in current organizational culture and practices, a prerequisite to improving your organization's capacity to sustain high performance is to perform an environmental audit:

- Ask your employees and your customers to evaluate your performance and your behaviors on the key dimensions of high performance.
- Identify your organization's current vulnerabilities and then define, design, and embed in your organization the processes and behaviors that will enable you to achieve the goal of sustainable high performance.

- Monitor progress toward shaping the behaviors and attitudes that contribute to high performance. One way to do this is to use a targeted pulse or dashboard type survey to regularly measure the effectiveness of ongoing change initiatives.
- Focus on performance improvement.
- Create a bias for action within the culture by rewarding and recognizing success.

Summary

In this paper, we have discussed the deterrents to high performance and the role of culture in enabling these deterrents. Next, we presented a model that describes the five factors that enable high performance and the symptoms that indicate these factors are out of alignment. Finally, we discussed a range of strategies for moving your organization up the performance curve toward high performance. We hypothesize that the outcomes of such efforts will be committed, competent employees, loyal customers, and superior business performance over the long haul.

References

Baum, J.R., Locke, E.L., and Kirkpatrick, S. (1998), "A longitudinal study of the relation of vision and vision communication to venture growth in entrepreneurial firms," *Journal of Applied Psychology,* Vol. 83, No. 1, pp. 43-54.

Buckingham, M., and Coffman, C. (1999), *First, Break All the Rules,* New York: Simon & Schuster.

Kotter, J.P., and Heskett, J.L. (1992), *Corporate Culture and Performance,* New York: The Free Press.

Mink, O., Esterhuysen, P., Mink, B., and Owen, K. (1993), *Change at Work,* San Francisco: Jossey-Bass.

Robbins, H., and Finley, M. (1996), *Why Change Doesn't Work,* Princeton, NJ: Peterson's.

Keith Owen and Ron Mundy are Senior Consultants with the Somerset Consulting Group, based in Austin, Texas (www.somersetcg.com), and associates with the Guild Group.

Will Guild and Robert Guild are Senior Consultants with the Guild Group, based in Austin, Texas (www.gldgrp.com), and associates with the Somerset Consulting Group.

Motivate Managers to Review Performance

Lin Grensing-Pophal

Effective and regular performance reviews are key to improving organizational and individual performance. But managers often avoid them or are negligent about them—particularly when performance management systems are imposed on them. This article discusses some problems with performance reviews and presents five recommendations for motivating managers to make the most of their reviews.

Giving an employee bad news during a performance review is tough enough. So why make the job any tougher by saddling managers with complicated appraisal systems?

Yet that's often what HR and top management do—create performance management systems that make managers procrastinate, hesitate or just plain resist because they see the system as a hassle, not a tool for developing and rewarding employees.

HR consultants and researchers say managers shun performance reviews for a number of reasons. The performance evaluation process is too complicated. They see no evidence that it affects the work quality of those whose performances are being reviewed. Many managers also fear possible legal challenges if the employee ties a negative review to a missed promotion or a denied pay raise.

Those fears translate into reviews that don't really help employees or employers, says John Grunseth, an HR consultant with Grunseth Connections in Green Bay, Wis.

To get more managerial buy-in for performance appraisals, say Grunseth and other experts, HR needs to involve managers in designing the performance system, train managers in performance management, show them why it matters to the employer and make appraisals part of managers' own performance goals.

Why Managers Balk at Appraisals

Busy managers have little incentive to devote precious time and energy to a process they consider difficult and filled with paperwork, says David Dell, research director of The Conference Board, a business research organization in New York.

"A lot of people find that the methodology itself is cumbersome," Dell says. The Conference Board surveyed HR directors and executives and found that 90 percent of respondents felt that their performance measures and management approaches needed reform. And if HR and executives—who do fewer reviews than many managers—don't like their performance systems, they can't convey a positive message about performance appraisal to the managers.

Managers also may feel that they lack control over the process because higher-ups dictate the results the system should give, says Lynda Ford, SPHR, president of The Ford Group, an HR consulting firm in Lee Center, N.Y. When that happens, managers get jaded.

She recalls working in a small company where the top rating was the number five. Managers could give only one employee each year the top rating, even if more deserved it. As a result, she says, "our manager would say, 'This year you're a three or a four,'" meaning that next year the employee would get the five. Managers simply passed the top rating around among employees.

In cases like this one, Ford notes, "If you back people up against the wall and force them to work in a system that they do not perceive is valuable, they'll figure out how to make it work to their advantage."

Managers also will give reviews short shrift when the connection between reviews and rewards is weak or nonexistent.

Leslie Kossoff of Kossoff Management Consulting in San Mateo, Calif., describes a client that had delays of up to two years on some of its performance evaluations, despite an expectation that managers would evaluate employees annually. Part of the problem, Kossoff found, was that managers didn't see a real link between performance evaluations and compensation.

When organizations falsely claim that merit increases are tied to evaluations, managers will know better and won't take those claims seriously, Kossoff says. Such a situation creates a "polite lie" because "everyone sort of treats the performance appraisal process with a wink and a nod."

Sloppy Reviews Dent Morale

Managers may not realize that employees are aware of the winks and nods. But when reviews are slapdash, employees notice.

A graphic designer in a university setting says, "The only time they do something remotely resembling a review is when my contract is about to expire. Whoever happens to be my boss at the time makes a mad dash to throw something together that says they're happy with my performance and recommend keeping me on. They call me into the office, they hand me the review and say, 'Do you want to talk about anything?'" The last time she received even that semblance of a review was nearly two years ago, she says.

Similarly, a utility industry engineer jumped into a new job where, she says, "I thought I was contributing within a few weeks." After seven months, she was eager for her year-end review, only to be told by her supervisor that all new employees received the same rating.

"I was shocked and mad," she says. "That sure didn't do anything for my motivation."

How to Motivate Managers

If you want to motivate employees to improve their performance, start by motivating managers to do a thorough job on reviews. Experts say that HR departments can improve managers' compliance with performance evaluation processes by taking these steps.

Make It Meaningful

"Part of the problem with performance appraisals," says Kossoff, "is the HR department tends to treat it as a management task, rather than as a management process" that incorporates recruiting, hiring and training, as well as evaluation.

Rather than looking back at what the employee did or did not accomplish, Kossoff suggests that managers and employees look forward and plan what the employees should do to move ahead.

HR also needs to impress on managers the importance of the process. "From the big picture perspective, it's probably the most important thing [managers] do," says Ronald Riggio, Henry R. Kravis Professor of Leadership and Organizational Psychology and director of the Kravis Leadership Institute at Claremont McKenna College in Claremont, Calif. "It's unfortunate that people don't give it enough attention."

Whatever the performance system used, the critical element is commitment at the top of the organization, says Curt Salisbury, HR manager at Carolina International, a truck sales and rental company based in Columbia, S.C.

"Management has to believe in the process," Salisbury says. "The boss, president, CEO or whoever needs to be in tune, obviously. If they aren't doing it, the motivation level is low for managers to do it."

Make Everyone a Player

Salisbury adds, "Get buy-in from the management team even if it means spending a good deal of time developing a customized performance measurement format."

"You need input from the managers themselves," Ford says. "Too many of these systems get developed in a vacuum with some senior leadership team and HR, and then it gets rolled out to the organization and they wonder why nobody likes it."

Carol Booz, PHR, president of Laurel Technologies Inc., a consulting firm in Nottingham, PA, agrees. "If you can get a couple of managers together and get them brainstorming, you'll find out what the roadblocks are and can work with the managers to overcome them."

Many managers complain about the complexity and length of performance evaluation forms. Through their experience in working with the forms, they may have excellent insights and suggestions on how to improve them, Booz says.

Keep It Simple

The more you can do to keep the process simple, the more likely you are to achieve compliance.

"One of the things that effective managers do for their people is remove the roadblocks" to performance, says Ford. "That's what HR should be doing for managers when it comes to performance evaluation."

Advance planning can help organizations simplify their performance appraisal processes. "If we haven't pre-determined as a department or an organization what aspects of performance we're going to look at," says Booz, "then it's very easy to get sidetracked and develop a form that's five or six pages long."

Train Your Managers

While training isn't the only solution for motivating managers, it certainly is an important part of the process. Booz notes, "If you can work with managers to help them find a system to keep track of all of the things their employees have done during the review period, they won't view the process as much of a chore."

Training also should incorporate the big picture. Show managers why the organization values performance appraisals, how individual performance benefits the organization and how managers can measure performance objectively.

Salisbury adds, "The best incentives for [managers] are educational and financial. HR needs to do our job and teach the managers the financial rewards of the system. Hit them with turnover costs in their department. Do some survey work and graph it out. Get some productivity reports or absenteeism reports and look for trends. Show them some numbers and follow it with the position that a performance system will add value to their margins. It's [managers'] responsibility to give feed back for the good of the organization."

Make It a Must

Experts agree that producing timely, effective performance evaluations should be a key component of any manager's job. Grunseth says managers should be held accountable for doing evaluations, and notes that some companies put a specific line item in managers' performance evaluations to rate their effectiveness at evaluating their employees.

"If you evaluate supervisors on the quality and the consistency with which they do their performance appraisals then you're pretty sure they'll be doing this and doing this consistently," Riggio says. "It also communicates to them the value to the organization. This is not just extra stuff. It's not something you do on top of your workload. It's a core component."

"The organization has to have a culture that encourages performance evaluation," says Booz. "If it's tied to a manager's compensation in some way, there will be a better incentive to make sure that it happens."

A manager of a small customer service information team adds that managers "should be rated on sticking to the process as well as on how often they are evaluating team members."

"HR offers training for managing the performance evaluation process, but managers don't apply it consistently," says the manager, who asked not to be identified. "Some managers stick to the goal-setting process and properly score work of their team members," she says of her workplace. "Other managers are very lax about the process. Some employees don't have individual goals. They apparently receive a rating based on the department or business unit success. How does that show the employee that individual contributions count? There's no real linkage."

Dick Grote, president of Grote Consulting, a performance management consulting firm in Addison, Texas, tells of a major oil company with a "shockingly simple" performance appraisal system he says is very effective at motivating managers.

"The CEO requires every person with supervisory responsibility in the organization—and there are a lot of them—to send him a memo each year saying one of two things: 'I conducted all of the performance conversations with my people' or 'I did not conduct all of the performance discussions with my people—and the reason is ....'"

That reason had better be good, Grote adds.

Lin Grensing-Pophal, SPHR, is a Wisconsin-based business journalist with HR consulting experience in employee communication, training, and management issues. She is the author of The HR Book: Human Resources Management for Business *(Self-Counsel Business Series, 1999).*

Serial Knowledge Transfer: How Groups Learn from Themselves

Nancy M. Dixon

This article is an excerpt from the book, Common Knowledge: How Companies Thrive by Sharing What They Know *(Harvard Business School Press, 2000). It discusses serial knowledge transfer initiatives by the U.S. Army, British Petroleum, and the Bechtel's Steam Generator Replacement Group. What's working and how are these organizations making the most of what their people know?*

One task of the U.S. Army troops that arrived in Haiti in 1994 was to remove guns and ammunition from the many rebel towns. After the first attempt, the unit assigned to do this held an After Action Review (AAR) to assess what had happened in order to improve the next attempt. During the meeting the soldiers recognized that their effort to disarm the town had been met with considerable resistance. One soldier noted that he had observed few dogs in the town. Someone else had noticed that the Haitians were fearful of the large German Shepherds that were used by the military police. That led a third person to suggest that the unit borrow some dogs from the military police so that in disarming the next town they could use the dogs out front with the hope of reducing the resistance.

After the next, and more successful, attempt to disarm a town, an AAR was again held and yielded additional ideas. In this AAR it was noted that the villagers were more cooperative when in their homes than when they were in the street. So in disarming the third town it was decided that most of the interaction should be held within the homes of the villagers. The next AAR produced yet another useful suggestion based on the observation that the Haitians were particularly respectful to women. The group decided to put a woman in charge of the team and to display particular deference to her in front of the Haitians, again as a way to more effectively and efficiently accomplish their mission.[1]

Adapted and reprinted by permission of Harvard Business School Press. From *Common Knowledge: How Companies Share What They Know* by Nancy M. Dixon, Boston, MA, March 2000. Copyright © 2000 by the Harvard Business School Publishing Corporation; all rights reserved.

The knowledge transfer described in this example is what I call *serial transfer*. It involves transferring the knowledge a team has learned from doing its task in one setting to the next time that same team does the task in a different setting. The repeated action and the knowledge gained from each action happen in a serial fashion.[2] The knowledge that the team gained during the first experience helps it to function more effectively the next time. But for that to happen, knowledge has to be transferred from individual team members to the team as a whole.

When a team is engaged in a task, (for example, drilling a well, developing a product, delivering a performance) each member of the team takes away from the experience a number of observations, among them:

- What actions the individual team member took (the term "actions" here includes what the person did physically, what the person said, what the person refrained from doing, etc.)
- How that team member's actions impacted the outcome
- What the team member noted about the actions that other team members took
- How the team member was impacted by the actions of other team members
- How the actions of other team members impacted the outcome
- What occurred in the environment, both expected and unexpected
- The impact of the environment on the team member and on other team members

All of these observations, and more, are held in the mind of each team member and are necessarily unique to each team member. Each team member can use the personal understanding gained from the experience to plan what to do differently during the next action. However, a team's action is more than the sum of individual parts. So for a team to perform more effectively the next time it takes the same action, much of what each team member has learned from the experience must be made available to others.

Serial transfer is a process that moves the unique knowledge that each individual has constructed into a group or public space so that the knowledge can be integrated and made sense of by the whole team.[3] But the transfer process is more complex than just team members reporting out their knowledge so that others in the group are aware of it. Individual team members are able to use what others have said to reinterpret how they themselves understand the situation. In the Haiti example, the soldier who "knew" that he had not seen many dogs in the village now "knows" that in a new way. The fact has not changed, but the way that fact relates to other facts has changed. This integration of ideas spawns the reconsideration of cause and effect, it produces the if/then that leads to new team action, it identifies discrepancies in the perception of what occurred, and it develops new generalizations that may guide future action. It is in this important sense that a transfer of knowl-

Teams Consider:
- actions each member took
- ways members' actions impacted each other
- how members' actions impacted the outcome
- environmental factors
- impact of environmental facts on members' actions and outcome

Team explores the relationship between action and outcome

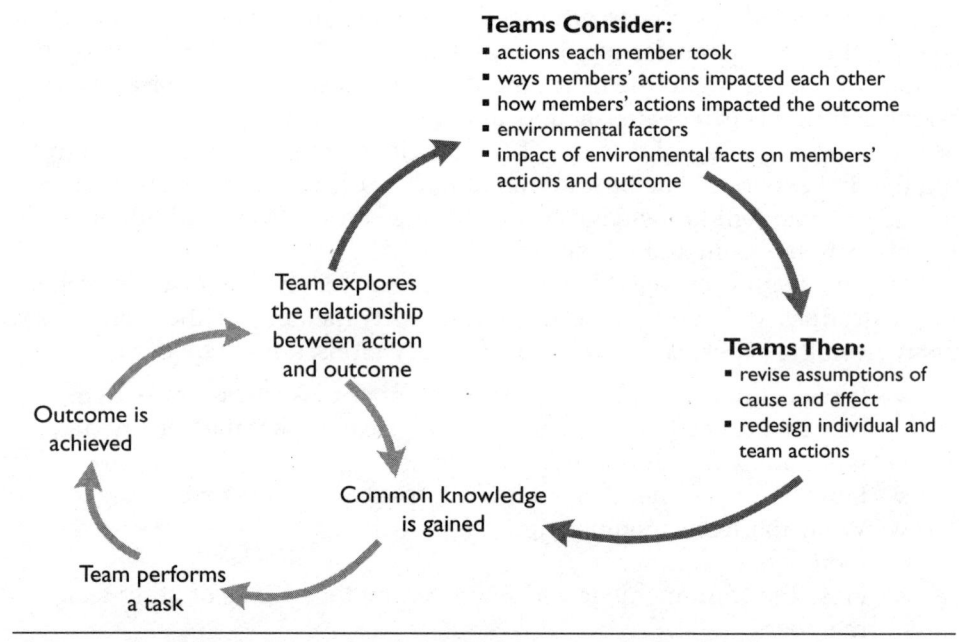

Teams Then:
- revise assumptions of cause and effect
- redesign individual and team actions

Outcome is achieved

Common knowledge is gained

Team performs a task

Figure 1. **Transferring member knowledge to team knowledge**

edge has occurred, from individual knowing to group knowing.

The whole team can then act on its shared knowledge the next time it takes action. The team may, of course, choose to change very little from its previous actions, particularly if the overall action was successful. Or the team may realize that it needs to alter a few of the actions of particular members or take an entirely new action in order to reach its goals. Figure 1 shows how the translation of experience into knowledge includes individual-to-group transfer.

It turns out that experience is a poor teacher because it requires interpretation of what are often confusing facts and events.[4] The relationship between cause and effect is often quite complex. Experience relies heavily on human memory, which is notoriously fallible. Moreover, most of the outcomes a team accomplishes have multiple causes, not just one, and teasing those causal relationships out of the experiences of ten or fifteen team members is a problematic task. The most functional way to deal with these barriers to creating useful and valid knowledge from experience is to use the checks and balances that multiple perspectives provide, especially when they are offered in the spirit of learning.

A team can, of course, leave the task of interpretation to the leader or to a member who is judged to be most expert. But when the available knowledge about actions and outcomes is distributed across team members, expertise does not result in drawing more accurate relationships between actions and outcomes. Expertise provides necessary input, but the relationships between actions and outcomes are more accurately drawn by a group that can correct, support and build on each other's insights.

Examples of Serial Transfer

The first example of serial transfer is the U.S. Army using the After Action Review process, described at the beginning of this chapter. The second comes from British Petroleum, which has modeled its system on the Army, and the third from Bechtel's Steam Generator Replacement Group.

U.S. Army—After Action Review

Probably the best-known example of leveraging knowledge within a team is the U.S. Army's use of After Action Reviews. The AARs are held at the end of any team or unit action with the intent of reusing what has been learned immediately in the next battle or project. These brief meetings are attended by everyone who was engaged in the effort, regardless of rank. The Army's simple guidelines for conducting AARs are (1) no sugar coating, (2) discover ground truth, (3) no thin skins, (4) take notes, and (5) call it like you see it. The meetings are facilitated by someone in the unit, sometimes the ranking officer but just as often another member of the team. The learning from these meetings is captured both by the members, who all write and keep personal notes about what they need to do differently, and by the facilitator, who captures on a flip chart or chalkboard what the unit as a whole determines that it needs to do differently in the next engagement. Army After Action Reviews have standardized three key questions: What was supposed to happen? What happened? What accounts for the difference? An AAR may last fifteen minutes or an hour depending on the action that is being discussed but, in any case, it is not a lengthy meeting.

Interestingly, AARs had their beginnings in training simulations as a way for a team that was engaged in a mock battle to gain as much learning as possible from the training event. They proved so useful to a team's effectiveness that gradually they began to be used in nontraining situations as well. Today, they have spread throughout the Army, not because someone at the top of the military hierarchy has required their use, but because the troops find them helpful in getting the job done. The first peacekeeping troops in Haiti in 1994 provide a useful illustration of how AARs can improve a team's next action.

It will probably not surprise anyone that the soldiers offered useful ideas that made the next action more effective. What makes AARs beneficial, however, is that this kind of collective knowledge pooling occurs not just once but over and over again. The speed, regularity and discipline with which AARs are held in the U.S. Army are the factors of most interest.

British Petroleum—AARs

Borrowing the AAR from the U.S. Army, British Petroleum has made it the middle step of its three-part knowledge management process. BP calls its practice of AAR "learning during." Along with "learning before" and "learning after" (more about these later), it gives BP a set of knowledge management practices that it can implement in a systematic way. The idea of an AAR is so uncomplicated that it takes little instruction to accomplish. BP has designed a simple, one-page flyer that explains what an AAR is, where it came from and how to do it. That basic explanation has been adequate to enable units in the field to implement the practice on their own.

The questions BP asks in an AAR are the same ones the U.S. Army uses, although the answers are, of course, very different. For example, the question "What was supposed to happen?" might yield, "We were supposed to install the new pump by the end of the shutdown period." Many projects in the oil industry take several months to complete, so AARs are held along the way, at the end of any "event" that has a definable beginning and end. During the course of a lengthy project, a BP team may hold, and benefit from, ten to fifteen AARs. On development wells, where teams often work around the clock, two AARs may be held each day, one for each shift. BP has found that if the team waits until the well is in to hold the AAR, much of the knowledge is lost. After a few days team members have forgotten what happened and, more important, the reasons for their actions. The only way to translate the experience of bringing in a well into knowledge that can be used on site for the next well is to hold frequent AARs.

Bechtel—Lessons Learned Meetings

Bechtel's Steam Generator Replacement Group also uses this practice, although it calls the meetings "lessons learned" instead of AARs. Bechtel is a multibillion-dollar international engineering, procurement and construction company engaged in large-scale projects, such as power plants, petrochemical facilities, airports, mining facilities and major infrastructure projects. Unlike other parts of Bechtel in which individuals work in ever-changing project teams, the Steam Generator Replacement Group is a small specialized unit that works on a lot of jobs together. Anything learned on one job can be immediately used by the team on the next job. The nature of its work leaves little room for error. The average window of time to replace a steam generator is seventy days or less, unlike the typical Bechtel project, which may last two years or more. This unforgiving schedule mandates that the Steam Generator Replacement Group learn from its own lessons, because even a small mistake can result in a significant delay to a project. The lessons are captured in two ways: first, supervisors are required to bring lessons learned to weekly meetings; then, at the end of each project, the project manager brings all players together for a full day to focus on the lessons learned.

The next section spells out what an organization needs to put into place in order to have an effective system for serial transfer. First, I apply the three criteria for selection of a transfer process to one of the examples; then I outline the design principles based on them.

Criteria Related to Serial Transfer

Serial transfer within a group is one of five kinds of knowledge transfer in organizations. The others are near transfer, far transfer, strategic transfer and expert transfer. *Near transfer* involves transferring knowledge from a source team to a receiving team that is doing a similar task in a similar context but a different location. *Far transfer* involves transferring tacit knowledge from a source team to a receiving team when the knowledge is about a nonroutine task. *Strategic transfer* involves transferring very complex knowledge, such as how to launch a product or make an acquisition, from one team to another that may be separated by both time and space. *Expert transfer* involves transferring explicit knowledge about a task that may be done infrequently. Designers of knowledge transfer systems can apply three criteria to determine which kind of transfer is appropriate to a particular situation and need:

1. Who the intended receiver of the knowledge is in terms of similarity of task and context
2. How routine and frequent the task is
3. The kind of knowledge that is being transferred

To illustrate the way those criteria can be used, I am going to do a bit of reverse engineering. Rather than apply the criteria to a fictional organization, I use the Bechtel Steam Generator Replacement Group, and pose the criteria questions (left-hand column) as though this team had determined that it should transfer the knowledge it gains from one action to its next action. The way that Bechtel would answer the questions regarding the knowledge it wants to transfer (right-hand column) leads to the conclusion that the most effective transfer process would be serial transfer. It would, therefore, in this reverse-engineered example, design a system based on the serial transfer guidelines outlined below.

Design Guidelines

Because the design guidelines that follow relate only to serial transfer, rather than to the many other possible "end-of" meetings that go on in organizations, I first want to differentiate serial transfer meetings from all-purpose debriefing techniques. For example, the familiar end-of-training evaluation meeting where participants are asked to offer the instructor ideas to improve the course is not serial transfer because those offering the ideas are not themselves responsible for changing the course. Only the instructors can act on the knowledge generated. End-of-course discussions then, as useful as they may be, don't meet the condition that those who generate the knowledge must also be those who can act on it.

Questions	Answers for Bechtel Steam Generator Replacement Group
Who the the intended receiver of the knowledge is in terms of similarity of task and context	
How frequently does this task occur? Daily? Monthly? Yearly?	The Steam Generator Replacement Group repeats its task every two to three months.
Is the task routine or nonroutine? Are there clear steps, or is each next step variable?	The Steam Generator Replacement Group's task has some routine elements. But it also has many nonroutine elements because each time it works at a new site, it faces differences in size, age of equipment, contract agreements, legal issues, so on. That makes each next step variable.
How routine and frequent the task is	
How similar are the task and the context of the receiving team(s) to those of the source team?	The task is similar for the Steam Generator Replacement Group because the knowledge is put to use by the same Group that generated it. However, the context changes with each new site.
Does the receiving team(s) have the absorptive capacity (experience, technical knowledge, shared language) to implement what the source team has developed?	The Steam Generator Replacement Group has the absorptive capacity because it builds its own knowledge base as it goes along.
The kind of knowledge that is being transferred	
Is the knowledge of the source team primarily tacit or explicit?	The knowledge that the Steam Generator Replacement Group transfers from one site to another is both tacit and explicit. The explicit parts can be written in procedures and regulations; the tacit parts must be constructed from the memory of team members as they address the new situation. In discussing the lessons learned from a just-completed project, the team members make their tacit knowledge explicit both to themselves and to other team members.
How many functional areas of the organization will be impacted by implementing the knowledge? One team? One division? The whole organization?	Although an entire plant is impacted by the speed with which the Steam Generator Replacement Group accomplishes its task, only the team itself is impacted by the knowledge it gains at one site and reuses at the next.

Table 1. **Illustration of how criteria can be used to determine appropriateness of serial transfer**

Another necessary condition of serial transfer is that team members are interdependent and working together toward an agreed-upon goal. Many teams are a team in name only; they are really a group of individual contributors who all happen to do the same type of work (perhaps for the same manager) but who do not depend on each other to get that work done. Such groups may benefit from occasional team meetings, but they are not engaging in serial transfer. But when the situation is one in which each member's effectiveness depends on the effectiveness of the other members, then serial transfer can work to increase the team's productivity.

Given those conditions the following guidelines create effective serial transfer.

Meetings Are Held Regularly

It is the discipline of the regularity of these meetings that makes them effective. Serial transfer meetings are held either at a scheduled time (for instance, every morning or every week) or at the end of a defined action. In either case they are not "called" meetings whose purpose is to address an exception, such as a problem that has occurred, or indeed even because a success was achieved. Rather they are a part of the way the work of the team gets accomplished—a work routine. To some extent the regularity also can reduce team members' anxiety that the meeting will be about placing blame—a concern that arises when meetings are held only after something has gone wrong.

Meetings Are Brief

Perhaps because of their regularity, serial transfer meetings are quick and to the point. At Bio-Tek Instruments they are called "standing meetings"—everyone stands rather than sits—as a kind of tacit assurance that the meeting will be short. Even "boring" meetings are tolerable if they last only twenty minutes.

In order to be brief, the meetings have to have a recognized format—a clarity about what is on the table and what should be left to other kinds of meetings. The three questions the U.S. Army uses, for example, provide that kind of format:

- What was supposed to happen?
- What happened?
- What accounts for the difference?

Everyone Involved in the Actions Participates in the Meeting

This is an important guideline of serial transfer for two reasons. First, the information and ideas of everyone are necessary to get a full picture; someone may well have seen or been aware of something that others did not see.

Second, the attendance of everyone is evidence of shared responsibility. Not to attend is a tacit statement that "The results were none of my doing," as in "I just give the orders" or "I just do what I'm told." No one is so unimportant as not to share responsibility for what happened and for making it happen more effectively the next time. No one is so important as not to need the insights of others.

There Are No Recriminations

The Army has a very clear rule: nothing said in an AAR can be used in any kind of personnel action. It is a hard rule to believe in, but a necessary one if people are to tell the truth, or at least their version of the truth, in the meetings. However, team members don't believe it just because someone says, "Speak your mind and there will be no recriminations." The only way that rule becomes believable is when some courageous team member says something like "What we lacked in this situation was clear leadership," and then waits for the response. If the response is a threat or a putdown, then others see that they can't trust the rule. If the response is lighthearted or an acknowledgment of fault by the leader, then others can begin to believe the rule. "No recriminations" is a rule that has to be experienced to be believed. But teams do not have to start with believability; it can grow over time.

Because the intent of these meetings is to understand more fully what happened and what needs to be done differently the next time, they are more descriptive than evaluative. But that does not lessen the need to "call it like you see it."

Reports Are Not Forwarded

In many of these meetings no written record is kept. In others, notes are taken but retained only for local use and distribution. At BP an administrative assistant may write up the notes from an AAR, but those notes are for the team's own use and review, and are not forwarded to any higher level. Likewise in the U.S. Army, the notes are for local use. In special situations in the Army, units are asked to send their AAR notes to the Center for Army Lessons Learned (CALL)—if, for example, Army officials have identified the area that unit is working in as one in which knowledge is needed for the whole (for instance, how to build a bridge in a particular type of terrain or how to achieve better cooperation between two branches of the service). But even under these special conditions the AAR notes are not sent through a reporting line but through a "knowledge line." More typically, notes from an AAR stay in the unit.

The policy of not forwarding reports up the organizational ladder or even laterally across the organization is a critical element in serial transfer. It avoids many of the concerns and fears that teams have about meeting to review their actions—concerns about "not wanting to air their dirty laundry" or that they will gain a bad reputation with others in the company. If a team is going to learn, it needs to be able to try out actions that may not work perfectly the first time, to thoroughly analyze those actions, to acknowledge misjudgments and to find ways to move forward. That is much easier and safer to do when the discussion stays with the group that is working on the problem.

This idea may seem contrary to the notion that teams can and should learn from other teams. The key to successful transfer of knowledge is knowing under what circumstances different types of knowledge can be shared, however. What a team learns from its repeated actions and reflections on those actions may well be shared at some later time, but it is not effective to do so through sharing the reports of each successive meeting.

Meetings Are Facilitated Locally

Serial transfer meetings are facilitated by a member of the team. The responsibility of the facilitator is to remind the group of the simple guidelines and to keep the discussion focused on the few critical questions. After repeated meetings the responsibility may become almost perfunctory. The facilitator role may rotate among members or may be taken by someone in the group who is recognized as having particularly good facilitation skills.

Local facilitation means that outside expertise is not required in order to hold a serial transfer meeting. The rules and guidelines are few and easily understood by everyone. Using local facilitators makes possible both the regularity and frequency of the meetings, as well as justifying the short duration. It would hardly be cost effective to bring in an outside consultant to run a fifteen-minute meeting.

Business Driver

The business driver for serial transfer is improvement in the team's outcome measures. That could be a way to get a task that is repeated accomplished more quickly, at lower cost, with higher quality, or with more satisfied customers. The way serial transfer gets the team to that goal is by carefully examining the relationship between the actions of members and the outcomes they have achieved.

Barriers and Problems

In this section I address some of the concerns that people raise when I talk about making serial transfer work.

Team Members Won't Take the Time to Meet

Team members have no reason to meet at the end of a project unless the meeting accomplishes something they value. For the teams that employ serial transfer what is valued is reaching an identified goat. The goat is evident in the

Army example, where life or death is a likely consequence of action. Likewise, the need to reduce the number of days that a generator is down is apparent to Bechtel's Steam Generator Replacement Group. BP establishes a best-in-class number for each step of the drilling process that the team tracks itself against. In each case AARs provide assistance in getting to the identified target.

In translating experience into knowledge (see Figure 1), which is what serial transfer does, being aware of the outcome is the second step. Team members cannot develop knowledge about the relationship between action and outcome if the outcome is unknown or, more accurately, if the outcome is unknown to those who are trying to construct the knowledge. A "known" outcome does not necessarily mean numbers or measures (for example, soldiers know the outcome if they have taken the hill), but for most organizational purposes, measures are a useful way to track progress toward a goal. Figure 2 shows how an identified target and outcome measures fit into the knowledge transfer picture.

For constructing knowledge, who "owns" the measures is a critical factor in their use. Team members "own" the measures that they themselves establish, track and report.[5] Moreover, these measures are primarily for their own

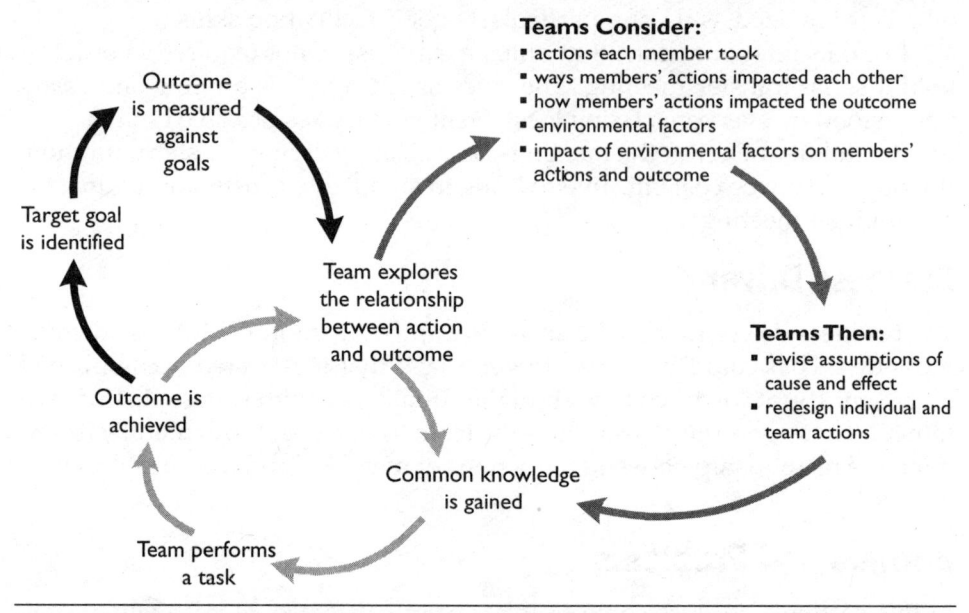

Figure 2. **How outcome measures facilitate the construction of common knowledge**

use rather than serving as a reporting mechanism. There may well be end-goal measures that are reported up through the organization, but the day-to-day measures that help the team continuously improve its task are not reported. It is difficult for the same set of numbers to serve both improvement and reporting functions; difficult, because if team members knew that the measures they were using to identify errors and problems in the team's processes were to be reported upward, they would be more likely to design measures that give a favorable impression rather than a useful assessment. Serial transfer requires that team members make mistakes together and clean up the mess together without recriminations from above. The measures they own help teams identify their mistakes.

Team Members Lack the Skills to Have Knowledge-Producing Conversations

When the type of knowledge being developed is on the explicit end of the explicit/tacit continuum, as in the Army and the BP drilling examples, few skills beyond normal communication skills are needed to translate experience into common knowledge. Having in place (1) a standardized format of questions, (2) a member of the team who serves as facilitator and who is familiar with the process, (3) basic norms of truth telling and (4) a no-recriminations policy is sufficient for serial transfer.

As the complexity of the knowledge increases, however, moving toward the tacit end of the continuum, a greater level of skill may be needed. Training team members in the communication skills of advocacy and inquiry can assist them in learning to provide the reasoning behind their conclusions, to examine their own assumptions, to inquire into the assumptions of others and to remain open to errors in their own reasoning. This set of skills, which behavioral scientist and business communication theorist Chris Argyris calls Model II, has long been associated with organizational learning and is a proven way to deal with the fallibility of human memory and the tendency to draw inferences based on scant data.[6]

Team Members Disperse Before the End of the Project

For projects that last over months, team members may come and go, moving on to other projects when they have made their contributions. So by the end of the project, team members may have dispersed across the organization and be fully engaged in new efforts. In this configuration, the same team does not do the next project together; rather, a new team is formed for each project. This situation is, of course, not serial transfer because the same team is not able to transfer its knowledge to the next site. It is, however, still possible for the organization to benefit from any serial transfer meetings in the following way.

Imagine each source team member carrying a suitcase of knowledge to the next team. Each suitcase is filled with the knowledge that team member drew out of his or her experience with the source team. If the source team held frequent serial transfer meetings to construct knowledge from its experience, then the suitcase that each team member takes to the next team is filled not only with his or her own knowledge, but with additional and more fully tested common knowledge developed in the serial transfer meetings. Each member's knowledge has been tested against the perceptions of others and in the process has been both corrected and enlarged.

The Team Is Virtual

Serial transfer works the same way with virtual teams as it does with face-to-face teams. It is, however, important that the same design guidelines be in place. Meetings should be:

- Held regularly
- Brief, with a set of standard questions or elements
- Participated in by everyone involved in the action
- Facilitated locally

BP, for example, has invested heavily in hardware and software to support its virtual teams, including desktop PCs equipped with videoconferencing capability and groupware. The company's initial pilot project for virtual teamwork also had a heavy involvement of behavioral scientists who helped team members learn to work effectively in a virtual environment. BP has been remarkably successful in accomplishing serial transfer in a virtual environment. An offshore exploration team, for example, may be made up of members who are out on the rig and others who are onshore. Morning meetings are frequently held between these two groups using videoconferencing. These virtual meetings have reduced the person-hours needed to solve problems between the land-based engineers and the offshore rig crews as well as decreased the number of helicopter trips to the offshore platforms. BP estimates that the videoconferencing system alone has produced a cost savings of over $30 million in its first year of operation.

The Power of Serial Transfer

Holding a team meeting to reflect on what has happened is certainly not new to organizations. The medical profession has a long tradition of holding "postmortems" when an unexpected death occurs. Safety organizations have often debriefed after a disaster or a near miss to find out what went wrong. But the meeting of team members for the purpose of constructing knowledge out of their experience is a relatively new way to think about such meetings.

Serial transfer places the focus on collective knowledge rather than individual knowledge. It assumes the capability of team members to construct knowledge themselves, rather than simply providing data or input for others to use. It focuses on the complexity of the relationship between action and outcome and assumes that team members can add a valuable perspective that helps make that relationship more accurate. This intentional effort to translate experience into common knowledge is an outgrowth of organizations' increasingly seeing themselves as knowledge intensive and viewing their employees as knowledge workers.

Endnotes

1. Lloyd Baird, John C. Henderson, and Stephanie Watts, "Learning from Action: An Analysis of the Center for Army Lessons Learned (CALL)," *Human Resource Management* 36, no. 4 (1997), pp. 385-395.
2. Nick Milton, "Knowledge with Shelf Life," *Knowledge Management* 2, no. 10. Nick Milton uses the term "serial transfer" in this article that describes BP's knowledge assets.
3. Nancy M. Dixon, "Hallways of Learning," *Organizational Dynamics* 25, no. 4 (Spring 1997), pp. 23-34.
4. Daniel A. Levinthal and James G. March, "The Myopia of Learning," *Strategic Management Journal* 14 (1993), pp. 95-112.
5. Christopher Meyers, "How the Right Measures Help Teams Excel," *Harvard Business Review* 72, no. 3 (May-June 1994), pp. 95-103.
6. Chris Argyris, *Knowledge for Action: A Guide to Overcoming Barriers to Organizational Change* (San Francisco: Jossey-Bass, 1993).

Nancy M. Dixon is an Associate Professor of Administrative Sciences at the George Washington University. In addition to Common Knowledge: How Companies Thrive by Sharing What They Know, *she has also written* The Organizational Learning Cycle: How We Can Learn Collectively *(McGraw-Hill, 1995),* Perspectives on Dialogue: Making Talk Developmental for Individuals and Organizations *(Center for Creative Leadership, 1996),* Dialogue at Work *(Lemos and Crane, 1998), and* The Organizational Learning Cycle: How We Can Learn Collectively *(Gower Publishing, 1999).*

Dare to Share: Using Extranets to Exchange Knowledge

Bill Roberts

Some pioneering companies are gaining a competitive edge by sharing knowledge they previously kept to themselves. They're using extranets to collaborate with customers and partners. As might be expected, it's not easy, but it can dramatically affect organizational performance. This article gives some examples of what companies are doing, as well as some recommendations and some cautions.

The scenarios are diverse. An electronics company divulges its closely guarded technology roadmap to its manufacturing partner. A furniture maker gathers consumer data from dealer showrooms. A chemical company allows customers to participate in its forecasts. A dozen large companies band together to share best practices for procurement.

A few daring companies are beginning to share knowledge they previously kept to themselves. The details vary, but all of them are using extranets—secure, limited-access networks running on the Internet outside the company firewall—as the vehicle for these innovative practices.

These pioneers understand that using the Internet to distribute marketing materials or automate basic processes doesn't even begin to tap its potential. The real power of an extranet is the capability it conveys to collaborate with customers and partners. Yet that collaboration presents a challenge. It consists of sharing what was once closely guarded information: design specifications, sales and market forecasts, inventory levels along the supply chain, profit goals, customer intelligence and best practices.

Because of this reluctance there aren't yet many detailed examples of companies using extranets for sharing knowledge. Most come from the electronics industry, where product cycles are so short that knowledge sharing is a survival tool. "Until other companies get a more thorough realization that extranets are going to be a major way we conduct business, it's going to be a challenge to get to deeper levels of information sharing," says Jason C. Watkins, senior manager of the Texas region for the Alexander Group Inc., a

Reprinted by permission of the publisher from *Knowledge Management*, November 2000. Copyright © 2000 by Freedom Technology Media Group. All rights reserved.

management consulting firm in Scottsdale, Ariz.

The problem is one part technology and three parts psychology, according to Cornelius Mendoza, managing director of the knowledge management practice at KPMG Consulting Inc. in New York City. Establishing a regular practice of sharing proprietary information demands behavioral changes. "When the IT department is asked to open up the firewalls to provide access to outside folks, it can take weeks just to reach internal agreement to do so," he says.

Companies can overcome resistance to sharing knowledge by building trust and adopting legal protections. For the former, it's important that all partners have a say in what knowledge will be shared, how and with whom. And a quid pro quo approach is necessary. "There's a lot of focus on who owns information," says Mendoza. "We try to get our clients to focus on dual ownership of information."

Because each company is different, there's no blueprint for extranet partnering. However, the relationships that Cisco Systems Inc. of San Jose is building with manufacturing partners come close. Cisco, developer of networking hardware and software, has been the poster child for e-commerce and knowledge sharing. Here are a few other examples.

Take My Roadmap—Please

Adaptec Inc. of Milpitas, Calif., develops hardware and software for managing data transfer in computers. The key to its success lies in designing innovative semiconductors. About three years ago, Adaptec faced a watershed decision: to speed up product cycles it would have to either build its own $2 billion semiconductor fabrication plant or find ways to collaborate faster with its fabrication partner, Taiwan Semiconductor Manufacturing Co. Ltd., and others in the supply chain.

In considering options, Adaptec saw that the most significant return on investment (ROI) would come from investing in collaborative processes, says Dolores Marciel, vice president of materials. Today Adaptec uses the Internet to share with TSMC and others information that used to be proprietary: its technology roadmap and design specs for chips under development. This lets the fab engineers work on manufacturing specs in parallel while Adaptec develops chips. The goal is to halve the time it takes to make new chips.

At first, the idea was a nonstarter. "We had to convince our own management that sharing this previously proprietary information would be critical to reducing cycle time," Marciel recalls. In return, partners were asked to share information about supply chain inventories and fabrication capacity; they balked. "There was definitely some resistance because the suppliers knew we would be working with some of their competitors as well," she says.

Engineers who would benefit from the idea loved it, and the CEOs were easily convinced. The roadblock was everyone in between. "Most people favor these ideas until they become affected by them," says Marciel. "There will continue to be challenges as we implement these programs because they change the ways people do things."

One tactic that helped to overcome this barrier was Marciel's unrelenting effort to market the idea both internally and externally. She also put together a team of stakeholders from all the partners involved and worked to make it effective. She made sure the partners understood that Adaptec would share its proprietary information, exposing itself to at least as much risk as they would. In addition, state-of-the-art encryption technology was adopted to protect and control access to all information.

Eventually the partners agreed on a yardstick: cutting cycle time by almost half. This measure created tangible reinforcement. "Overnight we were able to cut cycle time by 25 percent, making the goal of 48 percent seem much more attainable," says Marciel.

The Lowdown on Ups

The Rowe Companies, a furniture manufacturer in McLean, Va., was mired in obsolete methods. About two years ago, CEO Jerry Birnbach decided that Rowe needed to become customer-centric. First he hired new executives, including a CIO, a vice president of strategy and organizational development and a vice president of corporate development. Bolstered by these like-minded people, Birnbach moved forward.

New Internet technologies were available, but the executives realized that merely automating transactions was not enough to create the kind of enterprise they wanted to be. "If I can accept 500 purchase orders a day electronically, what does that mean?" says CIO Suzanne Krupa. "Yesterday I was processing 300 by fax and phone. Do I have the systems and manpower to address the other 200?"

To progress further, Rowe had to extend knowledge sharing practices throughout its own enterprise, which includes three manufacturing subsidiaries and two retail units. To accomplish that, the company is implementing a supply management system that will aggregate the necessary information and make it available on the company intranet. Rowe then wants to extend this information over an extranet to give dealers a window into the manufacturing and supply chain, especially a view of what's being made and what materials exist to allow other furniture to be made. These two types of information are called "available to promise" and "capable to promise"; presently they're derived from guesswork.

Rowe also plans to give dealers a tool with which to report what they're selling and to provide intelligence about what customers see as the hottest styles, fabrics and designs. Dealers are reluctant to share this knowledge with Rowe, but Krupa says their balkiness has less to do with its proprietary nature than with the haphazard way in which dealers collect information about their "ups"—that is, each time a salesperson on the floor gets up to meet a potential new customer. The ideal is to collect information on every up, whether or not a sale results.

Rowe has developed a tool to track ups that combines Internet and voice response technologies. It is implementing the system in its own two retail units, which compete with many of Rowe's other dealers. After rolling it out internally, Rowe plans to offer the tool to the top 50 of its 2,000 dealers. "The tool provides a competitive advantage for our own retail side right now," Krupa says. Management believes that whatever disadvantage its own retailers experience when others get the tool will be more than offset by the wider intelligence gained from input by more dealers.

It hasn't been easy to get Rowe's rank-and-file to accept all these changes. "From middle management on down there has been skepticism," Krupa admits. In response, a monthly newsletter, a Web site and closed-circuit television broadcasts in cafeterias are helping to put out the message that sharing is good. Since most Rowe employees work on a factory line, e-mail wouldn't work for getting feedback, so Rowe will install a voice response system instead. Executives also are evaluating employees, revamping job descriptions to fit new practices and revising the compensation system to establish incentives that support the new goals.

Forecasts for All

For years, Eastman Chemical Co. of Kingsport, Tenn., which makes fibers, plastics and chemicals found in a range of consumer products, was driven by manufacturing. The head of manufacturing decided how many of each product to make, and the sales force sold them. In the mid-1990s, the company decided it needed to be driven more by its customers.

The first step toward this goal was a new forecast method. Previously Eastman developed a short-term forecast every six months; based on historical data, that forecast was part of the annual operating plan. The company wanted to reverse the strategic forecasting process to be customer-driven.

To begin, it had to clean up its own internal act by aligning the long-term and short-term forecasts done separately by 40 divisions and the field sales force of 400. Toward this end, about two years ago Eastman provided a Web-based forecasting tool to divisional managers and later to field sales.

The next step wasn't as simple. Eastman did pilot projects with two strategic customers, letting them see the forecast data as it evolved, contribute their input and adjust to changes over time. The pilots lasted six months and produced more accurate forecasts than the company had ever seen.

The company continues to allow those two customers to participate but has not yet offered the option to other customers. "Eastman is still a traditional manufacturing-centric company," says Andrew White, vice president for product strategy at Logility Inc. of Atlanta, the developer of the supply chain

> ### EFFECTIVE EXTRANETS
>
> Jason C. Watkins, senior manager for the Alexander Group in Scottsdale, Ariz., offers the following pointers for setting up effective knowledge sharing extranets.
> - Define business requirements and processes before deciding which application best suits your needs.
> - Talk to partners who will be using the extranet to determine their needs and requirements.
> - Get buy-in from all parties, both internal and external.
> - Make sure the extranet application can be integrated with existing systems for forecasting, business planning, budgeting and other key processes.
> - Develop metrics for measuring the success of the extranet and keep a running scorecard of its performance.

planning software Eastman uses. "The head of manufacturing, who thought he was in charge, was the biggest barrier the company had to overcome. Then to go and say the customer is half the process is yet another big change."

What Eastman is trying to do is rare in any industry except electronics, says White. An unforeseen occurrence emphasized the cultural nature of such a change: the forecast manager who led the effort died unexpectedly, leaving the project without its champion. It remains uncertain what will happen to the initiative, says White.

Ganging Up for Goods

Textron Inc. of Providence, R.I., is a manufacturing conglomerate with independent subsidiaries that include Cessna Aircraft and Bell Helicopter. It has engaged in few coordinated activities across business units. A year ago, Textron decided to better coordinate procurement of indirect materials—goods and services essential to business in general but not to product manufacturing, ranging from pencils and notepads to PCs to janitorial services. Textron spends $2 billion on indirect materials each year.

"Coordinating indirect materials is a lot less emotional than operating materials," says Ed Arditte, vice president of e-business for Textron. "If we said we were going to coordinate spending on avionics for the cockpits of our aircraft, you'd see a lot more emotion from engineers and others."

Earlier, Textron had retained A.T. Kearney Inc., a Chicago-based management consulting subsidiary of EDS Corp., to help in streamlining its procurement procedures. A company can only slice so much out of the way it manages these processes; eventually the only way to achieve greater savings is to increase leverage on suppliers. One way to do that is to join with other companies to increase total buying power. Thus, when Textron heard about a

> ## COLLABORATION AND OPPORTUNITIES
>
> Larry Lapide, supply chain analyst at AMR Research in Boston, identifies the following areas of supply chains that knowledge sharing can improve.
> - Collaborative demand planning: Two or more companies figure out together how the supplier(s) will meet the needs of the procurer over time.
> - Synchronized production planning: Processes are automated so supplier(s) can deliver parts and materials as they are needed without human interaction.
> - Collaborative product development: The product developer and its suppliers work together on parts and components, electronically sharing CAD files and other information.
> - Collaboration with third-party logistics providers: Producers let transportation partners know what will be delivered to the warehouse or loading dock over the next two weeks.
>
> Lapide also identifies these levels of extranet collaboration:
> - Automated transactions: invoices, shipping notices and the like
> - Information sharing: finding out what one company needs and what the other can deliver
> - Joint planning and scheduling: a two-way effort to develop plans for what each party needs, what can be provided and when.

Web-based exchange Kearney was setting up, it wanted to know more.

EDS CoNext is a group of 12 noncompeting companies that collaborate on indirect procurement. Other members include, for example, Bethlehem Steel Corp. and Kellogg Co. The exchange, now owned by large systems integrator EDS, drives down costs by leveraging its buying power and collaborates on best practices, says Matt Lekstutis, a Kearney principal in Cleveland.

The consortium formed last year, and Textron joined this spring. Kearney has benchmarked indirect procurement best practices for dozens of companies, so it knew which were good candidates for the exchange.

EDS CoNext is structured to assure collaboration. On top there's a leadership council with an executive from each member company, on which Arditte sits. A second level is the day-to-day decision-making body, and a third level has individual stakeholders from each company in specific areas of procurement.

Textron set up a parallel three-tier structure internally. "The biggest issue for us is the cultural shift from complete independence to a bit of coordination," says Arditte. A committee of senior Textron executives from its various businesses provides governance. Procurement managers from each subsidiary provide day-to-day leadership. Separate teams of stakeholders from each subsidiary address each purchase area.

As for the consortium's ability to collaborate, Arditte is optimistic. "I think people are open and willing to do this," he says. "It's not revolutionary—we're talking about indirect supplies. The revolutionary step is more internal to Textron."

The First Wave

Marty Gruhn, vice president for Internet business solutions at Summit Strategies Inc. in Boston, calls exchanges like EDS CoNext the wave of the future. "This is a great example of how companies can come together and collaborate in a structural way to everyone's benefit," he says.

In her view, most business leaders embrace the Internet because they understand the need to build better knowledge sharing practices. "Every time I talk to CEOs, there is a slightly higher level of angst about what is going on," says Gruhn. "To participate in the digital revolution they have to dot-com their infrastructure—make information about inventory instantly available, etc., all those things that have been in house until now. And instead of one report a week, partners want a report every nanosecond."

The big problem isn't with executives, who know they must lower costs and improve efficiencies, she says, but with corporate bureaucracy. "People are threatened by this. They start circling the wagons," says Gruhn. "But the business benefits are so compelling the culture will have to realign."

Bill Roberts is a freelance writer in Los Altos, Calif., who covers business, technology, and management issues.

Companies Need Well-Defined Electronic Monitoring Policies

Carrie Garcia

We are all aware of the power of technology, of how e-mail and the Internet are changing our lives and improving organizational performance. But the power can be used in ways that undermine that performance, ways that can cause harm, inadvertently or intentionally. Here an attorney makes the case for policies to control how employees use e-mail and the Internet and outlines elements that every policy should include.

In this employee-friendly market, companies have been trying harder than ever to make their workplace one that attracts and retains employees. So is it possible in this world of dot-coms, casual everyday, telecommuting, flexible schedules, laptops, palm pilots, cellular phones, 401k matching, extra vacation and quality-of-life focus that these same employers are engaging in such seemingly Orwellean practices as employee monitoring?

When it comes to e-mail and the Internet, monitoring, or at least a policy regarding monitoring, is not only a reality, for many businesses it is a necessity. Why is it in every company's interest to know how its Internet and e-mail services are being utilized? What are employees' concerns with monitoring policies? What follows are some insights into how to design an e-mail/Internet usage and (yes) monitoring policy that protects your business and fits your corporate culture.

Employer Concerns

There is no question that e-mail and the Internet are essential tools in business. The power and speed with which the Internet works can be both empowering and, as seen by the recent "I Love You" virus, debilitating. Many employers, for good reason, entrust their employees with this valuable tool every day. However, many of their employees do not realize the risks that go along with such usage. The following concerns are among the many reasons

Reprinted with permission of the publisher from *Employment Review™ Online,* October 2000. Copyright © 2000 by Resource Communications, Inc. All rights reserved.

why employers have found it necessary to implement a meaningful Internet/e-mail policy.

Harassment Liability

E-mail provides employees with the opportunity to communicate with co-workers, clients, friends and relatives quickly and efficiently. There is no question, however, that e-mail is less personal and people feel less accountable when sending a quick message. Rarely do you see a group gathered around an employee while he tells a racist/sexist joke in the hallways, but often people do not think twice about forwarding an offensive joke received over e-mail to friends and co-workers.

Gone are the days (hopefully) where the centerfold is pinned up in a person's cubicle, but some employees have no problem visiting pornographic Web sites during office hours, downloading pictures from the Internet or even saving offensive images as screen-savers on their laptops. A supervisor may know better than to send love letters to the new, cute intern, but he may not think twice about sending her frequent, non-business-related e-mails. Such behavior is more than ill-advised and sophomoric—it could create a hostile environment. Employers who do not take measures to prevent the creation of such an environment or do not take quick action to remedy the problem may be faced with indefensible harassment claims. E-mails and Internet records are discoverable in litigation and can often serve as the proverbial nail in the employer's liability coffin.

Confidential Information/Trade Secrets

Many workers have daily access to the trade secrets or other confidential information of their employers. Many of those same employees also have daily access to millions of people via the Internet. It is not difficult to see how mistakenly addressed e-mail, or worse, one deceptive employee, could result in the trade secrets of the company ending up in the wrong hands. Employers spend millions of dollars to protect their trade secrets and confidential information; for many it is the lifeblood of their business. It is necessary for these employers to make sure that there are safeguards in place to protect these secrets from leaking out.

Copyright Violations

The trademark and copyright laws are complicated; certainly most workers are not intimately familiar with the intricacies. Employees could, therefore, unwittingly copy another's copyrighted material from the Internet and, as a result, violate the copyright laws. In certain situations, liability could attach to the employer for such violations.

Employee Productivity

Certainly e-mail and the Internet have made many workers much more efficient and their jobs easier. At the same time, it is no secret that some employees waste a significant amount of time on the Internet e-mailing friends, paying bills, shopping, chatting or simply surfing. Reasonable recreational use is certainly not harmful, and in many cases encouraged by employers (especially those that require long hours); however, such activities must be kept in bounds in order to ensure that valuable employee time is not wasted.

System Integrity

Viruses not only wreak havoc on a single employee's computer, they can debilitate entire networks, companies and sometimes countries. And as the world is now well aware, these villains can come in the form of an e-mail from a friend with a sweet, unsuspicious subject heading. It is becoming increasingly imperative that employers have the ability to detect and stop these "bugs" before they are even opened by their employees.

Autonomy and trust are extremely important to most employees. The obvious fear is that if their employer is monitoring their Internet and e-mail activities, these workers effectively will be stripped of both. Further, many employees believe that their e-mail communications and Internet activities are private and that their companies are invading that privacy by instituting a monitoring policy.

The bad news for workers is that, presently, the law does not appear to be on their side with respect to the privacy issue. Although this is an ever-evolving area of the law, most courts thus far have found that there is no reasonable expectation of privacy when an employee is using a company computer on company time. As employee and privacy advocacy groups become increasingly concerned with employee monitoring, this may change.

In 1993, the Privacy for Consumers and Workers act was introduced in Congress. This act would have required companies to notify employees when they were being monitored in the workplace. Although this legislation was not passed, it is very possible that in the future a similar bill may be introduced and passed. Furthermore, some believe that in order to stay in line with the Electronic Communications Privacy Act, employers must get the consent of their workers before monitoring personal communications.

Regardless of the current state of the law, many employers take the privacy concerns of their employees seriously. In order to promote job satisfaction and retention in their work forces, most companies struggle with balancing employee expectations with their own need to monitor activities. Although the balance may be difficult to strike, it is far from a losing battle.

Designing an Effective Policy

Every company's Internet and e-mail policies will differ, depending upon the needs and the culture of the company. Before designing a policy or copying a sample policy in its entirety, each organization must evaluate what concerns are most prevalent in its environment and what types of behavior it would try to prevent/detect through monitoring. Some, such as preventing harassment, should be universal. Others, such as productivity or trade secret issues, will be more or less important, depending upon the specific nature of the business involved. There are certain elements, however, which every policy should include.

Employees who understand the risks involved with e-mail and Internet use and realize that many of the reasons for monitoring are for their own protection and the protection of their work product will be less likely to take issue with a monitoring policy. When workers are aware that e-mail communications and Internet activities leave an electronic trail back to the company long after such activities are deleted or erased from the employees' own inboxes, they will be more likely to be careful and conscious of their own activities.

- **No Expectation of Privacy:** Employers should make clear to employees that their computer systems, including their e-mail and Internet, are company property and that no employee should have a personal expectation of privacy in communications conducted through these systems.
- **Describe Prohibited Conduct and Consequences of Violations:** Employers should not let ignorance be an excuse for violations of the e-mail/Internet policy. The policy should thoroughly outline what are considered illegal or impermissible uses of the Internet, including harassment, copyright violations, offensive or off-color jokes, distributing confidential information, etc. It should also be made clear that violations of the policy could result in loss of the privilege of Internet access or disciplinary action up to and including termination.
- **Reserve the Right to Monitor:** Even though an employer may legally have the right to monitor, the first step in establishing trust between employees and the employer is to actually tell them that the company may monitor, and under what circumstances such action would be taken. For example, if an employer does not plan to monitor at all times, it should be made clear to a worker that it may monitor occasionally for security and administrative reasons, including verification of compliance with the policy.
- **Employee Consent:** Employers should require each and every employee to read the Internet policy and expressly agree to its

terms by signing an acknowledgment form before access is granted to, or continued in, the companies' Internet services.

Conclusion

Although employers and employees alike may fear the idea of Internet monitoring, the risks of allowing free access to the "information superhighway" require that companies take the necessary precautions to protect their business and their employees. Some employers have found it necessary to monitor at all times. Others choose to do spot checks to ensure compliance with the policy. Still others monitor only when they believe there are problems.

The bottom line is that each company must institute and consistently apply a policy that fits its needs. Such policies do not have to be contrary to the corporate culture or the way that America is doing business today; rather, thoughtful, thorough Internet policies can promote better business practices in the increasingly technological 21st century.

Carrie Garcia is an attorney in employment law with the Chicago law firm of Goldberg, Kohn, Bell, Black, Rosenbloom & Moritz Ltd. Contact her at (312) 201-3998 or Carrie.Garcia@goldbergkohn.com.

Individual Performance

Reinforcing Professional Self-Management for Improved Service Quality

Baird K. Brightman

This article outlines the challenges of managing professionals and presents an approach called "managing by reinforcing self-management." This is an alternative for professionals in healthcare, education, and other fields to use to manage themselves and their work effectively. It examines the process of professional self-assessment and describes the approach to effective professional self-management. While it focuses on certain service occupations, the practices described can be useful when seeking to improve the performance of people in many other fields.

> That one can truly manage other people is by no means adequately proven. But one can always manage oneself.
> —Peter Drucker

As the market demands higher service quality at lower cost, organizations must adapt. As managers attempt to drive improved performance, they rapidly discover that standard approaches to management can create friction when applied to many of the individuals who select professional careers. If organizations fail to pay attention to the state of mind of the people who produce their goods and services, they may create an unintended decline in service quality rather than the desired quality improvement (Huselid, 1995).

Valuing most highly their own intelligence/skill and autonomy at work (Schein, 1993), professionals tend to chafe under management approaches with even a whiff of command-and-control. Historically, professionals have tended to view all management as *bad management,* as an intrusion into their sphere of professional control. The reflex reaction in this situation is to reject, resist and act against these management efforts. Yet in doing so, professionals end up rejecting and depriving themselves of any elements of *good management* (a paradox to the professional mind!). For purposes of this discussion, good management can be defined as processes and resources that are designed to help people do their best work for both individual and organizational gain.

While there has been some discussion of special management features and strategies that can be useful in dealing with highly trained professionals, the focus is still largely on what the manager needs to do with and to the professionals they are managing. However creative and appropriate those strategies may be, they still inevitably result in a management culture that can irritate and provoke resistance among professional personnel. Though this can never be entirely avoided (since modern realities demand that accountability and authority expand beyond the workbench), there are balancing forces that can be brought into the management equation to reduce the degree of clash between managerial and professional cultures (Brightman and Moran, 1999; Moran and Brightman, 2000; Vermaak and Weggeman, 1999).

Management strategies that vest decision-making responsibility in the professional will, by definition, reduce the resistance and antagonism generated by external controls. The most familiar strategy is the development of so-called self-managing teams (Becker-Reems, 1994) by which goals are set by managers and responsibility for achieving them is delegated to the team. This is clearly a step in the right direction of aligning management strategies with the special characteristics of those being managed. This article will discuss another approach to managing professionals which can generate good results: *managing by reinforcing self-management.* Strategies that increase a person's ability to effectively manage themselves and their work environment have been shown to increase personal well-being, professional satisfaction and performance effectiveness (Gist, 1987; Hollenbeck and Breif, 1987; Luthans and Davis, 1979).

The following self-management model is framed as an assessment and intervention program that professionals in business, healthcare, education and other fields can use to better cope with the work challenges they encounter. It can be adopted by organizations seeking to achieve critical outcomes by offering coaching and career management programs to their workforce.

Professional Self-Assessment

When doing their work, professionals generally perform a thorough evaluation (physical exam, blueprints, financial analysis) on which their activities will be based. It is also possible to conduct an evaluation of the core drivers of one's own professional satisfaction and performance. If provided with the right materials and information, it is a simple matter for most professionals to conduct this type of self-assessment as an important part of maintaining their professional balance. Optimal professional self-management over time should include a periodic "check-up" of these critical work factors, with appropriate intervention as indicated.

A thorough professional self-assessment should include an analysis of *who* we are, *where* we work, *how* we work and *what* kind of work we do (Keita and Sauter, 1992). Usually the major obstacles to professional satisfaction and effectiveness can be found in one or more of these areas. There are now time- and cost-effective methodologies available for assessing these critical professional sectors.

The Person

Everyone is not the same. While organizational efforts to recognize diversity have so far focused on factors such as gender and race, people also differ in other ways which have a powerful impact on their work behavior (McCrae and Costa, 1997). These individual variations include the following:

Who we are:

- health (personal and medical): I am strong enough to handle work demands;
- personal power: I can assert myself enough to have an impact at work;
- relationship style: I am comfortable with people, can get along;
- performance strategy: I am responsible and organized;
- skills and knowledge: I know what I need to know to perform well;
- priorities: I know what really matters to me at work.

Periodic assessment and improvement of these personal factors can have a beneficial impact on a professional's work (as well as on their personal and family life):

A senior executive had little time for herself between the demands of her clients and the firm's financial goals. In reviewing her professional life, she recognized that her family and cultural tradition of "respecting authority" made it difficult to question the way she was treated by clients, colleagues and others in her life. An adequate professional work-up, helped her to recognize that she was overworked, undersupported and silent, and to increase her ability to set limits and obtain needed resources.

The Work Environment

The structure of the work environment has a dramatic impact on employee health, morale and performance (Karasek and Theorell, 1990). By conducting periodic assessment of the following work environment factors and moving them to the positive side of the continuum, professional satisfaction and performance effectiveness can be enhanced.

Where we work:

- safety vs threat: I am secure at work;
- structure vs chaos: I have clear responsibilities, a manageable workload and enough control/influence at work;
- support vs deprivation: I get the resources I need to do my best work;
- growth vs stagnation: I am learning new things and making progress toward my career goals.

While the individual factors above can usually be managed independently, effective coping with the work environment issues will often involve effective negotiation and group problem solving:

A professional found that she was "drowning in paperwork." She often put in hours of overtime each day to catch up on documentation, which interfered with her music, sports and other interests. She believed that the organization had failed to invest in the support staff and technologies that would make her workload less onerous, and presented several detailed improvement proposals to the firm's partners. In addition to obtaining these resources, she negotiated to work four ten-hour days a week in order to carve out space for her avocational pursuits.

Task Management and Career Issues

To maintain a high level of professional and service quality, it is very important for people to evaluate how they manage their work demands, and re-define what kind of work they do at each stage of their career. Inefficient management of work tasks, or failure to make periodic adjustments in the structure of one's work over the course of a career, can erode both professional satisfaction and performance (Holland, 1997; Maslach, 1986; Pines and Aronson, 1988). Organizations that help people to manage their work and careers will derive a return on investment in the form of commitment to operational priorities.

How we work and what we do:

- handling work tasks: I know how to handle my workload in the most efficient manner;
- managing professional relationships: I am able to work well with people;
- dealing with problems and challenges: I can handle difficult work situations without losing my balance;
- job and career "fit": I have work that suits my interests, abilities and values;

- stage of career/life: At this point in my life, I have the right work/job.

A young surgeon was promoted to the chief's position over a number of older doctors. He had developed a reputation as a great doctor who could absorb any amount of work and do it well (he continued with a full surgical load in addition to his administrative duties). He rapidly discovered that his old strategy of "just work harder" could not possibly absorb the added workload he had inherited in his new position, and found it extremely difficult to manage the other surgeons, many of whom were former teachers/mentors and whom he still viewed as authority figures. After much deliberation and discussion with a physician mentor, he decided that his promotion was premature, and returned to his former staff position with much improved satisfaction.

Selecting a Focus for Change

Once the professional self-assessment clarifies which of the factors above are interfering with professional satisfaction and/or performance, it is then useful to select the optimal focus for effective problem-solving and action-planning. This can be done by rank ordering the following options in order of their estimated benefits/costs.

Change scenarios:

- change *nothing;* continue the status quo;
- change something *outside* of work;
- change how you *manage* your work;
- change your *position* (role, tasks, schedule, workload, etc.);
- change your *job* (where you work);
- change your *career* (what kind of work you do).

After defining where changes will be made, professionals can decide what changes to make and how to make them.

Professional Self-Management

Most professionals will work in their chosen fields for four to five decades, making significant career transitions every ten to 15 years. Therefore, professional self-management (PSM) is a marathon, not a sprint. Successful PSM requires adequate training and health maintenance, knowledge of the course to be run (terrain, challenge points, location of the finish line), and a race strategy that addresses course dynamics, competition and changing conditions.

Optimal PSM involves devoting adequate resources to periodic (e.g., annual) over the professional lifespan. After a professional has conducted an adequate professional work-up, it is imperative that they find a way to act on those findings that ensures *satisfying near-term gains in* professional satisfaction and performance. Otherwise the investment in the self-assessment will be experienced as generating few benefits, resulting in low motivation for further efforts and ultimately professional self-neglect. Individuals (and work groups) that are most successful in their PSM efforts tend to demonstrate a number of critical operating features; these efficacy attributes can be learned through instruction and practice.

Effective self-managers:

- they create a clear vision of desired goals/ results;
- they take action steps toward goal attainment that are clear and attainable in the short term;
- they work within their sphere of influence/control;
- their self-esteem is adequate to support the pursuit of a good professional life;
- obstacles to success are anticipated, and solutions are developed/refined;
- the benefit/cost ratio of change goals and strategies is continuously evaluated;
- skills and resources (people, information, things) needed for goal attainment are defined and online;
- reasonable limits ("bottom line") are clear and not violated.

Effective professionals remain actively engaged with what they can control and change, and they find ways to limit the negative impact of forces beyond their control (Lazarus and Folkman, 1984). They make maximum use of their cerebral cortex for developing creative solutions to work challenges, and they manage to avoid the "dark side" of the career marathon (fight-flight reactions, loss of work/personal balance, "burnout"). Certain self-management strategies are directed toward active coping with professional challenges.

Active coping strategies:

- define the specific problem(s) I'm facing; be objective;
- envision how I ideally want things to turn out;
- clarify my strategies/solutions for reaching my goal(s);
- anticipate potential obstacles and ways to overcome them;
- obtain needed resources (things/information/people);
- seek advise/consultation;
- communicate-negotiate effectively with other people.

Individuals who make good use of these active coping strategies are in general more satisfied and perform better at work. Most of us tend to favor certain of these skills while ignoring others; maintaining a dynamic balance among them can improve the likelihood of achieving important work goals:

After conducting a professional work-up, a talented professional in her 50s clarified that her work distress was driven by very specific personal (anxiety, shyness, perfectionism), workplace (safety, workload, resources) and interface (interpersonal style conflicts, gender barriers) factors. A good assessment is a significant part of the self-management process, for as she said: "I knew I was burning out, but it was just a vague sense of feeling bad about my work. I feel better just knowing what the causes are, since I know that will focus me in the direction of making things better." She discovered that while she was quite adept at using most of the active coping strategies when working with clients, she rarely used them when addressing her own work concerns. This recognition resulted in a marked improvement in her sense of focus and empowerment in coping with work and career issues. She found it most difficult to utilize the interpersonal skills (obtain resources, seek advise, negotiate) on the job because, as she put it, "people in this organization are supposed to be tough and independent, and women need to be more so." With practice she was able to expand her utilization of these critical active coping strategies with good results.

While it is generally healthy to seek and achieve mastery and influence where possible, there is a risk of putting an excessive emphasis on "being in control." While there is much that we can influence in our work and personal lives, there are areas that are simply beyond our control. Talented professionals can often be very strong in their active coping skills, but over time or when faced with situations that do not yield to their efforts to change them, they may experience increasing frustration and decline in morale and performance. The following self-management strategies can be viewed as the shock absorbers, bumpers and lubrication systems that permit high-performance professionals to maintain a winning pace without burning up or breaking down.

Energy conservation strategies:

- relax/remain calm;
- take care of my health;
- exercise to work off "stress";
- be patient;
- maintain a sense of humor;
- see the big picture, take the long view;
- engage in pleasurable activities.

When running a marathon, athletes need to know how to pace themselves (and even at times to slow down!). The runner who tries to maintain a "killing pace" over the entire course often ends up destroying only their own chances of winning:

A professional in his 40s sought professional consultation due to disappointment around his failure to be promoted to a management position. He explained that while he was widely respected for his technical abilities, he was consistently described by colleagues as "angry, critical, and controlling." He was told that in the current business environment, managers needed to be able to motivate and mentor people, and these were not viewed as his strengths. He had always prided himself on his ability to "work harder and be smarter than anyone," and viewed this as his strategy for success. In the process he had become alienated from his family, suffered from symptoms that his primary care physician attributed to "stress," and now had lost the prize he had worked so hard to attain. He decided to "conduct an experiment: let's see if these energy conservation skills do any good." He was pleased to find that his quality of life improved significantly within six months; he continued to be ambitious and productive, but "with less of an edge to it."

Professionals who fail to maintain a balance between active coping and energy conservation strategies in their PSM efforts are vulnerable to sliding into the "dark side" of coping. When a person is unable to find adaptive creative ways of handling work challenges, there is a tendency to resort to ineffective and ultimately self-defeating strategies such as fight and flight.

Fight and flight strategies:

- avoid thinking about the problem;
- use alcohol or drugs to "treat" stress;
- cry or yell at people;
- do risky things to "let off steam";
- withdraw from people;
- give up on efforts to solve the problem.

A reliance on fighting results in high levels of conflict with and alienation of the very people on whom one's professional quality and effectiveness ultimately depend. Excessive use of flight or withdrawal moves one away from the persistent engagement with people and tasks required for effective problem solution, and can result in a sense of isolation and futility:

A professional was very dissatisfied with his job, and after several attempts to improve the situation he concluded that "I can't do anything to make it better here, and I can't afford to leave." Over time, he noticed that he was becoming more short-tempered at work and home, had trouble falling asleep, and was increasing his use of alcohol. These symptoms resolved rapidly when he developed and implemented a PSM program with adequate dosage of active coping and energy conservation strategies.

Creative Problem Solving

One of the greatest obstacles to both professional satisfaction and service quality is cognitive paralysis, as in "I just cannot think of anything I can do to make things better." The absence of promising choices or solutions to work problems is a major contributor to deterioration of professional satisfaction and performance, and even the brightest and most capable professionals can occasionally find themselves in that predicament. Strategies that allow one to generate positive goals, choices and solutions can be a major contributor to professional improvement.

When we know what we do not know, it is a relatively simple matter to close those gaps by obtaining the relevant information by self-directed study/research, seeking advice, and formal learning or training. When we do not know what we do not know, it is difficult to close the gap independently; in these situations it is worthwhile to seek some form of coaching or mentoring. The information gaps that block most professionals are caused by their difficulty in accessing the knowledge, insights and creativity they in fact possess; that is, *they act as if they do not know what they know*! Chronic work strain is known to interfere with higher-level cortical functions such as creative problem-solving, and this can produce a negative work spiral. A number of learnable strategies can rapidly increase one's ability to generate promising pathways toward professional improvement. These strategies include the following:

Problem-solving strategies:

- *Brainstorming.* Make a list of all possible solutions and evaluate benefits/costs.
- *Reverse brainstorming.* Make a list of all possible ways to make your work situation worse, and then write the opposite and evaluate.
- *Giving advice.* Imagine what you would recommend to someone else facing the same problem you are trying to manage.
- *Polling method.* Imagine what ten people would recommend as a solution (you can also poll real people for advice).
- *Sensory methods.* Imagine watching a TV show, movie, or play; having a daydream; listening to a radio program; reading a book; something in what you see or hear will suggest new options and choices for professional improvement.
- *Genesis method.* Imagine you were just designing your organization to cope with current challenges. Would you set it up the way it is now? What would you change?
- *Time machine.* Imagine traveling forward in time one day, one week, one month, one year, one decade, etc. Envision that your work situation is better; focus on what has changed and how.
- *Hero/oracle method.* Imagine the person/organization you admire most and how they would cope with your current work dilemma (you can also benchmark for real quality indicators).

Armed with new insights, options and choices, professionals can move forward with action planning for professional improvement.

A third-year resident was struggling with the strain and exhaustion of medical training, and was having increasing difficulty in finding any meaning or purpose in his work. He was having active fantasies of abandoning his medical career despite considerable talent and promise in the field. Having little discretion or control over much of his profession, he tried to imagine how certain religious and military figures he admired would handle a similar challenge. He was able to rekindle the values of duty, honor and sacrifice that had initially attracted him to medicine, and to see his work as a battle against disease. He also spent more time imagining how good he would feel helping patients in developing countries after residency as part of his medical ministry.

Beyond "Time-Management"

A recurring theme in the workplace is "too much work and too little time." Many professionals learn in their early career to work long hours and put the job first, and to tolerate the personal and family costs of doing so. Given ever-increasing competition and downward cost pressures in the marketplace, there is little reason to believe that demands to do more with less will abate any time soon. And yet the negative impact of a workload that is perceived as chronically excessive is well known.

While generic "time management" programs can be useful, they often fail to recognize that problems with timely work completion can be driven by a wide variety of factors. The first step is for the professional to evaluate the contribution of a range of possible etiologies for difficulty completing work within a reasonable time frame.

Performance Obstacles

These include the following:

- *Procrastination.* I put work tasks off until the last possible moment, then panic and rush to do it.
- *Performance anxiety.* I feel nervous/scared that my work is not good enough, and I will be judged negatively by others.
- *Perfectionism.* I never feel my work is good enough, so I keep trying to make it "perfect."
- *Work-a-holism.* I just cannot stop working; it is my whole life.
- *Attention-concentration problems.* My mind wanders easily, so it takes longer to do the work.
- *Learning style issues.* I have had trouble with reading/writing or understanding spoken information since I was in school.
- *Excessive workload.* My job description includes too much work for anyone to complete on time.

- *Unclear work role.* I am not sure what I am responsible for, so I end up responsible for "everything."
- *Inadequate control.* I could do my work more effectively if I had more control/authority.
- *Inadequate resources.* I cannot get the help (people, information, things) I need to do my job efficiently.
- *Lack of interest.* I cannot get interested enough in my work to complete it.
- *Responsibility for others.* I have a management/supervisory position, so I am responsible for other people's work as well as my own.
- *Culture of working hard.* The norm in my organization is to work hard and long; I would be viewed as "lazy" if I did not work very long hours.
- *Lack of assertiveness.* I cannot say "no" when I am given extra work, even if it is not my responsibility.
- *Psychological disability.* I suffer from depression, anxiety, substance abuse or other disorder that interferes with my work performance.
- *Physical disability.* I suffer from an illness or disability that interferes with my work performance.
- *Skill-knowledge deficit.* I have competency gaps that undermine my work performance.

After pinpointing the primary obstacles to timely work completion, professionals can consider a range of interventions and strategies designed to improve their work efficiency. These include the following:

Task management strategies:

- *Prioritize.* learn to separate important from unimportant tasks, and spend less time on the latter.
- *Systematize.* create work processes that increase your efficiency, e.g., templates/ forms, decision trees, schedules/lists.
- *Synergize.* seek group solutions to shared work challenges.
- *Automate.* utilize technologies that perform work for you e.g. computers, contact/task managers and other artificial intelligence devices.
- *Delegate.* move work to more appropriate personnel.
- *Divide.* do the parts of tasks that contribute most to core mission or business strategy.
- *Dispose.* drop tasks that do not contribute to core mission or business strategy.
- *Problem-solving.* use cognitive strategies to develop novel solutions to workload management problems.
- *Learning.* Acquire knowledge/skills that increase effectiveness.
- *Treatment.* Address illness or disability that interferes with task management.

- *Coaching.* Seek advice/help in support of effective task management.
- *Job re-design.* Change roles, responsibilities, schedules, etc.; obtain reasonable accommodations; evaluate the benefits/costs of working less.
- *Job change.* Seek out new workplaces for better fit.
- *Career change.* Seek out new work for better fit.

One of the major sources of work strain/overload for the leadership team of a large organization was their frequent travel to various state and national customer sites. At first, the team could see no solution to this dilemma: "We just have to do all this traveling because there's no alternative." To stimulate their creative problem-solving talents, a consultant provoked them with the challenge to imagine what a better, smarter leadership team would do with this problem. The vice-president for management information systems (an avid *Star Trek* fan) immediately said with a laugh: "Well, we don't have the transporter yet, but it's ridiculous at the end of the twentieth century to send bodies across the country for every meeting. Let's think high-tech!" Building on that kernel of a new solution to an old problem, the group set this goal: to reduce its out-of-state travel by 50 per cent within three months by constructing a digital telecommunications suite. They followed up with a supporting strategy and budget. When the CFO warned of tough fiscal roadblocks ahead, the team wisely documented how the savings in airfare, hotels, etc., would pay for the suite in six months, and reduce the budget every month thereafter. The plan was approved, implemented and successful (Brightman, 1998).

Summary

As demands for productivity and change accelerate in the marketplace, organizations should invest in the capacity of their professionals to manage themselves and their work effectively. Teaching and reinforcing these proactive self-management strategies in daily work practice can enable talented professionals to maintain both high work satisfaction and service quality.

Strategies for professional self-management:

- define key obstacles to your professional satisfaction and effectiveness via focused assessment;
- choose the change scenario(s) with the best benefits for you;
- develop an action plan with specific change goals, steps and strategies for improvement; model the features of effective self-managers as you develop and implement your professional development campaign;
- maximize utilization of both active coping and balance strategies while minimizing fight/flight reactions;

- define and obtain needed skills and resources;
- evaluate obstacles to timely work completion and develop appropriate interventions;
- use creative problem-solving strategies to generate and refine choices, goals and strategies over time.

References

Becker-Reems, E. (1994), *Self-Managed Work Teams in Health Care Organizations*, American Hospital Association Press, Chicago, IL.

Brightman, B. (1998), "Achieving professional satisfaction and effectiveness: a case study," *The Health Forum Journal*, May/June, pp. 53-72.

Brightman, B., and Moran, J. (1999), "Building organizational citizenship," *Management Decision*, Vol. 37 No. 9, pp. 678-85.

Gist, M. (1987), "Self-efficacy: implications for organizational behavior and human resource management," *Academy of Management Review*, Vol. 12, pp. 472-85.

Holland, J. (1997), *Making Vocational Choices: A Theory of Vocational Personalities and Work Environments*, 3rd edition, PAR, Odessa, FL.

Hollenbeck, J.R., and Breif, A.P. (1987), "Self-regulation in the workplace: towards a unified approach to understanding worker attitudes and behaviors," in Schuler, R.S. (Ed.), *Readings in Personnel and Human Resource Management*, West Publishing, St Paul, MN.

Huselid, M. (1995), "The impact of human resource management practices on turnover, productivity and corporate financial performance," *Academy of Management Journal*, Vol. 38, pp. 635-72.

Karasek, R., and Theorell, T. (1990), *Healthy Work: Stress, Productivity and the Reconstruction of Working Life*, Basic Books, New York, NY.

Keita, G., and Sauter, S. (1992), *Work and Well-Being: An Agenda for the 1990s*, American Psychological Association, Washington, DC.

Lazarus, R.S., and Folkman, S. (1984), *Stress, Appraisal and Coping*, Springer, New York, NY.

Luthans, F., and Davis, T.V. (1979), "Behavioral self-management: the missing link in managerial effectiveness," *Organizational Dynamics*, Vol. 8 No. 1, pp. 42-60.

Maslach, C. (1986), "Stress, burnout and workaholism," in Kilburg, R., Nathan, P., and Thoreson, R. (Eds), *Professionals in Distress*, American Psychological Association, Washington, DC.

McCrae, R., and Costa, P. (1997), "Personality trait structure as a human universal," *American Psychologist*, Vol. 52, pp. 509-516.

Moran, J., and Brightman, B. (2000), "Leading organizational change," *Journal of Workplace Learning* Vol. 12 No. 2, pp. 66-74.

Pines, A., and Aronson, E. (1988), *Career Burnout: Causes and Cures*, Free Press, New York, NY.

Schein, E. (1993), *Career Anchors: Discovering Your Real Values,* Pfeiffer & Co., San Diego, CA.

Vermaak, H., and Weggeman, M. (1999), "Conspiring fruitfully with professionals: new management roles for professional organizations," *Management Decision,* Vol. 37 No. 1, pp. 29-44.

Baird K. Brightman, Ph.D., is President of Worklife Strategies in Sudbury, Massachusetts, an organization that helps talented professionals achieve satisfaction and success at work (www.wklf.com). He teaches at the Harvard Design School's executive education program and served for 20 years on the faculty of the Harvard Medical School. Contact him at info@wklf.com.

Emotional Intelligence: Training People to Be Affective So They Can Be Effective

Mike Bagshaw

Emotional intelligence is a powerful force in the workplace. Neglect it and the costs can be great. Low morale, bitter conflict, and stress all limit individual perfromance. There's also the financial cost of litigation over charges of bullying, intimidation, and exploitation. But you can use emotional intelligence to improve teamwork and customer service. The key to developing this force is appropriate coaching and training.

What Is Emotional Intelligence or EI?

Stability makes us feel secure. It gives a firm and safe base on which to build. Stability means we know what is going on, and what is likely to go on in the future and stability is something we have not got. Instead, we have one dramatic change after another. It feels frightening and out of control, and it's a natural reaction to keep things the same as much as we can, even when we acknowledge that that is going backwards. What we need to do is build, but we can not have the firm base of stability. We need to draw on inner resources to help us move forward.

One powerful resource is emotional intelligence (EI). Two psychologists—John Mayer, PhD of the University of New Hampshire, and Peter Salovey, PhD of Yale University—coined the term emotional intelligence in an academic paper which was published in 1989 (Salovey and Mayer, 1990). Psychologist and journalist Daniel Goleman, took Mayer and Salovey's theory and turned it into a best-selling book titled *Emotional Intelligence* (Goleman, 1996). Daniel Goleman defines this as "the capacity for recognising our own feelings and those of others, for motivating ourselves, and for managing emotions well, in ourselves and in our relationships." This is a bonus far beyond personal relationships. People with high EI cope well with their own emotions, and notice, and respond appropriately to, the emotions of other people. This makes it easier to harness their potential, and thereby the potential of the organization.

You can make a quick measure of your own EI by answering these questions:

1. Are you aware of the subtleties of your own feelings?
2. Do you usually know what other people are feeling, even if they do not say so?
3. Does your awareness of what others are going through give you feelings of compassion for them?
4. Can you carry on doing the things you want to do under distressing circumstances, so they do not control your life?
5. When you are angry, can you still make your needs known in a way that resolves rather than exacerbates the situation?
6. Can you hang on to long-term goals and avoid being too impulsive?
7. Do you keep trying to achieve what you want, even when it seems impossible and it is tempting to give up?
8. Can you use your feelings to help you to reach decisions in your life?

People with high EI will answer yes to these questions. However, self-assessment can only measure well for people who are self-aware. Therefore, the above test is only a good measure for those with the important EI quality of self-awareness. There are objective psychometric instruments, but they are still in the development stage.

Emotions at Work

Low emotional intelligence brings a plethora of negative emotions, like fear, anger and hostility. These use up a lot of energy, lower morale, absenteeism, apathy, and are an effective block to collaborative effort.

Emotions give us great energy. Negative emotions create negative energy and positive emotions create positive energy. We all know the tight knot in the stomach that comes with anger and resentment, and the primitive urges it brings to wreak revenge, or at least discomfort, to the one we see as opposing us. We also know the excitement of being involved in developing some project, be it an ambitious new product, or winning a football match. It is obvious in the extremes that emotions have a huge effect. They also have a steady, day to day effect.

It is easy to recognise low emotional intelligence in others. We are all guilty of sounding off about someone who gets our backs up, who bulldozes their way through opposition, so that somehow, their decision stands. We are not so quick to ponder on how we could exhibit high emotional intelligence.

There are insensitive managers who try to bulldoze their staff. They think that steady criticism, backed by a loud voice and veiled threats of redundancy, will spur staff on to greater efforts. This is certainly emotionally unintelligent. The typical reaction is for people to start huffing and puffing in corners, and occasionally have a showdown shouting match. This is also emotionally unintelligent.

The reasons for this behavior stem from emotions. Being badly treated by the manager rouses anger, antagonism, fear, desire to get your own back, and a general feeling of ill will. The manager probably behaves like that because of similar feelings, caused by past experiences or they are mimicking how their boss behaves. The behavior evokes bad reactions, which evoke bad behavior. Once emotionally unintelligent behavior starts, it creates a downward spiral of low morale, avoidance, and negative politics.

This situation is common, and the deleterious effects are obvious to anyone who has been there. Good work is not compatible with knotted stomachs and anxious looking over the shoulder. Yet managers are slow to realise the value of emotional intelligence in the workplace.

Logic is given more value. It is generally believed that a logical flow of information is the essential ingredient for new ideas. Emotions are supposed to be stowed away until the work is done. Exceptions might be made for artists and poets, as their creativity is considered emotional, but the "real work" comes from logic.

This staid point of view does not seem valid when you see and feel inspiration. It comes with a whoosh, seemingly from nowhere. Suddenly, one thought locks into another, a new connection is made, and we feel what is pithily known as the "Aha" experience. There is a rush of excitement as we see a dozen possibilities all at once, and can not wait to try them out. We write feverishly in case we forget, we rush into the next office to tell our colleagues. We phone up whoever we think can help us expand the ideas. Nothing will stop us. That is when ideas really develop. The careful step by step process gets ideas into action, but their first development comes from that heady rush of adrenaline. The logic is there in abundance, but it is fueled by emotional fervor.

The Case of Phineas Gage

Even logic can tell us this is true. We cannot expand knowledge purely with knowledge that already exists. There has to be an input of hunches, guesses, and intuition. These come more readily when we open the doors to emotional reactions.

Emotional intelligence is also essential in day to day work. This becomes obvious when you find someone who has not got it. An extreme case is Phineas Gage, a nineteenth century explosives worker who was considered thoroughly stable and well suited to such a dangerous job. However, he let off some explosives too soon and sent an iron bolt through his head. He survived for 13 years and, apart from the sight of one eye, he regained complete physical health. Even his logic seemed unimpaired. He could answer questions about the accident within the hour.

It was his emotional intelligence that died. He became hopelessly unreliable, insensitive, and incapable of even simple laboring jobs. The iron bolt had damaged the part of his brain that allowed emotions to take their part in his decisions. He no longer cared about the effect of his actions. It ruined his life and relationships.

The idea of different types of intelligence is not new. The psychologist, Thorndike, defined three types in 1927 (Thorndike et al., 1927). The type that is measured in IQ tests, that is, understanding and manipulating verbal and mathematical concepts, he called abstract intelligence. He gave the name of concrete intelligence to the understanding and manipulating objects and shapes. The third type, social intelligence, was in the area of what we call emotional intelligence. Thorndike defined it as the ability to understand and relate to people. This is clearly an asset in any type of teamwork. The concept of emotional intelligence takes this further.

Emotions have a part to play. The emotionally intelligent are aware of this. They are not constantly thinking about how they feel. They do not go to the extremes of letting it all hang out or hiding everything. They express what they feel when appropriate, so that molehills do not grow into mountains. They listen and empathise, but do not drown people with sympathy.

Sometimes there is a fine line between empathy and sympathy, between self-awareness and self-obsession, between confronting uncomfortable differences and nit picking. Part of emotional intelligence is making these judgements.

EI Competencies

As with other types of intelligence, emotional intelligence is difficult to measure. One way is to look at competencies. I have defined five of these, which can be remembered by using the mnemonic CARES in the sidebar on the next page.

Training for Emotional Intelligence

The good news is that unlike IQ emotional intelligence can be learned. However, emotional intelligence training is very demanding on trainers. To help them I have recently completed a pack for Fenman titled *Using Emotional Intelligence at Work*.

EI trainers need to be competent facilitators who can draw out discussion about experience and feelings. They need the sensitivity to deal with situations where strong emotions come to the surface. EI training is not meant to "open people up," but discussing inner feelings often has that effect. The

> ### THE CARES FRAMEWORK FOR EMOTIONAL INTELLIGENCE
>
> **Creative tension.** This involves managing the tension between managing the present and creating the future. It involves being able to defer immediate rewards for future goal achievement and investing time now to create the future.
>
> **Active choice.** This involves making decisions to act when faced with equally viable options and living with the decisions you have made. It involves working with your feelings to make choices. It is being proactive and not being overly anxious about the risks you have taken.
>
> **Resilience under pressure.** This involves managing your own stress reactions and destructive feelings and dealing with upsets. It means reframing how you view adversity and giving yourself time to relax and renew your energy stores.
>
> **Empathic relationships.** This involves investing in understanding before being understood, communicating authentically and assertively, and being able to develop relationships of trust and credibility quickly.
>
> **Self-awareness and self-control.** This involves being aware of your inner feelings, being honest with yourself. It is recognising when your reactions are exaggerated and non-productive and exercising self-control. It also involves feeling good about yourself and appreciating your personal qualities.
>
> Note: By kind permission of Trans4mation Training Ltd.

trainer should not simply set exercises and stand back, but move around groups and keep aware of any changes in the emotional atmosphere.

EI training is not meant to counsel individuals. It is meant to develop their sensitivity and to bring them new understanding of the emotional dimension. However if the facilitator has good counselling skills this can provide a strong foundation for being an effective EI trainer. EI skills are likely to improve the way people relate to others at work, so they become more involved. This will bring better customer service and satisfaction, and thereby value for money. We need to be affective to be effective.

Emotional intelligence draws on a range of materials and concepts which good people development trainers have experience of already, such as conflict management, active listening skills, assertiveness, and stress management. However EI enables these skills to be leveraged more effectively to achieve personal and business success. These skills, insights and beliefs need to be continuously honed throughout life. Emotional intelligence brings these topics under one umbrella in a powerful and compelling way.

To develop EI skills and awareness the following three factors are important for the effectiveness of EI training programs.

The Participants Must Be Ready

Discussing issues of emotional intelligence in an emotionally intelligent way is only possible when the participants are able to suspend their own concerns and discuss the concepts as concepts, not as personal problems. They may make revelations by way of example, but "opening people up" is completely inappropriate (and emotionally unintelligent). It would not be emotionally intelligent either to turn the group into a lot of cold fish. They may well be dealing with uncomfortable memories or current issues. EI training is much more likely to rouse emotions than most other topics. For this reason, you should make a point of being aware of any particular vulnerabilities in the group (such as a recent bereavement, redundancy, demotion etc.). Preliminary one-to-one sessions of a more counselling nature may be helpful. In any case, it is advisable to establish a confidentiality contract between all members of the group.

What Do You Need for Excellence in This Job?

There are a great many formal and informal ways of deciding EI requirements for a job, from detailed competency frameworks to simple observations. Emotional intelligence is rarely given the importance it deserves. A workforce that deals with problems, setbacks, and conflict in a productive way will avoid delays and prevent obstacles growing. It is an asset with a strong commercial benefit. So, decide beforehand what EI elements will make the difference in your place of work and focus on them using real world examples where possible.

Continuous Reinforcement

The importance of emotional intelligence should be emphasised, not just once, but continuously. It is not a separate quality from such factors as energy, willingness to work hard, expanding knowledge bases, and so on. Emotional intelligence is embedded in all areas of life and work. Therefore the principles should be reinforced, if only tacitly, in all development programmes.

Initial training starts people on the road to greater emotional intelligence. This can rapidly add to the value of the organization's emotional capital. It can bring change that is more profound if it becomes part of an ongoing cultural transformation programme, backed up by coaching, on-the-job learning, participative processes, and reinforcing of strong people-oriented values and vision.

Summary

To sum up, emotional intelligence is being able to harness emotions effectively, so that they play a role in business success. It is not emotionally intelligent to allow the heart to rule the head. It is no better to allow the head to rule the heart. The heart and the head must each play an intelligent role so that business relationships and business projects can both improve, side by side.

References

Goleman, D. (1996), *Emotional Intelligence,* Bloomsbury, London.

Salovey, P., and Mayer, J.D. (1990), "Emotional intelligence," in *Imagination, Cognition & Personality,* Vol. 9, pp. 185-211.

Thorndike, E., et al. (1927), *The Measurement of Intelligence,* New York Teacher's College Press, New York, NY.

Further Reading

Bagshaw, M. (2000), *Using Emotional Intelligence at Work,* Fenman, Ely, Cambridgeshire, England.

Cooper, R., and Sawaf, A. (1997), *Executive EQ: Emotional Intelligence in Leadership and Organizations,* Grosset/Putnam, London.

Crawley, J. (1992), *Constructive Conflict Management,* Nicholas Brealey Publishing, London.

Ellis, A. (1977), *Anger: How to Live With and Without It,* Citadel Press, New York, NY.

Fritz, R. (1984), *The Path of Least Resistance,* Butterworth Heineman, London.

Goleman, D. (1993), *Working with Emotional Intelligence,* Bloomsbury, London.

Seligman, M. (1998), *Learned Optimism,* Pocket Books, New York, NY.

Mike Bagshaw is Director of Trans4mation, an organization training and development firm in Evesham, Worcestershire, UK. Contact him at info@trans4mation.com or through the Web site, www.trans4mation.com.

The Key to Leadership Today

Marlene Caroselli

This original article by trainer and author Marlene Caroselli is an articulate reminder of what's really important when considering what leadership is all about: the ability to influence people to perform well and continuously improve. What's at the foundation of positive influence? That's the question the author addresses. It's not too complicated—it has to do with personal integrity and intelligent choices, but it's not so easy to achieve. That's why articles such as this are worth reading.

No less renowned a figure than Ken Blanchard has asserted that the key to leadership today is influence, not authority. Whether you're attempting to influence your team, your subordinates, your co-worker, your customers, your manager, or the larger culture in which you operate, you have a wide range of influence-choices available. Those choices impact the corporate vision, values or mission statement, which no doubt include a reference to integrity. The choices you make as you influence others microcosmically reflect the larger, macrocosmic culture. Make your choices wisely.

Use Definitions To Guide You

An ancient Buddhist proverb reminds us that anything you do is everything you do. Contained within your every action, your every communication, your every exchange is the potential to impact the organization's reputation positively or negatively. As you work to influence others, remember that it's easy to influence. It's much harder to influence with integrity. Whether you persuade for a living or you simply "sell" your ideas in the normal course of learning and living and working, you have already discovered influence techniques that work. Persuaders, in effect, are sellers. And vice versa. If you're attempting to improve your influence-power, know that you have some difficult choices ahead.

Part of the difficulty lies in the many possible definitions of key words, like "integrity." Is it, as the dictionary denotes, a question of honesty? Is it a matter of sincerity or of uprightness, as the dictionary also suggests? Would

> An ancient Buddhist proverb reminds us that anything you do is everything you do.

Reprinted with permission of the author. Copyright © 2001 Marlene Caroselli. All rights reserved.

you perhaps equate integrity with sound moral principles? If so, what exactly are those principles?

Some people regard integrity as the decision to live according to the Golden Rule: "Do unto others as you would have them do unto you." Is this your belief as well? And what if you were seeking to measure your degree of integrity as well as define it? Would you assess your actions as ethical ones if they brought improvement to existing situations? If not, what gauge would you use? The choices for determining what integrity means are multiple and mingled—they overlap with many other factors.

In the simplest sense, "integrity" means living according to specified values. But, of course, simplicity is usually deceptively complex. Living by specified values involves complex ramifications and interpretations. When you act with integrity, you are widening the sphere of influence, you are using power tools to achieve powerful benefits for those who "buy" your concepts or your commodities. If your actions are taken for your own advantage exclusively, you are following a narrow moral code, one that places your needs above all others. You no doubt operate within the letter of the law but perhaps not within the spirit of the unwritten laws that govern our behavior as human beings. If your actions are self-serving, you are not concerned with serving others. Consequently, your ethical influence is limited.

> In the simplest sense, "integrity" means living according to specified values. But, of course, simplicity is usually deceptivel complex.

Widen Your Sphere of Influence

On the other hand, when your actions benefit other people, you are operating from a higher-level moral code; you are living by and influencing others with generally accepted principles of correctness rather than your own interpretation of specific rules.

Unlike morality—which implies a codified sense of ethics, an acknowledged system to which many people subscribe—integrity is an individual consideration. Consequently, achieving clarity on integrity is much harder than achieving clarity on influence. But once you have made the choices that lead to clarity, you can consciously take ethical actions—actions that reflect the principles by which you wish to live. Having grasped what integrity is, you'll proceed to use it in your efforts to influence others in honorable ways.

Remember, though, the caveat issued earlier: "It's much harder to influence with integrity." Don't think that once you have managed to define "integrity," the definition will last a lifetime. Integrity, in truth, is a slow-moving target. Think about it. Over the years, haven't you shifted some of your views, in keeping with Emerson's insistence that "a foolish consistency is the hobgoblin of little minds"? Some of those views probably involved the definition of what it means to act with integrity.

The events or encounters that occur even after you have finally defined integrity to your satisfaction keep the target in a state of slow flux. These occurrences may be significant enough to force you to re-think your definition. You may have determined your personal set of principles, but when those principles are put to the test, you may find they are not steadfast after all. Or, you may find that your principles do not apply to other people. Or, that certain factors cause a given principle to recede in importance. You may even modify your definition to include certain behaviors that gained greater significance in your life. Having been betrayed by a friend or an employer, for example, you may now decide that keeping one's word is a critical aspect of integrity.

Resolve Cognitive Dissonance

Psychologists have a name for these below-the-surface rumblings in our mental terrain: "cognitive dissonance." In other words, you may have determined for yourself what actions fall within the acceptable realm as far as integrity is concerned. To be sure, it is important to make these determinations. Otherwise, you may find yourself in a state of emotional dis-equilibrium. But then you receive information that upsets what you've come to believe is true. You are thrown off balance, so to speak by the information that runs contrary to the belief system you've established. Your ethical "wholeness" now has a crack in it.

To illustrate, let's assume you have placed various individuals in either the acceptable or the non-acceptable area on the integrity spectrum, on the basis of their actions. Then you learn that someone you regard as a person of high moral character has done something you consider unethical. You actually have several options available to you in order to change your mental "dissonance" to "consonance." You can refuse to believe the story you are hearing, thus maintaining the image you have of this person. Or, you can relax your standards, perhaps even redefining what integrity means to you, in order to keep this person's behavior within the realm of acceptability. Finally, you could decide to shift your opinion of this individual from the high end of your integrity scale to the lower end. But, resolution of some kind is necessary. Otherwise, you'll continue to experience psychological discomfort.

Let's look at another example. If you were asked what core values you abide by, would you be able to express them without hesitation? Many people would find this question a challenging one, to be sure. Having lived through recent eras such as the Me Generation, the Greed-Is-Good Era, and a Scandal-in-Government era, you may find yourself wondering more than ever before how steady your moral compass really is. When you read that approval ratings for dishonest politicians continue to soar or that stock prices continue to climb despite charges of unethical practices against corporate leaders, you may even wonder if the integrity-component of the leadership personality is as important as you've always thought it was.

Current events force us to grapple with questions just like these. We choose our leaders in part because we believe them to be men and women

> Having lived through recent eras such as the Me Generation, the Greed-Is-Good Era, and a Scandal-in-Government era, you may find yourself wondering more than ever before how steady your moral compass really is.

who act with integrity, which in the eyes of many is an integral aspect of leadership. When we learn they are alleged to have done things we regard as unethical, perhaps even immoral, we have to make some tough choices. Do we still support such individuals? Do we revamp our opinions of them? Do we widen the borders surrounding appropriate behaviors? Do we remove certain actions from our previous definition, regarding them as unimportant after all? Do we decide that the person can still be an effective/successful leader despite his transgressions, because the economy is strong and/or because the nation is at peace?

Our basic moral foundation was formed early in our childhood. But experience and events cause it to undergo periodic revisions. Think of the childhood and young-adult experiences that shaped your ethical view of the world. Would you want your children growing up with the moral outlook that you depended on to guide your actions? In what ways has your belief system changed to accommodate today's world? Once you entered the world of work, did you find a fit between your beliefs and the culture in which you work? Depending on your answers to these and other questions, you make choices—important choices—about the way you choose to live and work. The choices bring you closer and closer to the target that represents your ethical core.

Let Questions and Answers Shape Your Choices

The choices, as we've mentioned, cannot be made collectively. Yes, you may be swayed by the results of polls, you may engage in discussions of these issues, you may read how others are learning. But in the end, you must decide for yourself what constitutes integrity. The decisions are seldom simple and almost never quick. But they must be made. Otherwise, you find yourself floundering in a sea of decisions each time a new scenario presents itself. You probably know some metaphoric boats that have capsized or sunk because there were cracks in the hull. In reference to the integrity of boats and individuals alike, the literal definition of "wholeness" or "soundness" is a good one to use.

As we've noted, choosing an operational definition of "integrity" is a personal matter. By contrast, when we work collaboratively and collectively, it's fairly easy to establish standards to govern us. As team members, for example, we have groundrules that promote ethical treatment of one another. As organizations, we have mission, vision, and values statements that guide our operations. As members of one religious group or another, we have holy books and golden rules that encourage ethical practices. As members of a reading community, we are able to purchase books that encourage us to adopt specific behaviors. While we can, as a society, as a nation, as a member of one group or another, establish agreed-upon principles that overarch our collective behaviors, it is much more challenging to know and articulate our own core values.

In addition to questions regarding integrity, you should explore questions regarding influence: What does it take for you to be influenced? How do you feel when someone has influenced you unethically? What led you to believe it was unfair or unethical? Do we have a right to influence those who hold onto their viewpoints as firmly as we hold on to our own? What role does "manipulation" play in ethical influencing?

Think of what life would be like if integrity did not govern the actions of those with whom you come in contact, especially those attempting to influence you. Speculate for a few moments about the results of a world in which ethical questions had not been answered, had not, perhaps, even been asked. Consider the products you buy, the services you receive, the work that you do, the community in which you live—if there were no moral premise governing decisions, the world would be in a sorry state indeed.

Build a Foundation of Business Success

Answering these and related questions requires effort. But the investment-effort produces an ethical return. As Peter Drucker, often referred to as the father of modern management science, notes: "Moral vision and commitment to social values are the foundation of enduring business success." Expending the time and energy to explore the issues surrounding integrity results in the formation of those sound moral principles that serve as a base of operations. Without this foundation, we lack the higher purpose that makes us feel good about what we do—as individuals, as corporate citizens, as citizens of even larger communities. As you study the questions and answers associated with influence and integrity, you'll be adding to your store of knowledge. And, the greater the array of choices on the shelves of that store, the more carefully and correctly you can select the ones allowing you to influence with integrity.

Marlene Caroselli is the head of the Center for Professional Development in Rochester, NY. She is the author of Leadership Skills for Managers *(McGraw-Hill, 2000) and* One-to-One in the Workplace: Scripts for Achieving Success in Business *(Alpha, 2001). She can be reached at MCCPD@aol.com.*

86 Your Appraisal Process?

Jonathan A. Segal

Performance appraisals are considered by many to be a necessary evil. In fact, some management experts claim that they're not even necessary. This article argues the contrary—that performance appraisals provide many important legal and other benefits—and takes on the criticisms one by one. Agree with it or not, this is an important topic that's not going to go away.

Performance appraisals have been getting negative reviews as of late. In fact, some individuals claim that performance appraisal systems are so fundamentally flawed as to be manipulative, abusive, autocratic and counterproductive.

If such labels are indeed accurate, the ineluctable conclusion would be to chuck the process altogether. A number of management gurus have come to this very conclusion and have called for the outright abolition of performance appraisals.

But such a reaction is far too strong—and, from a legal perspective, problematic for employers. Performance appraisals provide so many important legal and other benefits that employers should be loath to part with them entirely.

This is not to suggest, however, that there exists no room for improvement. Those who criticize performance appraisal systems raise valid and useful observations about a process that is undeniably imperfect.

But let's not throw out the appraisal with the bathwater. Such an approach would be inconsistent with the fundamental elements of HR. After all, when there are weaknesses in employees' skills and performance, we do not automatically toss them out on the sidewalk. Instead, we try to maximize their potential, reduce their weaknesses and build on their strengths.

It seems reasonable to do the same with the very tool we use to evaluate those employees. Rather than doing away with it entirely, why not evaluate the performance of our performance evaluation system, with an eye toward improving it?

Reprinted with the permission of the publisher from *HR Magazine*, October 1, 2000. Copyright © 2000 by the Society for Human Resource Management, Alexandria, VA. All rights reserved.

Discourage Teamwork Collaboration

A major and valid criticism of appraisals is that they tend to discourage collaboration. Performance appraisals undeniably focus on individual achievements and, therefore, produce self-focus rather than a team focus. This is particularly problematic in organizations that embrace Total Quality Management, of which teamwork is an important component.

But this problem can be fixed: if collaboration is essential, make it a criterion on which employees are evaluated. Appraisals that focus on—and reward—collaborative behavior will encourage teamwork. Conversely, appraisals that punish employees for working contrary to the team (e.g., withholding information) discourage anti-collaborative behaviors.

The problem, then, is not an endemic part of the performance appraisal system, but rather a function of how we use it. As seen above, appraisals can actually encourage teamwork.

Further, employers that do away with appraisals altogether, or that fail to focus on teamwork in the evaluation process, actually take on more legal risk if they later take adverse action against employees who do not display the desired teamwork skills. When employers do not clearly communicate the requirements for success (or how employees, fail to meet those requirements), any subsequent discharges will lack adequate foundation. That leaves the door open for employees to claim that the adverse action was based on illegal discrimination.

Inconsistencies

Critics also contend that appraisals are inconsistent. Evaluators often apply the same criteria in different ways or give different weights to the same criteria.

However, a good performance appraisal instrument increases the potential for consistency by ensuring that all similarly situated employees are evaluated on the same criteria. The abolition of appraisals increases the likelihood of inconsistency (and discrimination claims) by eliminating this common benchmark.

That being said, the critics are not entirely wrong—appraisals should be more consistent. This is a legal as well as a business imperative.

One way to improve consistency is to provide training for supervisors. For example, supervisors who plan to give subordinates a negative ranking should be taught to ask themselves: "Does any other employee whom I supervise have the same or a similar deficiency?" If so, the employee in the current situation should receive the same or a similar ranking.

In addition, where feasible, HR should review a draft of all supervisors' appraisals before they are finalized. This gives HR an additional opportunity to focus on the consistent application of the appraisal's criteria.

Human resources also should look for patterns on appraisals that may suggest conscious or unconscious bias. Clearly, rooting out such bias early, perhaps before it has an effect on employees, is advantageous from both a practical and a legal standpoint.

The review by HR also can help avoid the plaintiff's lawyer's dream: overevaluation of the substandard performer shortly before termination, which then makes the subsequent performance-based termination appear pretextual. In other words, if the draft appraisal does not reflect concerns previously expressed by the supervisor about the employee, HR can send the appraisal back for a reevaluation.

Employers also may wish to consider evaluating all their employees at the same time each year (as opposed to throughout the year on employees' anniversary dates). When evaluations are done at the same time, supervisors are more likely to apply consistently the same criteria or factors.

Valuable Only at the Extremes

Another criticism is that the appraisal process has value only at the extreme ends of the performance scale, for those who are exceptionally able or exceptionally poor performers. Critics claim that it is impossible to quantify precisely degrees of difference between acceptable levels of performance.

Even if the critics were correct and appraisal processes truly were this limited, they still would have tremendous value to employers. Why? Because most employment decisions are made not in the middle, but at the extreme. Performance appraisals can help justify promotional decisions for extremely good performers. And they can be equally helpful, if not absolutely necessary, when deciding whom to lay off. It is with regard to these situations that the appraisal is of critical value, if performance is to be the primary consideration of appraisals in setting the foundation for subsequent employment decisions. (Conversely, in the absence of appraisals, there are no clear benchmarks to distinguish among employees. In the absence of such benchmarks, subsequent promotional and layoff decisions are easier to attack.)

The value can be accentuated by including a comparator question in the appraisal instrument. Such a question might ask the following: "Is the employee's overall performance generally stronger than, the same as or weaker than others performing the same or similar tasks?"

This comparator question can be particularly useful in situations where supervisors rate all their subordinates as meeting expectations. The question forces supervisors to assign a loose ranking among subordinates who are performing satisfactorily, but to different degrees.

Finally, it should be noted that the appraisal is not without practical value in between the extremes. If sufficient detail is provided in the comments, the appraisal provides a map for middle-of-the-road employees by showing what they need to do to increase their standing within the organization or to avoid falling below expectations.

Short-Term Orientation

Another concern is that appraisals tend to encourage employees to achieve short-term goals. When this occurs, prudent risk taking is dangerously discouraged.

Undeniably, appraisals can focus employees on meeting short-term goals. But, once again, the problem is not with employees' reactions but with the focus employers establish.

As with collaboration, the key is to incorporate this value into the appraisal process.

Accordingly, the appraisal instrument should include both short-term and long-term goals for decision makers. Those who excel at one but not the other are not meeting expectations.

However, this solution does bring a potential risk because some employees may construe long-term planning to be a guarantee of long-term employment. Employers can minimize this risk by ensuring that all employees sign an application for employment with at-will language and that no express or implied guarantees are made in the appraisal process.

How do you achieve this? To be safe, when discussing long-range plans, always focus on the company, the department or the product line—not the employee. (For example, it is legally safer to say, "How should this process work in three years?" rather than "How will you be running this process in three years?")

This strategy will minimize—but not avoid—the legal risk. The only way to completely avoid legal risk is to avoid discussions of long-term plans, which is a greater risk.

With regard to encouraging prudent risk taking, supervisors may wish to ask subordinates prior to the appraisal for a list of innovations that they tried but that failed. If a subordinate has not failed, then he or she has failed.

Further, the appraisal process should be dovetailed with the compensation program. If we want appraisals to encourage employees to go after more than just short-term goals, we need to consider long-term commitment and planning when making compensation decisions.

Autocratic

Abolitionists see appraisals as wretchedly autocratic. The argument is that the supervisor has all the power in a supervisor-dependent relationship.

But removing the appraisal process will not change the balance of power. With or without appraisals, supervisors will judge their subordinates and through that process they will mold their behavior.

Further, eliminating the appraisal process will remove one of the few concrete mechanisms management has for measuring and checking a supervisor's use of power. Rather than eliminating the behavioral manifestation of management's power, we should make sure this power is not abused.

More specifically, one of the criteria on which supervisors should be appraised is how they appraise their subordinates. Supervisors are less likely to abuse their power or abdicate this responsibility altogether if they know that their professional growth hinges on how they manage and evaluate their subordinates.

While the appraisal process cannot be entirely equal, it should not be entirely one-sided either. It's a good idea to ask employees for their comments on their appraisals. This can help supervisors get a better idea of how employees perceive themselves; it also may be valuable if litigation later ensues.

After employees are discharged, they sometimes argue that their performance was substandard because they had a disability the employer did not accommodate or they were subjected to harassment that interfered with their ability to function effectively. When employees raise these concerns after being terminated—but fail to raise them on the appraisal instrument itself—their credibility suffers.

Employee comments should not be limited to written form. There should be an open dialogue between the evaluator and the employee evaluated. Too often the evaluation process is a paper process, not an interactive one. If the process is interactive, employees are more likely to understand their evaluations and supervisors are more likely to understand subordinates' perception of their evaluations.

There is a potential downside to encouraging increased spoken interaction, however: Because not every interaction between employee and supervisor is captured on paper, employees and their supervisors may easily disagree about what was said and how it was expressed. This can increase risk in litigation. However, this risk should be more than balanced by the potential gains of conducting a valuable, interactive performance appraisal.

Too Subjective

Critics also contend that appraisals are too subjective. There is no question that appraisals are necessarily subjective, but we should not eliminate the process because of this subjectivity. Rather, we should acknowledge that there is substantial subjectivity in appraisals, particularly at senior positions. We should then include safeguards to make sure this subjectivity is applied in a defensible way.

Employers can minimize the inherent but necessary risk of considering subjective factors by measuring achievement in terms of specific behaviors. In other words, employers can increase the objectivity of the appraisal process by focusing on specific employee behaviors, as opposed to general personality traits that flow from those behaviors.

This is an easier standard to articulate than it is to apply. To help supervisors apply this standard, give them guidelines to help them focus on the specific behaviors that are relevant to the criteria they are applying.

The Benefits of Performance Appraisals

Flawed as they may be, performance appraisals still provide employers with important benefits. For this reason, they should not be abolished. Here is a short list of same of the benefits that appraisal systems can provide:

Communicating deficiencies. The performance appraisal process requires supervisors to take note of deficiencies in employee performance at least once a year. Without this obligation, supervisors may be reluctant to undertake this difficult process—and employees might never be told that their work is sub par.

If underperforming workers are terminated without being given a chance to improve, they will perceive the discharge to be unfair. Of course, unfairness is not unlawful. But it can motivate employees to take legal action. And even the most pedestrian plaintiff's lawyer can turn an unfair treatment claim into a viable discrimination or wrongful discharge claim by arguing that the employee was fired for belonging to a protected group (e.g., age) or for engaging in a protected activity (e.g., complaining about harassment).

Ensuring consistency. Discrimination complaints often allege that employees with similar performance levels were handed dissimilar rewards or discipline. However, a good performance appraisal instrument increases the potential for consistency by ensuring that all similarly situated employees are evaluated on the same criteria.

Stated otherwise, in the absence of uniform criteria, there is greater potential for inconsistency.

Distinguishing among employees. Personnel decisions between similar candidates can be difficult to make and hard to justify. When choosing who will be promoted to influential positions—or who will be laid off in a downsizing—employers often must choose between individuals with very similar skill sets, experience and performance histories.

A properly conducted performance appraisal that is consistently applied throughout the organization can help employers pinpoint the strongest—and weakest—employees, It also can help justify in court, if necessary, any positive or negative personnel actions taken.

Recognizing valued performers. Even in the best companies, attitude surveys often show that employees complain about a lack of appreciation and recognition. In a labor shortage, this can quickly result in the loss of stellar employees, who are lured away by competitors.

The performance appraisal lets top performers know, in a concrete way, how much they are valued by the organization. As such, it is a necessary component of a comprehensive employee retention program.

> **Communicating strategic vision.** An important element of conducting a performance appraisal is establishing employee goals, which, ideally, should be tied to the organization's broad strategic aims. For example, an organization that values diversity can reflect this by evaluating supervisory personnel on their sensitivity to and appreciation of diversity.
>
> When properly executed, an appraisal instrument can become a powerful tool for establishing corporate culture and ensuring that employees understand and act on the organization's broad strategic goals.

For example, we can all agree that adaptability is essential to the success of an HR professional. In measuring whether an HR professional is sufficiently adaptable, we would want to look for specific behaviors that either confirm or contradict the employee's ability to:

- Deal with ambiguity.
- Shift gears quickly.
- See the big picture quickly.
- Make decisions without "perfect" information.
- Value diverse ways of handling problems.

Produce Emotional Anguish

Another concern about appraisals is that they produce emotional anguish—that employees worry about the process and are devastated by the results.

Employers should be humane with their appraisal processes and should minimize the adverse emotional impact on employees. As a result, appraisals should be conducted on time. The longer employees wait, the more anxious they become. Further, criticism should be delivered in a constructive, non-punitive way.

At the same time, we shouldn't avoid appraisals out of fear that some employees may not like what they hear. We should motivate employees to achieve excellence, not coddle them so that they are content with mediocrity.

To the extent appraisals create anguish in those that don't meet expectations, that's not a bad thing. It may stimulate them to leave on their own initiative. And employees who leave on their own are less likely to sue.

Conclusion

The critics of appraisals make good points. The problem is where their criticism leads them. It is easy to call for the abolition of something that is flawed. The problem is that the alternative is worse.

It is far more difficult to find solutions—even imperfect ones—but this is not new ground for HR. Just as human resource professionals strive to give sub-par employees the opportunities, guidance and training that may help them become productive workers, they also must work to improve the systems that appraise those employees.

It may not be easy, but it is worthwhile. And it is necessary if we are to derive the legal and other benefits that appraisals can provide, when they are structured properly.

Author's note: This article should not be construed as legal advice or as pertaining to specific factual situations.

Jonathan A. Segal, Esq., is a partner in the Employment Services Group of Wolf, Block, Schorr and Solis-Cohen LLP, a Philadelphia-based law firm. His practice concentrates on counseling clients, developing policies and strategic plans, and training managers to avoid litigation and unionization.

When Stress Won't Go Away

William Atkinson

Some stress is part of almost any job. So why try to reduce workplace stress? The American Institute of Stress reports that stress costs U.S. businesses between $200 billion and $300 billion a year in lost productivity, increased workers' compensation claims, turnover, and health care costs. Maybe it makes sense to take action to help employees and managers deal with the inevitable.

One day in late 1997, Carolyn Magura, vice president of HR for Wilsonville, Ore., shipyard Cascade General Inc., sat in her office weighing competing crises.

Two shipyard employees sat across from her arguing, wanting her to adjudicate their dispute. The owner of the company was on her cell phone. The head of the production department was on her office phone. And the safety director and an employee were yelling at each other outside her office, waiting for informal dispute resolution.

How did Magura react? To those arguing inside her office, she said, "Please be quiet for now; I'll be with you in a moment." To the two arguing outside, she said, "Please come back in an hour if you haven't solved the problem on your own." She told the manager on her office phone that she would call back soon. "Then I got on my cell phone to find out what the president wanted," she says.

Magura simply was doing what her job required. The word for her ability to handle the multiple unavoidable stresses of her job is resilience. Magura has it—but can other employees be trained to develop it? The answer is yes, according to some experts on workplace stress. Much work-related training focuses either on eliminating specific stressful conditions from the workplace or on alleviating stress after the fact. But another approach says that differences in employees, such as how they cope with stress, are more important in predicting stress than are specific job conditions.

If stress is just an inherent part of the job, why bother to examine how well employees cope with it? Because stress takes a bite from employers' bottom

Reprinted with permission of the publisher from *HR Magazine*, December 2000. Copyright © 2000 by the Society for Human Resource Management, Alexandria, VA. All rights reserved.

lines. The American Institute of Stress, a nonprofit research organization in Yonkers, N.Y., reports that stress costs U.S. businesses between $200 billion and $300 billion a year in lost productivity, increased workers' compensation claims, turnover and health care costs.

Stress You Can't Change

"The distress that a person may feel is not a result of what actually exists objectively in the job. It is a result of how the person perceives what is happening," says Al Siebert, a Portland, Ore.-based consultant and author of *The Survivor Personality* (Perigee Books/Berkley Publishing, 1996).

"If you had to handle 300 telephone calls a day from people wanting some sort of action from your company, would that be stressful? For most of us, it would, but the customer service reps at an insurance company I consulted with average over 400 calls a day. For them, 300 calls would be an easy day," Siebert says.

Siebert believes that "activities focusing on job stress reduction are often more harmful than helpful because they create the illusion that something called stress is 'out there,' constantly assaulting and harming us. In truth, what most people call stress is really an internal feeling of strain that they don't like."

"From a personal point of view, I believe that stress is very much a perception," says Danielle Shanes, an HR research consultant for The McGraw-Hill Companies, a publishing, financial and media services business in Hightstown, N.J. "For example, some people I know get very stressed when they are forced to work under deadlines; however, I tend to thrive when I work under deadlines."

Siebert cites another example: Fill half a room with older employees who are ready to retire and the other half with young employees right out of college. Then, announce that you're going to be introducing a new computer system. The older employees may groan and immediately feel stress. The younger employees likely will be excited about the new possibilities the system will offer.

Now assume that all of these employees work in the same office, and a major crisis hits one day. It's likely that the young employees will experience stress, never having dealt with a major crisis. The veterans most likely will take control confidently and show the younger employees how things are done. In each case, Siebert notes, the stress felt by one group of employees or the other is a reaction to a situation, and everyone reacts differently.

"Employees' self-management skills determine how they respond to and deal with circumstances in the workplace, including perceived stressors," adds Thomas J. O'Connor, director of PRS Disability Management, a training and consulting firm in Falls Church, Va. "Each employee brings his own set of these skills to the workplace and applies them. So the issue is how employees are behaviorally prepared to deal with and adapt to different stressors in the workplace."

O'Connor adds that while a first step toward containing workplace stress is to train managers to reduce as many sources of stress as possible, the next step is to realize that not all stress can be eliminated. "Certain things, such as market conditions, are out of an employer's ability to control," he says.

Shanes offers another example. "If a product line is struggling, management should emphasize to the employees that it is still committed to this line, if this is indeed the case. Management should also explain what steps the company is taking to try to address the impact of market conditions." Keeping employees in the loop with information like this can help calm fears, Shanes adds.

Employers: Check the Job Fit

Where jobs have inherent stresses, employers need to ensure that employees are in the right positions, Siebert and others note. A job that may be stressful for one employee may be sheer delight to another.

For example, a utility employee who loves being outdoors and climbing transmission towers might experience severe stress if he were required to sit in an office all day answering phone calls from customers. Conversely, an employee comfortable with being on the phone all day in an office might experience severe stress if he were required to work outside and climb transmission towers.

"You can hire someone who seems great, but six weeks later you may find that the person is miserable," observes Bob Largent, SPHR, president of HR Management Associates Inc., a consulting firm in Perry, Ga. "Often, the problem is he's in the wrong job. You may have placed him in a job that naturally increases stress for a person with his unique characteristics."

To reduce workplace stress, train managers "in how to place employees into job responsibilities where they can excel, based on their inherent strengths," Largent says. "Managers should learn to hire people for their individual characteristics, not the skills they have. Individual characteristics include how they communicate, what they like, what they find demotivating, etc. Just because someone has skills for a job doesn't mean they will thrive in that job."

"When talking with applicants, you don't want to come out and tell them that they will automatically experience stress on the job," Largent adds. "What is stressful for one person may not be the case for another. What you should do is provide clear details about job expectations and the requirements to meet those expectations."

For example, he recommends talking with applicants about specific expectations to find out how the applicants react to them. "If part of the job requires making 25 sales calls per week, one applicant might respond by saying, 'Only

25? That's great,' while another might respond with, 'I don't think I'm cut out for that kind of work,'" Largent says.

Shanes believes in getting to the root of job fit problems quickly. "When I find someone who is not working out in a job, I want to find out what is going on," she says. She explores what is working, what isn't, what kinds of help are available to the employee and whether the employee truly wants to succeed in that specific job. "If it becomes evident the employee isn't cut out for that job, then it is important to look for ways to make a transfer," she adds.

Management has to follow up by managing employees in ways that capitalize on their characteristics. "For example, a lot of employees like to work on their own; so, a micromanaging supervisor would be a big stressor," Largent says. "Other employees, though, like a lot of guidance and attention; so, a supervisor who fails to provide this would increase stress for these employees."

Employees: Learn to Identify Stress

While managers should have some responsibility for placing employees in the right jobs, employees also should take responsibility for identifying the jobs that will help them thrive.

"Employees should be trained in how to assess their individual characteristics and skills," suggests Shanes. To train employees to identify work-related stress, she says, have them ask themselves these questions:

- What skills that I enjoy using am I currently using in my job?
- What skills that I enjoy using am I currently not using?
- What skills that I don't enjoy using am I required to use?
- What skills that I don't enjoy using am I not required to use?

Assessing their own skills and preferences can help employees understand why they find some tasks or roles more stressful than others, Shanes says.

"It is important to help employees identify their behavioral limits in dealing with stressors," O'Connor says. He suggests that employees learn "how to take inventory of their coping skills in various situations. ... For example, if a supervisor tells his employees that they must accomplish a certain amount of work, some employees may say nothing and then get stressed out. However, others might engage the supervisor and try to negotiate another arrangement."

Situations for which employees should gauge their coping skills include relating to supervisors and co-workers, managing workloads, dealing with change and handling multiple responsibilities, O'Connor says. Stress-related training should cover those situations.

Employees also should be encouraged to assess how much stress they are placing on themselves, according to O'Connor. "For example, if they are working a lot of overtime, are they doing so because the company requires it or because they want to earn a lot more money?"

Should the manager, or the trainer, attempt to separate the resilient employees from those with less resilience and train just the latter? No, experts warn, because judging who is and who isn't coping well with a job's inherent stresses is difficult. Just because some employees don't seem to be stressed doesn't mean they're not experiencing it, O'Connor says.

"There is a stigma to admitting that you are struggling, especially when it comes to issues like stress and depression," he says. "Employees may feel pressure not to come forward and discuss their problems. As such, it is important to make the same training available to everyone."

According to Siebert, there are two types of employees: those who thrive on challenge and those who wither from it. Resilient people actually become stronger under pressure, he says. "These are the same situations that can cause less resilient people to file stress disability claims. Such people tend to be open to more information on how they can become even more resilient."

Less resilient people operate like victims. "When they experience strain and feel they can't handle certain situations, they blame something or someone else for these situations," Siebert says.

What Can You Control?

Blame wasn't on Magura's agenda when, in the late 1980s, the federal government closed the savings and loan where she was vice president of HR. "Those of us left in management realized that resilient people take control of their environments," she recalls. "They don't let their environments control them." That realization prompted her interest in resilience training.

First, the company's managers decided to partner with the government and succeed. "We wanted to create a business where, when the feds eventually sold us, we would have something worth selling," Magura recalls. "We told our employees that we wanted this to be the most exciting and positive experience of their careers."

She worked with Siebert to bring resilience training into the organization. They met with employees to allow them to vent their frustrations. Then Magura and Siebert asked employees, "What are the things you can control? And how can you control them?" Faced with a situation where some fundamental changes—like the government intervention—were beyond employee control, Magura steered employees to focus on what they could control, such as their contacts with customers.

Magura also made this promise to employees: "If you choose not to be resilient and work through this with us, I will personally help you find a new job." Not only did employees stay, but Magura actually ended up hiring even more people. The S&L made a profit and a bank bought it. "We didn't cost the taxpayers a penny," Magura adds.

Causes of Workplace Stress

While stress often stems from a person's reaction to a situation, more than from the situation itself, certain workplace situations—such as lacking control over decisions that affect them or working under unclear expectations—generally create stress for most employees, according to the National Institute of Occupational Safety and Health (NIOSH).

"Our research shows that certain things are stressors for most people," explains Terry Bond, vice president for research at the Families and Work Institute in New York, a research organization that assisted NIOSH with a 1999 report on workplace stress.

"For example," Bond says, "there is a positive correlation between working long hours and experiencing stress for the working population in general." The NIOSH report identifies several aspects of work that generate stress when handled poorly:

- **Task design.** This includes heavy work loads, infrequent rest breaks, long work hours, shift work and hectic or routine tasks that have little inherent meaning, do not use workers' skills and provide little sense of control.
- **Management style.** This can include poor communication, lack of family-friendly policies and workers' lack of participation in decision-making.
- **Personal relationships.** These include a poor social environment and lack of support from co-workers and supervisors.
- **Work roles.** Conflicting or uncertain job expectations, too much responsibility or having to "wear too many hats" are work role problems.
- **Career concerns.** Stress can result from job insecurity and lack of opportunity for growth, advancement or promotion. Another cause of career stress: rapid changes for which workers are unprepared.
- **Environmental conditions.** These can include unpleasant or dangerous physical conditions, such as crowding, noise, air pollution or ergonomic problems.

Attitude Check for Managers

As Magura and the other managers at the S&L found, helping employees become more resilient to stress can have significant benefits for management, especially in a crisis. "When workloads increase, managers value the employees who can handle the extra work without getting stressed out," says Mara Gottlieb, a New York-based training consultant.

Managers can be trained to understand individual differences in their employees and then help employees become more resilient to perceived stressful situations, as Magura did at the S&L.

Who's Tough Enough?

Some employees cope or even thrive under difficult conditions, while others fold. What makes some people tougher than others when a workplace crisis—or even everyday stress—hits? Author and consultant Al Siebert offers some identifiers of the resilient employee.

When resilient employees experience something upsetting, they identify things they can begin doing immediately to minimize its impact.

"This helps them avoid feelings of helplessness," Siebert says. "When less resilient people experience challenges, their first reaction is usually to get upset. Then, their second reaction is to try to find ways to calm down."

While resilient employees may experience a temporary emotional reaction to a problem, they immediately move to the problem-solving mode.

"One thing almost all resilient people have in common is a revitalization strategy," such as spending time with family or friends and having a "higher purpose," often related to church or community activities, Siebert says.

Resilient people also tend to take care of themselves physically, he adds. "These are not people who put themselves to sleep with alcohol or pills and then try to energize themselves in the morning with coffee."

"If something is not working, a lot of employees will find ways on their own to get it to work," notes Glen Fahs, director of training and organization development for Cascade Employers Association, a membership group of employers, based in Salem, Ore. "However, others will throw up their hands and assume nothing can be done. Managers should be trained to get together with these employees and say something like, 'If you find something is not working, let me know. Then, we'll sit down and find ways to fix it together.'"

Over time, these employees should gradually begin to see that they do have more control than they once thought—and having more control generally means less stress. (See the sidebar, "Causes of Workplace Stress.").

It is also important for managers to keep their own attitudes in mind. "Most managers with positive attitudes have negative attitudes toward people with negative attitudes," says Siebert. These managers need to develop a positive attitude about people with negative attitudes. "Managers must learn to assimilate the 'negative voice' into the workplace," he explains. "Don't insist on changing everyone. Just accept them."

One way Siebert recommends managers deal with people who seem to operate with "negative voices" is to put them in charge of, or allow them to specialize in, the areas where they have the most complaints. "Often, being given responsibility for things employees complain about helps them begin to shift from the negative to the positive," he says.

William Atkinson is a business writer based in Carterville, Ill. He specializes in safety, health, and workers' compensation issues.

Retaining Peak Performers by Individualizing Employee Recognition

Cindy Ventrice

For many employees, receiving acknowledgment for doing good work is more important than compensation in terms of performance and improvement. Recognition of excellent performance is more appreciated and more effective if it takes into account the differences among individual employees. This article argues cogently for individualizing recognition and offers some valuable recommendations.

Regardless of economic conditions, employers will always struggle with the issue of turnover and retention among their peak performers. Even in an economic downturn, high-performing employees have options. Keeping the best and the brightest requires employers to create a positive work environment. One of the tools that they use to do this is employee recognition. The problem is that these programs frequently fall flat.

Recognition programs can be successful. They can have a positive effect on employee turnover, morale and motivation, particularly among those employees that offer the greatest retention challenge, the peak performers. To keep peak performers and keep them happy, recognition must take two things into account.

1. Peak performers want to do work that matters. They want to know what the company values, and how their work personally contributes to the organization's goals. They want to be recognized for their individual contribution.

> An employee from IBM shares that his manager sends out a handwritten note on the anniversary of each employee's hire date. That note recounts the employee's contributions to the department. People in that manager's department look forward to receiving and sharing these notes with each other. This manager has their loyalty because he values both the employee and their contribution.

Reprinted by permission of the author from *Potential Unlimited*, 2001. Copyright © 2001 by Cindy Ventrice. All rights reserved.

> ### IMAGINE, LOOK, CONSIDER …
>
> *Imagine* the impact on morale, when every employee receives a potted plant on the anniversary of his or her hire date. The business office generates the purchase order, the florist delivers the plant, and employees wonder if the manager is even aware of the anniversary.
>
> *Look* at recognition from the perspective of the diabetic employee who receives a Mars candy bar as a symbol of appreciation for "out of this world" customer service. Clever idea … that shows disregard for the employee's needs and preferences.
>
> *Consider* the company that regularly hands out awards for "going beyond the call of duty." Sounds like a good idea, except that the employees at this company view the recipients of the award as "simply doing their jobs." They wonder if anyone would even recognize exceptional behavior if they saw it.

2. **Peak performers want their unique abilities and interests recognized.** They find recognition meaningful when it takes into account their unique offerings.

> A maintenance officer in the Air Force received an award that was both unique and meaningful. He received a hand drawn picture of the three types of aircraft he maintained, mounted with photos of the eighteen people who worked with him in that section. This was a one-of-a-kind award that had significant impact.

Personalize Recognition

To be effective, managers must personalize recognition. This is best done with a three-part process:

1. Identify how the employee can best contribute to achieving organizational goals and values.
2. Determine what the employee values in terms of recognition.
3. Recognize the employee's unique contribution with personalized rewards.

When a manager takes the time to get to know employees and what they value, they offer one of the most important forms of recognition. They understand the unique contribution and needs of each individual. The employee feels both *valued* and *valuable*.

The payoff to an organization is that when peak performers feel both valued and valuable—when they know that someone cares about them and their growth within the organization, they have greater job satisfaction and are more likely to want to stay with their current job and/or organization.

1. Identify How the Employee Can Best Contribute to Achieving Organizational Goals and Values

A manager should schedule at least one meeting per year with each employee in order to discuss how their job impacts the values and goals of the organization. The conversation should begin with the manager restating the organization's values and goals. This conversation can be something as simple as "Jeff, as you know, XYZ Corporation values innovation, quality, and adaptability. The company's three main goals for the coming year are to release one new product, upgrade our three most popular products, and find new markets for two products with declining sales." This statement of values and goals sets the stage for the questions that follow.

How does your work relate to these goals and values?

Use this question or something similar to help employees explore their job responsibilities and relate those responsibilities back to the values and goals of the organization. Make sure employees understand that you are not questioning whether or not their work has value, but are interested in discovering how they perceive the value of their contribution.

Jeff, of XYZ Corporation, might respond that, as a salesperson, the information he gathers from customers and clients is used to determine consumer preferences. This information helps the company to develop products that will be in high demand.

What tasks are you currently doing that don't support these organizational values and goals?

The purpose of this question has two parts. One, to uncover responsibilities that are not of value to the organization so that operations can be streamlined. Two, to help the employee understand how specific tasks do contribute to achieving the organization's values and goals.

Jeff might feel that the time he spends compiling statistics on lost sales is a waste of time.

Can theses tasks be modified to make them more relevant?

This question is used as a follow up to the preceding question. Allow the employee to make appropriate changes to how tasks are performed in order to help them contribute in a more meaningful way.

Maybe Jeff could also track why the prospect didn't purchase their product. This information might be used in development, upgrading, and expanding current markets.

What goals can you set for yourself that will allow you to contribute to an even greater extent?

Use this question to explore how an employee would make their contribution more relevant and impactful.

Jeff might want to work with R&D and facilitate a series of customer

> ### SOME RECOGNITION DOESN'T WORK
>
> Common recognition wisdom says that we should recognize the employee's family; acknowledge their contribution to the employee's success.
>
> One company chose to recognize the wife of a top salesman. She shares the impact of that recognition: "My husband's company sent me a big gift basket when he became the top salesman. I really resented that he had to work many overtime hours with no days off in order to make top salesman. I was actively lobbying to get him to change jobs at the time."
>
> The fruit basket was a reminder of all the hours her husband had spent away from the family. It had an impact, but not the one the company was hoping for.

focus groups that explore customer preferences in greater depth.

Employees who understand how their responsibilities affect their organization make a more meaningful contribution. When managers set aside time to help employees clarify and improve their role within the organization the positive impact on productivity and quality is measurable.

2. Determine What the Employee Values in Terms of Recognition

Some rewards can and should recognize the efforts of work groups, departments or even the entire organization. These rewards will be celebrations of achievement and won't take into account each individual's unique recognition preferences.

While group recognition has a place within the organization, most recognition should be directed to the individual. For individual recognition to have impact, it should be personalized. An employee of a high-tech company shares that an award of an overnight trip was memorable because "it was tailored specifically to what I like to do."

When it comes to rewards and recognition, everyone values something a little different. It is the manager's job to determine what each employee values and recognize their individual contribution with a reward that has special value to them.

No two people want to be recognized in exactly the same way. One loves the spotlight and would be thrilled to have their accomplishments announced at a pizza party given in their honor. Another prefers to stay in the background, receiving private praise and a thank you. One employee would like the opportunity to take a class; another wants the chance to teach it.

When asked about recognition that had a lasting impact, employees across the country had very diverse answers.

- One employee shared that being asked to take the president's place on a panel discussion was an honor she would never forget.

- An employee of a semiconductor manufacturer pointed to her manager's willingness to allow her to work whenever and wherever, as long as the work gets done.
- An employee of a large telecommunications company appreciated having her direct supervisor praise her work to the department head.

Recognition is most meaningful when it allows for the employee's personal preferences, needs and values.

Interviewing for Recognition Preferences

Everyone has different preferences. It is up to the manager to identify those preferences in order to recognize the individual in a way that will have meaning to them. The best way to do this is by asking good questions and listening to the employee.

Listed below are some open-ended questions about recognition preferences. The responses given are examples of what an employee might say, along with some hints regarding how the information might be used to motivate.

What do you love about your job? (Listen for hints about what they value.)
- *"I love that I can leave at 5:00 most evenings to be with my family."* In order to keep this employee, a manager shouldn't make a habit of asking them to stay late. A suitable reward might be time off, to be used at their discretion.
- *"I love the independence I have to do the job as I see fit."* If the job is getting done satisfactorily, a manager should make sure that this employee doesn't become restrained or restricted. Reward with increased autonomy.
- *"I love having the opportunity to learn and grow."* An astute manager will make sure that this employee doesn't keep the same duties for an extended period of time. Reward them with a new, challenging responsibility, or the workshop of their choice.

Asking, "What do you love about your job?" can provide specific information about tasks that the employee enjoys most. Use this information to reward them with more of what they enjoy, and less of what they consider drudgery.

As your manager, what could I do to make your job more satisfying? (This is not the time to debate; just listen and take notes.)
- *"You could allow me some flexibility in what hours I work."* Recognition for a job well done might include the freedom to leave early or come in late twice a week so long as the department has someone to answer the phones.
- *"I would like you to help me prepare for a promotion."* Recognize their efforts by introducing them to key managers or by providing a coach.

- *"You could provide more social opportunities for the department."* This employee values the social bonding of the group. Reward them with impromptu pizza parties, team-building activities at meetings, or put them in charge of celebrating birthdays.
- *"You could let others know how hard I work, so they don't try to dump their stuff on me."* This employee wants public praise.

Which would you prefer? (Offer only specific alternatives that are possible within the constraints of your organization.)

Which would you prefer?

to be recognized for your performance by being given control over a more prestigious project
or
receive a weekend getaway for two?

a sincere thank-you card for overtime on a special project
or
having your efforts recognized in front of your team?

a cash bonus for being the top sales performer during the quarter
or
a week in Hawaii presented at the quarterly sales meeting?

having your family present when you receive an award
or
having the VP personally recognize your achievement one to one?

the opportunity to telecommute one day a week
or
the opportunity to attend a professional development conference on the topic of your choice?

Combine these preference questions with those about goals and values. Together, they form the foundation of a recognition interview. The recognition interview helps a manager to learn more about what their employees value and how they want to be recognized.

A Final Thought on the Recognition Interview ...

It takes commitment to set aside the time to interview every employee. Effective managers make that commitment because they know that the time they spend with each employee demonstrates that they value both the person and their contribution.

Done well, the recognition interview itself is a significant form of recognition. Employees who have had a say in developing goals, who know that their manager is aware of what they value, and who believe that their manager cares about them personally, will experience greater job satisfaction.

Employees experiencing high-job satisfaction stay in their jobs longer, produce quality products, and provide quality service. Retaining these employees means managers need to spend significantly less time recruiting and training.

3. Recognize the Employee's Unique Contribution with Personalized Rewards

The information that the manager gathers during the recognition interview will provide most of what is needed in order to recognize an employee's contribution:

- **Measurable goals**—employees and the manager will have set measurable goals for performance. Recognize both achievement of these goals, and the behaviors that contribute to future achievement.
- **Insights into what employees value**—the manager will have insights into the work that employees see as valuable, and the forms of recognition they see as desirable. Use these to increase employee satisfaction with personalized opportunities and recognition.

Effective managers don't stop there, they:

- Track the recognition given, why it was given, when it was given as well as the employee's response. This information helps to tailor recognition even more.
- Attempt to give some form of recognition every week. When recognition is infrequent, they look into the cause. Is the employee off-track in meeting goals? Has past recognition been poorly received? Has the manager ceased to focus on recognition? The effective manager will take corrective action.
- Continue to learn more about employees, such as what kind of candy bar they like, whether they enjoy skiing, golfing, or photography, and they use that information to better show appreciation.

Recognition programs do have a place in retaining and motivating peak performers, provided they take into account key criteria. Gallup researchers Marcus Buckingham and Curt Coffman found that peak performers want to know what is expected of them at work, and that their work has meaning to the organization. They want to receive frequent recognition, and know that their supervisor cares about them as a person.

Recognizing performance is time-consuming. Recognizing performance in a personalized and unique way can be even more time-consuming. The over-burdened manager doesn't want to create more work for himself or herself. They want to reduce workload. The inclination is to dismiss recognition as an extra, but managers who focus on recognizing peak performance and peak performers reduce their workload by freeing up the time they would otherwise spend recruiting and training new employees.

Cindy Ventrice of Potential Unlimited Seminars in Santa Cruz, CA (www.potential-unltd.com), has been a consultant/trainer for the past 16 years. Potential Unlimited's seminars and workshops provide relationship-building solutions that improve morale, productivity, and profitability. She can be reached at CVentrice@potential-unltd.com.

The Manager's Role in Setting Goals

Lynn Summers, Diane Cox, and Jack Zigon

Goals are an important device for directing and improving performance—if they're properly articulated and monitored. This is a two-part article that explains how to prepare for and then discuss goals with employees. As a trainer or performance specialist, this kind of information can be especially valuable in helping you assist your managers in using goals and avoiding common mistakes in their development. The goal in all this, of course is to inspire and improve performance not undermine it.

Part 1. Preparing for the Goal Setting Discussion
Lynn Summers and Diane Cox

Perry Pharmaceuticals, like a growing number of companies, goes through a quarterly goal-setting process. At the beginning of each quarter, managers and their direct reports set goals. At quarter's end, they evaluate their performance against the results achieved. This whole exercise is given its sense of direction from a set of strategic objectives at the top of the company. These highest-level goals are owned by Perry's CEO and are cascaded out through the company, each successive level of management aligning its own goals to the goals of the level above. Eventually, each manager and individual contributor has his or her own compass for successfully navigating the quarter.

While the strategic objectives serve to direct the company's collective energy, talent, and know-how, another important collection of words gives purpose and guidance to this drive toward results. This voice of organizational conscience is the company's vision, mission, and values statement. Why is Perry striving to boost profitability, exceed customer needs, and develop its employees? (These happen to be three of its CEO's organizational goals.) Because its vision and mission statement expresses the intent to maintain and build further the company's reputation as a customer-oriented pharmaceutical. Why develop its employees? Because its values very strongly express the importance of maintaining a competitive edge by attracting and retaining talented employees.

Reprinted by permission of the publisher from *Performance Management Library*, Vol 4, Issues 8 and 10. Copyright © 2001 by Performaworks, Inc. All rights reserved. The *Performance Management Library* is maintained by Performaworks, Inc. and is available at www.performaworks.com.

The task of cascading goals throughout the company can be a daunting one. Imagine trying to coordinate everyone's goals and make sure that employees are working on things that contribute to the company's success—not at cross purposes, not on overlapping objectives, and not on organizationally irrelevant tasks. It is even more daunting, once everyone's goals are in place, to track progress toward goal achievement, troubleshoot problems employees might be having on certain key goals, and orchestrate any changes in priority that might occur during a quarter. Technology can drastically improve a company's ability to do all these things. In fact, Performaworks' own Internet-based eWorkbench product does just that. However, technology cannot substitute for sound management. Managers need to discuss goals with their direct reports. It's not something where they can flip a switch and watch everything get sorted out through some electronic wizardry.

This series of articles focuses on how managers can work "offline" with their direct reports to set goals while using technology as an aid to facilitate the process. The offline work, however, is prerequisite to flipping the switch and letting technology pull the heavy load in terms of tracking goal progress and measuring results. In this first article we consider how managers can prepare for a goal-setting discussion with their direct reports. A subsequent article looks at how the manager conducts the actual discussion.

The first piece of advice to managers is: Get your own ship in order! The goals that your direct reports work on will be dependent upon and inextricably intertwined with your own goals. As they ponder their goals they will need to know whence their goals come (they come largely from your goals). As they lay their goals into the system they'll use to track progress they'll need to know to which goals each is aligned (these, once again, would be your goals). We'll see some specific examples of this in the next article.

Now, here are some tips for preparing yourself and your direct reports for the goal-setting discussion. For each of the following five items, you'll want to give some thought from your own perspective as well as communicate some key things to your direct reports to enable them to think about their goals and prepare for the discussion.

1. The company's top level objectives

You: If your company has a vision, mission, and values statement and a set of strategic objectives that applies to the entire company, or to your division or business unit, make sure you are familiar with them. If there are levels of management between yourself and the top level, it's helpful to know what the chain of command above you is being held accountable for. Think about how your organizational goals align with these higher-level goals.

Your direct reports: Give them access to this information and ask them to think about how their work fits in and contributes to these higher-level objectives.

2. Your organizational goals

You: These are your goals. (Remember, get your ship in order first!) Think about those goals you'll need to delegate in order to achieve. (At Performaworks, we call these "organizational" goals. They are goals that you own, but you can have your direct reports create their own goals that contribute to yours.) Think about the relative priority of your organizational goals and the extent of contribution required from your direct reports to achieve the required results. Consider also how appropriate it would be to delegate a "chunk" of each goal to a particular direct report based on that person's position, experience, skills, and interests.

Your direct reports: Ask them to list ways they can contribute to the achievement of your organizational goals. Identify which goals it's most appropriate for each of them to contribute to, or the ones where you most need help.

3. Their key responsibilities

Usually key job responsibilities will translate readily into goals. Each quarter these *ongoing goals* will simply be extensions of the prior quarter's goals. It's a part of a sales person's job to meet a quota, for example. Work on this goal never ends. Progress on the goal is tracked throughout the quarter and measured "for the record" at each quarter's end. The goal remains the same although, more likely than not, the evaluation criteria are modified each quarter. For example, the quota one quarter might be $150,000 and $175,000 the next. There will also be projects that are associated with your direct reports' positions. *Project goals* have definite deadlines and, once completed, go away. Consider any projects that individual direct reports might need to take accountability for in order to fulfill the responsibilities of their position.

You: Make sure job responsibilities for your direct reports are clear. Any information regarding these matters that you can provide in advance of the actual discussion would be richly appreciated by your direct reports. If they are not clear on what their job responsibilities are (and you are), don't wait until the goal-setting discussion to spring this news on them! Also, if there are any goals that you know they will be responsible for, let them know in advance.

Your direct reports: They should refresh the list of goals from last quarter that are derived from their key job responsibilities, and revise them as necessary for the coming quarter. They should take any information you give them and begin to line up their goals as they understand them. They can also consider any projects that will need to be implemented this quarter as part of their jobs.

4. Competencies that apply to their positions

Competencies are the behavioral expectations pertaining to a job. Some companies have a single set of universal competencies that apply to all jobs, while others more finely tune their competencies to individual jobs or clusters of jobs. Competencies usually have two sources: They are descriptions of the day-to-day behaviors that reflect the company's values and that the company expects employees to adhere to. They are also specifications of the knowledges, skills, and abilities thought to be necessary for an individual employee in a given position to contribute effectively to the company's success.

You: If your company uses a competency model, it will be important to be familiar with the competencies that apply to your direct reports. This will become important during the upcoming discussion as questions arise about how to achieve the goals, what are the boundaries within which employees are free to exercise their own discretion, and what behaviors are rewarded, what behaviors are sanctioned.

Your direct reports: Make sure your direct reports have information about the competencies that apply to their jobs. As they prepare their thoughts on the goals they will be working on for the quarter, they should also give thought to which of the competencies will be most important for achieving these goals. They should consider whether the challenges for the coming quarter will call upon competencies they personally possess or lack, and how they can take best advantage of the situation.

5. Their development plans
You: You should be familiar with the development plans your direct reports have been working on. And, what are their development needs based on their performance in the most recent quarter? What competencies, if further developed, will enable them to better achieve the expected results?

Your direct reports: Your direct reports can think about how they can develop themselves to ensure more effective completion of their most important goals. Some factors to take into consideration include their performance in the past quarter, the requirements of anticipated high-priority goals for the coming quarter, and an understanding of the competencies that apply to their position.

If your organization is using eWorkbench, you can have your direct reports draft their goals online at their individual Workbenches. This will provide a structure that will make it much easier for them to prepare their goals, including aligning their goals with yours, establishing appropriate evaluation criteria, and setting up mileposts if necessary. Once they draft their goals at their online Workbenches, it becomes quite natural to conduct the goal-setting discussion in front of the screen, with your direct reports modifying their draft goals as the discussion proceeds.

Part 2. Conducting a Goal Setting Discussion
Jack Zigon

The first part of this series ended with the following tasks to be completed by the manager and the employees in preparation for a one-on-one discussion of the employee's goals:

Managers
- Review company's top-level objectives
- Identify which of your own goals should be divided up and delegated

- Clarify employees' key responsibilities and anticipate the goals you would expect them to set to back these responsibilities
- Review the competencies that apply to your direct reports' positions
- Review any development plans

Employees
- Understand the top-level objectives and their role in achieving them
- Think about how they contribute to the manager's organizational goals
- Refresh any goals from the prior performance period supporting key responsibilities
- Draft goals for any major projects
- Identify competencies that are important to achieving the goals
- Think about development needs

Assuming that these tasks are finished, the next step will be to conduct a goal setting discussion where the following tasks are completed:

1. Finalize the employee's goals for the coming performance period (quarter or year).
2. Agree on the competencies that are most critical to supporting the employee's goals.
3. Finalize any development plans that are needed to support the competencies and goals.

This article will guide you through these steps by addressing criteria for a successful result, a process for getting there, as well as common problems and their solutions.

What Do Good Goals Look Like?

If you've done a good job working with your employee, the results of your discussion should meet the criteria shown in Table 1 on the next page.

How to Create Goals

There are three ways to create goals:

1. Use the same metric as the higher-level goals. The easiest way to assure alignment is to use the same measure as a higher-level goal.

For instance, a top-level annual dollar sales goal of $5 million, might become a $250,000/year quota for a sales rep.

2. Borrow measurement ideas from other sources. Reviewing measures used by other organizations saves you from "reinventing the wheel." Asking colleagues for the measures they use or checking online or print sources of measures will save you time.

Criteria	Comments
The goals should be results-based	Each of the goals should measure the value-added outputs of the job, not just the activities.
The goals should be verifiable	Goals should not be vague. There should be a way to verify that the goals have been achieved.
There should be no more than 5-9 goals	Too many goals will cause the employee to lose focus.
The goals should be aligned with both the manager's and higher-level goals	The employee's individual success should visibly contribute to achieving these higher goals.
The competencies should directly support the goals	How to achieve the goals (that is, what competencies are required to be successful) should be as clear to the employee as the goals themselves.
The development plan should specify who should do what by when to improve the employee's competencies	Specific activities and new on-the-job behaviors must be detailed if the employee is to have a chance to really improve his/her competencies.

Table 1. **Criteria for effective goals**

For instance, accounts receivable might choose to support a top-level profit goal with an evaluation criterion of "no more than 5% of receivables will be over 90 days old," where the measurement idea of "% receivables over X days old" came from another industry.

3. Develop your own goals and evaluation criteria.
- Ask: "What does our customer need from us? What result do we leave behind that adds value to the customer?"
- When evaluating this result, do we care about quantity, quality, cost, timeliness or some combination of these factors?
- Some goals can be measured numerically: What number could we use to evaluate the quantity, quality, cost, timeliness?
- If a number can't be used, a descriptive measure should be agreed upon: Who will be able to judge the "goodness" of the result and what factors will the judge evaluate?
- How much of this result represents a good job? If a number can't be used, what would the judge see or hear that indicates that the result was a good one?
- How can we track progress toward the goal?

For instance, when evaluating a key responsibility of order fulfillment, the pharmaceutical warehouse knows that the sales reps they service need "accurately packed orders" from the warehouse. When evaluating this result, the reps care about a combination of quality and timeliness. The measures of "% perfect orders" and "order turnaround time" might lead to evaluation criteria of "99%-99.5% order accuracy, shipped within 24 hours of receipt of the order." This can be tracked using the dock's shipping manifest data.

When evaluating a project goal, a research team leader might decide that one of the results the company needs from her and her team is a "completed research project." While a budget criterion of "±3% budget variance" and a time criterion of "completed by the end of the 3rd quarter" could adequately measure cost and time, the quality of the work is best described, rather than quantified. Thus the quality criteria might read:

"The marketing and research managers agree that:
- *Experimental results are consistent, definitive and interpretable.*
- *The findings are scientifically novel, suggest new ideas to pursue, or identify a new application of a previous result.*
- *The team identifies an area of clinical usefulness.*
- *A more efficient research design wasn't possible."*

Note that the marketing and research managers have been identified as the judges of these descriptive evaluation criteria.

Get-Give-Merge

It is very likely that you and your employees will disagree about the content of their performance plan. Here is a negotiation model that gives you a way to understand the differences between your two separate views and begin to merge them. Using this model will encourage two-way communication and minimize confrontations in your goal discussions.

Get, give, and merge. These three words will cue you to get the employee's viewpoint, give your own and merge the two views. Here is what we mean by these terms:

- **Get**—Ask questions and restate what the other person has said, using your own words. Your employee will give you feedback to confirm that your understanding is accurate, or to let you know that you've misunderstood.
- **Give**—Explain your viewpoint in clear language, and then confirm that the other person understood you. You can do this by either asking a question or having the employee restate what you said in his/her own words.
- **Merge**—Resolve differences between your views and the employee's views.

While getting and giving are more self-explanatory, merging may be a new concept for some managers. There are four techniques used to merge or resolve differences. Their definitions and examples of each are listed below:

Type of Merge	Definition	Examples
Agree	You agree with the employee's viewpoint or the employee agrees with yours.	"You're right, we did forget to have a goal for 'customer satisfaction' on the original list. Let's add it."
Create	You and the employee create a totally new alternative that both of you can agree to.	"I want you to handle the customers' problems during their call, and you'd like the flexibility of handling them within an hour after the call. We've agreed that on each call, you'll ask the customers when they need an answer, and then you'll meet that mutually agreed-upon deadline."
Meet	You and your employee meet on a viewpoint somewhere between yours and the employee's.	"You'd like to shoot for 45 and I'd like the standard to be 25, but we'll both agree on 30-35 for the next six months. Then we'll re-negotiate."
Impose	You set the standard and require the employee to agree to agree with your viewpoint.	• "OSHA rules say that goggles and ear protectors must be worn in these circumstances. So that has to be one of the things I expect from you." • "The department budget for this project is $10,000, and so you have to have the same standard."

Table 2. **Four techniques for merging**

There is an order to the various types of merges. You can always impose your view or agree with the employee's views, but the best solutions usually come from creating a new alternative that is acceptable to both of you. Here's the recommended order for using these four merging techniques:

1. If the employee's idea is a good one, simply agree with it. He or she will probably do the same with some of your ideas.
2. If you disagree, create a new alternative that both of you can live with, or
3. Try to meet in the middle (especially if it is a numeric goal).

4. If an outside group such as upper management or a government agency is imposing a standard on your work, you will have no choice but to impose the same standard on your employee. When imposing, always explain why to lessen the bad feelings that may occur.

When conducting the goal discussion, recycle the steps of Get-Give-Merge for each goal before moving on to the next one. By doing so, you will maximize the employee's buy-in and commitment.

Common Problems and Their Solutions

Here are the kinds of problems you may encounter when you sit down with your employees to create their goals:

Common Problems	Examples	Solutions
Tasks disguised as goals	• Hold kickoff meeting by 9/1 • Meet with 15 clients per week • Review documentation for errors.	Ask, "If the kickoff is successful, what value will we add?" and then measure that result. For example, the result might be "buy-in to the new project" with an evaluation criterion of 10-15 locations volunteering to pilot the program."
Goals are too big or long range	Achieve division profitability in 5 years.	When a goal is too large and/or too far in the future to offer practical guidance on a near-term basis, identify interim goals that specify progress toward the longer-range goal. For example, achieving "$X revenue and $Y expenses by the end of the current year" could be an effective interim goal.
Goals for competencies	Setting a goal of "improving teamwork" while simultaneously evaluating a competency called "teamwork"	Decide which is more important, the end-result or the way of achieving the result. • If the result is more important, set a goal for it. • If the way of achieving the result is more important, evaluate only the competency and drop the goal.
Too many goals	List of 25 goals	Prioritize the goals in terms of effect on the organization and alignment with your goals and higher-level goals. Drop the low-priority goals or combine goals with similar intent.

Table 3. **Common problems with goal setting (continued on next page)**

Common Problems	Examples	Solutions
Not practical to track	• Answer the phone prior to the third ring. • No typos on any documents.	• Sample the work. • Switch to exception reporting where the two examples become "No complaints due to unanswered phones or errors in documents." • Drop the goals.
Vague or unverifiable evaluation criteria	• Do a good quality job. • Improve customer satisfaction.	Identify numeric measures and goals or switch to a verifiable descriptive measure. For instance, "improve customer satisfaction" could become "score 3.5 to 4.0 on customer satisfaction survey" or "customers say they are willing to recommend our product to their colleagues."

Table 3. **Continued**

Summary

Goal setting will go more smoothly if you prepare well and then hold meetings with your direct reports in which you:

- Set well-crafted goals that are results-based, verifiable, aligned, and have competencies and (as appropriate) development plans supporting them.
- Borrow measurement ideas from higher-level goals in the organization or from other functions or companies.
- Help the employee create goals based on the results his or her customers need. And use either numeric or descriptive measures to define the evaluation criteria.
- Negotiate goals by getting the employee's view first, giving yours, and then merging the two views.
- Merge your views in this order: Agree, Create, Meet in the middle, and Impose when you have to.

Lynn Summers is a co-founder of Performaworks and serves the company as Vice President of Research. His background includes more than 25 years of experience in industrial psychology, human resources, and training and management development.

Diane Cox is an associate at Performaworks.

Jack Zigon is president of Zigon Performance Group. He has published articles in Personnel Journal, Training, Performance Management, *and* Performance and Instruction Journal. *Contact him at info@zigonperf.com.*

PART FOUR

Implementing Performance Improvement Interventions

Part Four deals with successfully creating and delivering training and other performance improvement interventions. We've organized this part around the standard paradigm of analysis and design, delivery, and evaluation/validation of the interventions.

Analysis and Design

We've selected five articles for this section. The first, from Carolyn Thompson's book *Creating Highly Interactive Training Quickly and Effectively*, is titled "Design Training So People Learn Easily, Quickly, *and* with High Retention!" It includes a whole series of useful checklists for designing training programs of all types. The next article, "Build It Backwards: Begin with the Outcomes," comes from The Final Copy Group, Inc., a training and consulting firm. It reminds trainers to focus on goals for the training and not just content and provides techniques for assuring that the training you deliver gets the results you want. The other three articles include ideas for getting approval of training projects (a key step in analysis and design), the potential role of video in a training program, and, finally, an article outlining nine tips for planning and delivering effective training.

Training and Other Performance Interventions

Our goal is to include articles that deal with training as well as other interventions performance technologists may use to help people improve. In keeping with that goal, here's a sample of what's included in this section.

We've all heard about the new economy, which has had its problems but represents the direction all companies are going today. In that spirit, our first selection is "People Development Strategies in the New Economy" by Greg Wang. This article looks at the best practices of some leading firms, examining their strategies for attracting, developing, and retaining employees. We've included eight other articles here that look at a wide variety of techniques for delivering training and other interventions to help employees improve performance. Among those are "Time to Treat Learners as Consumers" by Stephen L. Cohen, David W. Dove, and Edward L Bachelder, which focuses on what makes employees want to learn and suggests ways to treat learners as consumers. Also included is "The Lighter Side of Learning" by Kathleen McLaughlin—about just what the title suggests. Another is "True Confessions: Adventures in Training" by Dave Zielinski, which looks at how some trainers have made the transition to e-learning. Yet another is "Tactics for the New Guerilla Trainer" by Phil Mershon. It looks at ways to make training a value-added activity outside traditional definitions. See the table of contents for a list of all of the eclectic ideas covered here.

Evaluation of Intervention Success

We've selected four articles for this section of Part Four. The first is "Measuring the Training Department" by Stanley E. Malcolm. In this piece, the author looks at a variety of metrics you can use to measure training department success. We follow this with "Liberating the Lamppost: Shedding Light on Training Evaluation" by Peter Bregman and Howie Jacobson, which posits that in evaluating training you need to use customer satisfaction as your measure, and it explains how to do this. Next we include Shari Caudron's "Evaluating E-Degrees." In this article, you will learn more about how to determine which types of degrees promise more for employees and what questions to ask about e-degrees to determine the quality. Finally we conclude this section with "Calculating Training Efficiency" by Scotty C. DeClue. This looks at how to compare different approaches to training in terms of costs versus benefits.

Analysis and Design

Design Training So People Learn Easily, Quickly, *and* with High Retention!

Carolyn B. Thompson

As the title of this article indicates, this excerpt from Creating Highly Interactive Training Quickly & Effectively *outlines a format for designing any type of training so that employees will learn in less time, with less effort, and with greater retention. It's a practical set of guidelines developed by the author, a well-regarded training specialist.*

Learners will love you when they have an *easy time learning* and are able to *retain what they learned*! You design lots of types and/or mediums of training—self-study (paper-based, video, audio, CBT/WBT) and/or facilitated (group, one-on-one coaching, OJT). Follow one simple, straightforward format for them all:

Training Systems, Inc. Learning Format

For the fastest learning and greatest retention, learning goes in this order:
1. Attention getting opening to get learners' attention off what they were doing before and onto this training.
2. Learners tell or write what they already know (to build confidence).
3. Facilitator tells or writes big objectives for this training.
4. Learners write, verbalize, and visualize specific individual objectives for

Reprinted with permission from the author from *Creating Highly Interactive Training Quickly and Effectively*. Copyright © 2000 by Carolyn B. Thompson and Training Systems, Inc.. All rights reserved.

this training *as though already achieved*. (Facilitator makes sure they're **SMART**—**s**pecific, **m**easurable, **a**ttainable, **r**elevant, **t**ime-based—and tells research on why objectives help learning.)
5. Facilitator tells all learning methods and times.
6. Facilitator and learners work on all learning methods needed to meet objectives. (Repeat cycle below for each learning method needed to meet all objectives.) (This is the bulk of the training time.)
   - Objective (boxed)
   - Intro (labeled)
   - Facilitator instructions and/or text (labeled)
   - Processing (labeled)
7. Facilitator reviews all that is learned.
8. Facilitator tells and shows resources to use for future.
9. Learners complete the Learning Action Plan.
10. Call to action closing that matches opening.

Overall you'll speed up learning with:

- Learning methods for all four learning styles (unless determined that training will not include all styles)
- Highly interactive learning, using the standard
  - Facilitator talks no more than 25% of time (including lecture, instructions, opening/closing, processing questions)
  - Learners doing 75% with facilitator as expert in room
- Use Fun Meter buttons as part of the learning.
- Learning that allows for the cycle of learning to be achieved
  1st: build community
  2nd: build knowledge
  3rd: build skill
  4th: build possibilities
- Learning method in group training to get learners involved with each other within the first 15 minutes
- Include at least one method to help learners *retain* what they learned
  - ✔ While learning imagine:
    - boss said they'd be giving a report on what they learned.
    - they have to do group training on what they learned.
    - they have to write book from new viewpoint.
  - ✔ Take breaks frequently.
  - ✔ Plan to review notes regularly after training three to four minutes each time—practice during training.
  - ✔ Create multi-sensory memories of each thing to remember.
  - ✔ Make visual images linked—especially if there's movement or humor.
  - ✔ Play music to stimulate emotional part of brain, where long-term memory is situated.

- ✔ Record what they want to learn and listen to it and music together.
- ✔ Organize material in related categories and label categories.
- ✔ Memory flashing—look at notes for a few minutes, then rewrite without looking at them, then compare the two sets. Keep doing this until both sets are the same.
- ✔ Flash cards for review.
- ✔ Create mnemonic device: three, five, or seven letters best.
- ✔ Let it sink in overnight after reviewing notes—brain uses sleep as time to file.
- ✔ Number the points.
- ✔ Whole learning—learn words, add sound, add movement.
- ✔ Fluency = mastery: continue learning it after already know it.
- ✔ Compress information into chunks and label each chunk, then make a mnemonic for the chunk words.

Start All Learning with an "Attention-Getting" Opening and End with a "Call to Action" Closing

People remember the first and last thing they see or hear. Since the facilitator is always going to say or do something first and something last, you might as well plan it so it will be attention-getting and call the learners to action. This is true in any type of training—group, OJT, self-study manual, video, audio, and computer/web-based. In training where there's no facilitator, the Attention-Getting Opening and Call to Action Closing are simply the first and last things said/done by the coach or written in the booklet or stated/done on the video or on the computer screen.

To design effective openings and closings:

- ■ Attention-Getting Opening and Call to Action Closing must fit the objective of the whole training. Choose the type of opening/closing to fit the learning's overall objective and the learners. Designers who choose a joke or story that doesn't fit the learners or the objective will always find they don't get anyone's attention.
  - ✔ Design the Attention-Getting Opening and Call to Action Closing to match each other. (If you start with a quote, end with a quote; if you start with a prop, end with a prop; and so forth.) This fits the learning into a neat package for the Learner. *Very effective!*
  - ✔ Examples include: question, statistic, video, story, music, role-play, case study, funny visual, prop, joke. Notice that telling the facilitator's name isn't in this list—unless the facilitator is someone famous, have him or her tell who they are *after* the opening so they have the learners' attention. Most of these examples work great in all types of training—choose which one works best based on the overall learning objective and the learners.

- *After* the Attention-Getting Opening, the facilitator needs to help people learn their name and possibly each other's names (if group training), amount of time for learning, learning objectives, how questions will be answered, and the methods used for learning. Within 15 minutes, get the learners involved in an interactive learning method to get the learners talking.
- *Before* the Call to Action Closing, be sure to handle reaction evaluations, summary activities, or other review method, any testing of skill/knowledge/attitude change, information about further resources, and their Learning Action Plan. Nothing should be said or done by the facilitator, seen on the screen, heard, or read after the Closing, or the Call to Action momentum will be lost.

Designing the Learning Between the Opening and Closing

In a full day of group training you'll have at least 15 objectives, in a half day seven objectives, in a video three or four objectives, in 15 minutes of OJT one objective, in a self-study manual few to lots. You'll need to plan the way you'll achieve each objective. Follow the steps below:

1. Write the learning objective of each method.
2. Write an example of a real situation that has to do with the objective.
3. Determine the best learning method to use by using 1 and 2 and your knowledge of the learners. *Choose from the list below:*
4. Write the introduction to the method using the ideas in the Attention-Getting Openings section above. (Each intro to a learning method is a mini Opening.) Be sure to make intros throughout the training attention-getting, so the learners will be able to take their minds off the last thing they were working on and focus on the next one.
5. Write instructions for the facilitator to use to conduct each method or instructions for the learners in the self-study manual, computer/web-based training, etc. (If the method is lecture, obviously instead of instructions this part is a combination of instructions and the actual words to say or the content they read if a book/web/CD.)
6. Write out the key processing question(s) or statement(s). This is designed to lead the learners directly to the objective. (For example, if the objective is "Learners see that they can write a training opening and closing in five minutes," then the key processing questions are "How many of you are finished?" and—assuming most raise their hands—then "Are you surprised?" and—assuming many say yes—then "Why could you do this in such a short time, what's different about today that allowed you to do it?") *For group training or OJT, always add potential answers for which the facilitator should be listening.*
7. Because we remember 80%-90% of what we see and do and only 10%-

PARTICIPATIVE LEARNING METHODS

Application Projects	Mentoring
Articles and Books	Metaphors
Audiotapes (music and speaking)	Newsletter
Book Groups	Participatory Lecture
Brainstorming	Planned Interruptive Lecture
Case Studies	Post-work
Chain Gang Lecture	Prep-work
Challenge Courses	Press Conference Lecture
Charts, Graphs, Posters	Programmed Instruction Lecture
Computer/Web-Based Training	Props
Concept Interference Lecture	Real-Time Video Tutorial Lectures
Concert Reading	Role-Plays
Confederate Lecture	Self-Analysis, Reflection
Continuing Learning	Sharing Best Practices
Demonstration	Simulation
Experiential Lecture	Story
Expert Call-in Lecture	Study Groups
Field Trips	Synergogic Lecture
Five-Minute Fables	Teach Back
Games	Team Quiz Lecture
Ice Breakers	TV and Videotape
Job Aids	Visualization
Lecture in a Fishbowl	Voice Mail, E-mail
Magic Tricks	

15% of what we hear, you'll need a variety of visuals in addition to the facilitator in group training or OJT. Be sure you apply this to the graphic look of your self-study manual, CBT/Web, video.

8. Determine the room setup, equipment and supplies needed.
9. Determine the number of people for which this will work best.
10. Determine how long the method will take.

Many designers do 8, 9, and 10 first and thus limit what they can do to help the learners learn quickly and effectively. Do these last and, if you realize that what you've just created is impossible, make modifications. You'll have a better end product.

I know you can already see people exhibiting the skills and using the knowledge after learning in this way. Their co-workers, staff, and bosses are bursting with happiness for the time well spent. Other people in your company—as well as your clients—are asking you how you got so smart.... *Make it a reality!*

This article is excerpted from *Creating Highly Interactive Training Quickly & Effectively* (TSI Publications, 2000), pages 9-14. The book can be ordered by calling 800 469-3560.

Carolyn B. Thompson is the President of Training Systems, Inc., and an experienced trainer and consultant knowledgeable in the challenging area of employee recruitment, inspiration, and retention. She is an exciting, inspirational trainer who leads people to learn. She's written articles for Safety & Health, Small Business Computing, Business Week, Working Woman, Redbook, *and* Inc. *magazines; she's also written chapters in several books. Contact her at (800) 469-3560 and visit her Web site at www.trainingsys.com.*

Build It Backwards: Begin with the Outcomes

The Final Copy Group, Inc.

This article stresses the importance of developing training around your goals rather than content. That's often difficult, the authors acknowledge, because some trainers naturally want to go with what they know and enjoy, because management is following popular trends, or because the objectives are "squishy." Although this article is not all about training, the other subjects and the style make it a piece that you can recommend to managers, so they can better understand why you insist on "building it backwards" and beginning with outcomes.

When asked to plan a documentation project, design a training course, or diagram a Web solution, many of us are tempted to start with content—the *stuff* that goes into the project.

Unfortunately, if you begin this way, you're probably heading down the wrong path. Why? Because you're building a content-driven solution, rather than an outcome-driven one.

Whether you're designing a manual, a seminar, or a Web site, you can miss by a mile if you don't begin by identifying the project's outcomes in terms of the intended audience. And these kinds of mistakes can cost you a lot of time and money.

Content-Driven vs. Outcome-Driven Design

What's the difference between content-driven and outcome-driven solutions? Imagine that you're traveling to an unfamiliar city—let's say, Chicago. You're renting a car at O'Hare, and you'd like to get driving directions to your hotel. How would you go about that? What's the first strategy that pops into your mind?

An Outcome-Driven Solution

You probably picked a strategy that started with the hotel. For example, you might call the hotel and ask for directions. If you have a map of Chicago handy, you might look up the hotel's address. If you use one of the Internet

Reprinted with permission from The Final Copy Group, Inc., FCG White Paper #0805. Copyright © 2000, The Final Copy Group, Inc. All rights reserved.

map services, you might type in the hotel's address, and get a map of the location.

What's common to all these approaches is that you start with the hotel the destination, or outcome. Then you work back from the hotel to the starting point—the airport. That's an outcome-driven solution.

A Content-Driven Solution

If you were to work this same problem with a content-driven strategy, you would start at O'Hare and simply pick one of the major routes out of the airport. Then you would start driving down various Chicago streets in the hope that you'd eventually come across the hotel.

Crazy? Sure it is. Nobody would ever use a strategy like that. Yet this is exactly what happens when we design training projects, manuals, or Web solutions by focusing on the content rather than the outcome.

Selecting Content

> The major problem with content-driven design is that it doesn't offer a useful benchmark for selecting content to include in the project.

The major problem with content-driven design is that it doesn't offer a useful benchmark for selecting content to include in the project. If we don't evaluate content in terms of its relevance to desired outcomes, then one piece of content is as good as another.

Let's look again at the Chicago hotel example. If the hotel location is the outcome of this hypothetical problem, then all the streets of Chicago are the content. How would you narrow down this content? That is, how would you decide which streets to drive down?

Well, you might select streets for your route based on perceived importance (*Don't miss State Street. It's famous.*), or on personal preference (*I like streets named after Presidents.*), or on familiarity (*My mother lived on Gunderson Avenue for years.*). But none of those choices is likely to get you any closer to your desired outcome.

How Come?

Why do we assume we can develop training, documentation, or Web sites without a clear sense of the desired outcomes? In the following sections, we look at some specific ways we've seen projects go awry because content prevailed over outcomes.

Training Projects

Ideally, any content that goes into a training project must be validated against the instructional objectives of the training (read outcomes). Content that clearly serves a specified outcome is in; any other content is suspect. For example:

If we're trying to show users how to install a lawn sprinkler, do we really need a module on the chemical properties of water?

A Crate Full of Content. Some people in the training business are fond of collecting magazine articles, jokes, Web pages, questionnaires, pithy sayings, book excerpts, videos, old textbooks, and anything else that looks like good fodder for a training course. Then, when it's time to design a course, they empty the crate on the table and try to assemble a training program from the disjointed bits of content.

There's nothing wrong with collecting these types of items, and some of them might very well fit into a course design (with the appropriate permission from copyright holders, of course). But every item in the crate still has to be measured against the learning objectives. If it doesn't fit, don't try to stuff it into the course.

Flavor of the Month. In some companies, the preferred management style changes almost on a monthly basis. Business buzzwords come and go, and—at least for a short while—they can become part of a corporate culture. The problem is not that these concepts are intrinsically bad, but that people go overboard with them. For example:

> *From now on, all training courses will include a module on Post-Transactional 360-degree Quality Circle Effectiveness Processes.*

This might be an admirable undertaking, but only if it serves the intended outcomes for the training. And if you haven't specified those outcomes clearly, then you better be ready to update your training every time the flavor of the month changes.

Squishy Objectives. In most cases, training people do mean well, and we do pay at least lip service to our objectives. Unfortunately, these objectives sometimes have more to do with the training writer or project manager than they do with the intended audience; e.g.:

> *The objective of this project is to provide information about the new, improved 2000 Gezortney.*

This may be a worthy project goal, but it has nothing to do with what learners should be able to do, think, or feel. In addition, this kind of "objective" is so broad that it's useless for screening content. Are we talking about engineering data for the Gezortney, manufacturing instructions, customer benefits, installation procedures, or maintenance guidelines? The objective is so "squishy" that it permits almost any type of content.

Manuals

User manuals, policy and procedure guides, and other types of technical documentation can also be sidetracked by content-driven designs. Manuals

---

In some companies, the preferred management style changes almost on a monthly basis.

should have clearly defined outcomes—things that readers will be able to *do* as a result of reading the manual.

Content that helps achieve these outcomes should be included. Extraneous content should be eliminated (or at least saved for another manual).

I Know This, So It Must Be Important. Most documentation writers rely on subject-matter experts (SMEs) to provide technical input. However, SMEs often provide much more technical detail than the intended audience will ever need. Writers often have to wrestle with SMEs who imply that certain information is important "because I know it."

The way out of this dilemma is to measure the content against the manual's outcomes. For example:

After reading this section, users should be able to change the battery in the flashlight. Do they really need an explanation of polarity to do that?

The Background Bog/Appendix Abyss. Many writers overcome their reluctance to include irrelevant content by saying, "Oh, we'll put that in the background section" or "That stuff can go in the appendix."

A certain amount of background information may be just fine (usually about half of what's actually included). And the appendix to a manual is a good place for important but seldom used reference material. However, beware of "bottomless pits" of trivial information.

If you have clear outcomes for your manual, judging the relevance of background or appendix information becomes much easier. For example:

To mix these two ingredients together, do readers really need a periodic chart of the elements?

Web Solutions

Although Web sites, portals, on-line stores, and other Web solutions are relatively recent phenomena, they too can suffer from the design mistakes of the past. Without clearly defined outcomes, Web sites can become confusing, boring, or otherwise ineffective. Before you plunge into developing a Web site, it's not a bad idea to ask, "What do I want visitors to do, think, or feel after they have visited this site?"

Shovelware. In their rush to "get on the Web," many companies assume they can simply shovel all their content from other sources—corporate brochures, PR pieces, annual reports, or press releases—onto the Web.

Unfortunately, most Web visitors have very little patience, and they simply will not wade through extraneous content. Visitors have reasons for visiting your site. If you've anticipated these desired outcomes, then you can tailor the content and navigation scheme so visitors can find what they want quickly. For example:

All I want to know is whether or not "appliance.com" sells the replacement part I need for my vacuum. Here, I'll look under "Parts."

BUILD IT BACKWARDS: BEGIN WITH THE OUTCOMES

Missions and Visions and Values, Oh My! If you do a good job specifying outcomes from a user's perspective, you'll have to admit that most people really don't visit a business Web site to check out a company's mission statement or read the latest speech by the company president. Yet many corporate sites feature this type of content prominently, at the expense of more user-oriented content.

A mission statement or a list of corporate values is certainly appropriate content for a business Web site. But an outcome-driven design will keep you from building a site that's focused more on the company than on its customers.

Tuck the mission statement away on an "About Us" page so users who want to read it can find it. But make sure the most prominent content is the stuff that serves your primary outcomes, such as selling products, demonstrating your customer solutions, or telling customers how to find your locations.

> Do yourself a favor. Find out what your target audience expects to do after using your materials. Then provide the content that helps them do it.

Conclusion

Although building projects backwards may seem counter-intuitive at first, starting with the outcomes will help you plan more focused training, more usable technical documents, and more effective Web sites.

Do yourself a favor. Find out what your target audience expects to do after using your materials. Then provide the content that helps them do it.

The Final Copy Group is a team of instructional designers, writers, electronic publishers, and computer professionals who share a common vision: communicate clearly. They create custom training programs, marketing communications, technical documents, and Web solutions that are designed from the user's perspective, developed to meet clearly defined outcomes, and produced using the most effective media available. Contact: The Final Copy Group, Inc., 27555 Ynez Road, Suite 130, Temecula, CA 92591, (909) 506-5316, www.finalcopygroup.com.

Seven Surefire Steps to Getting Approval for Training Projects

Peter Meyer

When you're trying to get approval for a training project, you're really entering into sales, a situation in which many trainers are relatively inexperienced and may be uncomfortable. That's why it makes sense to borrow a technique that was developed for salespeople. But it's not so much about selling as it is about communication and particularly about understanding needs.

People who are successful at selling their training programs tend to follow a pattern over time. That pattern has as its cornerstone a seven-step process that attacks every problem from the perspective of the people buying the training—your CEO, your department heads—and then finds a solution to that problem. Your training department is part of that solution, of course.

This seven-step process is the brainchild of Peter Meyer, co-founder of The Meyer Group, a consulting group in Scotts Valley, Calif. It was originally developed as a sales process but it adapts well to training because, indeed, what you're doing is selling your product.

A solution that has no problem. This situation creates an interesting scenario, Meyer points out. In fact, many of his clients use this premise on a corporate-wide basis, developing entire product lines that are great solutions with no problems. A lot of corporate training is that as well: a solution without a problem.

Here's how to use Meyer's seven steps to define the problem and then use your training programs as part of the solution.

1. Identify your target. The obvious person is the manager of the field being trained. That may not be right, Meyer believes. You may need to find someone who's two levels up to whom you can say, "Looking 12 months out, what keeps you up at night?"

Reprinted by permission of the publisher from *Managing Training & Development*, October 2000. Copyright © 2000 by the Institute of Management and Administration. All rights reserved.

Can't get access to the corner office? Try this: "We're designing next year's programs and the most important thing to us in designing them is finding out what keeps Chris (CEO, president, senior manager) up at night. Can I have 15 minutes of his time to ask him that question?" It works, Meyer declares.

2. Meet with that person. Say to Chris, "I'm here to listen." Then do that. Ask questions that flush out the top two problems that are keeping him up at night. Don't worry about trying to solve the problems. Don't drive solutions. Just understand the problems.

"Most people are not preconditioned to do this. Instead they feel they must present what programs they have that will accomplish X (increased productivity, teamwork, and the like.). The customer (CEO) doesn't want that."

Next ask, "How would you define success for that?" For example, if what's keeping your CEO up at night is figuring out how to move workers from a direct service model to an electronic service model, how do they define success for this?

This may take a whole lot longer than 15 minutes, Meyer admits. Never mind. Just write it all down. "At the end of the meeting, ask him who else needs to be part of the process because you need their answers to these questions as well. In this example, you would identify IT, telecommunications, sales people, and so on.

3. Survey the stakeholders. This is not a survey on training issues. It's a survey on business issues. This is a key step. The whole picture leads to the whole solution, Meyer stresses.

Remember to ask each stakeholder—IT, telecommunications, sales personnel—for their definition of success for the resolution of his or her problem.

Those success criteria will be part of the next step. *Caution:* No solutions in this phase. "If you flood people with idea after idea," Meyer warns, "they start losing their sense of responsibility for solving their own problems."

4. Conduct a design session. You now know more about the problem than anybody else does so you have a meeting to explain what you've discovered.

In the design session, you review what each of the involved groups has told you. The problem is you have many different answers and you need only one.

"Your stakeholders will come to an agreement on the definition of success, which you've pretty much been able to anticipate because you've been thinking about this."

You introduce a possible program that will achieve the success the group has defined. It will include training, of course.

You're not done, though. You tell the group that you're not sure the plan is exactly right, but it's a start and you need their help to refine it. Have a flip chart or a white board on which you identify all the components, the problems, the costs, and the benefits.

Your stakeholders are now involved in improving the program, Meyer explains. Resist the temptation to provide the answers. How much will it cost? "Well," you ask, "how much *will* it cost? I can do the training for X, but what about this cost?" Include everything down to postage stamps. "At that point they've taken ownership. If you want your training program to work, this is the best place to be, with the customer taking ownership."

Now you ask the group what the benefit will be and is it worth it to spend this much on a training program? An interesting thing will happen here, Meyer claims, which is how consultants get you to approve their plans.

You will have identified all the costs. The actual training cost, what you as an internal training provider will be charging, may be as much as $100,000. The actual cost of the project will probably be two to twelve times as much as that, say $600,000.

If the problem is one of the group's top two, they're probably going to decide that it's worth spending $600,000. They're not going to care that training is $100,000 or $110,000. Your costs and how you get it funded are going to be insignificant.

"The good news is you have a lot of flexibility," says Meyer. "The bad news is, training isn't really the driver for the program. And that's probably the way it *should* be. Their desire to fix the problem is the driver."

The next three steps follow very quickly, he adds. "If it's really important and they haven't been able to solve it and you've shown them the way, they're not going to want to sit around waiting for a game plan. They're going to ask you when you can start."

5. Document the meeting. This is your proposal. Expect to produce this quickly.

6. Get approvals. This can be a quick letter or memo, whatever method is the standard for your company. If this is a really critical problem, the approval process will be short-circuited. Guaranteed.

7. Do the work and follow up on it. In the follow-up, you review the initial success criteria and ask if you met them. Document your success and advertise it. Start over.

Peter Meyer is a founder and principal of The Meyer Group, an executive and management development firm based in Scotts Valley, CA, and the author of Warp Speed Growth. *He has spoken on management, technology, and strategies throughout the United States, in Europe, the Far East, and Australia and has published articles in* The Wall Street Journal *and business journals such as* The Canadian Business Review, Business Horizons, Internet Business Journal, Executive Female, *and* The Recorder. *Contact him at Info@MeyerGrp.com.*

Is a Video in Your Vision?

Betty Sosnin

In designing your training program, you may wonder if video is appropriate and feasible. Recent advances in technology have expanded the use of video in training, and for some purposes, it may be just the right medium for the message. But there are some questions to answer before deciding on video, and there are some points to consider in order to get the most out of any investment you might make in this medium.

For HR departments hoping to spice up their recruitment, orientation or training programs, a good video can be worth thousands of words. And you won't have to study scriptwriting, get behind the camera or understand computerized editing to produce a good one. But you will need to assemble a team of talented professionals and make sure they understand your goals and corporate culture. With their help, you can produce a blockbuster.

Before embarking on your video venture, however, you need to decide if it's the right format for what you want to communicate and whether it makes sense, dollarwise.

"Videos work best when you're trying to convey emotions or generate excitement," says Jim Carr, an Emmy and Peabody award-winning producer with Carr Communications in Atlanta.

Video also works well if you want to standardize your messages and the tone of their delivery. "Time and other factors may get trainers off track and result in an inconsistent message, but videos deliver the same message time and again," says Diana Osinski, a manager with KPMG Consulting and chair of the Society for Human Resource Management's Human Resource Development Committee.

For example, golf car manufacturer Club Car of Augusta, Ga., has a videographer record its corporate meetings and add a short "leader" in front that describes what the video is and where it was shot. The footage then is sent out unedited to branch locations. "This lets us personally welcome members and keep them in the loop without spending a lot of money," says HR manager Gary Holley.

Reprinted with the permission of *HR Magazine*, February 2001. Copyright © 2001. Published by the Society for Human Resource Management, Alexandria, VA. All rights reserved.

Video also works well for conveying compliance issues, adds Osinski. For example, DSM Chemicals North America in Augusta, Ga., uses a video to meet the requirement to present a basic safety orientation to everyone entering its manufacturing area.

Recent technological advances also have broadened the use of video. In addition to being shown on televisions, videos can be downloaded to CDs, used in computer-based training and webcast via the Internet. This lets you add an interactive element through chat rooms, message boards and online question-and-answer sessions.

Carr cautions, however, that videos "work poorly when you're trying to convey a large list of facts and figures. Print materials are better here because they can be read and reread." One way around this is to combine the two formats—kicking off a session with a video to garner interest and using print materials to provide the details.

Cost Considerations

Assuming you've decided that video is the right format, expect to pay, on average, $1,000 to $3,000 per finished minute for a high-end, script-to-screen project. With most videos running between five and 10 minutes, that's a budget range of $5,000 to $30,000. If you work with an independent scriptwriter, expect to pay $100 to $150 per finished minute of script, along with shooting and editing costs.

Even if you have deep pockets, shorter is generally better. At the outside, your video should be no longer than 15 minutes, no matter how much you can afford.

But if producing your own is beyond your means, consider generic videos, which are available on a variety of topics and can be considerably less expensive than customized productions. Holley says he often can buy a 20-minute video for $500, "which compares pretty favorably to a $1,000-a-minute customized production."

However, generic videos have drawbacks. "Each corporate culture is unique, and generic videos that try to be appropriate, for many audiences are generally watered down," says Osinski. Moreover, you won't really know if the video is effective until you've purchased and reviewed it.

Whatever the case, don't try to shoot your own video. Even a digital camera and a high-tech editing program will not give you a polished final product. You need a professional to produce a video that reflects a viable corporate image.

Taking the Plunge

Begin planning your video at least four to six months before you will need it. This time frame will allow you to think through what you want to convey and the image you want to project. You want to be able to clearly state the purpose

> *At the outside, your video should be no longer than 15 minutes, no matter how much you can afford.*

of the project. Don't try to produce a one-size-fits-all video and use it for everything. You'll end up with an unfocused production that doesn't work.

If your budget requires you to be more things to more people, consider producing more than one video at the same time. Don Mathews, a producer with Mass Media Marketing in Augusta, Ga., calls it the modular approach. "You can have the camera crew do all the shooting at once and use the same sections in more than one video when the information overlaps. There will be additional charges for writing and editing, but it'll be much less expensive than doing two or more entirely separate videos."

Being selective in your search for writers and producers is important because your video's success will depend largely on the experience and intelligence of the crew that produces it, especially the scriptwriter. Look for seasoned professionals, whether you use a production house for the entire project or hire a freelance writer to do the script separately. Most production houses and some television stations offer script-to-screen services for a fixed fee and employ narrators or work with radio personnel who freelance.

Once you've identified prospective writers and producers, interview them, review samples of their work and check their references. Ask the writers for samples of scripts they've written and screen them for crisp, clear writing done in a conversational tone.

Production people generally will show you a "demonstration" reel of samples, but Mathews says to be wary of these. "They may have been made by people who left the company several years back." He suggests asking for samples produced by the team that will work on your project.

If you decide to go with the crew of a television station, make sure the writer is experienced in doing video-length scripts. Many stations do not employ professional video scriptwriters; they often assign the work to someone accustomed to writing 30-second commercials. Or, the station may expect production people to cobble together a script. Don't let this happen.

"The script is the most important component of any video project," Carr says. It is the blueprint for the entire production.

When checking references, ask if the candidates finished the project on time and on budget, if they were easy to work with and if the client was happy with the final product. You don't want prima donnas who become defensive when you offer constructive criticism.

Once you've decided on your team, establish a production schedule that includes deadlines for the first and final drafts of the script, a pre-production meeting, shooting and a due date for the final video. Make sure everyone involved understands the schedule and can meet it.

Working with the Creative Team

To ensure success, make sure the writer and production team know where the video will be shown, the size and type of audience, what you want it to accomplish and how it fits into the big picture of your organization. Is it one component of your safety training, the backbone of your recruitment program or an introduction to diversity training?

DSM Chemical uses its safety-orientation video to deliver only basic safety information, such as procedures for entering its plants, emergency evacuation rules and required personal protective equipment. The writer and producer understood that more detailed information would be presented in a classroom setting and set the stage for that in the video.

Finally, discuss your corporate culture with the team and provide as much information as you can on the topic and the intended audience to help them understand the tone and style the video should have. An edgy e-commerce company and a conservative brokerage firm would probably take very different approaches to an orientation video for new employees.

Once the parameters are established, ask the writer for a treatment you can review. Treatments are brief descriptions that establish a conceptual framework for the video and outline its content. They state the purpose of the video, describe the audience, discuss the opening and closing shots, list important points to be covered and set the tone of the video, which is reflected in pacing, narration and music.

Pay particular attention to the pacing and make sure it matches the topic. If you're celebrating the introduction of a new product, you might want a fast pace that generates excitement. If you're producing a recruitment piece highlighting the natural beauty of your area, a slower pace might be more appropriate.

After you've agreed on a treatment, the writer will begin drafting the script, coordinating with production personnel as she works. The script also should describe the shots that will accompany each section of the narration—what the viewer will see as the narrator is speaking.

The final script should be clear, concise and flowing, with smooth transitions between topics. It should mention a topic once, cover it as needed and move on. It should not depend on humor or game show gimmicks or use nonactors to deliver dialogue. They usually come off as stilted and unprofessional.

As you read the script, ask yourself why you need each section of the video. Many videos open with a statement from the organization's CEO or president. These segments generally do little but slow the pace and bore the viewer. They also date the video if the person leaves. Such "talking heads," as they are known in the trade, should be avoided altogether unless the speaker has something truly interesting to say.

Other common video problems include the following:

- The script was not clear, concise and well structured.
- The video tried to convey too many facts and figures.
- The video lacked a thematic context that made the material more interesting.
- The video tried to accomplish too many missions.

Many videos open with a statement from the organization's CEO or president. These segments generally do little but slow the pace and bore the viewer.

Bringing the Script to Life

Limit the number of people who will review the script to those whose approval is required. (But, remember that it's much easier and less expensive to fix a paragraph of text than 30 seconds of video.) Have the writer make the necessary changes and submit a revised script.

Before shooting begins, your producer should hold a pre-production meeting to review the site, determine lighting needs, decide the sequence of shots and identify any potential problems. "A two-hour pre-production meeting can save a full day of expensive shooting," Mathews says.

Make sure a professional narrates the script, and let the topic determine whether you use a male or female narrator. When Canadian company PCS Nitrogen Fertilizer Ltd. of Saskatoon, Saskatchewan, produced a video on how those who live near its plants should respond to a chemical release, a female narrator was used to soften the impact of the message.

Also, make sure that any music used adds texture to your production. "If the music will play under narration, avoid melodic selections that induce humming," Mathews says.

Accompany the producer throughout the shooting period. Shots need not be taken in the order of their appearance in the final video. They are edited later to fit the script.

Adding Visual Interest

Much of the magic of a video takes place during editing. Sophisticated new equipment makes it easier to add special effects that help maintain viewer interest.

You also can enhance visual interest by shooting at related locations outside the workplace. If you are in an urban setting, a new employee orientation video can show scenes of your organization's immediate surroundings by taking the audience on a visual stroll around the block.

The *Florida Times-Union* in Jacksonville shot segments of its community-outreach video in a local classroom, at performances of various arts groups it sponsors and on a fishing pier. These images added human interest and linked the company to the community. This technique can be particularly useful to manufacturing companies that want to avoid a cold, industrial tone.

Updating Your Video

When editing was done on tape, it was difficult to change a video without affecting everything that came after the change. New editing systems make it much easier to change and update videos. When the production company presents the edited video for your review, minor changes or corrections usually can be made without additional cost, as long as the original scope of the work remains unchanged and no new shooting is required.

> Make sure a professional narrates the script, and let the topic determine whether you use a male or female narrator.

Also, it's wise to think about possible updates, even as you begin the project. Try to omit details that might change or date the video. If you must include material that might change, script it in segments that can easily be removed and replaced.

If you think you'll want to update the video, consider storing the raw footage on a CD or DVD or even paying the production company to keep it for you. "This may seem like an unnecessary expense up front, but it can save you lots of money down the road," says video producer Carr.

Once the video is ready, pop some corn, open a few sodas and invite your colleagues to the premier. With good planning and a talented production team, your video should win rave reviews.

Betty Sosnin is a professional freelance writer and a marketing and public relations consultant based in Augusta, GA. She writes brochures, video scripts, direct-mail packages, booklets, press releases, and magazine articles. She can be reached at (706) 736-7353.

General Tips for Training

Pete Blair

Analysis and design assumes the need for training and a sense of what kind of training will work best. So often the failures or successes of training initiatives can be tracked back to the start, to a crucial decision, to a wise move or to negligence. This article provides a list of tips and points to consider before making your final decisions about the nature of the training program that will work best in any situation.

Tip 1: Don't be too quick to select course delivery mode.

Don't jump to the decision on course delivery medium until you have complete and accurate definitions of three things:

- What the learner must be able to do at the conclusion of the training (performance objectives—obtained during task analysis).
- What the learner must know to be able to meet the performance objectives (identified during task analysis).
- What the learner already knows and can already do before the training begins (audience analysis).

For instance, if the worker must be able to operate a certain piece of equipment, then structured OJT or lecture/lab would be reasonable delivery systems, at least for the final part, of the worker's training. Lecture by itself, print-based, or computer-based training would fall far short. In short, select the delivery medium that permits adequate testing of the performance you expect of the learner at the conclusion of the course or training module. For many job tasks the only way to determine if the worker can actually perform the tasks in the job setting is to observe the performance, on the job. For that reason, structured OJT becomes a logical choice for at least part, if not all, of the worker's training. For knowledge level skills that support task performance, prerequisite training delivered by lecture, lecture/lab, print-based self-study, or CBT may, in some circumstances, be practicable. In other circumstances, it may be more prudent for workers to gain the required knowledge, at the job workplace while actually learning to perform the task. This is addressed further in the tip on task analysis.

Reprinted with permission of Pete Blair and Associates. Copyright © 2001 Pete Blair and Associates, http://pages.prodigy.net/pblair/ttthome.htm. All rights reserved.

Tip 2: Document the audience analysis and make it a part of the training design documentation.

When doing an audience analysis, concentrate on the characteristics of the new hire for the job, but don't completely ignore the workers who are currently performing the job. In many cases, job processes are simplified over the years and the incoming skill requirements for new hires change accordingly. Failure to look closely at the current new hire audience can result in a program that works well when tested on existing workers but falls flat on its face with new hires.

To conduct the audience analysis for a new-employee training program, start by examining the skills or experiences mandated by the human resource department for the job. However, investigate carefully to ensure that what is *documented* as hiring practices and *actual* hiring practices are the same. In some cases, documented hiring criteria simply cannot be met due to a tight labor market. Design training programs based on actuality and not on good intentions!

In many businesses, hiring practices seem to have a habit of changing over the years. And those changes can show up in training programs by lengthening the time required for a new worker to complete training. If, after a few years, the time required for new learners to become productive seems to lengthen, check the audience characteristics at that time against the audience analysis you originally documented to make sure that the original audience assumptions are still valid. If the audience changes, training will have to be revised or altered accordingly.

Tip 3: Make sure the task analysis is complete and accurate.

Simply stated, a task analysis is determining and listing all of the tasks performed by workers in the process of performing the job for which they were hired.

An accurate and complete task analysis is, in my estimation, the key to effective and efficient training. Weaknesses in the task analysis can result in wasted time, wasted money, and poor worker performance. Task analysis is not the place to cut corners! Training programs that fail usually have roots in erroneous or "fuzzily worded" tasks and performance standards.

Tons of paper have been devoted to task analysis methodologies, and I won't try to duplicate those writings here. I would suggest, however, that the general areas of responsibilities (duties) for a job be defined first and the tasks comprising each duty be developed next.

For some jobs, it makes more sense for a new worker to be trained and become proficient in one duty and then move to the next. In other jobs, a new worker might have to learn the tasks associated with multiple duties simultaneously.

Be consistent with your working definition of the word "task" and how you articulate task statements. For example,

GENERAL TIPS FOR TRAINING

- Tasks are usually considered meaningful units of work for which an employer is willing to pay.
- Tasks have beginning and ending points; for continuous process tasks, this might be the beginning or ending of a shift.
- Tasks are independent of each other, can usually be observed, and the task or its results can always measured.

For instance, changing the oil in an automobile can be considered a task. However, draining the old oil is not a task because it is part of the task of changing the oil and is not therefore done independently.

When doing the task analysis:

- Articulate all task statements with short sentences (usually two to seven words) that succinctly and accurately describe the observable, measurable performance; for example, "Produce widgets" or "Perform monthly maintenance."
- Don't include references to knowledge, training, skills, or attitudes in the task statement itself.
- Don't include modifiers unless absolutely necessary to ensure universal understanding. For instance, the second example, "perform monthly maintenance," contains the modifier "monthly." This would be appropriate in a situation where there might be multiple maintenance schedules, with "monthly" being one of those.
- For each task, develop as many statements of performance standards as necessary to explicitly describe the "yardstick" that an observer must use to determine if the task has been performed to the standards set by the company. Accurate statements of performance standards, including references to safety procedures, ensure that the same yardstick measures all workers. Don't use subjective terms such as "correctly," "in a timely manner," and "appropriately" that may be interpreted one way by one person and another way by someone else. This eliminates potential inconsistencies in training and worker claims of unfair evaluation.

When you think you have all of the performance standards listed for a task, ask yourself (or a subject matter expert) this simple question: "If the worker performs this particular task and meets all of these standards, do we know that that task has been done correctly?" If the phrase "Yeah, but ..." comes up in answer to that question, then the performance standards are not complete! Don't stop until the answer is an unequivocal "Yes."

After you are sure that the list of performance standards for each task is complete, ask the following question for each performance statement: "Is there any logical way that this statement could be interpreted one way by one person and another way by another person?" If you get any answer other than a solid "No," the standard of performance needs tweaking at best and a major overhaul at worst. Quality statements of performance standards are vital in ensuring consistency of training and evaluation.

- Develop a list of any particular safety precautions or procedures associated with the performance of the task to ensure that safety is included, in context, throughout the training program. Safety precautions should also be automatically included in the performance standards of respective tasks to ensure that everyone knows how to perform the task safely as well as efficiently.
- Develop a list of condition statements that describe the setting for either teaching or evaluating performance and include safety equipment, tools, materials, processing equipment, and supplies required for the task. Condition statements serve several purposes. In the structured OJT environment, they remind worker/trainers to make sure that all of the conditions are ready before teaching or evaluating the task.
- Rank each task as to:
  1. How difficult it is to learn
  2. How frequently it is performed
  3. How critical it is that the task be performed correctly (to the performance standards)

Use these rankings to identify where job aids or refresher training might be needed. These rankings will also help match development efforts to the real-world needs of the business. Another benefit might be a clue to the sequence of content for training, with simpler, non-critical tasks being taught before more complex and critical ones. However, keep in mind that in some structured OJT environments, training must follow the sequence dictated by the real-time events on the production floor.

- For each task, list the skills and knowledge that a worker must have before starting to learn how to perform the task in a hands-on laboratory or on-job environment (prerequisite skills and knowledge). This information, in conjunction with the knowledge/skill information identified in the audience analysis, dictates the learning experiences required *before* the worker can begin hands-on laboratory or workplace learning for this particular task.

Tip 4: Be specific when defining prerequisite skills and knowledge.

In many programs, prerequisite skills and knowledge are defined in such ambiguous terms or at such a high level that the prerequisite training developed (or purchased) is far more than is needed or prudent. Personal experience: after closely examining one prerequisite knowledge course that resulted from such ambiguity, one training manager exclaimed, "My goodness, we should be developing maintenance people, not brain surgeons!"

Ask the question, over and over, must this knowledge be gained *before*

GENERAL TIPS FOR TRAINING

"hands-on" or can it be incorporated *with* hands-on learning? Where possible, lean heavily toward incorporating knowledge with hands on. In many cases, knowledge courses must be scheduled administered so far ahead of hands-on training that content is forgotten by the time it's applied. Although my purpose here is not to reinvent nor dwell on learning theories, keep in mind that knowledge is retained when it is applied. If you learn a set of facts today but do not use those facts for a month or even a week from now, you've probably forgotten them by the time you need them!

Tip 5: Document course maintenance plans early in the design process.

In most businesses, continual process improvement is prerequisite to being in business tomorrow! Process improvement means that tasks, as well as task performance standards, must also change. These changes arbitrarily dictate corresponding changes to training.

A company's operating procedures, their training program, and the way they actually do things must be absolutely congruent or the training program has no credibility in the eyes of employees and trainees. In companies where absolute congruence is not maintained, training is considered a joke (and a rather expensive one at that) by most employees!

The following items are among the things that I recommend addressing when developing plans for training-program maintenance. While not a complete list of things you may wish to consider, it serves as a good starting point.

- Who or what department will be charged with the responsibility for training material maintenance? Will that department be a keystroking function that responds to input from someone else, or will it be charged with making content-type decisions?
- How will changes to the production process be communicated to those charged with course maintenance?
- Who will make the actual changes to the wording in existing material?
- Who will have review and approval rights for alterations to the training program? (Safety Department? Environmental Impact Department? Other departments?)
- When anyone proposes a change, how and to whom will that change be submitted, and who must approve and initiate the change?
- How will proposed changes be circulated to those who must review and approve?
- What resources such as computers, software, and personnel are required to maintain the training program? And where will those resources come from?
- What plans will be implemented to keep the training program lock-stepped with operating procedures in a controlled-document environment?

> Ask the question, over and over, must this knowledge be gained *before* "hands-on" or can it be incorporated *with* hands-on learning?

Tip 6: Make decisions, in the design phase, concerning document control.

If your company's operating procedures are controlled documents, the company will have to decide if trainee/trainer guides should be controlled documentation and how to implement and maintain control on these documents.

Tip 7: Plan, in the design phase, how to track training and certification.

This tracking system must be able to accommodate "update" training when production processes change. For companies that use standard operating procedures that are regularly revised, the tracking system must be able to tie task training to specific revision levels of operating procedures.

Tip 8: Plan how to handle training and/or certification of existing skilled workers.

Develop a strategy for how to handle employees who have been around for some time and are already performing the job. Do you "grandfather" all existing employees? Or do you force them to be retrained? Or do you require them to pass a task evaluation? The question of how to handle existing employees must be addressed early on to avoid serious personnel and attitude problems in your new training program. A word of caution: Beware, you can't bypass this one and it can be a barrel of snakes!

Tip 9: Continually monitor training quality.

Establish and maintain a system of collecting data, including trainee reaction, training times required, training efficiency, and training consistency. Monitor the training effort and detect any slippage in training quality. The longer the program is in place, the more this becomes an important issue. Left unmonitored, I can just about guarantee quality slippage.

Since 1991 Pete Blair has worked as an independent consultant, doing business as Pete Blair and Associates, in Raleigh, NC. He has also served as Director of Customer Training, DazzlerMax Division, MaxIT Corporation, since October 1999. Contact him at pblair@prodigy.net.

Training and Other Performance Interventions

People Development Strategies in the New Economy

Greg Wang

There are many different approaches to helping employees improve their performance. As the business world and society in general have been changing, the challenges that organizations are facing have led some to try new strategies for attracting, retaining, and developing employees and managing their performance. This white paper presents an overview of best practices.

> If you want one year's prosperity, grow rice. If you want 10 years' prosperity, grow trees. If you want 100 years' prosperity, grow people.
> —Chinese Proverb

This white paper presents alternative people development strategies and approaches from leading business organizations. It is not intended to place any value judgment on particular approaches. Rather, the purpose is to provide human resource development practitioners an overall insight into the best practices of people development strategies in businesses and industries.

Challenges from market pressures, technological innovations, and the increased importance of intangible assets as a percent of total corporate assets are the fundamental reasons for the corporate world's focus on people development. Due to these challenges, today's business leaders developed new visions of their employees, seeing them as knowledge resources, customers, and investors.

The best practices of business organizations in the areas of attraction,

Reprinted with permission of the publisher from *DPT Consulting White Paper 2000-2001*. Copyright © 2000-2001 DPT Consulting Group, Inc. All rights reserved.

retention, development, and diversity are presented to assist in benchmarking people strategies implementation. Two retention approaches, reservoir vs. river, are discussed as alternatives to retaining employees. Data on training investments by leading organizations is presented to demonstrate the organizational commitment to people development. Knowledge management systems, especially skills-based competency management systems, have become dominating performance management tools for many organizations.

Many leading business organizations have made corporate universities the ultimate solution for people development. The corporate university movement appears to be an effective approach to institutionalizing people development strategies and improving corporate images.

Introduction

The focus on people in the business world can be traced back to 1964, when Nobel laureate Gary Becker published *Human Capital*. Since Becker's time, many other alternative terms have been created to describe the important role that people play in the business world, such as intellectual capital and intangible assets. Leading business organizations increasingly emphasize people development with the growing rate of technological innovations and business knowledge expansions.

This white paper provides a summary and a benchmarking background on the core areas of people development strategies, such as attraction, retention, development, and diversity adopted by many leading organizations. Due to this purpose, this white paper does not cover the areas of technology-based learning and the technical side of people development. However, once organizations have developed appropriate people development strategies, choosing a platform to implement them will be a matter of cost-benefit analysis process.

Challenges

In today's business world, every organization has certain systems and/or processes for developing its employees, the most valuable asset as it appears in almost every annual report in all organizations. In general, people development strategies and approaches in business organizations are driven by multiple challenges brought on by the new economy:

Market Pressures

According to a survey of 16,000 U.S. businesses conducted by a national staffing firm, 24 percent of companies say they will hire more workers in the first three months of 2001, while only 10 percent forecast layoffs. At the same time, as the nation's unemployment rate holds at a three-decade low, the employment market, especially for IT related industries, is experiencing a much more competitive situation. The IT skills shortage costs U.S. employers $105.5 billion annually in salaries and sign-on bonuses. Various estimates predict 850,000 unfilled IT and Internet related jobs in the United States by 2002. This situation is caused by the fact that all organizations (government, private, not-for-profit) in all industries (manufacturing, financial, services, Internet) become competitors in the same labor market. They are all competing for the same, limited talents.

Technical Innovation

Rapid technological innovations in the IT industry have created another major challenge that has a double edge. On the one hand, the ever-changing technology requires existing employees to constantly acquire new skills and keep themselves updated. On the other hand, the implementations of new technologies are required to the same degree by competitions in the products/services market, creating even more demand on an already tightened labor market. The implication of technological innovations to IT organizations is: If IT professionals suspect their skills will soon be obsolete in current organizations, they will leave their positions at all costs.

Changes in Composition of Market Value

With increasing technological innovations and knowledge accumulation, the composition of market value has changed drastically with increased value in intangible intellectual assets. Table 1 lists the market values of some well-known companies, most consisting more of intangible assets than actual tangible assets.

Company	Equity (Net Tangible Assets)	Intangible Assets	Market Value
Microsoft	$8 Billion	$242 Billion	$250 Billion
IBM	$22.5 Billion	$31.5 Billion	$54 Billion
Ford Motor	$21.4 Billion	$8.6 Billion	$30 Billion
McDonald's	$6.2 Billion	$20 Billion	$26.2 Billion
Coca-Cola	$5.2 Billion	$73.4 Billion	$78.6 Billion

Table 1. **Compositions of market value for selected organizations**
(Note: data for Microsoft is from 1999. Data for all other companies from 1995)

Although some companies' intangible assets may include a large portion of brand name value, such as Coca-Cola and McDonald's, others may contain some stock market distortion; most intangible assets in the companies listed reflect the value of the knowledge the employees hold. The increasing value of knowledge makes organizations believe that business and market expansion can only be achieved to the extent that it is as good as the people they can attract and keep.

Buffeted by the interactions of a tight labor market, evolving technologies, and increasing intellectual assets, many organizations make precipitous work force decisions that sometimes take a toll in quality, morale, and risk. People development strategies and approaches are an urgent call that attempts to meet all three challenges in competitive markets: the product/services market and the labor market.

Philosophies on People Development Strategies and Approaches

Pressures represented by the above challenges have urged business leaders to change their mindsets and philosophies in people development. All business strategies implemented are rooted in the following philosophies. Several different, but similar, philosophies on people development exist in business organizations.

Employees as Knowledge Resources

A recent belief spreading across business leaders within knowledge organizations states that the biggest mistake a knowledge organization can make is to exclusively focus on its customers. Unlike manufacturing industries, knowledge organizations (such as IT organizations) cannot afford to focus too heavily on its customers alone. That is because knowledge organizations constantly compete in two markets: the market for key customers and the market for key employees. The best way to compete in the employee market is to develop existing employees.

Employees as Customers

A customer refers to the person with the greatest market leverage or power, the one with the most choices. Today's employment market has turned the situation around about who has market leverage over whom. The market advantage is to employees rather than employers.

Many leading companies ask themselves this question: This type of organization is pursuing employee satisfaction the same way the product/service markets pursue customer satisfaction.

Employees as Investors

Companies with this mindset believe that their employees are the organization's investors. This vision challenges the traditional "human assets" philosophy. It argues that people cannot be treated as assets because assets will depreciate over time, but the value of people will appreciate with accumulat-

"Suppose we are selling 'management and mentoring ability' to employees, what are some of the things they might want to buy in addition to the compensations that all other employers are offering?"

ed experience and organizational development strategies. Employees as investors are expecting increased returns from their investments. This is not only in the forms of salary and benefits, but also in individual competency development and career growth.

The philosophies on people development have one thing in common: the deep belief that compensation programs alone are not enough to retain talent, because it is too easy for other companies to match a salary in the labor market. The difference is the commitment an organization makes to develop its people. Realizing the challenges, companies are initiating more programs than ever to create a better workplace to retain their current employees and attract new ones.

> Employees invest their time, skills, talents, and creativity in the company's business activities and expect a high return.

Best Practices in People Development

In general, people development strategies in business organizations have been centered on the following four focal areas: attraction, retention, development, and diversity. This section will present the best practices in business organizations to benchmark people strategy.

No standard definition exists for "best practice." In general, "best practice" refers to the approaches that can be effectively used in an organization to help achieve business success. For instance, General Motors defines "best practice" as "information we can use." AMP deems practices as "best" if they are objectively better than AMP at a given practice.

In reality, attraction, retention, development, and diversity are components that closely interrelate to one another. No approach can focus only on one aspect without influencing the others. For instance, without an effective people development strategy, companies may appear less attractive to potential employees and have difficulty retaining existing ones. This situation may not be able to foster workforce diversity. For the purpose of benchmarking, the following discussion lists the four areas separately.

Attraction

Attraction is the first step in the people development process. It is a starting point for retention, development, and diversity. In other words, without attracting good employees, no base exists for retention and development, not to mention diversity.

Many organizations have launched multiple approaches to recruiting and attracting qualified candidates due to the tight labor market. In addition to regular college recruiting, the following strategies are commonly adopted by many organizations:

- Sponsors college scholarships or provide financial aid to attract graduates.

- Build partnerships with labor market institutions. Some companies have established an account management function within government employment agencies and different ethnic group employment agencies.
- Focus on different geographic regions and demographics—fishing in places that are more likely to produce something.
- Develop existing non-technical employees into technical careers and replace with new hires from a less competitive labor market. This internal strategy also reinforces retention because employees changing careers internally are more likely to remain with the organization.

Retention

Companies are developing various strategies in an attempt to retain their current employees. The implications are to retain their business knowledge and experiences and form the basis for further business and market expansions.

Basically, two types of retention strategies exist in business communities. Type one is analogous to tending a dam that keeps a reservoir in place. Type two is akin to managing a river.[1] The object is not to prevent water from flowing out, but to control its direction and speed.

Type one companies believe they can do better than the market to retain their existing employees. They are offering higher than average compensation packages to their employees, and frequently make counter-offers to employees who intend to leave with even higher compensation. This type of retention strategy results in the increase of general compensation value for certain positions.

Type two companies launch a "market-driven retention strategy." They develop retention action plans that project talent requirements and attrition rates. This allows companies to develop highly targeted retention programs and create cost-effective contingency plans for filling potential skill gaps.

In a variation of the type two strategy, some companies have found that the best way to deal with retention is to avoid the retention issue altogether by outsourcing and letting somebody else deal with it, such as outsourcing the entire technical operation. The downside of this approach is that business knowledge and experience are lost forever to the outsourcing part of the operation.

Another variation, taken by many companies in the IT industry, is to cooperate with competitors. Those companies began to "lend" teams of employees to their competitors after losing a bid for a contracting project. The team members remain employees of the first company and work on a specific project for the second company. This approach has its advantage for project-based companies in that it retains the lending company's investment in key employees, maintains its capability to bid on future contracts, and broadens the experience of its leased employees. The problem with this approach is that not all companies are suitable for the model.

Development

Compared with other focal areas of people development strategy, development is the core area, because it directly impacts the other three components. A company with strong commitment and a reputation in developing its people will not only be able to attract more talents, but will also retain existing ones.

In a recent American Society for Training and Development (ASTD) report, *2000 ASTD State of the Industry Report*, ASTD identified Training Investment Leaders among 1200 participating organizations. The following measures were used as criteria:

- Percentage of employees eligible for training who received training
- Total training hours per employee eligible for training
- Total training expenditures per employee eligible for training
- Total training expenditures as a percent of payroll.

Training spending. The Leaders devoted an average of 3.6 percent of their payroll to training in 1998 compared with an average of 2 percent for the rest of the 1200 organizations. The Leaders spent an average of $1,640 on training per eligible employee while the rest averaged less than $770. The dollar amount spent on training says nothing about the quality of the training, but it does indicate an organization's commitment to employee learning and development.

Number of employees that received training. The average companies provided training for about 76 percent of employees eligible for training. In comparison, the Leaders provided training for nearly 97 percent of eligible employees.

Amount of training employees received. On average, participating companies provided 29 hours of training per eligible employee per year. The comparable figure for the Leaders was 58 hours. Some companies established mandatory training hours (e.g., 40 hours per year) as a performance measurement to the employees.

Knowledge Management System

A logical question to the heavily invested training and development organizations is "How do they know what to train, to whom, and when?" Knowledge management (KM) is the answer. KM is the latest wave in the business world focusing on people, human capital development, and learning organizations. Knowledge management is defined as the art of creating value from an organization's intangible assets. Specifically, knowledge in the KM world refers to the knowledge of employees' competencies, business processes, and the market (customers, suppliers, and competitors). The first two components of knowledge in the KM scenario are all related to people and people development.

Many organizations have created skill-based competencies management systems as sub-systems of KM. A skill-based competencies management system enables the companies to develop an inventory of skills that are critical to business success. Most importantly, some organizations connect skill requirements to career pathing and provide employees clear pictures of their future advancement in the organization with specifically identified learning needs and training plans. All this can greatly motivate high performance, high retention rates, and, at the same time, boost productivity.

Numerous organizations, especially IT organizations, have established or are planning to establish such systems. According to a survey conducted by Gartner Group, 60% of IT organizations will implement skills management by 2002. 80% of those that proactively manage skills will have a 25% productivity advantage over those that do not.

Alternative Approaches to Skill-Based Competencies Management

Some organizations have developed alternative approaches to meet their businesses' human resources requirements. One such approach is called "experience-based attraction/retention strategy." The idea is to plan and identify the number of years experience required to perform certain projects or workloads within a business unit over a planning period. It follows a simple equation:

$$\text{Experience deficiency} = (\text{experience required by workload}) - (\text{current workforce experience})$$

For instance, a business unit may determine that they need an accumulated 95 years of experience to complete projects for the year 2001. They analyzed that they have a total of 10 years of experience deficiency/gap to perform required projects, because they lost 20 years of experience last year due to employee turnover and made up 10 years of experience by recent new hires. The 10 years of experience gap can be translated to training and/or recruiting activities. This approach has advantages because it is simple and easy to do, but the disadvantage is its inaccuracy. Organizations adapting this approach are relying heavily on internal/external expert opinions to estimate what job requires how many years of experience.

Other Development Approaches

"Manufacturing" future managers from an existing employee pool is a commonly used approach to develop and retain people. Many organizations have developed or adopted leadership and management development programs to attract, develop, and retain existing and college graduates. Through training, job rotations, and other assignments, the programs develop future business leaders for the organizations.

Diversity

Strictly speaking, diversity includes, but is broader than EEO and Affirmative Action compliance. Its meaning has expanded to allow for integration of an individual's differences in attitudes and values in the workplace, valuing these and extending beyond legal and social issues. In business reality, the diversity concept also includes diverse team composition, new ideas, different problem-solving approaches, wider selection pools, increased access to wider client bases, and a more multi-dimensional corporate image. In this aspect, the word "inclusivity" is often used interchangeably with diversity to refer to all the human differences.

Business organizations pursue diversity not only because "it is the right thing to do," but also because employees and customers demand it. Corporate diversity efforts are about money, business, and the bottom line. Organizations implement diversity programs because it saves them money, helps them retain good people, and meets and/or exceeds the expectations of their existing customers, while continuously winning new customers and employees.

Corporate University: A Comprehensive Solution

Realizing all people development related issues are closely connected to one another, corporations have recently shown a surge of interest in launching corporate universities as a strategic function and approach to address critical business issues of people development and employee learning. Today, corporate universities can be found in almost all businesses and industries, including government agencies. The number of corporate universities has increased from about 400 to more than 2500 in the last 10 years. This number is predicted to exceed the number of formal higher education institutes, which is about 3,700 nationally, during the next five years.

The major focus of corporate universities can also be found in the areas of attraction, retention, development, and diversity. Specifically, corporate universities focus on some or all of the following areas:

- Competency/skill-based, career development focus
- Initiative-driven
- Leadership/management development-driven
- Customer/supplier relationship management orientation
- Change-management

Many corporate universities are explicitly named as a "people university" to emphasize their focus on people, e.g., Southwest Airlines University for People. Take the example of financial and banking industries: about 60 percent of the companies have established some kind of corporate university that is distinctively different from traditional training centers. A corporate university in a well-known national bank represents many best practices in the industry. It has established several schools and colleges: School of Leadership

> The number of corporate universities has increased from about 400 to more than 2500 in the last 10 years.

Development, College of Customer Service, and College of Professional Development. Using a defined skills assessment system and career pathing approach, this corporate university has developed systems of learning events for tellers, IT professionals, and managers at all levels. Through this unique approach, the company was able to reduce the teller turnover rate from 200 percent to 25 percent. Similar corporate university functions can also be found at The First University of First Union Corporation, The Institute for Learning at Bank of Montreal, MasterCard University, MBNA Customer College, and Service Delivery University at Fidelity Investment.

Conclusion

To respond to the challenges presented by market and technological innovations in the new economy, organizations have initiated various approaches and strategies based on solid business philosophies to develop their employees. Many organizations have institutionalized people development initiatives through various forms of corporate universities. Through the institutionalization of people development, the following best practices have emerged:

- Competency-based career model
- Rich arrays of learning opportunities (e.g., e-learning, online collaborative learning, and ILT)
- Career options and advancement linked to core competencies
- Individual development plans linked to core curricula
- People development effectiveness measurement (ROI).

Notes

1. Peter Cappelli, "A Market-Driven Approach to Retaining Talent." *Harvard Business Review,* January-February 2000.

Greg Wang, Ph.D., is a principal of DPT Consulting Group Inc. (www.dptconsulting.com), which offers a unique combination of skills management, instructional design, ROI measurement, and other management consulting services to help organizations maximize human capital. Dr. Wang created and is moderating a free discussion group, ROInet (groups.yahoo.com/group/roinet), to advocate rigorous approaches for HRD and human capital measurement. He can be reached at gwang@dpt-consulting.com or (610) 206-0101.

Time to Treat Learners as Consumers

Stephen L. Cohen, David W. Dove, and Edward L. Bachelder

This article discusses focusing on how employees want to learn. The central question is "Why not treat learners as consumers with distinct preferences for what, how, and when they learn?" The authors propose assessing those preferences prior to creating learning solutions and training interventions. To do so, the authors recommend borrowing a statistical technique from market research, adaptive conjoint analysis.

One arena that has provided a significant contribution to the training field over the past several years has been that of learning styles. Not only does there appear to be decent evidence that there are a number of distinct learning styles, but also that they dramatically affect the way people go about learning.

Yet, there doesn't seem to be much evidence for how that knowledge is applied in a classroom, other than trying to create a learning environment that caters to all styles. Anyone who has either created or instructed learning programs realizes that this objective, more often than not, falls short of succeeding. At best, the learning experience is compromised by trying to please all of the people all of the time.

But perhaps catering to learning styles is the wrong approach. Is it important to know *how* learners learn, or is it important to know how they *want* to learn? It's a subtle, but important, distinction.

Wanting Versus Doing

Understanding how adults want to learn, not just how they learn, involves different issues. Though how adults learn has received the most attention, how they want to learn could potentially add more value to the learning experience. A lot is known about people's learning styles and approaches, but does that really help create a learning process that answers to a myriad of individual differences in styles and approaches?

That's why learner-driven solutions—whether delivered electronically or

Reprinted with permission from *Training & Development*, January 2001. Copyright © 2001 by the American Society for Training and Development. All rights reserved.

> ## How Adults Learn
> - How adults learn has received the most attention, but how they want to learn could potentially add more value to the learning experience.
> - Why not treat learners as consumers with distinct preferences for what, how, and when they learn? And why not assess those preferences prior to creating learning solutions and training interventions?
> - Adaptive conjoint analysis, a powerful statistical technique that deconstructs a product or service into a number of discrete elements, can provide insight on what, how, where, and when people want to learn and how likely they are to choose your training programs over others.

otherwise—are becoming so popular. In theory, they let learners determine when, and to some extent how, they want to learn. But, generally, learning styles appear only to provide some information on how people approach learning. They don't necessarily identify people's preferences for learning—not just the approach they take but the context in which they want to take it.

With continuously changing learner demographics and a new generation-type label per decade, it makes good business sense to check in relatively frequently on how learners prefer to learn. Rarely, however, are learners asked about their preferences. Instead, the training community often makes assumptions about what might work, what might be fun, and what might enhance the learning experience, and they hope that in addition to it working, participants will also like it.

It's usually more of a "choose your seat when you come" rather than "choose your seat before you decide to come" approach. In the product world, where consumers have choices and make purchase decisions, research on people's preferences is conducted as a matter of course. Companies need to know the particular attributes to build into a product if it is going to be attractive to their target market. Makes sense.

The question is, why has that kind of thinking escaped the radar screens of the training industry? Why not treat learners as consumers with distinct preferences for what, how, and when they learn? And why not assess those preferences prior to creating learning solutions and training interventions, instead of alpha or beta tests that evaluate what has already been created?

Just like marketers of consumer products, the goal is to get trial-and-repeat purchase behavior. But just what gets people to purchase in the first place? Taste, feel, price, packaging, convenience, availability—probably some combination of all of those factors and more. However, learners are often not treated in the same way. Assumptions are made about what they will like, based on what they have experienced and how well that has worked.

What if the process were reversed? What if learners were asked for their preferences prior to engaging them in a learning experience? Not ask them what skills and information they need to do their jobs (albeit important), but focus instead on how they want to go about accessing that knowledge in the first place.

A Consumer-in Approach

The approach that most people take to training is more product-out than consumer-in. That is, assessments and conclusions are made concerning the best way to deliver various skills and information learning, without the benefit of insight from consumers—the prospective learners. In the consumer products industry, consumer insight is critical, and few companies in that industry go to market without that type of assessment. There are, however, tried-and-true consumer research methodologies that can not only be readily applied to the training field, but also that can alter the entire mindset of how a learner is viewed as a potential buyer of learning programs and services.

What's more, learning initiatives are often sold through intermediaries such as HR departments, managers of the learners, senior executives, and so forth—all of whom mean well but impose their own perspectives and values on the buying behaviors of others.

For example, cereal companies don't rely entirely on what moms and dads say about the cereals their kids prefer; the cereal companies ask the kids directly. Car companies don't ask teenagers what cars their parents like most; they ask the parents. In the end, it's the end user—whether cereal eater, car purchaser, or trainee—who decides the fate of a particular product or service.

> The approach that most people take to training is more product-out than consumer-in.

A Page from Market Research

So, how can learning preferences be identified? There are many applicable techniques used by consumer product companies. One is called *adaptive conjoint analysis*. ACA is a powerful statistical technique that provides a means of deconstructing a product or service into a number of discrete elements, each with its own value. In doing so, ACA provides insight on the tradeoffs people make when choosing between various products and services. It measures the utility that consumers derive from various features, through the application of advanced fractional factorial experimental designs.

In its simplest form, ACA uses a forced-comparison methodology of preferences for any number of key factors—such as those that will influence the final purchase decision. For ice cream, that may mean brand, flavor, ingredients, fat content, package size, price, or other factor. For cars, it might include make or model (brand), performance characteristics, transmission options, gas consumption, and warranty.

As consumers, we make choices—whether for ice cream or cars—in the form of packages (or bundles) of attributes. If you want the performance and road-handling characteristics of a BMW, you'll have to make a tradeoff with other attributes, such as fuel economy or price. Similarly, if you want Ben & Jerry's ice cream, you have to make a tradeoff in package size; it typically comes only in pints. By asking people to choose from among various packages, each with a bundle of attributes, you can assign relative values (*utility* in conjoint terminology) to each attribute with remarkable validity.

The notion of adaptive conjoint makes this process even more powerful in that the choices presented to each consumer are different—generated incrementally by computer and based on prior responses or selections. In addition to easing the data-collection process, ACA drives to statistical validity with much smaller samples.

To use that methodology in the training field, some general assumptions must be made. First and foremost is the belief that employees are no different from buyers when it comes to the learning options they choose. They have their own preferences, interests, wants, and needs for learning. And though there are undoubtedly clusters of employees with similar learning preferences, there are also plenty of relatively unique combinations.

People also have deep-seated preferences for how they like to approach their personal development. Inherent in their preferences is a relatively universal attraction to event-based instruction that serves the natural human need for social interaction.

It's what we have been most used to throughout our lives. In fact, most of us were schooled in often-overcrowded classrooms. In other words, most adults are conditioned to learn *at* a place rather than *in* a space. There should be little surprise, then, that getting adults to recognize the potential benefits of online learning, for instance, will be difficult to achieve—particularly at any organization where the classroom tradition is well entrenched in the management development culture.

The Steps of ACA

The methodology for conducting ACA is fairly straightforward. The following steps outline how ACA would be applied to assessing learner preferences:

1. Define the product attributes to be tested. That is, define the critical factors that would be relevant to assessing learning preferences. Usually, that involves conducting a series of interviews with key internal stakeholders and experts in adult-learning principles to

- develop a robust list of consumer-learner decision factors and identify the specific product attributes used by the "buyers" when they choose a learning product. For learning purposes, the attributes might include such items as the subject matter or topic, where the learning takes place, how it's delivered, the time required for completing the learning experience, and so forth.

TIME TO TREAT LEARNERS AS CONSUMERS

- organize and map out key decision factors into independent dimensions or components, which are often referred to as "attributes."
- prioritize by distributing 100 points across those attributes.
- gather precise wording and vocabulary used to describe various differences in service offerings, which are often referred to as "levels."

2. Develop conjoint analysis survey. You do that by entering the information and definitions gathered in step 1 and constructing a set of product attributes and levels to be tested and by

- adding any segmentation questions or opinion questions that may be useful in interpreting the results.
- creating a survey using special computer software and testing it with the subject experts and stakeholders.
- refining and pilot testing the survey.

3. Administer the survey to the target audience. That involves

- using individual disks that contain the interviewing software and questions.
- compiling the surveys and analyzing the results.
- presenting the results to a subset of the respondents to ensure that the results were interpreted appropriately.

4. Document the survey results. You also should share the findings with the program managers. Conjoint analysis can provide data that can be used to identify what the optimal bundle of training looks like from the training customers' perspective: How long should it last? Where should it be done? What medium should be used?

ACA is a statistical technique that measures the utility that customers derive from various product and service features. ACA also provides insight into the tradeoffs that customers make when choosing a product or service.

In the Field

Following is some actual data collected from a group of more than 100 new supervisors asked to provide input on how they would most prefer to learn job-relevant information and skills for their new roles.

In this situation, the learning experience was deconstructed into five actionable attributes. Each attribute had a number of levels (or options) that were combined to create potential product combinations or learning offerings. Respondents were presented with 13 pairs of hypothetical product bundles and asked to indicate their preferences.

By repeating that process, it's possible to quantify which features a respondent likes and dislikes. It's also possible to determine the strength of someone's preferences. The result is a thorough mapping of a decision

	Attribute	**Levels**
Subject Area	• Problem solving • HR policy • Interpersonal skills	• Effective leadership • Corporate culture • Admin., forms, and info
Where Learning Can Be Accessed	• Home • Office	• Corporate training center
Medium	• Paper-based • Computer-based • Face-to-face	• Group interaction • Audio/visual tapes
Learning Method	• Simulation • Role play • Exercises • Self-assessment	• Case studies • Hear experienced managers • Traditional classroom
Time Required to Complete	• 1 hour • 2 hours • half-day • 8 hours over 3 months	• 16 hours over 3 months • 1 whole day • 2 whole days • 5 whole days

Figure 1. **Learning attributes and levels: first-line supervisors**

maker's utility or usefulness of each product attribute. The assumption is that utility values are additive. Therefore, it's possible to examine attribute tradeoffs and identify the impact on total package utility.

The results provide a quantitative basis for strategic product or, in this case, training decisions around the desired features and needs of targeted markets. Which target segments value which product bundles the most? The conjoint analysis can be used to examine the tradeoffs made by learners with respect to important dimensions identified by the management development team.

For example, the box shows the various attributes and respective levels used with these first-line supervisors to assess their learning preferences.

Conjoint analysis will also provide information about the relative importance of the attributes to learners. As shown in the bar graphs, for these supervisors the research identified that the learning medium and the subject area were most important. It also identified that the method used and the time required to complete the training were relatively less important.

Conjoint analysis can also permit a tradeoff analysis that will indicate that learners would be willing to study a certain subject area under certain conditions but not under others. An example of that is illustrated in Figure 3. These learners seem to value—that is, they are more interested in—studying effective leadership rather than administrative forms. Furthermore, when compared without reference to subject area, they also seem more interested in acquiring information in a learning center than in a home environment.

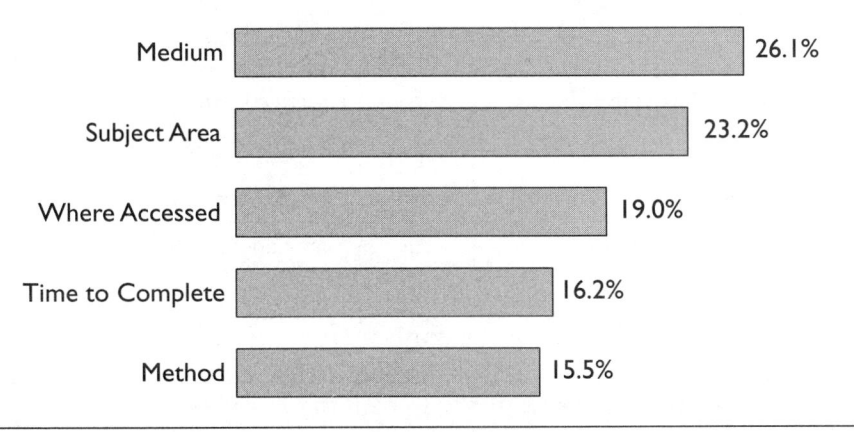

Figure 2. Relative importance of each attribute

Attribute	
Medium	26.1%
Subject Area	23.2%
Where Accessed	19.0%
Time to Complete	16.2%
Method	15.5%

Attribute	Levels	Utility Points	Delta
Subject Area	Effective Leadership Adminstrative Forums	38 5	+33 points
Where Learning Can Be Accessed	Learning Center Home	36 9	-25 points

Figure 3. **Example of one possible tradeoff**

The value of this type of analysis is that it offers the opportunity to combine attributes to create "most-preferred" or "desirable" learning scenarios, taking into account a number of tradeoffs that learners might be willing to make.

The example in the Figure 3 suggests that learners, given the choice, would more likely prefer studying effective leadership at home (note the additive utility points value of 38 + 9 or 47) more than learning administrative forms in a learning center (with an additive utility points value of only 36 + 5 or 41). The concept of utility points being additive makes it possible to see that some topics can be learned individually at home, while others would be more desirably taught in a group setting at a learning center.

Conjoint analysis also lets managers estimate how attractive various possible program structures would be to their staff. That can be done by combining various attribute levels into bundles and then summing the utility points to estimate which bundles would be more attractive.

The example in Figure 4 shows that from a product-offering preference perspective, conjoint analysis indicates that learners would derive more value (and thus be more interested in) training program bundle B than training program bundle A. Learners would see almost six times more value in

Attribute	Bundle A	Utility Points	Bundle B	Utility Points
Subject	Administrative Forms	5	Effective Leadership	38
Where	Home	9	Learning Center	36
Medium	Paper-based	9	Group Interaction	46
Method	Self-assessment	5	Experienced Manager	27
Time	1 hour	2	2 days	25
Total		30		172

Figure 4. **Utility points for two possible training bundles**

bundle B (172 utility points) than in bundle A (30 utility points).

In addition, it's important to ask traditional attitudinal and behavioral descriptor questions about the way people like to learn, the amount of time they spend in formal and informal training, and so forth. Last, demographic information is collected regarding their jobs, geographic locale, length of service, and so on to permit various cuts of the data in the analysis. Based on that information, you can create a paired comparison questionnaire and deliver it electronically to assess the overall preferences of a representative sample of learners.

So, a widely used market research tool can be helpful in the design and development of learning experiences. The ACA methodology enables a better understanding of just what learners would be willing to trade off for an optimal learning experience. It also provides a comparison of various learner program configurations and which ones learners prefer most.

What conjoint results are able to show is that learners have distinct preferences for what subjects they want to learn, how they want to learn, in what timeframe, and under what conditions.

A potential limitation to this approach, as might be expected, is the fact that in the absence of real long-term experience with certain types of learning experiences, most people would find it difficult to judge the actual value of a particular learning experience accurately. That is, it would be difficult to assess their preference for something they haven't truly experienced. Put another way, people don't know what they don't know. At best, they can only guess what that experience might feel like. As such, some conjoint results must be taken with a grain of salt until learners have had the experience.

On the other hand, this approach does offer the opportunity to assess exactly what the factors are that might prevent someone from evaluating a yet-to-be-experienced learning event accurately.

The value in treating learners as consumers by applying a technique used in consumer research is that it can offer valuable insight on configuring the most appropriate learning experiences for learners. If you believe that learners do indeed have points of view, then it would be prudent to conduct this or similar analyses if you want to know the best way to attract people to your training and learning experiences. Indeed, this type of information is invaluable for charting the learning strategies that an organization takes on to meet its performance improvement agenda.

Stephen L. Cohen is managing director of the Learning Solutions Group of Dove Consulting (www.consultdove.com), an international strategy and organizational effectiveness consulting firm; scohen@consultdove.com.

David W. Dove is chairman, CEO, and founder of Dove Consulting; ddove@consultdove.com.

Edward L. Bachelder is director of research for Dove Consulting; ebachelder@consultdove.com.

The Lighter Side of Learning

Kathleen McLaughlin

Training is a serious matter, but that doesn't mean that the training itself should always be serious. In fact, sometimes the more serious the situation, the more humor can help. This article reports on ways in which trainers are using humor to diffuse stress, stimulate creativity, and increase the impact of their intervention.

Stop me if you've heard this one. You know, the one about the trainer who uses humor to deliver serious messages about corporate downsizing and workplace diversity? If you haven't, you're overlooking a unique way of addressing sensitive issues without the requisite yawns, glazed eyes or even tears.

When Westinghouse terminated its super collider project two years ago, for instance, Ann Cox was brought in to help the company's stunned employees cope. Her method: improvisation and sketch comedy. "I walked in and told the group I was there to make them laugh and see the lighter side of the situation," says Cox, dean of fun at Humor University, an Austin, Texas-based provider of corporate "humor training."

"The attendees responded that they would rather laugh than cry," Cox continues, "And from there I built a rapport with them. Through the use of improvisational comedy, I helped them with the stress management relative to change and unpredictability."

Even getting fired can be treated with humor—once the initial trauma subsides, says Rebecca Rucker, a senior career specialist for CareerWorks, an Austin, Texas-based career development company. A humorous training session can provide new perspectives on the job loss and the corresponding job search, she explains.

"People are usually in shock and can't absorb what's being thrown at them. Humor is a way to let go of the feelings and psychological blocks created when they received the sudden news. Laughing allows people to start fresh and be more receptive to positive messages," Rucker says.

But training professionals like Cox and Rucker are not simply stringing a

Reprinted with permission from *TRAINING* Magazine, February 2001. Copyright © 2001 Bill Communications. All rights reserved.

series of one-liners together. In addition to keeping their audiences laughing, they're also using humor to help employees step into key problem-solving roles.

Engage Me

Have you ever wondered why hotel meeting-room lecterns always feature the name of the hotel? Those brass-plated signs are actually there so audiences will know where they are when they wake up, according to Humor University's Dean of Humor Terrill Fischer. He's joking, of course, but his message is clear: Training must be engaging to keep people interested and receptive.

> People's attention spans are shorter than they used to be, and humor is a way to keep them involved.

"People's attention spans are shorter than they used to be, and humor is a way to keep them involved," says Fischer. And while he acknowledges that interactivity can be created without humor, he believes that ultimately, "people learn better when they laugh."

And Fischer doesn't reserve the use of humor for stress management training and motivational speeches—improvisation also works well with more challenging topics such as downsizing and diversity, he says.

One of Fischer's techniques involves a game called Punch Line. Groups of participants are assigned an embarrassing or uncomfortable situation—related to the issue at hand—around which they must create a dialog. "Attendees find that by using humor in a nontraditional way they can work through awkward situations," Fischer says. When the situation calls for someone to be laid off, for instance, the group comes up with funny one-liners for the manager who must deliver the bad news.

Humor allows people to make mistakes and say the wrong thing, says David Granirer, president of Psychocomic.com, a Vancouver, British Columbia-based training firm that specializes in delivering humorous training programs. People inwardly groan at the mere mention of diversity and sensitivity programs, says Granirer. "They prepare themselves to be bored."

"Historically there have been bad diversity sessions in which trainers have crossed the line from training to therapy," Granirer continues. "Having people sit in a circle and talk about painful incidents on discrimination isn't an effective way to create a positive sense of diversity."

Rather than delivering the typical heavy presentation, Granirer thinks it's healthier to joke about diversity. He ends each session with an interactive game called One Word At A Time. The object of the game is to tell a story—you guessed it—one word at a time.

First, Granirer writes a sentence on an overhead projector: "What we will do differently is ... " The audience must complete the sentence—one word at a time. "The point isn't whether or not they come up with anything intelligent," Granirer says. "They've been placed in a group of relative strangers who have worked together and put aside differences to complete a task. Through cooperation and trust—the essence of diversity training—the objective is met."

Granirer recently presented the program to the Vancouver Crisis Centre, a volunteer-run crisis call center. "Volunteers must be sensitive and communicate effectively with people who have mental illness, live in severe poverty or are new to the community," says Robbin Jeffereys, Centre Program Director of Training and Operations, Distress Line. To provide volunteers with a clear definition of diversity, Granirer used historical Canadian events to show unfair treatment.

"We then looked at specific issues such as homophobia, racism and all the other -isms," says Jeffereys. "We focused on how to show empathy for someone in a situation that is different from your own."

Jeffereys is a true believer in the power of humor in diversity training. "It changes the energy in the room, keeps people interested, and helps them deal with heavy subjects," she says. "If we were ponderous about diversity, it would become too heavy and bog everyone down. In this situation, humor helps defuse the stress of the situation."

Teach Me

When employees are gently nudged or told outright to attend a leadership development or effective communication training session, they immediately think they are poor communicators or leaders, and the defensive wall soars, says Molly Cox of Out of the Blue, an Eagan, Minn., company that develops and delivers humorous training programs. "Humor loosens up people and gives them a greater perspective on themselves," adds her business partner, Mark Bergren.

Cox and Bergren were recently charged with helping engineers at 3M, St. Paul, Minn., better communicate with the rest of the company. "The goal of the training was to show that people should be seen as diverse individuals instead of collective groups, for example, engineers versus nonengineers," says Julie Coe, in charge of leadership development at 3M.

Engineers can be a fairly stodgy group, Coe continues. "They will roll their eyes and clearly show that they don't want to be there the minute a training professional enters the room. That's why it was so important to bill this session as fun and humorous, yet educational."

The program began with a parody of the blockbuster movie *Titanic*. Rose, the main character, held onto the bow of the ship and peered past the audience in the auditorium, claiming that she could see 3M buildings 275 and 224. The whole idea was that there's this great big world out there," says Coe. "Messages were subtle yet made a point in a humorous way." Another exercise required that the attendees split into groups, create a new product, name

Hospital Catches "FISH" Fever

A staff that laughs together works well together. And in the usually chaotic setting of a hospital, teamwork is particularly critical. So when Shari Bommarito, registered nurse and clinical education specialist, joined the neuro-renal floor at Missouri Baptist Medical Center in September of 1999, she immediately asked her co-workers how they would rate their team-building skills. She was alarmed by the survey results: The staff gave itself poor ratings for attitude, communication, mutual support and overall teamwork.

To give the team's morale a boost, Bommarito looked to the team building program called FISH. Created by ChartHouse Learning, a Burnsville, Minn., training firm, it is an entertaining yet enlightening video series that chronicles how a few fishmongers transformed a failing business into the world famous Pike Place Fish Market. The market is now a must-see Seattle tourist attraction. The FISH philosophy is based on four key principles:

PLAY. Encourages workers to have fun and be spontaneous.
MAKE THEIR DAY. Suggests doing something that will lift someone else's spirit.
BE THERE. Focuses on the person or task in which you are engaged.
CHOOSE YOUR ATTITUDE. Empowers people to look for the best and discover incredible possibilities.

When Bommarito introduced the FISH philosophy to her colleagues, the response was better than she had hoped. "And I have become their greatest cheerleader," says Bommarito. "Everyone in our unit wears a plastic fish on his or her badge. When we see something special or someone makes our day, we give them our fish. Patients, doctors and staff from elsewhere in the hospital are catching FISH fever and proudly wearing the fish that were given to them."

For more than a year, the Missouri Baptist Medical Center neuro-renal unit has been cultivating a FISH environment. The result is enhanced communication among team members, as evidenced by a big jump in the number of positive comments when Bommarito repeated her original team building survey eight months into the program (see sidebar, "Morale Off the Scale.") An even greater benefit is reduced turnover among staff.

"Sure, our floor has attrition; that's natural. But we have literally no turnover in a very high turnover industry," Bommarito says. "When people have fun in their jobs, they are motivated to do their best. We all have the power to choose our attitude and make a difference. Sometimes we just need to know its OK to do so!"

Reason enough for catching FISH fever.

MORALE OFF THE SCALE

Satisfaction ratings on these workplace characteristics soared for employees at the Missouri Baptist Medical Center after only eight months on the FISH program.

	Before FISH 1999	After FISH 2000
Teamwork	30%	75%
Positive team attitude	25%	75%
Communication among team members	33%	65%
Support for team members	25%	75%
Satisfaction working with the team	25%	75%
Have a say within the team	15%	65%

it, and write a jingle to present to the other groups ... all in 15 minutes.

Coe believes the training would have had a lot less impact without humor. "It was an effective way to engage the audience and deliver key messages," she says.

According to these proponents of learning through humor, almost any training situation can come alive with comedy—providing the appropriate comedy is used. After all, there is little more compelling than laughter.

Kathleen McLaughlin is features editor of Training. *Contact her at edit@trainingmag.com.*

Make New Employee Orientation a Success

Jean Barbazette

One of the key training sessions in any organization is employee orientation. Sometimes we don't think of that as training, but it is and it is an important intervention. How can an organization make sure that orientation results in an employee who adapts and begins performing well immediately? This article, by the author of Successful New Employee Orientation: Assess, Plan, Conduct, and Evaluate Your Program, *outlines 12 key factors derived from surveys that her company has conducted.*

New employee orientation is a planned welcome to the organization that usually is shared by the human resources (or training) department and the new employee's supervisor. There are 12 key factors that can contribute to the successful orientation of new employees.

The Training Clinic of Seal Beach, California, surveyed over 300 United States companies (in 1985, 1988 and 1990, 1993) that were conducting successful orientation programs. Here are the 12 factors.

1. **All effective programs view orientation as an ongoing process, not just a one-day program.** The process usually begins with the hiring decision and continues well into the first year of employment. New employee orientation (NEO) becomes the umbrella program for other programs that include performance reviews and training.

2. **Because orientation is an ongoing process, information is given to the new employee closest to the time it is needed.** For example, if the employee's health benefits vest 30 days from the start date, a benefits orientation is not needed during the first day or first week of employment. Many companies separated benefits from other orientation information. A separate meeting, if held in the evening, allows spouses to attend and participate in the selection of a specific health plan.

3. **The benefits of orientation are clear and visible to both the new employee and the organization.** The organization could identify such factors as

Reprinted with permission from *The Training Clinic*, 2001. Copyright © 2001 by The Training Clinic. All rights reserved.

reduced turnover or improved productivity as a few of the benefits of a systematic orientation. The employee felt valued and was able to "fit into" the new job more easily and quickly. Fewer mistakes were made by the new employee who was more relaxed.

4. **Successful orientation programs shared their "corporate culture" (philosophy, how to get along, how business is done, etc.).** New employees need to be told the organization's norms, customs and traditions. If a new employee knows informality is expected, then having coffee at your desk or leaving work out on your desk overnight is acceptable. However, if rules are strictly enforced, the new employee must know to follow the unwritten dress code and carefully adhere to accepted break and lunch times.

In some organizations all employees are addressed by their first names. In other organizations a strong sense of formality would demand using only surnames. Shared expectations and common definitions of "what's normal" can contribute greatly to the successful orientation process.

5. **The employee's first day is truly welcoming and helps the employee feel useful and productive.** This can be accomplished by being prepared for a new employee; desk, office, phone, and supplies are ready. How many times have new employees arrived at your organization and everyone is too busy to direct their activities or teach them the job? Several successful organizations set up a welcome, introductions and a tour that ends in the new employee's work area. The new employee is then paired with an experienced "buddy" to teach a specific task. This way a new employee can perform a simple task that contributes to the department's production on the first day of employment.

6. **The supervisor's role in NEO is clear and well executed with human resources department's or function's assistance.** Supervisors and the human resources department or function share responsibility for the successful orientation of the new employee. Supervisors need to identify what is best done by them and what information is more general and best given by the human resources department or function. The human resources department or function is usually best equipped to share organization policy, history and benefits. Supervisors usually prefer to explain safety rules, reporting requirements and job tasks. The division of tasks must be negotiated between supervisors and the human resources department or function if tasks are to be successfully shared.

7. **Orientation objectives in successful organizations are measurable and focus on specific knowledge, skill acquisition and influencing attitudes.** Too often poor orientation programs are an information overload—like drinking from a fire hydrant! Those programs that included some skills training (operating the telephone system or practice in using a fire extinguisher) found a balance of activity and pacing that made orientation interesting, not boring.

MAKE NEW EMPLOYEE ORIENTATION A SUCCESS

8. **Adult learning concepts are known and used to guide orientation.** If an organization wants its employees to use their initiative and exercise judgment, then a self-directed NEO is appropriate. Several successful NEO programs gave the new employee a list of tasks to accomplish, a deadline and the time and resources to complete the tasks. For example, a manufacturing organization gives the new hourly employee a checklist to be completed in five days. Items on the checklist include finding bulletin boards, safety and first aid supplies, and signing completed forms. Another organization gives its new middle managers and staff people a list of key co-workers to interview. A self-directed workbook suggests questions for the interviews. Sample questions are: 1) What do you expect from me when we work together? 2) What are your job and task goals and how do they affect me?

Many unsuccessful NEOs "spoon feed" all information to the new employee. This process often gives the impression to the employee that the organization will tell you everything you need to know ... just wait for it to come to you. If you want new employees to work independently, at least part of their orientation should be his or her responsibility.

> If you want new employees to work independently, at least part of their orientation should be his or her responsibility.

9. **Many NEO programs use guest speakers (live or on videotape).** Successful speakers are well prepared, present only essential information with specific objectives, and use good presentation techniques. The human resources department or function had frequently coached all speakers and even outlined or scripted their talks and provided professional looking visual aids. Guest speakers fail to meet their goals when they are ill prepared, ramble off their subject, or do not arrive on time (or not show up at all).

10. **Audiovisual components of successful NEO programs provide emphasis to the program and provide a positive message.** Frequently successful videos or slide tape presentations were used to describe the organization's culture, history and philosophy. Although the temptation is to put as much as you can on video, the content needs to be lasting. For example, benefits are best presented "live" if they are likely to change each year. The organization's history is not likely to change, but give the current executive group in written form on an organization chart. Guest speakers who deliver a consistent message and find attending every session of NEO are also good candidates for video.

11. **The NEO process is evaluated by participants, supervisors and the human resources department or function from bottom-line results.** Participants can give their reaction to NEO and offer suggestions to improve the process and validate the timing of content delivery. Supervisors can tell you if NEO information is used on the job and to what degree NEO needs revision. NEO should also be evaluated for results. A manufacturing organization was able to reduce turnover by 69% in the first three years by conducting a systematic NEO; a bank was able to reduce orientation and skills training of new tellers from six weeks to two weeks. Cost-benefit analysis is not easy to conduct, but worth doing to prove your results.

12. **Successful NEO programs provide information to the employee's family.** This included welcoming gestures and letters or organization newsletters to the family or a more inclusive program for spouses and families. Many companies welcomed families at work one day during the year. Others scheduled a benefits orientation during the evening. One unique approach involved a home visit by the corporate "welcome wagon."

These 12 elements suggest that NEO is a process that needs to be refined and customized for each organization. These 12 elements also need to be modified based on when orientation is first conducted and how many new employees are hired at one time.

Jean Barbazette is President of The Training Clinic in Seal Beach, CA, a training consulting firm she founded in 1977 (www.thetrainingclinic.com), and author of Successful New Employee Orientation *(Pfeiffer & Co., 1994; Jossey-Bass, 2001). Contact her at info@thetrainingclinic.com.*

True Confessions: Adventures in Training

Dave Zielinski

A lot of trainers have to make the transition from traditional classroom training to e-learning and all that encompasses. It's useful to know what others have done. Here are the stories of four training professionals who've succeeded in making that transition from traditional to virtual, with lessons learned from their trials and tribulations. Whether you're already an e-training expert or a novice or even still in the classroom, their stories should interest you.

As more and more training professionals move into cyber-training, they're finding they can take their classroom expertise with them, and flourish. Many not only survive the tsunami, but emerge with new titles, marketable skills, fresh perspectives on their chosen field and confidence in their ability to manage change.

And while there are many challenges, and even the occasional career casualty, the majority of training professionals overcome these obstacles successfully. The success stories profiled here offer insight into this career migration and a little advice for others on the cusp of such a leap.

The Invisible Trainer

John Geissler
Training Project Manager
OutlookSoft
Stamford, CT

Virtual instructors sometimes miss the richness of face-to-face interaction—the looks on students' faces after an "aha" moment, the compelling story enthusiastically received or the rush of shared debate and discovery.

But John Geissler, a 15-year veteran of classroom training, rarely gets sentimental about his past training life. At OutlookSoft—a seller of software for Web-based budgeting and performance analysis—he successfully conducts nearly all of his training online. He delivers synchronous Web-based training sessions to employees, clients and partners logging in from computers around the world.

Reprinted with permission from *TRAINING* Magazine, March 2001. Copyright © 2001 Bill Communications. All rights reserved.

Geissler uses Centra Software to teach those groups the ins and outs of his company's software products. Trainees log onto a Web site, where they hear streaming audio of Geissler walking them through Microsoft PowerPoint slides and observe demonstrations of software applications. This low-bandwidth delivery vehicle allows participants to "raise their hands" and pose questions via two-way voice-over IP.

Of course, Webconferencing saves travel dollars and reduces trainee time away from jobs. But for Geissler, it's also a reprieve from the wear and tear on trainers' bodies and a more concentrated use of time. "It's easy to be on your feet for six hours a day in a classroom environment, but now, sitting in front of a computer console, I can teach in about two hours something that might have taken six hours in the classroom," Geissler says.

In a physical classroom, it's common for students' 10-minute breaks to drift into 20 minutes, and for lunch hours to expand to 90 minutes. That time isn't lost in a virtual classroom, which features more tightly paced and closely scripted sessions, he says. Consequently, these shorter sessions ease the issue of trainee attention span.

However, there are trade-offs and significant adjustments with this new delivery medium, Geissler concedes. "The strangest thing is not being able to see students' faces or get visual cues."

Surprisingly, Webconferencing also can require more concentrated lung power from instructors than the classroom. Geissler likens it to being a radio talk show host with visuals. "Initially, it was hard for me to talk for two hours nonstop," he explains. "In these sessions there are few breaks and you really have to be 'on' all the time."

> Inflection and tone become even more important in a cyber-setting, where flat delivery can be tantamount to handing out sleeping aids.

Inflection and tone become even more important in a cyber-setting, where flat delivery can be tantamount to handing out sleeping aids. To keep trainees' attention, many organizations encourage their virtual instructors to go no longer than five or 10 minutes without a screen break or some form of interaction.

For Geissler, this means planning coursework and timing accordingly.

"Most of my development time goes into choreographing the entire event, figuring out in detail what's the best time to jump into application sharing, where quizzes should come in, and at what points I can make best use of interactive tools."

A Techno-Skeptic Converts

Dove Ferguson
Sales Training Project Manager
GE Global Exchange Services
Gaithersburg, MD

After 30 years as a training professional and performance technologist, Dave

Ferguson has seen plenty of new technology-delivered learning vehicles come down the pike, only to be marginalized by new innovations or misguided uses.

"I remember going to conferences when everyone had some form of black box between their PCs and monitors that LP-sized laser discs would run on, and that was the wave of the future," says Ferguson. "Now you couldn't find a training laser disc if you posted a $10,000 reward."

Given the skepticism, it's a bit surprising to find Ferguson designing technology-based training and information-sharing initiatives. But the self-proclaimed "techno-skeptic" discovered that e-learning vehicles not only reduce trainee travel costs and save time, they also create some extremely effective learning outcomes, too.

Ferguson's division was among the first in the General Electric empire to launch intranet-based product training that incorporates streaming audio and some video. His sales training group adopted these tools to deliver basic product training and update information to the GE salesforce—one that can ill afford time away from jobs for basic or prerequisite training.

In its first use of Web technology, Ferguson's group collaborated with sales managers to create a series of informational "Product 101" pages on the corporate intranet. Designed as short overviews, the pages familiarize salespeople with key selling features, pricing structures, targeted prospects, and a competitive landscape of the products to be sold.

In another application, Ferguson worked with an external Web design firm to build interactive training that uses Macromedia Flash software to help teach a sales process to new employees with the aid of audio and animation. Quizzes or "self-checks" are included to test comprehension and provide specific feedback.

Like many traditional instructional designers who experiment with new mediums, Ferguson's initial learning curve was steep. "I heard someone at a conference say that good judgment comes from experience, and experience comes from bad judgment," Ferguson says. "We've learned plenty about how to design, update and manage online content through our own experimentation and work with external vendors."

Although the department's Web authoring tools of choice are now Macromedia's Coursebuilder and Dreamweaver, Ferguson believed it was necessary for him to learn HTML, using a well-known tutorial from the Maricopa Center for Learning and Instruction. "I need to learn things from scratch, and I didn't want an authoring tool doing something for me until I fully understood its underpinnings," Ferguson says.

While he has no need or desire to become an expert in Web-authoring software, Ferguson does recognize the value of a designer who can credibly "talk the talk" with members of project design teams.

The viability of the Web or intranets as instructional tools rests in part on making clear distinctions between skills training and information sharing, Ferguson says. The goal shouldn't be to make the most extensive use of technology-delivered instruction, but to make good decisions about how to train or inform employees effectively in varying circumstances.

"When you slap hyperlinked text up on the Web, you don't automatically have training, you have reference material, informational updates or 'brochureware,'" he says. "That's OK for the purposes of disseminating information; just don't call it skills training."

Mixing It Up

Alicia Brown
National Director for Clinical Support
Sunbridge Healthcare Corp.
Albuquerque, NM

For many training professionals, the prospect of hitting the road holds a certain allure. Teaching in new locales promises new faces, new cities and the suggestion of a jet-setter's life. But veteran road warriors know it doesn't take long to get too much of a good thing.

Alicia Brown is among the new virtual instructors who embrace the travel-saving benefits of cyber-training. When her employer, Sunbridge Healthcare Corp., moved to videoconferencing, it proved to be something of a lifesaver. "I thought I'd love the traveling aspect of training, until traveling was all I did for most of three years," says Brown, director of clinical support. Now she is able to reduce what had become a daunting travel schedule, as well as master distance-learning technology.

Brown delivers training via videoconferencing systems about six times a week for Sunbridge—a subsidiary of Sun Healthcare Group International. She teaches both basic nursing skills and regulatory issues to some 300 employees around the country.

In one of Brown's typical 90-minute distance training sessions, up to 12 separate Sun facilities might take part in the videoconference. Sun uses InView Worldwide's bridging services to reach an average of two to four trainees or more at each site. To help enhance the effectiveness of each program, Brown sends copies of the presentations to each trainee before the videoconferences. She then uses a remote control fish-eye camera to zoom and auto-focus on visuals such as Microsoft PowerPoint slides and illustrations, as well as her own image.

Brown first received technology training from an internal technical support group as well as InView. And naturally, she continued to "learn lessons" from the earlier distance training sessions she conducted. Initially, for instance, she found that she kept her camera focused too long on supporting visuals. She hadn't fully grasped that distance learners need visual variety to stay engaged, as well as the humanizing touch of the instructor's image.

"If you don't mix things up after awhile, trainees will think you're not live, but on tape," she says. "So I project a different screen image at least every 10 or 15 minutes."

Then there's technology troubleshooting. Although Brown can phone internal technical support for help, there are some glitches an enterprising virtual instructor must learn to handle. "When I boot up my computer an hour before a session and there's a problem, or there are problems with ISDN lines connecting, no one's going to come running on-site to help me," she says.

Even more challenging for a virtual instructor is the choreography of sessions to ensure remote trainees stay engaged and interested. "I try to make all of my sessions interesting and humorous, but it's still difficult for participants not to feel simply 'talked to' because you can't create the same level of interactivity," Brown says. "But they still learn as well as in most comparable classroom settings according to our post-course evaluations."

To help her keep tabs on required interactivity levels, Brown recently acquired an auto scan feature, which allows her to simultaneously project the image of participants from six sites onto half her local screen (the other half shows her presentation). As the six sites pop up at different intervals, it helps her keep tabs on trainee reaction to, and comprehension of, content.

Still, Brown likes to combine her online instruction with occasional field training. "The job does become more alive and invigorating for me when I go out and train in person," she says. "You also get a better flavor of how a session is received when you're face to face. For me, it would be hard to be completely isolated and not get some chance to have that face-to-face experience."

Exiting Center Stage

Doug Young
Online Facilitator and Instructional Designer
Walden Institute
Bonita Springs, FL

Doug Young knew he'd face adjustments in the leap from classroom trainer to facilitator of Web-delivered courses. He understood that the computer keyboard would become his new "eyes and ears," and that the physical separation from students would, in the end, create certain instructional design challenges.

Online facilitators, while no less important to the learning process, operate far more in the shadows, necessarily assuming a hidden, backstage role to guide and nudge distance learners. Knowing that, Young was still surprised at how much he initially missed the "showmanship" role of the stand-up classroom environment.

"Distance learning can be tough at first, particularly when you see firsthand how that element of your personality no longer can carry you in the online world," says Young, who conducted classroom training for 20-plus years at the Federal Law Enforcement Training Center, Glynco, Ga., and later with the U.S. Department of Energy, Albuquerque, N.M. Now, he's a part-time online facilitator and instructional designer at Florida's Walden Institute, a "training the trainer" organization that teaches online instruction skills to training professionals and college faculty.

Although most students who enroll at Walden adapt well to the online teaching environment, some who previously thrived in classroom settings discover that they aren't yet prepared to give up that important part of their professional identity. "I had one person take an online instruction course from me, and he said that his key learning from the class was that he really didn't want to teach online," Young explains.

Those who stay with online facilitation often experience rewards in other ways. " Today I see my job as finding as many varied ways as possible to get students to interact more with each other and the content, and less with me," says Young. "In this medium, students should be more engaged by the quality of the content than by the personality of the instructor. Once I realized I was no longer the center of attention, I started seeking new ways to build that interaction, which usually resulted in a better learning experience for students."

Those new to facilitating online courses tend to be taken by surprise by workload issues, Young says of Walden enrollees. The time required to guide or monitor threaded discussions, post classwork summaries, answer e-mail questions, operate "virtual" office hours, grade final projects and troubleshoot technology can be demanding.

Consequently, Young gives fair warning on workload issues to his virtual instructors-in-training at Walden. As always, time invested on the front end is a function of the kind of learning experience the instructors want students to have. Young counsels eager new online instructors that it's important to pace themselves. Regardless of delivery format, he urges, "managing student expectations is still the key."

Dave Zielinski is a Minneapolis freelance writer. He is the editor of several books on training and e-learning, including The Best of Creative Training Techniques *(Lakewood Publications, 1996) and* Lessons Learned in Online Learning *(Lakewood Books, 1999). You can reach him at zskidoo@aol.com.*

Designing a Buddy Program

J. Leslie McKeown

Part of an employee orientation program or when giving employees new responsibility can be a buddy program, an effective way to transfer skills and knowledge. This original article explains how to set up such a program, including aims and objectives, how to pair up someone with a buddy, and more. It even includes a followup questionnaire to evaluate the program.

Orientation and retention are all about making your new employees feel at home. Along the way, that also means helping them understand your organizational culture and politics. A buddy program is a great tool to assist in both of these objectives.

It's tough being a new employee. You're not too sure what lies behind each door, there are enough acronyms and buzzwords to fill a book, and somebody keeps moving the photocopier!

These concerns pale into insignificance, however, compared with the sheer confusion of not knowing what's "normal" in the organization—what's "right" and "wrong" here—what's expected of me—what's the company's culture?

Not knowing the answer to these and similar questions makes every new employee feel like an "outsider"—at least for a while. Consequently, the typical new employee is less confident and somewhat insecure when it comes to relating with their colleagues—senior, peer or junior. Not knowing what's "right," or what's "accepted" here, can make the new employee hesitant, and confused in interpreting the responses of others.

A buddy program is a great way to accelerate the new employees ability to deal with these early disconcerting issues. By matching your new employees with a "buddy"—someone who has been in the organization for a while—you will not only assist in cultural integration and orientation. Done properly, your managers and supervisors will find that their interaction with new employees is much less about low level, operational issues, and much more about adding value.

What's the difference between a buddy, coach and mentor?

Reprinted with permission from the author. Copyright © 2001 J. Leslie McKeown. All rights reserved.

- A *mentoring program* seeks to assist the individual with his or her development, both personally and professionally;
- A *coaching program* seeks to increase the individual's job-related skills;
- A *buddy program* is solely involved with providing a one—point access to operationally necessary information. In essence, *the development of the individual* is not an expected output.

What should the structure of a buddy program be? We've designed the rest of this brief white paper as a briefing document that you might provide to prospective buddies. By using this method, you can see how the structure of a buddy program works.

Please note: the outline that follows is generic, and indicative only. The specific circumstances of your company may dictate a very different approach.

The Buddy Program: Buddy Briefing Document

1. Overview

[Company] has decided to implement a Buddy Program to assist new employees in the early months of their employment with us.

This document is primarily designed to brief those who will be the new employees' Buddies, but it will also help new employees, and the managers of both, understand more fully what the Buddy Program is, and what is expected of each party involved in the buddy relationship.

2. The Orientation Program

The Buddy Program is an integral part of the company's orientation program for new employees. It is strongly recommended that you read this document in that context. Please refer to: [list other materials that are available which will give an understanding of the wider context of the orientation program].

Buddies will be expected to occasionally attend the Company's other orientation activities, including the associated classroom training, to give an overview of the program to new employees. You will be contacted by [coordinator's name] regarding this in due course.

3. Outline of the Buddy Program

The Buddy Program matches new employees with employees who have been with the company for some time (typically 6-12 months), for a period of six months, with two goals:

- To provide the new employee with a point of contact for general queries regarding day-today operational issues, [such as the location of facilities, information processing requirements and relevant company policies] and
- To help the new employee integrate with the company by providing access to someone who is familiar with our culture, attitude and expectations.

The program is coordinated by [name of coordinator], and supported by the line managers.

4. Aims and Objectives
By providing such a relationship, it is intended that:

- The new employee will more quickly feel at home with the company;
- Relatively straightforward queries regarding basic operational issues will be dealt with in a timely and non-bureaucratic manner;
- The initial confusion and uncertainty faced by all new employees will be lessened;
- Other orientation activities, such as classroom and on-the-job training, can be related to actual real-world activities, and resulting basic queries can be resolved;
- Our new employees find out how best to "manage" us, the company, in a supportive and risk-reduced environment;
- Manger/supervisor time with new employees is freed up to deal with added value issues;
- The new employee begins to add value more quickly, leading to increased confidence and self-esteem;
- You, the buddy, are actively involved in make this a better place to work, and our new employees more productive.

5. Selection and Pairing of Buddies
Employees are nominated by departmental managers on the basis of two criteria:

- The employee's interpersonal skills; and
- Their understanding and commitment to the Company's vision and values.

Additionally, at the end of the buddy relationship, you will get the opportunity to nominate as a buddy the new employee with whom you have been working, if you feel he or she fulfills these criteria.

The program coordinator will allocate buddies to new employees. Where at all possible, buddies will be matched with new employees in their own department.

6. Role and Responsibilities of the Buddy
The primary aspects of the buddy's role and responsibilities are detailed in section 4 above.

The role of a buddy must be distinguished from that of a *manager, mentor,* or *coach*:

A *mentor* is someone, typically more experienced, who is involved with the all-round development of an individual in his or her business, personally, or both.

You are *not* being asked to act as your new employee's mentor—you are not responsible for his or her growth or development as an individual, and it is not part of the role of a buddy to take on such a responsibility. You will not be assessed on your success as a buddy by whether or not the new employee you work with develops as an individual during the six-month period.

A *coach* is someone tasked with developing an individual's job-specific skills. You are *not* being asked to act as your new employee's coach. Although your role as buddy may involve explaining some simple job-related issues, or explaining straightforward procedures, it is not your job to replace formal training processes. If you feel your new employee queries are too detailed or specialized for you to answer, direct them to the supervisor or manager.

You are not the new employee's manager or supervisor. Your role as buddy does not mean you will be held responsible for your new employee's *performance*. If queries arise regarding performance, disciplinary or policy matters, you are free to give your *opinion*, and advice on how to approach the matter, you are *not* in a position to adjudicate or resolve the matter. The new employee must be directed to a manager or supervisor for resolution of the relevant issue(s).

7. Meeting Your Buddy

After you have been notified of the name and other relevant information regarding the new employee you will be working with, it is up to you to make contact at the earliest opportunity. This may be on the employee's first day on site, or if he or she is involved in orientation training on day 1, you may wish to arrange to meet him or her for lunch or otherwise on that day.

Content of Meetings and Discussions. Your first meeting with your new employee should be introductory in nature. Give a tour of the department, introduce colleagues and show the new person where he or she will be working. Explain the operation of any equipment or systems needed in order to commence work. Be familiar with the content of the orientation training, so that you do not duplicate any training being provided there.

Explain to the new employee how to contact you during the day, and make it clear that you are available when required, but to use their discretion at all times. Explain that you will be meeting regularly (see below), and that non-urgent issues should be left until those times, but that anything that is materially hindering his or her work or performance can be discussed with you immediately.

Explain the difference between a mentor, coach and manager (see above), and clear any ground rules regarding contact outside working hours (see below). Ask if there are any initial queries or issues, and deal with them. Then leave the new employee to get on with his or her assignment! Remember, your role is to help the new employee get on with the task at hand—not to prevent them from doing so!

Frequency and Timing of Meetings. You should aim to meet regularly for at least 30 minutes, once a week during the first month and at least once a month thereafter. Use this meeting (often best held over lunch or in an informal setting), should to discuss any non-urgent issues the new employee may have.

During the working day, it may be reasonable to expect as many as 4 or 5 brief queries a day from the new employee in the first few days, tapering down to one or two a day thereafter. Although all new employees are different, after 2-3 months, you may hear little or nothing from them on a daily basis. *This is a good sign*. If you are still getting a large number of "urgent" queries after the first month, then the buddy program is not working, and you should speak to the program coordinator.

Within the parameters above, it is expected that you and the new employee meet within working hours (your manager will let you know if you are spending too much time on this). Some buddies and new employees agree to meet on a social basis, outside working hours. This is an entirely discretionary matter between you and the new employee. It is up to you to indicate to the new employee how you feel about being contacted regarding work-related issues outside of working hours.

The company has no policy on this. Many buddies have felt happy with being contacted outside working hours up to 9 p.m. on weeknights, but not on weekends. This is entirely up to you.

8. Expectations of the Relationship

Your relationship with the new employee should be open, confidential, positive and supportive.

Discussions between you and the new employee should be confidential. The company has no interest in knowing the details of any discussions between you and the new employee, and we are not involved in monitoring buddy relationships. We simply ask that you are supportive of the company and your co-workers. We discourage gossip and speculation within a buddy relationship, particularly as many new employees are not in a position to form an opinion on most issues during their early months with us.

9. Available Support

If you are having any trouble with the interpretation of these guidelines, or with any aspect of the buddy relationship, contact [program coordinator], who will be happy to give you guidance.

Making Your Buddy a Buddy

We would like to see the new employee you are working with become a buddy in turn. If you feel this person could fulfill such a role, find time in the last two months of the relationship to share with him or her any tips or techniques you feel would help this individual in performing such a role.

Give this person's name to your manager, and suggest he or she be considered as a buddy.

Termination of the Relationship

The buddy relationship between you and the new employee will be terminated if either six months expires or either party requests it.

The buddy relationship operates under a "no-fault" termination mechanism. This means that if either the buddy or the new employee so requests, the buddy relationship immediately ends. The new employee is assigned to another buddy, and the buddy is assigned to a different new employee.

No reasons will be sought or offered, no discussion will ensue; no blame will be apportioned. Contact the program coordinator if you wish to trigger this process.

Note: many buddies form separate, social relationships with the new employees that continue beyond the formal buddy program. This is entirely a matter for the employees.

Review of the Relationship

At the termination of the relationship, the program coordinator will ask you to fill in a brief questionnaire aimed at improving the Buddy Program. It does not involve the issues discussed between you and the new employee.

Other Topics That May Be Covered in This Document

- Frequently asked questions regarding the Buddy Program
- Questions frequently asked by new employees
- Intranet site address containing discussion group used by buddies

Questionnaire for Use at the Close of the Program

Introduction

Thank you so much for participating in our buddy program I sincerely hope you got a lot out of it personally, and that you will consider acting as a buddy again.

This brief questionnaire is intended solely to help us in the review and redesign of the Buddy Program, in order that it can best meet everyone's needs. The contents of the questionnaire are confidential, and are not used for any other purpose. Please return this questionnaire to   (name) by   (date).

Please indicate which of the following apply, by circling the relevant number:

1 = Strongly disagree; 2 = Disagree; 3 = Neither agree not disagree; 4 =

Agree; 5 = Strongly agree

I was satisfactorily briefed regarding my role as a buddy:
1   2   3   4   5

I was happy with the way in which I was allocated to my buddy:
1   2   3   4   5

My buddy seemed satisfactorily briefed regarding his/her role;
1   2   3   4   5

I was happy with the support provided by the program co-ordinator;
1   2   3   4   5

The frequency of our meetings was adequate;
1   2   3   4   5

The content of our discussions was appropriate;
1   2   3   4   5

The aims and objectives of the buddy relationship, as set out in point 4 of the Buddy Briefing Guide, were met*;
1   2   3   4   5

Note: it may be appropriate to have a separate question for each individual objective if you have multiple objectives.

J. Leslie McKeown is president and CEO of Yellowbrick Training and Consulting. He is author of The Complete Guide to Orientation and Re-Orientation, The Complete Guide to Mentoring and Coaching, The Complete Guide to Retention, Marketing to the Public, *and Yellowbrick's monthly e-mail newsletter,* Deliver the Promise. *His company's Web site may be found at www.deliver-thepromise.com.*

Tactics for the New Guerrilla Trainer

Phil Mershon

Training doesn't always have to be formal. In fact, it doesn't even have to be called training at all, but that doesn't mean someone isn't consciously trying to help employees improve their skills. This article lays out several tactics trainers can adopt to make training a value-added activity outside traditional definitions, even outside e-learning.

This is about going into the jungle, staging the foray, and being victorious. Let's use the example of call centers. Say that you've been brought in as the corporate trainer for a call center in a metropolitan area where such centers proliferate. Typically employing 50 to 500 people, call centers share a certain ambience: Decade-old coffee stains meld into abstract floral decorations on low-pile carpet, the original color of which was probably some mish-mash of pink and gray. The desks are old, wobbly, and shoved together. Each holds a phone and a computer, with the connecting wires dangling in a hopeless jumble.

The scent of perfume and cologne worn by the recruits of the call center army hovers (and smells) like napalm in the morning. The platoons—collections, customer service, technical support, telemarketing—have distinct uniforms just a few seasons out of date but, nevertheless, worn in the service of their company. As you scout the terrain, the impact of your new surroundings hits you like a mortar shell. How will you survive, much less thrive, in a place such as this?

Certainly not all call centers look like the one I just described. But many do, and some are even bleaker.

The employees in those underdeveloped empires often believe they are viewed by management as equivalent to full time employees. In fact, management tends to view those troops more as hired mercenaries, ready to sell out to the highest bidder and as dispensable as a busted headset. Though there is some small validity to both viewpoints, on the whole they are each only an interpretation of one side by the other and as easy to accept as they are wrongheaded.

Reprinted with permission from *Training & Development*, April 2001. Copyright © 2001 by the American Society for Training & Development. All rights reserved.

Both viewpoints are the direct result of an ideology held by the commanders-in-chief that their enterprises are somehow unique. Solutions, processes, and even simple rules that seem commonplace in a real business don't apply here. Or so believe the company architects, who came of age in the industries they now champion.

The CEOs of multinational corporations (through any combination of education, experience, and social heredity) may validate their effectiveness from one industry to the next, but the president of a company whose primary source of revenue comes from call center operations has spent most of his or her working life in that specific industry and would operate about as comfortably elsewhere as a tiger cub in a pool of piranhas. Given the economic volatility of their call center camps, the corporate officers quite naturally take solace in regarding their domains as impenetrable from the forces of progress. Conditions, therefore, almost never improve in any substantive way (other than by unplanned luck), and so employee desertion is the order of the day.

Make no mistake: These corporate leaders aren't stupid. After all, they hired you, didn't they? Besides that, they understand the impact of market forces, have a keen knowledge of what their clients want, and are as cognizant of the impact of employee attrition as the heads of, say, international technology concerns. Their handicap isn't one of intelligence but rather of vision. And the myopia predominates in the struggle to progress beyond the perimeters of things they've tried before. To that end, they would rather repeat a familiar method they know to be a mistake than take a chance on succeeding with something that is unfamiliar.

So, when a bright-eyed trainer like you approaches those leaders with such urgent concepts as return-on-investment, Six Sigma, and e-learning, you are as likely as not met with a patronizing smirk.

"That's all very nice," comes the response. "But at the moment, we have 20 people waiting for you to deliver new hire orientation."

Some trainers learn to accept restricted vision as a condition of continued employment. Others resist. That resistance may be motivated by company loyalty, personal integrity, or a fondness for goodhearted muckraking. Whatever the impetus for their actions, trainers who revolt at finding themselves stagnating in the quagmire of the status quo are in positions somewhat analogous to rebel insurgents in small, beleaguered third-world countries. In fact, those trainers are in the enviable position of being able to liberate the masses of call center employees and managers alike from the bloodless tyranny of boredom and frustration—surely two of the deadliest diseases endemic to an otherwise viable workplace. Though no single training department in and of itself can penetrate the walls of mediocrity, guerrilla training—using calculated, provocative attack-and-withdrawal techniques—can open minds to unimagined possibilities.

Here then (with perhaps fewer battlefield metaphors) are the requirements of a successful guerrilla training campaign in almost any industry:

Recognize that you are one of the best things that ever happened to your company. Your predecessor in all likelihood became a trainer based on experience in the specific industry rather than on experience in the training arena. That person no doubt spent the better part of the work day (except every other Wednesday, invariably missed due to court appearances for wrongful dismissals and similar claims) mindlessly reciting unrelated job skills and came to life only when sharing personal experiences that had nothing to do with work.

You, on the other hand, are a professional trainer. You have ideas. You have hopes and enthusiasm. You understand the solid as well as intangible values of your role. You have vision. You can see for miles. Once you understand those differences, make sure everyone else in your company understands them.

Become as knowledgeable about your industry as anyone alive. Being an outsider to this "unique" enterprise, you have zero credibility. The fact that you have this job is seen by many as proof that the company will hire anyone. People in your office are already placing bets on how long you'll last before something scares you off.

Don't let anything scare you off. Between classes, sneak out of the training room, walk out onto the call center (or shop) floor (or wherever) as if you own the place. Even take some calls. Interrupt people to ask about the differences between what you teach and what happens in the real world. Read books and magazine articles about your industry, and e-mail your reactions to people in operations and HR. During training downtime, sit with managers and find out how they do their jobs.

Reach out to the best people in the company, and remember that *best* doesn't necessarily refer to those with the most visibility. *Best* in this sense means intelligent, creative, daring people who are also borderline malcontents. These folks will rarely if ever be in HR or on Executive Row. You're more likely to find them occupying positions of frontline managers, who are frustrated about how good things could be if only staff were more competent. You'll also find them in information services, where they really do know how much better things could be.

Both groups are unwitting allies. Their skills are essential, they aren't easily replaceable, and their good opinions of you are vital to your political acceptance, which means the acceptance of your ideas. Invest time with those people. Give them hope.

Train as if your life depended on it. If you're training new employees, they must emerge from your programs with more than combat readiness and an arsenal of job-related skills. They must attack their new jobs with an enthusiasm that shakes the comfort zones of the veterans.

The challenge for you will be that in a call center (or similar) environment, many new employees have been recycled from alike positions with competitors. Novices will cling to your every word for guidance and inspiration, but the job hoppers want only to know how the computer works and what day they get paid.

Guerrilla training requires you to inform and enlighten both groups with all of your might. Stand up. Move around. Use props. Learn to dance, juggle, skate, sing, act. Samuel Johnson said that the purpose of art is to elucidate and entertain. Done properly, training—especially the guerrilla variety—is an art form.

If you're training managers (or anyone else not new to the company), workshops are the only way to go. Even if someone in attendance claims to enjoy a good lecture, remember that while sermons might prepare people for enlightenment, actions allow for the real thing. No matter what the stated issue of your workshop is, one underlying agenda must be to get people to believe in their collective potential. That revolutionary awareness won't cause managers to seek the overthrow of the company, but it will lead them to demand more from themselves and each other. Those feelings will be new, refreshing, and addictive. They must be maintained or your mission will be viewed as heretical.

Plan spontaneity. Use to your advantage the fact that most employees want to do a good job, regardless of how they behave. Visit one of the departments unannounced and ask employees questions you covered weeks earlier in training. Show that you recognize their correct answers. Ask them about their performance statistics. Congratulate the winners and encourage the rest. Fade back and reappear at irregular intervals.

The best managers—who, after all, have become your allies—will likely not only imitate your actions, but also improve on them. That's progress.

Be sincere. You are a force of radical change in the organization. You are in the messianic position of raising tired and trampled spirits from the slag heap of history. But if people see what you're doing as part of some sinister scheme, your hard efforts will come to naught. Therefore, you must understand your own motivation and hold it in view at all times. When someone asks what you're up to with all this training stuff, don't embark on a tirade about being dedicated to the ascension of an enlightened workforce. Just tell the truth; you don't have anything better to do.

Get the company to spend money on training. Make sure you have all of the supplies you need to do your job, and don't go out of pocket for anything. Chances are, there won't be a training budget, and you'll have to go to someone else (probably someone with short arms and low pockets) for everything you need. Who cares? The more the company invests in your department, the more it will expect in return. Make it expect a lot.

Perform as if your company were a real business. Shove ROI reports into people's hands. Propose computer-based training systems. Show managers the connection between quality assurance and employee empowerment. Rail against the "anyone with a pulse" approach to hiring.

Become the unofficial retention manager. Fight lethargy. Promote your aims with pride. Make a flag for your ragged army of soldiers to salute. Irritate the conformists. Soothe the restless. Never give up.

Phil Mershon is manager of training and development, Associated Creditors Exchange, Phoenix, Arizona; philm@ace-collects.com.

Teaching Diagnostic Steps vs. Teaching Situational Steps

Michael O. Thomas

This is a kind of "think" article, about the difference between training that focuses on situations versus training that focuses on cause-and-effect analysis. It is only when employees have these latter skills that they become true experts in their fields. The author makes a compelling argument as to why this is true, and this can be valuable information for anyone involved in planning and delivering training, whether on the job, in the classroom, or electronically.

An advertising executive for a large toy company had a question about the titles we use for our training sessions: "Why can't you use glitzier titles, like *Problem Solving with Phasers for the Captain Kirk's of Enterprise?*" she asked. She liked the humor and creativity she saw in our training, but wondered about the titles we had chosen for our sessions. As we talked with her, it became clear she had a professional concern that our titles would make our programs tougher to sell. You see, the titles we use reflect the cause-and-effect models used to build our programs. Each title represents a cause, i.e., Motivation problems, Ability problems, Emergent problems, etc. In the training industry, session titles provide a good clue as to how programs have been built. A different way to build a program would be around symptom similarity. Then each title would represent an application area, i.e., Violations of policy, Absenteeism and tardiness, Productivity problems, etc. Our titles emphasize similarities in causes, while these other titles emphasize similarities in application.

The advertising executive pointed out that it is easier to sell sessions that are grouped by application rather than by cause. Titles like, Dealing with Violations of Policy, sound more familiar than, Solving Motivation Problems. In addition, the approach seems more targeted: you can focus on the titles that match your symptoms. So why do we build programs around a cause-

Reprinted with permission of the publisher from *Pathway Learning*. Copyright © 2001 by Interact Performance Systems, Inc. All rights reserved.

and-effect model? Because a cause-and-effect model results in training that is simpler to learn, easier to remember, and better at matching the complexity of the real world.

Experts Use Cause-and-Effect Models

In 1978, Dr. Herbert Simon won the Nobel Prize in economics for his work on business decision-making. One of the key areas Simon studied is how experts make decisions within their fields of expertise. Early on, he showed that experts, people with 20,000 hours of successful work in their fields and rated highly by their peers, make decisions faster, more accurately, and with better bottom-line results than non-experts. The challenge that Simon set for himself was to figure out how the experts did it.

Simon studied experts in many fields: management, finance, economics, mathematics, and physics. Here is what he found. Experts are not better at the details: they don't do arithmetic any better, they are not more creative, and they don't jump to conclusions any faster. In fact, they take longer to think through problems before acting. The essential difference is in how experts define the problems they face.

Experts define problems in terms of underlying causal forces, while people with less experience describe problems in terms of application areas. Here is an example of one of his studies that used experts and non-experts in physics:

> Simon's experts in this study were physics professors. His non-experts were professors in other subjects who had never taken college physics. He gave each person a stack of physics problems written on 3X5 cards. Their task was to sort through the problems, and to group them into piles containing similar problems. Simon was interested in whether the experts and the nonexperts would use the same criteria to define which problems were "similar."

> Here is what he found: Nonexperts grouped problems based on where the problems took place—the area of their application. For example, they would group the problems dealing with boats in one pile, with planes in another pile, with outer space in a third pile, and so on. On the other hand, experts grouped problems based on the causal forces of physics. For example, they would group the problems dealing with friction in one pile, with refraction of light in another pile, with gravity in a third pile, and so on.

In this way, the experts completed a causal analysis as they sorted the problems. Simon found that this causal analysis focused their search for solutions. Instead of searching through the whole complexity of physics for their solutions, the experts could focus on one pile at a time knowing that all of the problems in the pile required a similar solution. For example, every problem

Experts define problems in terms of underlying causal forces, while people with less experience describe problems in terms of application areas.

in the "friction" pile required the 3 or 4 physics equations that deal with friction. Every problem in the "refraction" pile required the 3 or 4 physics equations that deal with refraction.

Defining problems in terms of underlying causes focuses the search for solutions, and makes solving problems easier and more accurate. Meanwhile, the non-experts were struggling. It turns out that similarities based on problem locations or application areas are a poor substitute for causal analysis. When Simon took a pile of problems that the non-experts thought were similar and gave it to the experts, the experts had to start their causal analysis from scratch. Every problem in the pile might deal with "boats," but the underlying causes of the problems were not similar at all. One boat problem might deal with electricity, another with wave phenomena, and another with acceleration, etc. Knowing that the application had to do with boats didn't narrow the search for solutions at all.

Cause-and-Effect Models are Easier to Learn

Modern science rests on the observation that you can explain a large number of diverse phenomena using a relatively small number of basic causes. Once you understand the basic causal mechanisms involved, you can compute the answer to any number of applications. For example, consider the principle: Rate times Time equals Distance. This equation captures a single causal relationship that explains an infinite variety of applications—as anyone who has had to do "story problems" can testify. Because there are always fewer cause-and-effect relationships than there are applications, it is easier to learn a program that begins with causes and effects and then moves to applications. In fact, this is a basic rule of instructional design: Teach cause-and-effect relationships before teaching applications.

> Once you understand the basic causal mechanisms involved, you can compute the answer to any number of applications.

Programs That Don't Use Cause-and-Effect Models Are Often Simplistic

Some training programs fall into a double trap that forces them to create too many modules and to make each module overly simplistic. The first part of this trap is the one we've already discussed. They base their programs on applications instead of on a cause-and-effect model. This trap forces them to create a session for every application that a participant is likely to face. The participant loses the advantage that a cause-and-effect model provides. Of course, the training company gains some advantages: the session titles give them an advertising edge and the extra sessions mean more sales for them.

The second part of this trap stems from treating problems that have similar effects as if they had similar causes. For example, they might teach six action steps for resolving quality problems, as if all quality problems stemmed from the same causes. This assumption confuses the effects of a problem with its causes. The only things that two quality problems might share are 1) the effect they both have on quality, and 2) the fact that they both must be solved. Their causes and solutions might be very different.

For example, we know that motivation, ability, or both can cause a quality problem that seems relatively simple on the surface. Most of the "action step" programs assume that the problem is always caused by motivation (a dangerous assumption), and most don't teach participants to find out for sure. If the problem is motivation, we know it can be caused by outcomes that the person doesn't know about, doesn't think are likely, or doesn't care about- and each of these causes requires a slightly different solution. The "action step" programs don't make this causal analysis at all. If the problem is ability, it can be caused by a skill that the person doesn't have or by an obstacle that the person is facing. Most "action step" programs don't even consider the potential ability causes of a quality problem. Given that each of these different causes requires a different solution, there is no way that 6 action steps can handle it.

This double trap produces programs that are both confusing and simplistic. At first people like the "targeted approach" that the modules seem to provide. Like the physics novices who feel comfortable with a category called "boat problems," participants feel comfortable spending a half-day on "quality problems." They also like the action-step approach. In addition, note that there is nothing wrong with action steps per se. We use them too. The problem is the use of action steps without any causal analysis or diagnostic skills to guide them.

The confusion begins as more and more sessions pile on. After 6 or 7 sessions, the action steps begin to blur together. Many of the sessions are repetitive, and the differences between one session and another are hard to justify and difficult to remember. When you add to this situation that the skills in the sessions are too simplistic to be truly effective, the costs of this approach become clear.

The Difference Between Basic Principles and a Cause-and-Effect Model

Many programs that don't teach any form of causal analysis still teach basic principles. These basic principles can be valuable, but should not be confused with a cause-and-effect model. Most "basic principle" sessions take one of two forms: they either, demonstrate and discuss the core values underlying the program or they outline the key responsibilities that compose the participants' job descriptions.

Programs should have core values at their basis and be effective at getting the job done, build strong working relationships, show respect for individuals, build esteem, and avoid manipulation or coercion. However, these values do not help a person figure out what to do or say when confronted by a problem. They do not constitute a diagnostic model, nor are they skills at all. *They are criteria for evaluating skills.*

Basic principles that outline key job responsibilities can also be useful. However, they are often either too general or a bit off target for many organizations. Our experience has proven it's best to have managers lead discussions of their specific business strategies when outlining job responsibilities. Job discussions are educational and inspiring to the extent that they are factual, specific, and rich with details and stories. There is no way an outside training company can provide this service better than a company's own management team.

Michael O. Thomas is the head of Pathway Learning (www.pathwaylearning.com) a training and consulting firm. Contact him at mike@pathwaylearning.com.

Expert Advice on Setting Up a Conflict Resolution Training Program

Editors, Managing Training & Development

Conflict hurts organizations in many ways, some very obvious and some hidden and perhaps even more damaging. Conflict resolution training can make a big difference—if it's done right. Here are some key points and valuable suggestions from an attorney, drawn from her book, The Power of a Good Fight: How to Negotiate Conflict, Confrontation *and* Consensus in the Workplace.

By some estimates, managers spend 20% of their time *in* conflict or managing it. A manager who earns $60,000 will be wasting, in profitability terms, $12,000 of that salary on conflict. If your company has 10 managers, that's a $120,00 hit to your bottom line. Add to that the costs of turnover or litigation and you have a strong case for developing a good conflict management training program.

What will be your plan for conflict resolution training? Here are some key strategies from Lynn Eisaguirre, founder and president of Workplaces That Work (Golden, Colo.) and author of *The Power of a Good Fight: How to Negotiate Conflict, Confrontation and Consensus in the Workplace.*

First, you must train managers to understand and own this prickly process, she told HR and training professionals attending the June 2000 Society for Human Resource Management (SHRM, Alexandria, Va.) conference in Las Vegas.

Understanding Conflict

A conflict, Eisaguirre explained, is the perception that two or more parties have different interests and needs and that all of their interests and needs cannot simultaneously be met.

Unresolved conflict deteriorates into a personality contest involving threats, intimidation, and blame for past actions. Allowed to continue, this

Reprinted with permission from *Managing Training and Development*, September 2000. Copyright © 2000 by the Institute of Management and Administration. All rights reserved.

negative spiral causes a change in psychological perspectives such that the parties will be unable to fairly perceive each other.

Conflict Styles: There Are No Real Grown-Ups

Under stress, people tend to fall into certain conflict styles. Some use more than one style or a combination of many, and each has advantages and disadvantages. Here's a primer on how to identify—and deal with—these conflict styles.

Pit bull. Attacks conflict, likes to argue and debate, threaten, and intimidate. Highly competitive. Avoids concessions.
Tips: Don't attack back. This will create a negative spiral of conflict. Listen and allow the other party to ventilate and restate. Try to determine their needs and interests and find agreement on common goals and criteria. Ask what standards and criteria the speaker is using to determine their position. Try humor.
Golden retriever. Usually accommodates. Can be extremely loyal and has a need to please and be liked.
Tips: Acknowledge their loyalty and cooperation. Recognize that they may have needs and interests that are different from yours or different ideas on how to solve the problem. Ask them to articulate their views.
Roadrunner. Avoids conflict. Can be difficult to pin down to determine interests. They tend to be thoughtful types as well, needing to think before they speak.
Tips: Don't chase. State the problem as clearly as possible and announce that you are ready to talk when they are. Meanwhile, act happy and productive. Occasionally ask if they're ready to talk.
Cobra. Triangulates conflict. Talks to other people rather than to the person(s) directly involved.
Tips: Confront the person directly and calmly with your observations about their behavior in triangulating the conflict, and not their personality. Ask them to talk with you directly. Ask what change in behavior they need from you for them to trust you enough to talk with you directly.
Eagle. Approaches conflict with skill and balance. Uses other approaches only when necessary and after much thought. Constantly applies the 10 steps of conflict resolution (see sidebar).
Tips: Observe eagles closely. Try to learn from their behavior.

A word of caution: Everybody uses all of these styles at one time or another. Each style has its pros and cons. It's not useful to use these as labels to harass employees embroiled in a conflict.

How to Communicate During Conflict

Here are some of the skills managers will need to incorporate into their conflict resolution toolbox:

1. Filter. Everyone hears what others say through a set of filters—assumptions, biases, personal history, experience. Arbitrators will do it and so will conflict participants.

2. Listen. Ask, "How would I listen to this person if I knew I were going to be called as an objective witness in court?"

3. Clarify. Ask open-ended (non-leading) questions to be sure you understand what the other person is saying.

4. Restate. Repeat what you think you've heard until the other person agrees that you understand his or her position.

5. Pause. Ask which conflict style you're dealing with and why. Identify the style *you're* using in response.

6. Summarize. An important part of the conflict resolution process is a summary of the conversation and an iteration of the required action, if any. Sometimes the situation requires only a venting of frustration.

7. Own. Those who will be dealing with conflict resolution must take responsibility for understanding what the conflict participants are saying and making their position clear as well.

8. Assume the best. Until they know otherwise, managers in charge of conflict resolution should assume there's a *misunderstanding,* not an intentional effort to undermine their efforts.

> Until they know otherwise, managers in charge of conflict resolution should assume there's a *misunderstanding,* not an intentional effort to undermine their efforts.

A Case Study on Conflict Resolution

Here's an example of how the conflict resolution process might proceed.

A CEO has retained Eisaguirre to "fix" an ongoing clash between the company's HR director (Harriet) and another department manager (Dawn) at a small organization. Dawn, although she is Harriet's direct report, consistently goes around her to the CEO (Dawn is a Cobra). This is undermining Harriet's authority in the company.

The real problem here, Eisaguirre notes, is the CEO. "Like many CEOs, he's a conflict avoider—a roadrunner." He has also created an untenable situation because he *allows* Dawn to step around Harriet, her boss, and come to him directly. Eisaguirre's conflict resolution plan is as follows.

First, she will meet with Harriet and Dawn, whose conflicts go back *years*, and work with them to uncover the real problems. They will all work together to clean up the past so that they can start fresh to work together.

They will then each identify specific, observable behaviors each needs

SETTING UP A CONFLICT RESOLUTION TRAINING PROGRAM

> ### 10 STEPS TO CONFLICT RESOLUTION
>
> 1. Prepare, prepare, prepare! Identify your own and the other party's walk away points.
> 2. Agree upon common goals and objectives and a written statement of the problem(s).
> 3. Identify needs and interests; avoid positions.
> 4. Attack the problem, not the person.
> 5. If you believe the problem is a personality conflict, focus on *behavior*, not personality.
> 6. Agree upon standards to solve the problem.
> 7. Brainstorm/invent and discuss many possible solutions.
> 8. Keep talking until you agree upon a solution that best meets the needs and interest of all parties. Tenacity works!
> 9. Agree on follow-up and next steps.
> 10. Consider committing your agreement to writing to avoid future conflicts.
>
> Source: Lynne Eisaguirre, *Workplaces That Work*

from the other. This has to be more than intangibles like respect or trust. It must be specific things they want the other person to say and do.

The final step is identifying what Eisaguirre calls "beyond" issues. These are issues that, in fact, Harriet and Dawn cannot resolve. Although they are policy matters that the CEO or executive management needs to address, these issues have become part of their ongoing conflict.

"By separating these out, identifying them as systemic," says Eisaguirre, "and getting the two people in the room to agree to that, it can create a huge breakthrough. Sometimes, it even unites them."

Then There's the CEO

Without saying that he's part of the problem, of course, Eisaguirre will then meet with the CEO to explain the steps he needs to take to help resolve the conflict.

A. Tell Harriet and Dawn that it's part of their job description to work well together. This is an accountability issue, Eisaguirre notes. The company needs to give them the tools and training to deal with conflicts, but ultimately it's they who must accept responsibility for this as part of their jobs.

B. Sort out who reports to whom and then respect the chain of command.

C. Admit to Harriet and Dawn his part in fostering the conflict by allowing Dawn to come to him directly and explain to them that it is going to stop.

This is an overview of the conflict resolution process, but identifying styles and knowing the steps to follow (see sidebar on previous page) can get you well on your way to designing a training program that will help managers and supervisors deal with conflict without becoming a Golden Retriever or Roadrunner themselves.

Resources

Other resources for building conflict resolution skills:

Getting to Yes: Negotiating Agreement Without Giving In, Roger Fisher (Penguin, 1991).

Getting to Peace: Transforming Conflict at Home, at Work, and in the World, William L. Ury (Viking Press, 1999).

Lynne Eisaguirre is the president and founder of Workplaces That Work (www.workplacesthatwork.com). Through speeches and seminars, she helps organizations improve productivity and profits. In addition to writing The Power of a Good Fight, *she has used her training and experience as an attorney to write* Affirmative Action: A Reference Handbook *and* Sexual Harassment: A Reference Handbook. *Contact her at lynne@workplacesthatwork.com.*

Evaluation of Intervention Success

Measuring the Training Department

Stanley E. Malcolm

This article suggests an approach for training and development professionals to use to develop "meaningful metrics." The approach is based on principles of business urgency and customer service. The author proposes them as appropriate for developing metrics "idiosyncratic to the organization being measured."

You've heard the old saying, "Everyone complains about the weather, but nobody does anything about it." You could say just about the same thing for measurement in the training field. I'd like to suggest how training and development professionals might approach development of meaningful metrics. The metrics themselves are beyond the scope of this article—since they will necessarily be idiosyncratic to the organization being measured. But the approach applies anywhere and is based on simple notions of business urgency and customer service.

Measurement can be approached at two levels: the "course" or event, or program, or initiative—call it what you will; and the department—training, training and development, etc. While my main purpose is to address measurement at the department level, I'll include a few words about course-level measurement as well since it is hardly possible to succeed at one without paying close attention to the other.

Reprinted with permission from *Performance Vision*. Copyright © 2001 Performance Vision. All rights reserved.

Measuring the Training Department

External and Internal Metrics

I find it useful to distinguish "external" from "internal" metrics. For me, external metrics are those that others (e.g., sponsors, customers) use to assess the training department's value. Internal metrics are those we in training use to assure ourselves that we're doing the right things—things which will serve as indicators of strong results to come on external metrics. Putting it another way, external measures may be thought of as *summative* while internal measures are primarily *formative*. Alternatively, you might think of external metrics as assessing *terminal* objectives while internal metrics address *enabling* objectives, or steps along the road to success.

Subjective and Objective Metrics

Note too that metrics can be objective or subjective—and we should look for a balance of both. In my opinion, there is sometimes nothing better than a good, subjective anecdote or two to build senior executive confidence in its training function. For instance, a senior sales representative who tells his VP, "I wouldn't have made that sale if I hadn't had such-and-such learning experience" can have enormous impact on management perceptions of the training department. I believe the effect is greater because a) it's coming from a business person versus training measuring itself, and b) the link to the bottom line performance is often more direct (even though anecdotal). (See sidebar, "Subjective versus Objective Measures," for more depth on this issue.)

Approaching Your Sponsors

How should the training department be measured? The best people to answer that question are our sponsors, the people whose money we're spending! I'd like to propose a radical step—let's ask them. Specifically, we need to ask what measures would assure them that they were receiving value in excess of what they were investing.

No, it's not quite that simple. We should first present some basic information to them in order to give context to the question. Otherwise, it is our own fault if they tell us they that want to know how many people we trained, the old "asses in classes" nemesis. Also, included in our presentation should be some suggestions for what we think they should expect of us. Following are some suggested bullet points for such a presentation:

- Statement of the problem: The training department wishes to adopt metrics that will demonstrate our value to the company. We need to determine which metrics to select, and then establish a measurement and reporting strategy. We would like you, our sponsors, to help in selecting appropriate metrics.

> In my opinion, there is sometimes nothing better than a good, subjective anecdote or two to build senior executive confidence in its training function.

SUBJECTIVE VERSUS OBJECTIVE MEASURES

Several key differences (besides the obvious one) and one important similarity need to be explored relative to objective versus subjective metrics.

Unlike objective metrics gathered by the training department, subjective metrics are generally reported serendipitously from employee to management. They're pretty much (but not entirely) outside of your control. I think that they're often more credible simply because Training isn't reporting them.

It doesn't take a lot of anecdotes to make a big impact on management perceptions. This works both ways: bad news travels fast too; faster probably.

Objective measures a) require interpretation and b) are reported routinely. Both a) and b) may diminish their impact.

The similarity is that you can influence both objective and subjective measures, though the means aren't always the same.

What can you do to affect the likelihood of generating good subjective anecdotes versus bad ones?

- You can set the seeds for a good impression through your communications strategy. Communications can set the stage for a self-fulfilling prophecy. (I don't mean just formal communications like a training department newsletter. Every meeting you have with an executive sponsor is an opportunity; as is every conversation a training administrator or instructor has with students and their supervisors.)
- You can avoid obvious turn-offs like making certain programs mandatory. You can reach the same audience by making the program "by invitation only," but instead of having people arrive angry that they're being forced to do something, they come pumped up at feeling they are part of a special "elite." People who feel "special" aren't very likely to bite the hand that gives them that distinction.

    Aetna's chairman, Ron Compton, had a knack for such incentive techniques. When we prepared to release our first EPSS, the AMP Facilitator, he suggested that we control distribution in such a way that we created a "high-visibility frenzy." We did so by placing the software first with people who were known to be on the fast track and likely to use the software where others would see them using it. It didn't take long for others to be clamoring for their copies.
- You can also create peer groups of participants ("alumni") who can a) increase your effectiveness in real ways by serving as coaches to subsequent groups while they b) serve as promoters of the program as much for the shared experience as for the real value they got from it. For example, at Aetna the "Group School" for health insurance sales executives retained a fantastic reputation (unfortunately, some would say, long after the school had diminished significantly in relevance).

> - Anything you do to ensure consistent, caring, customer service behaviors can go a long way towards generating good "press."
> - When someone reports a positive anecdote to you, you can ask them to share it with their senior management.

- Flaws with "traditional" measures of training: Classes offered and students attending them are measures of training volume. However, they say nothing about the appropriateness of training to closing business performance gaps or preparing for the future. In other words, the training department might be doing a lot of the wrong thing. Such measures may in fact further confuse the picture by a) acting against learning strategies that don't fit the measure, e.g., on-demand training without registration, electronic performance support systems, or structured on-the-job training; or b) concentrating trainers' activities on delivery versus development.
- Given this insight into the world of training measurement, how do you know if training is giving you an adequate return on investment? (Probe for objective and subjective measures.) Can you think of any anecdotes from your past, that is, training that you felt was particularly effective? How did you know?
- Finally, having engaged your sponsors in the question of metrics, suggest some or all of the following questions be the foundation for external metrics, supplementing the list with others specific to your environment if necessary.

External Metrics

Once again, by "external metrics" I mean measures valued by the training department's sponsors or customers, generally your company's senior executives. Your goal is to determine what metrics would assure the executives that the training department is providing them greater value than cost. Questions around which you might design external metrics include:

Are we addressing the most critical training needs?
All training needs are not created equal. Resources are finite at best, typically scarce, and never to be frittered away. Every dollar you spend had first to be earned through sales. Given these facts, it's critical that you determine what matters most to your company's success—and focus resources there. If some other, less critical things don't get done, there may be a few complaints but senior management will not likely be among the complainers.

Your job is to determine the most critical needs in terms of business urgency. Ask yourselves what keeps your executive sponsors up at night. Ask how they would define "X" in the sentence "If only we could do a better job at X, our business objectives would be achieved." Concentrate your resources on training needs associated with the "Xs."

If you can't achieve this kind of linkage with business strategy, you might as well stop here—it won't matter how successful you are on other questions. As for measuring your success on linkage to issues having business urgency, ultimately it is your executive sponsors who must answer the question. Your job is to feed them information on what you understand to be the company's priorities and what you are doing to address training needs associated with them.

Are we focusing training dollars on the right organizations?
Just as all training needs are not equal, all organizations are not of equal importance to a company's success. Some lines of businesses represent the rising stars that will provide tomorrow's profits, others are today's cash cows, providing the capital and profits for business growth and investor satisfaction, and other businesses may be past their prime, candidates for sale or dissolution.

Your executive sponsors should be able to tell you how they'd like to apportion resources among lines of business. Measurement is a simple matter of reporting how closely you were able to match actual spending by organization against their plan.

Is the training we support making a difference in performance on the job?
Training is about influencing business performance by improving individual and group performance. Learning is just a step along the way. My advice, which some would call radical, is not to bother measuring learning at all. If you can prove that you've influenced performance, you can infer that learning has occurred—but why bother since performance is the point? (See sidebar, "Measuring Courses," for more depth on this point.)

As with many of the questions you need to answer with regard to metrics, you need to build for success long before any measurement takes place. If you're going to measure performance, you need to design for performance! That means your designs should be based on action learning or problem-centered models. Wherever possible, they should be designed for intact work groups, not aggregations of individuals. As Barry Leskin, a former Head of Aetna Education, said (personal communication), "You can't put a changed individual into an unchanged environment and expect change to happen."

In my opinion, every training initiative should be designed to conform to this simple rule: The "event" (course, program, etc.) is not over until the skills have been successfully demonstrated on the job. If you're designing new product sales training, the event doesn't end in the classroom. It ends after a certain number of actual sales have been completed. In addition to designing the classroom (or CBT, or workbook ...) component, you must create a structure for the on-the-job component where skills get applied. Too often it seems that trainers abrogate responsibility for designing this element. Since they won't be there to "teach," it seems that skill application is "out of sight, out of mind."

With the right design in place, measuring improved performance is rela-

Measuring Courses

At the course level, the standard approach has been based on Kirkpatrick's four levels—with "smile sheets" at level one and assessment of organizational impact at level four. Most organizations use smile sheets to determine if students "liked" a course, that is, perceived it as worthwhile. Many test students to see what they learned. Few measure skill application on the job, and of those few, fewer still do so routinely. A very rare few indeed feel able to measure organizational impact and do so only rarely.

While, to a certain extent, measurements at Kirkpatrick's four levels tell course developers different things, by and large they represent a hierarchy of perceived difficulty to implement. They also represent increasing direct relationship to business impact, which, after all, is the point of training in a corporate setting. So, the things that seem easier to measure (perceptions and learning) say less about business impact than application and, well, impact.

Generally, training organizations have chosen to measure perception and learning while inferring application and impact. I contend that this satisfies nobody. Trainers have lingering doubts about the impact of their efforts. In the worst cases, they lose sight of the real point of the measures, contenting themselves with achieving "satisfaction" and learning. Business managers remain skeptical, often treating training as an expense to be cut—for if they "believed" in training's effectiveness, would they cut the budget?

The problem in measuring courses is not in Kirkpatrick's levels, it is in the design of the courses themselves. In "Reengineering Corporate Learning" (*Training*, August 1992, pp. 57-61), I estimate that over 80% of critical job learning happens on the job. If you're skeptical of that figure, just ask yourself where you learned the critical skills you apply every day. Did you learn them in a classroom? If less than 20% of critical job learning happens in our traditional courses, how can trainers be confident that they've made a valuable contribution to business success? After all, the trainers were "absent" when over 80% of the learning took place!

I propose a simple solution to the problem—design the entire 100% of learning, but continue to deliver only 20% or less by traditional means. The remaining 80% or more should properly be learned on the job—but in a way that has been designed or "structured" to make it consistent—from office to office, supervisor to supervisor, and day to day. Training's role is to provide the structure for learning, not to deliver it. The means might include coaching and assessment guides for supervisors, self-instructional materials for employees, and electronic performance support systems that embed business processes, advice, and learning granules accessible in the context of performing work. Our initiatives in the area of knowledge management are a response to the realization that most learning happens on the job, not in the classroom: we're learning all the time, and need to learn all the time to be competitive; and we don't just learn from "teachers."

> To drive home the point of how radically different the "100%" view is from our traditional approach to course design, let me propose the following simple rule: *The "course" isn't over until the learning has been successfully applied on the job.* For example, the sales course isn't over until the learner has sold 500 of the new model widgets. I ask you, how many of the courses you currently offer conform to that rule? If they did, wouldn't much of the frustration of measurement vanish?

tively simple—certainly much simpler than if you weren't expecting performance to be demonstrated "on your watch." Better still, the right people to measure improved performance are business managers. After all, the measures are business measures: improved sales, etc. Engage them in the measurement process.

Have we achieved the right balance between strategic and operational training?
The balance I speak of is that between the skills necessary for today's jobs and those you know your company will need in the future. Again, you'll need your executive sponsors' help in answering this question. With that information, measurement is a matter of dividing courses into strategic and operational categories and monitoring proportional utilization.

Are we offering employees an opportunity to grow and remain employable?
There's a new social contract between employer and employees. Companies aren't offering a job for life. Today's employees know they must develop the skills that will maintain their employability. An employer's obligation is to provide the means—courses and experiences—and opportunity by which employees can enhance their skills.

If you've done a good job assessing the performance goals of your company, chances are you've covered the "means" aspect of your obligation to employees. But do employees have the opportunity, generally expressed as a management commitment to some average amount of training per year? Are employees actually being released to attend that training? These are questions you should address through metrics. Does everyone have a learning plan? Are they progressing towards implementing it? If you don't have a goal, how can you reach it? Implementing a learning plan strategy assures that every individual has defined their learning goals. Furthermore, it means that you can roll those plans up in order to a) forecast volume, b) determine if the plans reflect your company's priorities (and if not, adjust the plans before they're implemented), and c) measure the degree to which plans have been achieved.

In my experience, learning or development plans are often an adjunct to performance appraisals and administered through human resources, not the training department. You need access to those plans! Better still, you should be in charge of the process of creating and monitoring those plans. Ideally, individual planning tools and plans should be accessible on your company's intranet, and linked to your training administration system and training history database.

Is training administered efficiently and is it easily accessible when and where needed?
When people need training, they generally need it now! Don't make them jump through hoops to get it. Technology can be a great tool in this area. Many companies are using their intranets to share training information, register students, provide on-line courses, and assure access to critical information and performance support resources.

Look for means to measure the elapsed time from when a training need is identified (for groups as well as individuals) until the training has been accomplished. In the case of group needs, note that you should measure the time it takes to close the underlying business performance gap for the entire group. Too often it seems that trainers concern themselves with the course development cycle time, that is, the time until the first course offering, ignoring the fact that it might take years to reach the entire population in need of training.

If you measure time, you'll probably also affect accessibility in terms of location. The further people have to travel to receive training, the longer it is going to take to arrange it. Look for means to serve people at or near their workstations and your results on your accessibility metric will improve dramatically.

How does your company's training compare with that of your competition, and of business in general?
This measure doesn't seem very important to me, but it can be to your executive sponsors. Often they'll want to know how their efforts compare to those of others. Humor them—and take the opportunity not only to determine how well others are doing, but how and what they're doing. In other words, use this metric to justify part of your travel budget. Get out there and visit peers at other companies.

Are you doing all this at a cost that is acceptable to your sponsors?
By all means track costs. But if you've done your homework on the questions above, the benefits you provide to your company should far exceed the resources you expend. Your executive sponsors should understand that they have received a bargain!

Internal Metrics

These are the training department's measures of ourselves: Are we focusing our energy on the right initiatives? Are we creating or buying effective designs? Have we the right balance between design and delivery? Are we communicating effectively? Is our delivery infrastructure (facilities and technologies) matched to our employee's ability to access them? We should look for a mix of design, delivery, and administrative measures.

Internal metrics should be designed with the external metrics in sight. If we are performing well on our internal metrics, the external metrics should fall into place. Again, view internal metrics as "formative" or "enabling."

In addition to indicating probable performance on external metrics, internal metrics should feed performance management discussions in one-on-ones and appraisals. In other words, we should be using these metrics both in aggregate and by individual.

In this case it wouldn't be appropriate to ask your executives for help in determining internal metrics. The best approach is still to ask—but in this case, ask the training department's staff.

Your guiding principle should be this simple statement: *We only measure those things that we care enough to act upon.*

Following are some questions around which a training department might develop internal metrics:

- Are we focusing our energy on the right initiatives? Are we doing enough?
- Are we creating or buying effective designs? (e.g., Action Learning; embedded skill application)
- Have we the right balance between design and delivery?
- Are supervisors anxious to send employees to training, and are employees anxious to attend? (i.e., do they value it?)
- Are people satisfied when the leave? (Do they recommend training to others?)
- Are people learning?
- Are people applying what they learn?
- Are we communicating effectively?
- Is our delivery infrastructure (facilities and technologies) matched to employees' ability to access them?
- Are training administrative staff able to give the right advice on a broad range of subjects to supervisors and employees?
- Have training staff, supervisors, and employees achieved the right balance of responsibilities for creating and implementing learning plans?

Stanley E. Malcolm, Ph.D., through Performance Vision in Marlborough, CT, serves as a coach to companies wishing to develop or review their strategies for performance support, learning technologies, and/or corporate learning issues generally. Formerly, he headed learning technologies and performance support initiatives at Aetna, Inc. He can be reached at Stan@Performance-Vision.com.

Liberating the Lamppost: Shedding Light on Training Evaluation

Peter Bregman and Howie Jacobson

Training and development professionals measure what is easiest to measure, instead of what is most important, according to the authors of this article, who propose a solution—"a cheap, quick, and easy way to measure meaningful results" that "involves one mind-bending assumption: the most important business result is customer satisfaction."

An old joke: A training manager is searching under a street lamp for a set of keys. A passerby offers to help. Together they search and search, in vain. Finally the passerby asks where the keys fell. The training manager points to the other side of the street. "Why are you looking on this side when you dropped them over there?" the incredulous passerby asks. The reply: "The light's much better here."

Training and development professionals have a problem. In theory, we believe in evaluating our work. In practice, however, we don't know how to do it. We measure what is easiest to measure, instead of what is most important. We search for the keys to effective training under the lamppost, instead of where they are. This article will examine the reasons for this misdirected effort and suggest a simple and inexpensive solution.

In Theory, It's a Good Theory

According to prevailing theory, we are supposed to evaluate training from four related points of view: what the trainees think, what they learn, how their behavior changes following training, and how those changes affect the business (the "Kirkpatrick Model"). That seems straightforward enough: trainees value training in useful new skills and behaviors. Because they are useful, those skills and behaviors will be used in the workplace. Therefore, the organization will benefit in tangible ways.

Reprinted with permission from *TRAINING* Magazine, August 2000. Copyright © 2000 Bill Communications. All rights reserved. Slightly revised by authors.

The purpose of the four-level evaluation is to test the training program against this theory. The rosy picture described above can break down anywhere. For example, trainees may react favorably at the end of an exciting program. A few days later, they realize that they haven't actually learned anything. When the jazzed feeling wears off, so does any perception of value. Or, most typically, trainees learn how to behave and why, but slip back into old behaviors on the job. "Raving fans," you hear the help desk technician growl through clenched teeth after three hours back on the job, "I'll give them something to rave about." Occasionally, the behaviors change, but the impact on the business is negligible. Customer service reps now practice active listening, but your networking software still crashes every time a user joins a chat room. As a training manager, you want to evaluate all four potential breakdown points. Only then will you understand how the training program relates to the desired results.

The three lower levels of evaluation (reactions, learning, and behaviors) are only of interest insofar as they serve business results. They don't matter by themselves. Here, in a nutshell, is the problem:

- Employee reactions to training are easiest and least expensive to measure. They are what you care about least.
- Business results due to training are most difficult and costliest to measure. They are what you care about most.

Training managers typically survey trainees immediately following the last training session and consider the program fully evaluated. It is easy to see why. We prefer looking for the keys directly under the lamppost, where the light is brightest. But we know the keys are not there. Current theory does not explain how to shine a light on the side of the street where there is something important to find. At best, we try to tilt the beam to shine dimly where we need it. How can we liberate the lamppost to move where we need it?

Leaning on the Lamppost

The 2000 American Society for Training and Development (ASTD) State of the Industry report found that 95% of surveyed organizations gauged trainees' reactions to training, 37% measured their learning, 13% tracked behavior changes following training, and only 3% accounted for business results of the training.

Since these organizations accept the need for a four-level evaluation process, what is stopping them from evaluating learning, behavior, and business results?

In a 1997 ASTD survey of human resources development professionals, respondents gave four answers most frequently:

- difficulty in determining the impact on financial performance
- time required for a proper evaluation

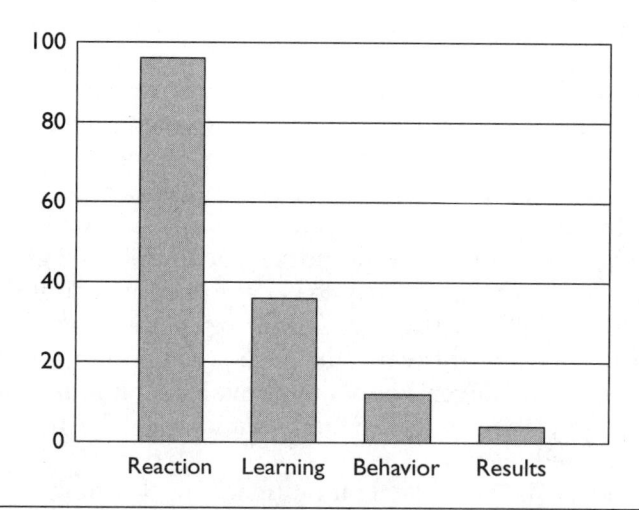

```
100
 80
 60
 40
 20
  0
      Reaction   Learning   Behavior   Results
```

Figure 1. **Percent of Surveyed Organizations Measuring Each Evaluation Level (ASTD, 2000)**

- inability to determine appropriate outcome measures
- cost of evaluation

The more important the outcome, the harder to measure. Let's examine why the four-level model is so difficult to use.

Reactions

Employee reaction to training is the easiest: Ten minutes before the end of the last session, the instructor hands out an evaluation questionnaire to each participant. Questions look like this: "How do you rate the subject? How do you rate the presenter?" After each question, participants are given a choice of "poor" to "excellent" and an invitation to give a comment or suggestion. That evening, the training manager takes all 49 questionnaires home (five new managers were sick on the last day, and six had to leave early) and tallies the responses over "Ally McBeal." The data, along with recommendations, are presented to headquarters the next day. The 11 absentees never give their opinions.

Reaction surveys require very little time to prepare, fill out, and tabulate. As measures of customer satisfaction, they provide immediate and often useful feedback to trainers. They are important *to the training function*, but not so much to the rest of the organization.

The major limitation of trainee surveys is that they cannot tell you if the training actually worked. If the responses are highly negative, the program probably didn't do the job (though it might have). But favorable responses don't mean that trainees will retain or act on the material. I always enjoy outdoor adventure-based workshops, even when I know that the lessons won't transfer to the office.

> The major limitation of trainee surveys is that they cannot tell you if the training actually worked.

Cynical trainers have dubbed these surveys "Smile Sheets." They are necessary, but not sufficient. You might still be wasting money on training that is more fun than a day at the office, but ineffective nevertheless.

Learning

Measuring learning is harder and more time-consuming than asking trainees if they liked the training. Employees often view tests as demeaning, as a lack of trust in their abilities. Often tests do not measure learning, but how well people take tests. Good tests are hard to construct, and can be time-consuming to take if they measure all aspects of the course content. Online assessment is beginning to simplify and streamline the process, but so far has done little to solve the above problems. Just because trainees learn new skills and behaviors does not mean that they will use them in the workplace.

> Measuring learning is harder and more time-consuming than asking trainees if they liked the training.

Behavior

Observing employee behaviors is more complicated than testing knowledge, and can also be more time-consuming. A test is an event, but behavioral observation is a process. Who should observe? How often? In what form should they record data? How is it fed back to employees? These questions are not simply matters of convenience and efficiency; companies run the risk of alienating employees who feel that Big Brother is watching them.

Training programs exist to change behavior. If behavior at work changes in desired ways, the training has been successful. It is at this level that most training programs fail: According to most studies of non-technical training (cited in *The Learning Alliance*, by Robert O. Brinkerhoff and Stephen J. Gill), about 90% of trainees will not be using the new skills six months later.

Business Results

Some training programs *do* change behaviors, of course. The question then becomes, How has our organization benefited from those changes? A group of senior managers learn a more efficient way to manage projects. They begin to manage projects in this new way. What results will interest the executive who paid for the training?

One obvious result is "efficiency of project management." But what does that look like? How can "efficiency" be observed? People meet deadlines. They complete tasks with less supervision. They spend less time on those tasks. But what if these "improvements" reduce customer satisfaction? Donald Kirkpatrick, in the second edition of *Evaluating Training Programs*, gives the example of a company that improved efficiency by waiting until trucks were full before sending them on runs, thus reducing transportation costs. In the short term, profits rose. But soon customers were complaining about less frequent deliveries.

Organizations are complex systems. Often something looks like an isolated improvement and actually proves disastrous for the system. Everyone knows that it is easier to do something oneself than teach someone else to do it. Suppose that increased efficiency was achieved through reduced delegation. In his excellent book, *Managing the Professional Service Firm*, David Maister points out that under-delegation of tasks can lead to morale and retention problems among junior associates. Focusing on discrete results can fool you into thinking that your training program is helping the whole business. The 1997 ASTD survey shows that many training managers do not know which results to measure.

Why not look just at financial performance? When businesspeople invest in something, they naturally want to know the return on their investment (ROI). Training managers feel pressure to demonstrate that training improves financial performance. But ROI is notoriously difficult to measure. Often, there are too many variables. When sales increase following training in communication skills, training may or may not have caused the increase. Perhaps a competitor went out of business. Maybe the increase is seasonal. Or the economy just got stronger. The 1997 ASTD survey found that human resource development professionals struggle to link training results to financial performance.

One solution is to craft a study using a similar control group: Group A receives training, while Group B does not. If the same conditions affect both groups, any differences in financial performance following the training must be caused by it. Most organizations, however, do not have the luxury of two identical groups operating in exactly the same environments. Studies that aggressively control the differences between two groups tend not to look like the real world. For example, if someone from Group A is transferred to Group B, the study loses validity. Most controlled studies take a lot of time and a lot of money to do well. As the 1997 ASTD survey shows, human resource development professionals view excessive duration and cost as challenges to adequate evaluation.

Moving the Lamppost

There is a cheap, quick, and easy way to measure meaningful results. It involves one mind-bending assumption: the most important business result is customer satisfaction.

Every employee in an organization has customers. Many employees serve internal customers: their managers, their direct reports, their peers on project teams, members of line units that rely on their work, and others. Some employees serve external customers as well: buyers, suppliers, business partners, clients, and others. Doing a good job means providing quality service to all of one's customers.

Every organization has internal and external customers. Employees and clients are both customers, evaluating how they are treated and whether their needs are being met or exceeded by the organization. As Maister points out, professional service firms must create super-satisfied employees and super-satisfied customers if they are to succeed financially. The ultimate bottom line (profits) depends on customer and employee satisfaction. Employee satisfaction is crucial, ultimately, for external customer satisfaction. Phil Terry, CEO of Creative Good, a New York-based Internet strategy firm, puts it succinctly, "Happy employees create happy customers."

Every business result that matters leads to improved customer satisfaction, either directly or indirectly. An event or process or attitude that does not make customers happy is bad for business, even if it improves efficiency or pads short-term profits. Recent books like *Net Ready*, by Amir Hartman, John Sifonis, and John Kador, and *The Cluetrain Manifesto*, by Rick Levine, Christopher Locke, Doc Searls, and David Weinberger, identify a key feature of the New Economy: a fundamental shift in power from companies to their customers. The days of Henry Ford's "Give 'em any color they want, as long as it's black" are over. To succeed, companies will need to partner with their customers to provide customized products and services.

> Every business result that matters leads to improved customer satisfaction, either directly or indirectly.

Why Customer Satisfaction Is Easy to Measure: Four Reasons

Changes in customer satisfaction due to training are easy to measure for four reasons.

First, we can use reaction surveys. As we have seen, they are easy and inexpensive to create, administer, tabulate, and interpret. They are also a reliable measure of customer satisfaction. We just administer them to a different population: the customers of the training participant.

Second, reaction sheets for customers get high response rates. Customers want to give feedback, especially if they believe it will be taken seriously. Most are delighted to offer an opinion that may help them get better service in the future, or that allows them to express frustration or appreciation. People care deeply about how they are affected by other people.

Third, it is easy to make a valid connection between the effects of training on an employee and how customers feel about that employee. By definition, a training program succeeds when it changes employees' behaviors *in ways that matter to their customers*.

- Customer service and sales reps receive training in active listening. Ask their customers and prospects whether their concerns are being addressed better than before.
- A manager learns to communicate performance feedback more effectively; ask his direct reports whether they understand better how they are doing and what they need to do differently, and whether the feedback motivates or discourages them.

- An associate learns to be more organized in her work; ask her manager and her clients if she meets her deadlines more consistently and produces better quality work.

Fourth, organizations that use 360° reviews already ask their customers to evaluate their employees' performance. To evaluate the effects of training, simply ask targeted questions about behaviors relevant to the training and ask at times that relate to the training schedule (i.e., pre/post/three-month follow-up).

Why It's Smart to Measure Customer Satisfaction: Four Additional Benefits

Evaluating training in this way confers four additional benefits.

First, asking external customers how happy they are with your services makes them happy. It shows that you are committed to improving your service, and that you value their patronage and don't take it for granted.

Second, it communicates to employees that their organization is serious about their development. That message can enhance the effectiveness of any training program.

Third, it communicates to employees that nothing they do is more important than increasing customer satisfaction. Competencies such as "Leadership" and "Analytical Thinking" are important, but only in the service of co-workers and external customers. In effect, organizations tell their people, "The most important job you have is making customers happy. To show you we mean it, we'll measure your success through your customer's eyes."

Fourth, it tells trainers that their work will be valued to the extent that employees do things differently after the training. For trainers accustomed to evaluation by smile sheet, this represents a revolution in accountability. Assessment drives instruction. Trainers will inevitably "teach to the test." The challenge is creating a test worth teaching to. What your customers think of you may be your ultimate business test.

Conclusion

We know where the keys are. Enough stumbling in shadows trying to locate them. Enough searching on the wrong side of the street. If our organizations embrace customer satisfaction as the principal business result of training, we can liberate the lampposts. Who knows? They might dance across the street to illuminate our search for the keys to effective development.

Peter Bregman is CEO and Howie Jacobson is director of voice for Bregman Partners Inc., a New York consulting firm (www.bregmanpartners.com). Reach them at pbregman@bregmanpartners.com and hjacobson@bregmanpartners.com.

Evaluating E-Degrees

Shari Caudron

As technology has expanded learning opportunities, a problem has emerged for HR professionals who make hiring decisions: How should they regard job candidates with online degrees? This article reports on differing perspectives in the growing debate and offers seven questions to ask when evaluating online degrees.

In many ways, Alex Zai is your typical online learner. As vice president of store operations and international development for PakMail Centers of America, Inc., Zai's job is too demanding for a traditional classroom education. Seeking an MBA program that could accommodate his extensive foreign travel schedule and give him a greater understanding of international business, Zai enrolled in the University of Phoenix Global MBA Program. The courses, which were offered entirely online, allowed him to complete his coursework after his kids were asleep, while waiting in airports, or while conducting business in other countries.

How does he describe the quality of education received? "Mediocre at best," he admits. Zai rarely received feedback on his work, there was no interaction with the other students, and he often felt that his writing skills were better than those of his instructors. "The only thing I gained from the online courses was a better understanding and use of the Internet," he explains.

Across the country, there are countless other working professionals just like Alex Zai. Pressed for time but faced with the need for ongoing education, more and more adults are choosing to enroll in online degree programs. According to a study conducted by Merrill Lynch, more than 2.2 million college students will be taking courses online by 2002, a huge jump from the 710,000 enrolled in 1998. Many if not most of these students are the working adults who now make up over 50 percent of post-secondary students.

In response to the growing demand for online education, colleges and universities are rushing headlong into the e-learning marketplace. There are currently more than 6,000 accredited college courses offered on the Web, and

Reprinted with permission from *Workforce*, February 2001. Copyright © 2001 by ACC Communications, www.workforce.com. All rights reserved.

84 percent of four-year colleges will be offering distance-learning courses in the next two years. In addition to the standard books-and-classroom universities, there are also a handful of universities that were born on the Web. These include Jones International University, based in Englewood, Colorado, and Capella University, in Minneapolis. The willingness of educators to embrace the Internet means it is now easier than ever to obtain a college degree without ever setting foot on a college campus.

But does the growing enrollment in online degree programs mean that they are as effective as a traditional classroom education, or is Zai's disappointing experience the norm? How should HR professionals who make hiring decisions regard online degrees? Are the candidates as qualified as those who lug briefcases full of books across campus?

As you might expect, in a new industry where the financial stakes are high but the experience level low, there are vigorous disagreements as to the effectiveness of online degree programs.

Online Versus the Classroom: Which Is More Effective?

A glance at some of the research indicates no significant difference between distance education—of any sort—and classroom-based instruction. In his book *The No Significant Difference Phenomenon* (North Carolina State University Press, 1999), Thomas L. Russell of North Carolina State University details results from 365 distance-education studies that show little if any difference in the quality of education received through distance learning versus the classroom.

"If you believe this research, which I do, there is no doubt that with very few exceptions, students in online degree programs are at least as good as comparable students in traditional courses," he says. "If I was doing the hiring, I would definitely give preference to the person with an online degree. They have to be more disciplined and work harder to achieve their goals."

John Losak, vice president of research and planning at Nova Southeastern University in Fort Lauderdale, agrees with Russell. Over the past six years, his department has conducted more than 24 studies comparing student performance in online courses with that of their classroom counterparts. The research analyzed rate of graduation, time to graduation, and knowledge acquisition, among other things. "Overall, students perform as well or better in online courses," he says.

But critics of such favorable reports emphasize that these studies are comparing online education with classroom-based instruction that was never very good to begin with. Roger Schank, chairman of Cognitive Arts Corporation, based in New York, is one of the most outspoken detractors. "You shouldn't be comparing online education with existing education because existing education is not that good," he says. "A lecture hall crammed with 1,000 students is not good education. Lectures themselves are not good education. People learn best by doing."

Schank, whose company is helping Columbia create its online university, is not a critic of online education overall, only of the way that most online courses are currently being offered. As he explains, in their zeal to create online offerings, most universities are simply slapping lecture notes and readings online, making what was a bad education to begin with even worse.

"It's like filming plays," he explains. "When movies came out in the 1920s, the first thought was to film plays because that was how people were used to delivering entertainment. You look at movies today, and they don't look anything like plays. As time evolved, people began to understand that the medium was different and thus what we could do with it was different. The same is true with education and the Internet."

So how should online education be evolving? Because adults learn best through interaction and experience, Schank says, online courses must be developed in such a way that learners can apply their new knowledge to real-life experiences as well as interact and seek feedback from others.

To be fair, there are some pioneers who are bringing together experts in subject matter, adult learning theory, and technology to design courses specifically for the Internet that are radically different from any you'd find in a classroom. These include Capella University, an accredited online institution that offers 12 degree programs, and Cardean University, a spin-off of UNext.com that has partnered with educational heavyweights such as Carnegie Mellon, Columbia, and Stanford. The most advanced courses being created by these universities use movie-like presentations, student-driven simulations, and asynchronous communication to facilitate interaction and experiential learning.

Because courses like this are designed from the ground up with technology, interaction, and simulation in mind, they are time-consuming and expensive to develop. In fact, some courses take as long as 18 months and cost as much as $1 million to create. By comparison, current development costs for most distance-education courses average less than $10,000, according to a report by Eduventures.com, Inc.

For instance, the University of Phoenix Online creates courses for less than $5,000. Because of the enormous time and cost involved in putting more experiential courses online, it is likely to be some time before the overall quality of online education improves. "There are great courses online now," Schank insists, "but it will be a while before there are great online degrees."

But What About Today's Job Candidates?

Does the fact that e-learning is still in its infancy mean that all graduates of online degree programs are receiving substandard education? Should HR

EVALUATING ONLINE DEGREES: SEVEN QUESTIONS TO ASK

1. Is the university accredited? Regional accreditation, which is provided by regional associations of schools and colleges (each named after the region in which it operates: Middle States, New England, North Central, Northwest, Southern, Western), means that a school has been recognized by the U.S. Department of Education, that the program is one of integrity, and that course units can be transferred from one campus to another.

2. What is the reputation of the institution? Because it is too early to determine the reputation and effectiveness of specific online degree programs, you'll want to consider the reputation of the institution offering the degree. "If the online program is from Duke University, you can bet Duke has invested a lot in it because the school is putting its reputation behind it," says Thomas Russell, director emeritus, office of instructional telecommunications, North Carolina State University.

3. What outcomes can the degree-granting institution demonstrate? How does the institution evaluate whether or not students have acquired skills and knowledge? "The issue of assessment has been given a high priority by the regional accrediting agencies," explains Claudine Schweber, associate vice president, distance education and lifelong learning, University of Maryland University College. Consequently, more online degree programs should be able to demonstrate outcomes.

4. How does the institution support or promote interaction in the online environment? "Anybody who is serious about educating people online will understand the importance of interaction among students and among students and faculty," Schweber says.

5. What are the faculty members' credentials? You'll want to take a look at their degrees, their experience in dealing with adult learners, and their understanding of online learning.

6. How does the institution keep courses current? This refers not just to course content but also to the resources used in the course. Does the institution provide access to digitized libraries and global online databases? How often are courses updated? "Almost every credible institution has an approval process to control the quality and currency of courses," Schweber explains.

7. How does the degree-granting institution promote experiential learning? Because adults learn best by doing, the best online programs are those that require students to apply the knowledge they've learned.

> **WHEN IS AN ONLINE PROGRAM A GOOD FIT?**
>
> If you or one of your employees is interested in online learning, here are some questions to ask:
> - Am I self-directed enough to handle distance learning?
> - Am I motivated enough to work on my own, or do I need the structure and accountability of a classroom to nudge me along?
> - Do I have the required technology and am I comfortable using it?
> - Are my writing skills sufficient to succeed online?

professionals stay away from current online grads in favor of employees with traditional degrees? Not necessarily. As with all hiring decisions, it depends on what you are looking for.

"Certain subjects are very conducive to online delivery," explains Jeff Creighton, founder and chairman of EduPoint Inc., which manages a Web site that provides centralized access to information about online education. "Information technology courses, for example, are ideally suited to the Web," he says.

HR professionals at high-tech companies appear to be in agreement with Creighton. According to a recent survey of hiring managers by Vault.com, the three industries most likely to hire candidates with online degrees are Internet and new media, technology, and high tech.

Aside from technical skills, the other competencies that online graduates typically demonstrate are discipline, motivation, good writing skills, the ability to work independently, and a high degree of comfort with the Internet. Why? Because all these characteristics are required in order to successfully complete an online program.

But in today's highly collaborative workplace, where joint decisions have to be made quickly, the best-prepared applicants might still be those who have acquired their abilities through traditional classroom programs.

"Measurable skills, such as whether or not a candidate can read a balance sheet or create a strategic plan, can typically be taught effectively both online and in the classroom," Creighton says. "But when it comes to qualitative abilities such as interpersonal skills, leadership qualities, and problem-solving, e-learning is not yet delivering because it doesn't provide the immersion and interaction required to change a student's paradigm. These attributes are still best developed through more traditional classroom-based education."

Alex Zai agrees. As a result of his disappointing experience with an online MBA program, Zai says if he were faced with the decision to hire an employee with an online degree versus an employee with a classroom education, he would choose the latter. "The interaction between students in a classroom is invaluable," he says.

Of course, when it comes to learning, it's important to keep in mind that adults do have different learning styles. Some adults like the social interaction of a classroom. Still others may thrive online because the medium is highly democratic—issues of age, race, gender, physical disabilities, and appearance rarely play a role.

Online courses also allow introverts time to formulate responses and contribute to class discussions. Such differences in learning style mean that people will be drawn to the learning modes that best fit their personalities and natural aptitudes. "As a result," Losak explains, "HR people might want to consider placing people into positions based on how the learning occurred."

But in the end, when it comes to evaluating a particular job candidate, it's important to remember that the degree itself is just one characteristic. A person's experience, enthusiasm, ideas, ability, and organization fit are equally—if not more—important.

Shari Caudron is a freelance writer in Denver and a contributing editor for Workforce. *She has also published in* Business Finance, Industry Week, Workforce, Training & Development, Black Enterprise, Controller, *and* Chief Executive *magazines. You can e-mail her at scaudron@aol.com.*

Calculating Training Efficiency

Scotty C. DeClue

Which type of learning environment delivers the highest return on investment? That's a question facing training managers in many organizations. Here's a rating system—CLUE (Concept Learning and Understanding Efficiency)—for calculating the true cost of training courses. It can also be used in forecasting annual training expenditures and negotiating with vendors.

Today's training managers are challenged to serve the customers in their organization with limited budgets. Limited budgets require justification of expenditures. As the Technical Training Manager at the Department of Energy's Savannah River Operations Office, my main responsibility was to provide technical training to engineers and scientists. I was faced with the dilemma of how to decide which type of learning environment delivered the highest Return on Investment (ROI).

One subject area was Electrical Theory and Distribution Systems. Several individuals expressed interest in some refresher training on this subject, so I conducted research to determine how to "get the best bang for the buck." My options included the following courses with similar learning objectives:

Course	Cost	Hours
Professional Engineering Licensing Examination Review Course	$295	5
Electrical Engineering Review	$995	40
Electrical Engineering Course at a Local University for 14 weeks	$1,200	42 (3 hrs per week)
Computer-Based Training	$8,000	16

Table 1. **Electrical theory and distribution system courses**

Reprinted with permission from *TRAINING* Magazine, February 2001. Copyright © 2001 Bill Communications. All rights reserved.

I developed the CLUE (Concept Learning and Understanding Efficiency) rating to compare the costs of college semester courses, one-day courses, 40-hour one-week courses and computer-based training courses.

The CLUE rating is calculated for each course by dividing the cost of the course by the number of students, times the number of hours of the course. This number is then multiplied by the reciprocal of the course rating to factor in the opinion of the learners. The CLUE rating formula is shown below:

$$\text{CLUE} = \frac{\$}{(N \times H)} \times \frac{1}{(CR)}$$

CLUE = Concept Learning and Understanding Efficiency rating
N = Number of Students
$ = Cost of the Course
H = Hours of the Course
CR = Course Rating

Courses with the lower CLUE rating are considered more efficient.

Using N = 10 and N = 25 employees for a planning basis for the course options, and applying the CLUE rating formula to the courses in Table 1, the Electrical Engineering review would be more economical for 10 people while purchasing the CBT would be more economical for 25 people

Course	N=10 Total Cost	N=10 Cost/Student x Hour	N=25 Total Cost	N=25 Cost/Student x Hour
PE Review Course	$2,950	59	$7,375	59
Electrical Engineering Review	$9,950	25	$24,875	25
University Course	$12,000	29	$30,000	29
CBT	$8,000	50	$8,000	20

Table 2. **CLUE ratings**

CLUE rating = ($2,950/(10 x 5)) x (1/1) =59 (sample calculation)

Course selection should not be made solely on the cost/student x hour ratio. This is where the course ratings become a factor. In the example above, the course ratings were assumed to be 1.0. But what if you have some histor-

CALCULATING TRAINING EFFICIENCY

ical background on the 40-hour electrical-theory course. Let's say an individual took the course last year and did not like the course and on his course critique; he rated the course as average (which equals a .5 on our Likert scale end-of-course critique form). By multiplying the cost/student x hour ratio by the reciprocal of the course rating, the CLUE rating for the Electrical Engineering Review course (N = 10) becomes higher, and the University Course would be more economical.

CLUE rating = ($9,950/(10 x 40)) x (1/0.5) = 50 (sample calculation)

The CLUE rating can also be used for budget purposes to forecast annual training expenditures. Table 3 lists sample courses that were offered in previous years to the Environmental Technical Staff at my location.

Course	Cost	N	H	CLUE
Air Pollution Control	$3,900	20	4	49
Water Pollution Control	$3,900	19	4	51
ISO 14000 Certification	$24,000	12	40	50
Waster/Wastewater Treatment Systems	$13,398	9	40	37
Groundwater and Contaminants	$10,000	8	40	31
Biological Principles of Environmental Engineering	$12,889	5	42	61
Average CLUE Rating = 41				

Table 3. **Environmental courses**

Using the average CLUE rating of 41, N = 50, and planning for 40 hours of annual training yields an estimate of $82,000 for an annual training cost to train 50 people.

Cost of Training = CLUE rating x N x H

Cost of Training = 41 x 50 x 40 = $82,000

The CLUE rating can be used to measure efficiency for the next year by negotiating with various vendors to reduce their costs to obtain a lower

CLUE rating. Now that you have been able to normalize the costs, you have leverage to negotiate with a vendor for a reduced training course cost.

The CLUE rating can also be used to decide when to cancel a scheduled course due to low attendance. For example, a manager wants you to contract with a vendor to bring a course to your site. The vendor has agreed to teach a 24-hour course for $20,000 at your location. Using a CLUE rating of 41, H = 24, $ = 20,000, the minimum number of students required for training to achieve your CLUE rating is 20. The course can be scheduled and advertised to the population, but if the minimum number of people do not sign up for the course by a set time (three weeks prior to the scheduled date), cancel the course because it would not be cost efficient (in comparison with your standards).

Number of Students = $/(CLUE rating x H)

Number of Students = $20,000/(41 x 24) = 20

Note: The numbers presented here are representative of actual costs but are not to be construed as actual costs spent by my organization. Use the CLUE rating equation to determine the costs for your organization based upon your historical cost data and course critique to set standards unique for your unique setting.

Scotty C. DeClue currently serves as a facility representative for the FB-Line facility at the Department of Energy—Savannah River Site. Prior to working for the Department of Energy, DeClue commanded a U.S. Army Special Forces Chemical Reconnaissance Detachment in the Gulf War, where he was decorated for valor during the rescue mission of the U.S. Embassy in Kuwait.

PART FIVE

Focusing on People to Drive Organizational Strategy

Organizational strategy and human performance are two sides of the same coin. Part Five is designed to affirm this statement and provide examples of how HR development and successful strategic initiatives are intimately related. What you'll see, among other things, in reading these articles is that:

- Strategies that take into account people, and indeed emphasize people, are key to succeeding today.
- You need to create a culture that brings out the best in people and there are specific ways to do this.
- You need to develop people who are open to change and new ways of doing things for the organization to survive and thrive.

In Part Five, you'll find seven articles that provide a number of different perspectives on the relationship between people and strategy. We start with "The Learning Organization in Practice: New Principles for Effective Training" by Mark Mallinger. A learning organization comes about as part of a management strategy to systematically learn from experience and improve the performance of individuals and the organization as a whole. This article describes how to facilitate learning, especially through the use of self-managed teams. Next we include the article "Beyond Training: Reconceptualizing Learning at Work" by Patricia Bryans and Richard Smith. These authors advocate the implementation of seven principles that will transform the organization and help bring people and organizational performance and strategic excellence in sync with one another.

Moving from the idea of the learning organization, you'll next find "Leadership DNA: The Ford Motor Story" by Stewart D. Friedman. Friedman is the head of the Leadership Development Center at Ford, and he describes the commitment Ford has made to building leaders who empower employees and imbue the company's vision throughout its culture. This is a great story and has lessons for many organizations. This is followed by another case study, "The Little Airplane That Could" by Sarah Fister Gale. In it she documents how people at the McDonnell Douglas Long Beach plant reinvented the way to manufacture a plane and took it from a money loser to a very profitable enterprise for the company.

We change gears again with "Managing Dispersed Work Effectively: A Primer" by John D. Adams. Telecommuting and employees dispersed in many locations are becoming more and more a part of the way companies operate. This article, based on a research project, describes the practices that work and those that don't.

The next article, "A Seat at the Table" by Kristine Ellis and Sarah Fister Gale, explains how training directors are becoming intimately involved in helping companies assess what skills and talents are necessary to achieve strategic goals.

And we conclude with "Turning Passion into Organizational Performance" by Richard Chang. Chang has written extensively on the notion of passion and commitment of people to the organization and the organization to its people. In this article he explains the connection between passion and performance.

The Learning Organization in Practice: New Principles for Effective Training

Mark Mallinger

How can training and development programs help promote organizational learning and personal growth? This article recommends a team-based, self-managed training (SMT) design. The author presents the results of an SMT program in a business unit of a large manufacturing organization. He concludes, "SMT responds to the demands of the turbulent business environment by emphasizing development of collaborative skills, encouraging teaming, promoting the value of information sharing, and reinforcing effective problem-solving techniques."

To survive and grow in the current business environment, organizations increasingly are required to be learning systems. Success, even survival, may be dependent on the extent to which the organization is able to learn, adapt, and change. Rapid changes in the business environment necessitate that organizations create training and development programs that enhance their employee's adaptive abilities. Technological advances require the development of new skills. Corporate restructuring places greater responsibility on fewer workers, and decision making is pushed to lower levels—often to self-managed teams. Cross-functional teams may be necessary for problem solving across functional boundaries. Empowered employees who are accomplished problem solvers are needed.

The question for Human Resources (HR), and particularly for Training and Development departments, is how to design a training program that will facilitate a firm's becoming a learning organization. A team-based, self-managed training (SMT) design is one model for doing this. SMT is a method for improving the delivery of training and development and can be applied to existing training content. It enhances collaborative skills, develops effective

Reprinted by permission of the publisher from *Graziadio Business Report*, Winter 2000. Copyright © 2000 by the Graziadio School of Business and Management, Pepperdine University. All rights reserved.

team members, emphasizes taking initiative, encourages information sharing, and produces long-term, rather than short-term, behavior changes.

Limitations of Traditional Training

As organizations commit more resources to the development of employees, cost/benefit analyses become critical. Value-added training designs must respond to the needs of a rapidly changing business environment. Traditional training methods do not pass this test for several reasons. They stress individual skills development rather than collaborative problem solving. The emphasis of most training programs is individual skill development (e.g., leadership, negotiation and communication). Although people may learn useful techniques and tools, they don't learn to work collaboratively.

Passive Listening Rather than Active Involvement

Participants are often relegated to asking questions or engaging in an occasional experiential exercise. They are seldom actively involved throughout the training experience.

Theoretical Problem Solving Rather than "Real" Organizational Problem Solving

They frequently rely on examples and cases that do not represent the culture or structure of the organization. Having participants focus on real, ongoing organizational problems is likely to be a more valuable learning tool.

Short-Term Learning Versus Long-Term Change

Without reinforcement, skills learned in training sessions are short-lived. The opportunity to practice and receive feedback on a continual basis is necessary for skills to "stick."

Skill Training Rather than Personal and Professional Development

Unless participants recognize the extent to which their personal styles may limit or augment their ability to use the techniques, the skills learned are not likely to be applied effectively.

Responding to the following questions will help in assessing your organization's return on investment in training and development.

1. To what extent do the lessons taught in training have long-term benefit? Frequently skill loss occurs because the training lab cannot recreate the conditions managers encounter when they leave that environment and reenter their work environment. The realities of the workplace and the lack of opportunity to reinforce the tools learned in training result in a return to old patterns of behavior.

2. To what extent is your organization a collaborative, cross-functional problem-solving entity? Building a learning community where members take the initiative to share information, transfer knowledge, and work together to solve cross-functional problems. This requires training sessions to be learning opportunities for participants to actually work collaboratively.
3. After completion of the training program, do employees place their training notebooks on the office shelf, never to be revisited? Many training interventions include creatively designed materials that raise participant interest, but when the session is completed, these notebooks become additions to the bookcase and ignored.
4. To what extent are lessons learned in the training process reinforced in the workplace? Without the opportunity to practice, on a continuing basis, the skills developed during the training intervention, the likelihood that employees will maintain those skills is greatly diminished.

Self-Managed Training

SMT is designed for organizations that want to become a learning organization and have a strategic commitment to training and development. Our consulting work demonstrates that collaboration is enhanced when members trust one another, are secure with their skill level, feel comfortable with the skills of others they work with, and establish a commitment to learning and continuous improvement. This attitude is reinforced when participants take an active rather than passive role in the training process, solve "real" organizational challenges rather than theoretical problems, and are provided the opportunity to apply group maintenance skills, and when the organization establishes an environment that encourages developmental feedback.

> SMT is designed for organizations that want to become a learning organization and have a strategic commitment to training and development.

Active vs. Passive Responsibility—Solving Real Problems

Passively sitting through a training session may allow the learner to be able to define terms, but it does little to help the participant integrate the knowledge that is necessary and to make the concepts real. The SMT model not only encourages active learning, it supports collaboration through the use of team interaction and the teaching of collaborative problem solving. In so doing, it leads to high levels of skill development as well.

The results of an SMT program in a Business Unit of a large manufacturing organization on the West Coast are instructive. Participants were initially reluctant to embrace the training model. The company had a history of introducing interventions that were promoted as the "ultimate training experience," only to have people disappointed by the short-term benefits that emerged. However, as participants began to recognize the impact created by the model and observed measurable results associated with the training, their reaction shifted toward optimism. Although a number of troublesome situations occurred, improvements in productivity and quality were experienced.

At the beginning of the training session, participants were placed in teams of four or five managers who had differing task responsibilities. These teams met throughout the formal training period. As an incentive to continue the working relationship after formal training was terminated, participants were given increases in their department training budgets if they demonstrated progress on the projects selected by their team. As they dealt with each other over time, the heterogeneity of their perspectives provided multiple perspectives in analyzing and working through issues. It enhanced the generation of alternative voices and, in so doing, improved the decision quality. The experience also allowed members the opportunity to observe colleagues and provide feedback regarding leadership style and effectiveness.

The role of the SMT trainer shifted from lecturer to resource manager. The facilitator started a session with an introduction of the module, then discussed the relevant conceptual framework that supported the topic. However, the majority of time in the training session was devoted to discussing cases, experiential exercises, and then solving real Business Unit problems.

Group interaction within teams was followed by dialogue between teams. The degree of interaction allowed for the expression of differing viewpoints and suggestions, which, in turn, led to more collaborative decision making both within and across teams.

Real Problems

Parts shortages were a nagging problem for the Business Unit. The ordering of parts was not the issue; rather it was the storage, retrieval, and coordination between departments. So, the training teams took on the challenge of solving the parts shortage enigma. The use of cross-functional teams provided a way for participants to understand underlying difficulties and, at the same time, develop creative solutions that would integrate the work of the departments.

Initially there was a considerable amount of finger pointing. Blame was placed anywhere that avoided ownership by the team member's department. The skills developed in the conflict management module, however, helped team members sort out issues. Internal customer/supplier relationships were nurtured and improvements in the dialogue between departments were made. Although the parts shortage problem was not completely resolved by the end of training, the dialogue that came out of training did result in recommendations that improved quality. Equally important, six months after the intervention, there were still reports of greater responsiveness to requests for information and greater accuracy of paper work, leading to improvements in productivity and quality.

Training does not operate in a vacuum. Organizational actions can both facilitate or hinder the process. In this case, a management decision to reduce

> Training does not operate in a vacuum. Organizational actions can both facilitate or hinder the process.

the amount of refreshments offered during training sessions resulted in a perception among participants that management's action to cut back the refreshment budget was a reflection of the low value they placed on the training. After some conversations with senior Business Unit managers, we were able to restore the quantity of refreshments offered during breaks. Commitment to be a learning system should be reinforced by both symbolic and structural messages that say that management supports the goals and the training.

Group Maintenance

Reinforcing Collaborative Skills

The teamwork that is required in SMT encourages collaboration, and processing issues that arise during training further reinforces collaboration. In this case, as the managers worked together on real business issues, control issues appeared. Providing time for the group to process these dynamics helped strengthen the skills necessary for collaborative problem solving.

Early on, competitive actions created conflict and got in the way of collaborative problem solving. Dominant personalities tried to gain control and aggressive behaviors by some caused others to shy away and reduce their contribution to group discussion. On numerous occasions during the training cycle, the facilitator used feedback exercises that incorporated communication and leadership skills learned in earlier modules. Using these exercises allowed the team to examine the behavior of members and develop action plans for change. Our experience suggests that heterogeneous teams are able to deal with these issues effectively after they have finished training because the managers have "lived" together throughout the training cycle. The development of a community within the team is likely to result in a commitment to resolve internal problems.

Personal Development

To be able to implement collaborative skills, people must be aware of their own behaviors and how well they interact with others. SMT training is a valuable tool in helping them analyze how they communicate, handle conflict, and express leadership. Continuous improvement in these areas is required, and the use of assessment tools that require participants to give feedback to team members is part of SMT.

With respect to the training intervention in the Business Unit, information was received more readily when participants had developed trust through the emergence of collaborative relationships. They were less defensive when receiving data that were confirmed by others. In these cases, quality feedback generally resulted in information that was meaningful and honored.

SMT: Value Added Training and Development

The rapid change occurring in most industries is likely to continue or even increase. To maintain a competitive advantage, organizations must be concerned about creating a learning environment where members can engage in collective thinking. SMT responds to the demands of the turbulent business environment by emphasizing development of collaborative skills, encouraging teaming, promoting the value of information sharing, and reinforcing effective problem-solving techniques. Because of active involvement and team learning, skills mastered in SMT are more likely to have long-lasting effect than is the case with traditional training. But, for long-term benefits, the organization must institutionalize the process and make it a part of the culture.

Mark Mallinger, Ph.D., is Professor of Organization Behavior in the Graziadio School of Business and Management at Pepperdine University. He has a B.S. and a M.S. from California State University, Northridge, and a Ph.D. from the University of Southern California. As a consultant, Dr. Mallinger specializes in management development and organizational change.

Beyond Training: Reconceptualizing Learning at Work

Patricia Bryans and Richard Smith

Organizational and individual performance improvement are related to organizational culture and the approach taken to coordinate people and strategy. This article suggests going beyond training, and in it the authors advocate for a conception of personal/personnel development that values thinking and feeling. To develop this new framework, they contend that seven fundamental principles will require attention: openness, uncertainty, complexity, relationships, reflection, reframing, and restoration.

There is a widespread view that existing versions of management and management theory are inadequate in our changing world: indeed, we are often said to be in the midst of a frenzied search for new approaches to management (Eccles and Nohria, 1992; Hamel and Prahalad, 1994). Many writers (e.g. Kets de Vries, 1995) identify as the basic flaw in current paradigms of management the essentially rationalistic or Cartesian cast of mind which thinks in terms of linearity, quantification, and command and control organization. This, sometimes identified as "Second Wave" management thinking, is often compared unfavorably with "Third Wave" theory in which issues of learning and knowledge management are taken as central.

In all kinds of contexts, when we offer people training we help them prepare to undertake a particular task or range of tasks. Teaching people to drive is a good example. The purpose and scope of the training is relatively narrow and well-defined, being typically short-term with outcomes that can be specified in a degree of detail, probably as competences or skills. Work-based training naturally focuses on the skills individuals need in their current employment; other forms of training may focus on the skills needed to secure employment, such as communication skills or the skills of information technology.

When we think of development, on the other hand, we are likely to have in mind considerations of wider personal growth and change. Here we may not be proposing any particular goal, instead sensing that the individual is capable of more than they are achieving in their current position. The frame of reference is longer-term and more open-ended: it is unlikely to be focused on their present employment and may well be connected only in the loosest way with the needs of the employing organization as a whole. We may encourage the individual to undertake a course of study (say, for an MBA), or attach them for a while to a different department to "broaden their vision." Those companies (such as Ford, through its EDAP scheme) which give their employees "learning credits" to learn a foreign language or whatever they would wish to learn are showing their commitment to this kind of development.

Training tends to presuppose that there is an answer—a problem that can be solved—rather than a difficulty that may have to be worked *with*, which the process of development by contrast may acknowledge. In being oriented to skills—to doing rather than being—it does not address the affective and other dimensions of the personal. Training is individualistic and does not attempt to do justice to the organizational, social or political (think of the way these will be ignored in "stress management skills" training).

Training is obviously necessary, and development is fashionable. Both notions underlie much of what is written about the Learning Society into which we are widely supposed to be moving. It is important to see that while training and conceptions of skill are vital in the kinds of fields to which they are appropriate they are damaging if applied in other areas of human learning. Talk of "personal relationship skills" or "listening skills" gets something very wrong. Who, in distress or difficulty, would want "listening skills" exercised on them?

Development, meanwhile, carries its own dangers. Often its vocabulary is that of "personal growth." This moves the focus of concern from the organization to the individual, with the corollary that where failure occurs it is the individual, exclusively, that is to blame. Investment in too *personal* a notion of development may be an excuse for not thinking about the contexts—political, organizational and economic—in which these "developed" people are going to live their lives in the future, in or out of work. Development is insouciant about the connection between people and their work: country hotels host all kinds of outdoor management development programmes, in the *faith* (by no means always misplaced) that this will be somehow beneficial back in the office, irrespective of what kind of office, what place of work that is.

We suggest that there is a need here for a reconceptualization of adult learning in order to give us a picture of the process that takes us beyond the relative narrowness of training but avoids the decontextualization of development. At the heart of this reconceptualization is the idea of *people in dialectical relationship with organizations*. That is to say, this way of thinking of adult learning foregrounds the importance of the connection between individuals and the organizations which in some sense or other they belong to, whether it is their workplaces, communities, social or leisure organizations or organizations of any other sort.

In a world where the great majority of the top *500 Fortune* organizations sell nothing but the ideas and knowledge of their people, these points apply with especial force.

The Knowledge Economy

One of the most familiar ideas of our time is that the Western world is rapidly moving towards a knowledge economy: an economy in which the development and application of knowledge replaces capital, raw materials and labor as the main means of production (Stewart, 1997). Knowledge management—the explicit and systematic management of knowledge and the associated processes of creating, gathering, organizing, diffusion, use and commercial exploitation—is foregrounded in the organizations of the knowledge economy. It requires, for example, transforming personal knowledge into corporate knowledge that can be widely shared throughout an organization and appropriately applied.

It is possible to identify some key themes and characteristic strategies in knowledge management (Nonaka and Takeuchi, 1995). Key themes include the importance of knowing what we know, and of releasing the existing (hidden) knowledge in an organization; enhancing tacit knowledge via strategies for improving interaction and (often but not always) converting tacit knowledge into explicit; making knowledge management an explicit function of the organization and encouraging employees to be self-conscious managers of knowledge, in addition to their other tasks. Characteristic strategies of an organization in the knowledge economy include the appointment of a knowledge leader, the development of knowledge bases (best practices, expert directories, market intelligence, etc.), the use of collaborative technologies, such as intranets or groupware for rapid information access, and the development of knowledge Webs, i.e. networks of experts who collaborate across divisions. We need to be alert to the danger that such strategies may drive us along the route of the management of information systems at the expense of working to support the *people* in whose heads the knowledge lies.

Beyond Training

This takes us beyond training. Training, which by its nature pre-specifies outcomes, inevitably forecloses on the *kinds* of knowledge that are taken to be relevant to the knowledge economy (this is a particular irony if the knowledge economy is premised on rapid and exponential change). The link between knowledge management and the learning organization emphasizes the contribution that personnel/personal development can make in the knowledge economy. But this is not development *in vacuo*. It is the dialectical relationship

> One of the most familiar ideas of our time is that the Western world is rapidly moving towards a knowledge economy.

between person and organization which we wrote of above. Guile and Fonda (1998) argue that the nature of work is changing and that a "process-based organization" made up of "flatter, partnership-based, customer-focused, team and project-orientated structures" is resulting. As a result, they argue that a new learning paradigm is required in which "organizational and individual development has to be seen as a single process of relationships" (Harrison, 1998).

We advocate the need to go beyond training and development because we recognize that neither is enough and each has its characteristic limitations. Development is too open, training not open enough. Training cannot cope with a world of uncertainty, while development may accept it to the point of giving no guidance in how to shape the world. Training cannot deal with a high degree of complexity: development does too little to bring order to complexity. We also advocate the need to go beyond the ideas of organizational development and the learning organization in ways which fundamentally tie together the organization and its members; for neither should be developed at the expense of the other, and neither operates successfully without the other. The frustration and sense of disappointment and pointlessness experienced by employees who are sent off on courses but are not allowed to implement or practice what they have learned when they return to their organizations is a huge waste.

A New Framework

To go beyond training, then, in the narrower sense, what is required is a conception of personal/personnel development which is richer and more responsive to the conditions of a knowledge economy and which moves us to a new paradigm: a way of valuing thinking and feeling. Organizations which take knowledge management seriously will share many of the characteristics of the "learning organization" familiar in literature and practice. They emphasize *openness* (knowledge needs to be seen as public property), the development of new knowledge and new *kinds* of knowledge, the importance of *awareness* (consciousness-raising) about knowledge as a product and process.

We propose that there are seven fundamental principles which require attention if this new framework is to be developed. *All are derived from consideration of the changing conditions which the knowledge economy brings*. They are the principles of:

- *openness*—as the starting point: recognizing and removing barriers, setting the tone which allows learning to happen.
- *uncertainty*—expecting uncertainty and helping people to cope with it because we cannot predict future knowledge.
- *complexity*—problems and solutions are complex in this world. Rushing to the latest "quick-fix" is not the answer.

- *relationships*—learning is a social activity and we must recognize the importance of building relationships to facilitate learning.
- *reflection*—allows us to "know what we know" so we must build systems to ensure that reflection has a recognized and valued place in the organization.
- *reframing*—involves thinking outside of the usual boundaries, thus aiding the development of both a long-term view and new knowledge.
- *restoration*—ensures that what we are good at is not lost but is preserved in a new harmony of purposeful relationships.

Openness

Openness means recognizing barriers and boundaries—personal, organizational and political—as a step towards removing them where appropriate. Openness is the starting point for any organization which hopes to go beyond training, for it is openness which allows learning to happen. To be open is to refuse to settle in advance what might be relevant to personal or organizational development. This may be a difficult concept for organizations which focus their measures of success on outcomes and their immediate impact on the bottom line. Even organizations held up as examples of good practice in their approaches to knowledge management may close down or "keep the lid on" development: "the company won't undertake any knowledge-sharing initiative unless there is a clearly-defined business or technical issue that needs to be solved" was the comment on BP's Connect initiative, a skills database (John, 1998). Knowledge-sharing does not just help us to *solve* business or technical issues. It helps us to realize that there may be issues of which we have not even been *aware* in the first place.

> To be open is to refuse to settle in advance what might be relevant to personal or organizational development.

The open organization is alert and attentive to the world and through analysis builds its capacity for critical awareness of itself in its environment. It seeks feedback in all kinds of ways; it likes to have a mirror held up to it, accepting that it is not possible to move on until you see where you are. Openness is not facilitated by mission statements, glossy brochures and other image management. Intranets and Web sites may be a substitute for it rather than a means towards it.

There are issues of gender and power (as well as other cultural ones) in openness, and the open organization and individual acknowledges them, for openness involves personal vulnerability. Senge (1993) emphasizes the importance of openness to the development of a learning organization, linking openness and vision as the antidote to organizational politics and game-playing. He saw two aspects to openness: the participative openness that comes from an organizational norm of "speaking openly and honestly about important issues" and the reflective openness that is the "capacity continually to challenge one's own thinking." Open organizations trust their employees to be concerned for themselves and for the well-being of the organization. At the least this is an instrumental concern; at best it is motivated by an understanding of the symbiotic nature of the individual/organizational partnership.

We have worked with a food manufacturing organization which was based in a run-down inner-city estate. Its workforce was mainly local and the factory mirrored the decay by which it was surrounded. Working practices barely met the most basic hygiene regulations, the work was routine for the majority of employees and they appeared to take no pride in it. There was no evidence that there was an awareness of these issues—everyone seemed to take it for granted that this was simply "the way things are around here." The company was due to move to new premises which were purpose-built in a newly revitalized area only a short distance away. Almost all its existing workforce would move to the new site. Would the old ways move with them?

A video camera was passed around to make a record of the old site. People enjoyed acting up for the camera. What started as a sentimental commemoration of years of history (which could have moved into company myth about the good old days) became a focus for cultural change, and it came from all levels in the organization. Watching themselves and the factory on film seemed to open up the ability to see themselves more clearly. The film was not threatening: everyone joked about "the state of the place," the dirty floor and the work surfaces cluttered with rubbish. The organization had opened itself to excited discussion about making it different and everyone was interested in the part they were going to play. This pride in themselves is still shared years on. New recruits to the company see the film and through it begin to share the sense of standards and the vision.

Openness can lead to a shared awareness of values and a new inclusiveness which facilitates powerful learning throughout the organization. A good starting point is through institutionalizing open communication: proving from the top of the organization that the intention is to open up the flow of information and knowledge. An organization administering pensions took this seriously by setting up a system to respond to the rumors which can spread when there is a period of change and uncertainty. Staff are encouraged to air the rumors they hear and misinformation is discouraged by swift, open and honest responses from management.

Uncertainty

Uncertainty is the most marked feature of the knowledge economy. The future grows less predictable, the foundations of knowledge less secure. Forms of knowledge are seen to be permeable and such knowledge as we achieve is provisional, our "best truth." We learn, in the knowledge economy, to live with doubt and uncertainty instead of supposing that every problem must have a solution. Risk becomes a constant reality. The individual or organization that can manage (not manage away) uncertainty is at an advantage.

Organizations are consistently urged to plan, set and fix their objectives and encourage their staff to do the same. The acronym SMART is often applied: objectives should be set which are Specific, Measurable, Achievable, Realistic and Timed, and the performance of staff can be monitored and corrected in line with their targets. Clearly this is a training model which can be helpful when appropriately applied. In the knowledge economy we must go beyond training by urging that objectives should not be slick and SMART but WISE or OPEN:

- **W** Workable (rooted in the complex realities of the workplace).
- **I** Intelligent (thoughtful and alert to a wide range of ideas and factors).
- **S** Situated (in the network of relationships in the organizational context).
- **E** Experimental (ready to take risks, try out new ways and formulate new aims).
- **O** Open (responsive to a wide range of ideas and influences).
- **P** Participative (emphasizing inclusivity and shared learning).
- **E** Experiential (seeing learning as rooted in reflection on experience).
- **N** New Knowledge (creating new knowledge rather than managing what is known).

Currently, engineering-based manufacturing organizations are coping with the huge impact of developments in technology. New knowledge is fundamentally changing jobs, not necessarily doing away with them. Globalization has impacted by moving jobs elsewhere in the world, never to return. In this context the members of the organization have to live with the uncertainty and build their knowledge to ensure their own future employability and the survival of the business.

When the automobile industry unveils its "concept cars" at the Motor Show it displays the results of coping positively with uncertainty. Designers have had the opportunity to think creatively and imaginatively. Their cars may never be seen on our roads, but their ideas will influence aspects of design for the future. However, at the start of the project there will have been little certainty of where they might end up and few tightly constraining objectives.

Complexity

That which is complex is densely woven. In the knowledge economy items of knowledge do not sit in discrete boxes but connect with one another and hold implications for each other in ways that are hard to predetermine. The need to share ideas and work together from different disciplinary backgrounds becomes paramount. The model of knowledge becomes perhaps the "rich landscape" rather than the list of separate and sequential points. The linearity of the list (whether of competencies, action-points, outcomes ...) is itself suspect. The landscape lends itself to "dwelling in" rather than "mastery."

The civil service of a small overseas territory was reeling from the impact of one new initiative after another. Our own program, focusing on the ideal of the "learning organization," threatened to become just one more such initiative. Consultants passed through in rapid succession: the civil service was to be "reinvented" on the principles of neo-liberal economics, senior staff were to focus on the "skills of people management," the whole service was to be re-shaped so as to express everything in terms of performance indicators. The only common factor in all these initiatives, as one head of department said bitterly, was that they all reduced your job security and diminished your sense of professional identity. Here the important thing seemed to be not to present our program as one more, competing, set of solutions. Accordingly we focused on how to *live with* constant change rather than how to implement it. It was notable how helpful participants in the program found it that we acknowledged, vigorously and repeatedly, the reality of their experience of rapid change.

We presented ourselves as people who had no particular, predetermined solutions to offer but who could at best work with the civil service to help them find their own piecemeal answers and accommodations. There was some initial discomfort at the idea that we had no shining solutions to bring out of the hat ("You've come all the way from England to tell us you have no solutions to offer us?") and what we felt as pressure to "turn on the tricks" and supply relief and Elastoplast in the form especially of skills training. After we had resisted this for some time and been very open about our own feelings at having no solutions to offer in a context where nevertheless we believed there were no solutions to be found, the atmosphere changed. Participants became able to speak about their own feelings about change ("I've never been able to say this to anyone, not in 11 years ... we only talk a kind of 'professional' language here and that's not enough, it's as if you leave really important bits of yourself behind when you come to work"). They began to think of ways they could use something like our approach with their own staff:

> I know I tend to try to help them find solutions when really there are no solutions, there are difficulties you have to work with and work around as best you can.

Relationships

It is important to see learning as significantly a function of the relationships between persons rather than something held as the "possession" of the individual. We may know truths together that we cannot know apart. Just as the collective intelligence of an organization may fluctuate with circumstance and according to its capacity for collaboration, living with complexity, etc., so may its capacity for sharing and generating knowledge. This will involve particular relationships between particular people and not just the "relational tone" of the organization as a whole. Paying attention to relationships can help the open organization to build trust, sociability, solidarity and commonality. These positive aspects of working life help create the conditions in which learning can occur, for learning is often pleasurable and effective when it is a social activity.

A large and immensely task-focused supplier of information technology software had finally accepted that high rates of absenteeism and illness, as well as of personal problems such as alcoholism, breakdown, divorce and so on, might be connected with the stressful working lives of its employees. Various training courses had attempted to equip people with the "skills of interpersonal relationships" and of course "stress management skills" of various sorts. During the progress of our lengthy contact with this organization, senior managers became more and more prepared to talk of the problems, not of relationships in the company in general, but of various particular relationships between particular individuals (and often ones where the success of the relationship was crucial in terms of lines of communication and responsibility in the organization as a whole).

Rather than focus directly on these relationships as if some organizational version of *Relate* was called for the company decided to set up a mentoring scheme for all employees. Everyone would have a mentor; many if not most would themselves be mentors to others. This, it believed, would require everyone in the organization to be more sensitive to issues of supportiveness, appropriate distance, acceptable criticism. Through being both mentor and mentee, people would become better at seeing matters from the other's point of view. An early problem was that the scheme was a victim of its own success ("Everyone's so interested in mentoring there's no bloody work getting done around here!"); following this honeymoon there grew up a perception that meetings were running better and key relationships were improving, particularly because employees were becoming more sensitive to power differentials and their effects ("My mentoring sessions have made me much more aware how things here look from two or three grades down ... it's too easy to think everyone shares your own outlook").

Reflection

The successful organization in the knowledge economy welcomes all opportunities to look at itself, since this is a source of vital knowledge. Processes of "mirroring" are consciously put into place. They may occur through celebration, festivity, shared mourning (e.g. for a defunct project) as well as in more familiar ways such as appraisal and review. Reflection is sometimes non-verbal (the foyer display, the cover of the in-house magazine). Such processes are kept distinct from image-management. Reflection allows us to "know what it is that

The successful organization in the knowledge economy welcomes all opportunities to look at itself, since this is a source of vital knowledge.

we know" and is the starting point for moving forward. It requires putting systems in place in our organizations to ensure that it happens, that it becomes second nature in individuals and institutionalized in our organizations.

A recent popular television program used these processes to help people to sell their houses when they had been on the market for a long time and no-one wanted to buy them. "Expert" advisors were brought in to advise, but in reality what they did was to help the homeowners see for themselves some very basic aspects of their homes which required attention. It does not take an *expert* to tell us that our houses would be more attractive to potential buyers if we tidied up our everyday clutter and made our rooms appear more spacious. But these *reflective processes* helped the owners to see what was all around them that they had stopped noticing.

Reframing

Reframing occurs where the organization questions and moves its established boundaries. This process allows a long-term view to be taken and promotes the development of new knowledge. The move to thinking in terms of the knowledge economy is itself a major piece of reframing. The organization welcomes "liminality," the experience of moving through a frame, and does not seek to hasten the process unduly since it is one richly productive of new knowledge and insights. "Training," in the sense described above, can be particularly destructive of reframing since it demands that the frame be fixed in advance.

Reframing the National Health Service (NHS) is an urgent priority if it is to survive into the twenty-first century. Increasing numbers of an ageing population and new demands on the service through advancements in knowledge, technology and the expectations of patients require managers to think in new frames of reference: to radically rethink what they are there for. Instead of trying to be endlessly more efficient and effective we have to take the radical step of rethinking basic ends and purposes. As those who have made the attempt have discovered, it may occasion discomfort and hostility.

Restoration

Restoration acknowledges that people need to have something "put back," restored to them through their daily work. This is especially true where the knowledge economy denies people the familiar satisfactions of predictability and of the regular production of tangible goods. More than any of the other six elements, restoration takes seriously the often-repeated idea that people are an organization's greatest asset. What *counts* as restoration may differ from person to person according to their "psychological contract" with their workplace. Parallels can be drawn between restoration and what Kessels (1996) in his work on the corporate curriculum calls "peace and stability."

It is particularly important after difficult times that an effort is made to restore. In the last eight years BT has more than halved its workforce. Against a background of concerns about morale and motivation it launched a new way of working called "... *for a better life.*" The aims were to improve customer-focus, motivate staff and live up to the public image it sold of the benefits of good communication by placing its emphasis on staff and customers, not technology. There was a desire to instill a new sense of excitement and belonging, to restore faith, trust and hope in a new kind of organization. Thus "... *for a better life*" is referred to as a crusade, rather than a program or an initiative (Mason, 1998) because it was intended to be a long-term investment which it was recognized might take years to embed into the culture of the organization. It is still "alive and well four and a half years after its inception."

Employee Development Programmes (along the lines of Ford's EDAP scheme which encourages employees to learn by funding their efforts, whether or not they are work-related or vocational), are becoming increasingly common. After a period of conflict and industrial disputes in their Peterlee factory was finally settled, Walkers Crisps began an EDAP scheme specifically in an attempt at restoration—giving something back to their staff which would help to restore relationships and harmony.

Restoration takes place on a different level when organizations give something back to their surroundings. There is some evidence to suggest that organizations are beginning to take seriously once again their responsibilities to the communities in which they are based. Many organizations are to be congratulated on the innovative ways they are developing their links with their locality, often in symbiotic partnerships which also contribute to the continuing development of their staff. One example of this is BT's "Roots and wings" campaign to mentor young people in schools in underprivileged areas (Mason, 1998).

When football clubs make efforts to link with their locality (for example by encouraging visits to the ground by local schools or by their players coaching local children) this is not just a matter of good public relations. There is an element of restoration, of giving something back to the area in which they are based. However, the club itself also benefits from these activities, since often they help to give the more wayward young players a sense of themselves as role models, with responsibilities to others. It is this which can encourage self-discipline of a sort which is more effective than any discipline the club can impose.

Conclusion

In a relatively known and predictable world rational solutions can be planned, for training as for anything else. A program can be organized and implemented so that a workforce acquires the skills it needs. These skills will be the possessions of individuals (and will vanish with them when they leave the organization): where else can learning be located but in the individual, whether in his or her head or hands? But perhaps we are beginning to see the limitations of this way of understanding things. To conceive learning objectives as WISE and OPEN (as stated) is to begin to transcend these limitations. They take us into a world where the old certainties and regularities are rapidly disappearing. They acknowledge the *social* nature of learning: that knowledge is created by people in combination with each other and also lives in social relationships (and so will not vanish with the employee). It is a function of persons in interaction and not a possession of individuals.

An article on training would, at this stage of its conclusion, clearly indicate (preferably with bullet-points) the way forward: it would signpost what the reader should do next. Of course this has its place. Yet this is the characteristic device of technical/rational thinking and, in its worst manifestations, is suggestive of the "quick fix." It would be ironic to adopt this device in an article intended to foreground a very different philosophy of personal and personnel development. That does not mean that there are no practical ways forward "beyond training." The social nature of learning, for instance, is rich in implications: for making places and spaces for people to meet, for giving them time to do so, for telling them (in all kinds of ways and not just the explicit) that talk and the sharing of ideas is valued.

And, finally, the organization which understands the value of going beyond training will pay attention to the seven principles of openness, uncertainty, complexity and so on, that we outlined. It will be prepared to initiate and sustain dialogue among its members on the state of these issues in their workplaces. It will perhaps consider appraising performance in ways which require people to set WISE and OPEN and not SMART objectives for themselves. Otherwise it is hard to see how organizations will develop the flexibility and creativity necessary for "a new economic order in which the daily work environment is an authentic learning situation that highlights the role of the learner" (Kessels, 1996) rather than that of the teacher, trainer or training program.

References

Eccles, R.G., and Nohria, N. (1992), *Beyond the Hype: Rediscovering the Essence of Management*, Harvard Business School Press, Boston, MA.

Guile, D., and Fonda, N. (1998), *Performance Management Through Capability*, IPD, London.

Hamel, G., and Prahalad, C.K. (1994), "Strategy as a Field of Study: Why Search for a New Paradigm?," *Strategic Management Journal*, Vol. 15, pp. 5-16.

Harrison, R. (1998), "Move with the Goal Posts," *People Management*, 22 January, Vol. 33.

John, G. (1998), "Share strength," *People Management*, 13 August, pp. 44-47.

Kessels, J. (1996), "Knowledge Productivity and the Corporate Curriculum," *Proceedings of the Fourth International ISMICK Symposium*, Rotterdam.

Kets de Vries, M.F.R. (1995), *Life and Death in the Executive Fast Lane: Essays on Irrational Organizations and Their Leaders*, Jossey-Bass, San Francisco, CA.

Mason, B (1998), "Switchboard," *People Management*, 29 October, pp. 46-48.

Nonaka, I., and Takeuchi, H. (1995), *The Knowledge-Creating Company*, Oxford University Press, Oxford.

Senge, P. (1993), *The Fifth Discipline: The Art and Practice of the Learning Organization*, Doubleday, New York, NY.

Stewart, T.A. (1997), *Intellectual Capital: The New Wealth of Organizations*, Doubleday, New York, NY.

Patricia Bryans is a Lecturer in the Centre for Professional Development, University of Durham, UK. Contact her at Patricia.Bryans@durham.ac.uk.

Richard Smith is a Senior Lecturer in the School of Education at the University of Durham, UK. Contact him at R.D.Smith@durham.ac.uk.

Leadership DNA: The Ford Motor Story

Stewart D. Friedman

Ford Motor Company has determined that leadership development is at the absolute center of all its efforts to succeed in the marketplace and as a corporate citizen. This article by the director of Ford's Leadership Development Center explains in detail why Ford has developed this center, and how it works. It is a great example of how one company has made its commitment to people development and strategic success one and the same thing.

We live in extraordinary times. Not a day goes by when we don't hear or read about a new discovery, invention, or business initiative that will ultimately affect all of our lives. New media are transforming virtually every aspect of human action. On top of the digital revolution, add new business models, globalization, and new labor market dynamics (such as increased diversity and fresh attitudes about work and one's personal life) and you have a different world than business leaders have ever seen before.

The underlying structure of the global economy is shifting, bringing with it a bewildering array of unprecedented challenges that require a new kind of leadership. Developing the next generation of leaders at a time of momentous change is a monumental task. Yet, those of us in the field of leadership development must continue to ask fundamental questions:

- How can we accelerate the identification of candidates for leadership positions?
- What methods should we use to enable our people to become competitive in the new economy?
- How can we challenge our leaders to contribute to the transformation of our company?
- How can we accelerate the preparation of our best leaders for senior executive roles?
- How can we drive our company's vision deep into its culture?
- How can we create a new leadership mindset that invests in the developing leader as a whole person, capable of contributing not only at work, but also at home and in the community?

Reprinted with permission from *Training & Development*, March 2001. Copyright © 2001 by the American Society for Training & Development. All rights reserved.

Ford Motor Company is facing those same questions; senior management has set the direction. In our 2000 Corporate Citizenship Report, chairman William Clay Ford Jr. writes: "We see no conflict between business goals and social and environmental needs. I believe the distinction between a good company and a great one is this: A good company delivers excellent products and services; a great one delivers excellent products and services and strives to make the world a better place."

In the same report, our CEO Jacques Nasser observes: "The transition from a traditional manufacturer to a 21st-century consumer company is critical for our long-term financial success. It requires a new mindset—one focused on connecting not only with our customers, but also with all of our stakeholders to make it work."

The DNA Revolution

Adopting a consumer mindset as well as one of environmental and social responsibility requires leadership. We need leaders who can make informed business decisions that will make our company better able to meet customer needs and increase shareholder value, as well as honor commitments to the world in which we live. Change like that is easy to talk about but difficult to implement. It will take nothing less than a massive shift in culture to create new leadership DNA. Nothing short of revolution will do.

And that is where our Leadership Development Center enters. Our vision is to be the center for the revolution, developing Ford Motor Company leaders to change the world. Our mission is to accelerate transformation to a consumer- and shareholder-driven business, to accelerate the identification and development of leadership talent, and to drive the company's mission, vision, and values deep into its culture.

How can we do that? We've developed a series of leadership programs centered around these core principles:
- Adopt a transformational mindset.
- Use action learning—learning by doing, leading, and teaching.
- Leverage the power of e-tools.
- Integrate work and life, what I call "total leadership."
- Generate business impact.

Let's examine the first two in depth and the others later on.

Adopt a Transformational Mindset

The chief way that Ford's Leadership Development Center is fomenting revolution is by creating transformational leaders—men and women who know how to get things done in ways that use the talents of their people for maximum business impact. Our leaders also learn to think "outside of the box" because our programs force them out of their comfort zones in everything

Adopting a consumer mindset as well as one of environmental and social responsibility requires leadership.

from selecting a project to working with new people. Participants return to their positions enthused and ready to look at familiar challenges with fresh eyes and to try new ideas that deliver results.

We nurture the transformational mind-set by consistently challenging participants to think of alternative possibilities. That push really begins before participants start the training. The workload of most programs isn't light, and the real work isn't done in the classroom but in the field of real business activity. Participants are expected to do work prior to the classroom phase—mainly, to choose a project and research feasibility. They must devise innovative ways to balance their usual workloads and assume responsibility for meeting program requirements. The challenge is to find ways to eliminate unnecessary tasks and obtain help. Many participants learn to empower their staff and to network with peers to delegate their day-to-day responsibilities. In itself, that is a significant opportunity for leadership lessons.

Transformational leadership at Ford is underscored, as reflected in our expected leadership behaviors, by these values: integrity, flawless execution, and the building of effective relationships with key stake-holders. In other words, while we're asking our people to think and behave differently, we are mindful of our company's culture and respectful of its rich cultural values.

Another aspect of the transformational mindset is the growing need to recognize the triple bottom line of financial success, environmental protection, and social responsibility. Our programs have community service aspects that serve to put our work as a company in the perspective of the larger social context in which we operate, and to which we must contribute. There is a growing realization that a company such as ours (indeed, most companies for that matter) can't continue with traditional business models into the 21st century. We're actively incorporating renewable resource technologies and developing alternatives to the internal combustion engine, for example. Such bold actions require equally bold leaders to implement them. Success in the new century requires the transformational mindset, one found in our new leadership DNA.

Use Action Learning

All of our programs feature action learning. Participants work individually or in teams with leaders at all levels on projects that challenge them to expand their creative abilities and refine their critical-thinking and execution skills—all in order to drive for improved business results.

Participants receive extensive feedback from multiple sources that enables them to improve and refine their leadership abilities. In addition, alumni of our programs serve as leader-teachers—a practice that helps participants and the instructor grow and develop new capacities for leadership.

It's also a critical feature of our strategy to "spread the word." Action learning creates business impact. The projects participants choose must have a business benefit in terms of customer satisfaction, cost reduction, or enhanced revenue. One of the most notable examples is the QIP—the Quantum Idea Project. It's the key to our New Business Leader program for first-time supervisors of salaried employees. The QIP, intended to drive revolutionary change at Ford, stretches an individual's capacity to think critically, innovate daringly, evaluate choices strategically, and support business objectives wisely. In the process, a manager begins to develop leadership skills that he or she can use every day.

The QIP process is organized according to key milestones, checkoffs, and evaluation processes inherent to a project. Biweekly, participants undergo a cycle of review that occurs in teams with a peer serving as co-strategist or advisor. Review also happens online on password-protected Websites. During these reviews, participants rate their projects as *green* (good to go), *yellow* (not quite sure), or *red* (stuck). Then, they receive feedback and support on how to maintain momentum and progress towards their goals.

Additionally, our programs instill a sense of accountability. Participants are evaluated on the outcome of their projects and how well they performed as leaders. For example, how did they interact with their peers? Did they network successfully? Did they learn new ways of doing things? Success as a leader depends on more than delivering results; it requires an ability to continually strengthen working alliances and a willingness to test new ideas. The feedback participants receive from multiple sources such as peers, clients, and supervisors adds to their sense of accountability. The feedback also becomes instructive in the development of a person's leadership style and capacity.

Four-Five Punch

At present, the Leadership Development Center at Ford Motor Company offers nine programs—four core and five strategic change initiatives. The four core programs play a significant role in the identification, selection, and development of Ford's next generation of leaders. For admission, candidates must be rated either as having high potential or recent high performance. The four core programs, targeted for specific leadership levels, are listed in ascending order:

1. *New Business Leader* teaches leadership through the pursuit of innovative ideas designed to transform the business. To date, participants have generated more than 600 QIPs (quantum idea projects), all of which aim for a specific business impact. Participants increase their leadership capacity by building skills in the 12 Ford leadership behaviors as they learn how to take their ideas from conception to implementation.

2. *Leadership for the New Economy* pioneers new ways to work. A primary goal is to enable leaders to deliver strong business results and enrich lives by using

> At present, the Leadership Development Center at Ford Motor Company offers nine programs—four core and five strategic change initiatives.

new economy tools and by taking what I call a "total leadership" perspective—integrating work, home, community, and self. The lessons emerging from this program are accelerating transformation as participants teach others throughout the company about how they've changed the way work is done.

3. *Experienced Leader Challenge* demonstrates how to deliver improved business results in the form of cost reduction and revenue generation by working in cross-functional teams. Participants improve their leadership capacity by working in an environment that develops new business knowledge and that leverages the strengths of broad, cross-functional networks for specific results.

4. *Capstone* prepares people moving into positions of senior leadership. Capstone projects are strategic in nature and are designed to expand leadership capacity to the next level. Corporate officers are sponsors for projects, and senior leaders are involved in teaching, coaching, and evaluating participants.

The Leadership Development Center lends its support through strategic change initiatives, which by nature cut across vertical and horizontal boundaries. At present, there are five change initiative programs underway:

1. *Leadership for Consumer-Driven, Six-Sigma* complements the technical training of Black Belt candidates by teaching the leadership skills required for successful execution of Black Belt projects.
2. *Ford/Supplier BLI* fosters collaborative partnerships with Ford's key suppliers to improve understanding, increase efficiency, and lower costs.
3. *BLI 3 Flawless Execution* builds business leadership competencies in vehicle line, cross-functional teams responsible for designing, engineering, and developing new cars and trucks.
4. *New Leader Impact* rapidly integrates newly hired executives by cultivating networks throughout the company and by reinforcing their role as agents of change.
5. *Global Leadership Forum* brings Ford's top 300 executives together on a quarterly basis to focus on key business initiatives and to strengthen connections among the key players in our company.

Those Who Can, Teach

Every program features extensive use of teachers. Graduates of our programs serve as leader-teachers, a practice that helps participants and the instructor grow and develop new capacities for leadership. The concept of leader-teacher isn't unique, but Ford places a high emphasis on teaching. The lesson begins at the top.

More than three years ago, CEO Jacques Nasser inaugurated the Business Leadership Initiative concept with himself as teacher. Now, thousands of managers are teaching other managers about everything from the basics of supervision to the intricacies of Six Sigma. Nowhere is the concept of leader-teacher more prevalent than in the *New Business Leader* program. The active participation of senior leaders in the Quantum Idea Project process is essential. Each QIP must have a senior leader sponsor who serves as a project mentor. The sponsor not only shepherds the project, but he or she also nurtures the leadership capacity of participants.

Another way that leader-teachers contribute is through feedback. Participants in all of our core programs receive extensive feedback from multiple sources to enable them to improve and refine their leadership abilities. The feedback is a two-way street; leader-teachers receive feedback on how they teach. That input is extremely valuable and gives them something to take back to the workplace.

Leader-teachers also create synergy throughout all of the action-learning programs. Graduates become teachers, sponsors, and mentors of participants. That creates cohesion in a spirit of revolutionary change and helps accelerate the transformational process that we're all engaged in.

The Power of E-Tools

If we're expecting people to work in the new economy, we need to give them tools to work more effectively. The global 24/7 reality makes working face-to-face often impossible; time zones and distance preclude it. Yet, we need people to work together. Thankfully, technology is making it possible.

The Internet and e-mail are the starting points; virtual collaboration is the next step. For example, in our *Leadership for the New Economy* program, participants work in virtual spaces called "e-rooms" six weeks prior to commencement of the first residential (classroom) session. They also begin working collaboratively in the e-room, using an online tool dedicated to their program sessions and monitored by faculty made up of Ford executives and outside faculty drawn from leading universities and consulting firms. Interestingly, the team set the standard in virtual collaboration as the program was designed and delivered by people who functioned as a virtual team during most of the development.

Taking e-tools to the next step—as a learning exercise as well as a way to have fun—participants took part in an online auction conducted by AutoXchange (later Covisint), bidding on the opportunity to meet individually with outside experts from joint-venture partners and other companies that could offer useful insight and information on specific projects. Not only did the bidding process teach participants lessons about online auctions, but it also enabled them to expand their network of information and resources.

In using e-tools, participants invest time and energy trying out new ways of working that leverage synergies among work, home, and community, thus taking a total leadership approach. That might involve experimenting with telecommuting, flexible schedules, reduced face-time for internal meetings (while making more intelligent use of face-time for customers and other

> In using e-tools, participants invest time and energy trying out new ways of working that leverage synergies among work, home, and community, thus taking a total leadership approach.

external stakeholders), and other new models for leadership.

To augment our e-leadership mindset, we launched a Web site devoted to leadership, with the intention to make it all things to all people at Ford who are interested in leadership. We consider it our virtual community for Ford leadership. Anyone at Ford can visit the site and learn how to gain insight into leadership best practices and get access to leadership materials, including self-nomination forms for admission to our programs. In addition, each program has e-rooms where participants can work independently or cooperatively on their projects.

Integrating Work and Life

We at Ford are pioneering a new dimension of leadership that seeks to integrate all aspects of a person's life. We call it "total leadership." Total leadership is similar to most leadership approaches in that it aims to achieve superior results. It's different from many prior leadership models because it starts with your life as a whole: your life at work, your life at home, and your life in the community. Total leadership recognizes that the stakeholder expectations in each of those domains can and do affect each other. Therefore, total leadership is about being a leader in all aspects of one's life.

New technologies, specifically the e-tools, permit us to integrate stakeholder domains and even create synergies among them. No longer is business leadership confined to the work domain. Boundaries between diverse domains of life are becoming more permeable and flexible, and leadership now must account for that emerging reality. Leaders will have to leverage resources—financial and human capital, technology, new business models, and so forth—to gain synergies across diverse stakeholder domains: work, home, community, and self.

The total leadership perspective allows for a faster, more agile means to achieve superior business results in the 24/7, global, anytime-anywhere economy. More specifically, because it deemphasizes face-time and focuses on results both within and across domains, the total leadership perspective offers the potential for reduced workload and better results, in all aspects of life.

Business results increase in the short term because of

- increased motivation and commitment
- greater efficiencies in work processes
- reduced cycle times
- lower costs (from less travel, for example)
- enhanced customer focus through explicit emphasis on performance impact across the value chain
- more active engagement by business leaders in home and community life.

With employees having greater control in arranging their life circumstances, long-term business benefits accrue—including greater attraction and retention of top talent in the new labor market, less burnout and stress (potentially related to health-care costs), and decreased down-time from poorly managed connections between work and other aspects of life.

That's the good news, the opportunity. As pioneers facing the frontier of a new economy, the challenge for us is to develop the total leadership capacity necessary to bring the opportunity to reality. It requires understanding more about how to leverage the resources inherent in new-economy tools and models. That means learning how to

- capture synergies across domains of life so that total achievement in life is greater than just the sum of efforts applied at work, at home, in the community, and for one's self
- make more conscious and strategic choices about allocation of time and energy towards valued goals
- rethink the means by which work gets done in ways that force a results-driven focus
- reduce reliance on traditional work methods—face-time and co-location of resources—and use them more wisely
- innovate to better meet performance expectations of key stakeholders at work, at home, in the community, and those you hold for yourself
- aggressively cultivate networks and partnerships that provide the support needed for flexibility and agility in and across domains.

We believe our programs need to continue to develop total leadership capacity further to stay ahead of the curve in the rapidly evolving economic and social environments of business in the 21st century. It isn't a stretch to say that without a total leadership perspective, our company will not be able to compete successfully in the future. Total leadership is essential to Ford's new leadership DNA.

> It isn't a stretch to say that without a total leadership perspective, our company will not be able to compete successfully in the future.

Generating Business Impact

All of the programs significantly impact business in two ways: financially and organizationally. Financially, each individual or team project must contribute to customer satisfaction, reduced costs, or increased incremental revenue. And we have some impressive statistics.

Participants in QIP programs have generated more than 600 projects, some with significant business impact such as tire recycling, vehicle customization, and new vehicle servicing models.

A recent *Ford Supplier/Business Leadership Initiative* program identified $300 in cost-reductions per vehicle, which is now in development. Three hundred dollars may not seem like much at first, but when you multiple it by thousands of vehicles, the savings is substantial.

Projects in the *Experienced Leader Challenge* program have identified more than $100 million in cost-savings and another $100 million in incremental revenue. Over the next three to five years, those numbers will likely climb to the billions in savings and earnings.

You can accurately declare that our leadership programs pay for themselves many times over. But that's only part of the story. The second business impact is the effect our programs are having on the organization. We're accelerating the process of creating leaders at every level by having emerging and experienced leaders work individually as well as collaboratively on projects of significant merit. We create synergies further among the programs that, in turn, further facilitate learning and speed the development of leadership capacities.

Bottom line: We are creating transformational leaders, men and women who know how to get things done in ways that use the talents of their people for maximum business impact. For that reason, I believe it's no exaggeration to say that the return on this organizational contribution is exponential. And in the new economy in which we face escalating customer demands, fluid market conditions, and global scale, exponential return is what is required.

Leadership development is an evolutionary process that changes as the needs of an organization change. Core principles, such as action learning or leader-teachers, may remain. But the what, why, and how of a program should change in response to emerging issues. As one who has taught leadership in an academic and now a corporate setting, I suggest these guidelines when creating a leadership development program:

Create a sense of urgency for leadership development. Leadership is not a nice-to-have; it's a must do. Success in the new economy, or any economy, will require men and women to adopt a transformational mindset that enables them to anticipate change, develop strategies to meet new demands, and continue to maximize growth opportunities. In a nutshell, all of that requires leadership.

Our CEO, Jacques Nasser, is brilliant at conveying urgency. Despite years of record earnings, Nasser has been galvanizing Ford to transform itself as quickly as possible in an effort to become a 21st-century company capable of meeting escalating demands and adapting to the rules of the new economy.

Develop a brand for your leadership-development strategy. Every successful consumer product has a readily identifiable brand. Same goes for services. Brand, put simply, is the sum of the attributes, aspirations, and perceptions associated with a product or service. At the heart of successful brands is a sense of trust between the provider and the consumer. That's the kind of trust we're trying to foster with Ford employees whom we encourage to join our programs. Therefore, it makes good sense to develop a strong brand image around the kind of transformational leadership we're trying to create.

Our brand image revolves around creating a new leadership DNA. We even developed a logo (a double helix) and gradually began attributing to it positive characteristics of leadership at Ford. Over time, we believe our brand will become synonymous with the kind of transformational mindset Ford is creating.

Communicate the results of leadership-development activities. Communication is central to leadership, so why would it be any different for a leadership-development program? Tom Grant, program leader for *New Business Leader*, often talks about the time in the not-too-distant future when applicants to the program will exceed its capacity to deliver. Grant is no glutton for excess work, but he understands that when more people want to participate, we'll have achieved a measure of success.

Demand is tied directly to communications, so it's important to use all available means to communicate about your programs: Web site, e-mail, video, print materials. Be certain you also communicate your brand in everything you do. Make the logo and its associated images ubiquitous. But a word to the wise: Keep senior leadership in the loop. Invite them to teach, and send them regular updates on what's going on in the programs. Solicit their feedback. Their active support is essential to the long-term health of your programs. Indeed, the Leadership Development Center at Ford isn't an HR initiative; it's owned by senior line management.

Celebrate achievements. Leadership programs should be targeted to achieve business results. When they do, publicize them. Let others in the organization know how the programs are affecting the bottom line. In this way, you can shift the perception of leadership development from a "cost" to a "revenue enhancer." More important, you will demonstrate that leadership development isn't something nice to have but a must-have that not only pays for itself, but also facilitates a mindset and culture that seek to build the business. Frankly, you can't put a price tag on that.

Promote your alumni as leaders of tomorrow. The ultimate measure of any leadership-development program is how well the alumni do. If graduates are moving up in the organization, it's an indication that the lessons of the leadership-development program are effective. As more graduates move up through our organization, the leadership message and example will become part of the culture and transformation process.

A leadership-development program can help its alumni achieve success in the organization in two ways. One, alumni make terrific teachers. Keep bringing them back to your programs.

They'll not only help your current participants, but they will also hone their own leadership skills. Two, create an alumni association (similar to what universities do) to help grads of the leadership development programs network with each other and senior leaders. The success of a program depends on its alumni. The more you can do for them, the better you will do for your leadership development efforts and the organization as a whole.

> Promote your alumni as leaders of tomorrow. The ultimate measure of any leadership-development program is how well the alumni do.

Make no mistake: The Leadership Development Center is no charm school. It's more like an obstacle course devised by the Marines to bring out the best in Ford's leadership talent by pushing, prodding, and stretching for results.

David Murphy, our vice president of human resources, says, "We aim to be seen by Wall Street as the best-led company in the world, with leaders at all levels, building leadership capacity faster than any other corporation. "We must become a company where leadership represents intellectual capital at such a level that it will out learn, out compete, and out lead all of the competition to ensure ongoing increases in shareholder value throughout the foreseeable future."

People who graduate from the Leadership Development Center gain improved customer focus, a renewed commitment to business results, and a greater understanding of their role in generating shareholder value. They become transformational leaders—ready, willing, and able to lead Ford Motor Company to meet future challenges. Perhaps the truest measure of our impact will be in the marketplace for talent when Ford is seen as *the* company to go to for the best leadership talent in the business world.

Stewart D. Friedman is the director of the Leadership Development Center at Ford Motor Company and co-author of Work and Family: Allies or Enemies? *(Oxford University Press, 2000).*

The Little Airplane That Could

Sarah Fister Gale

What do you do if a major product line is losing money and company morale and cooperation are low? Boeing faced that situation with its 717 program. As it reorganized its approach to this problem product line, training was essential. The company conducted a training event for representatives from four key groups: employees, union workers, support organizations, and stakeholders throughout the supply chain. It also provided leadership training and mentoring for managers.

When aircraft manufacturers Boeing and McDonnell Douglas merged four years ago, everyone expected the 717 program to crash. Like three other airplane programs housed at McDonnell Douglas' Long Beach, CA facility, the 717 was losing money like jettisoning fuel—millions of dollars, in fact, on each 100-seat commercial jet built. But unlike those other programs, Boeing executives didn't clip the wings of the downtrodden 717. Instead, they decided to fix it.

Today, the program that was expected to sell fewer than 200 planes in its lifetime is flying high with orders for more than 300 planes. And—unlike the 717s of four years ago—these planes earn Boeing a profit.

The Challenge: Building a Profitable Program

The layout of the 717 manufacturing process was inefficient, there was no cooperation between employees, union workers and suppliers, and the massive downsizing that came with the merger had created an overall negative attitude at the Long Beach facility. With the termination of the other three programs, the facility went from employing close to 6,000 people to 3,000 in less than two years, turning the 7.5 million-square-foot complex into an airplane hangar ghost town. Naturally, the remaining employees were fearful for their jobs.

"We seriously considered also shutting down the 717 program," says Boeing CFO Scott Carson. And few would have argued with that decision, except for the fact that the 717 filled the 100-seat, short-range-flight niche—a growing market with great appeal for Boeing. Carson saw the 717's tailspin

Reprinted with permission from *TRAINING* Magazine, December 2000. Copyright © 2000 Bill Communications. All rights reserved.

> ## WILD SUCCESS
>
> To kick off the strategic business transformation program for Boeing's ailing 717 airplane, The Belgard Group, along with Deloitte and Touche, hosted a five-day off-site training event for representatives from four key groups: employees, union workers, support organizations and stakeholders throughout the supply chain.
>
> "A strategic business transformation begins with the definition of the strategic imperative," says Bill Belgard, president. "We needed a goal that was highly desirable but currently out of reach."
>
> During the kick-off meeting, the group agreed that their strategic imperative was to become "wildly successful." In other words, they would reduce costs and sell more planes—to the benefit of each member. For employees, wild success would result in job security; for shareholders, an increase in earnings; for suppliers, financial wealth.
>
> "Wild success is at the center of our entire transformation," says Pat McKenna, director of the program management office at Boeing. "We want to sell 1,000 planes or more and make sure everyone makes a reasonable profit."
>
> In addition to defining 717 success, kick-off meeting participants determined seven key areas in which change was required to achieve that success: leadership, team-based culture, supplier alignment, overhead costs, relationship with labor, strategies and customer focus. For each of the seven areas, representatives from every part of the value chain formed a team with the goal of making the necessary changes, while communicating them with the rest of the organization.
>
> With these groups in place, the 717 team was ready for the real challenge: turning wild success into reality.

as an opportunity to rethink traditional airplane manufacturing methods, and make "a fundamental change in business processes." He wanted to see what would happen if traditional hardcore management tactics were replaced with empowered, educated teams and a lean, more entrepreneurial business approach. The goal: a profitable program that produced a highly salable airplane.

Though unorthodox, this wasn't a completely new concept for Boeing or Carson. The C17, an airlift aircraft built for the U.S. Air Force, faced similar quality and production problems in 1995. With the expertise of The Belgard Group, a Hillsboro, OR, change management organization, Boeing was able to make dramatic cultural changes and turn the C17 program from a loss generator into a profit center in less than a year. Ultimately, manufacturing costs were reduced by 50 percent, production increased two-fold, and the program eventually won the Malcolm Baldrige Award in 1998.

A witness to the C17 transformation, Carson believed that he could replicate that success with the help of Bill Belgard, president of The Belgard Group, and Ed Schaniel, Boeing's director of employee involvement and a key player in the C17 turnaround. The three agreed that implementing team-based management, lean principles and considerable training for all Long Beach facility employees would give the 717 program a fighting chance.

"The idea was to take a portion of a large airplane company and turn it into a small, fast entrepreneurial organization, increasing speed and flexibility," says Belgard. Isolated from the rest of Boeing's Seattle-based headquarters and responsible for only a single product, the 717 program was the ideal testing ground for this theory.

The 717 program was also a more cost-effective place to test the new business theories. "If you are going to learn lessons, it's better to experiment at the low end and then spread those lessons to other programs," explains Belgard. The 717 costs about $2.8 million, a relatively inexpensive product for the airplane industry.

> The idea was to take a portion of a large airplane company and turn it into a small, fast entrepreneurial organization.

The Plan: Redefining Responsibilities

"In the past we gave people authority without accountability," says Jim Michel, director of final assembly for the 717 program. "We needed teams that had freedom with responsibility."

To open lines of communication and eliminate waste, functionally aligned, self-managing work teams were formed, grouping employees according to their function, not their titles. For example, instead of housing all the engineers in a separate building, they grouped them in teams around specific tasks. Members in all functions of the organization—from finance and labor unions to engineering, and product support—were grouped together according to specific tasks such as interior design, final assembly, propulsion and product delivery.

With the new structure came new training. Employees learned about business concepts, including lean management principles, internal ROI and shareholder value—including how their actions could potentially affect overall costs or create a competitive advantage in the marketplace.

"Traditionally, each person did a single task and went home," says Schaniel. "Now they have a global view of the production cycle, from conception to design to manufacture and delivery."

And as the functional workgroups became more competent, they also became more efficient—and frugal. In the past, for example, the assembly department ordered parts for immediate delivery, regardless of whether or not that part was needed immediately—but a single rush order cost the company five times more than a five-day delivery request.

"They'd meet their own on-time goals but they didn't care what it cost," says Phil Rowberg, a senior manager on the program. "Now that they own that cost, they make smarter, more-educated business decisions."

Along with making the teams more effective, this "big picture view" has given employees enormous pride in the products they build. Carson, who once observed the Long Beach facility on the verge of closing, now sees workers applauding as new planes roll off the factory floor. "They are proud of the product and what they've accomplished," he says.

The "Lean" Physical Plant

To promote this newly adopted view throughout the actual manufacturing process, changes were needed at every stage along the production line. More than 5 million square feet of space at the facility was sold, and the 717 work teams were moved into a single space—Building 80, a 600,000-square-foot factory. Updates were made in the look and feel of the building and better lighting was installed. The workflow process was redesigned so employees work side by side on a full-moving production line—a first for a commercial airplane, says Carson.

"In this environment the person who designs the seats is next to the person who builds them, and he's next to the person who installs them," says Schaniel.

At each position on the new line, mechanics complete assigned tasks on the airplane—from joining the fuselage sections and wings, to adding control surfaces and engines, to installing the flight deck and cabin interior. Standard assembly line work is repeated on each airplane to boost efficiency; and drawings, parts and tools are brought in as-needed to the mechanics—as if they were surgeons and the airplanes were patients.

Concerns that workers would be upset by the move—especially after being "enthroned" in their own offices—were unfounded. Being close together in the factory setting actually motivated employees, says Carson. And because they work side by side to complete whole tasks, hours of time lost passing projects from designers to engineers to assembly, all of whom were housed in different buildings, were eliminated.

Within a few feet of the assembly positions, support teams are located in open factory-floor offices. The teams are equipped with everything they need to help keep airplanes moving, including specialists who inspect work while it's being done. Other resources were also relocated for easy access, including a quick-response parts fabrication shop, a team dedicated to meeting rapid equipment requests, and a parts-receiving and inventory area.

Now people see themselves as part of the whole process, says Schaniel. "They understand their impact on the product, and they know their personal contribution counts. They ask how they can make the process better—that's the most thrilling thing I hear."

More Cut Costs

While realigning the factory cut hundreds of hours and dollars from the manufacturing process, 70 percent of the cost of each plane still went to suppliers.

TOP-DOWN CHANGE

In the beginning, the strategic transformation of Boeing's ailing 717 airplane was viewed as just another "flavor of the month," says Arlene Rios, a union representative for employee involvement at Boeing. Employees were skeptical, having seen many "improvement programs" come and go, and were consequently hesitant to jump on board.

Convincing them required a change process that involved leadership training and mentoring for managers, which taught them the importance of modeling the behaviors and attitudes they expected on the factory floor. "We had to turn managers into team leaders," says Rios.

For managers who admittedly spent more time "fighting fires" than worrying about the future, Rios knew this would be a challenge. In the new environment, dealing with the problems of the day would only be a small part of a manager's job. As leaders of the 717 program, their new roles would include helping teams become aligned with the company's "value goals" and providing them with the tools to achieve those goals.

Before the rest of 717's employees even began training, managers participated in seven, four-hour leadership skills workshops. Over the course of three and a half weeks, they learned how to coach employees and generate commitment and enthusiasm. They also spent time at the Open Leadership Center in St. Louis, where they practiced envisioning value goals and looking at the big picture from a profit standpoint. In short, says Rios, "they were shown the difference between managing and leading."

Some cost cuts were made possible with a redesign of building elements, simplifying designs and re-evaluating purchases. For example, under the old production system only flex hoses rated at 3,000-psi were purchased for hydraulics components, even though the psi requirements were much lower for several uses. Now, purchases are adjusted to include only appropriately sized hoses for each need, with resulting cost savings. "It's a small example," says Michel, "but it counts."

They also asked suppliers to cut prices by 20 to 30 percent—a bold move when suppliers' prices were, admittedly, already competitive. According to Michel, not all of the suppliers embraced the request enthusiastically, but ultimately they agreed that if it didn't happen everyone would go out of business. "If they want us to be successful, it's in their best interest to participate," says Michel.

To make lowering prices more worthwhile for suppliers, Boeing agreed to work with a small number of key manufacturers, guaranteeing that they'd do more business with each of them. In addition, they outsourced as much work as possible to each supplier.

"In the past we built many of the plane's parts in-house," says Rowberg.

"It's a change in mind-set. Other people are more efficient than we are at manufacturing parts. We decided to focus on what we do best—designing, developing, integrating and assembling airplanes." And improved efficiency for Boeing means improved profits for its suppliers.

The Outcome: Dramatic Improvements Abound

Through the combined efforts of managers, employees, union laborers and suppliers, Boeing has significantly cut costs and delivery time-both established as key elements of "wild success." (See sidebar, "Wild Success.") Before the turnaround began, the company completed an airplane every six days. By last March they had trimmed that cycle time to one every four days—and improvements are still being made. By 2001, Schaniel believes that the assembly time will have improved by more than 50 percent since the program began.

"That's the difference between losing money and making money," says Belgard.

And the market is taking notice. This year, Boeing sold 19 of the 717s—versus only three of the comparably sized Air Bus A318s, sold by its competitor Airbus Industries, the Toulouse, France-based consortium of European aircraft manufacturers.

Perhaps even more telling is the fact that Carson no longer has to fight executives to keep the 717 program alive. In fact, Carson and Michel already are eyeing aircraft programs at the Seattle headquarters that will benefit from the lessons learned by the nearly grounded 717. "It's a change in paradigm of traditional airplane assembly," explains Michel. "Boeing is looking to us to be fast, flexible and highly successful." And that's exactly how they've put the 717 back on Boeing's radar screen.

Sarah Fister Gale is a freelance writer in St. Paul, MN. You can contact her at 952/915-4448 or sfister@mn.rr.com.

Managing Dispersed Work Effectively: A Primer

John D. Adams

Today a dispersed workforce is commonplace. It saves money and helps a company retain employees. However, unless such employees are well managed, it can compromise an organization's ability to attain its strategic goals. This article presents some recommendations for managing dispersed work more effectively. These practices are based on an action research project to determine which managerial practices tended to succeed and which tended to fail with dispersed workers.

The number of work groups whose members are *not* working most or all of the time in the same place is growing rapidly as changes in technology have enabled flexible work styles and created a truly global economy. It is not unusual for a manager to be in one location, and her/his team located in several other places around the world. In a rapidly growing number of organizations, *dispersed teams* are the norm, especially in sales and service functions. Assisting in the creation and building of such teams represents a huge opportunity for OD practitioners virtually everywhere in the world. The purpose of this article is to present some research-based recommendations for managing dispersed work as effectively as possible, for use by both OD practitioners and dispersed team managers.

Technology tools have enabled many additional forms of dispersed work, including: home offices, drop-in work centers, offices with fewer work spaces than employees, temporary task teams, and "virtual" team meetings. (See sidebar "The Varieties of Dispersed Work" on next page.)

While much has been written about "Virtual Teamwork" and the dispersed worker, (e.g. Bleeker, 1994; Duarte and Snyder, 1999; Faucheux, 1997; Lipnack and Stamps, 1997), relatively little has appeared so far that specifically supports the manager of a "virtual" or dispersed team. I recently had the opportunity to conduct an action research project to determine which managerial practices contributed to success, and which to failure, of dispersed work.

Over the course of three months, I interviewed thirty managers representing a variety of functions, levels, and locations across a large high-tech

> ### THE VARIETIES OF DISPERSED WORK
>
> **Home Office.** Many companies provide computing systems and high speed Internet connections for employees, to enable them to work from home some or all of the time. In some cases, fax machines, telephone lines, copiers, and other office equipment are part of the "work from home" package.
>
> **Drop-in Work Centers.** These are generally located near areas where many employees live in larger metropolitan centers. Centers support workers not having to commute during traffic rush hours. They ordinarily consist of cubicles with workstations and phones, plus copiers, faxes, group meeting spaces, etc. In some cases, these centers also have a receptionist/space manager to provide support and assist in allocating appropriate workspaces.
>
> **Unassigned Work Space.** In situations where many of the people assigned to a given location are away from the office for extended periods (e.g. consultants, sales force, service engineers), it is more cost effective to provide fewer workspaces than employees, allocating some proportion of the office to "unassigned" workspaces. These spaces are reserved much like a hotel room when the traveling employee is in the office. The most forward thinking versions of this concept provide a rich variety of unassigned individual and team workspaces—not just a "sea of cubes"—to support a wide range of in-office work needs.
>
> **Temporary Task Teams.** The nature and speed of today's complex projects often requires that people with specialized capabilities be assigned temporarily to one or more project teams. These teams often consist of employees from several functions and disciplines. Someone who is not the full time manager of any of the team members frequently manages these temporary teams.
>
> **Electronic Conferencing.** It is often necessary to hold meetings with many of the meeting attendees located remotely. In addition to the now ubiquitous conference call enabled phones, there is a huge range of products available to support dispersed meetings, including Internet-assisted meeting templates, interactive overhead projectors and whiteboards, and a variety of videoconferencing systems.

company. I also attended a workshop on "Virtual Teamwork" offered by the corporate education center, and followed up by holding telephone interviews with seventeen of the employees who had attended. The focus of all my interviews was on people's experiences with dispersed work and on identifying the best management practices for developing and maintaining successful dispersed teams.

The remainder of this article summarizes what I found to be the most important practices for the successful management of dispersed teams in the following five areas:

- Management Style
- The Remote Employee
- New Employee Orientation
- Meetings
- Teamwork

If you are a manager of a dispersed team, you are invited to use these ideas to self-assess your own performance. If you are an OD consultant, these guidelines should help you in coaching clients who are managing dispersed work.

Most of the suggestions and practices contained in this article are also essential for effective face-to-face teams. However, it is important to note that dispersed work magnifies the benefits of the presence, and also magnifies the difficulties caused by the absence, of the practices and qualities described below.

Management Style

One key finding was that whatever style a manager employed, the greater the degree of "dispersion" of her or his team, the more exaggerated that style became. Those who were thoughtful and systematic developed conscious practices to take the dispersion factor into account, and generally fared pretty well. Those who were haphazard usually experienced chaotic conditions and were unable to generate successful results from their dispersed teams.

Two of the most clear-cut overall findings about management style were never to *sit and wait* for things to "work themselves out" or for resources to "appear" and never to allow dispersed employees to be *taken by surprise*. Regular check-ins and updates are essential to keep the team working smoothly. In the absence of these, project management quickly regresses to "fire-fighting" and momentum disappears.

Coaching and Flexibility. In dispersed work, coaching is the recommended style of managing, for improving performance, leveraging strengths most effectively, stretching the attainments of high performers, and redirecting off-target performance. In all of the dispersed work situations I reviewed, coaching employees worked better than "telling" them.

Results Focus—Deliverables. Managing for results means that expected deliverables, deadlines, and results must be as clear as possible. Based on my findings, I urge managers to hold regular progress reviews, both individually and with the whole team. The amount of "face time" with employees is less critical than establishing clear goals and holding regular reviews. For example:

- These are your ten accounts.
- Here are the expected outcomes for each account.

> In dispersed work, coaching is the recommended style of managing, for improving performance, leveraging strengths most effectively, stretching the attainments of high performers, and redirecting off-target performance.

- These are the decisions you can make on your own.
- We will hold weekly team meetings and monthly one-on-ones to review progress and solve problems.
- Here are my telephone and pager numbers—call me when you need me.

Issues and Performance Problems. Problems must not be allowed to go unresolved, as "molehills" become "mountains" very rapidly in dispersed work situations. Since distance magnifies the complexity of an issue or a performance problem, it is essential to "clear the air" as soon as you realize that something is amiss. Remember also that sensitive and complex "discussions" are seldom concluded successfully by e-mail.

When a dispersed employee's performance is not meeting expectations, his/her manager should:

- Increase telephone contacts
- Increase number of one-on-ones
- Build and use informal networks to detect problems early
- Use face-to-face coaching to generate quicker results
- Explicitly track results
- Change the job and/or compensation

If performance continues below par, cancel the dispersed arrangement (such as discretionary telecommuting), bringing the employee into your immediate work area for a period of time for more direct supervision.

Technology Tools. Technology tools supporting dispersed work will continue to evolve rapidly. While it is not necessary to adopt every new tool invented, it is essential to ensure that everyone on your team can use whatever tools you have adopted: workstations, laptops, pagers, remote telephony, reservation systems, shared calendars, shared files, etc.

This area is an important one for OD people who have coaching relationships with managers of dispersed teams. The most usual result of helping a manager become more explicit in her/his practices is that team performance improves.

The Remote Employee

Much research has been conducted within corporations to ascertain what makes employees successful in dispersed work situations. My own research project confirmed what has been found by a number of studies (e.g., Bredin, 1996 and 1998; Curran and Williams, 1997; Jackson and van der Wielen, 1998; Nilles, 1998). (See sidebar "Remote Employee Success and Failure Factors" on next page.)

It is important that OD practitioners help client managers understand the traits that predict success for remote employees.

> ### REMOTE EMPLOYEE SUCCESS AND FAILURE FACTORS
>
> **Success Factors**
> *Those remote employee qualities that most often predict work success include*
> - Strategic direction is sufficient (i.e. big picture and clear deliverables)
> - Good communicator, maintains contact
> - Good at building relationships, committed to being a team player
> - Reliable and trustworthy
> - Disciplined, results-focused work style
> - Able to work independently, a self-starter—willing to "bite the bullet" and review consequences at next update opportunity
> - Problem solver and decision maker
> - Assertive and confident
> - Good time management skills
>
> **Failure Factors**
> *The remote employee qualities that most often predict work failure include*
> - Needs tactical direction (i.e. what to do next), uncomfortable with ambiguity
> - Poor at communicating and staying "in touch"
> - Too independent—not interested in the rest of the team
> - Haphazard style of remote manager
> - Unable to maintain focus on results
> - High needs for social inclusion
> - Inflexible approach to work
> - Doesn't push back
> - Blames others for problems with work
> - No access to technology tools or doesn't use them well

New Employee Orientation

When employees join a dispersed team (whether through being hired, an internal transfer, or a reorganization) if they are not familiar with the dispersed work "terrain," an explicit, high quality orientation is essential to get the person up to speed and contributing effectively. This is an area I found to be frequently overlooked. It is far too common that new, specialized resources are brought on board, and then left alone to pick up the team's ways of doing things "by osmosis."

Very strong "self starters" who have made a number of job changes, and who have worked previously in dispersed settings, may be able to get themselves functioning fairly quickly. Most people flounder for longer than is necessary, as their managers and team members have forgotten how different the work landscape looks when one is newly arrived.

In the hyper-fast pace of work today, many managers overlook the fact that new employees have particular needs when they join a new group, and that these needs are magnified when the new group is a dispersed one. OD consultants should help their clients work with the following points when selecting new employees for a dispersed team assignment.

Orientation for New Hires—Hiring Manager

It is essential that the hiring manager begin preparing for the arrival of a newly hired employee as soon as the job offer is accepted. This includes getting badges and security clearances ordered, stocking the person's workspace with basic materials, getting technology tools ordered and installed, and so on.

A detailed summary of the dispersed work environment should be given to the new hire prior to arrival, so that he or she can form clear expectations. A "guide" or mentor should also be assigned to the new hire before his or her arrival, to guide the new employee through the first month or so.

Finally, the manager is encouraged to contact the new hire a day or so before arrival to describe the agenda for the first day. This contact should not be delegated to an administrator.

During the first week, the manager should ensure that:

- All administrative procedures are completed
- All requirements, guidelines, and procedures are reviewed
- Appropriate training and meetings are scheduled
- Charter, deliverables, and how to stay in touch with key people are reviewed.

I have found that a majority of younger new hires do best in the long run if they are not placed in a remote or dispersed situation for the first month or so.

Orientation for New Hires—Mentor/Guide

The Mentor/Guide coordinates all meetings for the new hire for the first month or so, and facilitates the completion of all administrative procedures. In addition to making sure that the new hire gets to know all of the team members in residence, plus other people who are important to the team, the guide also ensures that all technology tools are in place, and that the new hire knows how to use them and what to expect from the dispersed working of the group.

The guide's most important role is to acculturate the new hire and explain who to go to and how to get things done. It is important that the guide check frequently for retention and understanding.

I found many cases in which bringing the new hire to the work location of the group's manager was not feasible at the time of hire. Frequently, another manager or specialist at the remote location served as the new hire's mentor. Additionally, it is exceedingly important that the remote new employee receive assistance in joining the appropriate "shared interest" networks (sometimes called "communities of practice") at the remote location. (Allee, 2000)

Meetings

Meetings are the times when dispersed teams "come together." Successful meetings are an exceptionally critical aspect of managing dispersed work. If team meetings are scheduled regularly, and are well planned to contribute to the essential work of the team, they can be one of the major success factors for the dispersed team's effectiveness. If meetings are haphazardly planned and do not contribute to the core work of the team, then there is a good chance that the team will fail. OD practitioners who have experience in designing and facilitating effective team meetings can make important contributions here.

> Successful meetings are an exceptionally critical aspect of managing dispersed work.

Face-to-Face Meetings. All team members should understand that meeting attendance is expected—in person. The most successful dispersed team managers held quarterly meetings at which attendance by everyone was required. These meetings were rotated, so that each team member's location was a meeting site on a regular basis—even if the site was quite remote and only a single team member was located there.

Informal "Water Cooler" Time. When team members are dispersed, the informal conversations that happen "around the water cooler," over informal lunches, or in the hallways are missing from at least some of the team members' work lives. These conversations are often catalysts for new ideas and breakthroughs. It is essential, when "all-hands" face-to-face meetings are called, that plenty of informal, unstructured time be built into the design of the meeting to allow for remote members to catch up socially. Dispersed team managers must fight the urge to schedule every minute with formal work. The unstructured time is where the best conversations often take place!

One manager in my study insisted that every full time teleworking employee conduct her/his work from the team "center" for one week every other month to allow for these remote team members to catch up on the team's social life and to benefit from at least some of the informal interactions.

Virtual Meetings—Conference calls, data conferencing, video conferencing. When some of the team members cannot be in the meeting room, there is a wide array of rapidly evolving technology tools available. When using conference calls, data conferencing (e.g. chat room), or video conferencing, it is essential that the agenda and ground rules for meeting behavior be made explicit in advance—especially prohibitions from "double-tasking" during the meeting. For example, during conference calls, a rule that all computer monitors be turned off may be needed, in order that all team members make themselves fully available for the meeting at hand.

Communications—E-mail. It is not possible to manage by e-mail! E-mail is a great medium for sharing information and making announcements. It is a very bad medium for handling difficult situations and attempting to resolve conflicts. Short, clear e-mails that utilize itemized lists and specify the kind of response expected are the most effective.

Communications—Threaded Conversations. There are many Web-based tools available that allow for team members to post items for discussion, and for responding to discussion items. These processes don't substitute for face-to-face handling of complex issues, but they allow for more complexity than e-mail.

Communications—Formalized. Formal practices should be adopted for providing each other with regular updates of progress and relevant information. Regular "Transfer of Information" sessions should be built into every meeting. This creates a regular mechanism for sharing what has been learned in each team member's "communities of practice" for the benefit of the rest of the team. The team should collectively decide how to best keep everyone informed—and then stick to it.

Communications—Knowledge Management. Regular "round-robin" sharing of highlights, challenges, and tips at regular group meetings is a good way to spread the "tacit" knowledge team members are acquiring from their work and from their networking with others outside the team.

Good knowledge management relies on team spirit and trust. When these are present, team members will be most likely to share their learning and insights. When team spirit and trust are absent, team members are more likely to withhold information and ideas that would be extremely helpful to others.

Each team should be aware of what its knowledge management needs are for:

- Capturing information
- Assuring *access* to this information
- Building team norms that nurture and reward knowledge *creation*
- Insure that each individual's knowledge and capabilities are *utilized* fully

Teamwork

Teamwork is talked about a lot these days, but is often ignored in the frenzy of fast-cycle environments. All too often, it is "individual heroics" that get the rewards, even though it is clear to us in OD that teamwork could generate even higher levels of creativity and breakthrough performance. In coaching managers of dispersed teams on teamwork, I have often made use of the old TQM adage, "Go slow to go fast." In most teams, especially dispersed ones, there are plenty of examples of how the individual heroics approach to group work has led to the need for major reworking of a project.

New Team Formation—Charter. Newly forming dispersed teams need to be clear about their charters and goals from the outset. A first team meeting should address at least the following:

- Team purpose
- Shared and individual goals
- Time lines for goal accomplishment
- Ground rules for functioning effectively as a dispersed team
- Information and knowledge sharing needs and norms
- Operational guidelines (meeting frequency, outcomes, agenda format, rules, and roles)

Team Development. Schedule regular one-on-ones and face-to-face meetings. Team identity can be built and enhanced by holding specific events to build the team (e.g. monthly team breakfasts, social outings, team building retreats), and by creating subgroup tasks that require people to work together. Follow up on all action items and agreements to engage in new practices reached at team development sessions. Dispersed teams are even less likely than face-to-face teams to carry out "off-site agreements" back on the job.

It is also important in dispersed teams that every member understand the roles, responsibilities, deliverables, and challenges of every other member. One way this has been accomplished is through job rotations, in which every team member does her/his job from another location within the team for two weeks every year. The manager must also locate him/herself temporarily in the various dispersed locations on a regular cycle.

> It is also important in dispersed teams that every member understand the roles, responsibilities, deliverables, and challenges of every other member.

High Performance Virtual Teams. In my research, I found several qualities that were almost always present in acknowledged high performing dispersed teams. Use these qualities as a checklist for assessing your team's readiness to be a high performing dispersed team:

- Relentlessly customer-centric (including "internal" customers)
- Clear purpose to which all team members are committed
- Understood and agreed-to specific goals
- Shared understanding of the team's guiding principles
- Clear and agreed rules and procedures for decision making and problem solving
- Explicit procedures for ensuring regular information flow and knowledge management
- Use of effective project management tools
- Everyone's roles, responsibilities, and deliverables understood by all
- Coaching/facilitating approach to performance management
- Continuous learning through regular reviews of what's working and what could be improved in the team's operations
- High levels of team spirit, trust, and mutual respect

Summary

As mentioned earlier, dispersed work tends to "magnify" the impact of every manager's approach to managing. Effective face-to-face managers, with consistent and clearly articulated supervisory practices, generally fare pretty well when they move to a dispersed team format. Managers with haphazard approaches to their supervisory duties (which is *not* a rare occurrence!) generally have a great deal of difficulty when they try to manage in a dispersed work situation.

While all of the practices reported in this article would most likely make a positive contribution to managing a face-to-face team, they become increasingly important as the amount of dispersion (number of remote people, frequency of absences from the assigned workplace) in a team increases.

I found that many managers take their management skills for granted, and then are puzzled when their dispersed teams don't function the way they expected them to. The most frequent response is to try harder with the same managerial procedures that aren't working, with the hope of different results (this is often referred to as a definition of "madness"). As OD professionals in a rapidly deploying world, there are many contributions we can make to ensuring that dispersed work is as effective as it can be.

References

Allee, Verna. (2000). Knowledge Networks and Communities of Practice. *OD Practitioner.* 32(4).

Bleeker, Samuel E. (1994). The Virtual Organization. *The Futurist*, March-April 1994, pp. 9-14.

Bredin, Alice. (1996). *The Virtual Office Survival Handbook: What Telecommuters & Entrepreneurs Need to Succeed in Today's Non-Traditional Workplace.* Rexdale, Ontario, Canada: John Wiley & Sons Canada, Limited.

Bredin, Alice. (1998). *The Home Office Solution: How to Balance Your Professional and Personal Lives While Working at Home.* New York: John Wiley & Sons.

Curran, Kevin, and Williams, Geoff. (1997). *Manual of Remote Working.* New York: Gower Publishing Company.

Duarte, Deborah L., and Snyder, Nancy Tennant. (1999). *Mastering Virtual Teams.* San Francisco: Jossey-Bass.

Faucheux, Claude. (1997). How Virtual Organizing Is Transforming Management Science. *Communications of the ACM*, 40 (9), September 1997, pp. 50-55.

Jackson, Paul J., and van der Wielen, Jos M. (1998). *Teleworking: International Perspectives: From Telecommuting to the Virtual Organisation.* New York: Routledge.

Lipnack, Jessica, and Stamps, Jeffrey. (1997). *Virtual Teams: Working Across Space, Time, and Organizations with Technology.* New York: John Wiley & Sons.

Nilles, Jack M. (1998). *Managing Telework: Strategies for Managing the Virtual Workforce.* New York: John Wiley & Sons Inc.

John D. Adams, Ph.D., is Director of the Organizational Systems Ph.D. Program at Saybrook Graduate School and is a faculty member at The Union Institute. His consulting practice is in individual work effectiveness and large-scale organization change, with priority given to organizations that are committed to building a sustainable future.

A Seat at the Table

Kristine Ellis and Sarah Fister Gale

Part five of this yearbook is all about strategy and human resource development. Here's an article that deals with this subject very directly, looking at the operational role of the training director in helping companies assess what skills and talents are necessary to achieve strategic goals. You'll read more about this trend here along with descriptions of various companies where this is happening now.

As employees increasingly become "human capital" and knowledge is recognized as an asset to be managed, there's a growing appreciation in the boardroom for the direct impact training can have on profitability. Consequently, today's training professionals have been catapulted into highly visible and pivotal roles, leading cross-functional teams assembled to address real business issues and create solutions that are strategically linked to the bottom line.

In the past two years alone, more has happened to change the trainer's job than in the previous decade, according to Tom Kelly, director of worldwide training for Cisco Systems, San Jose, Calif. "This is our chance to actually achieve strategic partnerships within the organization."

For training professionals like Kelly, it's no longer enough to provide training to employees. Rather, it's about creating solutions that affect the success of the business—solutions that are, in many cases, unrelated to training and development. Chris Vasiliadis, for example, now uses his educational and technical background to help his company Breakaway Solutions improve organizational performance—which may or may not require "training solutions."

"Training is only one of the many options provided by my group," says Vasiliadis, director of performance improvement for the Boston-based provider of collaborative e-business enterprises. When senior management comes to him with a request for training, Vasiliadis and his group first facilitate a discussion to evaluate whether or not training is the correct solution to the business problem at hand. "Sometimes," he says, "we need to prove that training would not provide the value that management seeks."

Reprinted with permission from *TRAINING* Magazine, March 2001. Copyright © 2001 Bill Communications. All rights reserved.

Becoming a Consultant

As the country's third-largest cable company, Philadelphia-based Comcast Cable Communications faces a common problem for fast-growing companies: In the aftermath of a merger or acquisition, how do you merge company cultures and develop employee understanding of the big picture?

That's just one of the objectives that Shawn Doyle, Comcast's vice president of learning and development, is charged with as he builds an umbrella training and development organization for the company. With 180 trainers employed around the country, the best way to achieve that goal, he says, is to share resources through the Comcast University.

Since joining the company last fall, Doyle and Filemon Lopez, president of the university, have taken on several projects and roles, but perhaps the largest one is that of "performance improvement consultants," explains Doyle. "We work closely with the business unit leaders to quantify the value of training. First, we identify the major issues and the required evidence that would prove to the business unit leaders that those issues were resolved. Then we ask the leaders to assign a dollar value to that resolution."

As business unit leaders begin to better understand the value of training, they begin to consult with Doyle's department much earlier in the cycle. "While education about the performance improvement and consulting capabilities of our department is still necessary," he admits, "I think we'll end up being valued and strategic partners in helping the business units meet their objectives."

Joining strategic discussion sessions is one of the many new tasks becoming commonplace for training and HR departments, and these sessions represent perhaps the most powerful opportunities to effect change and prove training's value across the board.

"We don't just concentrate on the traditional training objectives anymore," explains Patty Settles, training and development specialist for Metro Wastewater Reclamation District, Denver. "We sit down with management and help them identify strategic goals and objectives and the skills and knowledge needed to achieve them. Then we work together to identify whether or not our staff has these skills and knowledge, and when they don't, that's when we discuss training needs."

And often, it is not the training or HR specialist who determines that training is the answer. Increasingly, it's business unit leaders who raise the warning flag when time-sensitive, skills-based training is needed. And that's exactly what Martin Hand, senior director of reservation operations for Continental Airlines, did as technology-based operations like Web reservations became the norm.

In an industry in which companies must rely so heavily on customer satisfaction, training has never been a hard sell for anyone at Houston-based

> Joining strategic discussion sessions is one of the many new tasks becoming commonplace for training and HR departments....

Continental Airlines. With increasing amounts of Web bookings, the connection between training and profitability is even more pronounced, Hand says.

"Our technology has been changing for the past two to three years, and it has changed significantly in just the last six months, so we're doing even more training than in the past," he says. Previously, reservation agents were responsible for just one service function, such as phone reservations. But new technological tools bring automation and generalization of functions, and as a result, agents are handling a broader range of services.

For instance, in addition to taking reservations, an agent might also handle calls regarding One Pass, the company's frequent flyer program. In doing so, the agent probably uses a computer telepathy integration system that automatically gives on-screen data about the customers. Although agents who answer questions regarding Web-based bookings still speak with customers via the phone, e-mail support is already being implemented in some areas and text chats will be possible in the near future. Enter more training.

Currently, Continental agents receive an average of six hours of training per month, and Hand doesn't expect that to decrease any time soon. "The technology will continue to evolve," he says, "so we'll continue to make sure that our folks are trained to help our customers."

> But what happens when actual customer profiles—not just technology—change? Entire training objectives are transformed.

But what happens when actual customer profiles—not just technology—change? Entire training objectives are transformed. At least that's what happened at Panalpina, an international shipping and logistics company in Morristown, N.J. Seven years ago, training was pretty much confined to Panalpina's management level, explains Anja Marquardt, vice president of business processes and quality assurance. "Now, everyone in the company participates in a wide range of training programs."

"It's simply a must," she continues, "given the changes in the industry over the past few years." Panalpina's customer base now includes global companies from the automotive, electronics, telecommunications, energy and chemical industries. Not only do these multinationals expect Panalpina to know the ins and outs of international logistics, they also want complete supply chain management solutions.

"We are now expected to provide services that, in the past, were taken care of by other vendors," Marquardt explains. "Our customers need integrated logistics—from handling inventory for just-in-time delivery to tracking, tracing and transparency all the way through the process."

Given the demand for broader and more complex customer solutions, Panalpina devised a plan for a mandatory industry overview training program last year. "The courses give a broad overview of what we do and how our industry is changing, but we already see that we're going to have to get more in-depth," she says. "Given the feedback, we are going to take it further and break the program down into different segments, with different levels of training in different areas."

Training for Sales

Carey Winters faced challenges similar to Marquardt's when he joined Minneapolis-based Medtronic less than two years ago as manager of sales performance development. He was hired to oversee the Cardiac Surgery division's sales training, and he was surprised at what he found: Despite Medtronic's ranking as one of the world's largest medical device companies, its training programs focused on little more than product knowledge.

"The change since then has been significant," says Winters. "There is a recognition now that training and development are crucial to our long-term success."

One of the results of that awareness meant pulling training and development out of the marketing department. Winters now reports to the division's vice president of sales, tying his work directly to the line of command most concerned with bottom line performance.

Winters has several key initiatives planned for the next few years. First, he wants the sales organization to become more process-oriented, focusing on training processes aligned with the fundamentals of selling. Second, he intends to incorporate new technologies that will help the salespeople manage their territories as businesses. One such pilot in the works is a program with MedSchool.com, which provides Web-based medical and technical training programs.

"We're going to be migrating a lot of the medical and technical knowledge that our salespeople need onto the Web. This will help our reps get away from the idea that training is an event that happens in Minneapolis and see that learning and development are ongoing processes," he explains.

Winters' third planned initiative is to standardize the division's training and development processes around the world. And finally, he plans to build ownership among the field managers responsible for implementing the programs. "If the people who are responsible for implementing training don't buy into it, you might as well not bother," he says. "So all the new programs we roll out will include training for the managers on coaching and developing their salespeople."

It's the role of the salesperson that has changed for Columbus, Ohio-based Ashland Chemicals Co., says Bill Christian, manager of sales training. "Salespeople now need to be much more focused on the company's return on investment, the quality of the business they do, and the company's profitability, as well as have more technical knowledge."

As a result, the focus of Ashland's extensive nine- to 12-month sales trainee program has changed. "We've continued to massage it and keep it updated," he says. Recent additions to the program include new training tools to help sales associates quantify the value-added advantages for customers. "We're not just selling products to our customers anymore,"

Christian explains. "We can help our customers be profitable in a variety of ways, but our salespeople have to be the ones to sell that. With proper training, we can show them how."

Christian predicts that e-commerce will be the biggest factor in sales training in the near future. "There will still be a number of customers who prefer to deal with salespeople face-to-face," he says, "so e-commerce will become an adjunct territory—another ball in the air that our salespeople and sales managers will have to juggle." And that, too, he says, will require more training.

Kristine Ellis is a freelance writer in Helena, MT kellis@mcn.net.

Sarah Fister Gale is a freelance writer in St. Paul, Minn. sfister@mn.rr.com.

Turning Passion into Organizational Performance

Richard Chang

This article posits that passion and organizational success can be and often are intimately related. Developing passion for the organization's mission and its role in society is about turning on the people in the organization and creating an environment that engenders true commitment to goals and not just compliance with management. It is a people thing, and it requires leaders who believe in what they're doing and provide their employees with the wherewithal to believe and act as well. Learn more here.

What does your organization have that makes it better than the competition? How does it distinguish itself in an increasingly complex and competitive economy? Does it exude enthusiasm to clients and customers? Are your clients and customers excited about and loyal to your products and services? Does it attract and retain high-performing employees and strategic partners? If not, then it may be missing out on the greatest competitive advantage an organization can claim: passion.

Though skeptics will argue that a solid business plan and high-profit margin are of greater benefit, they are wrong. Certainly, both are critical to an organization's success. But while many companies have the technology and financial backing to succeed, few have the sheer emotional force to be the best. Essentially and fundamentally, passion is the competitive advantage that an organization can't buy. Passion can help turn good organizations into great ones.

Passion is the underlying force that fuels our strongest emotions. It is the intensity we feel when we engage in activities that interest us deeply. It fills us with energy and enables us to perform at our peak. Just as people can be guided and inspired by their personal passions, so can organizations be driven and defined by their collective passions. Organizations that are driven by the collective passion of their associates reap those same rewards.

Reprinted with permission from *Training & Development*, May 2001. Copyright © 2001 by the American Society for Training and Development. All rights reserved.

> Passion is the underlying force that fuels our strongest emotions. It is the intensity we feel when we engage in activities that interest us deeply.

A number of private and public-sector organizations that have incorporated passion as a key ingredient in their business strategy are featured in my new book, *The Passion Plan at Work: Building a Passion-Driven Organization* (Jossey-Bass: A Wiley Company, 2001). Consider the examples offered by Ben & Jerry's Homemade and Southwest Airlines. Both have achieved tremendous success because their businesses are passion driven. They acknowledge the importance of tried-and-true business principles, but they focus on the forces that truly motivate them rather than those that might seem more logical. These companies prioritize passion over protocol and are unwilling to compromise it to earn a quick buck or gain the approval of critics.

Passion in Action

Ben & Jerry's Homemade. When Ben Cohen and Jerry Greenfield opened their first ice cream shop in 1977, they wanted to create something different. They hoped to establish a profitable business, but, more important, they wanted to make a difference in the world. They wanted to give something back to their community. They started small by throwing a local festival and giving away free ice cream cones. As their business grew, they expanded their efforts by donating an unparalleled percentage of profits to charity, forming partnerships with minority suppliers, and developing environment-friendly packaging.

Ben's and Jerry's unrelenting passion for social responsibility shaped all aspects of their business. From product development to marketing to human resources to operations, the company's leaders are guided in their decision making by the social impact of their efforts, even when doing that meant slimmer profit margins. The results were remarkable. The business that began in an old gas station in Vermont sold hundreds of millions of dollars worth of ice cream every year and was recently named by the *Wall Street Journal* as one of the most respected U.S. companies.

Southwest Airlines. This company's passion also defied conventional business wisdom. Founders Rollin King and Herb Kelleher agreed that the major airlines were charging far too much money for what was poor service. So, they decided to create an airline that would charge markedly lower fares and offer friendly, fast service. Despite an onslaught of legal battles from their larger, more powerful competitors, Southwest prevailed and opened up the skies to thousands, if not millions, of people who had previously considered air travel too expensive.

Employees of Southwest Airlines are united and driven by their passion for freedom. Not only do they provide it to customers, but they also nurture it within the company. Everyone from senior executives to baggage handlers has the freedom to make on-the-spot decisions. Employees are encouraged to be creative and "color outside the lines" in their work. They make improvements on their own initiative, serve customers in their own unique ways—singing, dancing, and cracking jokes—and shun the rigid formality of their competitors. Guided by its passion for freedom, Southwest turns a profit even when other airlines post huge losses.

Organizations like Ben & Jerry's and Southwest are just two examples of the spectacular results a passion-driven organization can achieve. When the members of an organization are united by a common passion—whether for technological innovation, unparalleled customer service, or creating the ultimate product—they perform at a heightened level, putting forth tremendous effort but enjoying themselves in the process. They exude an excitement that attracts customers and employees and wins their loyalty. Quite simply, they are great places that are accomplishing great things.

You might be surprised by the idea that emotion can be the driving force behind a solid business strategy. We often think of business—especially "big business"—as cold and heartless. But consider business from the human perspective. A business exists only when there are people to run it and purchase its products and services.

Employees and customers have feelings that compel them to act the way they do. People don't check their personalities at the office door and become organizational automatons; their performance is predicated on their feelings toward their work. Customers don't buy just anything; they often make purchasing decisions based on emotional responses to products and services, and to the organizations that provide them.

> Consider business from the human perspective. A business exists only when there are people to run it and purchase its products and services.

Seven Steps to Passion-Driven Success

Regardless of where your organization is, it can make the changes necessary to become passion driven. Here are seven steps toward that transformation. Many organizations have taken one or two of these steps but have failed to fully align their businesses around passion. Until they address each step, their efforts will be limited.

Step 1: Start from the heart. For passion to be effective, it must be the foundation of the organization. It's not a technique for improvement but the starting point from which all else emanates. Purpose, vision, culture, strategy, policies, and practices must all reflect the underlying passion of the organization.

Step 2: Discover core passions. Once the organization has acknowledged the importance of passion, it must identify the ideas and activities that inspire its performance. Those forces, which matter most to the organization and give it life, are its core passions.

Step 3: Clarify purpose. Many organizations have identified one or more purposes for existing. Often, however, those purposes don't reflect the underlying passions of the organization. Leaders and associates must have a clear definition of where the core passions will lead the organization. If they don't share the same sense of purpose, their passion may lead them in divergent directions and compromise the stability of the organization.

Step 4: Define actions. To ensure that being passion driven will be productive, organizations must create strategies and plans that target passion as the catalyst for change and the source of future excellence. The action plan the organization creates should outline strategies for capitalizing on existing passions and nurturing new ones.

Step 5: Perform with passion. Once a plan is in place, the organization can begin acting on its passions. That will be liberating for leaders and associates alike. People who are aligned around the passions and purpose of the organization and excited about them will begin to perform at a higher level as passion enters their work. The organization will become self-motivated and increasingly capable, with little need for outside guidance or inspiration.

Step 6: Spread excitement. The organization that acts with passion gains notice from the outside world, spreading its excitement to customers, colleagues, potential employees, and even critics. Internal learning and development programs can help employees identify personal passions and put them to work on the job. External communication programs and marketing efforts can expose customers and colleagues to the organization's core passions and give those people an opportunity to build personal enthusiasm around the organization's efforts.

Step 7: Stay the course. Passion-based change is exhilarating. Once the organization has cleared the initial hurdles of fear and caution, it discovers that passion-based change is energizing. However, passion-driven organizations also take measures to ensure that they don't lose sight of the passions that made them great. They recognize that if their enthusiasm went unchecked, it might lead them in counterproductive directions.

Passion in the Workplace and Marketplace

Passion must start with leadership. Surely it can emanate from other sources, but in building a passion-driven organization, it has to come from the top. The leaders must live and breathe the passions they profess. Could Southwest's employees embrace freedom if they weren't allowed to make decisions without the permission of supervisors? Obviously not. If leaders don't exude their organization's core passions, associates will have no reason to believe the passions are real or worth embracing.

Although passion in leaders is essential, it's meaningless if not shared by associates at all levels. Without their support, the goals established in the action plan are mere wishes. Associates' energy and commitment are the foundation of the organization's performance and the key to its progress. To ensure the achievement of desired organizational performance results, lead-

> Leaders must live and breathe the passions they profess.

ers must immediately and systematically seek to align associates with the core organizational passions they've identified.

One of the most important and effective practices leaders can adopt in aligning the organization around passion is to establish clear and constant communication. Associates can't be expected to share a passion they aren't aware of or don't understand. Beyond the basic forms of communication, organizations can create programs for the express purpose of educating associates about their core passions. As efforts are made to increase employees' awareness of their organization's core passions, there will be some people who won't share them. In such cases, the people not on board with the organization's passions will usually choose to leave.

The leaders of McLeodUSA realized that the greatest enabler, but also the greatest obstacle, to their success was people. Its growth in terms of technology and opportunity was limitless, but McLeodUSA knew it couldn't achieve its goals if it couldn't find the appropriate people to fuel progress. The company needs people who can support its core values—growth, integrity, relationships, and passion—and truly appreciate the opportunities the company wants to offer them. To accomplish that, McLeodUSA's recruiting and interviewing efforts immediately convey the company's core passions, and candidates are screened on their perceived ability and dedication to uphold those passions.

Ben & Jerry's has found that because it's so vocal about its passions outside the bounds of the company, it attracts people who already share its passions. Recognizing the critical importance of shared passion in employees, Southwest's CEO Herb Kelleher has been quoted as saying, "We can teach the job; we can't teach the attitude."

Another critical part of deploying passion in an organization is creating the conditions in which passion can thrive. Not surprisingly, that includes the physical environment. Businesses that hinge on creativity aren't the only ones that can capitalize on passion by creating stimulating work environments. Manufacturing plants are spaces that must meet strict safety requirements and traditionally aren't viewed as hotbeds of innovation. Wainwright Industries, a past Malcolm Baldrige National Quality Award winner in the Small Business category, discovered that there's emotional value in the seeming limitations of a manufacturing environment. Its facility reflects the firm's passion for safety and serves as a constant reminder to employees of their shared commitment to safety. All employees, including the CEO, wear the same white uniforms. Floors and machines are spotless. Workspaces are clearly delineated and well lit, in contrast to the cave-like atmosphere that characterizes many factories. Clearly, as demonstrated through Wainwright's successes, passion as a strategy for achieving organizational performance isn't limited by an organization's size, scope, or revenues.

All approaches—communication, education, environment, policies, and

> Ben & Jerry's has found that because it's so vocal about its passions outside the bounds of the company, it attracts people who already share its passions.

practices—contribute to building a passionate outlook within an organization. When passion permeates all aspects of the organization, associates at all levels become excited about core passions and perform in accordance with them. They develop faith in leadership and enthusiasm for performance goals. They stop finding excuses and start looking for effective solutions.

The Brazosport Independent School District in Texas is a powerful example. In 1991, there was a wide disparity in student performance (a key indicator of success for K-12 educational institutions) between ethnic and economic groups. One set of test scores indicated that minority and economically disadvantaged children were achieving at much lower levels than white, middle-class students at BISD. That may not be a big surprise, but many educators (and businesspeople) are willing to accept the status quo as the best that can be done. They accept problems and performance limitations as the way things are and try to make the best of them.

BISD turned things around by defining a new organizational core passion to teach and empower all children in its care and by identifying a purpose that every student can learn. From 1991 to 1998, the proportion of economically disadvantaged students who passed the Texas Assessment of Academic Skills in reading rose from 60 percent to 91 percent, in math from 54 to 93 percent, and in writing from 57 to 90 percent. The results for minority groups are equally impressive. The numbers aren't just data; they're a reflection of the shared passion that resulted from a change of heart of the district's leaders and associates—a passion that ultimately produced improved organizational performance.

Passion Alignment Through HRD Efforts

When employees are passionate about their work, their organizations thrive. Once passion is present and reinforced throughout an organization, it becomes contagious. All organizational stakeholders—employees, partners, and customers—sense it and respond to it. Passion wins support, inspires loyalty, and gains invaluable energy as associates from each stakeholder group share in the excitement passion creates.

Given the current challenges that organizations face in the economy worldwide, it's vital that they harness the power of their people's vitality, creativity, and energy—in a nutshell, their passions. According to the human resources champion of development at Clarke American, "The key to our success, now and in the future, is our people. Our competitors can duplicate our technology, they can duplicate our products, and they can duplicate our processes. But they can't clone our people."

To truly benefit from passion, organizations must help employees grow in their passion. That includes helping them more fully understand and experience the organization's core passions and find ways to incorporate their personal passions into their work. The bottom line is that if organizations want associates to be passionate about their work, they must be passionate about helping them. Each of the organizations profiled in *The Passion Plan at Work* has either established internal universities or specific training programs to promote and strengthen passion in their employees.

At the Disney Institute, the training organization of Walt Disney World, leaders go to extreme lengths to make sure employees (who are called Cast Members) gain experience from the perspective of a Guest (as Disney World visitors are called). For example, new reservationists are invited to stay at the resort as a Guest so they understand what they're selling to customers. One institute leader explains the motivation behind that practice: "It would be a false expectation to think that people could stay passionate about something but then not let them try it themselves.... We just think it's really important that our Cast Members stay connected to who we are and what we do so they can communicate that passion to our Guests."

Training can help employees develop skills and discover the emotional forces they need to perform at their peak and derive fulfillment from their work. At Southwest's University for People, employees can take classes in leadership, customer service, career development, team performance, and personal development. The leadership classes focus on the company's history, its values, and its passions, but they also help employees identify their own strengths and potential areas for growth.

PSS/World Medical also operates an internal university, with curriculums on job-related skills and assessments that help people gain a window into themselves. For example, an occasional sales recruit may realize that selling isn't a core personal passion and decide to pursue a different career path. Similarly, someone who enters the university's leadership school may find that despite the initial appeal, a leadership role doesn't tap into his or her core passions or may even be passion draining. Yet, PSS/World Medical doesn't give up on those people. It subscribes instead to right-fit placement, putting people in jobs that best match their passions and abilities. From a passion-management perspective, that's a critical and necessary practice. Sharing or believing in an organization's core passions doesn't guarantee employees' performance success. To excel, they must also be passionate about the roles they fulfill.

When people are excited about their organization and passionate about what they do, the benefits are tremendous. Because they're invested emotionally, they're also loyal. Their relationship goes beyond the transactional to a deeper level of organizational commitment.

Given the right desire and commitment, almost any organization can be transformed into a passion-driven one. Minor adjustments can bring improvement, but major changes aimed at aligning the organization around passion can bring phenomenal success. That success may be measured in dollars, but it can also be measured in more significant terms—in fulfillment of

> Training can help employees develop skills and discover the emotional forces they need to perform at their peak and derive fulfillment from their work.

potential and in the value and quality of experience. Passion-driven organizations, and the people that form them, are raising the standard by which we judge goods, services, and employment. Simply put, passion makes things better. Doesn't your organization deserve to enjoy the many benefits of being driven by passion?

Richard Chang is CEO of Richard Chang Associates, a performance improvement consulting, training, and publishing firm headquartered in Irvine, California. He has written more than 20 books on business and personal development, including The Passion Plan at Work, The Passion Plan, *and* Performance Scorecards; *www.richardchangassociates.com or www.thepassionplan.com.*

PART SIX

Training and Performance Resource Almanac

We have created *The ASTD Training and Performance Yearbook* as an anthology to keep you current with what's going on in your field. However, we also want to provide you with additional resources for improving your own performance. Parts One to Five of this book are the anthology. Part Six is resources. All the material included in this section of the yearbook has been completely updated from past editions. Here's what you'll find:

- **Training and Performance Resources Online.** The Internet has become a tremendous repository of information on every subject as well as a communication medium. It has certainly taken hold in the human resources field. There are hundreds of Web sites in cyberspace that deal in one way or another with training and performance management issues. To help you identify those that may be useful to you, we include this annotated directory that provides a representative sampling of what's available on the World Wide Web as well as e-mail discussion groups and newsgroups. We have sought to make this the most comprehensive and current directory of such resources you'll find anywhere in print.
- **Directory of Magazines, Journals and Newsletters.** Here we provide another annotated directory of periodicals that cover training and performance issues as well as general and industry periodicals that will be of interest to readers of this annual. You'll find information on how to get in touch with the publishers and how to subscribe.

- **A Glossary of Performance Management Terms.** We recently became aware of this glossary prepared by performance specialist Lynn Summers and found it to be a valuable resource. It's more than just a glossary in that each term is defined in enough detail to almost make this a mini-textbook on performance management and improvement concepts.
- **Directory of Training and Performance Associations and Organizations.** This directory provides a descriptive listing of professional organizations and associations that people in the training and performance improvement field should know about. This has been completely updated for 2002, and includes information on how to find out more information as well as the purpose of each organization, its publications, and, if available, its meetings.
- **Calendar of Conferences and Events, 2002.** This is a review of conferences and events of interest to those in HR development for 2002, including dates, locations, and how to find out more information on the Web.

Training and Performance Resources Online

Prepared by Robert Magnan

The Internet is an excellent source of information resources on virtually everything, including training and performance. The purpose of this part of our yearbook is to provide a good sampling of what's out there on the 'Net in this area.

Since most World Wide Web sites have links to other sites, with the sites listed below you're just a click or two away from many more sites. The same is true of discussion lists and newsgroups: you're often just a query away from other lists, through suggestions by cyber colleagues. At the end of these lists, in "Going Beyond These Resources," we provide more help so you can find other discussion lists, newsgroups, and Web sites.

What You'll Find Here

Our directory consists of five categories of online resources:

- **Discussion Lists.** These are free mailing lists that usually allow members (subscribers) to send e-mail messages to a central location, which then copies the messages to all members of that group. Some mailing lists are for distribution only: they send members information (usually publications or other resources), but don't allow members to post messages. Many of these lists have archives, which can be valuable resources.
- **Newsgroups.** These are informally managed, open forums, unlike discussion lists, which are by membership. Each is like a bulletin board, where anybody can post a message of any sort for anybody else to read. Although the term is "newsgroups," the content is often ads and chatty conversations, but the groups allow you to connect with people who can provide information and opinions about virtually anything in the world.
- **E-publications.** Also called "e-letters," these are resources that show up in your mailbox, regularly or sporadically. The number

of free e-pubs is growing rapidly, so there are a lot of choices. Many provide content (often mixed with marketing); others are simply notifications of new content on a Web site.
- **World Wide Web Sites.** These are sites hosted by associations, companies, and other organizations. You access these sites using a Web browser such as Netscape Navigator or Microsoft Internet Explorer.
- **Going Beyond These Resources.** This is a list of Web sites that can help you find more discussion lists, newsgroups, and Web sites.

The Internet has something for everybody and information to meet every need—if you can find it.

Some of the discussion groups bring together experts and we can gain a lot from their exchanges; others are more like discussions around the water cooler. There are many Web sites that are treasures, while others are basically infomercials or have a high "fluff-to-stuff" ratio.

Also, discussion groups and Web sites are time-sensitive. The groups are like any other types of association: the value to any member depends on what the other members are contributing at any given time. Many of the sites suffer from inadequate maintenance as they age; some move to other addresses or just disappear, while others come into being.

We can't possibly list even all of the best lists, groups, and sites. We've simply tried to mention some of the better resources out there for you to explore. Good luck!

If you'd like to recommend a list or a site that we haven't included here, please e-mail us at jwoods@cwlpub.com.

Discussion Lists

There are two ways to join discussion lists—through a Web site or by e-mail. If you join through a Web site, the site generally provides easy instructions, although you may be required to register. If you join by e-mail, you send a message to the computer that maintains the list. The message varies according to the computer program used to administer the list (usually listserv, listproc, majordomo, or mailbase) and the wishes of the list owner/moderator. For each of the groups below, we give the Web site URL and the e-mail address and specific message to send.

When you subscribe to a list, you should receive an introductory message that describes the purpose of the group, what you can expect, and how to participate. This message will also tell you how to leave the list if you don't find it of value. Save this message: it takes up very little space on your hard drive or printed out, but it can help you avoid embarrassment and frustration.

TRAINING AND PERFORMANCE RESOURCES ONLINE

Accelerated Learning Exchange (accelerated learning: "facilitation and training that produces measurable bottom-line results")
Web site: groups.yahoo.com/group/alexchange
E-mail: alexchange-subscribe@yahoogroups.com
Message: (blank)

Adaptive (adaptive learning systems)
Web site: www.topica.com/lists/adaptive
E-mail: adaptive-subscribe@topica.com
Message: (blank)

AEDNet (Adult Education Network)
E-mail: listserv@list.nova.edu
Message: subscribe aednet firstname lastname

BPMI (business process management and improvement)
E-mail: majordomo@quality.org
Message: subscribe bpmi

CBT (computer-based training)
Web site: groups.yahoo.com/group/cbt
E-mail: cbt-subscribe@yahoogroups.com
Message: (blank)

CBTMM (computer-based training using multimedia)
E-mail: listproc@neiu.edu
Message: subscribe cbtmm firstname lastname

Change (challenge of navigating major organizational transformation)
Web site: www.topica.com/lists/change
E-mail: change-subscribe@topica.com
Message: (blank)

CorpEd (all aspects of corporate education, training, and development)
Web site: groups.yahoo.com/group/corped
E-mail: corped-subscribe@yahoogroups.com
Message: (blank)

Crea-CPS (creativity and creative problem solving)
E-mail: listserv@nic.surfnet.nl
Message: subscribe crea-cps
or
crea-cps-subscribe@topica.com
Message: (blank)

Downsizing (effects of corporate downsizing on personnel and processes)
E-mail: majordomo@quality.org
Message: subscribe downsizing

EICoach (using coaching and emotional intelligence competencies to create a high-performance culture)
Web site: groups.yahoo.com/group/EICoach
E-mail: EICoach-subscribe@yahoogroups.com
Message: (blank)

Employee Training (helping small businesses develop and train employees)
Web site: clubs.yahoo.com/clubs/employeetraining

EPSS (planning, designing and developing electronic performance support systems)
Web site: groups.yahoo.com/group/EPSS
E-mail: EPSS-subscribe@yahoogroups.com
Message: (blank)

ERNet (employee relations, research and practice)
E-mail: listserv@perc.net
Message: subscribe ernet e-mail address

Grp-Facl (group facilitation, practice and theory)
E-mail: listserv@listserv.albany.edu
Message: subscribe grp-facl firstname lastname

HRD-L (human resources planning and development)
E-mail: hrd-l-on@hr.trends.ca
Message: (blank)

HRIS-L (human resources information systems)
E-mail: hris-l-on@hr.trends.ca
Message: (blank)

HRNet (exchange of ideas among human resource professionals)
Web site: groups.yahoo.com/group/hrnet
E-mail: hrnet-subscribe@yahoogroups.com
Message: (blank)

HRSolutions (HR professionals "peer consulting")
Web site: groups.yahoo.com/group/hrsolutions
E-mail: hrsolutions-subscribe@yahoogroups.com
Message: (blank)

Human_Resource (human resource management)
Web site: groups.yahoo.com/group/human_resource
E-mail: human_resource-subscribe@yahoogroups.com
Message: (blank)

ISAGA (discussion of simulation and gaming methodologies)
Web site: groups.yahoo.com/group/isaga
E-mail: isaga-subscribe@yahoogroups.com
Message: (blank)

Learning-Org (forum on learning organization concepts and shared experiences)
E-mail: majordomo@world.std.com
Message: subscribe learning-org

Lone Wolves of Training ("solo performers" of training)
Web site: groups.yahoo.com/group/LoneWolvesofTraining
E-mail: LoneWolvesofTraining-subscribe@yahoogroups.com
Message: (blank)

Mentor-Center (development, implementation, maintenance, and improvement of mentoring programs)
Web site: groups.yahoo.com/group/mentor-center
E-mail: mentor-center-subscribe@yahoogroups.com
Message: (blank)

MOP-Group (measuring organizational performance)
E-mail: majordomo@quality.org
Message: subscribe mop-group

NAGTAD (National Association for Government Training and Development)
Web site: www.usd.edu/nagtad/listserv.shtml
E-mail: nagtad-request@iglou.com
Message: subscribe

OB-HR-Net (research and teaching of organization behavior and human resource management)
Web site: groups.yahoo.com/group/ob-hr-net
E-mail: ob-hr-net-subscribe@yahoogroups.com
Message: (blank)

ODNET (Organization Development Network)
Web site: www.odnetwork.org/listsinfo/odnet.info.html

ODNET-Coach (coaching professionals)
Web site: www.odnetwork.org/listsinfo/odnet-coach.info.html

Online Facilitation (skills, techniques, and issues of online facilitation in Internet online environments and virtual communities)
Web site: groups.yahoo.com/group/onlinefacilitation
E-mail: onlinefacilitation-subscribe@yahoogroups.com
Message: (blank)

OrganizDev (professionals in organizational development, strategic planning, and human resources fields)
Web site: groups.yahoo.com/group/organizdev
E-mail: OrganizDev-subscribe@yahoogroups.com
Message: (blank)

OrgDyne (research, exploration, and understanding of group and organizational dynamics, as supported by systemic and psychodynamic thinking)
Web site: groups.yahoo.com/group/orgdyne
E-mail: orgdyne-subscribe@yahoogroups.com
Message: (blank)

Orientation (concepts for new employee orientation)
Web site: groups.yahoo.com/group/orientation
E-mail: orientation-subscribe@yahoogroups.com
Message: (blank)

PERFMGT (performance management, appraisal, and improvement)
Web site: groups.yahoo.com/group/perfmgt
E-mail: perfmgt-subscribe@yahoogroups.com
Message: (blank)

Performance-Management (performance management)
Web site: groups.yahoo.com/group/performance-management
E-mail: performance-management-subscribe@yahoogroups.com
Message: (blank)

PI-L (performance improvement)
E-mail: listserv@listserv.uark.edu
Message: subscribe pi-l firstname lastname

ROInet (evaluation, measurement, and return on investment of HRD interventions, including OD, KM, quality initiatives, e-learning, EPSS)
Web site: groups.yahoo.com/group/roinet
E-mail: roinet-subscribe@yahoogroups.com
Message: (blank)

TRAINING AND PERFORMANCE RESOURCES ONLINE

SyncTrain (synchronous Internet training: live online learning)
Web site: groups.yahoo.com/group/roinet
E-mail: synctrain-subscribe@yahoogroups.com
Message: (blank)

TeamNet-L (teamwork and topics related to collaborative systems)
E-mail: majordomo@mail.cas.unt.edu
Message: subscribe teamnet-L

Trainer Network (training professionals networking for information, requests, referrals, and any other training-related matters)
Web site: groups.yahoo.com/group/TrainerNetwork
E-mail: TrainerNetwork-subscribe@yahoogroups.com
Message: (blank)

TrainersAreUs ("everything for the Trainer and Training Manager")
Subscribe through Web site: groups.yahoo.com/group/trainersareus
E-mail: trainersareus-subscribe@yahoogroups.com
Message: (blank)

Training Design and Development (trainers and instructional design professionals)
Web site: clubs.yahoo.com/clubs/trainingdesignanddevelopment

TRDEV (training and development)
Web site: groups.yahoo.com/group/trdev
E-mail: trdev-subscribe@yahoogroups.com
Message: (blank)

VirtEd (virtual reality and education)
Subscribe through Web site: maelstrom.stjohns.edu/archives/virted.html
E-mail: listserv@maelstrom.stjohns.edu
Message: subscribe virted firstname lastname

WBTOLL-L (Web-based training and online learning)
E-mail: listserv@hermes.circ.gwu.edu
Message: subscribe wbtoll-l firstname lastname

WorkComm (communication in the workplace)
Web site: groups.yahoo.com/group/workcomm
E-mail: workcomm-subscribe@yahoogroups.com
Message: (blank)

WorkCon (prevention, management, and resolution of conflict in the workplace)
Web site: groups.yahoo.com/group/workcon
E-mail: workcon-subscribe@yahoogroups.com
Message: (blank)

WorkLearning (all aspects of learning at work, including learning organizations and training)
Web site: groups.yahoo.com/group/worklearning
E-mail: worklearning-subscribe@yahoogroups.com
Message: (blank)

ZPG Performance Measurement (creating useful, practical performance measures, goals, and feedback systems)
Web site: groups.yahoo.com/group/perfmeas
E-mail: perfmeas-subscribe@yahoogroups.com
Message: (blank)

Newsgroups

alt.education.distance
distance education

alt.training.technology
effective application of technology within training

bit.listserv.edtech
educational technology (mirrors EDTECH listserv)

bit.listserv.nettrain
training about and over networks (mirrors NETTRAIN listserv)

misc.business.facilitators
facilitation skills, techniques, and tips (mirrors GRP-FACL listserv)

misc.education.adult
adult education

E-Publications

ChangeMentor
Web site: groups.yahoo.com/group/ChangeMentor
E-mail: ChangeMentor-subscribe@yahoogroups.com
Message: (blank)

TRAINING AND PERFORMANCE RESOURCES ONLINE

Corporate Coaching News
Web site: www.corporatecoachingnews.com
E-mail: subscribeccn@coachville.com
Message: (blank)

Corporate University Review
Web site: www.traininguniversity.com

Distance Learning (About.com GuideSite^{TM})
Web site: distancelearn.about.com/education/distancelearn

e-Learning News
Web site: www.e-learninghub.com/freenews.html

Human Resources (About.com GuideSite^{TM})
Web site: humanresources.about.com/careers/humanresources

Intentional Learning Newsletter (learning orientation research and the application of theories, models, design, and technology to personalize learning)
E-mail: Maggiez00z@cs.com
Message: subscribe to newsletter

Lguide (e-learning)
Web site: www.lguide.com

Quick Training Tips
Web site: www.quicktrainingtips.com/QTT-Main.htm
E-mail: loretta@panix.com
Message (in Subject line): subscribe QTT

Spice of the Month (creative ideas for training)
Web site: www3.sympatico.ca/thetrainingoasis/sprack.htm

TechLearn Trends (e-learning, e-training, e-collaboration)
Web site: www.masie.com/list

TrainingWorld (training and development, leadership, performance)
Web site: groups.yahoo.com/group/trainingworld-subscribe
E-mail: trainingworld-subscribe@yahoogroups.com
Message: (blank)

Virtual University Gazette ("Internet University movement")
Web site: www.geteducated.com/vugaz.htm

Work Team Coaching
Web site: workteamcoaching.home.att.net/index.html
E-mail: subscribewtc@worldnet.att.net
Message: (blank)

Work911 ("variety of work issues")
E-mail: listmanager@burstmail.com
Message: subscribe work911

World Wide Web Sites

This listing includes a sampling of World Wide Web sites centered around training and performance and related areas.

About: The Human Internet
about.com
About offers dozens of theme sites, including human resources (humanresources.about.com), distance learning (distancelearn.about.com), and adult education (adulted.about.com). Each site consists of articles, links, and other resources—including a human guide.

Active Learning
www.active-learning-site.com/vark.htm
Although this site is primarily for college and university faculty, this page focuses on learning styles, a topic that should be of interest to most trainers.

Activity Page
www.du.edu/~citin/activitypage.html
Christian Itin, an experiential educator from Rochester, created this page as a resource for those who use activities in their practice. Visitors are encouraged to contribute activities.

Adult Education Network (AEDNET)
www.nova.edu/~aed/newhorizons.html
AEDNET publishes *New Horizons in Adult Education*, a refereed electronic journal, on this site.

Advanced Distributed Learning Network
www.adlnet.org
The Advanced Distributed Learning (ADL) initiative was launched by the government in November 1997 to ensure access to high-quality education and training materials that can be tailored to individual learner needs and made available whenever and wherever required. This site features news, a calendar of events, a library, and links.

AllTheTests.com
www.allthetests.com
"The online test search engine and your guide through the jungle of different tests on the Internet," this is a good site to visit for IQ tests, EQ tests, personality tests, and many more. The listings include the name and URL of the site, a brief description, a rating, and an indication of how long the test takes.

ALN Web: Asynchronous Learning Networks
www.aln.org
This is the home of *ALN Magazine* and *Journal of ALN* and a source of information about asynchronous learning, including the International Conference on Asynchronous Learning Networks. It hosts online discussions and features a directory of online courses.

American Productivity and Quality Center
www.apqc.org
APQC offers benchmarking, training, and other resources in such areas as quality, knowledge management, measurement, customer satisfaction, and productivity.

American Society for Training and Development
www.astd.org
This site is comprehensive, with articles from *Training & Development* and the new online magazine *Learning Circuits*, other information related to performance and training issues, and links to other sites. In addition, there are "learning communities"—areas with specialized resources and focused discussion.

America's Learning eXchange
www.alx.org
This is a marketplace for training and education resources. Users can search for classroom courses, distance learning opportunities, Web- and computer-based training, educational programs, apprenticeship programs, conference workshops, and seminars.

Big Dog's Bowl of Biscuits
www.nwlink.com/~donclark/index.html
This is an eclectic collection of training and performance resources compiled by Don Clark, with links to other sites dealing broadly and specifically with related areas.

Brandon Hall
www.brandon-hall.com
Brandon Hall has been providing information about using technology for learning since 1993.

Business Potential
www.businesspotential.com
"Life-long learning resources," this site features articles and other learning resources for personal and career development, categorized by topic.

Business Process Reengineering Online Learning Center
www.prosci.com
ProSci provides articles, tool kits, information on consultants and other resources, and addresses for BPR and related mailing lists.

Center for Accelerated Learning
www.alcenter.com
In addition to lists of resources on accelerated learning, this site features *Accelerated Learning Tips and Techniques,* an online newsletter of ideas for trainers.

Center for the Study of Work Teams
www.workteams.unt.edu
This site features information on conferences, educational resources, research projects, the work teams newsletter, and the Teamnet discussion list, as well as external papers and editorials, conference proceedings, and Web links.

Copyright Web Site
www.benedict.com
This site provides "real-world, practical, and relevant information" on copyrighting written materials, music, or whatever.

CWL Publishing Enterprises
www.cwlpub.com
This is the home of the company that produces this yearbook. It features selected articles and links to many training and performance sites. There's also information on books produced by this company.

Distance Education Clearinghouse
www.uwex.edu/disted/home.html
This site, maintained by the University of Wisconsin, covers distance education and related areas.

e-LearningHub
www.e-learninghub.com
This site—created by Brooke Broadbent, author of a new book on e-learning—is to help people use e-learning successfully.

TRAINING AND PERFORMANCE RESOURCES ONLINE

epss.com!
www.epss.com
Devoted to "innovative approaches to the analysis and design of software systems that result in improved business performance," this site provides a guide to terminology, hosts a forum, features industry news, and lists books, articles online, organizations, and conferences.

EPSS InfoSite
www.epssinfosite.com
This site has been judged "the best place on the Web for finding and sharing information, ideas, and opinions about planning, designing, and developing electronic performance support systems."

ERIC Clearinghouse on Adult, Career, and Vocational Education
ericacve.org
The site features the Trends and Issues Alerts as well as a searchable database of ERIC publications.

Explorations in Learning & Instruction: The Theory Into Practice Database
tip.psychology.org
Created by Greg Kearsley, an instructional designer, this site is "a tool intended to make learning and instructional theory more accessible to educators." There are summaries of 50 theories of learning and instruction, each consisting of overview, scope/application, example, principles, and references.

Extranet—A Reference Page
www.viktoria.informatik.gu.se/~kerstinf/extranet.htm
If you're interested in extranets—"the third wave of Internet evolution"—this site is the place to begin. The creator, Kerstin Forsberg, follows the development and application of Internet technologies, but particularly this emerging concept.

The Facilitator
www.thefacilitator.com
This site features articles from *The Facilitator*, a quarterly newsletter, as well as tips, a calendar of events, and other facilitation resources.

Gerrit Visser's HRD Page
gervis.net
This site provides links to "250 HRD sources," including performance technology. The choices are eclectic. If you can understand Dutch, there's a lot more of value here.

geteducated.com
www.geteducated.com
This site includes information on distance education/learning. Of particular interest is *The Virtual University Gazette*, a free monthly electronic publication, with archives of the most recent issues.

Globewide Network Academy
www.gnacademy.org
GNA is an educational non-profit organization that maintains an online distance education catalog listing more than 25,000 courses and programs.

Group Facilitation Resources
www.albany.edu/cpr/gf/group_facilitation_resources.html
Maintained by the group facilitation discussion list, this site features a wide array of links.

HR.com
hr.com
With the hybrid look and feel of a newspaper and a bulletin board, this site offers news and a wide range of resources, including sample forms and policies.

hr-esource.com
www.hr-esource.com
This site is a portal for HR professionals, with news, information, and products.

HRfree.com
www.hrfree.com
This site features news and a reading list.

HR Hub
www.hrhub.com
A "digital marketplace for the human resources industry," this portal offers news, information, links, and discussion forums.

HRIM Mall
www.hrimmall.com
This site, "Your Internet Portal to Human Resources," serves as a one-stop shopping center for HR needs—featuring products and services, articles and white papers, events, information on HR-related discussion lists, and links to associations and other HR Web sites.

HR One
www.hrone.com
This site was created with the goal of becoming a "Virtual HR Department." It features articles and advice as well as products and services.

HRWorld
www.hrworld.com
This site, an information service for human resource management, is primarily "for members only," but some levels of membership are free. It features forums, information, resources, and opportunities.

Human Performance and Achievement Resources
www.superperformance.com
This site features articles and annotated links to sites "relating to improving human abilities, skills, and performance in a variety of areas."

Human Resource Development
humanresourcedevelopment.start4all.com
This portal offers the basic assortment of news, information, and links.

Human Resource Learning Center
www.human-resources.org
This site, hosted by ProSci, features links, information on benchmarking and best practices, and references to articles and books.

Human Resource Management
hrm.start4all.com
This portal offers the basic assortment of news, information, and links.

Human Resource Management Resources on the Internet
www.nbs.ntu.ac.uk/depts/hrm/hrm_link.htm
This site was long known as Ray's List of HRM Connections, after the late Ray Lye, who created it. This site provides categories of links that can be useful, including publications, organizations, mailing lists, and more.

Human Resource Professional's Gateway to the Internet
www.hrprosgateway.com/index2.html
This site, created by Eric R. Wilson in 1995, includes a good variety of links and information on HR management.

Instructional Technology Research Online
www.gsu.edu/~wwwitr
InTRO provides professionals in instructional technology with an electronic forum to disseminate, discuss, and advance research in instructional technology and related fields.

International Association of Facilitators
www.iaf-world.org

This site offers good virtual libraries in English and Spanish and extensive links.

International Personnel Management Association Assessment Council
www.ipmaac.org/index.html

The IPMA is the main association for public personnel professionals, primarily those who work in federal, state, or local government. This page provides information on IPMA's assessment council and includes links to other sites.

International Society for Performance Improvement
www.ispi.org

This site features the organization's publications and other benefits, discussion lists, and a calendar of events.

Internet Business Technology Portal
www.brint.com/interest.html

This site provides very useful links and news.

John Sleigh: Achievement Learning
www.johnsleigh.com.au

Here's a colleague who believes in sharing his tricks, tips, and techniques—all in pursuit of his mission: to make learning fun.

justanotherhomepage (Martin Ryder)
www.cudenver.edu/~mryder/martin.html

Created by someone with "an unending itch to understand how we learn and grow together as thinking individuals in this rapidly changing culture that we are now creating," this site links to pages devoted to instructional design, instructional technology, and performance technology.

Learnativity.com
www.learnativity.com

This site—"where adult learning, productivity, creativity, and activity meet online"—is a great resource for information on organizations in the U.S. and around the world, online resources, and periodicals and books.

Learning Organizations
learningorganizations.start4all.com

This portal offers the basic assortment of news, information, and links.

Learning Styles
www.namss.org.uk/lstyles.htm
This page of the National Association for Managers of Student Services site offers more than two dozen links to resources on learning styles.

Lguide: Guide to E-Learning
onlinelearningguide.com
This site features ratings and reviews of online courses, but it also offers in the Resource Room articles, links, information on e-pubs, and a calendar of events.

Loretta's Training Resource Center
www.quicktrainingtips.com
This is the home of *Quick Training Tips* (a free e-mail newsletter), *The Microcomputer Trainer*, and other resources "for everyone who teaches people to use computers."

The Masie Center
www.masie.com
"The Technology and Learning ThinkTank," this site features a "TechLearn" bookstore and online learning resources. Of particular interest is the searchable database of links.

McGraw-Hill Publishing: Training Games
www.books.mcgraw-hill.com/training/toolchest/games.html
This page features free training activities.

MeaningfulWorkplace.com
www.meaningfulworkplace.com
At this site, formerly meaningatwork.com, Tom Terez offers "strategies and tools for bringing out the best in people at work."

National Association for Government Training and Development
www.usd.edu/nagtad
This site promotes NAGTAD and its quarterly newsletter, *Government Training and Development NewsBriefs*, but there are also some very good links here for training and development professionals in any sector.

OD Learning Group
www.learninggroup.org
Created by the Massachusetts Bay Organization Development Learning Group, this site serves as a resource on various areas related to organization development, including *The Executive Coaching Handbook*.

Online Course Delivery Software Products
www.marshall.edu/it/cit/webct/compare/comparison.html
If you want succinct comparisons of course software, this is a great place to start.

Online Educational Delivery Applications
www.ctt.bc.ca/landonline
"This site is designed to help educators evaluate and select online delivery software. ... The analysis describes and compares the most viable applications in use in Canada."

OnlineFacilitation.com
www.onlinefacilitation.com
This news site is "devoted to sharing information on online facilitation, moderation, and community hosting."

Online Learning Magazine
www.onlinelearningmag.com
This site, devoted to the publication that replaced *Inside Technology Training*, allows access to articles from both publications and features a discussion forum.

Organization Development Institute
members.aol.com/odinst
This site features news and links, primarily about the Institute.

Organizational Development Network
www.odnetwork.org
This site provides information about the ODN and supports a number of email lists. It also has a resource section that includes assessment tools, large group interventions, and organizational learning.

Peer Resources: Coaching/Mentoring Resources
www.peer.ca/coaching.html
This page offers an organized collection of annotated resources for coaching or mentoring.

Performance Measurement Resources
www.zigonperf.com/performance.html
One-stop shopping for information on performance measurement, this site includes how-to articles, examples of measures, links to measurement-related Web sites, and an annotated bibliography of books and articles related to performance measurement.

Professional Society for Sales and Marketing Training
www.smt.org
This site describes the society and includes some resources for Sales and Marketing Training.

Prometheon
www.onlearning.net
The goal of this "Learning Resource Network" is to provide "easy access to the world's best learning resources." It offers a wide variety of resources—speakers, articles, forums, courses, training forms, a store, and links.

Resources for Moderators and Facilitators of Online Discussion
www.emoderators.com/moderators.shtml
This page of the Berge Collins Associates site offers a variety of resources "for moderators and moderators-to-be of online discussion in both academic and non-academic settings."

Ron Tillotson's List of Training, Performance Improvement, HR, & OD Sites
www.michaelgreer.com/tillotson_list.htm
This is a page of links compiled by the principal of Performance Improvement Systems, a training and organizational development consulting service.

Self-Directed Work Team
users.ids.net/~brim/sdwth.html
This is a source for examples, books and other resources, bibliographies on the Web, and links to sites that cover the basics and team skills.

Seminar Finder
www.seminarfinder.com
Check out this site to locate and register for "public seminars, continuing education courses, and online learning on a variety of topics ... throughout the world."

Society for Human Resource Management
www.shrm.org
This site gives lots of information about the society and *HR Magazine*, its official publication. There are also daily news updates, online publications, and links. SHRM members can also access a library of research papers and a bulletin board area.

Society for Organizational Learning
www.solonline.org
SOL is "a global learning community dedicated to building knowledge about fundamental institutional change."

Square Wheels and Lost Dutchman
www.squarewheels.com
This site offers "tools and information on team work, creativity, change management, and leadership development ... 500+ pages of workshops, training tools, exercises, jokes, teambuilding ideas and creativity tools, immediately useful for consultants, trainers, and managers interested in facilitation and active experiential learning."

Suite101.com: Training and Development
www.suite101.com/welcome.cfm/training_and_development
This page of a site devoted to "real people helping real people" features articles, links, and discussions. The focus is primarily on online training.

Teaching Tips Index
www.hcc.hawaii.edu/intranet/committees/FacDevCom/guidebk/teachtip/teachtip.htm
Although intended for college and university faculty, the resources on this page can be of considerable value in training.

Team Builders Plus Training Links
www.teambuildersplus.com/links.htm
If you're using teams, this page of links should be on your list. The links are classified according to topic, but you'll want to skim through all the descriptions. The variety is impressive.

Technical Training Tips
pages.prodigy.net/pblair/ttthome.htm
Pete Blair—a very experienced trainer and independent consultant—offers suggestions for designing and developing technical training. These basics are a good place to begin.

TECHtionary
www.crosstouch.com/techtionary
TECHtionary is touted as "the world's first animated online dictionary on telecommunications, data networking, and Internet technology.

Trainer's Warehouse
www.trainerswarehouse.com
This is a mail-order company that provides products and ideas for "anyone who does presentations."

TRAINING AND PERFORMANCE RESOURCES ONLINE 427

TRAINET.com
www.trainet.com
The North American Training and Development Resource Center is a site for people selling or seeking training services, promoted as "the most comprehensive database known of training related products and services."

Training and Development Community Center
www.tcm.com/trdev
This comprehensive site maintained by Eric Snyder has all kinds of information and links to sites dealing with training issues, including a list of Internet discussion groups related to training and a multitude of sites for training and development and/or human resources professionals, plus glossaries of terms and acronyms.

Training and Seminar Locator
www.tasl.com
This site—proclaimed "The Ultimate Education & Training Portal for Career Development"— allows searches for events, products, and providers on many business topics.

Training by Design
www.trainingbydesign.com
This site features short articles on "timely topics," tips and ideas, and annotated links.

Training Forum
www.trainingforum.com
The purpose of this site is to offer training organizations, HR professionals, and trainers "a comprehensive resource of premium training products and services." It features databases of courses, speakers, training resources, seminars and conferences, and organizations.

Training Media Review
www.tmreview.com
This site provides help for business training and management development, along with several search engines. The site features a selection of past reviews, the current TMR Top 20, news, and opinion. Most of the resources are available only through paid subscriptions.

Training Place
www.trainingplace.com
The focus of the resources featured here is on e-learning, adaptive learning, and learning orientations.

Training Professionals
www.prossentials.com/trainingpro
This portal for training professionals on the PROssentials site offers a variety of reasons to visit regularly.

Training Registry
www.trainingregistry.com
This is a directory of training courses, trainers, training products, classroom and training facility rentals, business and consulting services, professional speakers, and books.

Training SuperSite
www.trainingsupersite.com
This site by Bill Communications features selected articles from *TRAINING* and *Online Learning*, a career center, a discussion board, and links to training-related Web sites.

TRDEV
groups.yahoo.com/group/trdev
TRDEV is the best list for training professionals and the archives and other resources available to members are all the more reason to join this list.

Virtual Communities
virtualcommunities.start4all.com
This portal offers the basic assortment of news, information, and links.

Web-Based Training Information Center
www.filename.com/wbt/index.html
This nonprofit site provides information on training via the Web: articles, tools, theory, style guides, events, and links to WBT sites. It also has a primer on Web-based training, discussion forums, and surveys about WBT and WBPSS.

Work 911/Bacal & Associates
www.work911.com/performance
"Everything You Need to Know" about performance management and appraisal from Robert Bacal, author of *Performance Management*, this site offers a lot of resources. There are discussion lists on such topics as performance management and appraisal, workplace conflict resolution, workplace communication, learning@work, and other topics of interest to HRD/T&D professionals.

Workforce
www.workforce.com
This site is an online, partial version of *Workforce* magazine, with a "community center" of discussion forums, peer groups, and live chats.

Workforce Commerce Center
www.mediabrains.com/client/workforcema/BG1/search.asp
This buyer's guide is a "comprehensive directory of HR products and services," with searching by category, company name, or keyword.

workindex.com
www.workindex.com
This "gateway to human resource solutions" covers many work-related areas, including training and development and human resources.

Workshops by Thiagi, Inc.
www.thiagi.com
This site, created by Sivasailam "Thiagi" Thiagarajan, is dedicated to making training fun and to eclectic approaches. Promising "more content, less fluff," he offers "freebies and goodies" and a variety of links.

Work Team Coaching
workteamcoaching.home.att.net/index.html
This site, "dedicated to making the world a better place to work," features *Work Team Coaching*, an e-zine for work team coaches and executive facilitators and The Coach's Bookshelf.

Going Beyond These Resources

Give someone a fish and he will eat for a day. Teach him to fish and he will eat for a lifetime. That's the essence of helping people improve themselves, so any listing of Internet resources in a yearbook devoted to training and performance should include some instructions on 'Net fishing, so you can find other discussion lists and Web sites to meet your specific needs.

To find other *discussion lists*, you can use the search functions of the following Web sites:

groups.yahoo.com
www.topica.com
paml.net
catalog.com/vivian/interest-group-search.html
tile.net/lists
www.lsoft.com/lists/listref.html

To find other *newsgroups*, we recommend the following Web sites:

groups.google.com
tile.net/news

To find other *Web sites*, you can use any of dozens of search engines. Search engines use varying protocols, but are basically similar, at least for less complex searches. The following search sites are among the best at this time:

www.google.com
www.altavista.com
www.search.com
www.alltheweb.com
hotbot.lycos.com
www.yahoo.com
www.dogpile.com
www.all4one.com
www.excite.com
www.lycos.com
www.webcrawler.com

Directory of Magazines, Journals, and Newsletters Dealing with Training and Performance Issues

This section presents a comprehensive but not exhaustive list of magazines, journals, and newsletters that will be of interest to those involved in training and performance improvement. Some of these cover training and performance issues as a matter of course, and some cover these issues along with many others. Many organizations offer newsletters that are not listed here because they are only sent to members. Check the Directory of Training and Performance Associations and Organizations to find out more about those. Also, a major change over the last few years is that many publications are also or only available online.

We have divided this directory into two parts:

1. Magazines, journals, and newsletters directly related to training and performance
2. General business and management publications of interest to people involved in training and to HR managers

Each listing gives addresses, phone numbers, fax numbers, e-mail addresses, and World Wide Web URLs. You'll also find subscription information (current as of April 2001); prices are in U.S. dollars and rates are annual, unless indicated otherwise. (Prices change, so we advise checking the Web site to verify.) We also provide a brief description of each periodical.

Often with specialized journals and newsletters you can get a sample copy by contacting the publisher. For those in which you have an interest but not enough to subscribe, use this directory as a guide to what you might find at your local college or university library.

If you have any recommendations for publications we should list in the next edition of this annual, or to update our information, please e-mail us at jwoods@cwlpub.com.

Magazines, Journals, and Newsletters Directly Related to Training And Performance

Adult Education Quarterly
Published quarterly by the American Association for Adult and Continuing Education, 1200 19th Street, NW, Suite 300, Washington, DC 20036-2422, phone: (202) 429-5131, fax: (202) 223-4579, e-mail: Anna_Darin@dc.sba.com (Anna Darin, Association Manager), Web: www.cdlr.tamu.edu/tcall/aaace.

Subscriptions: Free to AAACE members. Nonmembers: U.S., $39; Canada, $44; elsewhere, $49.

This is a refereed journal committed to the dissemination of research and theory in adult and continuing education. It publishes reports of research, philosophical analyses, interpretive reviews of the literature, book reviews, and theoretical formulations, primarily for professors, researchers, and students.

Adult Learning
Published six times a year by the American Association for Adult and Continuing Education, 1200 19th Street, NW, Suite 300, Washington, DC 20036-2422, phone: (202) 429-5131, fax: (202) 223-4579, e-mail: Anna_Darin @dc.sba.com (Anna Darin, Association Manager), Web: www.cdlr.tamu.edu/tcall/aaace.

Subscriptions: Free to AAACE members. Nonmembers: U.S., $29; Canada, $34; elsewhere, $39.

This publication covers cross-cutting issues with an emphasis on practical solutions to problems faced by all adult educators from secondary and post-secondary education, business and labor, military and government, and from community-based organizations.

ALN Magazine
Published semiannually by the Asynchronous Learning Network, John Bourne, Editor-in-Chief, P.O. Box 1570, Station B, Nashville, TN 37235, phone: (615) 322-2118, fax: (615) 343-6449, e-mail: john.nourne@vanderbilt.edu, Web: www.aln.org.

Subscriptions: Free.

This magazine is devoted to topics in Asynchronous Learning Networks that do not fit the traditional journal format. These topics include reports of uses of technology, experiences with ALN courses, reports of activities on various campuses or in industry, and summaries of ALN activities. The aim is to make it more news- and method-oriented than a formal journal.

American Journal of Evaluation
Published in three issues by the American Evaluation Association, 505 Hazel Circle, Magnolia, AR 71753, phone/fax: (888) 232-2275 or (870) 234-7433,

e-mail: aea@kistcon.com, Web: www.eval.org. Subscriptions: Elsevier Science, Regional Sales Office, Customer Support Department, P.O. Box 945, New York, NY 10159-0945, phone: (888) 4ES-INFO (437-4636) or (212) 633-3730, fax: (212) 633-3680, e-mail: usinfo-f@elsevier.com, Web: www.elsevier.com/locate/ameval.

Subscriptions: Free to members. Otherwise, individuals $106 and institutions $258.

This journal, formerly *Evaluation Practice,* covers topics of current interest, provides information about upcoming conferences, and includes book reviews.

Bob Nelson's Rewarding Employees
Published in 10 issues by Nelson Motivation, Inc., 12245 World Trade Drive, Suite C, San Diego, CA 92128, phone: (800) 575-5521 or (858) 487-1046, fax: (858) 487-0259, e-mail: info@nelson-motivation.com, Web: www.nelson-motivation.com/newsletter.cfm.

Subscriptions: $149.

This newsletter provides recognition ideas and techniques, insights into the recognition practices of leading organizations, experts in the field, fresh ideas, and book and product reviews.

Compass: The Magazine of Peer Assistance, Coaching, and Mentoring
Published quarterly by Peer Resources, 1052 Davie Street, Victoria, BC V8S 4E3, Canada, phone: (800) 567-3700 (in Canada) or (250) 595-3503, fax: (250) 595-3504, e-mail: rcarr@islandnet.com, Web: www.peer.ca/Compassinfo.html.

Subscriptions: Free to members of the Peer Resources Network (CDN$53.50 for individuals, CDN$107.00 for institutions and organizations).

This magazine, launched in Winter 1999, shares insights and information about issues, innovations, research, resources, and practices related to mentorship, peer assistance, and coaching in business, education, and community settings.

Corporate Universities International Newsletter
Published bimonthly by Corporate University Xchange, Inc., 381 Park Avenue South, Suite 601, New York, NY 10016, phone: (800) 946-1210 or (212) 213-2828, fax: (212) 213-8621, e-mail: info@corpu.com, Web: www.corpu.com.

Subscriptions: Free to members ($199).

This newsletter provides information on trends in corporate university funding, management, and marketing and strategies for using learning technology.

Corporate University Review See *New Corporate University Review*
Creative Training Techniques Newsletter
Published monthly by Bill Communications, Inc., 50 S. Ninth Street, Minneapolis, MN 55402, phone: (800) 707-7749 or (612) 333-0471, fax: (612)

340-4819, e-mail: circwork@billcom.com or bobpikectt@aol.com, Web: www.trainingsupersite.com/publications.

Subscriptions: U.S., $99 per year; Canada, $109 *plus 7% GST or 15% HST* (#123705485); all other countries, $119.

This newsletter presents lots of easy-to-learn and inexpensive tips, tactics, and techniques to make trainers more effective, entertaining, and creative.

Critical Linkages II Newsletter
Published five times a year by Sager Educational Enterprises, 21 Wallis Road, Chestnut Hill, MA 02167, phone: (617) 469-9644, fax: (617) 469-9639, e-mail: cs@carolsager.com, Web: www.carolsager.com.

Subscriptions: U.S., $40; other countries, $46.

The mission of this newsletter is "to support and promote the growth and continuous improvement of Learning by building *Critical Linkages* across traditional occupational, professional, and academic boundaries."

Customer Communicator
Published monthly by Alexander Communications Group, Inc., 215 Park Avenue South, Suite 1301, New York, NY 10003, phone: (800) 232-4317 x 100 or (212) 228-0246, fax: (212) 228-0376, e-mail: info@alexcommgrp.com, Web: www.alexcommgrp.com/csg/tcc.html.

Subscriptions: 10 copies, in North America, $200; elsewhere, $290.

This is a training and motivation newsletter for frontline service representatives.

Education Technology Research and Development
Published quarterly by the Association for Education Communications and Technology, Inc., 1800 North Stonelake Drive, Suite 2, Bloomington, IN 47404, phone: (877) 677-AECT or (812) 335-7675, fax: (812) 335-7678, e-mail: aect@aect.org, Web: www.aect.org/Publications.

Subscriptions: AECT members, $35; nonmembers in U.S., $55; elsewhere, $63 (surface mail) or $83 (airmail).

This is a refereed, scholarly journal dealing with research and development in educational technology and instructional design at the school, higher, and adult education levels. Articles tend to be a blend of theory and application. It includes book reviews.

Educational Media International
Published quarterly by the International Council for Educational Media/Conseil International des Médias Educatifs, ICEM General Secretariat, Hanns-Fay-Strasse 1, D-67227 Frankenthal Germany, phone: NA, fax : +49 6233 46355, e-mail: secretariat@icem-cime.com, Web: www.icem-cime.com.

Subscriptions: Free to members. Otherwise, individuals, $85; organizations (three categories), $135-$275.

The primary objective of ICEM is "to provide a channel for the international exchange and evaluation of information, experience and materials in the field of educational media as they apply to pre-school, primary and secondary education, to technical and vocational, industrial and commercial training, teacher training, continuing and distance education."

Educational Technology

Published bimonthly by Educational Technology Publications, Inc., 700 Palisade Avenue, Englewood Cliffs, NJ 07632-0564, phone: (800) 952-BOOK(2665) or (201) 871-4007, fax: (201) 871-4009, e-mail: edtecpubs@aol.com, Web: bookstoread.com/etp.

Subscriptions: U.S., $119; other countries, $139.

Subtitled "The Magazine for Managers of Change in Education," this publication is aimed at both education and training, with a blend of theoretical and practice-oriented articles dealing with the use of electronic technology, including computers, video, and multimedia.

e-learning Magazine

Published bimonthly by Advanstar Communications, Publishing Office, 201 Sandpointe Ave., Suite 600, Santa Ana, CA 92707, phone: (714) 513-8400, fax: (714) 513-8632, e-mail: kgallagher@advanstar.com (Keith T. Gallagher, publisher), Web: www.elearningmag.com. Subscriptions: Superior Fulfillment, 131 W. First Street, Duluth, MN 55802, phone: (218) 723-9299, fax: (218) 723-9377, e-mail: fulfill@superfill.com.

Subscriptions: Free to qualified applicants in U.S. and Canada. Otherwise, U.S. $35, Canada or Mexico, $45, other countries, $55.

"The Magazine of Distributed Learning" aims to educate executive decision-makers in the public and private sectors on the benefits of learning tools, programs, and applications.

Employee Assistance Quarterly

Published quarterly by The Haworth Press, Inc., 10 Alice Street, Binghamton, NY 13904-1580, phone: (800) HAWORTH or (607) 722-5857, fax: (800) 895-0582 or (607) 722-6362, e-mail: getinfo@haworthpressinc.com, Web: www.haworthpressinc.com.

Subscriptions: Individual: U.S., $60; Canada, $81; elsewhere, $87. Institutional: U.S., $125; Canada, $169; elsewhere, $181. Library: U.S., $425; elsewhere, NA.

This journal offers a compilation of theoretical and practical information for EAP administrators, counselors, or consultants.

Employee Assistance Report
Published monthly by Impact Publications, Inc., E3430 Mountain View Lane, P.O. Box 322, Waupaca, WI 54981, phone: (715) 258-2448, fax: (715) 258-9048, e-mail: impact@gglbbs.com, Web: www.gglbbs.com/impact.

Subscriptions: $189.
This newsletter provides information to help EAP and HR professionals get the most out of their programs.

Employee Responsibilities and Rights Journal
Published quarterly by the Council on Employee Responsibilities and Rights. Subscriptions: Plenum Publications, Kluwer Academic Publishers Group, 233 Spring Street, New York, NY 10013-1578, phone: (800) 221-9369 or (212) 620-8027, fax: (212) 463 0742, e-mail: info@plenum.com, Web: www.wkap.nl/journalhome.htm/0892-7545.

Subscriptions: Individual, $62 / EUR 61.50. Institutional: $275 / EUR 274.50.
This is an international journal of interdisciplinary studies on the changing balance of rights and responsibilities between employers and employees.

Employment in the Mainstream
Published quarterly online by Mainstream, Inc., 6930 Carroll Avenue, Suite 240, Takoma Park, MD 20912, phone/TTY: (301) 891-8777, fax: (301) 891-8778, e-mail: info@mainstreaminc.org, Web: www.mainstreaminc.org/eitm.html.

Subscriptions: Free.
This magazine is dedicated to moving people with disabilities into the workplace.

Employment Management Today
Published quarterly by the Employment Management Association, Society for Human Resource Management, 1800 Duke Street, Alexandria, VA 22314-3499, phone: (703) 548-3440, fax: (703) 535-6490, e-mail: custsvc@shrm.org, Web: www.shrm.org/ema.

Subscriptions: Free to EMA members; otherwise, $35 (U.S. only).
This is the magazine of the Employment Management Association, a professional association representing those involved in recruitment and employment issues. The magazine focuses on issues related to hiring and retaining staff.

The Facilitator
Published quarterly by Nurre Ink, P.O. Box 670705, Dallas, TX 75367-0705, phone: (972) 243-1356, fax: (972) 243-1357, e-mail: snurre@thefacilitator.com, Web: www.thefacilitator.com.

Subscriptions: U.S., $35; other countries, $40.
This newsletter, "written by facilitators for facilitators," is practical, covering techniques, tools, materials, and exercises.

DIRECTORY OF MAGAZINES, JOURNALS, AND NEWSLETTERS

Group Facilitation: A Research and Applications Journal
Published semiannually by the International Association of Facilitators, 7630 W. 145th Street, Suite 202, St. Paul, MN 55124, phone: (612) 891-3541, fax: (612) 891-1800, e-mail: office@iaf-world.org, Web: www.iaf-world.org/Journal/iafjournal.htm.

Subscriptions: Free to IAF members.

This publication focuses on the art and science of group facilitation. The aim is to increase understanding of group facilitation and its implications for individuals, groups, organizations, and communities and to advance knowledge of group facilitation. This journal is intended for facilitators, mediators, organizational development and training specialists, researchers, and others who seek to use facilitation skills.

HR Focus
Published monthly by the Institute of Management and Administration, Subscription Department, 29 West 35th Street, New York, NY 10001-2299, phone: (800) 401-5937 or (212) 244-0360, fax: (212) 564-0465, e-mail: subserv@ioma.com, Web: www.ioma.com.

Subscriptions: $259; Web discount rate, $209.

This publication covers a variety of issues and news items of interest to HR managers.

HR Magazine
Published monthly by the Society for Human Resource Management, 1800 Duke Street, Alexandria, VA 22314-3499, phone: (703) 548-3440, fax: (703) 535-6490, e-mail: hrmag@shrm.org, Web: www.shrm.org/hrmagazine.

Subscriptions: Free to SHRM members; nonmembers: U.S., $70; elsewhere, $125.

This magazine features a wide variety of well-written articles that deal with training and performance issues, often in depth. It includes many columns, departments, and buying guides.

Human Performance
Published quarterly by Lawrence Erlbaum Associates, Inc., 10 Industrial Avenue, Mahwah, NJ 07430-2262, phone: (800) 9–BOOKS–9 or (201) 236-9500, fax: (201) 760–3735, e-mail: orders@erlbaum, Web: www.erlbaum.com/Journals/journals/HP/hp.htm.

Subscriptions: U.S. and Canada, $60 (individual) or $350 (institutional); elsewhere, $90 (individual) or $380 (institutional).

This scholarly journal publishes research investigating the nature of performance in the workplace and applied settings, with information going beyond the study of traditional job behavior.

Human Resource Development International
Published quarterly by Taylor & Francis Group, 325 Chestnut Street, 8th Floor, Philadelphia, PA 19106, phone: (215) 625-8900, fax: (215) 625-2940, e-mail: info.journals@routledge.com, Web: www.tandf.co.uk/journals/routledge/13678868.html.

Subscriptions: Institutional, $343 or £207.

The mission of this publication is to promote all aspects of practice and research that explore issues of individual, group, and organizational learning and performance, "questioning the divide between practice and theory, between the 'practitioner' and the 'academic,' between traditional and experimental methodological approaches."

Human Resource Development Quarterly
Published quarterly by Jossey-Bass, 350 Sansome Street, San Francisco, CA 94104, phone: (800) 956-7739 or (415) 433-1740, fax: (800) 605-2665 or (415) 433-0499, e-mail: webperson@jbp.com, Web: www.jbp.com/JBJournals/hrdq.html.

Subscriptions: Individual: U.S., Canada, or Mexico, $58; other countries, $82. Institutional: U.S., $130; Canada, $170; other countries, $204.

A joint project by the American Society for Training & Development and the Academy of Human Resource Development, this publication is intended to be "the first scholarly journal focused directly on the evolving field of human resource development."

Human Resource Executive
Published in 16 issues by LRP Publications, 747 Dresher Road, Suite 500, Horsham, PA 19044-0980, phone: (215) 784-0910, fax: (215) 784-0870, e-mail: jviola@lrp.com (Joan Viola, administrative assistant), Web: www.hrexecutive.com.

Subscriptions: Free to qualified applicants; otherwise, U.S., $89.95; Canada and Mexico, $101.95, elsewhere, $133.95.

This magazine provides vice presidents and directors of human resources with news, profiles of HR visionaries, success stories of human resource innovators, and coverage of all areas of human resource management. The November issue includes an annual Purchasing Resource Guide.

Human Resource Management
Published quarterly by John Wiley & Sons, Inc., Customer Service, 605 Third Avenue, New York, NY 10158-0012, phone: (212) 850-6645, fax: (212) 850-6021, e-mail: subinfo@wiley.com, Web: www.interscience.wiley.com/jpages/0090-4848.

Subscriptions: Individual: U.S. and Canada, $460 (Canada, add 7% GST).

Institutional: U.S. and Canada, $225 (Canada, add 7% GST); other countries, $249.
This journal covers the broad spectrum of human resource management, informing managers and academics on the latest concepts, tools, and practices in this field and exploring issues of societal, organizational, and individual relevance.

Human Resource Planning
Published quarterly by the Human Resource Planning Society, 317 Madison Avenue, Suite 1509, New York, NY 10017, phone: (212) 490-6387, fax: (212) 682-6851, e-mail: info@hrps.org, Web: www.hrps.org.

Subscriptions: $120 (including postage).
The focus is on current theory, research, and practice in strategic human resource management, particularly on HR practices that contribute to making organizations more effective. At least one special issue a year focuses on a single key topic, such as globalization, executive resource planning and development, or service quality and organizational effectiveness.

Human Resource Professional
Published bimonthly by LRP Publications, 747 Dresher Road, Horsham, PA 19044, phone: (800) 341-7874 x 274 or (215) 784-0860, fax: (215) 784-9639, e-mail: custserve@lrp.com, Web: www.lrp.com/Human/hrnm.htm#Hum.

Subscriptions: U.S., $110 plus $15 shipping and handling.
This newsletter presents tips, strategies, and solutions, covering such areas as performance appraisals, electronic monitoring, harassment, reengineering, health issues, substance testing, benefits, and compensation policies and practices.

Incentive
Published monthly by Bill Communications, Inc., 770 Broadway, New York, NY 10003, phone: (646) 654-7649, fax: (646) 654-7650, e-mail: doldenburg@incentivemag.com (Donna Oldenburg, publisher), Web: www.incentivemag.com.

Subscriptions: Free in U.S. to qualified applicants; in other countries, call (646) 654-7649.
The publishers call this magazine "the only publication devoted exclusively to motivation and performance improvement through the use of incentives."

Industrial and Commercial Training
Published in seven issues (four dispatches) by MCB University Press Ltd., 60/62 Toller Lane, Bradford, West Yorkshire, England BD8 9BY, phone: +44 (0) 1274 777700, fax: +44 (0) 1274 785200, e-mail: help@mcb-usa.com, Web: www.mcb.co.uk/ict.htm.

Subscriptions: $7999 for North and South America. Other areas: check rates on Web site.

The editorial intent is to show how to put training theory into action. Featuring selected ideas from research and practice, this journal is meant to be a practical, informative training information resource.

Info-line

Published monthly by the American Society for Training and Development, 1640 King Street, Box 1443, Alexandria, VA 22313-2043, phone: (703) 683-8100, fax: (703) 683-8103, e-mail: info@astd.org, Web: www.astd.org/virtual_community/infoline.

Subscriptions: U.S. $119 per year (ASTD members, $79); rest of world, $159 per year (ASTD members, $119).

This magazine consists of 16- to 20-page issues focused on a single topic. Topics include performance improvement, training basics, ISD, management development, training technology, career development, and workplace enhancement.

Innovations in Education and Teaching International

Published quarterly by Taylor & Francis Group, 325 Chestnut Street, 8th Floor, Philadelphia, PA 19106, phone: (215) 625-8900, fax: (215) 625-2940, e-mail: info.journals@routledge.com, Web: www.tandf.co.uk/journals/routledge/14703297.html.

Subscriptions: Individual, $68 or £39. Institutional, $244 or £148.

Formerly *Innovations in Education and Training* International, the journal of the Staff and Educational Development Association (SEDA), newly merged with the Association of Education and Training Technology, provides perspectives and contributions on new developments in educational technology, for teaching staff, staff developers, and managers in higher and further education, continuing education, and training organizations.

Interactive Learning Environments

Published in three issues by Swets & Zeitlinger Publishers, North America Office, P.O. Box 582, Downingtown, PA 19335-9998, phone: NA, fax: NA, e-mail: orders@swets.nl, Web: www.swets.nl/sps/journals/ile1.html.

Subscriptions: Institutions: Dfl. 388 / US$ 205.Individuals: Dfl. 143 / US$ 79. This journal was founded in 1990 to provide "an archival repository of research and a forum for all individuals working towards changing education through learner-centred use of information technology." It has since broadened its scope to cover technologies such as Internet, groupware, and multimedia and their impact on education, training, and lifelong learning.

International Journal of Business Performance Management
Published quarterly by Inderscience Enterprises Ltd., (Order Department), World Trade Center Building, 29 route de Pré-Bois, Case Postale 896, CH-1215 Geneva 15, Switzerland, phone: NA, fax: +44-1234-240515 or +41 22-7910885, e-mail: subs@inderscience.com, Web: www.inderscience.com/ejournal/b/ijbpm/indexijbpm.html.

Subscriptions: $340; outside Great Britain, add $30 shipping and handling.
This journal covers various areas of performance management, both theory and practice: benchmarking, productivity and quality, outsourcing knowledge management, business process reengineering, organizational learning, virtual teams, and use of information and communication technologies to improve performance.

International Journal of Training and Development
Published quarterly by Blackwell Publishers, 350 Main Street, Malden, MA 02148, phone: (781) 388-8200, fax: (781) 388-8210, e-mail: subscrip@blackwellpub.com, Web: www.blackwellpublishers.co.uk/asp/journal.asp?ref=13603736.

Subscriptions: Americas, $56 (individual) or $256 (institutional) (Canada, add 7% GST, #130130412RT). Elsewhere, £56 (individual) and £212 (institutional).
This journal was founded to meet "the growing need for an international forum for the reporting of high-quality research, analysis, and debate for the benefit of the academic and corporate communities as well as those engaged in public policy formulation and implementation."

IOMA's Pay for Performance Report
Published monthly by the Institute of Management and Administration, Subscription Department, 29 West 35th Street, New York, NY 10001-2299, phone: (800) 401-5937 or (212) 244-0360, fax: (212) 564-0465, e-mail: subserv@ioma.com, Web: www.ioma.com.

Subscriptions: $279; Web discount rate, $229.
This publication provides information on improving productivity through the use of variable pay and bonus programs for all types of employees, with benchmarks and surveys to help keep employees motivated and the company competitive.

IOMA's Report on Managing Training and Development
Published monthly by the Institute of Management and Administration, Subscription Department, 29 West 35th Street, New York, NY 10001-2299, phone: (800) 401-5937 or (212) 244-0360, fax: (212) 564-0465, e-mail: subserv@ioma.com, Web: www.ioma.com.

Subscriptions: $249; Web discount rate, $199.
This newsletter provides information on building and maintaining state-of-the-art training programs, reducing costs, and automating learning and performance development.

Journal of Asynchronous Learning Networks
Published online by the Web of Asynchronous Learning Networks, John Bourne (editor), P.O. Box 1570, Station B, Nashville, TN 37235, phone: (615) 322-2118, fax: (615) 343-6449, e-mail: john.bourne@vanderbilt.edu, Web: www.aln.org/index.htm.

Subscriptions: Free.
The journal features research articles, including experimental results.

Journal of Educational Technology Systems
Published quarterly by the Society for Applied Learning Technology and the Learning Technology Institute, 50 Culpeper Street, Warrenton, VA 20186, phone: (540) 347-0055 or (800) 457-6812, fax: (540) 349-3169, e-mail: info@lti.org, Web: www.lti.org.

Subscriptions: SALT members, $60. (Membership required.) Outside North America, add $18 for shipping.
The journal deals with systems in which technology and education interface and is designed to inform educators who are interested in making optimum use of technology.

Journal of European Industrial Training
Published in nine issues (five dispatches) by MCB University Press Ltd., 60/62 Toller Lane, Bradford, West Yorkshire, England BD8 9BY, phone: +44 (0) 1274 777700, fax: +44 (0) 1274 785200, e-mail: help@mcb-usa.com, Web: www.emeraldinsight.com/jeit.htm.

Subscriptions: U.S., $9999. Other areas: check rates on Web site.
This journal covers developments in training and examines concepts, models, tools and processes.

Journal of Experiential Education
Published three times a year by the Association for Experiential Education, 2305 Canyon Boulevard, Suite 100, Boulder, CO 80302-5651, phone: (303) 440-8844, fax: (303) 440-9581, e-mail: info@aee.org, Web: www.aee.org/publications/journal/aeejourn.html.

Subscriptions: Free to AEE members. Nonmembers: U.S., $50; Canada, $56; elsewhere, $65.
This is a professional journal publishing practical articles on subjects such as outdoor adventure programming, service learning, experiential-based school programming, environmental education, internships, research and development, and the creative arts.

Journal of Instruction Delivery Systems

Published quarterly by the Society for Applied Learning Technology and the Learning Technology Institute, 50 Culpeper Street, Warrenton, VA 20186, phone: (540) 347-0055 or (800) 457-6812, fax: (540) 349-3169, e-mail: info@lti.org, Web: www.lti.org.

Subscriptions: SALT members, $40; others, $60. Outside North America, add $18 for shipping.

The journal is devoted to enhancing productivity through appropriate applications of technology systems in education, training, and job performance and to heighten awareness of technology-based learning.

Journal of Interactive Instruction Development

Published quarterly by the Society for Applied Learning Technology and the Learning Technology Institute, 50 Culpeper Street, Warrenton, VA 20186, phone: (540) 347-0055 or (800) 457-6812, fax: (540) 349-3169, e-mail: info@lti.org, Web: www.lti.org.

Subscriptions: SALT members, $40; others, $60. Outside North America, add $18 for shipping.

This publication provides instructional systems developers and designers with "important perspectives on emerging technologies and design methodologies."

Journal of Management Development

Published in 10 issues (five dispatches) by MCB University Press Ltd., 60/62 Toller Lane, Bradford, West Yorkshire, England BD8 9BY, phone: +44 (0) 1274 777700, fax: +44 (0) 1274 785200, e-mail: help@mcb-usa.com, Web: www.mcb.co.uk/jmd.htm.

Subscriptions: $8399 for North and South America. Other areas: check rates on Web site.

The purpose of this journal is to serve as "an international communications medium for all those working in management development whether in industry, consultancy, or academia."

Journal of Organizational Behavior Management

Published quarterly by The Haworth Press, Inc., 10 Alice Street, Binghamton, NY 13904-1580, phone: (800) HAWORTH or (607) 722-5857, fax: (800) 895-0582 or (607) 722-6362, e-mail: getinfo@haworthpressinc.com, Web: www.haworthpressinc.com.

Subscriptions: U.S., $60; elsewhere, $87.

This journal focuses on improving the quality of life for employees and helping them perform better.

Journal of Workplace Learning: Employee Counselling Today
Published in eight issues (four dispatches) by MCB University Press Ltd., 60/62 Toller Lane, Bradford, West Yorkshire, England BD8 9BY, phone: +44 (0) 1274 777700, fax: +44 (0) 1274 785200, e-mail: help@mcb-usa.com, Web: www.mcb.co.uk/jwl.htm.

Subscriptions: $4799 for North and South America. Other areas: check rates on Web site.

This journal covers all aspects of workplace learning, including formal and informal learning interventions, knowledge management, learning skills, learning styles, training effectiveness, learning organizations, personal development plans, self-directed work teams, new technology, and appraisal.

Leadership & Organization Development Journal
Published in eight issues (four dispatches) by MCB University Press Ltd., 60/62 Toller Lane, Bradford, West Yorkshire, England BD8 9BY, phone: +44 (0) 1274 777700, fax: +44 (0) 1274 785200, e-mail: help@mcb-usa.com, Web: www.mcb.co.uk/lodj.htm.

Subscriptions: $9399 for North and South America. Other areas: check rates on Web site.

The editorial purpose of this journal is to help readers further their understanding of the tough challenges facing today's leaders, develop people who can lead effectively in complex situations and master uncertainty and disruptive change, access details of the latest leadership research, and keep track of the issues that affect leaders and those responsible for developing them.

Learning Circuits
Published monthly online by the American Society for Training and Development, 1640 King Street, Box 1443, Alexandria, VA 22313-2043, phone: (703) 683-8100 or (800) 628-2783, fax: (703) 683-1523, e-mail: learningcircuits@astd.org, Web: www.learningcircuits.org.

Subscriptions: Free (online).

This online publication, created in January 2000 to replace *Technical Training*, covers e-learning. It presents feature articles, departments, columns, and peer interaction that help its readers understand workplace e-learning and bring it into their organizations.

Learning Decisions
Published in 11 issues by the Masie Center, P.O. Box 397, 95 Washington Street, Saratoga Springs, NY 12866, phone: (518) 350-2200, fax: (518) 587-3276, e-mail: kristin@masie.com (Kristin Barton, editor), Web: www.learningdecisions.com.

Subscriptions: $195.

This "interactive newsletter" presents data from subscribers on how they are implementing or changing training. Subscribers automatically become members of "the Learning Decisions community."

The Learning Organization: An International Journal

Published in five issues (four dispatches) by MCB University Press Ltd., 60/62 Toller Lane, Bradford, West Yorkshire, England BD8 9BY, phone: +44 (0) 1274 777700, fax: +44 (0) 1274 785200, e-mail: help@mcb-usa.com, Web: www.mcb.co.uk/tlo.htm.

Subscriptions: $1099 for North and South America. Other areas: check rates on Web site.

This journal aims to bring ideas, issues, and case studies to practitioners, consultants, researchers, and students, to promote a broader understanding into the concept of the learning organization.

LERN Magazine

Published in 10 issues by the Learning Resources Network (LERN), P.O. Box 9, River Falls, WI 54022, phone: (800) 678-5376, fax: (888) 234-8633, e-mail: info@lern.org, Web: www.lern.org.

Subscriptions: Free to members.

This magazine represents a recent consolidation of eight newsletters, including *Lifelong Learning Today*, from this international association of lifelong learning programming. It contains departments on seminars and conferences, contract training, association education, program analysis, credit and degree programs, demographics, training, and marketing programs online.

Managing Training and Development See *IOMA's Report on Managing Training and Development*

Measuring Business Excellence

Published in seven issues by MCB University Press Ltd., 60/62 Toller Lane, Bradford, West Yorkshire, England BD8 9BY, phone: +44 (0) 1274 777700, fax: +44 (0) 1274 785200, e-mail: help@mcb-usa.com, Web: www.mcb.co.uk/mbe.htm.

Subscriptions: $229 for North and South America. Other areas: check rates on Web site.

This journal presents research papers and case histories to provide international insights into non-financial ways to measure business improvements, apply best practices, implement innovative thinking, and learn how to use different improvement tools.

The Microcomputer Trainer
Published monthly by Systems Literacy Inc., 6 Saint Lo Place, P.O. Box 1032, Hopatcong, NJ 07843, phone: (973) 770-7762, fax: (973) 770-2205, e-mail: loretta@panix.com (Loretta Weiss-Morris, editor and publisher), Web: www.microcomputertrainer.com/MCTmain.htm.

Subscriptions: U.S. $265; Canada and Mexico, add $15; elsewhere, add $25.
This newsletter promises "solutions and strategies for the professionals responsible for building end-user skills."

Military Training Technology
Published in eight issues by Kerrigan Media International, Inc., 10209 Bentcross Drive, Building 2, Potomac, MD 20854, phone: (888) 299-8292 or (301) 299-5566, fax: (301) 299-5585, e-mail: kmi@kerriganmedia.com, Web: www.mt2-kmi.com.

Subscriptions: Free to government and military officials. Otherwise, U.S., $45; elsewhere, $65.
This magazine covers simulation training systems, modeling, interactive distance learning, wireless nets, training platforms, courseware, outsourcing, and more.

New Corporate University Review
Published bimonthly by HRevents, International Quality and Productivity Center, 150 Clove Road, P.O. Box 401, Little Falls, NJ 07424-0401, phone: (800) 882-8684 or (973) 256-0211, fax: (973) 812-5669 or (973) 256-0211, e-mail: info@traininguniversity.com, Web: www.traininguniversity.com.

Subscriptions: Free to members of the Corporate University Collaborative: U.S., $295, elsewhere, $395.
The mission of this publication is "to supply training executives with the thinking, the knowledge, and the skills required to make training a results-focused activity."

New Directions in Program Evaluation
Published quarterly by the American Evaluation Association, 505 Hazel Circle, Magnolia, AR 71753, phone/fax: (888) 232-2275 or (870) 234-7433, e-mail: aea@kistcon.com, Web: www.eval.org/Publications/NDE.htm. Subscriptions: Jossey-Bass, 350 Sansome Street, Fifth Floor, San Francisco, CA 94104, phone: (800) 956-7739 or (415) 433-1740, fax: (800) 605-2665 or (415) 433-0499, e-mail: webperson@jbp.com, Web: www.josseybass.com/JBJournals/nde.html.

Subscriptions: Free to AEA members. Individuals: U.S., Canada, Mexico, $66; elsewhere, $90. Institutions: U.S., $130; Canada, $170; elsewhere, $204.
This journal publishes original papers about the methods, theory, practice, and findings of evaluation.

OnlineLearning Magazine

Published monthly by Bill Communications, 50 S. Ninth Street, Minneapolis, MN 55402, phone: (612) 340-4809 (editorial) or (800) 328-4329, fax: (612) 340-4819 (circulation) or (612) 333-6526, e-mail: editor@onlinelearning.mag.com or circwork@billcomm.com, Web: www.onlinelearningmag.com.

Subscriptions: Free to qualified applicants in U.S. and Canada; otherwise, $89; elsewhere, $129.

Formerly *Inside Technology Training*, this magazine focuses on e-learning, including concepts like knowledge management, performance support and virtual collaboration.

Organization Development Journal

Published quarterly by the Organization Development Institute, 11234 Walnut Ridge Road, Chesterland, OH 44026, phone: (440) 729-7419, fax: (440) 729-9319, e-mail: DonWCole@aol.com, Web: members.aol.com/odinst/subjrnl.htm.

Subscriptions: Free to ODI members. Nonmembers: $60.

This practical, peer-reviewed journal covers organization development and how to create more effective organizations by working with people.

Organization Development Practitioner

Published quarterly by the Organization Development Network, 71 Valley Street, Suite 301, South Orange, NJ 07079-2825, phone: (973) 763-7337, fax: (973) 763-7488, e-mail: membership@odnetwork.org, Web: www.odnetwork.org.

Subscriptions: Free to ODN members. (Membership: U.S., $140; Canada and Mexico, $155; other countries, $160.)

This journal offers information and articles on current developments in the OD field as well as insights and teachings from practitioners.

Pay for Performance Report See *IOMA's Pay for Performance Report*

People Management

Published bimonthly by Personnel Publications Ltd., 17 Britton Street, London EC1M 5TP, United Kingdom, phone: +44 (0) 20 7880 6214, fax: +44 (0) 20 7336 7637, e-mail: editorial@peoplemanagement.co.uk, Web: www.peoplemanagement.co.uk.

Subscriptions: UK, £88; Europe, £140; elsewhere, £155 (surface mail) or £210 (airmail).

This magazine, produced by the Chartered Institute of Personnel and Development, is committed to providing personnel and development professionals with the information, advice, stimulation, and support they need in order to contribute effectively to their organizations.

Performance Improvement Journal
Published in 10 issues by the International Society for Performance Improvement, 1400 Spring Street, Suite 260, Silver Spring, MD 20910, phone: (301) 587-8570, fax: (301) 587-8573, e-mail: info@ispi.org, Web: www.ispi.org.

Subscriptions: Free to ISPI members. Nonmembers: $69.
This journal includes articles on a variety of topics related to training and performance improvement in the workplace written by practitioners.

Performance Improvement Quarterly
Published quarterly by the International Society for Performance Improvement, 1400 Spring Street, Suite 260, Silver Spring, MD 20910, phone: (301) 587-8570, fax: (301) 587-8573, e-mail: info@ispi.org, Web: www.ispi.org.

Subscriptions: ISPI members, $40. Nonmembers: $50.
This journal serves as a vehicle for "the scholarly publication of studies reflecting cutting-edge research in the field of human performance technology" and a forum for discussion among professionals in the field of issues related to human performance, instructional design and development, and learning.

Personnel Psychology
Published quarterly by Personnel Psychology, Inc., 520 Ordway Avenue, Bowling Green, OH 43402-2756, phone: (419) 352-1562, fax: (419) 352-2645, e-mail: ppsych@personnelpsychology.com, Web: www.personnelpsychology.com.

Subscriptions: U.S., $65; elsewhere, add $8.50 for surface mail or $32.00 for airmail.
This journal publishes research on personnel problems facing public and private sector organizations: selection and recruiting, training and development, job analysis, performance appraisal and feedback, compensation and rewards, legal issues, labor relations, work attitudes, motivation, and leadership.

Pew Learning and Technology Program Newsletter
Published monthly electronically by the Pew Learning and Technology Program, Center for Academic Transformation, Rensselaer Polytechnic Institute, Dean's Suite, Pittsburgh Building, 110 8th Street, Troy, NY 12180-3590, phone: (518) 276-6519, fax: (518) 695-5633, e-mail: bartp@rpi.edu (Patricia A. Bartscherer, Program Manager), Web: www.center.rpi.edu/PewHome.html.

Subscriptions: Free.
This electronic newsletter highlights ongoing examples of redesigned learning environments using technology and examines issues related to their development and implementation. Each issue includes an in-depth case study of a redesigned learning environment, reports on redesign develop-

ments in higher education, and announcements of conferences, workshops, and publications directly related to this topic.

Presentations
Published monthly by Bill Communications, Inc., 50 S. Ninth Street, Minneapolis, MN 55402, phone: (800) 707-7749 (circulation) or (612) 333-0471, fax: (612) 340-4819 (circulation) or (612) 333-6526, e-mail: circwork@billcom.com, Web: www.presentations.com.

Subscriptions: Free to qualified applicants in U.S. and Canada. Otherwise, $50. This publication is all about creating and delivering presentations and the technology available for presentations.

Public Personnel Management
Published quarterly by the International Personnel Management Association, 1617 Duke Street, Alexandria, VA 22314, phone: (800) 220-IPMA (4762) or (703) 549-7100, fax: (703) 684-0948, e-mail: publications@ipma-hr.org, Web: www.ipma-hr.org/pubs/ppmlist.html.

Subscriptions: Free to IPMA members. For nonmembers, U.S. and Canada, $50; elsewhere, $75 (airmail).
This journal features articles on labor relations, assessment issues, comparative personnel policies, and governmental reform.

Research-Technology Management
Published bimonthly by Industrial Research Institute, Inc., 1550 M Street, NW, Suite 1100, Washington, DC 20005-1712, phone: (202) 296-8811, fax: (202) 776-0756, e-mail: information@iriinc.org, Web: www.iriinc.org/web/rtm.cfm.

Subscriptions: U.S., Canada, and Mexico, $65 (individual) or $150 (institutional).
This journal, formerly *Research Management*, presents ideas and information that will help industrial R&D/technology managers run their operations more effectively, with an emphasis on "real-world" experience that can be put to use by practitioners across a broad spectrum of industries.

Simulation & Gaming: An International Journal of Theory, Practice, and Research
Published quarterly by Sage Publications Inc., 2455 Teller Road, Thousand Oaks, CA 91320, phone: (805) 499-0721 or (800) 818-SAGE(7243) (customer service), fax: (805) 499-0871, e-mail: info@sagepub.com, Web: www.sagepub.com.

Subscriptions: Individual, $75. Institutional, $355.
This journal—a joint publication by the Association for Business Simulation and Experiential Learning, the International Simulation and Gaming Association, the Japan Association of Simulation and Gaming, and the North

American Simulation and Gaming Association—provides an international forum for the study and discussion of simulation and gaming methodologies and their applications in education, training, consultation, and research.

Smart Workplace Practices
Published monthly by Employers of America, 520 S. Pierce Avenue, Suite 224, Mason City, IA 50401-2749, phone: (800) 728-3187 or (641) 424-3187, fax: (641) 424-1673, e-mail: employer@employerhelp.org, Web: www.employerhelp.org.

Subscriptions: Free to members.
This newsletter provides guidance for employers to cut costs and boost profits by working better with their employees.

Staff Leader
Published monthly by Aspen Publishers, Inc., 200 Orchard Ridge Drive, Gaithersburg, MD 20878, phone: (800) 234-1660 or (301) 417-7500, fax: (301) 695-7931, e-mail: customer.service@aspenpubl.com, Web: www.aspenpub.com.

Subscriptions: $153.
This practical, informal, 12-page newsletter is a guide to personnel issues for nonprofit administrators.

Supervision
Published monthly by the National Research Bureau, Inc., 320 Valley Street, Burlington, IA 52601-0551, phone: (319) 752-5415, fax: (319) 752-3421, e-mail: national@willinet.net, Web: NA.

Subscriptions: $56.55.
The purpose of "The Magazine of Industrial Relations and Operating Management" is to help supervisors achieve their goals and objectives and strengthen their management skills by providing guidance, resources, and "right now" solutions for the types of problems they face.

The Systems Thinker
Published 10 times a year by Pegasus Communications, Inc., 1 Moody Street, Waltham, MA 02453, phone: (781) 398-9700, fax: (781) 894-7175, e-mail: editorial@pegasuscom.com, Web: www.pegasuscom.com/tstpage.html. Subscriptions: P.O. Box 2241, Williston, VT 05495, phone: (800) 272-0945 or (802) 862-0095, fax: (802) 864-7626, e-mail: customerservice@pegasus-com.com.

Subscriptions: North America, $89; elsewhere, $119.
This newsletter helps managers and leaders put systems thinking to work in their organizations, by introducing the basic tools and concepts of systems thinking and building expertise in this essential component of management literacy through a variety of approaches.

Team Leader

Published biweekly by Dartnell Corporation, 360 Hiatt Drive, Palm Beach Gardens, FL 33418, phone: (800) 621-5463, fax: (561) 622-2423, e-mail: teamldr@dartnellcorp.com, Web: www.dartnellcorp.com.

Subscriptions: $74 plus $10 shipping/handling.

This four-page newsletter keeps team leaders up to date on team-leading techniques, provides solutions to common team-oriented problems, and offers motivational ideas.

Team Performance Management

Published on the Internet by MCB University Press Ltd., 60/62 Toller Lane, Bradford, West Yorkshire, England BD8 9BY, phone: +44 (0) 1274 777700, fax: +44 (0) 1274 785200, e-mail: help@mcb-usa.com, Web: www.mcb.co.uk/tpm.htm.

Subscriptions: $549 for North and South America. Other areas: check rates on Web site.

This international journal, which incorporates *Journal of High-Performance Teams*, aims to contribute to the development and exploitation of team performance for the benefit of organizations, teams within those organizations, and individual team members by providing a forum for the sharing of experience and learning, leading to stimulation of thought and transfer of ideas.

Teamwork

Published biweekly by Dartnell Corporation, 360 Hiatt Drive, Palm Beach Gardens, FL 33418, phone: (800) 621-5463, fax: (561) 622-2423, e-mail: teamwk@dartnellcorp.com, Web: www.dartnellcorp.com.

Subscriptions: $245.70 plus $34 shipping/handling (five copies).

This newsletter offers employees practical solutions to common team problems, so they can work better in small groups and in groups outside their areas. (There's a special edition for manufacturing.)

Tech Trends: For Leaders in Education and Training

Published bimonthly by the Association for Educational Communications and Technology, 1800 North Stonelake Drive, Suite 2, Bloomington, IN 47404, phone: (812) 335-7675, fax: (812) 335-7678, e-mail: aect@aect.org, Web: www.aect.org/Publications.

Subscriptions: AECT members, free; nonmembers: $30.

This is a peer-reviewed periodical for practitioners that features practical articles about technology and its integration into the learning environment. Regular departments include news items, new products, copyright, ethics, new books, and software.

Technology for Learning (Lakewood Report on Technology for Learning)
Published monthly by Bill Communications, Inc., 50 S. Ninth Street, Minneapolis, MN 55402, phone: (800) 707-7749 or (612) 333-0471, fax: (612) 340-4819, e-mail: circwork@billcom.com, Web: www.trainingsupersite.com/ publications.

Subscriptions: U.S., $189 per year; Canada, $199 plus 7% GST *or* 15% *HST* (#123705485); other countries, $209.

This newsletter, subtitled "Practical Ideas for Creating a Wired, Retooled and Networked Learning Organization" and incorporating the *Multimedia & Internet Training Newsletter,* provides practical ideas, how-to case studies, and product reviews that can help trainers accelerate learning in their organizations.

T.H.E. Journal
Published in 11 issues by THE Journal, 17501 East 17th Street, Suite 230, Tustin, CA 92780, phone: (714) 730-4011, fax: (714) 730-3739, e-mail: editorial@thejournal.com or subscriptions@thejournal.com, Web: www.thejournal.com.

Subscriptions: Free to qualified applicants. In Canada, add $29 for mailing. In other countries, add $95 for mailing.

This journal, formerly *Technological Horizons in Education*, covers applications of technology in learning.

Thiagi GameLetter
Published in 10 issues by Jossey-Bass/Pfeiffer, 350 Sansome Street, Fifth Floor, San Francisco, CA 94104, phone: (888) 378-2537 or (415) 433-1740, fax: (800) 605-2665 or (415) 433-0499, e-mail: webperson@jbp.com, Web: www.josseybass.com/catalog/isbn/TGL.

Subscriptions: U.S., $99.

This is a newsletter of "seriously fun activities for trainers, facilitators, and managers," to help make learning more effective and enjoyable. Each issue presents a complete, reproducible four-page game, as well as icebreakers, energizers, closers, product reviews, puzzles, Q&A with Thiagi (editor Sivasailam Thiagarajan), contests, and meeting management tips.

Today's Supervisor
Published monthly by the National Safety Council, 1121 Spring Lake Drive, Itasca, IL 60143-3201, phone: (800) 621-7619 or (630) 775-2056, fax: (630) 285-1315, e-mail: customerservice@nsc.org, Web: www.nsc.org/pubs/today.htm.

Subscriptions: NSC members, $21; nonmembers, $27.

This publication addresses the many problems and issues confronting the first-line supervisor and provides supervisors with short, concise, and easy-to-read articles on incident prevention, occupational health, management principles, and human relations.

DIRECTORY OF MAGAZINES, JOURNALS, AND NEWSLETTERS 453

TRAINING
Published monthly by Bill Communications, Inc., 50 S. Ninth Street, Minneapolis, MN 55402, phone: (612) 333-0471 (editorial) or (800) 328-4328 (subscriptions), fax: (612) 333-6526 (editorial) or (612) 340-4819 (subscriptions), e-mail: edit@trainingmag.com (editorial) or circwork@billcom.com (subscriptions), Web: www.trainingmag.com.

Subscriptions: U.S., $78; Canada, $88 plus 7% GST or 15% HST (#123705485); all other countries, $99.

This magazine covers issues of interest to corporate trainers and managers in general, on all aspects of training, management and organizational development, motivation, and performance improvement.

Training & Development
Published monthly by the American Society for Training and Development, 1640 King Street, Box 1443, Alexandria, VA 22313-2043, phone: (703) 683-8100 or (703) 683-4323 (TDD), fax: (703) 683-8103, e-mail: info@astd.org, Web: www.astd.org/virtual_community/td_magazine.

Subscriptions: U.S., $85; elsewhere, $165.

This premier journal in the field of training and performance includes articles on a wide variety of topics relating to training, human resources, performance, and management issues.

Training and Management Development Methods
Published in five issues by MCB University Press Ltd., 60/62 Toller Lane, Bradford, West Yorkshire, England BD8 9BY, phone: +44 (0) 1274 777700, fax: +44 (0) 1274 785200, e-mail: help@mcb-usa.com, Web: www.mcb.co.uk/tmdm.htm.

Subscriptions: $6399 for North and South America. Other areas: check rates on Web site.

A loose-leaf publication, this "toolkit" provides best training practices devised from real-world learning situations adapted in formulas for use outside the original organization.

Training Journal
Published monthly by Fenman, Clive House, The Business Park, Ely, Cambridgeshire, CB7 4EH, United Kingdom, phone: +44 (0) 1353 665533, fax: +44 (0) 1353 663644, e-mail: service@fenman.co.uk, Web: www.trainingjournal.co.uk.

Subscriptions: United Kingdom, £92; elsewhere, £106 (airmail).

Known as *Training Officer* until January 1999, this publication offers training professionals regular news, book reviews, feature articles, and commentary from practitioners in the field of training and human resource development.

Training Media Review
Published bimonthly by TMR Publications, P.O. Box 381822, Cambridge, MA 02238-1822, phone: (617) 489-9120 or (877) 532-1838, fax: (617) 489-3437, e-mail: customerservice@tmreview.com, Web: www.tmreview.com.

Subscriptions: U.S., $229 for print edition or $189 for online edition.
This is a comprehensive source for objective evaluations of media-based business training materials.

Training Strategies for Tomorrow
Published in six issues by MCB University Press Ltd., 60/62 Toller Lane, Bradford, West Yorkshire, England BD8 9BY, phone: +44 (0) 1274 777700, fax: +44 (0) 1274 785200, e-mail: help@mcb-usa.com, Web: www.mcb.co.uk/tst.htm.

Subscriptions: North America, $899. Other areas: check rates on Web site.
This journal covers management development, customer service training, outdoor training, evaluation of training programs and strategies, lifelong learning, participation and empowerment, training for quality, teambuilding, career development, performance appraisal, self-development, leadership skills training, selection and use of multimedia programs, and the impact of training and development on organizational performance.

Training Technology Monitor
Published eight times a year by Carswell, Thomson Professional Publishing, 1 Corporate Plaza, 2075 Kennedy Road, Scarborough, ON M1T 3V4, Canada, phone: (800) 387-5164 or (416) 609-3800, fax: (877) 750-9041 (Canada) or (416) 298-5082, e-mail: customercare@carswell.com, Web: www.carswell.com.

Subscriptions: CDN$150 or US$103.45.
This newsletter covers practices, trends, and issues related to the use of technology in delivering training for the workplace. It features profiles of innovative projects and individuals, features on new software and hardware, summaries of research focusing on technology-assisted learning, and a calendar of conferences, seminars, and workshops.

Virtual University Business Digest
Published monthly by geteducated.com, LLC, 4 Carmichael Street, #2160, Essex Junction, VT 05452, phone: (802) 879-1379, fax: (802) 288-1083, e-mail: info@geteducated.com, Web: www.geteducated.com/vubd/vubd.htm.

Subscriptions: U.S., $265; other countries, $295.
Launched in March 1999, this newsletter focuses on "the Internet-enabled, for-profit, e-education industry." It is aimed at "executives, deans, analysts, and suppliers who are building or servicing for-profit, Internet-enabled, adult education enterprises." It covers new products and platforms, mergers, partnerships, funding sources, acquisitions, and emerging market leaders.

What's Working in Human Resources
Published semimonthly by Progressive Business Publications, 376 Technology Drive, Malvern, PA 19355, phone: (800) 220-5000 or (610) 695-8600, fax: (610) 647-8089, e-mail: customer_service@pbp.com, Web: www.pbp.com/human-res.html.

Subscriptions: $299.
This newsletter provides information to help companies better manage their human assets and increase profitability and keeps human resource executives up to date on employment law and discrimination, harassment, and disability issues.

Workforce
Published monthly by ACC Communications, Inc., 245 Fischer Avenue, B-2, Costa Mesa, CA 92626, phone: (714) 751-1883, fax: (714) 751-4106, e-mail: mailroom@workforcemag.com, Web: www.workforceonline.com. Subscriptions: *Workforce* Magazine, P.O. Box 55695, Boulder, CO 80322-5695, phone: (800) 444-6485 or (303) 604-1464, fax: (303) 604-7455, e-mail: sekasa@workforcemag.com.

Subscriptions: U.S., $59; all other countries, $99 (Canada: GST #R126520766).
This magazine covers a broad range of topics of interest to HR professionals, including training and performance issues.

Working Together
Published biweekly by Dartnell Corporation, 360 Hiatt Drive, Palm Beach Gardens, FL 33418, phone: (800) 621-5463, fax: (561) 622-2423, e-mail: worktog@dartnellcorp.com, Web: www.dartnellcorp.com.

Subscriptions: $245.70 plus $34 shipping/handling (five copies).
The subtitle, "A Bulletin of Ideas & Inspiration for Achievement-Minded People," expresses the purpose of this newsletter succinctly.

Workplace Today
Published monthly by the Institute of Professional Management, Suite 2210-1081 Ambleside Drive, Ottawa, ON K2B 8C8, Canada, phone: (613) 721-5957, fax: (613) 721-5850, e-mail: pascal@workplace.ca (Brian W. Pascal, publisher and editor), Web: www.workplace.ca/magazine/index.html.

Subscriptions: CDN$96.
This magazine provides managers and supervisors legal information, detailed case studies, and reports on labor trends.

WorkSpan
Published in 11 issues by WorldatWork, 14040 N. Northsight Boulevard, Scottsdale, AZ 85260, phone: (877) 951-9191 or (480) 951-9191, fax: (480) 483-8352, e-mail: customerrelations@worldatwork.org, Web: www.worldatwork.org.

Subscription: Free to members.
This is a news magazine by the association formerly known as the American Compensation Association.

WorldatWork Journal
Published quarterly by WorldatWork, 14040 N. Northsight Boulevard, Scottsdale, AZ 85260, phone: (877) 951-9191 or (480) 951-9191, fax: (480) 483-8352, e-mail: customerrelations@worldatwork.org, Web: www.worldatwork.org.

Subscription: Free to members.
This journal from WorldatWork (formerly American Compensation Association) contains in-depth articles by professionals on topics such as pay at risk, competencies, broadbanding, changing roles for compensation professionals, the future of health care, stock options and work/life issues.

General Business Periodicals of Interest to Training and HR Managers

Across the Board
Published in 10 issues by The Conference Board, Inc., 845 Third Avenue, New York, NY 10022-6679, phone: (212) 759-0900 (editorial) or (212) 339-0345 (subscriptions), fax: (212) 980-7014, e-mail: atb@conference-board.org, Web: www.conference-board.org.

Subscriptions: Conference Board members, $39; nonmembers, $59.
A thoughtfully edited general interest business magazine for all managers, this publication occasionally includes articles directly related to training and performance.

Business Horizons
Published bimonthly by the Indiana University Graduate School of Business and JAI Press (Elsevier). Editorial: Business Horizons, Indiana University, IU Research Park, Suite 1, 1309 East 10th Street, Bloomington, IN 47405, phone: (812) 855-6342, fax: (812) 856-4971, e-mail: organ@indiana.edu (Dennis Organ, editor), Web: www.kelley.indiana.edu/Horizons. Subscriptions: Elsevier Science, Regional Sales Office, Customer Support Department, P.O. Box 945, New York, NY 10159-0945, phone: (888) 4ES-INFO (437-4636) or (212) 633-3730, fax: (212) 633-3680, e-mail: usinfo-f@elsevier.com, Web: www.elsevier.com/inca/publications/store/6/2/0/2/1/4/index.htt.

Subscriptions: All countries except Europe and Japan, $96 (individual) or $252 (institutional). Other areas: check rates on Web site.
This journal publishes articles that range widely, covering such areas as strategic management, trends in global business, marketing, executive edu-

cation, environmental management, human resources, information and communications, business and society, corporate law, operations management, and accounting and finance.

California Management Review

Published quarterly by the University of California, F 501 Haas School of Business #1900, University of California, Berkeley, CA 94720-1900, phone: (510) 642-7159, fax: (510) 642-1318, e-mail: cmr@haas.berkeley.edu, Web: www.haas.berkeley.edu/News/cmr.

Subscriptions: U.S., Canada, and Mexico, $65 (individuals) and $90 (institutions); elsewhere, $105.

This is a serious journal with a practical orientation, often including in-depth articles on management, sometimes related to HR issues. Intended to serve as "a vehicle of communication between those who study management and those who practice it," the journal is somewhat academic, as most contributors are professors.

Harvard Business Review

Published in 10 issues by Harvard Business School Publishing, 60 Harvard Way, Boston, MA 02163, phone: (617) 783-7410, fax: (617) 783-7483, e-mail: hrb_editorial@hbsp.harvard.edu, Web: www.hbsp.harvard.edu/hbr/index.html. Subscriptions: Harvard Business Review, Subscriber Services, P.O. Box 52623, Boulder, CO 80322-2623, phone: (800) 274-3214, fax: (303) 661-1994, e-mail: hbursubs@neodata.com.

Subscriptions: U.S., $118; Canada and Mexico, $128. (Canada rate includes 7% GST, #12473845). All other countries, $165.

This journal features in-depth articles on management techniques in all functional areas by "the leading business thinkers around the world." It's worth perusing, then keeping on hand as a reference.

IIE Solutions

Published monthly by the Institute of Industrial Engineers, 25 Technology Park, Norcross, GA 30092-2988, phone: (800) 494-0460 or (770) 449-0461, fax: (770) 263-8532, e-mail: cs@www.iienet.org, Web: www.iienet.org/period1g.htm.

Subscriptions: Free to IIE members; nonmembers, U.S., $60; elsewhere, $77. (For airmail, add $72.)

This is the official member publication of the IIE. Although described as "exclusively for managers and engineers responsible for reducing operating costs, increasing efficiency, and boosting productivity in business, industry, and government," it regularly includes articles that deal with issues related to many management issues, including human resource development in manufacturing settings.

Industry Week
Published biweekly by Penton Media, Inc., P.O. Box 901979, Cleveland, OH 44190-1979, 1300 E. 9th Street, Cleveland, OH 44114, phone: (800) 326-4146, (216) 696-7000, or (216) 931-9188 (customer service), fax: (216) 696-6413 (customer service), e-mail: subscriptions@penton.com, Web: www.industryweek.com.

Subscriptions: Free to qualified applicants in the U.S. and Canada. Otherwise, U.S. $65, Canada $85 (add 7% GST), elsewhere $105. (Discounts through Web site.)

More oriented to line management issues, this magazine is a general business publication focused on the unique management challenges faced by the executives of global manufacturing enterprises. Its mission is to cover, analyze, and present management best practices to executives in the manufacturing sector and its supporting service industries.

Journal for Quality and Participation
Published bimonthly by The Association for Quality and Participation, Executive Building #200, 2368 Victory Parkway, Cincinnati, OH 45206, phone: (513) 381-1979 or (800) 733-3310, fax: (513) 381-0070, e-mail: journal@aqp.org, Web: www.aqp.org/pages/jqp.

Subscriptions: Free to AQP members. (Membership: U.S., $150; Canada and Mexico, $180; other countries, $225.)

This publication focuses on implementing quality and promoting employee involvement.

Journal of Business Strategy
Published bimonthly by Faulkner & Gray, Inc., 11 Penn Plaza, 17th Floor, New York, NY 10001, phone: (800) 535-8403 or (212) 967-7000, fax: (212) 967-7155, e-mail: faulknergray@msn.com, Web: www.faulknergray.com/jbs.htm.

Subscriptions: $98, plus $4.95 for shipping and handling.

Each issue has a special focus article, with several pieces on this subject, and a cover story. Intended for senior executives and corporate strategists, this journal covers new product development, forecasting, strategic restructuring, sales, and marketing.

Journal of Organizational Excellence
Published quarterly by John Wiley & Sons, 605 Third Avenue, New York, NY 10158-0012, phone: (212) 850-6645, fax: (212) 850-6021, e-mail: subinfo@jwiley.com, Web: www.interscience.wiley.com/jpages/1531-1864.

Subscriptions: U.S., Canada, Mexico, $399 (Canada, add 7% GST).

The mission of this journal, formerly *National Productivity Review*, is to provide "timely information on the techniques and strategies that organizations around the world are using to excel—that is, to effectively enhance their performance and competitive position in a global economy—while providing a rewarding work experience for their employees."

DIRECTORY OF MAGAZINES, JOURNALS, AND NEWSLETTERS

Quality Digest
Published monthly by QCI International, 40 Declaration Drive, Suite 100, Chico, CA 95973, phone: (530) 893-4095, fax: (530) 893-0395, e-mail: info@qualitydigest.com, Web: www.qualitydigest.com.

Subscriptions: Free within U.S., Canada, and Mexico. Other countries, contact for rates.

This magazine features how-to articles and pieces on how organizations implement quality management in both technical and people/training-related areas. It also includes monthly columnists such as Ken Blanchard and A. Blanton Godfrey (Juran Institute), plus software reviews, book reviews, and other information.

Quality Progress
Published monthly by the American Society for Quality, Inc., 611 E. Wisconsin Avenue, Milwaukee, WI 53202, phone: (800) 248-1946 or (414) 272-8575, fax: (414) 272-1734, e-mail: cs@asq.org, Web: www.asq.org/pub/qualityprogress.

Subscriptions: Free to ASQ members. Nonmembers: U.S., $60; elsewhere, $95. Institutions: U.S., $120; elsewhere, $130. (Canada rate includes 7% GST #128717618.)

This is the foremost magazine dealing with quality management topics, including HR, training, and teamwork. The articles are nearly always practical and provide valuable perspectives. It includes event calendars and reviews.

Sloan Management Review
Published quarterly by the MIT Sloan School of Management, Room E60-100, 77 Massachusetts Avenue, Cambridge, MA 02139-4307, phone: (617) 253-7170, fax: (617) 258-9739, e-mail: smr@mit.edu, Web: mitsloan.mit.edu/smr/index.html.

Subscriptions: U.S., $89 (individual) or $148 (institution); Canada, $99 (individual) or $192 (institution); elsewhere, $125 (individual) or $214 (institution). This influential journal features practical, yet thoughtful articles and case studies on a variety of issues of direct interest to managers. Articles are usually fairly long and only occasionally relate to HR issues. There's a good book review section.

strategy+business
Published quarterly by Booz-Allen & Hamilton, 101 Park Avenue, New York, NY 10178, phone: (212) 551-6222, fax: (212) 551-6008, e-mail: editors@strategy-business.com, Web: www.strategy-business.com. Subscriptions: strategy+business, P.O. Box 548, Lewiston, NY 14092-0548, phone: (888) 557-5550 or (203) 341-7450 or (877) 280-3001, fax: NA, e-mail: service@sbsubscriber.com.

Subscriptions: U.S., $38; other countries, $48.

This magazine features articles and book reviews by prominent researchers, executives, and Booz-Allen consultants. The content is often relevant to training and HR professionals.

Strategy & Leadership

Published bimonthly by MCB University Press Ltd., 60/62 Toller Lane, Bradford, West Yorkshire, England BD8 9BY, phone: +44 (0) 1274 777700, fax: +44 (0) 1274 785200, e-mail: help@mcb-usa.com, Web: www.mcb.co.uk/sl.htm.

Subscriptions: North and South America, $239. Other areas: check rates on Web site.

This magazine, formerly published by Strategic Leadership Forum, offers thoughtfully written articles by prominent consultants, professors, and executives, as well as in-depth profiles, analyses of trends, theories, and case studies in strategic planning. The articles often deal with issues of interest to those HR and training.

A Glossary of Performance Management Terms

Lynn Summers

What's the difference between a goal and an evaluation criterion, between a development plan and an action plan? Why is an organizational survey an element of performance management? This article from the *Performance Management Library* offers an annotated collection of words and phrases from the realms of individual and organizational performance management.

Action Plan The specification of what is going to be done about a particular concern or result that is identified in an organizational survey. In a well-planned survey project, results are "cascaded" down through the organization, so that managers can see the results that apply to the part of the organization they have responsibility for. Managers can meet with their teams, identify strengths and weaknesses highlighted by the survey, and select a few high-priority areas of concern to work on. To deal with a particular concern, the team may first collect more information to supplement the survey findings and to more clearly define the problem and identify the root cause. At this point, actions can be proposed and agreed upon, and the action plan initiated. Within Performaworks' Workbench system, the action plan becomes a goal, owned by one person, perhaps with sub-goals spun off to other team members. (Contrast with "development plan.")

Anonymity When you are a rater in multisource feedback (MSF) or a respondent in an organizational survey, being assured anonymity means that no one in your organization will be able to tell what specific input was provided by you. It is one of the safeguards built into the rating process to ensure that the information gathered is candid and accurate. Anonymity can also serve to protect feedback givers against retaliation for offering negative feedback. Ratings given without anonymity tend to be more positive than ratings given anonymously. Anonymity in MSF is assured by averaging together the individual ratings within a particular rater group (direct reports, coworkers, etc.) and assuring that ratings for a group won't be reported unless the number of raters actually responding in that group exceeds some preset threshold (usually 3 raters). In an organizational survey, anonymity is similarly assured—responses are averaged together and the results for any department or unit within the company are not reported unless the number of respondents exceeds some threshold number (usually 5 respondents, but sometimes as high as 10). (Contrast with "confidentiality.")

Balanced Scorecard "As companies ... transform themselves for competition that is based on information, their ability to exploit intangible assets has become far more decisive than their ability to invest in and manage physical assets. The balanced scorecard supplements traditional financial measures with criteria that measure performance from three additional perspectives—those of customers, internal business processes, and learning and growth. It therefore enables companies to track financial results while simultaneously monitoring progress in building the capabilities and acquiring the intangible assets they would need for future growth."[1] It is used to align individual, organizational, and cross-departmental initiatives and to identify entirely new processes for meeting customer and shareholder objectives, as well as to evaluate the performance of top executives.

Behavior Behavior is what people do, the actions they take, the things they say. Behavior is observable by others, so when people rate you in MSF, it is your behavior they are rating. Behavior is what produces results, so when you miss a goal it is behavior you want to focus on in order to figure out how to do better at achieving that goal. Behavior is the outcome of competencies, so as you strengthen or develop a competency the more effective your behavior becomes. Organizational processes (communication, customer service, etc.) are the aggregated behaviors of the employees in the organization, so changing the collective behaviors of employees can result in changes in the effectiveness of organizational processes.

Behaviorally-Anchored Rating Scales (BARS) "Graphic performance rating scales with specific behavioral descriptions defining various points along each scale. Each scale represents a dimension, factor, or work function considered important for work performance. Typically, both raters and ratees are involved in the development of the dimensions and the generation of behavioral descriptions."[2] For example, the competency "Group Facilitation" might have "Asks quiet members of the group for their input" as the behavioral anchor for the "4" on the rating scale and "Imposes own ideas on group without asking for suggestions" as the "1." BARS are good in that they clarify the behavior represented by each point on the rating scale. However, they are time-consuming to develop, tedious to use, and do not provide any psychometric advantage over other types of rating scales.

Coach (1) What every good manager is supposed to be. The manager provides periodic feedback, counsels to improve performance, gives recognition for good or improved performance, and assists the direct report in creating and executing development plans. (2) In development-only MSF programs, a coach is often used to help deliver the feedback and help ratees identify their development needs and prepare development plans. This type of coach is usually a consultant (internal or external) who specializes in MSF coaching. (3) Executive coaches are a special breed of consultant, almost always from outside the organization. They work closely with an executive over an extended period of time to challenge the assumptions and decisions that internal staff are usually reluctant to address.

Competency A cluster of related knowledges, skills, and abilities (KSAs). Organizations might develop competency models to specify what KSAs are required for successful performance in a job, group of jobs, or organization—and also to reflect the espoused values of the organization ("The customer comes first," "We are a caring company"). Competencies are thus helpful (a) in employee selection (they tell you what attributes to look for in a candidate) and (b) for managing employee performance (they tell you attributes you should evaluate and provide feedback on regularly). Examples of competencies: Leadership, Communication, Influence, Decision Making, Teamwork, Flexibility, Initiative. A typical competency model will include, for each competency, a definition and some behavioral examples. In the Performaworks model of performance, competencies represent the "how" side of the performance coin; it is their competencies that enable employees to achieve their goals (which represent the "what" side of the coin). (Compare to "goal.")

Competency Modeling The process of defining the competencies for an organization. There are 3 approaches to competency modeling:[3] (a) research-based—a rigorous process often involving critical incident interviews, focus groups, and structured surveys with subject-matter experts (people familiar with the jobs under study), (b) strategy-based—which attempts to capture the attributes that will be needed to contribute to the organization's future success, and (c) values-based—the least rigorous method that might consist of a discussion with the CEO to clarify the values that are important to the company. Competency modeling has become very fashionable. However, not everyone loves competency modeling. Traditionalists argue that competency modeling is nothing more than old-fashioned (also tedious and boring) job analysis stripped of its methodological rigor, spiffed up, and marketed under a sexy name. Competency modelers argue that the process takes in a broader range of things (such as attributes relating to organizational culture and other "contextual" factors) and is more nimble (which is more appropriate for fast-changing, flexible organizations) than job analysis.

Confidentiality Confidentiality is concerned with the question of who sees what. The greater the confidentiality, the fewer the people who get to see the confidential thing. When MSF is conducted for development-only purposes, for example, the ratee and a coach are often the only people who have access to the ratee's results. When it is conducted for administrative purposes, "confidential" is defined in broader terms to include the ratee, the chain of command above the ratee, and the HR staff. Once confidential material is distributed to the appropriate parties, its continuing confidentiality depends on the behavior of those who hold the material. Ratees sometimes share their own results with their staff, a practice that is encouraged by most MSF professionals. However, the decision to "go public" with this information is the ratee's to make; others who hold the confidential information are obligated to maintain its confidentiality. (In contrast, compare to "anonymity," which has to do with who knows who said what.)

Development Need A gap between how a person is currently performing and how the person needs (or wants) to perform. Sometimes development needs arise from a person failing to achieve a goal, sometimes from the recognition that a particular competency must be more fully developed or refined.

Development Plan Also referred to as an individual development plan (IDP), it is a plan for addressing a development need, whether to become better at doing the job you're doing now, to make better use of an underused strength, or to prepare to take on greater or different responsibilities in the future. It is a plan that focuses on changing your behavior in a way that will enable you to better achieve the goals for which you are accountable. It should also result in improvement in the ratings you receive on the competency that is most closely related to your development need. Behavior change is the primary focus of a development plan. If your behavior doesn't change, then there is no difference between you as you were before and you as you are after embarking on your development efforts—development has not occurred. (Contrast with "action plan.")

Evaluation Criteria The standards you will use to determine if a goal has been successfully achieved. For example, a sales goal might have "Achieve $1.5M in booked sales" as one of its evaluation criteria. A goal regarding completion of a major project might have criteria such as "Within budget" and "Meets customer's requirements." It is not unusual for a goal to have multiple evaluation criteria. The criteria can encompass positive results to be achieved ("Increase number of prospects by 10%"), undesirable results to be avoided ("Keep unqualifiable prospects below 25%"), resources to be conserved ("Stay within budget"), and resources to be fully utilized ("Involve Creative Department").

Feedback "Information, provided to a person, which addresses the prior behavior of the person or the results of their behavior. If provided by another person, feedback is usually intended either to reinforce behavior or to suggest changes. The term may also be applied at the group or organizational level. Examples include operational feedback on the total performance of an organization or its subunits, customer feedback to service organizations by means such as surveys, or feedback to a work group from quality inspection of products for which all members of the group are responsible."[4] Feedback can be a powerful stimulus for change, provided that it creates energy (tells you that something important to you is not as it should be), that you are able to focus the energy constructively (toward using the data to identify and solve problems vs. to deny or fight the data), and that you can access resources to turn the energy into action.

Goal A desired (or required!) future outcome that you strive to achieve. At the designated time in the future, the results you actually achieve are compared to the original goal (and the specified evaluation criterion) to determine your success. In the Performaworks model of performance, this process of setting goals and working toward their achievement represents the "what" side of the performance coin. That is, goals are specifically *what* it is that you are trying to achieve, while competencies are *how* you go about pursuing them or the knowledges, skills, and abilities you bring to bear in their pursuit.

Goal Alignment The linking of a goal at one level of the organizational hierarchy to a goal at the next higher level within Performaworks' Workbench system. The system reinforces the logic of delegation. In practice, managers take "big" goals they are held accountable for, break them into delegatable pieces, and pass on the accountability for achieving those pieces to their direct reports. The Workbench creates a convenient feedback loop by having the direct reports align the pieces of the higher-level goal they have been delegated back to the higher level goal.

Goal Setting A theory of motivation, in fact, the most effective such theory and the one with the greatest empirical support. Goals are intentions that serve to direct and energize behavior. The two major findings from extensive goal-setting research are that higher performance levels are achieved by (a) setting specific goals (vs. general goals) and (b) setting difficult goals (vs. easily attainable goals). These findings hold up so long as the following two conditions are met: (a) you get feedback on how well you are progressing toward your goal and (b) you accept (are committed to) the goal.

Industrial Psychology The study of the behavior of people at work. Industrial psychology has been around for over 100 years. Actually, it is now called "industrial and organizational psychology" or simply "I/O psychology." The "I" focuses on individual behavior and such things as the prediction of individual job performance, while the "O" focuses on how the individual influences and is influenced by the group and the larger organization. Industrial psychologists are "scientist-practitioners," meaning that they are trained both to conduct rigorous research in the quest for general principles (scientist role) and to help client organizations solve practical problems relating to individual and group performance (practitioner role).

Instrument Any kind of device that is used to collect information in a structured, systematic way. Examples of instruments are tests, performance evaluation "forms," and survey questionnaires.

Management by Objectives (MBO) A structured approach to goal setting used by many companies. MBO was suggested by management guru Peter Drucker in the early 1950s. MBO programs were very popular for a time but tended to be rigid and administratively burdensome in their implementation (which was not Drucker's intent!) and hence fell out of favor. However, most performance management systems even today include a section on goals or on results expected, although few actually use the term "MBO." The problems with MBO included: quantitative goals tend to get emphasized at the expense of goals that are more difficult to quantify, top management must actively and continuously support the process, users have to know how to set goals and communicate with each other. "MBO ... is a superb tool if the objectives are (1) simple, (2) focused on what's important, (3) genuinely created from the bottom up (the objectives are drafted by the person who must live up to them, with no constraining guides), and (4) a 'living' contract, not a form-driven exercise."[5]

Mileposts Date-based checkpoints that can be set and used to ensure a goal is on track. They are the major action items or steps an individual needs to take to achieve a goal. For example, for the goal "Revise company policies," a milepost might be "Get sign-off from Legal Dept."

Multisource Feedback (MSF) A process in which feedback is obtained (in whatever format) from more than one source. The feedback is usually about a person's job-related behavior. Sources can include the self, manager, coworkers, subordinates, customers (internal or external), and anyone else who is in a position to give job-related feedback to the person. The feedback is provided to the person to trigger individual development activity. Sometimes a coach is involved in giving the feedback and helping the person craft a development plan based on the feedback. More and more organizations are using MSF not only to foster employee development, but for administrative purposes. In such cases, the MSF results are provided to the person's supervisor as well as to the person him/herself, and the results are typically available to any manager in the chain of command and to the HR department. MSF is also called 360-degree feedback, multirater assessment, multirater feedback, full-circle feedback, upward feedback, and a host of other names, both trademarked and in the public domain.

Norms (1) The "way things are around here," or the informal rules that operate within a work group. "Norms are enforced to help the group more readily achieve its goals, to protect the group from potential external threats, to simplify and make predictable what behaviors are expected from group members, to help the group avoid embarrassing interpersonal problems, and to express and clarify what the central values of the group are. Individuals who repeatedly or flagrantly violate group norms are typically sanctioned by other group members."[6] Organizational surveys often try to detect what kinds of norms are in place and how strong they are. Action plans might then focus on how to strengthen or spread constructive norms (such as "around here, we do whatever it takes to deliver uninterrupted service") or how to "fix" dysfunctional norms (such as "it's us against management"). (2) Any time a psychometric instrument is used to measure some attribute, it may be possible to compare the results you get with results that apply to some relevant comparison group. In multisource feedback, your feedback report might present norms alongside your results so that you can see how you "stack up" against others similar to you who have participated in MSF. Organizational survey results can also be compared against normative data. It should be noted, however, that the value of normative information is warmly debated. There are plusses and minuses associated with their use and, as you might imagine, there are several rules of thumb regarding what kinds of normative data are appropriate in different situations.

Objective A desired (or required!) future outcome that you strive to achieve. For our purposes, objectives are synonymous with goals. Some people and some organizations make very precise distinctions between goals and objectives, as well as among several other terms (e.g., tactics, targets, etc.). Usually the distinctions have to do with the level at which the goal is set—strategic objectives are at the top, followed by tactical goals and operational goals. And sometimes the distinctions are functional—objectives are what must be achieved, tactics are the methods for achieving them. Whatever, Performaworks does not fuss over these distinctions—they are all "goals."

Organization Development (OD) "OD is the theory and practice of bringing planned change to organizations. These changes are usually designed to address an organizational problem or to help an organization prepare for the future. … [I]nterventions are the techniques that OD practitioners use to bring about change."[7] Most OD interventions are intended to improve organizational performance, place emphasis on changing the collective behaviors of employees (including managers), and use methods derived from the social sciences. One form of OD, for example, uses surveys to collect data about the organization's current functioning and then uses the results to direct the change efforts—a practice sometimes called data-based OD. Some of the *managerial* behavior changes that might result from a successful OD intervention include encouraging more participation, leading by providing a vision, functioning strategically rather than simply in response to situations, promoting the flow of information, and fostering employee development. Similarly, *employee* behavior changes might include communicating more openly, collaborating more effectively, taking more responsibility, maintaining a shared vision, solving problems more effectively, showing more respect and support for others, interacting with each other more effectively, being more inquisitive, and being more open to experimentation and new ways of doing things.

Organizational Survey A way of measuring what is going on in an organization or how the organization is performing. Information is collected via a questionnaire (sometimes interviews are also conducted), the information is processed, and the results are fed back in order, ideally, to achieve some purpose. The purpose is usually to identify strengths and weaknesses in the organization and to guide improvement efforts. Surveys can be traditional employee opinion surveys that ask about the work itself, coworkers, supervision, communication, pay, benefits—usually from the standpoint of how satisfied employees are with these things. Surveys can also measure the organization's climate or culture, looking at things like how effectively the organization (or department, or work group) handles conflict, makes decisions, gives people freedom to do their work, maintains high standards for the work, and so on. Surveys may also be strategic in nature (more and more organizations are conducting these kinds of surveys). A strategic survey contains items that seek to determine how well the company is living up to its mission, vision, and values. Survey results can be used ineffectively (they sit on the administrator's desk and never are shared with anyone), moderately effectively (they are used by top management to "fix" something organization wide, such as the benefit plan), or impressively (they are cascaded down through the organization and managers take responsibility for "owning" the results for their part of the organization).

Outlier In MSF, a rating of an individual item by one rater that lies far outside the normal range of ratings given that item by other raters. Outliers can be due to a rater (a) providing a legitimate but unique perspective on the item in question (the rater is a "maverick"), or (b) inadvertently entering the wrong rating (thinking the low end of the scale is positive, or just making a clerical error in selecting this one response), or (c) deliberately trying to slam or whitewash the ratee (the rater is an "out-and-outliar"). Because it is difficult to tell what the cause of an outlier is, the decision regarding what to do with outliers is not an easy one. Performaworks uses a very conservative statistical definition of an outlier (it really has to be way out) and recommends that outliers be eliminated. Outlier detection and elimination are accomplished after data collection is complete (you have to have all the ratings in before you can detect the outliers).

Performance Appraisal The formal discussion that managers conduct with their direct reports to review the direct report's performance over the past performance period, acknowledge achievements, identify development needs, justify a salary decision, and set business goals for the upcoming performance period. In earlier times, this was referred to as the "performance appraisal interview." It has never been a popular event as it often entails having to deliver bad news to the employee but, when handled effectively, can be a very positive and constructive experience. There have been many recommendations concerning how to make the discussion more effective, including splitting out the administrative function (justifying salary) from the coaching function (discussing past and future performance).

Performance Evaluation This refers to the full process, of which the performance appraisal discussion is one part, of looking back over the past performance period to determine whether goals and behavioral expectations were met. It includes integrating all the information needed to complete an accurate evaluation, filling out "the form," handling other administrative aspects of the process (often the form must be submitted to HR and approved, especially if a merit increase or bonus payout is involved), and planning for the next performance period. Reasons for doing performance appraisals or evaluations: (a) feedback—to let employees know where they stand, motivate continued performance, give employee a pat on the back, (b) compensation—to determine the size of merit increase to be awarded, determine bonuses, (c) assignment—to assist in deciding who gets promoted, transferred, assigned to a special project, (d) termination—to "justify" firing an employee, assist in identifying whom to lay off, (e) development—to assist in identifying what an employee needs to work on for developmental purposes, help in career planning discussions with employees, (f) performance counseling—to correct performance problems, and (g) succession planning—to assess employees' potential for advancement.

Performance Journal In performance management, the performance journal is where "critical incidents" related to an employee's goals and competencies are documented. Documentation can be made by either the employee or the manager. What is documented could be instances where the employee has done something particularly effectively or ineffectively. The notations could be related to a goal ("Experiencing difficulty getting needed resources from Layout Dept.") or a competency ("Conducting focus group, was able to get candid information from participants by first doing some self-disclosure"). In traditional performance management, such documentation makes it easier to complete the summary evaluation at the end of a performance period. This is important because, without the documentation, managers must rely on memory, which can be notoriously selective when writing up the review at the end of a year. Within Performaworks' Workbench system, such journal entries foster real-time, open communication between employee and manager, thus making it easier for the manager to coach.

Performance Management (PM) "There is no universally accepted definition of performance management, and it is sometimes used simply to refer to performance appraisal or to performance related pay. However, it is increasingly coming to mean a general, integrated human resources strategy that seeks to create a shared vision of the purpose, aims, and values of the organization, to help each individual employee understand and recognize their part in contributing to them, and in so doing to manage and enhance the performance of both individuals and the organization. Typically, elements of such a strategy will include developing the mission statement and business plan, objective setting, and other methods of performance measurement, appraisal, performance related pay, and various approaches to enhancing internal communications. Two of the attributes that differentiate performance management from other systems (such as management by objectives or appraisal) are: (1) that it is supposed to be line management-owned and driven; personnel departments have a mainly facilitative role; and (2) that it seeks to combine and integrate the various elements into a coherent set of procedures."[8]

Psychometrics The quantitative science of measuring individual differences in abilities, behaviors, attitudes, preferences, and a bevy of other attributes. The instruments used in performance management to measure individual performance (performance evaluation "forms," multisource feedback "surveys") can—and *should*—be studied from the psychometric perspective. This is the way to determine how good the instruments are at measuring what they are supposed to measure. (See "reliability" and "validity.") Organizational surveys are also psychometric instruments, as they measure people's perceptions of organizational performance.

Ratee A participant in MSF who is being rated. This individual will receive feedback on the results of the MSF and be able to identify behaviors for improvement and behaviors that represent strengths.

Rater A person who is either nominated or required to provide feedback during a MSF process. This person should be someone who has worked with the ratee during the last year and can provide appropriate feedback to the individual on the competencies being evaluated. To encourage candid feedback, raters (with the exception of the ratee's manager) are usually assured anonymity.

Rating Scale A structured way for a person to respond to items on an instrument. The most popular type of rating scale is the Likert scale. It provides the rater or respondent a numeric scale, each point of the scale anchored by some descriptive term. For example, respondents can indicate their degree of agreement with a series of statements by selecting the appropriate point on a scale that runs from "5 = strongly agree" to "1 = strongly disagree." Each of the statements has the same scale attached to it, making it easy for respondents to use (they don't have to read a set of unique options for each item). In addition, when data are processed, dimension (or competency) scores can be easily computed for groups of related items by simply averaging the numeric values of the responses.

Reliability Reliability goes hand in hand with validity. Instruments, such as personnel tests, performance measures, and organizational surveys, must be reasonably reliable before they can be valid—that is, you can't have validity without reliability. Using the yardstick analogy: a rigid, wooden yardstick is a reliable measure of length. You measure an object five or six times with it, and you probably get the same result each time within an eighth of an inch or so. But suppose you have an elastic band with a yardstick printed on it. Each time you measure the object you get a wildly different result. The elastic yardstick is not reliable; the measures you get when using it contain a lot of "random error." Reliability of a test or performance measure is determined statistically. There are different approaches: for example, you can compare measures taken of the same thing at different times (test-retest), ratings of the same thing made by different raters (inter-rater), or compare the scores on the different items that make up your measure (internal consistency). Reliability is usually reported as a reliability coefficient, the higher the better; in general, it's good if it is in the high .70s or above (reliability coefficients range from .00 to 1.00). A very popular measure of reliability is the coefficient alpha (a measure of internal consistency).

Respondent In an organizational survey, a person who completes a survey. Respondents are usually assured anonymity in order to encourage candid ratings and comments.

Root Skill A skill, ability, or area of knowledge for which there exists a collection of developmental suggestions (techniques, tricks, methods, principles, or repository of knowledge) that help the user work on a development need. Root skills are, in essence, a way of categorizing developmental suggestions. They are called root skills because they operate in the same way as root causes. Think of it this way: If you encounter a problem (floor is wet), you solve it by first determining the root cause (roof is leaking vs. a water line is broken, etc.) and then taking corrective action that focuses on that cause (patch the roof). Similarly, if you have a development need (weak in leadership), you address it by determining the appropriate root skill (poor listening vs. lack of vision, etc.) and then engaging in developmental actions that seek to strengthen the root skill in question (eye contact, paraphrasing, etc.).

Straight Ticket A form of rating bias in which the rater uses the same response option on the rating scale for all (or most) of the items on an instrument. For example, you might complete an MSF by giving the ratee all 5s (on a 5-point scale, where 5 is the most positive rating). This is not likely to be accurate (few ratees are perfect) and it does not provide the ratee with very useful information (it doesn't help identify strengths and weaknesses). The rater's motivation for making a straight ticket might be: it's a real time-saver to click all the same options so you don't really have to read the items, or you may just want to be lenient, or middle of the road, or severe in your rating of this individual. Because straight tickets diminish the accuracy and discriminability of ratings, it is a good thing to try to reduce their prevalence. Performaworks' MSF actually interacts with raters when they are completing their evaluations by detecting the straight ticket pattern and encouraging raters to reconsider their ratings. The straight ticket concept, by the way, also applies to organizational surveys.

Strategic Objectives "Broadly defined target or future end results set by top management. Such goals typically address issues relating to the organization as a whole and may sometimes be stated in fairly general terms.... Peter Drucker suggests that organizations need to set goals in at least eight major areas. These areas encompass a number of aspects that are important to the health and survival of most profit-making organizations."[9] Drucker's suggested major areas for strategic goals are: market standing (desired share of present and new markets, service goals aimed at building customer loyalty), innovation (innovations in products and services as well as in the skills and processes required to supply them), human resources (supply, development, performance, attitudes, labor relations), financial resources (sources of capital supply and how it will be used), physical resources (facilities and how they will be used in production of goods and services), productivity (efficient use of resources relative to outcomes), social responsibility (community, ethical behavior), profit requirements (indicators of financial well-being).

Succession Planning "Succession planning refers to the process and actions that aim at identifying and developing a pool of potential successors for senior or key jobs in the future. Unlike replacement planning, succession planning is more strategic, proactive, long-term oriented, and development-focused. It ensures the continual supply of qualified executive talent to lead and support business growth."[10] An important distinction is that, whereas performance evaluations typically rate a person's past and current performance, effective succession planning requires predicting future performance, often in a job situation that the person has yet to experience.

Validity Validity has to do with how sound your conclusion is when you base the conclusion on the scores from a personnel test, performance evaluation, or survey questionnaires. In other words, if you use a yardstick to measure the height of a cubicle wall and conclude that its height is 6 feet, you probably have made a valid inference or conclusion. But if you used a butcher's scale to measure its height, whatever conclusion you arrived at about height based on that would certainly not be valid—what you measured is *not* height. In performance management, we use instruments (analogous to yardsticks, butcher's scales) to measure how effective a person is on each of several competencies and whether they have achieved their goals or not. If the instrument is valid, it means that when we get a score on "leadership," the score really does represent the person's standing on an actual thing called "leadership." Organizations want to use valid personnel tests, performance evaluation methods, and organizational surveys, and sometimes they are required to demonstrate their validity (as when employees sue the company claiming unfair discrimination in their performance review which prevented them from being considered for a promotion). To establish the validity of the instruments you can make sure that the content of the instrument makes sense (the "leadership" competency is made up of behavioral items that sound pretty much like leadership), that the leadership measure has statistical integrity (scores on the behavioral items making up this competency "hang together" when you conduct a factor analysis), that scores employees get on this measure of "leadership" are correlated with scores on other accepted measures of "leadership," or that employees rated high on "leadership" become acknowledged leaders sometime in the future. Validity goes hand in hand with reliability.

Weight (1) Used to signify that some competencies and goals are more important than others. Showing differential weights is a useful way to clarify priorities (a goal with a weight of "10" is more important than one weighted with a "7"). It is also a way to give more weight to the more important goals and competencies when a person's performance is evaluated at the end of a performance period. For example, poor performance on a very important goal can be the primary determinant of the person's overall summary evaluation even if the person did an outstanding job on a couple of goals that carry much less weight. (2) Furthermore, weights are used to lend greater influence to goals over competencies (or vice versa) in the computation of a person's overall summary evaluation. For some jobs, for example, a company might want achievement of goals to account for 60% of a person's overall summary evaluation and competencies to account for 40%. (3) In Performaworks MSF, weights can also be applied to rater groups. For example, the manager's ratings might carry 50% of the weight and all other raters carry the remainder of the weight.

Note: Thanks to Anne Doster, Elizabeth O'Keefe, and Diane Cox for assistance in preparing this glossary.

Notes

1. Robert S. Kaplan and David P. Norton. "Using the Balanced Scorecard as a Strategic Management System." *Harvard Business Review,* January-February, 1996.
2. John Bernardin's entry for "BARS" in Lawrence Peters, Charles R. Greer, and Stuart A. Youngblood (eds.), *Encyclopedic Dictionary of Human Resource*

Management. Oxford, UK: Blackwell, 1997.

3. Jon P. Briscoe and Douglas T. Hall. "Grooming and Picking Leaders Using Competency Frameworks: Do They Work? An Alternative Approach and New Guidelines for Practice." *Organizational Dynamics,* 28(2) (Autumn 1999): 37-52.
4. Maury Peiperl's entry for "Feedback" in Nigel Nicholson (ed.), *Encyclopedic Dictionary of Organizational Behavior.* Oxford, UK: Blackwell, 1998.
5. Tom Peters. *Thriving on Chaos.* New York: Knopf, 1987.
6. Daniel C. Feldman's entry for "Group Norms" in Nigel Nicholson (ed.), *Encyclopedic Dictionary of Organizational Behavior.* Oxford, UK: Blackwell, 1998.
7. Robert D. Smither, John M. Houston, and Sandra A. McIntire. *Organization Development: Strategies for Changing Environments.* New York: Harper Collins, 1996.
8. Clive Fletcher's entry for "Performance Management" in Nigel Nicholson (ed.), *Encyclopedic Dictionary of Organizational Behavior.* Oxford, UK: Blackwell, 1998.
9. Kathryn M. Bartol and David C. Martin. *Management* (3rd ed.). New York: McGraw-Hill, 1998.
10. Arthur K. Yeung's entry for "Succession Planning" in Lawrence Peters, Charles R. Greer, and Stuart A. Youngblood (eds.), *Encyclopedic Dictionary of Human Resource Management.* Oxford, UK: Blackwell, 1997.

Lynn Summers is co-founder and VP of Research at Performaworks, Inc., an outsource provider of Web-based performance management, measurement, and development services. He holds a doctorate in industrial and organizational psychology from the University of South Florida. Prior to the startup of Performaworks in 1997, he served as staff psychologist at Baltimore Gas and Electric Co., VP of training and management development at Hardee's Food Systems, and head of the HR program at Peace College. Performaworks is headquartered in Raleigh, NC, and may be found on the Web at www.performaworks.com.

Directory of Training and Performance Associations and Organizations

What follows is a comprehensive directory of associations and organizations in the areas of training and performance improvement. What you'll find here is the association or organization name, contact (if known), address, phone and fax numbers, e-mail and Web page, along with a brief description of what the organization does, to give you an idea of its potential value to you with regard to training and performance.

If there are organizations that you think we should include here, please let us know about them. Just e-mail us at jwoods@cwlpub.com and then we'll get more information about the organization to include in future editions of this yearbook.

Academy of Human Resource Development
P.O. Box 25113
Baton Rouge, LA 70894-5113
Louisiana State University
Old Forestry Building, Room 142
Baton Rouge, LA 70803
Phone: (225) 334-1874
Fax: (225) 334-1875
E-mail: office@ahrd.org
Web: www.ahrd.org
AHRD was founded to encourage the systematic study of human resource development theories, to disseminate information about HRD, to encourage the application of HRD research findings, and to provide opportunities for social interaction among individuals with scholarly and professional interests in HRD, from various disciplines and from around the world. AHRD publishes the *Human Resource Development Quarterly* and *The Forum* (also quarterly), as well as an annual collection of articles, *Human Resource Development International: Enhancing Performance, Learning and Integrity*.

Accrediting Council for Continuing Education and Training
1722 N Street, NW
Washington, DC 20036
Phone: (202) 955-1113
Fax: (202) 955-1118
E-mail: rjwilliams@accet.org (Roger J. Williams, Executive Director)
Web: www.accet.org
ACCET is a group of educational organizations affiliated to improve continuing education and training. ACCET has developed and refined the accreditation evaluation process to more closely align with the operational characteristics of progressive private sector training organizations, corporate training departments, and professional associations. ACCET accreditation functions as an independent validation of performance management for the continuous improvement of training services, both for internal assessment and external assurance.

Adult Education Network
Adult Education Program
Programs for Higher Education
Fischler Center for the Advancement of Education
Nova Southeastern University

1750 NE 167th Street
North Miami Beach, FL 33162-3017
Phone: (954) 262-8530
Fax: NA
E-mail: aedmod@fcae.acast.nova.edu
Web: www.nova.edu/~aed

AEDNET is an international network of individuals interested in adult education, connected through a discussion list. AEDNET publishes *New Horizons in Adult Education*, a refereed electronic journal that's accessible on the Web site, and maintains the AEDNET e-mail discussion list.

Alliance of Work/Life Professionals
Clarion Management Resources, Inc.
515 King Street, Suite 420
Alexandria, VA 22314
Phone: (800) 874-9383, (703) 684-5570
Fax: (703) 684-6048
E-mail: ksharbaugh@clarionmr.com
Web: www.awlp.org

This is a membership organization for professionals who work in business, academia, or the public sector to promote a healthier balance between work and personal life.

American Association for Adult and Continuing Education
1200 19th Street, NW, Suite 300
Washington, DC 20036-2422
Phone: (202) 429-5131
Fax: (202) 223-4579
E-mail: Anna_Darin@dc.sba.com (Anna Darin, Association Manager)
Web: www.cdlr.tamu.edu/tcall/aaace

The mission of AAACE is to promote adult learning and development. AAACE works to unify adult education practitioners and to foster the development and sharing of information, theory, research, and best practices. The association holds an annual conference and publishes books, the bimonthly *AAACE Newsletter*, and several journals: *Adult Learning*, *Adult Education Quarterly*, and *Adult Basic Education*.

American Center for the Study of Distance Education
College of Education
The Pennsylvania State University
110 Rackley Building
University Park, PA 16802-3202
Phone: (814) 863-3764
Fax: (814) 865-5878
E-mail: acsde@psu.edu
Web: www.ed.psu.edu/acsde

The Center was established to promote distance education research, study, scholarship, and teaching and to serve as a clearinghouse for the dissemination of knowledge about distance education. It publishes *The American Journal of Distance Education*, *Readings in Distance Education*, and *ACSDE Monographs*. It also sponsors the Distance Education Online Symposium.

American Council on Education
1 Dupont Circle, NW
Washington, DC 20036
Phone: (202) 939-9300
Fax: (202) 833-4760
E-mail: web@ace.nche.edu
Web: www.acenet.edu

ACE is the nation's umbrella higher education association and a forum for the discussion of major issues related to higher education and its potential to contribute to the quality of American life. ACE maintains the Business-Higher Education Forum to bridge the gap between corporations and the campus and the Center for Adult Learning and Educational Credentials.

American Council on International Personnel, Inc.
NY Office
515 Madison Avenue, 15th Floor
New York, NY 10022
Phone: (212) 688-2437
Fax: (212) 593-4697
E-mail: info@acip.com
Web: www.acip.com

ACIP was established in 1972 as a not-for-profit organization dedicated to facilitating the movement of international business personnel. It comprises over 300 member organizations.

American Evaluation Associaton
505 Hazel Circle
Magnolia, AR 71753
Phone/Fax: (888) 232-2275, (870) 234-7433
E-mail: aea@kistcon.com
Web: www.eval.org

AEA is an international professional association of evaluators devoted to the application and exploration of program evaluation, personnel evaluation, technology, and many other forms of evaluating the strengths and weaknesses of programs, policies, personnel, products, and organizations to make them more effective. AEA publishes *American Journal of Evaluation* (three issues a year) and a quarterly journal, *New Directions for Evaluation*, and runs an e-mail discussion list.

American Management Association
1601 Broadway
New York, NY 10019-7420
Phone: (212) 586-8100, (800) 262-9699
Fax: (212) 903-8168
E-mail: cust_serv@amanet.org
Web: www.amanet.org
AMA provides educational forums where members and their colleagues learn practical business skills and explore the best practices of world-class organizations through interaction with each other and expert faculty practitioners. The association publishes books (as AMACOM) and an online *Management Review* for members only. It also provides seminars and sponsors several annual conferences and meetings.

American Marketing Association
311 S. Wacker Drive, Suite 5800
Chicago, IL 60606
Phone: (800) AMA(262)-1150, (312) 542-9000
Fax: (312) 542-9001
E-mail: info@ama.org
Web: www.ama.org
AMA is the world's largest and most comprehensive professional society of marketers, with nearly 45,000 members in 100 countries and 500 chapters throughout North America. It sponsors numerous national and regional conferences and is actively involved in the training of marketing professionals, especially through its regional chapters. It publishes eight business magazines and scholarly journals as well as books.

American Productivity & Quality Center
123 N. Post Oak Lane, 3rd Floor
Houston, TX 77024-7797
Phone: (800) 776-9676, (713) 681-4020
Fax: (713) 681-1182
E-mail: apqcinfo@apqc.org
Web: www.apqc.org
APQC is a nonprofit education and research organization that helps companies and the public sector change and improve. It runs the International Benchmarking Clearinghouse, focusing on benchmarking and the development of best practices, and offers training and other resources in many areas.

American Society for Healthcare Human Resources Administration
1 N. Franklin Street
Chicago, IL 60606
Phone: (312) 422-3725
Fax: (312) 422-4579
E-mail: ashra@aha.org
Web: www.ashhra.org
The mission of ASHHRA is "to advance excellence and increase competency in Human Resources Management within health care organizations."

American Society for Quality
600 N. Plankinton Avenue
Milwaukee, WI 53202
P.O. Box 3005
Milwaukee, WI 53201-3005
Phone: (800) 248-1946, (414) 272-8575
Fax: (414) 272-1734
E-mail: cs@asq.org
Web: www.asq.org
ASQ is the leading quality improvement organization in the United States, with over 130,000 members from every industry. It provides education and training programs in various fields. It publishes books and seven journals, including *Quality Progress* and *Quality Management Journal*.

American Society for Training and Development
1640 King Street
P.O. Box 1443
Alexandria, VA 22313-2043
Phone: (800) 628-2783, (703) 683-8100
Fax: (703) 683-1523
E-mail: csc4@astd.org
Web: www.astd.org
ASTD is the world's premier professional association for workplace learning and performance, with more than 70,000 members in more than 100 countries. Its mission is to help individuals, organizations, and society to achieve work-related competence, performance, and fulfillment. ASTD provides information, research, analysis, and practical information. ASTD publishes *Training & Development* (monthly), *Info-Line*, and *ASTD's Buyer's Guide & Consultant*

Directory and sponsors two annual conferences—the International Conference and Exposition and TechKnowledge^{SM}.

American Teleservices Association, Inc.
1620 I Street, NW, Suite 615
Washington, DC 20006
Phone: (202) 293-2452, (877) 779-3974
Fax: (202) 463-8498
E-mail: ata@moinc.com
Web: www.ataconnect.org
ATA is a not-for-profit trade association representing the providers and users of teleservices in the United States and around the globe. ATA holds an annual convention, lobbies for legislation, and provides an online newsletter, *E-Connections*.

Association for Applied Interactive Multimedia
Jared A. Seay, President
Robert Scott Small Library, Reference
　Department
College of Charleston
66 George Street
Charleston, SC 29424
Phone: (843) 953-1428
Fax: NA
E-mail: info@aaim.org, seayt@cofc.edu
Web: www.aaim.org
AAIM was founded in 1992 to support professionals using and developing multimedia. The organization includes professionals from business and industry, higher education, K-12 education, military, medicine, hardware and software producers and manufacturers, suppliers, and government.

Association for Business Simulation and Experiential Learning
Hugh M. Cannon, Vice President and
　Executive Director
Department of Marketing
Wayne State University
5201 Cass Avenue, Suite 300
Detroit, MI 48202-3930
Phone: (313) 577-4551
Fax: (313) 577-5486
E-mail: hughcannon@email.com
Web: www.towson.edu/~absel
ABSEL is a professional association whose purpose is to develop, promote, and assess the use of experiential techniques and simulations in business education and development. Members include game designers and trainers interested in business gaming, experiential learning in higher education, and professional training at the national and international levels. ABSEL co-sponsors *Simulation & Gaming: An International Journal of Theory, Practice, and Research* (quarterly), sponsors *Developments in Business Simulation & Experiential Exercises* (the annual association proceedings), and maintains a discussion list.

Association for Career and Technical Education
1410 King Street
Alexandria, VA 22314
Phone: (800) 826-9972, (703) 683-3111
Fax: (703) 683-7424
E-mail: acte@acteonline.org
Web: www.acteonline.org
ACTE (formerly American Vocational Association) is the largest national education association dedicated to the advancement of education that prepares youth and adults for careers. Its mission is to provide educational leadership in developing a competitive workforce. It provides a wide variety of programs to advance vocational-technical and school-to-careers education. It publishes *Techniques* (magazine, eight issues yearly) and *Career Tech Update* (newsletter, twice monthly) and offers other professional publications, videos, and materials to promote workforce education.

Association for Continuing Higher Education, Inc.
Trident Technical College
P.O. Box 118067, CE-M
Charleston, SC 29423-8067
Phone: (843) 574-6658
Fax: (843) 574-6470
E-mail: zpbarrineaui@a1.trident.tec.sc.us
Web: www.charleston.net/org/ache
ACHE is an institution-based organization of colleges, universities, and individuals dedicated to promoting lifelong learning and excellence in continuing higher education. Its annual conference provides a blend of theoretical and hands-on programs. ACHE publishes the *Journal of Continuing Higher Education*, the proceedings of its annual meeting, and a newsletter, and hosts a discussion list.

Association for Educational Communications and Technology
1800 N. Stonelake Drive, Suite 2
Bloomington, IN 47404
Phone: (877) 677-AECT or (812) 335-7675
Fax: (812) 335-7678
E-mail: aect@aect.org
Web: www.aect.org

AECT is an international organization representing instruction technology professionals working in schools at all levels and in corporate, government, and military sectors. Its mission is to provide leadership by linking professionals interested in the use of education technology. AECT publishes a quarterly journal, *Educational Technology Research and Development*, and a bimonthly magazine, *TechTrends*. It also sponsors an annual national convention and an annual professional development seminar.

Association for Experiential Education
2305 Canyon Boulevard, Suite 100
Boulder, CO 80302-5651
Phone: (303) 440-8844
Fax: (303) 440-9581
E-mail: info@aee.org
Web: www.aee.org

AEE is a not-for-profit, international, professional association with roots in adventure education, committed to the development, practice, and evaluation of experiential learning in all settings. AEE's professional group is made up of practitioners of experiential and adventure training methods with organizations and businesses. The AEE publishes books and periodicals, including *The Journal of Experiential Education* (three issues a year), and hosts an e-mail discussion list.

Association for International Practical Training
10400 Little Patuxent Parkway, Suite 250
Columbia, MD 21044-3510
Phone: (410) 997-2200
Fax: (410) 992-3924
E-mail: aipt@aipt.org
Web: www.aipt.org

AIPT is a nonprofit organization that promotes international understanding through cross-cultural, on-the-job, practical training exchanges for students and professionals. AIPT offers U.S. businesses the opportunity to internationalize.

Association for Media and Technology in Education in Canada
3-1750 The Queensway, Suite 1318
Etobicoke, ON M9C 5H5
Canada
Phone: NA
Fax: NA
E-mail: membership@amtec.ca
Web: www.amtec.ca

AMTEC is Canada's national association for educational media and technology professionals, representing K-12, postsecondary, government, and business/industry sectors. It provides national leadership and advocacy through annual conferences, publications, workshops, and consulting. It publishes *Canadian Journal of Educational Communication* (three issues/year) and maintains an e-mail discussion list.

Association for Multimedia Communications
P.O. Box 10645
Chicago, IL 60610
Phone: (312) 409-1032
Fax: NA
E-mail: amc@amcomm.org
Web: www.amcomm.org

ACM membership consists of individuals, small businesses, corporations, and educational institutions involved in interactive multimedia and the Internet as communications tools, including training and education.

Association for Quality and Participation
Executive Building #200
2368 Victory Parkway
Cincinnati, OH 45206
Phone: (800) 733-3310
Fax: (513) 381-0070
E-mail: aqp@aqp.org
Web: www.aqp.org

AQP is an international not-for-profit membership association dedicated to improving workplaces through quality and participation practices. It sponsors annual conferences and a series of courses and workshops. It also publishes *The Journal for Quality and Participation*, a monthly e-newsletter (*AQP Inbox*), a member newspaper (*News for a Change*), and books. In addition, it sells books from other publishers and provides training programs throughout the United States in teamwork, quality management, and related topics.

Association for Worksite Health Promotion
60 Revere Drive, Suite 500
Northbrook, IL 60062
Phone: (847) 480-9574
Fax: (847) 480-9282
E-mail: awhp@awhp.org
Web: www.awhp.org

AWHP is a not-for-profit network of work site health promotion professionals dedicated to sharing the best-of-practice methods, processes, and technologies. Its mission is to advocate the value of work site health promotion to business and government leaders throughout the world through education and by providing resources. The association sponsors an annual conference, publishes the quarterly journal *AWHP's Worksite Health*, and provides other resources in this field.

Association of Career Management Consulting Firms International
204 E Street, NE
Washington, DC 20002
Phone: (202) 547-6344
Fax: (202) 547-6348
E-mail: aocfi@aocfi.org
Web: www.aocfi.org

AOFCI, formerly the Association of Outplacement Consulting Firms International, is the trade association for the career management industry. Members provide a wide range of services: career management, human resource consulting, executive coaching, leadership development, succession planning, outplacement, workforce deployment, and assessment. AOFCI provides industry publicity and statistics, sponsors an annual conference, and publishes a quarterly newsletter.

Association of Management/International Association of Management
Maximilian Press Publishing Company
P.O. Box 64841
Virginia Beach, VA 23464-0841
920 South Battlefield Boulevard, Suite 100
Chesapeake, VA 23322
Phone: (757) 482-2273
Fax: (757) 482-0325
E-mail: aomgt@infi.net
Web: www.aom-iaom.org

AoM/IAoM is a nonprofit professional organization of academicians and practitioners of management founded in 1975 to advance the theory and practice of management in a wide range of fields and to promote the personal and professional growth of its members. AoM/IAoM hosts an annual conference, provides leadership and service opportunities, publishes five journals, and maintains more than a dozen e-mail discussion lists.

Association on Employment Practices and Principles
Richard Fitzpatrick
School of Business
Manhattan College
Riverdale, NY 10471
Phone: (718) 862-7221
Fax: (718) 862-8032
E-mail: RFitzpat@manhattan.edu,
    main@aepp.net
Web: www.aepp.net

AEPP is an international organization of scholars and practitioners dedicated to providing a forum that encourages conceptual and empirical research, evaluates existing and new methods, and promotes concrete problem solving to bridge the gap between organizational concepts and practices in the effective managing of organizations, people, and performance.

Canadian Association for Distance Education/Association Canadienne de l'Éducation à Distance
260 Dalhousie Street, Suite 204
Ottawa, ON K1N 7E4
Canada
Phone: (613) 241-0018
Fax: (613) 241-0019
E-mail: cade@csse.ca
Web: www.cade-aced.ca

This is a national association of professionals committed to excellence in providing distance education in Canada. It holds an annual conference, using video, satellite, and teleconference technology. It also publishes a magazine, *Communiqué*, and a refereed semi-annual journal, *The Journal of Distance Education*.

Canadian Council of Human Resources Associations/Conseil Canadien des Associations en Ressources Humaines
P.O. Box 1227, Station B
Ottawa, ON K1P 5R3
Canada

DIRECTORY OF TRAINING AND PERFORMANCE ASSOCIATIONS AND ORGANIZATIONS

Phone: NA
Fax: NA
E-mail: mmcpherson@trakkerinc.com
Web: www.chrpcanada.com
The Council is a collaborative effort of 10 provincial and specialist human resources associations that represent the interests of 18,000-plus professionals across Canada.

Canadian Human Resource Planners/L'Association des Planificateurs en Ressources Humaines du Canada
Ian Hendry
P.O. Box/C.P. 769
Station/Succursale B
Ottawa, ON K1P 5P8
Canada
Phone: NA
Fax: NA
E-mail: ihendry@chrp.ca
Web: www.chrp.ca
CHRP is a nonprofit, volunteer-run network of senior human resource planning and development professionals, line managers, and others who provide leadership within organizations on effective human resource management practices.

Career Planning and Adult Development Network
Administrative Office
P.O. Box 1484
Pacifica, CA 94044
Phone: (650) 359-6911
Fax: (650) 359-3089
E-mail: network@psctr.com
Web: www.careernetwork.org
The Network is a nonprofit international organization of professionals serving the information needs of career counselors, human reource specialists, educators, and researchers who work with adults in career transition. The Network publishes the monthly *Career Planning and Adult Development Newsletter*, with information on activities and resources of interest to career counselors and trainers, and a quarterly, *Network Journal*.

Center for Nonviolent Communication
P.O. Box 2662
Sherman, TX 75091-2662
Phone: (903) 893-3886
Fax: (903) 893-2935
E-mail: cnvc@compuserve.com,
   staff@texoma.net
Web: www.cnvc.org
This is a nonprofit organization founded in 1984 to help people connect compassionately with themselves and one another through Nonviolent Communication[SM], a process created by Marshall B. Rosenberg, Ph.D.

Center for Quality of Management
1 Alewife Center, Suite 450
Cambridge, MA 02140
Phone: (617) 873-8950
Fax: (617) 873-8980
E-mail: cqm_mail@cqm.org
Web: www.cqm.org
CQM is a nonprofit organization founded by senior executives to promote mutual learning through educational programs, advising services, research initiatives, and networking events. It publishes *The CQM Journal* and produces videotapes and the CQM Quality Improvement Toolkit.

Center for the Study of Work Teams
Melanie Bullock
University of North Texas
Terrill Hall Room 330
Avenue C & Mulberry
P.O. Box 311280
Denton, TX 76203-1280
Phone: (940) 565-3096, 940 565-2198
Fax: (940) 565-4806
E-mail: workteam@unt.edu, melanieb@unt.edu
Web: www.workteams.unt.edu
The Center is a nonprofit organization for research and education on collaborative work systems. The Center creates learning partnerships that support the design, implementation, and development of collaborative work systems to maximize individual and organizational effectiveness. The Web site features TeamTalk, an open forum for discussing any aspect of teams. The Center also hosts TeamNet, an e-mail discussion list.

Center for Workforce Development
Anastasia Bogushevskaya, Senior
   Administrative Assistant
Education Development Center, Inc.
55 Chapel Street

Newton, MA 02458-1060
Phone: (617) 618-2370
Fax: (617) 969-4902
E-mail: abogushevskaya@edc.org
Web: www.edc.org/CWD
CWD, a nonprofit organization affiliated with the Education Development Center, conducts worldwide research into tools, strategies, and design elements for effective workforce development.

Center on Education and Work
School of Education
University of Wisconsin-Madison
1025 W. Johnson Street, Room 964
Madison, WI 53706-1796
Phone: (800) 466-0399, (608) 263-3696
Fax: (608) 262-9197
E-mail: cewmail@education.wisc.edu
Web: www.cew.wisc.edu
The mission of the Center is "to enhance the quality of career-related learning for all individuals in schools, colleges, and the workplace." The focus is particularly on initiatives in the areas of school-to-work, tech prep, and coordinated workforce development.

College and University Personnel Association for Human Resources
1233 20th Street, NW, Suite 301
Washington, DC 20036-1250
Phone: (202) 429-0311
Fax: (202) 429-0149
E-mail: lramey@cupahr.org (Lisa Ramey, Customer Service Supervisor)
Web: www.cupahr.org
CUPA-HR serves more than 6,500 human resource administrators at nearly 1,700 colleges and universities worldwide, as well as others interested in the advancement of human resources in higher education, including students and human resource service providers.

Council for Adult and Experiential Learning
55 E. Monroe Street, Suite 1930
Chicago, IL 60603
Phone: (312) 499-2600
Fax: (312) 499-2601
E-mail: cael@cael.org
Web: www.cael.org
CAEL is a national nonprofit organization devoted to expanding lifelong learning opportunities for adults. CAEL focuses on working with employers to help them implement learning programs for their employees. CAEL publishes books and the *CAEL Forum and News* (three issues a year).

Council for Hotel and Restaurant Trainers
P.O. Box 2835
Westfield, NJ 07091
741 Carleton Road
Westfield, NJ 07090
Phone: (800) 463-5918
Fax: (800) 427-5436
E-mail: chart@chart.org
Web: www.chart.org
CHART is a learning organization for the hospitality industry. Its mission is to help hospitality training professionals improve operational performance by developing people. It provides its members with an open forum for sharing best practices and offers conferences, training programs, and networking opportunities for training hospitality personnel.

Distance Education and Training Council
1601 18th Street, NW
Washington, DC 20009-2529
Phone: (202) 234-5100
Fax: (202) 332-1386
E-mail: detc@detc.org
Web: www.detc.org
DETC is dedicated to promoting sound educational standards and ethical business practices within distance education programs. The nationally recognized accrediting agency for distance learning programs worldwide, DETC publishes *Directory of Accredited Institutions* and *Accredited Distance Education Courses for Employee Training and Development* and serves as a clearinghouse of information about distance study.

Employee Assistance Professionals Association, Inc.
2101 Wilson Boulevard, Suite 500
Arlington, VA 22201
Phone: (703) 387-1000
Fax: (703) 522-4585
E-mail: info@ eap-association.com
Web: www.eap-association.com
EAPA is the largest organization for professionals in employee assistance programs. Its mission is to work

to develop and maintain workplace relationships. It represents more than 7,000 individuals and organizations around the globe.

Employee Assistance Society of North America
230 E. Ohio Street, Suite 400
Chicago, IL 60611-3265
Phone: (312) 644-0828
Fax: (312) 644-8557
E-mail: easna@bostrom.com
Web: www.easna.org

EASNA is an international group of professional leaders, with competencies in such specialties as workplace and family wellness, employee benefits, and organizational development. Its mission is to provide a standard of care for employee assistance programming in affiliation with other workplace groups through accreditation processes, peer review, and staff development and training opportunities.

Employee Benefit Research Institute
2121 K Street, NW, Suite 600
Washington, DC 20037-1896
Phone: (202) 659-0670
Fax: (202) 775-6312
E-mail: info@ebri.org
Web: www.ebri.org

EBRI, established in 1978, is the only nonprofit, nonpartisan organization committed exclusively to data dissemination, policy research, and education on economic security and employee benefits. Its mission is to advance knowledge and understanding of employee benefits and their importance to the economy.

Employee Involvement Association
525 S.W. 5th Street, Suite A
Des Moines, IA 50309-4501
Phone: (515) 282-8192
Fax: (515) 282-9117
E-mail: eia@assoc-mgmt.com
Web: www.eia.com

The mission of this nonprofit service association is "to be the leader in optimizing the effectiveness of organizations through employee involvement processes."

Employee Services Management Association
2211 York Road, Suite 207
Oakbrook, IL 60523-2371
Phone: (630) 368-1280
Fax: (630) 368-1286
E-mail: esmahq@esmassn.org
Web: www.esmassn.org

ESMA is a nonprofit association that serves as an information resource network for over 3,000 members, who are responsible for implementing and maintaining a diverse range of employee services. The members of ESMA are "individuals in companies that strive to enhance the quality of life for employees by implementing social activities, cultural events, sports leagues, discount programs, travel programs, convenience services, etc. for employees" or suppliers of products or services for such purposes.

Employers Council on Flexible Compensation
927 15th Street, NW, Suite 1000
Washington, DC 20005
Phone: (202) 659-4300
Fax: (202) 371-1467
E-mail: info@ecfc.org
Web: www.ecfc.org

ECFC is a nonprofit membership association established in 1981 "to create and maintain the most favorable legislative, regulatory, and public opinion environment for flexible compensation." The nearly 3,000 members are plan sponsors, corporations, governments, unions, colleges and universities, hospitals, and clinics that provide cafeteria and 401(k) plans and actuarial, accounting, insurance, and consulting firms that design and administer flexible plans.

Employment Management Association
1800 Duke Street
Alexandria, VA 22314-3499
Phone: (703) 535-6233, (800) 283-7476 x 6233
Fax: (703) 535-6490
E-mail: rhastings@shrm.org
Web: www.shrm.org/ema

Part of the Society for Human Resource Management, EMA "provides high-quality employment-related programs, services, and networking opportunities to members who have staffing-related accountabilities." EMA publishes *Employment Management Today*, a quarterly magazine, and *EMA Reporter*, a bimonthly newsletter, and it hosts a recruitment and employment discussion area on its Web site (for EMA and SHRM members only).

Employment Policy Foundation
1015 15th Street, NW, Suite 1200
Washington, DC 20005
Phone: (202) 789-8685
Fax: (202)-789-8684
E-mail: info@epf.org
Web: www.epf.org
EPF is a small, nonprofit, nonpartisan public policy research and education foundation that focuses on workplace trends and policies. Its mission is "to shape public policy outcomes by providing policymakers and the public with the highest quality economic analysis and commentary on U.S. employment policies affecting the competitive goals of American industry and the people it employs."

ERIC Clearinghouse on Adult, Career, and Vocational Education
Center on Education and Training for
   Employment
College of Education
The Ohio State University
1900 Kenny Road
Columbus, OH 43210-1090
Phone: (614) 292-7069, (800) 848-4815 x 2-7069,
   TTY/TDD (614) 688-8734
Fax: (614) 292-1260
E-mail: ericacve@postbox.acs.ohio-state.edu
Web: ericacve.org
One of 16 Educational Resources Information Center clearinghouses, ERIC/ACVE provides comprehensive information, publications, and services in adult and continuing education, all aspects of career education, and vocational and technical education, including work force preparation. The Web site provides access to AskERIC, a personalized Internet-based service that provides information on request. There are also links to other Web sites. ERIC/ACVE maintains an electronic distribution list that provides information of value to the adult, career, vocational, and technical training communities.

Experiential Training and Development Alliance
P.O. Box 12485
Portland, OR 97212
Phone: (866) 733-7607
Fax: NA
E-mail: info@etdalliance.com
Web: www.etdalliance.com
The ETD Alliance is a not-for-profit association composed of 19 organizations whose primary services center around experiential-based professional and organizational development, skills training, and/or organizational consulting services. Since 1997, the members of the ETD Alliance have been working to define exemplary practices in experiential training and development, to educate consumers, and to ensure that its members provide the highest-quality training and development solutions to their clients.

Foundation for Enterprise Development
2020 K Street, Suite 400
Washington, DC 20006
Phone: (202) 530-8920
Fax: (202) 530-5702
E-mail: fed@fed.org
Web: www.fed.org
FED is a nonprofit organization dedicated to helping entrepreneurs and executives use employee ownership and equity compensation as a fair and effective means of motivating the workforce and improving corporate performance.

Human Factors and Ergonomics Society
P.O. Box 1369
Santa Monica, CA 90406-1369
Phone: (310) 394-1811
Fax: (310) 394-2410
E-mail: info@hfes.org
Web: hfes.org
HFES was founded to promote the discovery and exchange of knowledge concerning the characteristics of human beings that are applicable to the design of systems and devices of all kinds. It publishes a quarterly peer-reviewed journal (*Human Factors*), a quarterly magazine (*Ergonomics in Design: The Magazine of Human Factors Applications*), and *HFES Bulletin* as well as books and brochures.

Human Resource Planning Society
317 Madison Avenue, Suite 1509
New York, NY 10017
Phone: (212) 490-6387
Fax: (212) 682-6851
E-mail: info@hrps.org
Web: www.hrps.org
HRPS is a nonprofit organization of more than 3,000 human resource and business executives committed

to providing current perspectives on complex and challenging human resource and business issues. HRPS publishes the quarterly *Human Resource Planning* and books, hosts an annual conference, provides workshops and programs, and schedules chat room discussions.

Information Technology Training Association, Inc.
Rachel Cheeseman, Executive Director
450 East 22nd Street, Suite 230
   Lombard, IL 60148-6158
Phone: (702) 839-0975
Fax: (630) 268-1384
E-mail: rcheeseman@comptia.org
Web: www.itta.org

The IT Training Section of CompTIA is the trade association for professionals and companies involved in the IT Training Industry. The organization was formed in 1994 from the merger of the International Computer Training Association and the Association of Technical Education Centers. It has taken an active leadership role in legislative efforts, professional development and business management conferences, and setting industry standards. It has more than 350 member companies and holds educational conferences and focus seminars around the world.

Instructional Systems Association
12427 Hedges Run Drive, #120
Lake Ridge, VA 22192
Phone (703) 730-2838
Fax (703) 730-2857
E-mail: info@isaconnection.org
Web: www.isaconnection.org

ISA, comprising over 125 member companies, is "dedicated to the transfer of learning and knowledge for work-related performance needs." It pursues this mission by encouraging and facilitating the exchange of ideas, perspectives, and information among CEOs and other senior management of member companies.

Interactive Multimedia & Collaborative Communications Alliance
P.O. Box 756
Syosset, NY 11791-0756
Phone: (516) 818-8184
Fax: (516) 922-2170
E-mail: staff@imcca.org
Web: www.imcca.org

IMCCA is an organization of people "who share a common interest in fostering and promoting people to people communications and learning throughout the industry." Its mission is "to foster industry growth by facilitating nonprofit industry organizations to coalesce around promoting the technology and the uses of collaborative communications globally."

International Association for Continuing Education and Training
1620 I Street, NW, Suite 615
Washington, DC 20006
Phone: (202) 463-2905
Fax: (202) 463-8498
E-mail: iacet@moinc.com
Web: www.iacet.org

IACET is a voluntary membership organization that provides guidance and direction for the development and use of the Continuing Education Unit (CEU). The mission is to promote and advance quality continuing education and training through research, education, training, and resource dissemination. The association publishes materials to facilitate the development of effective continuing education programs.

International Association for Human Resource Information Management, Inc.
401 N. Michigan Avenue
Chicago, IL 60611
Phone: (312) 321-5141
Fax: (312) 527-6636
E-mail: moreinfo@ihrim.org
Web: www.ihrim.org

IHRIM ws formed in 1996 to enable its members to achieve strategic objectives through the integration of information technology and human resource management. Membership consists of practitioners, vendors, and consultants. IHRIM publishes *IHRIM.link Magazine* and the quarterly *IHRIM Journal*, as well as surveys, white papers, and conference proceedings.

International Association of Career Management Professionals
204 E Street, NE
Washington, DC 20002
Phone: (202) 547-6377
Fax: (202) 547-6348
E-mail: iacmp@iacmp.org
Web: www.iacmp.org

IACMP is a nonprofit, incorporated association devoted to meeting the collaborative needs of career management professionals.

International Association of Correctional Training Personnel
P.O. Box 780278
Orlando, Florida 32828-0278
Phone: (407) 482-6624
Fax: (407) 482-1690
E-mail: iactp@aol.com
Web: www.iactp.org

IACTP is a professional association of correctional trainers, administrators, and educators representing all fields of corrections. IACTP sponsors annual training conferences, presents the Awards of Excellence in Correctional Training, and publishes *The Correctional Trainer*.

International Association of Facilitators
7630 W. 145th Street, Suite 202
St. Paul, MN 55124
Phone: (952) 891-3541
Fax: (952) 891-1800
E-mail: office@iaf-world.org
Web: www.iaf-world.org

IAF exists to promote, support, and advance the art and practice of ethical facilitation, through providing resources, interchange, and opportunities for professional development. It publishes *Group Facilitation: A Research and Applications Journal*.

International Association of Information Technology Trainers
PMB 451
6030-M Marshalee Drive
Elkridge, MD 21075-5935
Phone: (410) 290-7000 or (888) 290-6200
Fax: (603) 925-1110
E-mail: member@itrain.org
Web: www.itrain.org

ITrain is a nonprofit international association of more than 5000 information technology professionals in 158 countries. It provides its members access to resources and support services and publishes two newsletters, *Responsible Training* and *ITinfo*.

International Board of Standards for Training, Performance and Instruction
c/o PERQ Publications
509 W. Main Street
Barrington, IL 60010
Phone: (800) 236-4303, (847) 304-5571
Fax: (847) 304-5553
E-mail: prc@prcinc.net
Web: www.prcinc.net/ibstpi.htm

IBSTPI is a not-for-profit standards-setting board founded in 1984. Its mission is to promote high standards of professional practice in the areas of training, performance, and instruction for the benefit of individuals and organizational consumers through research, definition, and measurement of competencies. As administered by PERQ Publications, IBSTPI publishes books on standards for instructional design, training manager competencies, and related material.

International Coach Federation
1444 I Street, NW, Suite 700
Washington, DC 20005
Phone: (888) ICF(423)-3131, (202) 712-9039
Fax: (888) 329-2423, (202) 216-9646
E-mail: icfoffice@coachfederation.org
Web: www.coachfederation.org

ICF is a nonprofit professional organization of personal and business coaches. Its mission is to build the profession through education and promotion, to foster the spirit of community among its members, and to preserve the integrity of the coaching profession. ICF has chapters in almost every state in the U.S. and in more than 10 countries. It sponsors the Coach Referral Service, produces a monthly e-newsletter (*ICF Coaching News*), and hosts an annual conference.

International Communications Industries Association, Inc.
11242 Waples Mill Road, Suite 200
Fairfax, VA 22030
Phone: (800) 659-7469, (703) 273-7200
Fax: (703) 278-8082
E-mail: kward@iciahq.org (Kim Ward, Membership)
Web: www.icia.org

ICIA represents for-profit individuals and organizations that derive revenue from the commercialization or utilization of communications technologies. ICIA ensures the credibility and desirability of its members' products and services through education programs, workforce development activities, industry technology updates, publications, Internet presence, market research, industry certification programs, government relations, and participation in national and international expositions.

International Consortia of Business Coaches
Mike R. Jay
The Leadwise Group, LLC
Mitchell, NE 69357
Phone/Fax: (800) 823-1251
E-mail: infowww@i-cbc.com
Web: i-cbc.com

This group was founded in 1999 to create a global network of business coaches and generate opportunities for collaboration and teaming.

International Council for Educational Media/Conseil International des Médias Educatifs
ICEM General Secretariat
Margo Van Sluizer, Secretary General
Hanns-Fay-Strasse 1
D-67227 Frankenthal
Germany
Phone: +49-6233-46051
Fax: +49-6233-46355
E-mail: secretariat@icem-cime.com
Web: www.icem-cime.com

The primary objective of ICEM is "to provide a channel for the international exchange and evaluation of information, experience and materials in the field of educational media as they apply to pre-school, primary and secondary education, to technical and vocational, industrial and commercial training, teacher training, continuing and distance education." ICEM publishes a quarterly journal, *Educational Media International*.

International Customer Service Association
401 N. Michigan Avenue
Chicago, IL 60611
Phone: (800) 360-4272, (312) 644-6800
Fax: (312) 245-1084
E-mail: icsa@sba.com
Web: www.icsa.com

ICSA is dedicated to promoting the development and awareness of the customer service profession through networking, education, and research. It offers a professional certification program, leading to the designation Certified Customer Service Professional. ICSA publishes *ICSA News* and *ICSA Journal*.

International Federation of Training and Development Organisations, Ltd.
David A. Waugh, Secretary General
1800 Duke Street
Alexandria, VA 22314-3499
Phone: (703) 535-6011
Fax: (703) 836-0367
E-mail: iftdo@shrm.org
Web: www.iftdo.org

IFTDO is a worldwide network committed to identifying, developing, and transferring knowledge, skills, and technology to enhance personal and organizational growth, human performance, productivity, and sustainable development. It is the leading global HR organization, with member organizations in more than 50 countries, representing more than 500,000 HR professionals. IFTDO co-sponsors the annual International Performance Improvement Conference and Exposition with the International Society for Performance Improvement.

International Foundation of Employee Benefit Plans
18700 W. Bluemound Road
P.O. Box 69
Brookfield, WI 53008-0069
Phone: (262) 786-6700
Fax: (262) 786-8670
E-mail: infocenter@ifebp.org
Web: www.ifebp.org

IFEBP is a nonprofit, nonlobbying educational association serving the employee benefits field by providing programs, services, and information of interest to benefits professionals. Membership consists of 35,000 individuals representing 8,400 multi-employer trust funds, corporations, public employee groups, and professional advisory firms throughout the United States and Canada.

International Mentoring Association
Office of Conferences and Institutes
Western Michigan University
A-115 Ellsworth Hall
1201 Oliver Street
Kalamazoo, MI 49008-5161
Phone: (616) 387-4174
Fax: (616) 387-4189
E-mail: cedu_ima@wmich.edu
Web: www.wmich.edu/conferences/mentoring

IMA promotes and supports mentoring in various environments and the exchange of information about the theory and practice of innovative mentoring. IMA publishes a quarterly newsletter, *Mentoring Connection*, and hosts an electronic network for discussion of mentoring issues and access to a bibliography of mentoring publications.

International Organization Development Association
IODA Secretariat
P.O. Box 40323
Providence, RI 02940-0323
Phone: (401) 826-1340
Fax: (401) 827-8806
E-mail: ioda212016@aol.com
Web: www.ioda.de
IODA is an international association of OD professionals. IODA provides opportunities for having a global impact on the development and change processes used by organization development practitioners through an international learning community environment that enhances sharing, openness, and creatively supporting the continual development of global communities.

International Personnel Management Association
1617 Duke Street
Alexandria, VA 22314
Phone: (703) 549-7100
Fax: (703) 684-0948
E-mail: ipma@ipma-hr.org
Web: www.ipma-hr.org
IPMA is a non-profit membership organization for agencies and individuals in the public sector human resources field. Its mission is to provide human resource management leadership, education, information, and representation services to advance organizational objectives and quality in the public sector. IPMA sponsors conferences, publishes the quarterly *Public Personnel Management* journal and monthly *IPMA News*, and hosts an e-mail discussion list for IPMA members.

International Quality & Productivity Center
150 Clove Road
P.O. Box 401
Little Falls, NJ 07424-0401
Phone: (800) 882-8684, (973) 256-0211
Fax: (973) 256-0205
E-mail: info@iqpc.com
Web: www.iqpc.com
IQPC is dedicated to providing practical, detailed information through conferences.

International Simulation and Gaming Association
Jan Klabbers, General Secretary
Oostervelden 59
6681 WR Bemmel
Netherlands
Phone: +31 481 462455
Fax: +31 481 461828
E-mail: jklabbers@kmpc.nl
Web: isaga.pm.it-chiba.ac.jp
Founded in 1970, ISAGA is an organization for people working on and using simulation/gaming and related methodologies—computerized simulation, policy exercises, role-play, experiential exercises, play, case studies, structured experiences, game theory, operational gaming. ISAGA publishes a journal, *Simulation & Gaming: An International Journal of Theory, Practice and Research*.

International Society for Performance Improvement
1400 Spring Street, Suite 260
Silver Spring, MD 20910
Phone: (301) 587-8570
Fax: (301) 587-8573
E-mail: info@ispi.org
Web: www.ispi.org
ISPI is dedicated to improving productivity and performance in the workplace. Founded in 1962, it has more than 10,000 members throughout the U.S., Canada, and 40 other countries. Most of its members are performance technologists, training directors, HR managers, instructional technologists, change agents, human factors practitioners, and organizational development consultants. ISPI publishes the *Performance Improvement Journal* (10 issues a year) and *Performance Improvement Quarterly*, plus books and *News & Notes*, a society newsletter. It also sponsors a yearly International Conference and Expo.

International Vocational Education and Training Association
IVETA Secretariat
Oregon State University

129 Education Hall
Corvallis, OR 97331-3502
Phone: (541) 737-2962
Fax: (541) 737-2040
E-mail: iveta@ccmail.orst.edu
Web: www.cord.org/iveta
This is an organization and network of vocational educators, vocational skills training organizations, business and industrial firms, and other individuals and groups interested or involved in vocational education and training worldwide. The aim is to promote the development of a network of institutions around the world. IVETA publishes a quarterly newsletter and a biannual refereed journal, the *International Journal of Vocational Education and Training*. It sponsors an annual conference in conjunction with the Association for Career and Technical Education.

Job Accommodation Network
West Virginia University
P.O. Box 6080
Morgantown, WV 26506-6080
Phone: (800) 526-7234 (accommodation information), (800) ADA-WORK (232-9675) (ADA information)
Fax: (304) 293-5407
E-mail: jan@jan.icdi.wvu.edu
Web: janweb.icdi.wvu.edu
The Job Accommodation Network (JAN) is an international toll-free consulting service that provides information about job accommodations and the employability of people with disabilities. JAN also provides information regarding the Americans with Disabilities Act (ADA).

Learning Resources Network
P.O. Box 9
River Falls, WI 54022
Phone: (800) 678-5376, (715) 426-9777
Fax: (888) 234-8633, (715) 426-5847
E-mail: info@lern.org
Web: www.lern.org
LERN is an international association offering information and resources to providers of lifelong learning programs, including business classes, conferences, contract training, seminars, consulting, staff training, and continuing professional education. LERN has more than 4,000 members in eight countries.

Learning Technology Institute
50 Culpeper Street
Warrenton, VA 20186
Phone: (540) 347-0055
Fax: (540) 439-3169
E-mail: info@lti.org
Web: www.lti.org
The Learning Technology Institute was founded in 1975 as a non-profit public interest corporation devoted to research, development, organization management, and education activities in connection with the use of technology and computers in knowledge engineering, systems design, and technology-based information delivery systems.

Mainstream, Inc.
6930 Carroll Avenue, Suite 240
Takoma Park, MD 20912
Phone: (301) 891-8777 (voice/TTY)
Fax: (301) 891-8778
E-mail: wlink@mainstreaminc.org
Web: www.mainstreaminc.org
Mainstream, Inc. is a national, nonprofit organization dedicated to improving competitive employment opportunities for people with disabilities. Mainstream provides specialized services and acts as a bridge that links people with disabilities, employers, and service providers. Founded in 1975 by Harold E. Krents, the organization works to identify and implement cost-effective programs and services that will benefit all three of its constituencies.

Masie Center, Inc.
95 Washington Street
P.O. Box 397
Saratoga Springs, NY 12866
Phone: (518) 350-2200
Fax (518) 587-3276
E-mail: emasie@masie.com
Web: www.masie.com
The MASIE Center is a think tank dedicated to exploring the intersection of learning and technology.

Meeting Professionals International
4455 LBJ Freeway, Suite 1200
Dallas, TX 75244-5903
Phone: (972) 702-3000
Fax: (972) 702-3070

E-mail: feedback@mpiweb.org
Web: www.mpiweb.org
MPI is the world's largest association of meeting professionals, with more than 18,000 members in 64 countries. It serves as an educational, technological, and peer-interaction resource for the meeting industry. MPI publishes a monthly magazine, *The Meeting Professional*.

National Alliance of Business
1201 New York Avenue, NW, Suite 700
Washington, DC 20005-6143
Phone: (800) 787-2848, (202) 289-2977 (TDD)
Fax: (202) 289-2869
E-mail: info@nab.com
Web: www.nab.com
The Alliance is "a national business organization singularly focused on increasing student achievement and improving the competitiveness of the workforce." Its 5,000 members include companies of all sizes and industries, their CEOs and senior executives, educators, and business-led coalitions.

National Association for Employee Recognition
1805 N. Mill Street, Suite A
Naperville, IL 60563
Phone: (630) 369-7783
Fax: (630) 369-3773
E-mail: naer@recognition.org
Web: www.recognition.org
NAER is "dedicated to the enhancement of employee performance through recognition, including its strategies and related initiatives." It provides a forum for exchanging information, sharing best practices, and educating.

National Association for Government Training and Development
Ed Klee, President
Governmental Services Center
State of Kentucky
KSU, 4th Floor, Academic Services Building
Frankfort, KY 40601
Phone: (502) 564-7455 x 231
Fax: (502) 564-2732
E-mail: eklee@mail.state.ky.us
Web: www.usd.edu/nagtad
NAGTAD is the only professional association serving leaders in government training and development and helping public sector training and development professionals prepare for career challenges. NAGTAD provides a membership directory and a nationwide information exchange on government training programs, holds annual conferences and an awards program, offers vendor discounts, and publishes a quarterly newsletter.

National Association for Industry-Education Cooperation
Donald M. Clark, President & CEO
235 Hendricks Boulevard
Buffalo, NY 14226-3304
Phone/Fax: (716) 834-7047
E-mail: naiec@pcom.net
Web: www2.pcom.net/naiec
NAIEC's mission is to promote collaboration to improve education and workforce preparation with an emphasis on career education. The NAIEC serves as a national clearinghouse for information on business/industry involvement in education and assists in the development of industry-education collaboration. It publishes the *NAIEC Newsletter* (six issues/year).

National Association of Workforce Development Professionals
1620 I Street, NW, LL 30
Washington, DC 20006-4005
Phone: (202) 887-6120
Fax: (202) 887-8216
E-mail: nawdp@aol.com
Web: kaisergrp.com/nawdp/index.htm
NAWDP is a professional association for individuals working in employment and training and related programs. The association publishes *Advantage*, a monthly newsletter for members, and manuals on workforce development topics.

National Career Development Association
c/o Creative Management Alliance
10820 East 45th Street, Suite 210
Tulsa, OK 74146
Phone: (918) 663-7060, (866) 367-6232
Fax: (918) 663-7058
E-mail: dpenn@ncda.org (Deneen Pennington, Executive Director)
Web: ncda.org
The mission of NCDA, a division of the American Counseling Association, is to promote the career development of all people over the life span. It pub-

DIRECTORY OF TRAINING AND PERFORMANCE ASSOCIATIONS AND ORGANIZATIONS

lishes the *Career Development Quarterly* and an on-line newsletter, *Career Developments*, holds an annual conference, and hosts more than a dozen discussion lists on areas of career development.

National Center for Employee Ownership
1736 Franklin Street, 8th Floor
Oakland, CA 94612
Phone: (510) 208-1300
Fax: (510) 272-9510
E-mail: nceo@nceo.org
Web: www.nceo.org
NCEO is a private, nonprofit membership and research organization that serves as a source of information on employee stock ownership plans (ESOPs), broadly granted employee stock options, and employee participation programs.

National Dissemination Center for Career and Technical Education
1900 Kenny Road
Columbus, OH 43210-1090
Phone: (800) 678-6011 or (614) 292-9931
Fax: (614) 688-3258
E-mail: ndccte@osu.edu
Web: nccte.com
This is half (with the National Research Center) of the National Centers for Career and Technical Education, a consortium of institutions, agencies, organizations, experts, and consultants. It operates from two centers to conduct research and provide information to advance career and technical education in the United States.

National Environmental Training Association
5320 North 16th Street, Suite 114
Phoenix, AZ 85016
Phone: (602) 956-6099
Fax: (602) 956-6399
E-mail: neta@ehs-training.org
Web: www.ehs-training.org
NETA is a non-profit international organization of environmental, health and safety, and other technical training professionals. NETA is the network for academic, government, industrial, utility, and consulting trainers and training managers responsible for protecting public health, workers, and the environment. It provides EH&S training information and programs to industry, supports the professional development of its members, and defines competency standards.

National Human Resources Association
c/o Judy Huschka
JH Association Management
6767 W. Greenfield Avenue
Milwaukee, WI 53214
Phone: (414) 453-7499
Fax: (414) 475-5959
E-mail: nhra@humanresources.org
Web: www.humanresources.org
NHRA, established in 1951, is a nonprofit organization of about 1,500 professionals, managers, and executives engaged in human resources management and related fields. Its goals are to provide programs and services for HR professionals, to advance the interests and development of HR professionals, and to provide a forum for the exchange of information and ideas related to human resources management. It publishes a quarterly newsletter, *Connections*.

National Labor Management Association
P.O. Box 819
Jamestown, NY 14702-0819
1093 East Second Street, Room 340
Jamestown, NY 14701
Phone: (800) 967-2687
Fax: (716) 665-8060
E-mail: nlma@nlma.org
Web: www.nlma.org
NLMA is a national membership organization devoted to helping management and labor work together for constructive change, fostering labor-management partnerships through education and training.

National Management Association
2210 Arbor Boulevard
Dayton, OH 45439-1580
Phone: (937) 294-0421
Fax: (937) 294-2374
E-mail: nma@nma1.org
Web: www.nma1.org
NMA is a professional management and leadership development association dedicated to the personal and professional development of America's workforce. NMA develops managerial and leadership skills through its books, training programs, and magazines.

National Occupational Competency Testing Institute
500 N. Bronson Avenue

Big Rapids, MI 49307
Phone: (800) 334-6283, (231) 796-4695
Fax: (231) 796-4699
E-mail: nocti@nocti.org
Web: www.nocti.org
NOCTI produces occupational competency tests, with more than 150 technical tests.

National Research Center for Career and Technical Education
1954 Buford Avenue
St. Paul, MN 55108-6197
Phone: (800) 322-9664 or (612) 624-3000
Fax: (612) 624-7757
E-mail: nrccte@tc.umn.edu
This is half (with the National Dissemination Center) of the National Centers for Career and Technical Education, a consortium of institutions, agencies, organizations, experts, and consultants. It operates from two centers to conduct research and provide information to advance career and technical education in the United States.

National Restaurant Association Educational Foundation
250 S. Wacker Drive, Suite 1400
Chicago, IL 60606-5834
Phone: (800) 765-2122, (312) 715-1010
Fax: (312) 715-0807
E-mail: info@foodtrain.org
Web: www.edfound.org
The Educational Foundation is a not-for-profit organization that serves as the primary source of education, training, and professional development for the foodservice industry. The Foundation publishes a quarterly *Best Practices* magazine and offers more than 100 educational products and services, including textbooks, student manuals, instructor guides, training, seminars, and certification programs.

National Skill Standards Board
1441 L Street, NW, Suite 9000
Washington, DC 20005-3512
Phone: (202) 254-8628, (877) THE-NSSB (843-6772)
Fax: (202) 254-8646
E-mail: information@nssb.org
Web: www.nssb.org
NSSB was established by Congress as an independent group of business, labor, education, and civic leaders, to help America's workers—current and future—better prepare for their jobs. It publishes a newsletter, *Skills Today*.

National Society for Experiential Education
1703 N. Beauregard Street, Suite 400
Alexandria, VA 22311-1714
Phone: (703) 933-0017
Fax: (703) 933-1053
E-mail: info@nsee.org
Web: www.nsee.org
NSEE is a membership association committed to all forms of experiential learning—in the classroom, in the workplace, or in the community. "NSEE is a strong advocate of partnerships that contribute to more dynamic classrooms, a stronger workforce, and thriving communities." It publishes the *NSEE Quarterly* and books. It also provides consulting services.

National Speakers Association
1500 S. Priest Drive
Tempe, AZ 85281
Phone: (480) 968-2552
Fax: (480) 968-0911
E-mail: information@nsaspeaker.org
Web: www.nsaspeaker.org
NSA is the organization for experts who speak professionally, including trainers, educators, and consultants. NSA provides resources and education to improve the business skills and platform performance of professional speakers.

North American Simulation and Gaming Association
P.O. Box 78636
Indianapolis, IN 46278
Phone: (888) 432-GAME(4263), (317) 387-1424
Fax: (317) 387-1921
E-mail: info@nasaga.org
Web: www.nasaga.org
NASAGA promotes the use of simulation and games for educating and training. Its members are primarily academics, trainers, consultants, and facilitators. NASAGA co-sponsors a refereed publication, *Simulation & Gaming: An International Journal of Theory, Practice, and Research* (quarterly). NASAGA holds an annual conference and hosts a discussion forum on its Web site.

Ontario Society for Training and Development
80 Richmond Street West, Suite 508
Toronto, ON M5H 2A4
Canada
Phone: (416) 367-5900
Fax: (416) 367-1642
E-mail: info@ostd.ca
Web: www.ostd.ca

OSTD is the largest association in Canada dedicated to the profession of training and human resource development. OSTD acts as a public relations and advocacy group for its members. It publishes *The Canadian Learning Journal*, a quarterly magazine for training and learning professionals, and other materials, such as *Training Competency Architecture* and an accompanying toolkit.

Organization Development Institute
Donald W. Cole, President
11234 Walnut Ridge Road
Chesterland, OH 44026-1299
Phone: (440) 729-7419
Fax: (440) 729-9319
E-mail: DonWCole@aol.com
Web: members.aol.com/odinst

ODI is a nonprofit educational association organized in 1968 to promote an understanding of the field of Organization Development. It publishes *The Organization Development Journal* (quarterly), *Organizations and Change* (monthly newsletter), and *The International Registry of O.D. Professionals and O.D. Handbook* (annual). The Institute also holds two conferences a year.

Organization Development Network
71 Valley Street, Suite 301
South Orange, NJ 07079-2825
Phone: (973) 763-7337
Fax: (973) 763-7488
E-mail: odn@odnetwork.org
Web: www.odnetwork.org

This network is a values-based community that supports its members in human organization and systems development. Its members are some 2500 practitioners, academics, managers, and students employed or interested in organization development. It holds an annual conference and publishes a quarterly journal, the *OD Practitioner*.

Positive Employee Relations Council
Doug Kalish
4226 Long Branch Court, NE
Atlanta, GA 30319-1735
Phone: (770) 454-9130
Fax: (770) 454-9781
E-mail: dkalish@perc.net
Web: www.perc.net

The PERC Network is composed of about 1100 individuals in professional employee relations, legal, or management positions in more than 800 companies around the world. The Web site is intended as a "complete on-line service for positive employee relations policies and practices for proactive employers." PERC also maintains an e-mail discussion list, ERNET.

Professional Society for Sales and Marketing Training
P.O. Box 995
Fayetteville, GA 30214-0995
Phone: (770) 719-4SMT
Fax: (770) 719-8SMT
E-mail: gconnor@smt.org
Web: www.smt.org

The Professional Society for Sales and Marketing Training is committed to improving sales, marketing, and customer relations through excellence in training. It offers programs and publishes training manuals and other materials.

Project Management Institute
4 Campus Boulevard
Newtown Square, PA 19073-3299
Phone: (610) 356-4600
Fax: (610) 356-4647
E-mail: pmihq@pmi.org
Web: www.pmi.org

Established in 1969, PMI is the leading nonprofit professional association serving the project management profession, with more than 70,000 members worldwide. PMI provides consultants and trainers opportunities to stay current through seminars, local chapters, specific interest groups, monthly magazines, quarterly journal, and an annual seminar and symposium.

Scanlon Leadership Network
Scanlon Plan Associates
2875 Northwind Drive, Suite 121
East Lansing, MI 48823-0509

Phone: (517) 332-8927
Fax: (517) 332-9381
E-mail: office@scanlonassociates.org
Web: www.scanlonassociates.org
Founded in 1964, the Scanlon Plan Associates—"The Nonprofit Association Whose Members Pioneered Gainsharing, Goalsharing, Labor-Management Cooperation, Employee Involvement, Open-Book Management, and Servant Leadership—consists of organizations dedicated to the Scanlon Principles and Processes.

SHRM Global Forum
1800 Duke Street
Alexandria, VA 22314
Phone: (703) 548-3440
Fax: (703) 535-6490
E-mail: forum@shrm.org
Web: www.shrmglobal.org
Formerly known as the Institute for International Human Resources, the Global Forum is a division of the Society for Human Resource Management that provides its more than 6,500 members in over 70 countries with information and support in developing their expertise to meet the challenge of managing a global workforce.

Society for Applied Learning Technology
Raymond G. Fox, President
50 Culpeper Street
Warrenton, VA 20186
Phone: (540) 347-0055
Fax: (540) 349-3169
E-mail: info@lti.org
Web: www.salt.org
SALT is a nonprofit professional membership organization founded in 1972 for professionals whose work requires knowledge and communication in the field of instructional technology. It has about 68,000 members worldwide. The society sponsors meetings and conferences, special interest groups, and publishes a quarterly newsletter and three journals, *Journal of Interactive Instruction Development*, *Journal of Educational Technology Systems*, and *Journal of Instruction Delivery Systems*.

Society for Human Resource Management
1800 Duke Street
Alexandria, VA 22314-3499
Phone: (800) 283-7476, (703) 548-3440, (703) 548-6999 TDD
Fax: (703) 535-6490
E-mail: shrm@shrm.org
Web: www.shrm.org
SHRM is the leading voice of human resource professionals, representing the interests of more than 130,000 members from around the world, with more than 450 chapters across the U.S. SHRM provides its members with education and information services, conferences and seminars, government and media representation, and publications, including *HR Magazine*, a leading publication in the HR field. The Web site provides information about the society and includes an extensive listing of links to other sites.

Society for Industrial and Organizational Psychology
Lee Hakel, Office Manager
SIOP Administrative Office
P.O. Box 87
Bowling Green, OH 43402-0087
Phone: (419) 353-0032
Fax: (419) 352-2645
E-mail: lhakel@siop.bgsu.edu
Web: www.siop.org
SIOP is a scientific, professional, and educational organization founded to promote human welfare through the various applications of psychology to all types of organizations providing goods and services. It's a division of the American Psychological Association and an organizational affiliate of the American Psychological Society.

Society for Technical Communication
901 N. Stuart Street, Suite 904
Arlington, VA 22203-1822
Phone: (703) 522-4114
Fax: (703) 522-2075
E-mail: stc@stc.org
Web: www.stc.org
STC is dedicated to advancing the arts and sciences of technical communication. Its 25,000 members include technical writers, editors, graphic designers, multimedia artists, Web and Intranet page information designers, translators, and others whose work involves making technical information understandable and available to those who need it. It publishes a quarterly journal, *Technical Communication*, and a magazine, *Intercom*, and holds an annual conference.

Society of Consumer Affairs Professionals in Business
801 N. Fairfax Street, Suite 404
Alexandria, VA 22314
Phone: (703) 519-3700
Fax: (703) 549-4886
E-mail: socap@socap.org
Web: www.socap.org
SOCAP aims to be "the champion and service leader for the bottom-line impact of customer satisfaction and loyalty." Membership is open to "all professionals who are in some way responsible for creating and maintaining customer loyalty." It publishes a quarterly magazine, *Customer Relationship Management*.

Society of Insurance Trainers and Educators
2120 Market Street, Suite 108
San Francisco, CA 94114
Phone: (415) 621-2830
Fax: (415) 621-0889
E-mail: socinstred@aol.com
Web: www.insurancetrainers.org/index.htm
SITE was founded in 1953 to promote education and training in the insurance industry. It is "dedicated to providing performance improvement opportunities to Society members through programs, networking, and services." It hosts an annual conference and publishes a biannual journal.

Society of Professionals in Dispute Resolution
1527 New Hampshire Avenue, NW, 3rd Floor
Washington, DC 20036
Phone: (202) 667-9700
Fax: (202) 265-1968
E-mail: spidr@spidr.org
Web: www.spidr.org
SPIDR is an international association established to advance the highest standards of practice and ethics for those who resolve disputes.

United States Distance Learning Association
John G. Flores, Executive Director
140 Gould Street, Suite 200B
Needham, MA 02494-2397
Phone: (800) 275-5162, (781) 453-2388
Fax: (781) 453-2389
E-mail: jflores@usdla.org
Web: www.usdla.org
A nonprofit organization formed in 1987, the USDLA promotes the development and application of distance learning for education and training at all levels. The USDLA publishes a monthly journal, *ED, Education at a Distance*.

U.S. Foundation for Performance Measurement
Phone: (202) 251-7676
Fax: (202) 318-0665
E-mail: usfpm@fpm.com
Web: www.netmain.com/usfpm
The Foundation, established in 1992, is a membership association of educators, business, government, and consultant specialists interested in improving organizational performance.

Vocational Evaluation and Work Adjustment Association
202 E. Cheyenne Mountain Boulevard, Suite N
Colorado Springs, CO 80906
Phone: (719) 527-1800 (also TDD)
Fax: (719) 576-1818
E-mail: info@vewaa.org
Web: www.vewaa.org
VEWAA is a national nonprofit professional association whose members work with people to match them with training, careers, and employment. It promotes professional development through workshops, conferences, training programs, and position papers and other publications, including *VEWAA Bulletin* and *VEWAA Newsletter*.

Wellness Councils of America
9802 Nicholas Street, Suite 315
Omaha, NE 68114
Phone: (402) 827-3590
Fax: (402) 827-3594
E-mail: wellworkplace@welcoa.org
Web: www.welcoa.org
WELCOA is a national nonprofit organization whose mission is to enhance the well-being of employees, improve productivity, reduce absenteeism, and contain escalating health care costs. WELCOA publishes a newsletter for employees of its member companies, *The Well Workplace*, and sourcebooks.

Work in America Institute, Inc.
700 White Plains Road
Scarsdale, NY 10583

Phone: (800) 787-0707, (914) 472-9600
Fax: (914) 472-9606
E-mail: info@workinamerica.org
Web: www.workinamerica.org
Founded in 1975, WIA is a not-for-profit workplace research organization with support from business, labor, and government. Its mission is "to advance productivity and the quality of working life through the principles of sound human resource practices which are applicable in all industries."

Workforce Excellence Network
200 Constitution Avenue, NW, Suite C-4318
Washington, DC 20210
Phone: (202) 693-2990
Fax: (202) 219-8503
E-mail: WENwebpage@doleta.gov
Web: www.workforce-excellence.net
The purpose of the Workforce Excellence Network (formerly the Enterprise Organization) is to "engage state and local workforce development organizations in a voluntary process of pursuing performance excellence."

WorldatWork
14040 N. Northsight Boulevard
Scottsdale, AZ 85260
Phone: (877) 951-9191, (480) 951-9191
Fax: (480) 483-8352
E-mail: customerrelations@worldatwork.org
Web: www.worldatwork.org
"The Professional Association for Compensation, Benefits, and Total Rewards," WorldatWork (formerly American Compensation Association and Canadian Compensation Association) is a 45-year-old global not-for-profit professional association dedicated to knowledge leadership in disciplines associated with attracting, retaining and motivating employees. It publishes the *WorldatWork Journal* (quarterly), *workspan* (a newsletter), and books.

Calendar of Conferences and Events, 2002

To help you plan for 2002, the following list provides information about some events of interest to professionals in areas of training and performance, with Web sites that you can check for details. Since we cannot include every event of potential interest, you might also want to visit the Web sites listed in the Directory of Training and Performance Associations and Organizations.

January

The Center for Lifelong Learning & Design
CSCL Computer Support for Collaborative Learning 2002: Foundations for a CSCL Community
January 7-11, 2002
Boulder, CO
www.cscl2002.org

Meeting Professionals International
Professional Education Conference
January 20-22, 2002
Honolulu, HI
www.mpiweb.org/pec

Center for Distance Learning Research, Texas A&M University
9th Annual Distance Education Conference
January 22-24, 2002
Austin, TX
www.cdlr.tamu.edu

University Forum for HRD
EURESFORM
Academy of HRD
3rd Conference on HRD Research and Practice Across Europe: Creativity and Innovation in Learning
January 25-26, 2002
Edinburgh, Scotland
www.lums.lancs.ac.uk/ufhrd/events/euroconf3.htm

February

American Society for Training and Development
ASTD TechKnowledge Conference & Exposition
February 4-7, 2002
Las Vegas, NV
www.astd.org

Alliance of Work/Life Professionals
6th Annual Conference
February 6-9, 2002
San Francisco, CA
www.awlp.org

Huey B. Long, College of Education, University of Oklahoma
16th Annual International Self-Directed Learning Symposium
February 7-9, 2002
Boynton Beach, FL
sdlglobal.com

Intermedia Exhibitions & Conferences
2nd European E-Learning Expo & Conference
February 13-14, 2002
Paris, France
www.elearnexpo.com

VNU Business Media
Training 2002 Conference and Expo/Presentations 2002 Conference and Expo
February 18-20, 2002
Atlanta, GA
www.trainingconference.com

Flagg Management
2002 HumanAssets.org: 3rd Annual Show & Conference
February 25-26, 2002
New York, NY
www.humanassets.org

Academy of Human Resource Development
International Research Conference 2002
February 27-March 3, 2002
Honolulu, HI
www.ahrd.org

CALENDAR OF MEETINGS AND EVENTS, 2002

March

VNU Business Media
OnLine Learning 2002 Europe
March 5-6, 2002
London, United Kingdom
www.vnulearning.com

Council of Hotel and Restaurant Trainers
Spring 2002 Conference
Seattle, WA
March 10-13, 2002
www.chart.org

Association for Quality and Participation
24th Annual Spring Conference & Resource Mart: "Thriving Through Teamwork"
March 11-13, 2002
Las Vegas, NV
www.aqp.org

International Technology Education Association
64th Annual Conference: "Positioning Technological Literacy in the Mainstream of Education"
March 14-16, 2002
Columbus, OH
www.iteawww.org/D.html

Association for the Advancement of Computing in Education
SITE 2002 (Society for Information Technology & Teacher Education)
March 18-23, 2002
Nashville, TN
www.aace.org/conf/site

Association for Business Simulation and Experiential Learning
29th Annual Conference (ABSEL 2002): "New Learning Techniques for the New Times"
March 20-22, 2002
Pensacola, FL
www.towson.edu/~absel

Human Resource Planning Society
24th Annual Conference
March 24-27, 2002
Miami (South Beach), FL
www.hrps.org

LRP Publications
4th Annual Public Human Resource Management Conference and Expo
March 25-27, 2002
Arlington, VA
www.lrpconferences.com/calendar.html

April

International Mentoring Association
15th Annual Diversity in Mentoring Conference
April 4-6, 2002
Fort Worth, TX
www.wmich.edu/conferences/mentoring

Higher Colleges of Technology, United Arab Emirates
International Vocational Education and Training Association
IVETA-TEND 2002 International Conference: "Bridging the Divide: Strategies for Change"
Dubai, United Arab Emirates
April 7-9, 2002
www.iveta.org

Advanstar Communications Inc.
E-Learning 2002 Conference & Expo
April 8-11, 2002
Washington, DC
www.elearningexpos.com

Center for Internet Technology in Education
3rd Annual CiTE Conference: The Evolution of eLearning
April 10-12, 2002
Denver, CO
www.cite.ecollege.com

Distance Education and Training Council
76th Annual Conference
April 14-16, 2002
Denver, CO
www.detc.org

Society for Human Resource Management Global Forum
25th Annual Conference & Exposition
April 15-17, 2002
New York, NY
www.shrmglobal.org/conference/index.html

Employment Management Association
33rd Annual Conference & Exposition
April 17-19, 2002
San Francisco, CA
www.shrm.org/ema

Association for Computing Machinery, Special Interest Group on Computer-Human Interaction
CHI 2002 Conference on Human Factors in Computing Systems
April 20-25, 2002
Minneapolis, MN
sigchi.org/sigchi/chi2002

International Federation of Training and Development Organizations
Bahrain Society for Training and Development
31st World Conference and Exposition: The New Frontiers of HRD
April 21-24, 2002
Manama, Bahrain
www.iftdo.org

International Society for Performance Improvement
Annual Conference and Exposition
April 21-25, 2002
Dallas, TX
www.ispi.org/services/conf.htm

American Management Association
34th Global Human Resource Management Conference
April 22-24, 2002
Lisbon, Portugal
www.amanet.org

Council on Employee Benefits
Spring 2002 Conference
April 28-May 1, 2002
San Antonio, TX
www.ceb.org

May

Employee Assistance Society of North America
14th Annual Professional Development Institute
May 1-4, 2002
Quebec City, QC, Canada
www.easna.org

National Association of Workforce Development Professionals
13th Annual Conference
May 5-8, 2002
San Juan, Puerto Rico
kaisergrp.com/nawdp/index.htm

Richmond Events, Inc.
4th Annual Human Resources Forum
May 9-12, 2002
New York, NY
www.hrforum.com/aboutevent

WorldAtWork
2002 International Conference
May 12-15, 2002
Orlando, FL
www.worldatwork.org

VNU Business Media
OnLine Learning 2002 Asia
May 14-16, 2002
Singapore
www.vnulearning.com

Employee Services Management Association
61st Annual Conference and Exhibit
May 19-23, 2002
San Diego, CA
www.esmassn.org/conference

Organization Development Institute
32nd Annual Information Exchange
May 21-24, 2002
Wheeling, IL
members.aol.com/odinst/confrnce.htm

Center for the Study of Work Teams
10th Annual Symposium on Collaborative Work Systems
May 22-24, 2002
Denton, TX
www.workteams.unt.edu

International Association of Facilitators
Worldwide Conference 2002: "The Art and Mastery of Facilitation—The Quest for Transformation"
May 23-26, 2002
Fort Worth, TX
www.iaf-world.org/iafconferences.htm

World Federation of Personnel Management Associations
Asociación Mexicana en Direccion de Recursos Humanos
North American Human Resource Management Association
9th World Congress on Human Resource Management
May 27-29, 2002
Mexico City, Mexico
www.wfpma.com/mex02.html

American Society for Training & Development
ASTD 2002 International Conference & Exposition
May 31-June 6, 2002
New Orleans, LA
www.astd.org

June

Society of Insurance Trainers and Educators
2002 Conference
June 8-12, 2002
San Antonio, TX
www.insurancetrainers.org/index.htm

International Association for Human Resource Information Management
IHRIM 2002 Spring Conference: "Transcend Boundaries"
June 9-12, 2002
Orlando, FL
www.ihrim.org

VNU Business Media
18th Annual Training Director's Forum
June 9-12, 2002
Las Vegas, NV
www.trainingdirectorsforum.com

National Association of Employee Recognition
4th Annual Human Resources & Recognition Forum
June 10-13, 2002
Chicago, IL
www.recognition.org

Society for Human Resource Management
53rd Annual Conference and Exposition
June 23-26, 2002
Philadelphia, PA
www.shrm.org

Association for the Advancement of Computing in Education
ED-MEDIA 2002—World Conference on Educational Multimedia, Hypermedia & Telecommunications
June 24-29, 2002
Denver, CO
www.aace.org/conf/edmedia

Advanstar Communications Inc.
Collaborate! Conference & Expo 2002: Solutions & Strategies for Enterprise Collaboration
June 25-27, 2002
Boston, MA
www.elearningexpos.com

July

International Consortium of Educational Developers
4th ICED Conference
July 1-7, 2002
Perth, Australia
www.csd.uwa.edu.au/iced2002

National Speakers Association
Convention
July 13-16, 2002
Orlando, FL
www.nsaspeaker.org

Organization Development Institute
22nd Organization Development World Congress
July 22-27, 2002
Sogakope, Ghana
members.aol.com/odinst/confrnce.htm

Society for Applied Learning Technology
Education Technology 2002 Conference
July 24-26, 2002
Arlington, VA
www.salt.org

August

Council of Hotel and Restaurant Trainers
Summer 2002 Conference
August 11-14, 2002
Montreal, QC, Canada
www.chart.org

September

National Human Resources Association
52nd Annual National Conference
Fall 2002
Rochester, NY
www.humanresources.org

International Foundation of Employee Benefit Plans
Annual Conference
September 21-25, 2002
Toronto, ON, Canada
www.ifebp.org

VNU Business Media
Online Learning 2002 and Performance Support 2002 Conference and Exposition
September 23-25, 2002
Anaheim, CA
www.vnulearning.com

Human Factors and Ergonomics Society
46th Annual Meeting
September 23-27, 2002
Pittsburgh, PA
hfes.org

LRP Publications
HR Technology Conference & Expo
September 25-27, 2002
Chicago, IL
www.lrpconferences.com/calendar.html

BenefitNews.com
15th Annual Benefits Management Forum and Expo
September 29-October 2, 2002
Dallas, TX
www.benefitnews.com/expo/home1.html

October

International Organization Development Association
17th IODA World Conference 2002
October 7-11, 2002
Santiago/Maitencillo, Chile
www.ioda.de/ioda_2002.htm

Employee Assistance Program Association
31st Annual Conference
October 27-31, 2002
Detroit, MI
www.eap-association.com

November

GOAL/QPC
18th Annual Conference
November 2002
Boston, MA
www.goalqpc.com

American Evaluation Association
Evaluation 2002
November 6-9, 2002
Washington, DC
www.eval.org

Association for Experiential Education
30th Annual International Conference
November 7-10, 2002
Saint Paul, MN
www.aee.org

Asynchronous Learning Networks Center
8th International Conference on Asynchronous Learning Networks (ALN 2002)
November 8-10, 2002
Orlando, FL
www.aln.org

Association for Educational Communications and Technology
International Convention
November 12-15, 2002
Dallas, TX
www.aect.org

Index

A

Adaptive conjoint analysis (ACA), described, 273-275
Adams, John D., on managing dispersed work, 381-391
After Action Reviews (AAR), described, 151
Aldrich, Clark,
  on training, 76-77
  quoted, 83
American Society for Training and Development (ASTD), on state of training, 13-26
Analysis and design, cases and practices, 235-260
Appraisal processes, case for, 200-207
Arditte, Ed, quoted, 166
Ashland Chemicals Co., 395
Associations, of training and performance, 475-496
Atkinson, William, on stress, 208-214

B

Bachelder, Edward L., on how employees want to learn, 271-279
Bagshaw, Mike, on training people to be affective, 188-194
Barbazette, Jean, on new employee orientation practices, 37-41, 285-288
Bechtel, AAR at, 152-153, 154
Belgard, Bill, quoted, 377
Ben & Jerry's, 398, 399
Bereiter, Carl, quoted, 110
Birnbach, Jerry, quoted, 164
Blair, tips on training, 255-260
Blanchard, Ken, 195
Boeing, training at, 375-380
Booz, Carl, quoted, 146
Brazosport Independent School District, 402
Bregman, Peter, on training evaluation, 326-332
Brightman, Baird K., on reinforcing professional self-management, 174-187
British Petroleum, AAR at, 152
Brown, Alicia, training experience, 292-293
Brown, John Seely, 86
Bryans, Patricia, on personal development, 351-363
Buddy programs, how to design, 295-301

C

Calendar, conferences of, 497-506
Capella University, 334
Caroselli, Marlene, on leadership, 195-199
Carr, Jim, quoted, 249, 251, 254
Caudron, Shari, evaluating e-degrees, 333-338
Chang, Richard, on passion for organizational performance, 397-404
Christian, Bill, quoted, 395-396
Cisco, 392
  training at, 101-102
Clarke American, 402
Cohen, Stephen L., on how employees want to learn, 271-279
Comcast Cable Communications, trainers at, 393
Computer-based training (CBT)
  compared to e-learning, 56;
  e-learning a new twist on, 99-103
Conferences, calendar of, 497-506
Conflict resolution training, how to set up programs on, 312-316
Content, role with Internet, 87-89
Corporate, training at described, 77-78

Corporate universities, 269-270
Cox, Ann, quoted, 280
Cox, Diane, on setting goals, 223-232
Cox, Molly, quoted, 282
Cree, Lisa H., on telecommuting, 52-55
Cronbach, Lee, quoted, 109
Culture, improving corporate, 125-142
Customer resource management (CRM), 77-78

D

Dawson, David, 103
    quoted, 99
DeClue, Scotty C., calculating training efficiency, 339-342
Dell, David., on why managers balk at appraisals, 143-144
Delphi Group
    e-learning market, 56-71
    on integrating e-learning with business goals, 92-98
    on training trends, 3-12
Design
    cases and practices, 235-260
    e-learning, 104-114
    trends in training, 40-41
Directory, of training and performance organizations, 475-496
Discussion lists, online for training and performance, 408-414
Disney Institute, 403
Dixon, Nancy M., on how groups learn, 148-161
Dove, David W., on how employees want to learn, 271-279
Doyle, Shawn, quoted, 393
Drucker, Peter F., 174
    on learning and training, 81-82
    online, 75
    quoted, 199
Dyson, Esther, 86

E

E-degrees, evaluating, 333-338
E-learning
    cases and practices, 73-121
    on transition from traditional training to, 289-294
    trends, 30-12, 56-71
E-publications, bibliography, 414-416
E-tools, at Ford Motor, 369-370
Eastman Chemical Co., knowledge sharing at, 165-166
Eisaguirre, Lynn, quoted, 312, 314-315
Electronic monitoring policies, need for, 169-173
Ellis, Kristine, on role of trainers, 392-396
Emotional intelligence, described, 188-194
Employees
    cases and practices, 343-404
    development of, 261-270
    how they want to learn, 271-279
    new orientation programs for, 385-387
    personal development of, 351-363
    training spending by type of, 28-30
    training trends, 42-47
    trends in orientation for new, 37-41, 285-288
Enterprise e-learning, defined, 5
Enterprise resource planning (ERP), training and, 77-78
Evaluations, of interventions, 317-342
Extranets, to share knowledge, 162-168

F

Fahs, Glen, quoted, 214
Feola, Christopher, quoted, 85, 87
Ferguson, Dove, training experience of, 290-292
Final Copy Group, Inc., on training design, 241-245
Fischer, Terrill, quoted, 281
Ford, Lynda, quoted, 144
Ford, Jr., William Clay, quoted, 145, 365
Ford Motor Company, leadership development, 364-374
Friedman, Stewart D., leadership DNA, 364-374

G

Galagan, Patricia, on revolution in e-learning, 75-82
Gale, Sarah Fister
    on role of trainers, 392-396
    training at Boeing, 375-380
Gaps, in performance, 130-141
Garcia, Carrie, on electronic monitoring policies, 169-173

INDEX

Gayeski, Diane, quoted, 78-79
Geissler, John, training experience, 289-290
Gelertner, David, quoted, 86
Glossary, performance management terms, 461-474
Goals, how to set, 223-232
Gottlieb, Mara, quoted, 213
Gottlieb, Marvin, on implementing e-learning, 83-91
Granirer, David, quoted, 281, 282
Grensing-Pophal, Lin, on motivating managers, 143-147
Grote, Dick, 147
Gruhn, Marty, quoted, 168
Guild, Robert, on high performance organizations, 125-142
Guild, Will, on high performance organizations, 125-142

H

Hale, Brandon, quoted, 100, 103
Hand, quoted, 394
Holley, Gary, quoted, 249
Humor, in training, 280-284

I

IBM
  employee recognition and, 215
  training in, 101
Industry, training trends by, 45, 73-121
Information Technology (IT) skills, spending on, 25, 27
Internet
  use in training, 73-121
  Web-based learning and, 56, 66-67, 407-430
Interventions
  for performance improvements, 233-342
  in training, 261-316
ISD, evolution of, 78-80

J

Jacobson, Howie, on training evolution, 326-332
Jeffries, Paul, quoted, 100
Jeffries, Robbin, quoted, 282
Jobs, growth areas in, 4
Jones International University, 334

Just-in-time learning, 11

K

Kelleher, Herb, 398, 401
Kelly, Tom, quoted, 392
King, Rollin, 398
Kirkpatrick, Donald, 329
Knowledge management, 353
Krupa, Suzanne, 164

L

Lanier, Jaron, quoted, 86
Lapide, Larry, quoted, 167
Largent, Bob, quoted, 210-211
Lasak, John, quoted, 334
Leadership
  development at Ford Motor, 364-374
  role of, 195-199
Learning
  Drucker on, 81-82
  how groups do it, 148-161
  how it changes using online techniques, 105-109
  methods for, 235-240
Learning management systems (LMS), 102
Linde, Karen Vander, quoted, 79

M

Magnan, Robert, online resources for training and performance, 407-430
Magura, Carolyn, quoted, 208, 212
Maister, David, ideas, 330
Malcolm, Stanley E., on measuring training department, 317-325
Malcomb Baldrige Award, winner of, 376
Mallinger, Mark, on promoting organizational learning, 345-350
Management
  in reviewing performance, 143-147
  on setting goals, 223-232
  reinforcing self-, 174-187
Marciel, Dolores, quoted, 163, 164
Marlboro College, mission statement, 10-11
Marquardt, Anja, quoted, 394
Martinez, Margaret, on designing e-learning, 104-114

MASIE Center, 30
Mathews, Don, quoted, 251, 253
McKeown, J. Leslie, on designing buddy programs, 295-301
McLaughlin, Kathleen, on humor in training, 280-284
McLeodUSA, 401
McLuhan, Marshall
    ideas of, 87
    quoted, 89
McMillen, Steve, quoted, 101
Measurements
    of e-learning, 80-82
    of training departments, 317-325
    of web-based training, 115-121
Meetings, managing, 387-388
Mendoza, Cornelius, quoted, 163
Mentoring, designing buddy programs for, 295-301
Mershon, Phil, on informal training, 302-306
Methods, training trends, 30-34
Meyer, Erick, quoted, 85
Meyer, Peter, on gaining approvals for training, 246-248
Michel, Jim, quoted, 377, 380
Miller, Joe, quoted, 79
Mundy, Ron, on high performance organizations, 125-142

N
Nasser, Jacques, 372; quoted, 365
Newsgroups, online resource, 414
Nilles, Jack, invented phrase "telecomputing," 52

O
O'Connor, Thomas J., quoted, 209-210, 211
Organization
    amount of training delivered, 13-20
    how they learn, 345-350
    improving performance of, 125-173
    strategies, cases, and practices, 343-404
Osinski, Diana, quoted, 249
Outcomes, designing training to, 241-245

Outsourcing, in training trends, 22-25
Owen, Keith, on high performance organizations, 125-142

P
Passion, for organizational performance, 397-404
People
    cases and practices, 343-404
    role in training trends, 42-47
Performance
    glossary of terms, 461-474
    improvement cases and practices, 123-232
    interventions, 238-342
    motivating managers to do reviews of, 143-147
    recognizing employees for, 215-222
    resource almanac, 405-506
    success factors, 126-130
Problem solving, 181-183
Processes, need to understand, 6
PSS/World Medical, 403
Public education, crisis in, 4
Publications, directory of, 431-460

Q
Quantum Idea Project (QIP), described, 367

R
Recognition, peak performance and, 215-222
Resources, on training and performance, 405-506
Retention, 266; training in support of, 235-240
Riggio, Ronald, quoted, 145
Roberts, Bill
    on CBT and e-learning, 99-103
    on using extranets to exchange knowledge, 162-168
ROI, for e-learning, 102
Rossie, Janeen, on tracking Web-based training, 115-121
Rucker, Rebecca, quoted, 280
Russell, Thomas L., quoted, 334

S
Salisbury, Curt, quoted, 145, 146
Schaniel, Ed, quoted, 377

INDEX

Schank, Roger C.,
  ideas on training, 76
  quoted, 334-335
Schwartz, Jeff, quoted, 77-80
Scordamalkia, Marlene, 110
Segal, Jonathan A., on appraisal processes, 200-207
Self-management, reinforcing, 174-187
Serial knowledge, how groups learns, 148-161
Settles, Patty, quoted, 393
Shanes, Danielle, quoted, 209, 210-211
Siebert, Al., quoted, 14, 209, 212
Simon, Herbert, ideas of, 308-309
Skills
  e-learning and, 59-65
  reinforcing collaborative, 349
Skinner, B.F., ideas of, 84-85
Smith, Richard, on personal development, 351-363
Software, for e-learning, 115-121
Sorenson, Richard C., on telecomputing, 52-55
Sosnin, Betty, on video in training, 249-254
Souders, Bill, quoted, 102
Southwest Airlines, 398-399
Spending, trends in training, 25-28, 42-47
Stoll, Cliff, quoted, 86
Stress, on managing, 208-214
Summers, Lynn,
  glossary of performance management terms, 461-474
  on setting goals, 223-232

T

Teamwork, role of, 388-389
Tears, effect of appraisals on, 201
Technology, trends in training, 33-34
Telecomputing, research findings, 52-55
Terry, Phil, quoted, 331
Thomas, Michael O., on types of training styles, 307-311
Thompson, Carolyn B., on designing training, 235-240
Trainers
  experience with e-learning instruction, 289-294
  role of, 392-396
Training
  calculating efficiency of, 339-342
  compared to e-learning, 6-12
  delivery trends, 21-36
  Drucker on, 81-82
  evolution of techniques, 326-332
  evolution to e-learning, 289-294
  getting approval for, 246-248
  intervention cases and practices, 261-316
  on informal, 302-306
  practice trends, 34-36
  resource almanac, 405-506
  retention and, 235-240
  role of humor in, 280-284
  situational vs. cause-and-effect, 307-311
  technologies cases and practices for, 73-121
  tips on, 255-260
  tracking web-based, 115-121
  trends in, 1-71
TRAINING Magazine, spending survey, 42-51
Trends, in training, 1-71

U

U.S. Army
  learning activities of, 148-149, 151, 156
  use of e-learning by, 99-100
U.S. Bureau of Labor Statistics (BLS), on future jobs, 4
University of Phoenix Online, 335

V

Value chains, e-learning and, 96-98
Van Buren, Mark E.
  on state of training, 13-20
  quoted, 100
  skeptical on e-learning ROI, 102
Vasilliadis, Chris, quoted, 392
Ventrice, Cindy, on retaining peak performance, 215-222
Video, in training, 249-254

W

Wainwright Industries, 401
Wang, Greg, on developing people, 261-270

Watkins, Jason C., quoted, 162
Web-Based Education Commission, quoted, 4
Winters, Carey, quoted, 395
Work, managing dispersed, 381-391
Workers, on identifying learners, 93-95
World Wide Web (WWW), training and performance sites, 416-429

X

X-economy, defined, 9-10

Y

Young, Doug, training experience of, 293-294
Youngman, Henny, quoted, 89

Z

Zai, Alex, quoted, 333, 337
Zielinski, Dave, on transition to e-learning, 289-294
Zigon, Jack, on setting goals, 223-232
Zittrain, Jonathan, quoted, 86